Uncollected Works of Abraham Lincoln

Two thousand and fifty copies
of the first volume of The
Uncollected Works of Lincoln
have been printed.   This is
copy number..
and is signed by

Uncollected Works of
Abraham Lincoln

His Letters, Addresses and Other Papers

Assembled and Annotated by

RUFUS ROCKWELL WILSON

Assisted by Other Lincoln Scholars

A Supplement to and Revision of

THE COMPLETE WORKS OF LINCOLN

by NICOLAY *and* HAY

VOLUME I—1824 to 1840

THE PRIMAVERA PRESS, INC.
610 West Church Street
Elmira, N. Y.

1947

To *CARL W. SCHAEFER—*

Devoted member of the Lincoln
fellowship, whose reverent regard
for a great man's memory has
made possible the publication of
the present and its sister volumes

TABLE OF CONTENTS

AIMS AND ACKNOWLEDGMENTS

The present volume is the first of a series in which it is proposed to assemble and annotate letters, speeches and other papers of Abraham Lincoln that have come to light in the forty-one years that have elapsed since in 1905 Nicolay and Hay published an enlarged and final edition of their Complete Works of Abraham Lincoln. To the new material thus collected notes are added which, it is hoped, read in order, will afford a full and sympathetic account not only of Mr. Lincoln's career from early manhood until his death but also of the personal contacts and friendships, and the march of events that helped to shape that career.

The twelve volumes of Nicolay and Hay contain 2243 items. The present work will include more than 1600 items of greater or lesser importance and meaning not found in that collection, part of it heretofore inaccessible and out of reach. William Henry Herndon was Mr. Lincoln's law partner from 1844 until the day in February, 1861, when the President-elect left Springfield for Washington. When the President died Herndon, with signal zeal and thoroughness, began to collect the reminiscences of those who had known Mr. Lincoln, along with manuscripts and documents of every sort relating to him.

When Herndon in turn passed away, this unique collection became the property of Jesse W. Weik who had aided in the composition of his well-known life of Lincoln, and following the death of the younger man it was sold to a New York dealer from whom in 1941 it was purchased by the Library of Congress. Before that time only a few students enjoyed access to a collection which includes upward of 600 legal documents written in whole or in part by Mr. Lincoln between 1836 and 1860, and which for the first time afford full and convincing proof of his untiring industry and range and capacity as a lawyer.

Micro-films of these documents have been secured from the Library of Congress, and, with painstaking care, have been or are being transcribed for the present work by John Henry Cramer of Cleveland, who is also tracing with infinite labor, so far as it may be determined, the history of each action in which the documents had a part. Moreover, in July, 1947, the papers of Mr. Lincoln bequeathed by his son to the Library of Congress under the terms of the latter's will are to become available for inspection and publication. Such of these papers written by Mr. Lincoln, as were not used by Nicolay and Hay and so remain unpublished, will be included in an appendix to the final volume of the present work, which will also contain an informing chapter on bogus Lincoln letters, some of which have a curious history, and another on important and unusual letters known to have been written by Mr. Lincoln, but which are now lost, seemingly past recovery.

Mr. Lincoln as a drafter of legal documents, particularly in his earlier years at the bar, was much given to erasures and interlineations, now and again with confusing results. He had also his own ideas of punctuation, spacing and underscoring which at times tax the skill and patience of those who seek to determine his exact meaning. Thus the writer can not hope for complete immunity from the fault-finding that generally waits upon the discharge of a difficult and delicate task. However, it has been at every stage his chief concern by devoted and patient effort to seek and find the exact form and purpose Mr. Lincoln had in mind in each instance; to faithfully reproduce his spelling and punctuation, and where he or another underscores a word or phrase to indicate that fact by the use of Italics.

Seconded by friendly officials of the several courts of the old Eighth Circuit diligent effort has been made to recover, whenever possible, a full and accurate history of the cases in which Mr. Lincoln had a part. The editor must also record his very real obligation to many learned members of the Lincoln fellowship who, in the process of labors that began when the century was young, have generously aided him with pertinent facts and timely suggestions. These include Oliver R. Barrett of Chicago and Dr. F. Lauriston Bullard of Melrose Highlands, Massachusetts, both enminent for a knowledge of every phase of Mr. Lincoln's career as all-embracing as it is exact, and Dr. Louis A. Warren of the Lincoln National Life Foundation, Fort Wayne, Indiana, whose revealing researches into the ancestry, parentage and childhood of Mr. Lincoln have made present and future students his debtors.

Thanks are also due to Dr. Harry E. Pratt, former executive secretary of the Abraham Lincoln Association of Springfield; to J. Harry Hopper and Frank P. Vickery, present clerks of the Sangamon Circuit Court for making easy searches for facts regarding Mr. Lincoln's early cases before it; to Jay

Monaghan and Margaret Flint of the Illinois Historical Society; to Drs. Robert B. Kincaid and R. Gerald McMurty of Lincoln Memorial University, Harrogate, Tennessee; to Dr. John E. Washington of Washington, sterling representative of the race Mr. Lincoln helped to set free; to F. Ray Risdon of Los Angeles and the writer's old friend, Thomas O. Marvin of Portsmouth, New Hampshire; to his typist, Mrs. Lillian Buckholtz Paganelli, tactful in pointing out shortcomings that call for correction, and finally to his wife, Otilie Erickson Wilson, whose love for things that are gracious and of good report and ready and quickening courage in face of obstacles that lengthen an arduous task, have made it possible for this volume to come into being.

There is an ancient saying, not without its message of cheer for the honest craftsman, that "the end crowns the work;" and if some of those entitled to speak with authority find here a worthwhile contribution to the history of the Lincoln era and its central figure, the writer will feel that he has abundant reward for his labors.

Rufus Rockwell Wilson

Elmira, N. Y., November 28, 1946.

LINCOLN CHRONOLOGY, 1809-1840.

February 12, 1809—Abraham Lincoln, son of Thomas and Nancy Hanks Lincoln, is born three miles south of present day Hodgenville on Nolin River, Kentucky.

Spring of 1811—Thomas Lincoln moves his family from Nolin River to a farm on Knob Creek, north and east of Hodgenville and on the highway leading from Louisville to Nashville—a location clearly remembered by Abraham Lincoln in after years.

Autumn of 1815 and Winter of 1816—Lincoln and his sister Sarah attend for short periods ABC schools kept in turn by Zachariah Riney and Caleb Hazel. This school was on the site of the present town of Athertonville, two miles from the Lincoln farm.

Autumn of 1816—Abraham Lincoln is saved from drowning in Knob Creek by Austin Gollaher, as related by the latter to William H. Herndon in 1865.

December, 1816—Thomas Lincoln moves his family from Kentucky and settles in an unbroken forest in what is now Perry County, Indiana, Abraham Lincoln being then in this eighth year.

October 15, 1817—Thomas Lincoln enters at the government land office at Vincennes the farm upon which he was living.

———1818—Abraham Lincoln in his tenth year is "kicked by a horse and apparently killed for a time," an incident which he later told Herndon he regarded as one of the remarkable events of his life.

September, 1818—Thomas Sparrow and his wife, Elizabeth Hanks Sparrow, aunt of Nancy Hanks Lincoln, die of "milk" sickness.

October 5, 1818—Nancy Hanks Lincoln also dies of "milk" sickness and is buried near the Sparrows.

December 2, 1819—Thomas Lincoln and Sarah Bush are married at Elizabethtown, Kentucky.

Winter of 1820—Abraham and Sarah Lincoln attend a school kept by Andrew Crawford.

Autumn and Winter of 1822—Abraham Lincoln attends for about four months a "blab" school kept by James Swaney, four miles from the Lincoln home. John Hanks, a cousin of Nancy Hanks Lincoln, is then a member of the Lincoln household.

————1824—Abraham Lincoln attends for about six months a school kept by Hazel Dorsey.

March 1, 1826—Abraham Lincoln writes this date on a page of his "Book of Examples in Arithmetic."

August 2, 1826—Abraham Lincoln's sister Sarah becomes the wife of Aaron Grigsby.

————1827—For nine months during this year Abraham Lincoln works for James Taylor as a farm hand and at the ferry at the mouth of Anderson Creek. It is at this time that he earns his first dollar ferrying passengers to a steamer in the Ohio River.

June 6, 1827—Thomas Lincoln receives a patent to eighty acres of land signed by President John Quincy Adams.

January 20, 1828—Sarah Lincoln Grigsby, sister of Abraham Lincoln, dies in childbirth.

Spring of 1828—Abraham Lincoln and Allen Gentry make a flatboat trip to New Orleans for the latter's father, James Gentry. This trip which began at Rockport, Indiana, occupied three months and gave Abraham Lincoln perhaps his first arresting contact with slavery.

————1829—Abraham Lincoln works in the store of James Gentry at a place later named Gentryville.

February 20, 1830—Thomas and Sarah Lincoln sell their eighty-acre farm for $125 to Charles Grigsby.

March 1, 1830—Thomas Lincoln moves from Indiana to Illinois at the head of a company of thirteen, which included his own family and those of Mrs. Lincoln's two sons-in-law—Dennis Hanks and Squire Hall.

March 14, 1830—The Lincoln caravan of three wagons, two drawn by oxen and one by horses driven by twenty-one year old Abraham Lincoln, camp in the village square of Decatur, Illinois, which then consisted of "less than a dozen log houses set in the heart of a grove of oaks."

March 15, 1830—Thomas Lincoln locates on a tract of land ten miles from Decatur and on the north bank of the Sangamon River, selected for him by John Hanks, who had preceded the Lincolns to Illinois.

Spring of 1830—Lincoln begins with four yoke of oxen to break forty-five acres of land. He and Charles Hanks also split the rails which were to play a picturesque part in the presidential campaign of 1860.

Summer of 1830—Lincoln makes his first political speech in Illinois at a campaign meeting in Decatur, advocating the improvement of the Sangamon River for purposes of navigation.

Winter of 1930-31—Lincoln splits 1,000 rails for Major William Warnick and freezes his feet in the process.

March, 1831—Lincoln with John Hanks and John D. Johnston begin to build a flatboat on the Sangamon, the trio having been employed by Denton Offutt to fill it with produce and float it to the New Orleans market.

April 19, 1831—Lincoln has his first view of New Salem, when the progress of his flatboat is temporarily barred by Rutledge's mill dam at that place.

April to July, 1831—Lincoln and his companions are on the way to and from New Orleans.

Late July, 1831—Lincoln arrives at New Salem to clerk in Offutt's store which opens for business in September.

August 1, 1831—Lincoln casts his first vote and serves unofficially as election clerk at New Salem at the same time winning a reputation as a story teller.

March 9, 1832—Aided by Mentor Graham and John McNamar, Lincoln writes his platform as a candidate for the Illinois Legislature.

March-April, 1832—Lincoln serves as one of the pilots of the steamboat Talisman in its round trip on the Sangamon from Beardstown to Portland five miles north of Springfield.

April 21, 1832—Lincoln volunteers for service in the Black Hawk War, and is elected captain of his company.

April 28, 1832—Captain Lincoln's company is enrolled in the state service.

May 9, 1832—Captain Lincoln's company is mustered into the federal service at Ottawa, and he re-enlists for a twenty-day period in the company of Independent Rangers (mounted) commanded by Captain Elijah Iles.

June 16, 1832—The company of Captain Iles is mustered out of service at Fort Wilbourn by Lieutenant Robert Anderson and Lincoln re-enlists for thirty days as a private in the Independent Spy Corps commanded by Captain Jacob M. Early.

July 10, 1832—Captain Early's company, including Private Lincoln, is mustered out of service at Burnt Village.

July 15, 1832—Lincoln begins return journey to New Salem to resume his canvass for the Legislature.

August 6, 1832—Lincoln is defeated for the Legislature, running eighth in a field of thirteen candidates.

May 7, 1833—Lincoln is appointed postmaster at New Salem by President Andrew Jackson.

Fall of 1833—John Calhound, Sangamon County surveyor, appoints Lincoln as his deputy for the New Salem section of the county. Lincoln accepts and under the guidance of Mentor Graham quickly masters the rudiments of surveying.

January 14, 1834—Lincoln writes the description of his first known survey—a tract for Russell Godbey six miles north of New Salem.

April 19, 1834—In the Sangamo Journal Lincoln announces that he is again a candidate for the Legislature.

July, 1834—During the legislative canvass John T. Stuart, who had served with Lincoln in the Black Hawk War, advises the latter to study law.

August 4, 1834—Lincoln is elected to the General Assembly, running second among the thirteen candidates. He borrows books from Stuart and begins the study of law.

December 1, 1834—Lincoln at Vandalia takes his seat as a member of the lower house of the General Assembly.

February 14, 1835—Lincoln returns to New Salem and to his duties as postmaster and deputy surveyor, also resuming his law studies.

August 25, 1835—Ann Rutledge, "beloved of Abraham Lincoln," dies after a six weeks illness, at the Rutledge farm a few miles from New Salem.

September 10, 1835—Thomas M. Neale, having succeeded John Calhoun as county surveyor, appoints Lincoln as one of his deputies.

December 7, 1835—Lincoln is present at the opening of a special session of the General Assembly called by Governor Duncan, and takes an active part in its proceedings.

January 18, 1836—The General Assembly adjourns and Lincoln returns to New Salem.

February 17, 1836—Lincoln certifies that he has surveyed the town of Petersburg.

March 19, 1836—Lincoln announces that he is a candidate for re-election to the General Assembly.

March 24, 1836—Lincoln's name is entered on the record of the Sangamon Circuit Court as "a person of good moral character," the first of the three steps then required in order to become a lawyer in Illinois.

May 30, 1836—The New Salem postoffice is discontinued and Lincoln receives $19.48 for his last three months service as postmaster.

July 11, 1836—Lincoln takes part in Springfield in his first political debate.

August 1, 1836—Lincoln receives the highest vote of the candidates for the General Assembly.

September 9, 1836—Lincoln is licensed by two justices of the Supreme Court to practice law in the courts of Illinois, the second step then demanded of applicants for admission to the bar of that state.

October 5, 1836—Lincoln files his plea in his first law suit, Hawthorn vs. Woolridge.

November 7, 1836—Lincoln votes for Hugh L. White for President.

December 5, 1836—Lincoln attends the opening of the Tenth General Assembly at Vandalia.

February 11, 1837—Lincoln as the leader of the Long Nine, the nickname given the Sangamon delegation to the General Assembly, shrewdly directs a contest for the removal of the state capital from Vandalia to Springfield.

February 28, 1837—As the result in large part of Lincoln's clever management the General Assembly selects Springfield as the future capital of Illinois.

March 1, 1837—Lincoln enrolls on the record of the clerk of the Supreme Court, his third and final step in becoming a member of the Illinois bar.

March 3, 1837—Lincoln and Dan Stone enter their protest against an anti-abolitionist resolution adopted by the General Assembly on January 20—the former's first recorded declaration as to the injustice of slavery.

March 6, 1837—The General Assembly adjourns and Lincoln returns to New Salem.

April 15, 1837—Lincoln settles in Springfield and becomes the law partner of John T. Stuart.

April 27, 1837—Lincoln attends a three-day term of the McLean Circuit Court at Bloomington, and so begins the circuit riding which was to end in 1860.

May 25, 1837—A prolonged and bitter controversy between Lincoln and James Adams, a fellow lawyer of Springfield, over a tract of land claimed by Adams and the heirs of Joseph Anderson, has its inception at this time.

June 14, 1837—Lincoln closes his accounts as postmaster of New Salem, and writes the first of a series of letters, signed Sampson's Ghost and published in the Sangamo Journal, in which he sets forth at length the alleged misdeeds of James Adams.

June 22, 1837—Lincoln and associates file the suit of Jané Anderson and her son against James Adams for recovery of ten acres north of Sprigfield title to which, it is alleged, Adams has procured by fraud.

July 11, 1837—Licoln takes his seat in the General Assembly at Vandalia called in special session by Governor Duncan and by general consent of his party associates exercises Whig leadership in the House.

July 22, 1837—The General Assembly adjourns and Lincoln returns to Springfield.

August 5, 1837—Lincoln issues a hand bill setting forth the history of the Anderson-Adams controversy.

August 7, 1837—James Adams, ending weeks of turmoil, is elected probate justice of the peace over Dr. Anson G. Henry, Lincoln's devoted friend.

August, 1837—About this time Mary Owens rejects Lincoln's offer of marriage.

September 4, 1837—Lincoln writes and files the bill of complaint in his first divorce suit.

September 30, 1837—A note signed "An Old Settler" and believed to have been written by Lincoln appears in the Sangamo Journal, the first of a series accusing James Adams of irregularities in securing title to certain lots in Springfield.

December 7, 1837—Lincoln writes a friend that he and his assocates regard Stephen A. Douglas as "a small matter."

January 27, 1838—Lincoln delivers an address before the Young Men's Lyceum of Springfield on "The Perpetuation of Our Political Institutions" in which he forecasts his thinking and public utterances in later years. The same day a letter signed "A Conservative," one of a series believed to have been written in part by Lincoln, appears in the Sangamo Journal.

February 24, 1838—The Sangamo Journal again announces Lincoln as a candidate for the General Assembly.

May 10, 1838—During this week Lincoln substitutes for his partner in a debate at Bloomington with Douglas, who is contesting with Stuart for a seat in Congress—the first of many tests of quality between them which were to span a score of years.

August 6, 1838—Lincoln is elected to the General Assembly for the third time—first in a field of seventeen candidates and Stuart defeats Douglas for Congress by thirtysix votes in a total of 36,495.

September 29, 1838—Lincoln speaks at a barbecue of 2,000 Whigs who thus celebrate Stuart's election to Congress.

October 9, 1838—Lincoln participates in the defense of Henry B. Truett charged with the murder of Dr. Jacob M. Early.

October 13, 1838—Truett is acquitted in part as a result of Lincoln's closing plea to the jury.

November 3, 1838—Lincoln in an editorial in the Sangamo Journal urges the Whigs to pass up Clay and Webster and nominate Harrison for President.

December 3, 1838—Lincoln attends the opening of the Eleventh General Assembly at Vandalia, and as the Whig nominee for speaker is beaten on the fourth ballot by W. L. D. Ewing, 38 to 47 votes, but continues as Whig leader on the floor of the House.

January 16, 1839—Lincoln drafts a bill establishing the counties of Menard, Logan, and Dane, which in due course is amended and passed by both branches of the General Assembly.

January 17, 1839—Lincoln from the finance committee reports a plan to pay for internal improvements by the purchase and resale of Federal lands, but the report is tabled to be later referred to a special committee of which Lincoln is made chairman.

February 27, 1839—At an evening meeting of Whigs Lincoln suggests a committee of nine to draft an address to the people arraigning in detail the misrule of the Van Buren administration. His suggestion is adopted and he is made a member of the committee.

March 2, 1839—The General Assembly adjourns and Lincoln returns to Springfield.

April 23, 1839—At Carthage Lincoln participates in the defense of William Fraim charged with murder. The jury convicts Fraim.

June 24, 1839—Lincoln is elected to succeed Samuel H. Treat on the town board of Springfield, and serves until April, 1840, when Springfield begins to operate under its city charter.

September, 1839—Lincoln meets Mary Todd, cousin of his partner, John Todd Stuart and his future wife.

October 8, 1839—The first Whig state convention, which had assembled the previous day chooses Lincoln as a presidential elector and appoints him to a state central committee of five members, thus making him a leader of Whig activities in Illinois.

October 19, 1839—Lincoln requests a summons in his first case in the United States Circuit Court to which he is admitted to practice by Judge Pope on December 3.

November 2, 1839—Stuart leaves to take his seat in Congress, and his partner cheerfully enters in the firm's fee book, "Commncement of Lincoln's Administration."

November 18, 1839—Beginning of a week of political debate between Whig and Democratic leaders which is closed by Lincoln on December 26 in a carefully framed address of which he makes large use in the presidential campaign the following year.

December 9, 1839—Called in special session by Governor Carlin the General Assembly meets for the first time in Springfield and Lincoln is again Whig leader in the House.

December 23, 1839—Lincoln writes Stuart that Douglas is in town but is "not now worth talking about."

February 1, 1840—The first of seventeen numbers of The Old Soldier, a Whig campaign sheet of which Lincoln is one of the editors, is published from the office of the Sangamo Journal.

February 3, 1840—The General Assembly adjourns, and Lincoln writes Stuart that "it has done nothing of importance."

February 10, 1840—Lincoln addresses a Whig mass meeting at Peoria, the first of three score speeches for Harrison he is to deliver during the campaign.

March 14, 1840—The Sangamon County Whig convention nominates Lincoln for another term in the General Assembly.

March 17, 1840—Lincoln and Douglas argue the issues of the day at Jacksonville.

May 23, 1840—At Clinton Lincoln successfully defends Spencer Turner indicted for murder and receives for his fee a ninety-day note for $200.

June 13, 1840—As a member of the Whig State Central Committee Lincoln helps to prepare an address to the people of Illinois in behalf of Harrison which is published in The Old Soldier and then issued as a pamphlet.

June 18, 1840—Lincoln makes one of his first arguments before the Illinois Supreme Court, appearing for the defendant in the suit of Scammon vs. Cline.

August 3, 1840—Lincoln is re-elected to the General Assembly, but by a reduced majority.

November, 1840—Lincoln and Mary Todd after a hectic courtship enter into an engagement to marry.

November 2, 1840—Harrison is elected President, but the Democrats, to the chagrin of Lincoln and the joy of Douglas, who has wrought valiantly for his party, carry Illinois.

November 23, 1840—Lincoln attends the opening of a called session of the General Assembly.

December 5, 1840—For party reasons Lincoln and his friend Joseph Gillespie by jumping out of a window strive unsuccessfully to prevent a quorum and an adjournment of the Legislature.

December 7, 1840—Lincoln attends the meeting of the House for the second session of the Twelfth Gneral Assembly and again is Whig leader on the floor.

UNCOLLECTED WORKS OF ABRAHAM LINCOLN

CHAPTER I

THROUGH YOUTH TO MANHOOD

SURVEY OF PERIOD

Born on February 12, 1809, in what is now La Rue County, Kentucky, the son of Thomas and Nancy Hauks Lincoln, Abraham Lincoln was taken by his parents to Indiana at the age of seven, and in the latter state he secured such scanty education as fell to his lot prior to 1830 when the Lincolns migrated to Illinois. The story of Mr. Lincoln's first twenty-one years is set forth with brevity and restraint in the third-person autobiography which he gave to John Locke Scripps in June, 1860, shortly after his nomination for the Presidency. "Before leaving Kentucky," he wrote, "he and his sister were sent, for short periods to A.B.C. schools, the first kept by Zachariah Riney, and the second by Caleb Hazel. . . . Abraham now thinks that the aggregate of all his schooling did not amount to one year. He was never in a college or academy as a student, and never inside of a college or academy building till since he had a law license. What he has in the way of education he has picked up. After he was twenty-three and had separated from his father he studied English grammar — imperfectly of course, but so as to speak and write as well as he now does. He studied and nearly mastered the six books of Euclid since he was a member of Congress. . . . When he was nineteen, still residing in Indiana, he made his first trip on a flatboat to New Orleans. He was a hired hand merely, and with a son of the owner who, with other assistance, made the trip. March 1, 1830, Abraham having just completed his twenty-first year, his father and family, with the families of the two daughters and sons-in-law of his stepmother, left the old homestead in Indiana and came to Illinois." (Mr. Lincoln earlier records that a year after the death of his mother in 1818 his father married at Elizabethtown, Kentucky, Mrs.

Sarah Johnston, a widow with three children, and that "she proved a good and kind mother" to him.)

The Lincoln migration to Illinois was made in wagons drawn by ox-teams. Young Lincoln drove one of the teams, and there has come down to us a characteristic incident of the journey which remained vivid in his memory after thirty years. While in attendance in May, 1860, at the Republican state convention at Decatur which proposed him as a candidate for President, Mr. Lincoln was introduced by Jesse K. Dubois to Peter Smith of Lawrence County, Illinois. What he said to Smith was set forth in a letter which the latter on July 17, 1860, addressed to an Ohio cousin, J. Warren Kiefer, and which is now owned by the Abraham Lincoln Life Foundation of Fort Wayne, Indiana. "Lincoln gave me a very cordial greeting," Smith wrote his kinsman, "and entered into conversation as an old friend and acquaintance. After conversing a while said I to him, 'Lincoln there is a rumor in circulation in our region about you and I want you to tell me all about it.' 'Well' said he, 'what is it?' 'About thirty years ago rumor says that Abraham Lincoln was seen walking barefoot driving an ox team with ox waggon moving a family through our town of Lawrenceville — is that true?' . . . . " 'In part' says Lincoln. 'About 30 years ago I did drive my father's family through your town of Lawrenceville and I was afoot but not barefoot. In my younger days I frequently went barefooted but on that occasion I had on a substantial pair of shoes — it was a cold day in March and I never went barefoot in cold weather. I will remember that trip thro' your Country as long as I live. I crossed the Wabash at Vincennes and the river being high the road on the low prairie was covered with water a half mile at a stretch and the water covered with ice — the only means by which I could keep the road was by observing the stakes on each side placed as guides when the water is over the road.

" 'When I came to the water I put a favorite fist (fice) dog I had along into the waggon and got in myself and whipped up my oxen and started into the water to pick my way across as well as I could — after breaking the ice and wading about ¼ of a mile my little dog jumped out of the waggon and the ice being thin he broke through and was struggling for life. I could not bear to lose my dog and I jumped out of the waggon and waided waist deep in the ice and water, got hold of him and helped him out and saved him'."

"His father and family," Mr. Lincoln wrote in 1860, *"settled on the north side of the Sangamon River, about ten miles westerly from Decatur. Here they built a log cabin, . . . and made sufficient of rails to fence ten acres of ground, fenced and broke the ground, and raised a crop of sown corn upon it the same year."* The succeeding winter, the winter of the deep snow, *"Abraham, together with his step-mother's son, John D. Johnston, and John Hanks, hired themselves to Denton Offutt, to take a flatboat from Beardstown to New Orleans, and for that purpose were to join him — Offutt — at Springfield as soon as the snow should go off. When it did go, which was about the first of March, the country was so flooded as to make traveling by land impracticable; to obviate which difficulty they purchased a large canoe and came down the Sangamon River in it. They found Offutt at Springfield, but learned from him that he had failed in getting a boat at Beardstown. This led to their hiring themselves to him for twelve dollars per month each, and getting the timber out of the trees and building a boat at Old Sangamon town, seven miles northwest of Springfield, which boat they took to New Orleans.*

"During this boat-enterprise acquaintance with Offutt, who was previously an entire stranger, he conceived a liking for Abraham, and believing he could turn him to good account, he contracted with him to act as clerk for him, on his return from New Orleans, in charge of a store and mill at New Salem. Hanks had not gone to New Orleans, but having a family, and being likely to be detained from home longer than at first expected, had turned back from St. Louis." Meanwhile Thomas Lincoln and his wife had *"removed from Macon to Coles County. John D. Johnston, went to them, and Abraham stopped indefinitely, and for the first time, as it were, by himself at New Salem. This was in July, 1831, and here he rapidly made friends and acquaintances."*

While he still dwelt in Indiana young Lincoln had become an eager and constant reader of the newspapers, a habit that was to remain with him at New Salem, Vandalia, and Springfield on the circuit and in Congress, and until the end of his days as President. Thus in February, 1837, before he set out for Illinois, he must have read of the great debate the previous month between Webster and Hayne in the Senate at Washington, and taken to heart the uplifting pledge of the deep-voiced senator from Massachusetts — *"Liberty and Union, now and*

*forever, one and inseparable" — a pledge that, as the years were
to bear witness, was to shape his own political creed.*

YOUTHFUL DOGGEREL

*The earliest writing of Abraham Lincoln, which has been
spared by time, dates from his brief and interrupted school days
in Spencer County, Indiana. It was the surmise of Dr. William
E. Barton that the first of the two youthful jingles given below—
written by Lincoln no less than five times—he learned from his
father, Thomas Lincoln, who had been employed to guard one
James Wilson, when the latter was awaiting trial in Kentucky on
a charge of counterfeiting. Wilson, who used this jingle, was
held not guilty of the charge against him, and his daughter later
married John Hanks who in 1830 split rails with Abraham Lincoln, in Macon County, Illinois, an association which thirty years
later was to have a memorable sequel. The second jingle, dated
1824, was written on a torn page of Lincoln's Sum Book.*

Abraham Lincoln,
His hand and pen
He will be good,
But God knows when.

Abraham Lincoln is my name
And with my pen I wrote the same;
I wrote in both haste and speed
And left it here for fools to read.

YOUNG LINCOLN'S BOOK OF EXAMPLES
IN ARITHMETIC, 1824-1826

*It is probable that a page from an old arithmetic copybook
made by Abraham Lincoln when attending school in Indiana,
contains the earliest known signature of the future President.
This homemade copybook has had wide dispersal, and it is now
possible to locate only a few of its mutilated pages. "I was collecting the facts of Mr. Lincoln's life in 1865-6," William Henry
Herndon, Mr. Lincoln's partner and future biographer, wrote
to a friend on November 9, 1881, "and went into Coles County,
Illinois, to see his step-mother; found the motherly, good old*

lady, and took down her testimony, etc. as material of his life. During her examination she let drop in her conversation, the fact that Mr. Lincoln when a boy had two copyboooks, in (one of) which he wrote down his sums worked out, and wrote out in his literary one what seemed to him strong, beautiful or good. We, the Lincoln family and myself, commenced the search, and found the arithmetical book, but not the other; it is gone, and gone forever."

The arithmetic book consisted of nine-by-twelve pages of plain paper, sewed together with a string on one of the longer edges, and probably once contained as many as a hundred pages. However, when Mr. Herndon first saw the book there were only a few pages remaining, and he was told by Mr. Lincoln's stepmother that "originally it contained more leaves but that the greater number had been lost or destroyed." According to one tradition, Thomas Johnston, a son of John D. Johnston, Mr. Lincoln's stepbrother, "sold part of it at least, page by page, during the war."

Be this as it may, Mr. Herndon took with him when he returned to Springfield from his visit with Sarah Bush Lincoln all that was left of the book, and the dispersal of this remnant began without delay. One page was given by Mr. Herndon to Charles Henry Hart of Philadelphia, and a second he presented on November 9, 1881, to the Soldiers' Memorial Association of Englewood, Illinois. Prior to 1884, Isaac Newton Arnold of Chicago, devoted friend of Mr. Lincoln and another of his biographers, became the owner of several pages. When the Lincoln Memorial Collection was exhibited in Chicago in 1886 its printed catalogue of manuscripts acquired listed three pages of the sum book. And on July 22, 1893, the New York Times mentioned John E. Remsburg of Atchison, Kansas, as the owner of two pages. But the greater number of pages distributed by Mr. Herndon, perhaps a full half dozen, went to Jesse W. Weik, who was associated with him in the preparation of his biography of Mr. Lincoln. There follows, substantially in the order of their appearance in the original book, all that is known of the present whereabouts of a majority of the pages given to Mr. Herndon by Sarah Bush Lincoln:

1 Leland (a) — This leaf, presented to Charles Henry Hart by Mr. Herndon, bears the title, "Multiplication 1824", and on both sides of it appears the full name of Abraham Lincoln, in all probability his earliest extant autograph. Major Lam-

bert and other Lincoln collectors were successive owners of this page before it passed into the hands of Wilfred C. Leland, Jr. of Detroit.

2. Library of Congress — This page has the caption "Substraction of Long Measure" and at the bottom, "Abraham Lincoln, his hand and pen he will be good, but God knows when". This page appears to have passed from Herndon to Weik and finally through Gabriel Wells of New York to the Library of Congress.

3. Barrett (a) A half-page fragment, now owned by Oliver R. Barrett of Chicago, contains the familiar phrasing "Abraham Lincoln, his hand and pen", to which is added a few lines beginning, "Time what an Empty Vapor 'Tis."

4. Barrett (b) A page also owned by Mr. Barrett, formerly in the possession of James W. Keyes and sold at the auction in 1894 of the Lincoln Memorial Collection, has on one side the caption "Compound Multiplication", and on the reverse side "To Exercise Multiplication" with the printed form "ABRAHAM LINCOLN, HIS BOOK" at the bottom of the page. A written example on this page suggests young Lincoln's use of Daboll's Arithmetic, Page 52.

5. Brown University — Another half-page fragment has on one side the caption "The Single Rule of Three", and on the reverse side questions and answers about proportion.

6. Chicago Historical Society — One of the pages formerly owned by Isaac Newton Arnold which has on one side the caption "Interest on Money" and on the other side "Discount March 1, 1826". The page on discount is one of the best examples of young Lincoln's use of Daboll as one of the sources of his copy book, its rules and definitions being very like those found on Page 135 of Daboll's Arithmetic. Although none of the pages under discussion reveals a close similarity to the later penmanship of Mr. Lincoln, this page has the closest resemblance to his handwriting in his manhood years.

7. Leland (b) This page was once owned by Major Lambert and was included in the auction of his famous collection, passing finally to the late Henry Leland and then to his son, Wilfred C. Leland, Jr. It gives as a caption on one side "Examples in Compound Interest", but the contents of the reverse side are unknown.

8. Columbia University — Photostat of what is believed by many students to have been the first page of the copybook.

One side is headed "Multiplication 1824" and the reverse side "Multiplication Continued". Both sides have been said to contain the name of young Lincoln, but the copy of the page now in the Columbia University Library bears no sign of a name, and it is possible that the "Abraham Lincoln Book" of the reverse side may be his earliest known autograph.

Al of the pages and half-pages here considered indicate that Mr. Lincoln's mathematical inclining as a boy was out of the ordinary, and had not a little to do with his success as a surveyor in later years. They make it clear that he was familiar with the contents of the text books of both Pike and Daboll, but, except in one or two instances, he does not make exact use of them; all of which indicates that the examples in his copybook first had been arranged and presented by his teacher. There has been selected for reproduction in this place the page of the copybook headed Subtraction of Long Measure.
See Lincoln Lore, No. 596, September 9, 1840.

Subtraction of Long Measure

L   M   f   P   y   f   I   B
71—1—3—10   48—0— 1—2
44—2—5—16   12—0— 3—1
———————   —————————
21—1—5—34   36—0—10—1
                     Subr.

———————   —————————
71—1—3—10   48—0—1—2

of Land Measure

———————   ———————   ———————

———————   ———————   ———————

A   R   P   A   R   P   A   R   P
    4   40   4   40   4   40
————————   ————————   ————————
12—1—10   17—3—17   28—1— 7
5—3—17   12—3—23   19—1—28
————————   ————————   ————————
6—1—33   4—3—34   8—3—19
————————   ————————   ————————
12—1—10   17—3—17   28—1—7

of Dry Measure

Ch	B	P		C	C	p		g	B	P
36	—	4		36	—	4		8	—	4
17	—2	—1		40	— 1	—2		19	—1	—1
10	—1	—3		16	— 5	—1		12	—7	—2
7	—0	—2		23	—32	—1		6	—1	—3
17	—2	—1		40	— 1	—2		19	—1	—1

Which are the Denominations of long measure

A

3 Barley cnns. or Bc makes	1 Inch	in
4 Inches	1 hand	hd
12 Inches	1 foot	ft
3 feet	1 yard	yd
6 feet	1 fathom	yd
5 yards ,and 1 half	1 Rod pole or pearch	
408 poles	1 furlong	fu
8 furlongs	1 mile	M
3 miles	1 league	1
60 miles	1 Degree Deg	

M	F	P		Y	F	T
17	—7	—19		14	—2	— 7
16	—1	—14		16	—0	— 4
19	—1	—16		19	—1	—10
17	—1	—19		16	—2	— 4
12	—1	—11		14	—2	— 5
18	—1	—16		14	—2	— 1
19	—7	—14		31	—1	— 3
16	—6	—26		11	—0	— 1
136	—4	—15		139	—0	—11
118	—4	—36		124	—1	— 4
136	—4	—15		139	—0	—11

17	2	6	14		16	1	10	0
12	1	1	18		14	2	4	1
16	2	1	16		17	1	11	2
19	2	7	11		13	2	7	1
19	0	1	31		16	1	4	2

17	2	1	12		17	1		1
12	1	2	14		19	2	0	2
19	1	1	14		19	2	1	2
36	2	2	10		36	0	10	2
115	2	3	36			0	10	2
133	2	2	10			0	10	0

THE CHRONICLES OF REUBEN

During Lincoln's last days in Indiana one of the few personal enmities of his career had issue in a ribald and lusty lampoon to which he gave the title The Chronicles of Reuben. In January, 1828, Lincoln's sister Sarah, who in August, 1826, at the age of nineteen had married Aaron, the son of Reuben Grigsby, a leading farmer of the neighborhood, died in childbirth, and the brother, grieving sorely at her death, declared it had been due in large measure to the neglect of her husband and his family. Thus was bred an antagonism which took on a sharper edge when in the spring of 1829 two sons of Reuben Grigsby, Reuben, Jr. and Charles, were married on the same day to Betsy Ray and Matilda Hawkins, and Lincoln was not invited to the wedding or the infare that followed it.

In hot anger twenty-year old Abraham, with a confederate, planned a confusion of brides and grooms to follow the wedding festivities and to be set right as soon as the joke was known to the guests. All befell as contrived and Lincoln wrote an account of the wedding, infare and mixup, phrased in imitation of Old Testament narrative, which he dropped by the roadside and which was found, as the writer purposed, by a member of the Grigsby family. News of its contents spread swiftly through the countryside to be talked over and laughed about and to be committed to memory by neighbors who delighted to repeat it, when opportunity offered, as long as they lived. The victims of the satire however, were able in time to recall its contents without resentment. "Yes, they did have a joke on us," Betsy Ray in 1865 informed Herndon. "They said my man got into the wrong room, and Charles got into my room. But it wasn't so. Lincoln wrote that for mischief. Abe and my man often laughed about it."

It is to be noted in closing that another of the individuals for whom the writer harbored just resentment had a place in The

Chronicles of Reuben. "Chief among them all was Josiah, blowing his bugle," had reference to the unsightly nose of farmer Josiah Crawford, the same Crawford who once loaned young Lincoln a copy of Weems' "Life of Washington." When rain came in at the chinks of the loft of the cabin, where the borrower read and slept, soaking through the book, to pay for it, young Lincoln, for two days, pulled fodder for Crawford—an over liberal measure of compensation that long had an unpleasant place in his memory.

Now there was a man whose name was Reuben, and the same was very great in substance; in horses and cattle and swine, and a very great household. It came to pass when the sons of Reuben grew up that they were desirous of taking to themselves wives, and being too well known as to honor in their own country they took a journey into a far country and there procured for themselves wives. It came to pass also that when they were about to make the return home they sent a messenger before them to bear the tidings to their parents. These, enquiring of the messenger what time their sons and wives would come, made a great feast and called all their kinsmen and neighbors in and made great preparations. When the time drew nigh they sent out two men to meet the grooms and their brides with a trumpet to welcome them and to accompany them. When they came near unto the house of Reuben, the father, the messenger came on before them and gave a shout, and the whole multitude ran out with shouts of joy and music, playing on all kinds of instruments. Some were playing on harps, some on viols, and some blowing on ram's horns. Some also were casting dust and ashes toward heaven, and chief among them all was Josiah, blowing his bugle and making sound so great the neighboring hills and valleys echoed with the resounding acclamation. When they had played and their harps had sounded till the grooms and brides approached the gates, Reuben, the father, met them and welcomed them to his house. The wedding feast being now ready they were all invited to sit down and eat, placing the bridegrooms and their wives at each end of the table. Waiters were then appointed to serve and wait on the guests. When all had eaten and were full and merry they went out again and played and sung till night, and dispersed, each going to his own home. The family then took seats with their waiters to converse while preparations were being made in an upper chamber for the brides and grooms to be conveyed to their beds. This being done the waiters took the two brides upstairs, placing one in a bed at the right hand of the stairs and the other on the left. The waiters came down, and Nancy the mother then gave directions to the waiters of the bridegrooms, and they took them upstairs but placed them in the wrong beds. The waiters then all came downstairs. But the mother being fearful of a mistake, made enquiry of the waiters, and learning the true facts took the light and sprang upstairs. It came to pass she ran to one of the beds and exclaimed, "O Lord, Reuben, you are in bed with the wrong wife." The young men, both alarmed at this, sprang up out of bed and ran with such violence against each other, they came near knocking each other down. The tumult gave evidence to those below that the mistake was certain. At last they all came down and had a long conversation about who made the mistake, but it could not be decided. So endeth the chapter.

PETITION SIGNED BY LINCOLN FOR CHANGE
OF POLLING PLACE

In August, 1941, Edwin Davis discovered in the office of the county clerk at Decatur, Illinois, an election petition dated May 26, 1830, and granted on June 7, 1830 by the Commissioners of the Macon County Court, which contains among the forty-five signers the signature of A. Lincoln—his earliest known writing as a citizen of Illinois and the earliest signature after he became of age that has been spared to us. A few weeks before, March 15, 1830, Thomas Lincoln, coming from Indiana, had located on the north bank of the Sangamon River, ten miles southwest of Decatur, and with relatives of both his first and second wives residing close at hand. The signatures of several of them, along with that of Abraham Lincoln, appear on the petition requesting a more central location for the polling place in Decatur Precinct.

One of the things about which Illinois people were talking in the late May days of 1830, when young Lincoln signed this petition, was the resolute manner in which President Jackson was thwarting South Carolina's threat of secession under the inspiration and leadership of John C. Calhoun. Perhaps the newcomer to Illinois then read for the first time newspaper accounts of the ringing toast offered by Jackson at a Jefferson Day dinner in Washington on April 15, 1830—"Our Federal Union; it must be perserved," a pledge which helped to shape Lincoln's political

*creed, and which a generation later was to be the foundation
stone of his policy as President.*

PETITION

To the Hon County Comm Court for the County of Macon

We the undersigned, qualified voters in Decatur Precinct,
earnestly request your honor to change the present place of holding Elections in said Precinct from Permenias Smallwoods to
the Court house in Decatur.

26th May 1830

David Miller	James Martin
Thomas Law	H. I. Armstrong
Saml. D. Dewees	Henry Ewing
D. H. Stewart	Joseph Stevens
S. R. Sheppard	John Grimsley
John Miller	Andrew W. Smith
M. C. Shaw	Thomas Cowan
Charles Lewis	I. C. Pugh
S. Sinnett	James Miller
Robert Stewart	Philip D. Williams
John Dickey	Buel Stevens
William Dickey	David Florey
William Hall	Moses Hand
J. B. Brown	David Owen
Squire Hall	Randolph Rose
William Hanks	Isaac Miller
Thomas Cole	Jas. Johnson
John Biglow	John Ballard
Landy Harell	Phillip Ballard
Alfred Hall	John Hanks
William F. Horen	John D. Johnston
John Pettyjohn	A. Lincoln
Reuben Brown	
Endorsement	

Granted the 7th
June 1830

Filed this 7th June
1830

Change of place of
voting in Decatur
precinct

LINCOLN'S FIRST POLITICAL SPEECH IN ILLINOIS, DECATUR, JULY OR AUGUST, 1830

Lincoln made his first political speech in Illinois during a campaign meeting held in Decatur in July or August, 1830. Lincoln passed the greater part of 1830 at the Macon County home of his kinsman Charles Hanks, helping the latter with a double team of oxen to break prairie. He was thus engaged when William L. D. Ewing and John F. Posey, candidates for the Legislature, came to Decatur to speak, and Hanks and Lincoln took time off to listen to them. The rest of the story is told in the campaign life of Lincoln by William Dean Howells, which, in due time, won its author the post of consul at Venice.

Posey writes Howells "in violation of venerable precedent and sacred etiquette, failed to invite the sovereigns to drink something. They were justly indignant, and persuaded Lincoln to reply, in the expectation that he would possibly make himself offensive to Posey. Lincoln, however, took the stump with characteristic modesty, and begging his friends not to laugh if he broke down, treated very courteously the two speakers who had preceded him, discussed questions of politics, and in his peroration eloquently pictured the future of Illinois. There was sense and reason in his arguments and his imaginative flight tickled the State pride of the Illinoisans. It was declared that Lincoln had made the best speech of the day; and he, to his great astonishment, found himself a prophet among those of his own household, while his titled fellow orators cordially complimented his performance."

A few weeks after the Howells volume came from the press Lincoln, at the request of a friend—Samuel C. Parks of the town of Lincoln—went carefully through its pages and with a pencil made marginal corrections of occasional errors, but he made no change in or addition to its account of his speech in front of Renshaw's store in Decatur. Macon County pioneers, however, long held to the belief that his remarks included an earnest plea for the inprovement of the Sangamon River for purposes of navigation—a significant detail which prompts regret that Lincoln, less fortunate than Dr. Johnson, in the summer of 1830, had no Boswell at hand to report him.

APPRAISAL OF AN ESTRAY SIGNED BY LINCOLN, DECEMBER 16, 1830

The document reproduced below, bearing the signature of Lincoln, was discovered in the archives of Macon County, Illinois, in the summer of 1941 by Edwin D. Davis. In Illinois a century ago whenever an animal strayed from its owner, and was found, the person taking possession of the stray went before a justice of the peace and a full description of the animal was recorded and advertised. The value of the stock was also estimated by some disinterested party. It was in the capacity of appraisers that Lincoln and Reed signed the following affirmation.

A few days before Lincoln and Reed appraised the mare taken up by J. B. Brown, the elder Francis P. Blair on December 7, 1830, had founded the Washington Globe, a journal a few years later most carefully and prayerfully read by the postmaster of New Salem. And in time to come the founder and editor of The Globe was to have an intimate and now and again influential part in shaping Mr. Lincoln's course as President.

We the signers having been called to appraise an Estray Mare Taken up by Jonathen B. Brown on Monday the 12th day of Dec. 1830. Do find horse to be four years old next Spring a bright bay 14 hands high a Small blaze and a stripe in her face, right foot white right fore foot with a white stripe down the hough and white hairs around the edge of the hough no brands perceivable black mane and tail appraised to 30 Dollars. Sworn under our hands this 16th day of December 1830.

A Lincoln
John W. reed

CHAPTER II — LINCOLN IN THE YEAR 1831

SURVEY OF PERIOD

Aside from the trip to New Orleans with its second arresting contact with slavery, and settlement in July at New Salem with its contact with a larger world, its new and helpful friends and its early entrance into politics, Abraham Lincoln's twenty-third year brought other events of personal or general import which were to help shape his own career and the history of an eventful period. The year was marked by the winter of the deep snow, long to remain a poignant memory with Illinois pioneers, while in Boston on January 1, William Lloyd Garrison, four years older than Abraham Lincoln, with paper bought on credit and type set by his own hand, issued the first number of The Liberator, and began his long and unrelenting fight against slavery. It is doubtful if copies of The Liberator ever reached New Salem; it never won more than a modest circulation, and it was kept afloat through the years by gifts from wealthy supporters. Moreover, Garrison, narrow of outlook and harsh of speech, had an unrivalled gift for the making of new enemies rather than the retention of old friends of moderate inclining; but he was a natural journalist and for a generation never for a moment stayed his efforts to arouse the people of the North to the mood, which in the end brought the creation of the Republican Party and the election of Abraham Lincoln to the Presidency. And in making final estimate of men and measures, it is well to recall that in the days that tried men's souls the troubled occupant of the White House had no more loyal nor understanding friend than William Lloyd Garrison.

May, 1831, brought to these shores a gifted young Frenchman, Alexis de Tocqueville by name, whose acute and penetrating study in two volumes of Democracy in America, duly translated into English, was to be read and pondered by Abraham Lincoln and his partner, William Henry Herndon. On August 21, 1831, came the insurrection in Southampton County, Virginia, led by the bondman Nat Turner, which, with its heavy destruction of property and loss of innocent lives, shook slavery to its foundations, and alarmed and startled the people of the North as well as of the South. And in the newspapers which came to New Salem, young Abraham Lincoln, with sober earnestness, must have read how on December 12, 1831, the vener-

able John Quincy Adams had presented fifteen petitions against slavery to the lower house of Congress, and set afoot with growing determination his long fight, not against human bondage but for the right of petition.

Finally at a convention in Baltimore, also on December 12, 1831, the National Republican Party which three years later, at the instance of James Watson Webb, was to take the name of Whig, nominated for President Henry Clay, the leader long most admired by Abraham Lincoln.

PETITION FOR CONSTABLE, MARCH 11, 1831

The appended petition which appears to have been drawn by its first signer, Hiram Watson, presents an interesting if minor Lincoln problem. It seems to have been intended for presentation to the commissioners of Sangamon County in March, 1831, but Lincoln made his first appearance in New Salem in late April or early May of that year, when with his employer, Denton Offutt, and his kinsmen, John Hanks and John D. Johnston, he halted there on the first stage of a memorable flatboat journey to New Orleans. This journey accomplished, he returned to New Salem in late July, 1831, to become a clerk in the store Offutt had decided to set up in that village. Therefore it must have been in March, 1831, while at a point on the Sangamon a few miles northwest of the hamlet of Springfield Lincoln was engaged in building a boat for the New Orleans trip, that he signed his own and the names of Hanks and Johnston to this petition to the Sangamon Commissioners for the appointment of a constable. There were in all twenty-nine signers and Lincoln's name is the twenty-fourth on the list—his second known signature to a document after his removal to Illinois. The original of this petition is now in the Illinois State Historical Library at Springfield.

The Honorable the county commissioners Court of Sangamon County at the March term for 1831—

We the undersigned citizens would represent to your Honorable body that whereas it (is) represented to us that there is a vacancy in the office of constable in the Springfield district, and whereas the statute in such cases made and provided authorises your Honorable Court to fill such vacancy up on petition—

We therefore request you to fill said vacancy with some suitable person.

LINCOLN WITNESSES A BILL OF SALE, OCTOBER 20, 1831

On October 20, 1831, a few weeks after his settlement in New Salem, Lincoln signed as witness the following bill of sale by which James Richardson conveyed to John Ferguson the New Salem ferry which a short time before he had taken over from William Clary.

This is to certify that I have sould all my Rite and title to the New Salem ferry to John Ferguson this 20th of October 1831.

James Richerson

A. Lincoln, witness

EARLIEST LEGAL DOCUMENT LINCOLN IS KNOWN TO HAVE WRITTEN

It was in late July, 1831, that Abraham Lincoln, then in his twenty-third year, settled in New Salem as clerk in the grocery store of Denton Offutt. He was soon called upon to perform services of various sorts for residents of the village and neighborhood, and one of these services was the drafting on November 12, 1831, of an agreement between James Eastep and Solomon Teter, perhaps with the aid of a book of forms loaned him by his friend Bowling Green, justice of the peace. The original of this, the earliest legal document which Lincoln is known to have written, is now owned by Mrs. Gussie Samuell of Chicago.

Know all men by these presents that I James Eastep am held and firmly bound in the penal sum of twenty Dollars unto Solomon Teter for the conveyance of a certain tract or parcel of land it being the part of a certain tract (situated in St. Clair County and State of Illinois) which falls to my wife as an heir of Abraham Teter deceased.

The condition of the above obligation is such—If the said James Eastep shall make a good and lawful patent to said Teter for the aforesaid parcel of land by the twelfth day of November in the year of our Lord one thousand eight hundred and thirty-six the above obligation is to be null void and of no effect— Otherwise to Remain in full force and Virtue at law.

In testimony whereof the said James Eastep has hereunto

set his hand and seal this twelfth day of November in the year of our Lord one thousand eight hundred and thirty-one.

James Easter (Seal)

Attest
A. Lincoln

CHAPTER III — LINCOLN IN THE YEAR 1832

SURVEY OF PERIOD

The year 1832, in which fell the twenty-fourth birthday of Abraham Lincoln, was to prove for him another period of broader outlooks and widening experiences. Early in the year the store and milling ventures of young Lincoln's visionary employer, Denton Offutt, ended in failure and Offutt's managing clerk was out of a job; but the latter promptly turned to other modest means of support; borrowed and read every book he could find within a radius of a dozen miles, and on March 9, 1832, prompted by some of the good friends he had made during his seven months in New Salem, announced himself as a candidate for a seat in the lower branch of the Illinois Legislature, setting forth his claims in a hand bill in which he championed improvement of the Sangamon River and more and better schools.

Young Lincoln had just begun his canvass for the General Assembly when he was selected as one of the pilots of the steamboat Talisman in its slow and difficult passage up the Sangamon from Beardstown to a point near Springfield, in a widely advertised effort to prove it a navigable river. The undertaking brought bankruptcy to its projector and disappointment to the hundreds who hoped for its success, but it won for Pilot Lincoln a fresh contingent of helpful friends. His canvass for the Legislature, however, was unexpectedly interrupted by the uprising of Black Hawk and his warriors, and a period of military service which lasted until the end of July. Then he resumed it with energy, speaking with effect at various rallies, and, although at the election August 6, a fortnight after his return from the field, he stood eighth in a list of thirteen candidates for the General Assembly, he received all but seven of the votes cast in New Salem.

Young Lincoln's feet were now firmly planted on the first rung of the political ladder, and his interest in politics was quickened by what, with a growing sense of their significance, he read in the journals that came to New Salem, of developments in Washington where, during 1832, Jackson's masterful Presidency reached a climax in his veto of a bill to renew the charter of the Bank of the United States, his swift and stern rebuke of South Carolina's attempts to nullify federal laws, and his own triumphant election over Henry Clay to a second term. But for young Abraham Lincoln in New Salem the outstanding event of 1832 was the beginning of his friendship with Major John Todd Stuart, who induced him to study law and in due course was to make him his partner — an association that was to have an important and shaping part in his future activities.

LINCOLN WRITES BILL OF SALE FOR JOHN FERGUSON

The original of this bill of sale, all in Lincoln's handwriting except the signature, is now in the Illinois State Historical Library. Ferguson was one of half a dozen men who in quick succession owned and operated the ferry across the Sangamon at New Salem. He was also one of the redoubtable fighting men who dwelt in and about New Salem in that village's palmy days. Thomas relates that "Sam Hill, a small man himself, once offered a set of dishes to Ferguson—if he would whip Jack Armstrong, with whom Hill had had a quarrel. Ferguson accepted, and, being larger than Armstrong, finally won; but he took such punishment that he later declared that the dishes would have been dear at half the price." See Lincoln's New Salem by B. P. Thomas (Springfield, 1934), Page 26.

During the month in which this bill of sale was written word came to New Salem that at Baltimore on December 12, 1831, the National Republicans, soon to become the Whig Party, had nominated for President, Henry Clay, the leader for long most admired by young Mr. Lincoln. Perhaps more significant of future events, on the same day in the House at Washington, John Quincy Adams presented eighteen petitions from Pennsylvania asking for the abolition of slavery in the District of Columbia.

Know all men by these presents that I John Ferguson for and in consideration of the sum of thirty-five dollars have given granted bargained and sold all my right and title in and to the New Salem ferry in Sangamon County unto Alexander Trent.

In testimony whereof I have hereunto set my hand this 25th January 1832

John Ferguson

RECEIPT TO JAMES RUTLEDGE

This receipt was posted by a later owner on the fly-leaf of the copy of Kirkham's Grammar—English Grammar in Familiar

Lectures by Samuel Kirkham, Cincinnati, 1828—studied by Lincoln. The book was by him given to Ann Rutledge, and in turn studied by her and other members of her family.

Those were eventful times, and two days after this receipt was written an expedition led by Nathaniel Jarvis Wyeth left Boston to travel overland to Oregon and to play a decisive part in the settlement of that State.

> "Mr. James Rutledge please to pay the bearer
> David P. Nelson thirty dollars and this shall
> be your receipt for the same
> "March 8th 1832
> > A. Lincoln
> > for D. Offutt"

RECEIPT TO WILLIAM SAMPSON

The original of this interesting reminder of Lincoln's association with Denton Offutt is owned by James W. Bollinger of Davenport, Iowa.

> Received of William Sampson in full of all
> demands up to this day April 21, 1832.
> > A. Lincoln
> > for D. Offutt

MUSTER ROLL OF CAPTAIN A. LINCOLN'S COMPANY, MAY 27, 1832

On this muster roll appear the names of a number of men who had intimate association with Lincoln's New Salem days. The first sergeant of the company was Jack Armstrong of Clary's Grove, then and always his unswerving friend, and one of the corporals was William F. Berry, who after their return to New Salem was to become his partner in business with disastrous results. In the ranks were David M. Pantier, son of Lincoln's good friend in the hour of need, Uncle Jimmie Pantier, and David Rutledge, brother of Ann and afterward a leading lawyer of Petersburg.

Twenty-three year old Abraham Lincoln began his brief military career as captain of a company and ended it a private in the ranks. When the company of volunteers of which he was elected captain on April 21, 1832, was mustered out of service on May 27th he enlisted as a private in the company of Mounted

Rangers commanded by Captain Iles.   The mustering-in officer
was Lieutenant Robert Anderson with whom the young man from
New Salem was to have historic association in future years.
When the company of Mounted Rangers was in turn discharged
from service, Lincoln re-enlisted for thirty days as a private in
the Independent Spy Corps commanded by Captain Jacob M.
Early, New Salem preacher and physician, whose career was to
have an early and tragic end.   One of Lincoln's fellows in the
Early company was James Clyman who in one of the intervals
of his outstanding career as a mountain man resided for a time
in the New Salem neighborhood.   Clyman had been born in 1792
on a Virginia farm owned by George Washington and in their
campfire talks no doubt his New Salem comrade was told that
he had more than once seen the father of his country in the flesh.

Muster Roll of Captain A. Lincoln's Company of the 4th
Reg. of the Brigade of Mounted Volunteers commanded by Brig.
Gen. Samuel Whiteside Mustered out of Service at the Mouth
of Fox River May the 27th, 1832.

No.	Names	Rank	When Enrolled	Where Enrolled	Remarks
1	Abraham Lincoln	Captain	April 21	Sangamon City	
2	Samuel M. Thompson	1 Lieut.	April 21		Resigned 30 April
3	John Brannen	2 Lieut.	April 21		Absent on extra duty
4	John Armstrong	1 Serg.	April 21		
5	Tavner B. Anderson	2 Serg.	April 21		
6	George W. Foster	3 Serg.	April 21		Transferred to a foot company April 29
7	Abadiah Morgan	4 Serg.	April 21		Absent on furlough
8	Thomas Comb	1 Corp.	April 21		
9	John Plaster	2 Corp.	April 21		
10	William F. Berry	3 Corp.	April 21		
11	Alexander Trent	4 Corp.	April 21		
12	John Erwin	Private	April 21		Promoted to 3rd Sergeant in room of G. W. Foster April 29
13	John H. Houghton	Private	April 21		
14	Thomas Pierce	Private	April 21		
15	Samuel Tibbs	Private	April 21		
16	Henry Hadley	Private	April 21		
17	Samuel Dutton	Private	April 21		
18	Calvin Pierce	Private	April 21		
19	Joseph Tibbs	Private	April 21		

20	Wm. Kirkpatrick	Private April 21	Promoted from the ranks April 30th
21	Cyrus Elmore	Private April 21	
22	Elijah Pierce	Private April 21	
23	Lewis W. Farmer	Private April 21	
24	Bordry Matthews	Private April 21	
25	Ep. Sullivan	Private April 21	
26	Valentine Crete	Private April 21	
27	Charles Sulivan	Private April 21	
28	James Simmons	Private April 21	
29	Hugh Armstrong	Private April 21	Promoted to 1st Lieutenant April 30th
30	Allen King	Private April 21	
31	Joseph Dobson	Private April 21	
32	David Rankin	Private April 21	Transferred to a foot company May 19
33	Urbin Alexander	Private April 21	
34	Henry Cox	Private April 21	
35	Merritt M. Carman	Private April 21	
36	Royal Potter	Private April 21	
37	David M. Pantier		Absent on furlough
38	Joseph Hohimer	Private April 21	
39	George Warburton	Private April 21	
40	Evan T. Lamb	Private April 21	
41	Colardey Barnette	Private April 21	
42	John M. Rutledge	Private April 21	
43	William Cox	Private April 21	
44	Usil Meeker	Private April 21	Promoted from the ranks May 2nd
45	Richard Jones	Private April 21	
46	Charles Pierce	Private April 21	
47	James Clement	Private April 21	
48	John Y. Lane	Private April 21	
49	Richard Lane	Private April 21	
50	Royal Clary	Private April 21	
51	Pleasant Armstrong	Private April 21	
52	James Yardley	Private April 21	
53	David Rutledge	Private April 21	Absent without leave
54	Michall Plaster	Private April 21	Absent without leave
55	John Mounce	Private April 21	
56	Wm. Hohimer	Private April 21	
57	Isaac Anderson	Private April 21	
58	Wm. Marshall	Private April 21	
59	Wm. Cummins	Private April 21	Absent without leave
60	John Jones	Private April 21	
61	Travice Elmore	Private April 21	Transferred to a foot company April 29
62	Wm. Foster	Private April 21	

63	Nathan Drake	Private April 29	Beards-town	
64	Robert S. Plunkett	Private April 29	Beards-town	
65	Wm. T. Sprouce	Private April 29		Promoted from the ranks May 2
66	Wm. Clary	Private April 29		
67	Jacob Heaverer	Private April 29		
68	Isaac Guliher	Private May 19	Dixons ferry	

I certify on honour that this Muster Roll exhibits a true Statement of Captain A. Lincoln's Company of Mounted Volunteers of Illinois Militia on this day and that the remarks set opposite the names are accurate and just.

A. Lincoln, Capt.

REPUTED FIRST POLITICAL SPEECH OF LINCOLN, JULY, 1832

On November 5, 1864, the Illinois State Journal of Springfield printed the following paragraph probably written by William H. Herndon:

"The President of the United States made his maiden speech at Pappsville (or Richland) in the year 1832. He was then a Whig and was a candidate for the Legislature of this state. The speech is short and sensible. To understand why it is so short, the following facts will show: First, Mr. Lincoln was a young man, say 22 years of age, and timid. Secondly, his friends and opponents in the joint discussion had rolled the sun nearly down. Mr. Lincoln saw that it was not then a proper time to discuss the question full, and hence he cut his remarks short. The time according to W. H. Herndon's informant—who has kindly furnished this valuable reminiscence for us—was 1832; it may have been 1834. The President lived at the time with James A. Herndon, at Salem in Sangamon County, who heard the speech, talked about it, and knows the report to be correct."

Herndon printed this speech in the first edition of his Life of Lincoln, stating that it was delivered on the occasion of a public sale at Pappsville, a hamlet eleven miles west of Springfield. In those days candidates were always present at a public sale, and those in attendance counted on a series of speeches after the "vandoo", when aspirants for office took the auctioneer's place. The brevity of Lincoln's maiden effort at Pappsville, as indicated by the Illinois State Journal, was probably due to the fact that he spoke at the end of a long afternoon of oratory. Nicolay and Hay did not include it in the early editions of their Complete Works of Lincoln, perhaps because of their dislike for Herndon, and one may reasonably doubt if, either in public or private, Lincoln ever referred to himself as "humble Abraham."

An anecdote of Lincoln's appearance at Pappsville, preserved by Ida M. Tarbell, deserves a place in this note. While he was on the stand, she writes, "a fight broke out in his audience, and, observing that one of his friends was being worsted, he bounded into the group of contestants, seized the fellow who had his supporter down, threw him, according to tradition 'ten or twelve feet,' mounted the platform and finished his speech." The James A. Herndon referred to in the Illinois State Journal paragraph was a brother of J. Rowan Herndon, Lincoln's stout friend over a long period of years. "Row" Herndon attended the Pappsville sale—held in late July, 1832, after Lincoln's return from the Black Hawk War—and being set upon by friends of a man whom he had recently whipped was saved from disaster in the manner related by Miss Tarbell. See The Life of Abraham Lincoln by Ida M. Tarbell, New York, 1900, Volume I, Page 90, and Lincoln's New Salem by Benjamin P. Thomas, Springfield, 1834, Page 58.

It was also in the summer of 1832, July 13 to be exact, that Henry Rowe Schoolcraft reached and named Lake Itasca, and so effected discovery of the source of the Mississippi.

Fellow citizens, I suppose you all know who I am. I am humble Abraham Lincoln. I have been solicited by many friends to become a candidate for the Legislature. My politics are short and sweet, like the old woman's dance. I am in favor of a national bank. I am in favor of the internal-improvement system and a high protective tariff. These are my sentiments and political principles. If elected I shall be thankful; if not it will be all the same.

LINCOLN SPEAKS IN SPRINGFIELD,
AUGUST 4, 1832

On August 4, 1832, Lincoln and other candidates made their closing speeches of the campaign in the old court house in Springfield. There is no contemporary record of what Lincoln

said on this occasion, but on July 6, 1875, Stephen T. Logan, his
sometime partner and life-long friend, in an interview with
William H. Herndon gave arresting memories of the gift of
speech of the young man from New Salem at this period of his
career. "I never saw Lincoln," Logan told Herndon, "until he
came up here to make a speech . . . He was a very tall and
gawky and rough looking fellow then—his pantaloons didn't
meet his shoes by six inches. But after he began speaking I
became very much interested in him. He made a very sensible
speech. It was the time when Benton was running his theory
of a gold circulation. Lincoln was attacking Benton's theory
and I thought did it very well . . . The manner of Mr. Lincoln's
speech then was very much the same as his speeches in after
life—that is the same peculiar characteristics were apparent then,
though of course in after years he evinced both more knowledge
and experience. But he had then the same novelty and the
same peculiarity in presenting his ideas. He had the same in-
dividuality that he kept up through all his life."

The manuscript record of Logan's talk with Herndon is now
owned by the daughter of John Hay, Mrs. Alice Hay Wadsworth
of Geneseo, New York.

ELECTION RETURN WRITTEN BY LINCOLN AS CLERK, SEPTEMBER 20, 1832

The first civil office ever held by Lincoln was that of elec-
tion clerk, and the return made by him here reproduced was his
first offical document. The original is now on file in the county
clerk's office at Springfield. Nearly all of the men whose names
appear on it had intimate association with Lincoln during his
New Salem days or in after years. John Clary, who led the poll
for constable, was a resident of Clary's Grove, to which he gave
his name, and the first settler within the area of the present
Menard County. Clary's principal contestant John R. Herndon,
was "Row" Herndon, who sold his store to Berry and Lincoln,
and with whom Lincoln boarded for a time. James Rutledge
was one of the founders of New Salem and the father of Ann
Rutledge. Bowling Green, local Democratic leader and justice
of the peace, was also an unfailing and helpful friend of Lincoln,
before whom the latter prior to his admission to the bar argued
minor cases.

At an election held at the house of John McNeil in the New
Salem precinct in the County of Sangamon and State of Illinois

on the 20th day of September in the year of our Lord one thousand eight hundred and thirty-two the following named persons received the number of votes annexed to their respective names for Constable—

John Clark had Forty-one   Votes for Constable
John R. Herndon had Twenty-two   Votes for Constable
William McNeely had Thirteen   Votes for Constable
Baxter B. Berry had Nine   Votes for Constable
Edmund Green had Four   Votes for Constable

James Rutledge ⎫
Hugh Armstrong ⎬ Judges of the election
James White ⎭

Attest

A. Lincoln ⎫
William Green ⎬ Clerks of the election

I certify that the above Judges and clerks were qualified according to law.

Bowling Green, J. P.

September 20, 1832

CAPTAIN LINCOLN CERTIFIES TO THE SERVICE OF ONE OF HIS MEN

This certification was a printed form filled in by Captain Lincoln.

I certify, That Lewis W. Farmer volunteered and served as a private in the Company of Mounted Volunteers under my command, in the Regiment commanded by Col. Samuel M. Thompson, in the Brigade under the command of Generals S. Whiteside and H. Atkinson, called into the service of the United States by the Commander-in-Chief of the Militia of the State, for the protection of the North Western Frontier against an Invasion by the British Band of Sac and other tribes of Indians, —that he was enrolled on the 21st day of *April* 1832, and was Honorably Discharged on the *7th day of June,* thereafter, having served 48 days.

Given under my hand this 21st day of September, 1832.

A. Lincoln, Capt.

CAPTAIN LINCOLN CERTIFIES TO THE SERVICE OF ANOTHER OF HIS MEN, SEPTEMBER 26, 1832.

Once again the certification of service is a printed document filled in and signed by Lincoln as captain of militia. He penned the following words: "David M. Painter, as a private, 21st April,

7th June 48 days, 26th and September." His rank was printed on the form used, and it will be noted that in affixing his signature he omitted the use of a period, either single or double, after the letter "A". David was the son of James Pantier, an eccentric worthy, whose stout friendship for Lincoln began in the latter's New Salem days and endured until his death. The elder Pantier was a "faith doctor" noted for his ability to cure snake bites. He was also a constant and devout attendant at camp-meetings and political rallies, and Henry B. Rankin affords an amusing glimpse of him in after years at a Whig gathering in Petersburg where Lincoln was the speaker, and where welcomed to a seat on the platform, he found difficulty in safely stowing his battered hat, and, before he finally settled in his seat, anxiously remarked, "Abe! I forgot to ax you how Mary and the babies were." To all of which was returned the reassuring reply: "All well when I left them yesterday morning, Uncle Jimmie. All very well, thank you" (See Rankin, "Intimate Character Sketches of Abraham Lincoln," Philadelphia, 1924, Page 44-48.)

I CERTIFY, that David M   Pantier   volunteered and served as a private in the Company of Mounted Volunteers under my command in the Regiment commanded by Col. Samuel M. Thompson in the Brigade under the command of Generals S. Whiteside and H. Atkinson, called into the service of the United States by the Commander-in-Chief of the Militia of the State, for the protection of the North Western Frontier against an Invasion of the British Band of Sac and other tribes of Indians, that he was enrolled on the
        21st day of April 1832, and was HONORABLY DISCHARGED on the 7th day of   June   thereafter, having served   48 days
    Given under my hand this   26th day of   September, 1832
                        A Lincoln   Capt.

CAPTAIN LINCOLN CERTIFIES TO THE SERVICE OF YET ANOTHER OF HIS MEN

The words underscored in this document were written by Lincoln. The remainder is a printed form.

I certify, That Travice Elmore volunteered and served as a private in the Company of Mounted Volunteers under my command, in the Regiment commanded by Col. Samuel M. Thompson, in the Brigade under the command of Generals S. Whiteside and H. Atkinson, called into the service of the United

States by the Commander-in-Chief of the Militia of the State, for the protection of the North Western Frontier against an invasion of the British Band of Sac and other tribes of Indians, —that he was enrolled on the 21*st day of April* 1832, *and was* HONORABLY DISCHARGED on the *7th day of June* thereafter, having served 48 days

Given under my hand, this 29th day of September 1832,

A. Lincoln, Capt.

NOTE GIVEN BY LINCOLN AND NELSON ALLEY TO JAMES D. HENRY, OCTOBER 20, 1832

A long-remembered event in the early history of New Salem and Springfield was the attempt to prove that the Sangamon River could be navigated by vessels of moderate draught. This attempt was promoted by Captain Vincent A. Bogue, an enterprising citizen who owned several mills along the Sangamon. In the winter of 1832 Bogue announced that he had chartered the steamboat Talisman, and would make a trip from Cincinnati along the Ohio and Mississippi and up the Sangamon as soon as the last named stream was free from ice. Leading citizens and business men pledged subscriptions to defray the attendant expenses, and in March the Talisman and Captain Bogue arrived at Beardstown, where they were given a noisy and hearty welcome.

Thence young Abraham Lincoln, who had come down to Beardstown for the purpose, at the cost of much patient and difficult labor, piloted the Talisman to and over the mill-dam at New Salem and on to Bogue's mill-dam near Springfield. The citizens of the town celebrated its arrival with a dance at the court-house and innumerable dinners in tavern and private homes. But at the end of a week, receding waters caused Pilot Lincoln many an anxious moment on the return trip to Beardstown, where he collected his pay of $40. and then returned on foot to New Salem. As a whole the venture had proved a disappointing and costly one for Bogue and his backers, and before the year's end the Talisman caught fire at a St. Louis wharf and burned to the water's edge.

This loss completed the financial downfall of Bogue, who shortly departed from the Sangamon country leaving his creditors to quarrel over his doubtful assets. It is probable that Lincoln and Nelson Alley, who was then landlord of the Rutledge Tavern at New Salem, had made a joint pledge of funds for the Talis-

man's voyage. At any rate on October 30, 1832, Lincoln and Alley gave the note reproduced below to James D. Henry, sheriff of Sangamon County, who was collecting Bogue's assets for distribution among those to whom the doughty captain owed money. This note was not paid when it matured, and on August 10, 1833, suit was filed for recovery, the first civil action against Lincoln in the Sangamon Circuit Court. No defense was offered and on September 13 a default judgment was entered for the plaintiff. Lincoln met this claim as he did all others springing from his good-natured but mistaken optimism as a New Salem business man. He paid it in six instalments, including $11.75 added for costs, the last payment being made on January 28, 1834. It is interesting to note that the attorney for the plaintiff in this action was George Forquer, with whom a little later Lincoln was to have a memorable passage at arms. See William H. Townsend, Lincoln the Litigant (Boston, 1925), Pp. 46-53.

$104.87½

Six months after date we or either of us promise to pay to J. D. Henry, Sheriff of Sangamon County, or order, (for the benefit of the creditors of V. A. Bogue) the sum of one hundred and four dollars eighty-seven ½ cents, value received this the 30th Oct., 1832

Nelson Alley
A. Lincoln

SUMMARY BY LINCOLN AS CLERK OF VOTE AT NEW SALEM, NOVEMBER 5, 1832

Lincoln on November 5, 1832, voted for presidential electors for the first time, and again served as clerk of election in the New Salem precinct.

At an election held at the house of Samuel Hill in the New Salem precinct in the County of Sangamon and State of Illinois on the fifth day of November in the year of our Lord one thousand eight hundred and thirty-two the following named persons received the number of votes annexed to their respective names for the following described offices (to Wit)

Daniel Stooker had one hundred and eighty-five votes for elector of President and Vice President

Abner Flack had one hundred and eighty-five votes for elector of President and Vice President

James Evans had one hundred and eighty-five votes for elector of President and Vice President

Adam Darling had one hundred and eighty-five votes for elector of President and Vice President

John C. Alexander had one hundred and eighty-five votes for elector of President and Vice President

William B. Archer had seventy votes for elector of President and Vice President

Leonard White had seventy votes for elector of President and Vice President

James B. Moore had seventy votes for elector of President and Vice President

Elijah Iles had seventy votes for elector of President and Vice President

Pierre Menard had seventy votes for elector of President and Vice President

James Rutledge ⎫
Bowling Green ⎬ Judges of the election
Hugh Armstrong ⎭

A. Lincoln ⎱
William Green ⎰ Clerks of the election

CHAPTER IV — LINCOLN IN THE YEAR 1833
SURVEY OF PERIOD

*Abraham Lincoln's twenty-fifth year, 1833, was a period
of testing and endurance for the best liked young man in New
Salem. After Denton Offutt's failure his late clerk set up as a
merchant on his own account, but his store, as he long after
whimsically put it, speedily, "winked out,' leaving him with a
burden of debt of which he did not see the end for upward of
a dozen years. "Many young pioneers," as Logan Hay has
pointed out, "failed in the frontier towns and villages," and,
blaming their failure "on the community in which they happened
to be living pulled up stakes and moved on. Not so Lincoln.
He realized that if he could not make a success at New Salem,
he could not make a success anywhere. He therefore determined
to stand his ground and to attack the problem of making a living
in New Salem."*

*To meet his modest needs young Lincoln split rails, chopped
wood and worked as a field hand on the farms about New Salem. Meanwhile, he continued to read every available book and
to study grammar under Mentor Graham, the village school-
master. On May 7, 1833, he was appointed postmaster of New
Salem by Andrew Jackson, thus linking his own career with
another of great and enduring service, and in the weeks that
followed found time, again with Mentor Graham, to study geometry and trigonometry in preparation for his work as a deputy
surveyor of Sangamon County, a post that shortly came his way.
The year 1833 was a year of testing for young Abraham Lincoln, and he triumphantly met the test.*

*And as a devoted Whig and follower of Henry Clay, in the
newspapers that came to the New Salem postoffice he followed
with absorbed attention the progress of events in Washington
— the stern measures taken by Jackson to meet South Carolina's
defiance of an obnoxious tariff, and the bitter opposition, not
always a just one, of the Whigs in Congress led by Clay to Jackson and all his works. He must have taken careful note of the
fact that in this opposition Clay had been joined by Calhoun,
who had resigned the vice presidency and returned to his seat
in the Senate to defend the course of his state. A series of resolutions, which Calhoun introduced in the Senate on January 22
and expounded in a speech of great ability, became a text-book
for those who championed the doctrine of states rights and a*

little later, absolute non-intervention with slavery, and also had their part in the political education of Abraham Lincoln.

When on February 12, 1833, Clay, in the role of peace maker and seeking to abate South Carolina's grievances, introduced a compromise tariff measure into the Senate, Postmaster Lincoln approvingly watched its swift progress through Congress and enactment into law. The force bill having also passed House and Senate, President Jackson on March 2 signed both pieces of legislation; a scant fortnight later South Carolina repealed its nullification ordinance, and the final issue of a dispute that threatened to disrupt the Union was postponed for a generation.

MORTGAGE OF WILLIAM GREEN, JR., TO REUBEN RADFORD DRAWN AND ATTESTED BY LINCOLN, JANUARY 15, 1833

On January 15, 1833, William C. Green, Jr., purchased for $400 the store of Reuben Radford in New Salem, giving in payment $23 in cash and two notes, each for $188.50, secured by a mortgage—drawn and attested by Lincoln and reproduced below —on the west half of Lot 5, North of Main Street in New Salem. On the same day the lately formed firm of Berry & Lincoln purchased the Radford store from Green for $750, paying $265 cash and assuming payment of the two notes given by Green to Radford. The balance of $108 due under this arrangement Berry cancelled by transferring to Green a horse, saddle and bridle of which he was the owner. Thus in a single day Green made a profit of $240. and one horse, and Lincoln incurred the second of a series of unlucky obligations final payment of which was to trouble him for nearly a score of years. The original of the Green mortgage is now in the possession of the Illinois State Historical Society. See Lincoln's New Salem by B. P. Thomas (Springfield, 1934), Pp. 70 to 74.

A week after Green gave this mortgage to Radford John C. Calhoun, then a member of the Federal Senate from South Carolina, presented a series of resolutions to that body in which he set forth with cogency and force the doctrine of states rights. Young Lincoln must have read these resolutions as printed in the newspapers which reached New Salem, and that reading, along with Jackson's bold championship of an inseparable Union, had its place, and a major one, in his political education.

William Green, Jr. to Reuben Radford

Know all men by these presents, that I, William Green Jr., of the County of Sangamon and State of Illinois, for and in consideration of the sum of Two hundred dollars, to me in hand paid, the receipt whereof I do hereby acknowledge, have given, granted, bargained and sold, and by these presents do give, grant, bargain and sell, all my right title interest and estate in and to

The West half of lot number five, North of Main Street, in the first survey, in the town of New Salem, in the county and State aforesaid.

Together with all and singular the appurtenances thereunto belonging, or in anywise appertaining thereunto—Reuben Radford, his heirs, and assigns forever.

In testimony whereof I have hereunto set my hand and seal this fifteenth day of January in the year of Our Lord, One Thousand Eight Hundred and Thirty Three.

William Green Jr. (Seal)

Attest: A. Lincoln

The condition of the above obligation is such, if the said William Green Jr. shall comply with the requisites of two promissory notes, made and executed on this day for the sum of one hundred and eighty-eight dollars and fifty cents each, payable to the said Reuben Radford, the above Deed of bargain to be null and void and of no effect. But if the said William Green Jr. shall prove insolvent, and utterly unable to comply with the demands of said notes, the above Deed of bargain is to remain in full force and virtue at law.

In testimony whereof the said William Green Jr. and Reuben Radford have hereunto set their hands this 15th of January, 1833.

William Green Jr (Seal)
Reuben Radford (Seal)

State of Illinois
to-wit
Sangamon County

This day personally appeared before the undersigned a Justice of the Peace in and for said County, Abraham Lincoln whose name appears signed as a subscribing witness to the annexed Deed of Conveyance, the said Abram Lincoln, being personally known to me to be the person whose name appears subscribed to the said Deed, and the said Abram Lincoln, after being duly sworn deposeth and saith that the said Deed was executed and delivered in his presence by William Green, whose name appears subscribed to the said Deed, that the said William Green whose name appears subscribed to the said Deed is the real person who executed the same, and that he, the said Abram Lincoln, subscribed his name as a witness in his presence, and at his request.

Given under my hand and seal this 10th day of July 1833. Recorded August 1, A. D. 1833—Robert Cownover, J. P.

(Seal)

BOND OF RUTLEDGE, GREEN AND LINCOLN DRAWN BY LINCOLN, JANUARY 31, 1833

This bond was one of the earliest legal documents drawn by Lincoln and the lot therein mentioned adjoined on the east the Rutledge Tavern at New Salem. B. P. Thomas in his Lincoln's New Salem observes that David Rutledge was at that time a minor and had no title to the lot, but adds that "on the frontier circumstances such as these were often of little consequence." It is probable that Rutledge, who was about to become a student at Illinois College, Jacksonville, desired to sell this lot in order to raise funds for his tuition and other expenses, and that Lincoln, a possible suitor for his sister Ann, gladly did what he could to help him. Be this as it may, on August 26, 1833, delivery not having been effected, the Trents sued Rutledge, Green and Lincoln in the Sangamon Circuit Court for $150; but three weeks later, September 16, an agreed order was entered in the case dismissing the suit and providing that "each party pay half of the cost."

Lincoln did not fare so easily in freeing himself from the heavier obligations he had incurred as a New Salem storekeeper —obligations to which in after years he often humorously alluded as "the national debt." Herndon records that as late as 1848 his partner was sending him part of his salary as congressman to be applied on his debts; but in the end they were paid in full. Moreover, Lincoln as President proved his gratitude to "Uncle Jimmie" Short, well-to-do farmer of the New Salem neighborhood, who, because he "liked Abe Lincoln," when the latter's horse, saddle, bridle and surveying instruments were levied on and sold, bought and returned them to him, for when in turn reverses overtook Short, who in old age had removed to the Farther West, Lincoln appointed him supervisor of the Round Valley Indian Reservation in California at a salary of $1800 a year.

Know all men by these presents that we David Rutledge William

Green, Jr. and A. Lincoln are held and firmly bound unto Alexander Trent and Martin S. Trent in the penal sum of one hundred and fifty dollars well and truly to be paid unto them—
as witness our hands and seals this 31st of Jany—1833—

David Rutledge (Seal)
William Green (Seal)
A. Lincoln (Seal)

The condition of the above obligation is such If the above bounded David Rutledge shall make a good and lawful deed of conveyance to the said Alexander Trent and Martin S. Trent for the East half of Lot Number five South of Main Street in the first survey in the town of New-Salem—on or before the first day of July next the above obligation is to be null and void and of no effect—otherwise to remain in full force and virtue of law.
In testimony whereof the said David Rutledge Alexander Trent and Martin S. Trent have hereunto set their hands and seals this 31st day of January 1833

David Rutledge (Seal)
A. Trent (Seal)
M. S. Trent (Seal)

PLEA TO THE COUNTY COMMISSIONERS OF SANGAMON COUNTY DRAWN AND SIGNED BY LINCOLN, FEBRUARY 9, 1833

This petition gives evidence of the early established custom of the citizens of New Salem to seek Lincoln's services in the matter of petitions. The original is now in the Illinois State Historical Library. See "The Genesis of Lincoln the Lawyer" by Dr. Harry E. Pratt, Bulletin of the Abraham Lincoln Association, September, 1939, Page 10.

To the County Commissioners Court for the County of Sangamon when met at their March term for the year 1833
We the undersigned citizens of Sangamon County being personally acquainted with Benj. Elmore (who also is resident in said County—) and knowing him to be insane and wholly unable to earn a livelihood either by labour or any other employment—and to have no relatives who can be lawfully made chargeable for his maintenance Therefore we respectfully request that his case be taken into consideration by your honorable body—
New Salem Feb. 9—1833—

Signed by twenty-six citizens, Lincoln included. All but six signatures are in Lincoln's handwriting.

RECEIPT WRITTEN BY LINCOLN AND SIGNED
BY RICHARD LARIMORE, MAY 7, 1833

On May 7, 1833, the receipt, reproduced below and now in the files of the Sangamon Circuit Court, was written by Lincoln and signed by Richard Larimore. On the same day Lincoln was appointed by President Jackson to succeed Samuel Hill as postmaster of New Salem, the first postoffice established in what is now Menard County. Lincoln was then and for nearly a score of years thereafter an ardent supporter of Henry Clay, but he recalled in a later time that he owed his appointment by a Democratic President to the fact that the office was "too insignificant to make its politics an objection." Nelson Alley and Alexander Ferguson signed Lincoln's $500 bond, and he served as postmaster until the removal of the office to Petersburg on May 30, 1836. His position gave him an opportunity to scan all newspapers delivered at the New Salem postoffice and confirmed him in the habit of diligent newspaper reading which remained with him through life. It also brought him in friendly contact with most of the settlers in the New Salem region, and contributed in no small measure to the success of his first campaigns for the Legislature. See "Lincoln the Postmaster" by Benjamin P. Thomas, Bulletin of the Abraham Lincoln Association, June, 1833.

It is also worthy of record that when young Lincoln was postmaster at New Salem, John Brown, who a quarter of a century later was to achieve disputed immortality at Harper's Ferry, was serving in like capacity the people of the village of Randolph, Pennsylvania.

John Close, appellee
     vs
John Ritter, appellant

Received of John Close Two dollars and fifty cents being the amount of fees due me for attendance as a witness in a suit in the Sangamon circuit court—John Close vs John Ritter.

    May 7, 1833.   Richard Larimore

The above is all in Lincoln's handwriting except the signature.

PROMISSORY NOTE OF ABRAHAM LINCOLN,
OCTOBER 19, 1833.

When young Captain Lincoln returned from the Black Hawk War on July 5, 1832, he found himself for the moment a member of the army of the unemployed. At first he considered becoming a blacksmith and then planned to begin the study of law, but for the moment decided not to adopt the latter course because of his faulty education. Instead he purchased a half interest in the Herndon Brothers' store in New Salem. William F. Berry, son of Reverend John M. Berry, who had served as a corporal under Lincoln in the Black Hawk War, had purchased a half interest in this store, giving his note in payment. In the same easy manner Lincoln became the owner of the other half interest. In January, 1833, the partners bought from its latest owner, William Green, the store of Reuben Radford who had found his career as a New Salem merchant a troubled one. Two months later Berry & Lincoln were granted a license by the county commissioners to operate a tavern. It appears that Berry took out the license and signed Lincoln's name to the bond. It is possible that this caused a dissolution of partnership in April, 1833, when Lincoln disposed of his interest in the store to Berry who managed to keep the business alive for another year. When Berry died in January, 1835, his estate amounted to little more than $100. The physicians who attended him in his last illness took half of this estate against which Lincoln had failed to file a claim. The promissory note here reproduced was given on October 19, 1833, to complete purchase of the Radford store. Lincoln and Berry paid $125.00 in cash, leaving a balance due of $254.82. Radford assigned a part of this note to Peter Van Bergen who on April 7, 1834, sued its makers for $500.00 and $50.00 damages. Green was the only defendant served. Upon April 29, 1834, he failed to appear. Judgment was given against him and upon November 19, Lincoln and Berry were made parties to this judgment. The balance then due was $154.00, all owed to Van Bergen. Lincoln and Berry were unable to pay and the sheriff levied against their personal possessions including Lincoln's horse, saddle and bridle, and his surveying instruments. When these were sold upon execution, as related elsewhere, James Short, a close friend, bid them in and returned them to the young surveyor. Van Bergen at a later date became a client of Lawyer Lincoln, proving that the suit had caused no ill-will upon the part of either man.

One day after date we or either of us promise to pay Reuben Radford Three hundred & seventy nine dollars and eighty two cents—for value received, as witness our hands and seals this 19th day of October 1833—

W. Berry   (Seal)
A. Lincoln (Seal)
Wm. Green   (Seal)

APPRAISAL OF NEW SALEM LOTS

The original of this appraisal is in the files of Sangamon County.   Only the signature is written by Lincoln.   The lots appraised were put up for sale to satisfy a judgment, but there were no bidders for them.   The store of Berry & Lincoln stood on one of them.

We the Subscribers being summoned & sworn by D. Dickinson Deputy Sheriff of Sangamon County to Value Lot No. 5 North of Main Street, in first Survey and Lot No. one in Second Survey of the Town of Salem, Levied on as the property of Henry Sinco to satisfy an Execution in favor of Nelson Alley, do Value Lot No. 5 to $100 & Lot No. one to $50.   Given under our hands and Seals this 25th day of October 1833.

> Test
>
> > A. Lincoln
> > H. Armstrong
> > J. Clement

CHAPTER V—LINCOLN IN THE YEAR 1834

SURVEY OF PERIOD

Abraham Lincoln's twenty-sixth year, 1834, brought him, besides his appointment as deputy surveyor, which called for many surveys in the country adjacent to New Salem, and his duties as postmaster and professor of odd jobs, his second candidacy for and election to the Legislature. His name appeared on April 19 in the list of candidates published in the Sangamo Journal, but he made no declaration of principles. This was perhaps due to the fact that, although known to be a Whig, he entered the field largely as a result of the urging of Bowling Green and other Democratic friends. He made an energetic canvass and at the election on August 4 was elected one of the four representatives from Sangamon County, running within fourteen votes of John Dawson, who received the highest vote. In the third person autobiography, which Mr. Lincoln gave to John Locke Scripps in 1860, he makes this reference to an important sequel to the election of 1834:

"Major John T. Stuart, then in full practice of the law, was also elected. During the canvass in a private conversation he urged Abraham (to) study law. After the election he borrowed books of Stuart, took them home with him, and went at it in good earnest. He studied with nobody. He still mixed in the surveying to pay board and clothing bills. When the Legislature met, the law-books were dropped but were taken up again at the end of the session."

During 1934, prompted by young Lincoln's improving fortunes, some of his creditors sought to collect what was due them as the result of his disastrous store-keeping venture. Thus in November Peter Van Bergen secured a judgment against him and his former partner Berry for $154. and the sheriff seized his horse and surveying instruments. But his good friend Uncle Jimmie Short bid in all the property and loaned the hapless surveyor the money with which to repay it. And when the time came for the meeting of the General Assembly at Vandalia, another good friend, Coleman Smoot, loaned him $200 with which to pay a Springfield tailor for a new suit of clothes, and to meet his expenses at the capital until he received his salary as representative from the state. And so, on a late November day, young Lincoln, pressing debts paid and properly clad, took at New Salem the stage for Vandalia to begin his career as a law-maker.

Both a diligent reader of the newspapers and an ardent Whig —the name adopted by the opponents of Jackson in 1834—young Lincoln continued to take careful note of the progress of the political battle at Washington. On March 28, after three months of debate in which Clay, Benton and Calhoun played leading parts, the Senate censured Jackson for removal of the public deposits from the Bank of the United States, and on April 27 the President recorded his protest in a message, admirable in form and content, which the Senate rejected on May 7, after a debate waged with a violence and harshness up to that time without a parallel in the history of Congress. More abiding in its effects than this war of words was a bill championed by Benton and passed on June 28 regulating the coinage of gold and silver on a basis of 16 to 1, a measure which appealed to men of goodwill, and by starting a new flow of gold to the government mints gave welcome relief to those who bought and sold. And young Lincoln must have approved a bill passed two days later by Congress which provided for the purchase by the nation of the papers of George Washington whose old comrade-in-arms, Lafayette, had passed from life in his native France on May 20, 1834, at the ripe age of seventy-six years.

And as a token of westward expansion on April 28, 1834, Nathaniel Jarvis Wyeth left Independence on the expedition in the course of which he was to build Fort Hall, the first settlement in what is now Idaho, while on June 21, 1834, Cyrus Hall McCormick received a patent for the reaper which was to hasten the settlement of the Middle West. Finally across the Atlantic, at the year's end, the first ministry of Sir Robert Peel heralded the coming of a broader and easier future for the common folk of England.

CERTIFICATE OF SURVEY MADE BY LINCOLN

It was in the latter part of 1833 that Lincoln secured employment as a deputy to John Calhoun, then surveyor of Sangamon County. Calhoun was an active and prominent leader of the Jackson forces in and about Springfield, and Herndon later surmised that Lincoln owed his appointment to Pollard Simmons, a Democratic friend. He knew nothing of surveying but from Calhoun he borrowed copies of Robert Gibson's "Theory and Practice of Surveying" and Abel Flint's "Treatise on Geometry, Trigonometry and Rectangular Surveying," and, enlisting the aid of

Mentor Graham, he began with these texts to fit himself for his new duties. "Hr studied day and night," writes Thomas. "Often he and Graham were up until midnight interrupting their calculations only when Mrs. Graham ordered them out for a fresh supply of wood for the fire. But he mastered the books, obtained a horse on credit, procured a compass and chain, and by the end of the year was ready to start work." He had been assigned the northern part of Sangamon County—now Menard and the southern part of Mason—and on January 14, 1834, performed for Russell Godbey the earliest of his surveys of which there is record, receiving for his labor two buckskins which Hannah, the wife of Jack Armstrong, "foxed" on his trousers to protect them from briars. The tract surveyed for Godbey was six miles north of New Salem and one mile east of the Sangamon River.

When in 1835 Thomas M. Neale succeeded Calhoun as county surveyor he continued Lincoln as deputy, and there is evidence that the latter did not cease to make surveys until a few months before he left New Salem for Springfield. He had skill as a surveyor, and from the first his work was highly regarded by those called to pass upon it. He surveyed the towns of Albany, Bath, Huron, Lincoln and New Boston, and in February, 1836, resurveyed Petersburg. Roads that he surveyed, "are still in use, and the boundaries of many Menard and Mason County farms were originally run by him." There are also records of surveys by Lincoln of three roads, three school sections and many pieces of farm land. Later Lawyer Lincoln's experiences and knowledge as a surveyor were of great use to him in the conduct of chancery cases in the courts. See "Lincoln's New Salem," by B. P. Thomas, (Springfield, 1834), Pages 68-69 and 74-75.

1834.   Surveyed for Russell Godby—the West half of the
Jan. 14   North East quarter of Section 30. in Township 19 North
of Range 6 West. Begining at a White Oak 12 inches in diameter bearing N 34 E 84 Links a White oak 10 inches S 58 W. 98 Links—Thence South 40 chains to a White oak 12 inches N 73 E 20 Links—Thence East 20 chains to a black Oak 12 inches S 54 W 16 Links—Thence North 40 chains to a Post & mound. —Thence 20 chains to the begining chainmen.

J. Calhoun S S C

Hercules Demming   By A. Lincoln

REPORT OF PUBLIC MEETING AT NEW SALEM, MARCH 1, 1834, SIGNED BY LINCOLN AS SECRETARY

This report of a public meeting held at New Salem on March 1, 1834, and printed two weeks later in the Sangamo Journal, recalls the career of an unusual man who, had length of years been granted him, would no doubt have played a large part in the history of Illinois. James Dougherty Henry was born in Pennsylvania in '1797, in his youth served as a private in the second war with Great Britain, learned the trade of shoemaker in Delaware, and, removing to the West, in 1820 settled in Edwardsville, Illinois. Up to that time he never had had a single day's schooling, but in Edwardsville he worked at his trade by day and attended school at night, in this way securing a fair education. After 1826 he was a merchant in Springfield, and, having a gift for winning and keeping friends, he was twice elected sheriff of Sangamon County. Henry's master ambition, however, was to win success as a soldier. In 1827 he served as adjutant in the Winnebago War, which for a time threatened the safety of the Galena mining district, and a few years later in the Black Hawk War, he was in turn lieutenant-colonel and colonel, commanding a brigade at the battles of Wisconsin and the Bad Axe, his success in both winning him great popularity. Peace restored, he was in 1832 for the third time elected sheriff, and two years later a growing army of friends began to work for his nomination and election as governor. But exposure as a soldier had induced a disease of the lungs, and vainly seeking in the South a restoration to health, he died at New Orleans on March 5, 1834, four days after the meeting in New Salem which Lincoln served as secretary. When on March 15 the Sangamo Journal printed a report of this meeting, General Henry had been more than a week in his grave. See, "A Forgotten Hero," by Frank E. Stevens, Transactions of the Illinois State Historical Society for 1934, Pp. 77-120.

At a respectable meeting of the citizens of New Salem, held pursuant to public notice on Saturday, first March, 1834, for the purpose of nominating a suitable person to fill the office of Governor of this state, Bowling Green, Esq. was called to the chair and A. Lincoln appointed secretary. The object of the meeting being explained by the chair, Dr. John Allen and Messrs. Nelson Alley and Samuel Hill, were appointed a committee to draft a preamble and resolutions, expressive of the sense of the meeting who, after an absence of a few minutes, presented the following, which were unanimously adopted:

"Whereas, the election of our executive officer, is always interesting to the people and should at all times demand their deliberate and serious consideration.

"And Whereas, the financial and infantile situation of this state is such, as to demand more than ever the deliberate attention and united efforts of its inhabitants for the election of a Chief Magistrate who is free from and above every party and sectarian influence; who respects the rights of his fellow citizens and who has wisdom to devise and energy to execute such laws as are conductive to the political happiness of the people and to the development of the great resources of our state.

"And Whereas, there is at this time no candidate for that high and responsible office before the people to whom we can, or to whom in our opinion the people in this section of the country, will give a cordial and hearty support.

"And Whereas, we have the most implicit confidence in the honor, integrity and firmness of our fellow citizen, General James D. Henry; therefore,

"Resolved, That the patriotic services, discreet and unaspiring character of Gen. James D. Henry, are such as to merit the confidence of the people of this state and to place his title to the gubernatorial chair paramount to that of any of the candidates now before the people.

"Resolved, That we will use every honorable effort to promote the election of Gen Henry to the first office in the gift of the people of this state at the next August election. We recommend him to our fellow citizens, as a suitable person for the office, believing that by choosing him, they will confer due honor on an individual and advance the permanent welfare of the state.

"Resolved, That the proceedings of this meeting be signed by the chairman and secretary and forwarded to the editors of the Sangamo Journal for publication."

And, on motion, the meeting adjourned.

Bowling Green,
Chairman.

A. Lincoln, secretary.

PETITION TO THE COUNTY COMMISSIONERS' COURT OF SANGAMON COUNTY, MARCH 3, 1834

The board of viewers petitioned for in this document seems to have been a one-man affair, as Lincoln made the cash deposit required by law, surveyed the route, plotted the road and wrote the report.

March 3, 1834. Reuben Harrison presented the following petition: We, the undersigned, respectfully request your honorable body to appoint viewers to view and locate a road from Musick's ferry on Salt Creek, via New Salem, to the county line in the direction of Jacksonville.

And Abram Lincoln deposited with the clerk $10., as the law directs. Ordered, that Michael Killion, Hugh Armstrong, and Abram Lincoln be appointed to view said road, and said Lincoln to act as surveyor.

RETURN OF LINCOLN AND MENTOR GRAHAM AS CLERKS OF AN ELECTION HELD IN THE NEW SALEM PRECINCT, MAY 5, 1834

Lincoln and Mentor Graham served as clerks in the New Salem precinct at an election on May 5, 1834, to choose a successor to James D. Henry as sheriff of Sangamon County. The original returns in Lincoln's handwriting are now in the Illinois State Historical Library at Springfield. Dr. Garrett Elkin, the successful candidate, received 84 of the 165 votes cast in the New Salem Precinct, but Lincoln and Graham voted for David Dickinson; so also did Pollard Simmons, John M. Rutledge, Peyton Harrison, Bowling Green, James Pantier, and Jack Kelso, Lincoln's poetry loving friend. On May 6 Lincoln returned the poll book of this special election to Springfield, and on June 3 the County Commissioners' Court allowed him $1.00 as clerk of the election and $2.00 for returning the poll book.

At an election held at the house of William F. Berry the New Salem Precinct in the county of Sangamon and State of Illinois on the fifth day of May in the year of our Lord one thousand eight hundred and thirty four the following named persons received the number of votes annexed to their respective names for the following described offices to wit
Garrett Elkin had eighty four votes for sheriff
David Dickinson had seventy seven votes for sheriff
Zachariah Peter had four votes for sheriff

Certified by us

Bowling Green ⎫
Hugh Armstrong ⎬ Judges of the election
David Whray ⎭

A. Lincoln ⎫
Mentor Graham ⎬ Clerks of the election

I certify that Hugh Armstrong, David Whray, Mentor Graham and A. Lincoln were qualified by me according to law as judges and clerks of the election.

Bowling Green

I certify that Bowling Green was qualified by me according to law as Judge of the election.

Mentor Graham

REPORT TO THE COUNTY COMMISSIONERS' COURT OF SAGAMON COUNY SIGNED BY LINCOLN, JUNE 2, 1834

Under a law passed by the Legislature of Illinois on February 19, 1827, surveyors were permitted to charge $3. a day for road work. A later law passed by the Legislature provided that a surveyor should record all surveys made by him in "a well bound book," but if Lincoln kept such a book it has not been found. The John A. Kelso, who served as chain-bearer in the Musick's ferry survey, was the New Salem idler, fisherman and poetry lover who introduced Lincoln to Shakespeare and Burns.

We, the undersigned, being appointed to view and locate a road—beginning at Musick's ferry on Salt Creek (via) New Salem, to the county line in the direction of Jacksonville—respectfully report that we have performed the duties of said view and location as required by law and that we have made the location on good ground, and believe the establishment of the same to be necessary and proper—

The inclosed map gives the courses and distances as required by law—

Michael Killion
Hugh Armstrong
A. Lincoln.

Indorsement in pencil, also in Lincoln's handwriting:

A. Lincoln, 5 days at $3.00, $15.00. John A. Kelsoe, chainbearer, for 5 days at 75 cents, $3.75. Robert Lloyd, at 75 cents,

$3.75. Hugh Armstrong, for services as axeman, 5 days at 75 cents, $3.75. A. Lincoln, for making plot and report. $2.50.

On Map.

Whole length of road, 26 miles and 70 chains. Scale, 2 inches to the mile.

RECEIPT OF LINCOLN TO CHARLES R. MATHENY, JUNE 3, 1834.

(Photostat in Lincoln Life Foundation Scrapbook Files)

The receipt here reproduced appears to have been penned by Matheny, but was signed by Mr. Lincoln with his characteristic, A.. Lincoln. Matheny, as elsewhere noted, was an early settler in Springfield who served as recorder of Sangamon County from 1821 to 1827, and from 1821 until his death in 1839 as clerk of the county commissioners' court. He signed the certificate of Lincoln's first election to the Illinois Legislature, and in return received the votes of Lincoln, as did his son Noah who succeeded him as clerk.

The year in which he signed this receipt was a period of present and future meaning for Abraham Lincoln. He was serving as postmaster of New Salem and late in the preceding year, with Mentor Graham's aid, had qualified for the post of deputy surveyor of Sangamon County under John Calhoun. He was also busy with the plans that on April 19, 1934, caused the Sangamo Journal to include his name in the list of candidates for the Legislature, and on August 4, brought his election to that body. And a little later he may have read in the journals which came to the New Salem postoffice that slavery was about to come to an end in the British possessions, Parliament having awarded owners a compensation of twenty million pounds—a condition that thirty years later no doubt profoundly affected the thought and course of President Lincoln in his efforts to save the Union.

And the postmaster of New Salem may or may not have heard in the summer of 1834 that in the preceding February, 1834, at Cincinnati, the students of Lane Theological Seminary, drawn both from the South and North, for eighteen consecutive nights had hotly discussed the slavery question, and then had formed one of the first anti-slavery societies to come into being in the Middle West. Whereupon the shocked and angry trustees of Lane, a fortnight after young Mr. Lincoln's election to the Legislature, had expelled upward of fifty of the members of the student body, who had refused to forego their right to inquire into slavery. Then these half a hundred young men with minds of their own, headed by one of their professors and a protesting trustee, flocked off to Oberlin to make that lately founded institution an abolition center, and to champion the opinions which, in the fulness of time, led to the organization of the Republican Party and the nomination and election of Abraham Lincoln to the Presidency.

Recd of C. R. Matheny Clerk $10. 00
deposited by me at the last Term of
com court on application for a road
June 3rd 1834

A. Lincoln

CAPTAIN LINCOLN MAKES AFFIDAVIT REGARDING A HORSE LOST BY ONE OF HIS MEN, JUNE 29, 1834.

(Photostat from National Lincoln Life Foundation

With the exception of Justice of Peace Anderson's attesting to the swearing of the affidavit, this entire paper was penned by Mr. Lincoln. It will be observed that he was already using the extra spacing characteristic of his later legal documents. It will be also noted that he used the spellings "verrily" and "verry," a form common in his early legal papers. "Apraisement" in place of the more correct, "appraisement," was one of the errors common to frontier spelling.

State of Illinois
Sangamon county

Abraham Lincoln being first duly sworn, states on oath that he was the Captain of one of the companies Illinois volunters, on the expedition directed against the Sac & Fox Indians in the year 1832, that Isaac Anderson was a volunteer in said company, that said Anderson had a horse mustered into the service of the United States, and valued, (as affiant verrily believes speaking from memory only, the original apraisement roll, being lost, mislaid or destroyed so that affiant, after diligent search has not been able to find it) at forty-five dollars, that said horse was turned out to graze in consequence of sufficient forage not being furnished by the United States, and was thereby lost, that said horse was lost about the tenth of May 1832, and without any fault or negligence on the part of said Anderson. The army was marched from Dixons

Ferry on Rock River, that being the point where said horse was lost, verry shortly after the loss of said horse— The affiant makes the above statements from memory only, but feels confident they are substantialy correct—

A.. Lincoln

Sworn to & subscribed before me
This 29th Day of June 1834 (?)

M. K. Anderson, J.P.

RETURN BY LINCOLN OF ELECTION AT NEW SALEM, OCTOBER 27, 1834.

William L. May, who led the ,New Salem poll on this oc-casion, was ,a pioneer lawyer, who at an early day came from Kentucky to Edwardsville. President Jackson in 1829 appointed him receiver of public moneys for the land office at Springfield, which then became his home, and later he served two terms in Congress. He passed his last years in California. Benjamin Mills, who opposed May for Congress in 1834, was a Galena law-yer of parts. Seventy-two voted at the New Salem election, Lin-coln and Mentor Graham being among the last to cast their ballots. The County Commissioners' Court at its next meeting allowed Lincoln and Graham $1.00 each for clerking this election.

At an election held at the house of William F. Berry in the New Salem precinct in the county of Sangamon and state of Illinois on the twenty-seventh day of October in the year of our Lord one thousand eight hundred and thirty-four the following named persons received the number of votes annexed to their respective names for the following described office (to Wit)
William L. May had Seventy-two votes for Representative to
    Congress
James Turney had one vote for Representative to Congress
Benjamin Mills had three votes for Representative to Congress

Certified by us.

James Pantier
Pollard Simmons   Judges of the election
William Janes

Attest   A. Lincoln
         Mentor Graham
Clerks of the election

I certify that the Judges and Clerks of this Election was Sworn according to Law.
New Salem, October 27, 1834

                                        Bowling Green, J. P.

and John Clary
Served as Constable

REPORT OF ROAD SURVEY, NOVEMBER 4, 1834

To the County Commissioner's Court for the County of Sangamon:
    We, the undersigned, being appointed to view and relocate a part of the road between Sangamon town and the town of Athens, respectfully report that we have performed the duty of said appointment according to law—and that we have made the said relocation on good ground—and believe the same to be necessary and proper.

                            JAMES STROWBRIDGE,
                            LEVI CANTRALL,
                            A. LINCOLN.

Athens, Nov. 4, 1834.
    Herewith is the map—The court may allow me the following charges if they think proper—1 day's labor as surveyor $3.00
                            Making map .... .50
                                                    _____
                                                    $3.50

                            A. Lincoln.

LINCOLN AND SAMUEL HILL APPRAISE AN ESTRAY FILLY

This estray notice is in the handwriting of Bowling Green, who filed it with Charles R. Matheny, clerk of the County Commissioners' Court in Springfield. Matheny then advertised the estray in the newspapers according to law.
Taken up by Thos. Dowel at his farm in Claries (Clary's) Grove one two year filly Dark bey or Rather Brown fourteen hands high Star on her forehead no brands Appraised to Thirty Dollars by A Lincoln & Saml Hill
November 14, 1834

                            Bowling Green J P

FIRST BILL INTRODUCED BY LINCOLN IN THE ILLINOIS LEGISLATURE, DECEMBER 9, 1834

On November 28, 1834, Lincoln traveled by stage to Vandalia, capital of Illinois, John Todd Stuart, John Dawson and William Carpenter, the other members of the Legislature from Sangamon County, keeping him company. He wore the best suit of clothes he had owned up to that time. It had been made for him by a Springfield tailor, and he had borrowed money with which to pay for it from his friend Coleman Smoot, a well-to-do farmer of the New Salem neighborhood. He found Vandalia a village of 600 souls perched on a bluff sixty feet above the west bank of the Kaskaskia River. It had a public square and unpaved streets eighty feet wide, and could boast several grist mills, half a dozen public houses and two weekly newspapers; but the greater number of its hundred-odd buildings were log cabins, and there were only two brick structures in the town. One of these, formerly used by the bank, was now devoted to state offices.

The other was the State House, a two-story building erected in 1824 but already wearing an air of age and neglect. The hall of the House with a lobby for spectators occupied a part of the ground floor, and above was the Senate chamber and lobby. In this building at 10 o'clock in the morning of Monday, December 1, 1834, Lincoln for the first time took his seat as a member of the lower house of the General Assembly of Illinois. Of his fifty-four fellow members, ten had served as officers and many more as privates in the Black Hawk War. More than half of them were farmers and a fourth were lawyers. A majority were natives of Kentucky and Virginia, and only one of Illinois.

There were among them, many men of ability, education and social charm, some of whom had brought with them to Vandalia their wives, sisters and daughters. Vandalia offered a sharp contrast to New Salem, and Thomas shrewdly observes that Lincoln's "first term in the Legislature was a liberal education, more valuable than anything he could learn in books." Other students stress the vital part Lincoln's Vandalia sojourns played in his development. "One wonders," writes Dr. Louis A. Warren, "if Vandalia was not a much more important influence in the life of Abraham Lincoln than New Salem . . . . a better understanding of Lincoln's intellectual advancement might be acquired by paying more attention to historically prominent people with whom he was associated at Vandalia instead of placing so much em-

phasis on a few rather obscure characters who lived in the legendary and folk lore atmosphere of New Salem."

Lincoln was appointed one of seven members of the Committee on Public Accounts and Expenditures, received in due course assignments to other committees, and, while the session was still young, faced his new duties with growing confidence and competence. On December 9, he introduced a bill for "an act to limit the jurisdiction of Justices of the Peace"—his first attempt at law making. "The justice of the peace bill," writes Pratt, "was probably the fruit of his many discussions with Bowling Green, who had held that office at New Salem since the founding of the settlement. The bill proposed that a justice of the peace should not have jurisdiction of any civil case unless it be in the precinct in which the defendant resided, or in which the contract on which the suit was brought was made and entered into, or made payable . . . . The bill did not please the select committee that took it in charge and they reported a substitute bill. Attempts to amend the substitute on the floor of the House brought its reference to a second select committee . . . This committee wrote a new bill which passed the House, but was tabled in the Senate." See B. P. Thomas, "Lincoln's New Salem," Pp. 78-80; Lincoln Lore 635, and Pratt "Lincoln Day by Day," 1809-1839, (Springfield, 1941), Pp. xxxvi, and 32-33.

An Act to limit the jurisdiction of Justices of the Peace.

Be it enacted by the people of the State of Illinois, represented in the General Assembly That Hereafter Justices of the Peace shall not entertain (sic) jurisdiction of any civil case whatever unless it be in the precinct in which the defendent (sic) resides or in which the contract on which suit is brought was made and entered into, or made payable—any thing in former laws to the contrary notwithstanding.

This act to be in force from and after the first day of June next.

MORTGAGE OF NICHOLAS BRYAN TO THOMAS E. PAYNE, DRAWN DECEMBER 8, 1834

The mortgage and notations here reproduced were not drawn by Mr. Lincoln who was then in Vandalia, but the "(A)" on the cover for the mortgage is in his hand, and he refers to exhibit "A" in the bill of complaint in the suit of Payne vs. Bryan which he filed in the Sangamon Circuit Court on February 14, 1838. This mortgage was the basis of that litigation, and is therefore included as part of a case in which Mr. Lincoln represented the defendant. It was Thomas M. Neale, the justice of the peace before whom Bryan executed the mortgage, who, when he became county surveyor in 1835, continued Mr. Lincoln one of his deputies.

I, Nicholas Bryan of Sangamon County and State of Illinois have this day Morgaged to Thomas F. Payne of St. Louis of the State of Missouri the following property to wit one waggon three yoke of Oxen with three yokes and chains four head of horses for head of Milch Cows and Calves forty head of Sheep three plows and gear for three horses one press one bureau four beds bedding and steads too doz Chares too doz plates too doz spoons too sets Knives and forks too doz cups and saucers one pair pitchers three pots three ovens too skillets one iron kettle one brass Kettle one tea Kettle three buckets too flatirons too (too) wayters too Glasses three bbls too tables seventeen head of hogs too thousand lbs. of new bacon thirty lbs. of corn too sacks of hay too stacks of Oats too axes too wedges one saddle and bridle and all other personal property that I own at this time together with all my wright title and interest that I have now or may hereafter have to a certain tract of Land which I bot of William L. May Lying on Spring Creek in Sangamon County—adjoining to Mr. Lasswell and Mr. Crowder containing seventy four acres the express understanding is that the sd Bryan is to have the wright to get his fire wood off of the sd tract of land the above named Property is Mortgaged to sd Payne in order to secure him in a Debt and by note for Seventeen hundred and one dollars Now it is expressly understood that if sd Bryan does pay sd note and Interest thereon that the above named property shall be released otherwise be legally applied to pay the Debt Witness my hand and seal this 8 day of Decr. 1834

Albert John Elliott　　　　　　　　Nicholas Bryan (Seal)

State of Illinois 　)
Sangamon County)

Be it known that on this day Nicholas Brian of said County & State appeared before me the undersigned Justice of the peace and acknowledged that he executed the within Mortgage for the purposes therein expressed
Given under my hand & seal January the 2d 1835 　　T. M. Neale J P D S

Mortgage
Thomas J. Payne
    Filed for Record
        Jan 3d 1835
            fee Paid 75
                (A.)

State of Illinois   )
Sangamon County)   Recorders office Jan 8 1835
I Edward Mitchell Recorder of Sangamon County do hereby
Certify that this Mortgage is Recorded in this office in Book
H Page 88

                        E. Mitchell R SC
                        By Charles Arnold D S

NOTICE BY LINCOLN OF A BILL HE INTENDS TO INTRODUCE IN THE LEGISLATURE, DECEMBER 9, 1834

On December 9, 1834, the eighth day of his first term in the Legislature, Lincoln gave the subjoined notice, copied from the original in his handwriting, of his intention to presently introduce a bill authorizing Samuel Musick to build a toll bridge across Salt Creek, in Sangamon County. Musick, who operated a ferry across Salt Creek, contended that increased travel on the road from Springfield to Peoria warranted the building of a bridge, and Lincoln, moved by his habitual desire to serve a friend, on December 15 introduced the bill of which he had given notice. It was amended in minor details by a select committee to which it was referred and of which Lincoln was a member. The amended bill passed the House on December 20, and in due course became a law.

Mr. Speaker: I now give notice that Thursday next, or some day thereafter I shall ask leave to introduce a bill entitled an act to authorize Samuel Musick to build a toll bridge across Salt Creek in Sangamon County.

MOTION BY LINCOLN TO CHANGE THE RULES OF THE HOUSE, DECEMBER 11, 1834

An unsuccessful effort by Lincoln to change the rules of the popular branch of the Illinois Legislature is thus recorded in the House Journal for 1834-35, Page 103.

Mr. Lincoln moved that the following be added to the rules of the House, viz:

"It shall not be in order, to offer amendments to any bill, after its third reading;"
Which was not agreed to.

LINCOLN SPEAKS IN LEGISLATURE ON BILL TO LIMIT JURISDICTION OF JUSTICES OF THE PEACE, DECEMBER 24, 1834

On December 27, 1834, the Illinois Advocate of Vandalia published the subjoined record of the proceedings of the lower branch of the Illinois Legislature on December 24. But no trace can be found of the speeches which the editor promised to give in a later issue.

McHenry from select committee reports the bill to "limit the jurisdiction of justices of peace, with an amendment thereto, striking out all after the enacting clause."

Link offered an amendment, giving the pltf. power to sue in civil cases, either in the precinct where the contract was made, or where the deft. resides.

McHenry moved the report & pro. amendment be tabled until July 4. On report and motion to amend, & to table an animated debate took place, Messrs. Link, Thomas, Webb, Lincoln & McHenry.

The speeches will hereafter be given.

CHAPTER VI—LINCOLN IN THE YEAR 1835
SURVEY OF PERIOD

Lincoln's twenty-seventh birthday, February 12, 1835, found him in Vandalia beginning his career as a law maker. The General Assembly of Illinois was then made up of twenty-six senators and forty-five representatives. Many of the senators and representatives, as noted elsewhere, brought their wives and daughters with them to Vandalia, and in contacts with them the new member from Sangamon began a belated and much-needed training in the social amenities. The Legislature convened on December 1, 1934 and adjourned on February 13, 1835. Sunday excepted, the House met on each weekday during this period. There were roll calls on all but eight days, and the records show that Mr. Lincoln was present and voting on every roll call.

A new member, Mr. Lincoln's only assignment to the standing committees of the House was to the minor one of public accounts and expenditures; but he was appointed from time to time to several select committees; introduced various bills of concern only to his constituents, and took a keen and intelligent interest in the proceedings of the House. He roomed with Major John Todd Stuart, who was serving his second term as a member of the House, and who a few months before had advised young Lincoln to study law, and during his weeks at Vandalia began his acquaintance with other members with whom he was destined to soon have close association in politics and at the bar. Then began his friendship with Edwin B. Webb, who was to become his rival for the hand of Mary Todd, and like enduring and helpful association with Archibald Williams, Jesse K. Dubois, Jesse W. Fell, William Fithian and John J. Hardin. These first weeks at Vandalia in truth played a vital part in shaping the career that then lay ahead of Abraham Lincoln. When they were ended he went back to New Salem, to his duties as postmaster and deputy surveyor and to study of the law books he was borrowing from Stuart and Dummer.

Meanwhile, in the newspapers that came to New Salem its postmaster found recorded events which he must have noted as of present or future import. Thus, significant of the trend the anti-slavery movement soon was to take in the Middle West, early in February, 1835, the trustees of the lately founded college at Oberlin, Ohio, not only declared for the training of both sexes, but also that "the education of people of color shall be encouraged and sustained." The first year only one of the 277 Oberlin students was colored, but without delay this lone student was joined by others of his race. In the end a fifth of the population of the town was negro, and it became a great station on the Underground Railroad.

It is probable that copies of the New York Herald, which James Gordon Bennett founded on May 6, 1835, rarely if ever reached New Salem, but twenty-five years later its Scotch editor, a law unto himself, was first to oppose and then to give ungrudging support to the policies of President Lincoln who had learned how, in trying times, to turn an enemy into a friend. And a fortnight after the founding of the Herald, on May 20, 1835, the Democratic National Convention at Baltimore nominated Van Buren for the Presidency and adopted the two-thirds rule which in years to come was to play havoc with the ambitions of its nominee and of more than one other Democratic leader, Stephen A. Douglas, Lincoln's long-time rival, among them.

The second Seminole War, which was to last for five years, began on November 1, 1835, and a little more than six weeks later, on December 16, an anti-Masonic convention chose as its candidate for President, William Henry Harrison who in the following year demonstrated such strength with the voters that in 1840 politicians concerned for the success of their party—Thurlow Weed and Abraham Lincoln were two of them—put aside Henry Clay to make Harrison the Whig nominee. More important in its bearing on the future of Abraham Lincoln, of New Salem, the popular branch of Congress on December 7, 1835, chose for its speaker James K. Polk of Tennessee who, a dozen years later as President, was to extend our national boundaries to the Pacific, determine the destiny of the vast area lying west of the Louisiana Purchase, call forth the Wilmot Proviso—and cost the sole Whig representative of Illinois a second term in Congress. And also in mid-December, 1835, William Ellery Channing published his reasoned book on Slavery, a copy of which later presented by Jesse W. Fell to his friend, Abraham Lincoln, was read and pondered by the latter with far-reaching results. Truly, 1835 was a pregnant year for the postmaster of New Salem.

SPEECH BY LINCOLN ON A SURVEYOR FOR
SCHUYLER COUNTY, JANUARY 6, 1835

In its issue for January 17, 1835, the Sangamo Journal printed the summary given below of one of Lincoln's earliest speeches, perhaps his first, in the Legislature, delivered on January 6, 1835. It would appear that the Assembly had appointed a surveyor for Schuyler County when no vacancy existed in that office.

Mr. Vandeventer gave notice that, although a surveyor had been appointed by the two houses for Schuyler County, there had been no vacancy. Mr. Webb said the last appointment then was a nullity.

Mr. Lincoln said, that if, as appeared to be the opinion of legal gentlemen, there was no danger of the new surveyor's ousting the old one so long as he persisted not to die—he would suggest the propriety of letting matters remain as they were, so that if the old surveyor should hereafter conclude to die, there would be a new one ready made without troubling the legislature.

Stuart offered an amendment to Lincoln's resolution striking out all after the word Resolved and inserting a provision requiring the House to rescind their nomination to that office and requesting the Senate to rescind their appointment. Said amendment was concurred in, and on the motion of Mr. Thomas the resolution was laid on the table.

RESOLUTION OFFERED BY LINCOLN IN THE

ILLINOIS LEGISLATURE, JANUARY 10, 1835

This resolution manifests the lively interest then taken by the people of Illinois in the disposition of public lands belonging to the United States. It was, however, promptly laid on the table.

Mr. Lincoln proposed for adoption the following resolution, viz:

RESOLVED BY THE GENERAL ASSEMBLY OF THE STATE OF ILLINOIS, That our Senators be instructed, and our Representatives requested to use their whole influence in the Congress of the United States, to procure the passage of any law relative to the public lands, by the operation of which, the State of Illinois, would be entitled to receive annually, a sum of money not less in amount than 20 per cent upon the amount annually paid into the Treasury of the United States, for public lands lying within the limits of the said State of Illinois.

RESOLVED, That the Governor of this State be requested to forthwith transmit a copy of these resolutions to each of our Senators and Representatives in Congress.

Mr. Thomas moved to refer said resolutions to a committee of the Whole House and make them the order of the day for Tuesday next: which was not agreed to. On motion of Mr. Ficklin, said resolutions were laid upon the table.

SUMMARY OF SPEECH BY LINCOLN IN THE LEGIS-LATURE DISCUSSING COMMITTEE ON APPRO-PRIATION PROPOSED BY JESSE B. THOMAS, JR, JANUARY 21, 1835

The subjoined article from the Illinois Advocate of Van-dalia, January 28, 1835, gives a summary of one of Lincoln's first speeches in the Legislature. Jesse B. Thomas, Jr., whose preamble and resolution prompted it, was the nephew of a more widely known namesake. A native of Ohio and a lawyer by profession, he entered the Illinois Legislature in 1834, and quickly became one of the Democratic leaders in that body. Before his term ended he was appointed attorney-general. Later he served as a circuit judge and in 1843 succeeded Stephen A. Douglas as an associate justice of the Supreme Court of Illinois. He died in Chicago in 1852 at the age of forty-four.

Thomas offered a preamble and resolution, requiring the appointment of a joint select committee to report a bill fixing the ratio for an apportionment of representation for this state, adapted to the census to be taken in the present year.

Thomas said, the apportionment could be fixed before the census was taken, by saying what number of inhabitants should have a representative, a senator; and it would save the state the great expense of having no representation for four years. The only difficulty which suggested itself to his mind, was that of fixing the senatorial districts. But this, he thought, could be regulated so as to answer all necessary purposes; and if there should be some defects as regards the inequality of represeta-tion in the Senate, they could be remedied in the next session. Mr. Vandeventer moved to lay said res. on the table until July 4.

Mr. Lincoln said, the reasons offered by the gentleman from Madison would certainly induce him to go against the resolution.

"The gentleman had said that there would be a difficulty in fixing the Senatorial districts; and, sir, in my humble opinion, there would be an insurmountable difficulty. The districts cannot be arranged, and with a full knowledge of this fact, I have no doubt the House will lay the resolution on the table until the 4th day of July—at least I will vote in that way."

Vote was taken on tabling until the 4th & tabled, ayes 35, nays 16.

BILL INTRODUCED IN THE ILLINOIS LEGISLATURE, FEBRUARY 12, 1835

Success attended Lincoln's second effort as a lawmaker. This bill, which appointed three of his friends commissioners to locate the first section of the Springfield-Lewiston road, became a law on February 12, 1835.

Sec 1 Be it enacted by the People of the State of Illinois represented in the General Assembly.

That Reuben Harrison, John Clary and Tandy James be and they are hereby appointed commissioners to view, mark and permanently locate so much of the State road, leading from Springfield in Sangamon county to Lewiston in Fulton county, as lies between Springfield and George G. Miller's ferry on the Sangamo river.

Sec 2 Said commissioners or a majority of them shall meet at the town of Springfield on the second Monday in March next or as soon thereafter as practicable and after being duly sworn by some officer authorized to administer oaths shall proceed to perform the duties required of them by this act; avoiding as much as possible the injury of private property.

Sec 3 The said commissioners shall as soon thereafter as convenient, cause to be filed with the clerk of the county commissioners' court of Sangamon a report and complete map of said road—which report and map shall be preserved and shall form a part of the record of said court. Said road when so established shall be kept in repair as other State roads are.

Sec 4 The county commissioners court of Sangamon county shall allow to said commissioners, out of the county treasury, such compensation, as to them shall seem just and reasonable.

LAND SURVEY BY LINCOLN FOR WILLIAM McNEELY, MARCH 10, 1835

All of this survey is in Lincoln's handwriting.

Surveyed for William McNeely a part of the of the (sic) South West fractional quarter of Section 30 in Township 18 North of Range 7 West. Beginning at the middle of Gum's branch where the Eastern boundary line of said fraction crosses the same at an Ash 7 inches in diameter bearing N 28 W 48 links. Thence North 18 chains to the North East corner of said fraction at an Overcup 10 inches S 42 E 92 links. Thence West 8 chains & 95 links to a White Oak 10 inches S 36 E 43 links. Thence South 17 chains & 57 links to the middle of the aforesaid branch at a Hackberry 7 inches N 28 W 48 links. Thence up the branch with the meanderings to the beginning.

Also, the West half of the South West quarter of Section 21 in the aforesaid Township. Beginning at the South West corner of the same at a Post & Mound. Thence East 20 chains to a Post & Mound. Thence North 20 chains to a Post & Mound. Thence West 20 chains to a Post & Mound. Thence South 40 chains to the beginning.

John Calhoun S.S.C.
By A. Lincoln

LAND SURVEY BY LINCOLN FOR ARCHIBALD KINCAID, MARCH 24, 1835

All of this survey is in Lincoln's handwriting.

Surveyed for Archibald Kincaid the North West fourth of the North East quarter of Section 33 in Township 18 North of Range 6 West—Beginning at the North West corner of the same at a White Oak 12 inches in diameter bearing N 85 E 17 Links. White Oak 13 inches S 66 W 7 58 Links— Thence S 88 E 20 chains & 21 Links to a White Oak 9 inches S 25 W 27 Links—Thence South 20 chains to a White Oak 24 inches East side corner—Thence N 88 W 20 chains & 21 Links to a Spanish Oak 20 inches—corner—Thence North 20 chains to the beginning—

J. Calhoun SSC
By A. Lincoln

POSTMASTER LINCOLN FRANKS AN ENVELOPE FOR M. S. MARSH, SEPTEMBER 22, 1835.

(Photostat from Lincoln National Life Foundation)

Postmaster Lincoln franked this letter completely in his own hand. It was sent to a brother of M. S. Marsh of New Salem, who wrote that Postmaster Lincoln left the office open and unattended, a careless thing in the eyes of Marsh, and he added that there were no high charges for postage by the New Salem postmaster. An interesting note in this franked cover is the frequent use of the double period after abbreviations of words, a thing that would lead to the conclusion that the "A" in "A.. Lincoln" was not the only letter to receive a double dot from the future President.

Free   A.. Lincoln P.. M..
               New Salem, Ills
               Sept 22
Mr. Gee   M.   Marsh
               Portsmouth
               N..   H..

NOTE TO BLAIR & RIVES

In 1835 Francis P. Blair, Sr., and John C. Rives were publishers of the Washington Globe, stout champion of Jackson and his policies. Twenty-five years later Blair and his two sons took an effective part in the nomination and election of Lincoln to the Presidency.

                         New Salem, Ills.
                         Nov. 3, 1835

Mesrs. (sic)

Your subscriber at this place John C. Vance, is dead, and no person takes the paper from the office.

                      Respectfully,
                      A.. Lincoln, P. M.

Blair & Rives

LINCOLN TO JOSEPH DUNCAN, NOVEMBER 10, 1835.

No doubt Lincoln and Davis began an enduring friendship while the former was serving his first term in the Leisglature. Davis was state auditor from 1835 to 1846, and later was for many years a prominent and successful lawyer in Alton, Illinois.

He was appointed auditor six days after Lincoln wrote Governor Duncan in his behalf.

New Salem, Nov. 10th, 1835

His Excellency Governor Duncan
Dear Sir

Understanding that Mr. Levi Davis of Vandalia, is an applicant for the office of Auditor of Public Accounts, I take the liberty to say to you, that his appointment to that office would be entirely satisfactory to me, and, I doubt not, to most others who are the friends of qualification and—merit—

Your Obt Servt
A. Lincoln

RESOLUTION BY LINCOLN TO BUILD A CANAL IN THE SANGAMON RIVER VALLEY, DECEMBER 11, 1835

Lincoln's advocacy of internal improvements was frequently in evidence during his entire period of service in the Legislature. The subjoined entry in the House Journal for 1835-36, Page 34 bears witness to this fact.

On motion of Mr. Lincoln,

Resolved, That a select committee of five be appointed to inquire into the expediency of incorporating a company to construct a canal upon the valley of the Sangamon river, and that they report by bill or otherwise.

Ordered, That Messrs. Lincoln, Brown, Gordon, Carpenter of Sangamon, and Trower, be that committee.

BILL BY LINCOLN INCORPORATING THE BEARDSTOWN AND SANGAMON CANAL COMPANY.

On December 12, 1835, Lincoln reported to the lower house of the General Assembly a bill to incorporate the Beardstown and Sangamon Canal Company, one of a score of similar projects which then found advocates in Illinois. This bill Lincoln reported from committee on December 16. It was duly passed by the House and, the Senate assenting, on December 28 became a law. Lincoln wrote Section 13 of the bill, the original of which is now in the Illinois State Archives at Springfield. Due to the panic of 1837 and other causes the Beardstown and Sangamon Canal never passed the initial stages of promotion.

Sec. 1. Be it enacted by the people of the State of Illinois, represented in the General Assembly, That Archibald Job, Francis Arenz, Thomas Wilbourn and Benjamin Sutton, of Morgan County; and John Taylor and Charles Broadwell, of Sangamon County; and all such persons as shall become stockholders, agreeably to the provisions of this act, are hereby constituted a body corporate, by the name of the "Beardstown and Sangamon Canal Company;" and shall continue for the term of fifty years, from and after the passage of this act.

Sec. 2. The corporation shall have the right and power to construct, and during its existence, to maintain and continue, a canal from Beardstown, on the Illinois river, to a point in township number nineteen north, of range number seven west, on the Sangamon river; from thence to improve the waters of said river, by canal or otherwise, through Sangamon county, into Macon county, as shall or may be agreed on by said company, to transport, take and carry, persons and property on the same; to have, hold, use, and enjoy the same, and the tolls and profits thereof, for and during the period aforesaid.

Sec. 3. The capital stock of said company shall be three hundred thousand dollars, with liberty to increase the same, from time to time, by new subscriptions, in such manner and form as they shall think proper, if such increase shall be deemed necessary by the company, to fulfill the intent of this act;—which said capital stock shall be divided into shares of one hundred dollars each, which shall be deemed personal property, and transferable in such manner as the said corporation shall direct.

Sec. 4. That Archibald Job, James Arenz, Thomas Wilbourn, Thomas Beard, Benjamin Sutton, Allen F. Lindsey, John Taylor and Charles Broadwell, are hereby appointed commissioners, the duty of whom or a majority of them, shall be, within one year after the passage of this act, to open books, at some suitable place in Beardstown, Springfield and Decatur to receive subscriptions to the capital stock of said corporation, and to do such other things as in their opinion is best calculated to get stock taken; thirty days public notice shall be given by said commissioners of the time and place of the opening of said books, in one or more of the public newspapers in each of the said places. The said commissioners shall receive no subscriptions, unless five dollars on each share subscribed, be paid at the time of subscription; and as soon as the whole of the stock, or twenty-five thousand dollars thereof, shall be subscribed, to give a like notice for a meeting of the stockholders, to choose five directors; and such election shall then and there be made, by such stockholders as may attend, either in person or by proxy; and persons having the highest number of votes, shall be duly elected: each share of capital stock, owned ten days previous to an election, shall entitle the owner to one vote. The commissioners who receive subscriptions of stock, shall be inspectors of the first election, and shall certify under their hands and seals, the names of those elected directors, and deliver over the moneys, books and papers to said directors. The first meeting of the directors shall be held at Beardstown, within ten days after the election.

Sec. 5. That in case the capital stock in whole, or twenty-five thousand dollars thereof, shall not have been subscribed, at the places named in the foregoing section, after the books have been kept open ten days, then the said commissioners shall be authorized to re-open said books for the subscription of stock, at such times and places, and in such manner, and after such notice, and under the direction of one or more, as a majority of them shall direct. And in case a greater amount of capital stock shall be subscribed for than necessary for construction of the whole, or such part of the canal as the directors shall designate, the excess shall be taken from each subscriber in proportion to the amount subscribed.

Sec. 6. At the first meeting of the directors after an election, they shall choose one of their own body as president; and the directors first elected, shall continue in office until the first Monday in June, next after their election, and until others are chosen: and elections shall be held annually thereafter, on the first Monday in June, at such place as the directors shall designate. Each subsequent election shall be held under the direction of three stockholders, not being directors, who shall previously be appointed for that purpose, by the directors. All elections shall be by ballot. No person shall be a director, who shall not at the time of the election, own one hundred dollars of stock. In case an equal number of votes shall at any time be given for two or more persons for director, those having a plurality of votes shall determine, by ballot, who shall be entitled to the office.

Sec. 7. In case it shall at any time happen, that no election shall be held for directors, at the time required by this act, the said corporation shall not thereby be dissolved; but the directors in office shall continue until their successors are elected.

Sec. 8. The said directors shall cause such examinations and surveys to be made, as may be necessary to the selection by them, of the most advantageous line, course, or way for the said canal, from Beardstown to such point or place on the Sangamon river, as they shall designate, for the termination of the same; and shall locate the same on the most advantageous route; and after such location, shall make a map thereof, and certify under their hands and seals, upon such map, the courses and distances of the route selected, describing the land through which it passes, and file one copy of such map and certificate with the recorder of each county through which said canal is intended to pass: and the said company shall be authorized to construct and make the said canal on the route so located.

Sec. 9. The said corporation shall have the power to purchase, receive and hold, such real estate as may be necessary and useful in the accomplishment of the objects of its creation; and shall be authorized to have and hold, any and all lands which may be given, granted or donated to the same, by the United States, or by any person, or body politic, and to sell and convey the same. It shall also be authorized to enter upon, and use any and all lands, over and upon which said canal may pass, and so much of said land as may be necessary to the construction of the canal, and the convenient use and enjoyment of the same; also to take and use timber, stone, and such other materials as may be indispensible to the construction and maintenance of said canal; Provided, That said company shall pay to the owner or owners of land, entered upon and used as aforesaid, the damages sustained by such owner or owners; and also the owner or owners of timber, stone, and materials, the value thereof, before entering upon and taking the same. And if said company and owner or owners, shall be unable to agree upon the damages sustained by the entering upon and using land and real estate, or the value of timber, stone and materials, such damage, or the value of materials aforesaid, shall be ascertained under, and according to the provisions of the act, entitled "An act concerning the right of way, and for other purposes," approved 28th February, 1833.

Sec. 10. The said company shall be authorized to use the waters of the Sangamon river, to supply the canal, or otherwise; and to make such dams or locks as may be necessary to procure a sufficient quantity of water for the use of the canal, or otherwise; Provided, No dam or lock shall be constructed across said river, as to injure the navigation thereof; And Provided, also That said company shall be responsible for all damages sustained by the overflowing of any lands, by the owner thereof; and also for all damages sustained by the making dams or locks upon the land of any person or persons whatsoever. In case the said canal shall cross any water course, or public road, the same shall be so constructed as not to injure the use of such water course, or road.

Sec. 11. The directors of said company shall have power to transact all the business of said corporation, and to this end may appoint such agents, clerks or servants, engineers, and other persons, as may be deemed necessary to attend to, and manage the business of the company. They shall also have power to prescribe all such rules, and to adopt all such bye-laws, touching the management and disposition of the stock, property, and estate of the company, and touching the conduct and duties of all persons employed by the company, as may be necessary, and not inconsistent with law. They shall also have power to require payment by the stockholders, of the stock subscribed, at such times, and in such proportions, as the same may be needed in the construction of the canal, or for any other purpose authorized by this act; and shall, from time to time, give public notice of the payments thus required, and of the time and place of payment, in some newspapers published in Morgan and Sangamon counties, Illinois, and such other papers as may be selected—such notices to be published at least four weeks previous to the day appointed for such payment. And the directors are authorized, in case any stockholder shall fail to make payment as required, to cause the stock of such stockholders to be sold at public auction, and apply the proceeds of such sale, to such payment, or to provide for the forfeiture of such stock to the company.

Sec. 12. A majority of the board of directors shall constitute a quorum to do business; and shall have, and exercise all the powers conferred upon the company; Provided, That the directors may, by their bye-laws, require the presence of all the directors, on the transaction of such business, as the directors may think should require such presence. The said company is hereby declared able, and capable in law, to sue and be sued, to plead and be impleaded, in all courts of law, and in chancery; to contract and be contracted with, as fully and completely as a natural person.

Sec. 13. The state, or the counties through which the said canal shall pass, at any time after ten years shall have elapsed, for the completion of said canal, have the privilege of purchasing the same, by paying said company the original cost, together with any deficiencies which have accrued by a failure of said canal to produce twelve per cent, per annum, from the time of its completion, upon the original cost.

Sec. 14. The canal to be constructed by said company, shall be of sufficient width and depth, to admit the passage of canal boats of the ordinary kind; and the company shall be responsible for all accidents and delays, occasioned by the negligence or inattendance of its agents. Said company shall also permit all persons to pass upon said canal with boats, persons and property, whenever the same is passable, upon payment of such tolls as may be fixed upon by the directors: Provided, That the tolls shall be uniform.

Sec. 15. If any person or persons shall wilfully, or negligently, do or cause to be done, any act or acts whatsoever, whereby any building, construction, or work of the said corporation, or any boat or other things pertaining to the same, shall be weakened, impaired, or destroyed, every such person shall forfeit and pay to said corporation treble the amount of damages sustained, to be recovered by action of debt, in the name of said corporation, in any court, or before any justice of peace, having jurisdiction thereof, with cost of suit; and such person or persons shall also be subject to indictment, and punishment by fine or imprisonment.

Sec. 16. Unless the said corporation shall commence the construction of said canal within three years from the passage of this act, and complete so much thereof as lies within the county of Morgan, within six years, the powers and privileges hereby conferred shall cease, and the said corporation shall be dissolved.

Sec. 17. The mode of suing such corporation, shall be by summons, and a copy of the summons delivered to the president of the board, the secretary, or treasurer, shall be sufficient service of process, to require the corporation to answer, and to authorize any court to proceed to judgment.

BILL BY LINCOLN TO RELOCATE A PART OF THE STATE ROAD FROM SPRINGFIELD TO LEWIS-TOWN, DECEMBER 15, 1835

Lincoln introduced the subjoined bill. He was chairman of the select committee that drafted it, and the original is in his handwriting. The bill was duly passed and approved by the Governor.

An act to relocate a part of the State Road leading from Springfield to Lewistown.

Be it enacted by the People of the State of Illinois represented in the General Assembly: That Samuel Berry, James Pantier, and John Jones, Sen. be and they are hereby appointed commissioners to view, mark, and relocate so much of the State Road leading from Springfield to Lewistown as lies between the Southern boundary line of Township 19 North of Range 7 West, and the residence of the said John Jones Sen.

The Said commissioners shall meet at the house of Samuel Berry on the first Monday of May next, or some convenient day thereafter, and after being duly sworn, shall proceed to make said relocation, and shall make return thereof to the county commissioners court for Sangamon county at their next term.

The said county commissioners court, shall allow said commissioners such compensation as they may deem reasonable.

LETTER TO THE SANGAMO JOURNAL BELIEVED TO HAVE BEEN WRITTEN BY LINCOLN, DECEMBER 19, 1835

Lincoln had been settled only a short time in New Salem before he began to make friends in the growing town of Springfield, which in 1821 had been made the county-seat of the lately organized county of Sangamon. One of the earliest of these was Simeon Francis. Born in Wethersfield, Connecticut, in 1796, Francis learned the printer's trade in New Haven, and removing to Illinois in the fall of 1831 began publication of the Sangamo (now the Illinois State) Journal in which he championed the policies and candidates of the Whig Party. He conducted the Journal until 1855, when he sold it to other parties. Then he founded and for three years published the Illinois Farmer. In 1859 Francis removed to Portland, Oregon, where he was in turn the founder of the Oregon Farmer and of the Portland Oregonian. Through the years he maintained an intimate friendship with Lincoln, who in 1861 made him a paymaster in the regular army with the rank of major. He served in that capacity until 1870, when he retired on half-pay, dying two years later in Portland.

James H. Matheny (Weik Mss., no date) is authority for the statement that Lincoln soon after meeting Francis began at New Salem to write pieces for the Journal, and there is little doubt

*that he continued this practice when late in November, 1834, he
went to Vandalia to begin his first term of service in the popular
branch of the Illinois Legislature. Beveridge believes that this
letter from Vandalia which appeared in the Journal of December
19, 1835, was written by Lincoln. See "Simeon Francis" by
Harriet Ramsey Taylor, Transactions of the Illinois State Historical Society for 1907, Pp. 329-331, and Abraham Lincoln by
Albert J. Beveridge, (Boston, 1928), Volume I, Page 171.*

It was at this time that Mr. Lincoln, as he recalled in 1860,
had the first of many meetings with Stephen Arnold Douglas,
four years younger than himself, who, though not a member of
the Legislature, was at Vandalia and on February 10 was elected
state's attorney for the Morgan County judicial district over John
J. Hardin, for whom Lincoln cast his vote. Born in Vermont,
the son of a country doctor, Douglas studied law for a brief
period in New York, and at the age of twenty drifted to the
West, poor in pocket but resolutely intent on winning his way.
His travels ended in the late November of 1833 at the hamlet of
Winchester, Illinois, where he hoped to find pupils for a subscription school and where his swift adjustment to new surround-
ings was not unlike that of Mr. Lincoln three years earlier at
New Salem. The second day after his arrival in Winchester
Douglas was asked to serve as clerk at an auction sale, and in
discharging this task proved his gift for making on the instant
devoted and helpful friends. Soon he had secured forty pupils
for his prospective school at three dollars and a quarter for each
pupil, and the path to an uncommon career in law and politics
lay clear before him.

Douglas had a long body and short legs which, in after years,
prompted Thomas H. Benton, a man always keenly aware of his
own importance, to declare with a sneer that "he could never be
President because his coattails were too near the ground." But
a man of great ability wedded to tireless ambition, Douglas was
also dominated from his first to his last years by his vision of
a united and closely welded nation stretching from ocean to
ocean and from the Great Lakes to the Gulf; and he had the
power to shape men and measures to that end. It is now the considered judgment of history that, after his longtime rival, Lincoln, he was the public man who, in a fateful era, most influenced
his country's destiny.

The late Logan Hay, addressing the Abraham Lincoln Association in 1936, recalled the helpful conditions under which the

newcomer at Vandalia gathered material for his letters to the
Sangamo Journal. Mr. Lincoln throughout the session roomed
with Major John Todd Stuart with whom he had become ac-
quainted during the Black Hawk War and with whom he was
to form a partnership in 1837 immediately after his admission
to the bar. "Stuart's important position in the House organiza-
tion," said Mr. Hay, "caused his room to be a meeting place for
the leaders of the House. There took place much of the informal
discussion regarding pending legislation. There, more intimately
than elsewhere, Mr. Lincoln saw forceful men in contact with
each other, agreeing, disagreeing, compromising their differences.
He saw that legislation was shaped by personal influence as well
as by the merits of the measure." Thus at Vandalia in the winter
of 1834-35 "he saw the democracy of the frontier in action and
took his freshman course in government, politics and statsman-
ship."

From a Member of the Legislature to His Friend in This Place

Vandalia, Dec. 7, 1835.

Dear Sir:

On this day the Van Buren Democratic Convention met.
For me to undertake to give any thing like a true account of its
splendor, would be presumption. It presented, really, a true
picture of disinterestedness. O, if you only had witnessed it, you
would immediately have wished yourself a real Van Buren democrat. Stock in the ranks of democracy has risen fifty per cent
up to 9 o'clock this evening. A large amount of it has been disposed of. They have engrafted some of it into the clouds of
Morgan. There is beauty in this democracy. It is of all shades
and colors. You had better come down immediately while stock
can be obtained. You have nothing to fear from your past of-
fences. No questions will be asked as to your past conduct.
You will only be requested to swear allegiance to Martin Van
Buren. I have said come, you have nothing to fear. My opinion
is founded upon the fact of their disposing of a large amount
to A. W. Cavarly, the ring leader of Websterism in this State.
Col. J. M. Strode, a true disciple of Clay—the same Col. S.
formerly of Sangamon County—and who swore so bitterly when
Adams and Jackson were candidates for the Presidency, that if
General Jackson was elected, he would leave the United States;
for if he was compelled to live under a monarchial government,
he would prefer Old England. I could give you the names of a

number of like characters composing this most august assemblage, and then throw in a British deserter for all I know for good count. Since I arrived here, I feel sorry that I have been born to die so soon, for I find that man is continually gaining information. I have seen of late what I thought could not be performed by any man, or set of men. On Sunday evening about ten o'clock the leaders of this disinterested Convention inoculated a Mr. .... with a little of the Van Buren democracy and next morning at sun-rise he had brought forth ten little democrats. Who would not wish to live forever when they can see such almost impossibilities performed? Gov. Jenkins did digress a little—not so little either. He certainly did wrong, and I believe he will be paid for it. Those good and obedient fellows were for electing Semple President.—They urged as a reason that the precedent had been set them by the Baltimore Convention, by electing Stevenson former speaker of the House of Representatives of Congress, and furthermore, Mr. Semple was chosen the night before by at least seven democrats. Here Jenkins done wrong in opposing dictation. He boldly denied the right of a few of the leaders getting together and appointing a President for him. He did wrong for the reason that this is the Van Buren policy, and, sir, who dare say to the contrary?

Your's with respect.

AMENDMENT PROPOSED BY LINCOLN TO THE SUPPLEMENTAL ACT INCORPORATING THE SUBSCRIBERS TO THE BANK OF ILLINOIS AT SHAWNEETOWN, DECEMBER 22, 1835

On January 6, 1836, the Illinois Advocate of Vandalia printed the account given below of a debate in the House on December 22, 1835, in the course of which Lincoln proposed an "amendment to an act supplemental to an act to incorporate the Subscribers of the Bank of the State of Illinois"—at Shawneetown, which was promptly voted down.

The engrossed bill entitled "An Act Supplemental to an act to incorporate the Subscribers to the Bank of the State of Illinois." was read a third time.

Mr. Lincoln moved to amend the bill by striking out the reservation in the 3rd section and adding the following as an additional section, viz: "Sec. 5. The said corporation shall at the next session of the General Assembly, and at each subsequent

general session, during the existence of its charter, report to
the same the amount of debts due to the same, the amount of
specie in its vaults, and an account of all lands then owned by
the same, and the amount for which such lands have been taken,
and moreover if such corporation shall at any time neglect or
refuse to submit its books, papers and all and everything neces-

sary to a full and fair examination of its affairs, to any person
or persons appointed by the General Assembly for the purpose
of making such examination, the said corporation shall forfeit
its charter."

AMENDMENT PROPOSED BY LINCOLN TO THE ILLINOIS AND MICHIGAN CANAL BILL

In the Illinois House of Representatives on Dec. 21, 1835,
Lincoln moved to amend the Eighth Section of the Illinois and
Michigan Canal Bill, by adding: "The Governor, during the recess
of the General Assembly, for any good cause, shall have power
to remove any or all of the said commissioners from office, and
to supply vacancies occasioned by such removal, which appointments shall continue until other appointments are made by the
General Assembly."   The motion fails.   House Journal.

RESOLUTION BY LINCOLN LOOKING TO THE PUB-LICATION OF GENERAL LAWS IN THE NEWS-PAPERS, DECEMBER 26, 1835

*Perhaps Lincoln had in mind the interests of his friend,
Simeon Francis of the Sangamo Journal, when he introduced the
subjoined resolution which was adopted by the Legislature.*

On motion of Mr. Lincoln,
Resolved, That the committee of Public Accounts and Expenditures, be instructed to enquire into the expediency of
authorizing the publishing of the State laws, of a general nature,
in the public newspapers, and that they report by bill or other--
wise.

CHAPTER VII—LINCOLN IN THE YEAR 1836

SURVEY OF PERIOD

The opening days of 1836, in which fell Abraham Lincoln's twenty-eighth birthday, again found him in Vandalia. In response to Governor Duncan's call the Ninth General Assembly began a second session on December 7, 1835, and so the member from New Salem was at the capital until it adjourned on January 18, 1836. In his call the Governor had urged a legislative reapportionment and the enactment of measures to hasten the construction of the Illinois and Michigan Canal. Bills for both of these purposes were promptly introduced and had the support of Mr. Lincoln, who was already known as a champion of better transportation. He gave his vote to various measures affecting the well-being of the State Bank; supported a proposal that Congress permit Illinois, in furtherance of its internal improvement program, to enter up to 500,000 acres of government land on credit; and as a good Whig was ready with pointed argument and shrewd maneuver when state and national politics claimed a place in the discussions of the Legislature.

When the Legislature adjourned, Mr. Lincoln went back to New Salem and to his law books and surveying; among other jobs that came to him laid out the towns of Petersburg and Huron; bought two lots in Springfield; entered a forty-seven acre tract on the Sangamon; engaged in a tepid courtship with Mary Owens, a young woman who had come from Kentucky to visit her sister in New Salem, and on April 2, 1836, announced in the Sangamo Journal that he was again a candidate for the Legislature. Two months later he published a platform in which he favored among other things the admission of all whites to the right of suffrage, by omission barring negroes but "by no means excluding females," and closed with the pledge: "If alive on the first Monday in November I shall vote for Hugh L. White for President."

This pledge recalls an interesting phase of Jackson's second and final contest for the Presidency. Late in January, 1833, Clay and his associates in the Senate, struck at the President through one of his most trusted advisers and by the casting vote of Calhoun, then Vice-President, rejected the appointment of Van Buren as minister to Great Britain—a political error, as it was to prove, of the first class. Calhoun, who for reasons of his own hated Van Buren, is recorded by Benton as saying to a doubting friend: "It will kill him, sir, kill him dead. He will never kick, sir, never kick." But Benton himself proved a better prophet. "You have broken a minister," he declared, "and elected a Vice President," while another shrewd observer remarked to William Cullen Bryant, "That makes Van Buren President of the United States."

Events quickly confirmed this prediction, for Van Buren's rejection fired the irate Jackson with an unswerving resolve to make him first Vice President and then President. Some of Jackson's ablest followers looked upon Van Buren with little favor and opposed his advancement; but all to no purpose. In due course Van Buren became Vice President and in May, 1835, the Democratic nominee for President. To prevent his election the Whigs nominated several candidates of local strength—among them White of Tennessee, Harrison and McLean of Ohio and Webster of Massachusetts—hoping in this way to throw the election into the House of Representatives. Jackson and White had been close friends for a generation, and the latter, a man of ability and a devoted public servant, had good cause for the conviction that he and not Van Buren should be the next President; but when the Tennessee Legislature followed by those of Alabama and Illinois, in defiance of Jackson's wishes, nominated White for President, their friendship changed on the instant to bitter and unrelenting enmity, while nothing came of the Whig plan to throw the election into the House, for Jackson's popularity with the people, assured both the nomination and election of his successor. True to his pledge Abraham Lincoln voted on November 1, 1836, for the White electors in Illinois, an example followed by young Andrew Johnson in Tennessee; but when the final returns were in it was found that the Tennessean had carried only Georgia and his own state, and that Van Buren had a substantial majority both of the popular vote and in the electoral college.

In the newspapers, which came to New Salem in the tense months of 1836, Abraham Lincoln read of the death on June 28 of James Madison, last of the makers of the republic, whose sunny disposition in old age had endeared him alike to Jackson and Clay; and he noted in intent and reflective mood that at last the future of slavery had become a dominant and insistent issue both in and out of Congress. Thus on the opening day of 1836, James Gillespie Birney, a lawyer of Kentucky and Alabama who *had freed his slaves, became an anti-slavery editor in Ohio and began the career which was to resolve the solution of a vital issue into a contest between parties.*

Again, in a formal speech on March 9, 1836, Calhoun, once more a member of the Senate, championed non-interference with slavery—a doctrine which, vitally affecting the career of Abraham Lincoln, was to lead to the Kansas-Nebraska bill and the Civil War. And on May 23, 1836, the venerable John Quincy Adams in a five-hour speech in the House—a speech no doubt read with care by New Salem's law student and surveyor—in which he championed the right of petition, grimly predicted a time when the federal government would be compelled to interfere to emancipate the slaves. Adams spoke at the moment without avail, for three days later the House, moved thereto by the report of a special committee headed by Pinckney of South Carolina, adopted what soon came to be known as the "gag resolution:" "That all petitions, memorials, resolutions, propositions or papers relating in any way or to any extent whatever to the subject of slavery or the abolition of slavery shall, without being either printed or referred, be laid upon the table and that no further action whatsoever shall be had thereon." Thus men of the South, backed by men of the North who wanted no interference with the established order of things, sought to silence opposition and in so doing lighted fires that only war could put out.

And while at Vandalia and New Salem, Abraham Lincoln watched the trend of events, in New York City, Theodore Dwight Weld, six years Lincoln's elder, born in Connecticut and reared in Western New York, under the auspices of the American Antislavery Society was training a band of seventy young men— most of whom in the Great Revival of those years had been converted by Finney to religion—to preach the freedom of the slave in the Middle West, a mission discharged with such zeal and effect that in Ohio and its sister states they bred another great revival, a revival in abolitionism, which a quarter of a century later made the men of that section active and powerful in the contest to preserve the Union. Weld was a man of consuming earnestness and of exceptional gifts as a writer and speaker. Among those whom he early brought to his own way of thinking were James Gillespie Birney whom he advised to quit a profitable place at the bar to labor for the slave, and Joshua Reed Giddings of the Western Reserve, who in 1838 began in Congress his long battle against human bondage. Weld from the first was governed by a fixed purpose to keep in the background, and so largely escaped public notice and the flood of abuse poured on Garrison, who was rarely if ever averse to the limelight; but until 1843 he more than any other shaped the activities of the American Anti-Slavery Society, and, although after the year named he lived in self-sought retirement, when he died in 1895, at the great age of ninety-two, he was honored as the last survivor of the little group of devoted men whose foresight and vision had directed the course of the anti-slavery movement to wise and enduring ends.

And as a herald of coming storm on February 16, 1836, the Virginia Legislature by resolution urged on non-slaveholding states the forcible suppression of abolition societies, then fast increasing in number—a gesture which a year later was to prompt Mr. Lincoln to the first public announcement of his position on the slavery question. Again, later in the year, Postmaster Lincoln must have read in the newspapers of the death on September 6, at the great age of ninety-eight, of Moses Brown of Providence, who in his early middle years had turned Quaker and freed his slaves; who in 1789 had persuaded Samuel Slater to come to America and so led in the founding of the cotton mill industry in New England, and whose generous gifts in part caused the name of Rhode Island College to be changed to Brown University. It should also be recorded that the president of Brown University for a generation following 1827 was Francis Wayland, whose firm yet measured stand on the slavery issue must have caused Abraham Lincoln to regard him as a man to be honored and admired.

NOTE OF CLIFTON R. GARRETT TO VON PHUL AND MC GILL, JANUARY 1, 1836
(Herndon-Weik Collection)

This note is not cited as part of a case, and has no definite marks except the date, but the "Dam 250" in the lower left corner is in the hand of Mr. Lincoln. The Record shows no citation of such a case as Von Phul & Mc Gill vs. Garrett.

Mr. Clifton R. Garrett
        To   Vonphul &McGill   dr..
1836
    Jany 1.   To Balance a/c Rem ? to date   177.04
                     Interest to 1st oct. 1837   18.69
                                                        ————————
Dam 250 $ 196. 33

LETTERS TO THE SANGAMO JOURNAL BELIEVED TO HAVE BEEN WRITTEN BY LINCOLN, JANUARY 16, 1836

John Dawson of Sangamon who offered the amendment referred to in the letter of January 6, had been elected to the Legislature as a Democrat, but about this time became a Whig, as did many other Democrats who did not relish the methods of those who supported the Presidential candidacy of Martin Van Buren and opposed that of Hugh L. White. The Speaker, James Semple, who on each vote here recorded supported the cause of Van Buren, and who later was to serve as United States Senator, was a native of Kentucky; and it is interesting to note that of the more than one hundred men who in 1836 served in the House and Senate of Illinois not one was born in the state of his adoption. Dawson had removed from Virginia to the West. John Todd Stuart, the best known member of the House, who had already begun his long and close friendship with Lincoln, had moved eight years before from Kentucky.

Vandalia, Jan'y. 6, 1836

Dear Sir—

In my last I mentioned the introduction into the House, of a set of resolutions approving the Baltimore nominations. On yesterday evening they were taken up; and I herewith send you a copy of the Journal, so far as relates to the vote on their final passage; and to all proposed amendments; and the votes taken on them respectively. I have not been able to get a copy of the original resolutions, though they are substantially, as above stated.

The situation in which the slaves of the magician, have placed themselves, by their votes upon these proposed amendments, is, by no means enviable.

By a reference to the Journal it will be seen that Mr. Dawson offered an amendment in these words: "Resolved by the House of Representatives that we believe the above preamble and resolutions to be foreign to the duties of the Representatives of a free people: not calculated to harmonize legislation; but to destroy its usefulness to the people we represent."

To this amendment, the three following were offered as amendments and adopted by the vote attached to each.

1st. Resolved that every man who is eligible to an office within the gift of the people, has an undeniable right to become a candidate for the same; and that the people have a right to support him without the sanction of a Caucus or convention. Yeas 47, nays 4. Those voting in the negative are Able, Buckmaster, Porter, and Tunnell.

2nd. Resolved that we believe with General Jackson, that Public officers should not attempt to influence elections; because they hold the power and influence and the people's money, by which they are enabled to establish presses, support conventions, and organize secret parties to sustain their power, even against the interests of the people, and the Democratic principles of this government. Yeas 44, nays 7. Those voting in the negative are Able, Buckmaster, Carpenter of Sangamon, Craig, Oliver, Tunnell, and Speaker Semple.

3rd. Resolved that the price of public lands ought to be reduced. Resolved that all white male citizens of the age of 21 years and upwards, are entitled to the privilege of voting, whether they shall hold real estate or not.—Resolved that the elective franchise should be kept free from contamination by the admission of colored voters. Resolved that we approve of the granting of preemption rights to settlers on the public lands. Yeas 35, nays 16.—Those voting in the negative are Able, Blackford, Blockburger, Bowyer, Carpenter of Sangamon, Craig, Hackelton, Hughs, Hunter, Oliver, Outhouse, Porter, Turney, Tunnell, Wyatt, and Speaker Semple.

These having been adopted, and thereby become a part of Dawson's proposed amendment, the question came up upon adopting the whole as an amendment to the original preamble and resolutions, which was negatived. Yeas 19, Nays 32. Those voting in the negative are Able, Blackford, Blockburger, Bowyer, Buckmaster, Carpenter of Hamilton, Carpenter of Sangamon, Cloud, Craig, Dunn, Frezer, Hackelton, Harris, Hughs, Hunter, Manly, Murphy, Nunnally, Oliver, Outhouse, Owens, Pace, Porter, Smith, Tunnell, Turney, Van Deventer, Wood, Wren, Wyatt and Speaker Semple.

Here we have recorded evidence, not of what Van Buren and his party support; but of what they oppose.

The last vote above stated, was taken upon the nine following propositions, en masse:

1st. President-making is foreign to the duties of legislation.

2nd. President-making is calculated to destroy the harmony of legislation.

3rd. Every man who is eligible to an office has an undeniable right to become a candidate for the same.

4th. The people have a right to vote for whom they please, without the sanction of caucuses or conventions.

5th. Public officers should not attempt to influence elections.

6th. The price of Public Lands ought to be reduced.

7th. In the admission to the right of suffrage, no property qualifications ought to be required.

8th. Colored persons ought not to be admitted to the right of suffrage.

9th. Pre-emption rights ought to be granted to actual settlers upon the Public Lands.

These nine propositions, as may be seen by any one who will refer to the Journal, were at once negatived by the whole Van Buren party in the House: and that too, when they stood wholly unconnected with any other propositions whatever. From what they oppose, it is easy to infer what they support. Hence it is, that we are enabled to draw up a correct code of their political doctrines, which is as follows, viz.

1. President-making is not foreign to the duties of legislation.

2. President-making is not calculated to destroy the harmony of legislation.

3. Every man who is eligible to an office has not an undeniable right to become a candidate for the same.

4. The people have not a right to vote as they please without the sanction of Caucuses or conventions.

5. Public officers should attempt to influence elections.

6. The price of Public Lands ought not to be reduced.

7. In the admission to the right of Suffrage, a property qualification ought to be required.

8. Colored persons ought to be admitted to the right of suffrage.

9. Pre-emption rights ought not to be granted to actual settlers upon the Public Lands.

It cannot be said that the party were deceived, or did not vote understandingly; for Webb who proposed the amendment embracing the four propositions relative to the reduction of the price of Public Lands, the requiring of a property qualification, the admission of colored voters, and the granting of pre-emption rights, upon offering it, stated briefly, that he understood the object of the Preamble and resolutions to be, to make a President of Martin Van Buren, and that he knew, as well as he knew there was such a man, that Mr. Van Buren was, and had by his votes so proved himself, opposed to every principle contained in his proposed amendment, and that he had offered it for the express purpose of ascertaining whether, his party was prepared to avow and sustain his doctrines. After this explicit explanation, the party did avow, they did sustain them. Here, then, we have the political code of the party, first promulgated by the great Generalissimo, Mr. Van Buren himself, then acknowledged, and responded to, by his partizans in the Legislature; and now, it only remains to be seen, whether the People will ratify it. It has long been known, by many, that these were the doctrines of Mr. Van Buren, and the great difficulty has been, that his partizans here, have ever heretofore, denied them: but now, that they have come forth boldly, and told the people, that they and their master, are opposed to reducing the price of Public Lands, that they are opposed to granting Pre-emption rights to actual settlers, that they are opposed to any man's voting who does not hold real estate, that they deny the right of every eligible man to become a candidate for office, that they deny the right of the people to vote for whom they please, without the sanction of caucuses or Conventions, that they are in favor of Public officers attempting to influence elections, and that they are in favor of admitting Indians and Negroes to the right of suffrage— I say, as they have thus boldly thrown off the mask, if the people be found prepared to sustain them, let the lamp of freedom be blown out, and henceforth remain in the darkness forever, and let the rights of man, in all time to come be spoken of, like the Phoenix, as only ideal and not reality.

Vandalia, Ill. 7th Jan. 1836

I am gratified in being able to inform you that the canal bill, introduced into the house by Dawson of your county, and which passed that body with amendments, was this morning returned to the house from the senate, with the amendments struck off. Mr. Turney labored hard to restore his amendments and to lay the bill on the table. In all his plans he was most completely foiled by the powerful appeals made to the good sense of the house by Messrs. Stuart and Dunn. The question on concurring with the senate, was decided in the affirmative—yeas 38, nays 14. And thus at last justice is meted out to the North, by the united action of all parts of the state. The northern members in general have done their duty. Some few Vannies have endeavored to prejudice the best interests of the work, by making efforts to secure the offices of canal commissioners to partizans of their own party. Notwithstanding their majority in the house, they have in all their attempts to legislate for the benefit of party, been boldly met and defeated. Their zeal to serve their friends, and to take the appointing power from the Governor and senate, has taken their attention so much, that they have suffered a total defeat.

The thing most of all desired by the North, is at last accomplished. The North is under the strongest obligations to the untiring zeal of Mr. Stuart of your county, who has spared no pains, in a high minded and honorable way, to secure the accomplishment of this great work. The bill provides to borrow $500,000 on the credit of the state; and to sell the Chicago lots on the 20th of June, to raise a fund to pay the interest of the loan. Under this arrangement the state is secure, and the treasury will not be called on to pay the interest on the money borrowed.

PETITION DRAWN BY LINCOLN FOR AN INCREASED ALLOWANCE FOR BENJAMIN ELMORE, FEBRUARY 3, 1836

The original of this petition is in the Illinois State Historical Library at Springfield. It was drawn by Lincoln and his name heads the list of signers, among whom were many well-known residents of the New Salem section including Bowling Green, Bennett Abell, Dr. Francis Regnier, James Purkapile, Samuel Hill, Hugh Armstrong and Dr. John Allen. Travice Elmore, the father of the insane man, lately dead, had served under Lincoln in the Black Hawk War, and the former captain's interest in the Elmore family was a lively and practical one. After the passing of Travice Elmore his widow Jemima, with her children, for a time farmed a little tract of land on what shortly became the site of the town of Petersburg. When Lincoln surveyed and laid out the town he gave one of its thoroughfares a meandering course. Had he not done so the house of Jemima Elmore and her family would have stood squarely in the middle of that particular street.

To the County Commissioners' Court for the County of Sangamon

We the undersigned being severally acquainted with the insane son of Travice Elmore for whose maintenance an allowance from the county treasury has already been made believe that the allowance is much too small and therefore recommend that it be increased to a fair compensation for the maintenance and management of an absolute mad man.

ADDRESS BY LINCOLN AT PETERSBURG, FEBRUARY 13, 1836

The subjoined item appeared in the Sangamo Journal February 20, 1836. The address it promised was not printed in its next issue. The Journal of February 27 gave space to a "Communication" stressing the need for subscriptions to the stock of the canal company, but there is nothing to indicate Lincoln's connection with it.

On Saturday, the 13th inst. there was a large collection of citizens at Petersburg, in this county—on which occasion the Charter of the Beardstown and Sangamo Canal Company was publicly read and an address delivered by A. Lincoln, Esq. We shall give the address next week.

STRAYED OR STOLEN NOTICE, SANGAMO JOURNAL, MARCH 26, 1836

No doubt the disaster here recorded befell Lincoln at the end of one of his frequent trips from New Salem to Springfield. There is also little doubt that as a result of it Lincoln was compelled a few months later to make on foot his third canvass for a seat in the Legislature.

Strayed or Stolen

From a stable in Springfield, on Wednesday, 18th inst., a large bay horse, star in his forehead, plainly marked with harness, supposed to be eight years old; has been shot all around, but is believed to have lost some of his shoes, trots and paces. Any person who will take up said horse, and leaves information with the Journal Office, or with the subscriber at New Salem, shall be liberally paid for their trouble.

A. Lincoln.

LINCOLN TO LEVI DAVIS

New Salem Ills, April 4th, 1836

Dear Sir

You will confer a favour on me by examining the Record kept by the old State Recorder, and ascertaining whether a deed for N. W. quarter of section 23. in Town 10 North Range 5 West

in the County tract, made by Williamson Trent to Michael
Medierman has ever been recorded in that office, and if so,
whether the record shows that the land has been transfered to
Medierman, and if it has, who is the present owner under him.
Also please to give me all the information in *your* office in regard
to sales of said land for taxes, and who is the present owner
by tax title.

Very Respectfully,
Your Obt. Servt.
A. Lincoln

ATTESTATIONS OF A SURVEY BY LINCOLN, MAY 10, 1836

*The following attestations accompanied by a plot were filed
with the commissioners of Sangamon County on May 10, 1836.
When the survey was made Lincoln was serving as deputy to
Thomas M. Neale who had succeeded John Calhoun as county
surveyor. Neale was a native of Virginia and a lawyer by profession who settled in Illinois in 1824, and surveyed and laid out
into lots the land donated by certain owners to assure the selection of Springfield as the county seat of Sangamon County. He
was three times elected county surveyor, holding that office at the
time of his death in 1840.*

I certify that the foregoing are an accurate Plot and Field
Notes for Section 16 in Township 17 North of Range 6 West
of the 3rd Principal Meridian as surveyed by me.

A. Lincoln
for T. M. Neale, S. S. C.

May 10, 1836

We certify that the foregoing is an accurate plot and valua-
tion of section 16, Town 17 north of range 6 west of the 3rd
principal meridian given under our hands this 10th of May 1836

Matthew Moorehead ⎫
Fleming J. Hall   ⎬ Trustees
Benjamin Wiseman   ⎭

LINCOLN CERTIFIES TO MAP OF THE TOWN OF HURON, SURVEYED BY HIM, MAY 21, 1836

*On May 21, 1836, Lincoln filed for record with the clerk of
Sangamon County a plot of his survey of the town of Huron*

*attached to which was the certification reproduced below. Huron
was situated at Miller's Ferry on the south bank of the Sangamon, a dozen miles northwest of New Salem, and was promoted
by several prominent business men of Springfield, among them
Ninian W. Edwards, Dr. Gershom Jayne, Simeon Francis and
Edward D. Baker, all friends of the surveyor.*

I hereby certify that the annexed is a correct map of the
town of Huron, and that the requisites of the statutes in such
cases made and provided, have been complied with.

A. Lincoln
for Thomas M. Neale,
Surveyor of Sangamon
County

May 21, 1836.

REPORT OF ROAD LOCATED BY LINCOLN FROM COUNTY LINE TO COUNTY LINE, JUNE 2, 1836

To the Honourable County Commissioner's Court for the
County of Sangamon

The undersigned having been appointed to view and locate
a road from the county line near Watkins mill via Miller's ferry
to the county line in the direction of Pekin report that they have
made the location and recommend the opening of said road. The
above is a Plot of said road. (Plot appears above this report.)

June 2nd 1836

Robert Conover
Wm. G. Jeter
A. Lincoln

Make us an allowance for one day and a half each.

CERTIFICATION OF SURVEY AND MAP OF THE TOWN OF ALBANY BY LINCOLN, JUNE 16, 1836

*Survey and map of the town of Albany were filed at Spring-
field on June 21, 1836, by Surveyor Lincoln who paid a recording
fee of $2.50. The proposed townsite was located near Rocky
Ford in Sangamon County. Six of the eight lots included in it
belonged to John Wright and John Donavan.*

I hereby certify that the above is a correct map of the town
of Albany as surveyed by me.

A. Lincoln
For T. M. Neale, S. S. C.

June 16, 1836.

THE PAPERS IN MR. LINCOLN'S FIRST CASE
AS A LAWYER, JUNE 27, 1836

The first suit in which Mr. Lincoln is known to have figured, following his admission to the bar and partnership with John T. Stuart, was that of Hawthorn v. Woolridge in the Sangamon Circuit Court. This suit began on June 27, 1936, and ran through its first stages while Lincoln was still a resident of New Salem. It was an action or rather three actions—one an action on assumpsit or breach of contract, another for trepass vi et armis and a third in replevin—brought by one, James P. Hawthorn against David Woolridge.

Hawthorn claimed damages alleging that Woolridge had agreed to furnish him two yoke of oxen to break up twenty acres of prairie sod-ground, and to allow him to raise a crop of corn or wheat on a certain piece of land, but had failed to perform in both instances. He also claimed that he had been violently assaulted by Woolridge, and for "consequent illness, injuries, loss of time and expense for medical attention" he demanded "damages in the sum of five hundred dollars and other proper relief." Finally in the replevin suit Hawthorn demanded the return of "one black and white yoke of steers, one black cow and calf, and one prairie plow" together with twenty dollars for their unlawful detention.

A race for Congress in the summer of 1836 absorbing the time and energies of Stuart, it speedily devolved on Lincoln to safeguard the interests of their client, Woolridge, and the younger man proved equal to the demands on him. Thus on October 6, he filed an affidavit of his client contending that, as the plaintiff was a young man without family or property, he should be required to furnish a bond for costs; and when on the following day, to the surprise of the defendant and his counsel, the required bond was executed and filed, Lincoln countered with an account, which promptly became a part of the record, and which included sundry items sufficient, if allowed, to serve as an offset to Hawthorn's demand on assumpsit. Below are reproduced affidavit and counter claim.

The fall term of the Sangamon Circuit Court adjourned without this suit coming to trial, but the peacemaker was at work during the months that followed, and on March 17, 1837, the parties by their counsel reported to the court the settlement of all pending litigation, and asked that the case be dismissed. This was promptly done, and so ended Lincoln's first lawsuit.

Jesse W. Weik, long-time associate of William H. Herndon, asserts that the case was settled by judgment being entered against Hawthorn for the costs in the assumpsit phase, against Woolridge in the replevin case and by dividing costs in the trespass case. J. W. Weik, The Real Lincoln, Boston, 1922. Lincoln: The Prairie Years, I, 217 states that the costs were divided. The same view is taken by Albert Woldman in his Lawyer Lincoln (Boston, 1936), except that he limits himself to the statement that the case was settled by a compromise agreement. Herndon, in his biography of his partner (Volume I, Page 182), asserts that Lincoln's first appearance as a lawyer was for the plaintiff in Hawthorn vs. Woolridge, but this is contradicted by the summons of September 29, 1836, which names Hawthorne as plaintiff and Woolridge as defendant. Finally Dr. Harry E. Pratt in his Lincoln Day by Day, (Springfield, 1941), Page 72, citing the court records in the case states that Hawthorn paid the costs in replenin, and that Woolridge paid the costs in the action in assumpsit. It is to be noted that Mr. Lincoln gave the case as James P. Hawthorn vs. David Woolridge. It is also interesting to recall that when in the summer of 1836 Mr. Lincoln was busy with his first lawsuit, his future secretary of state, William H. Seward was already a lawyer of note in Auburn, N. Y.; Salmon P. Chase, who was to serve him as secretary of the treasury, as a member of the Cincinnati bar was attracting notice by his defense of runaway negroes, and Edwin M. Stanton, his future secretary of war, had just begun practice in Cadiz, Ohio.

Praecipe in the Case of Hawthorn vs. Woolridge, June 27, 1836

James P Hawthorn ⎫
        vs   ⎬ Assumpsit
David Woolridge ⎭

The Clerk of the Sangamon Circuit will issue process in the above case returnable to the next Term of said Court.

Damages $100.00——

June 27th 1836   Walker & Hewett

Jno L Hawthorn, John Hawthorn, John Johnson, Thomas Lockerman, Stanley Lockerman. A. Bowling

J. P. Hawthorn
      vs
D. Woolridge

Precipe

Filed June 27th 1836
Wm Butler Clk.

This precipe is in the hand of Walker or Hewett, attorneys for Hawthorn, while the names below appear to have been penned by each man whose signature is given. The date of filing was penned by Butler, and other cover notations by Walker or Hewett, but the document is included as a part of the history of Mr. Lincoln's first case at law.

Declaration of the Plaintiff in the Suit of Hawthorn vs. Woolridge, July 1, 1836

State of Illinois ⎱ July Term of the
Sangamon Couty Sc't ⎰ Sangamon Circuit Court, 1836

James P Hawthorn complains of David Woolridge, being in custody &c of a plea of Trespass on the case upon promises, For that whereas, heretofore, towit on the 15th day of June A.D. 1835 at the County of Sangamon and State aforesaid, in consideration that the said plaintiff, at the special instance and request of the said defendant would break up for the said defendant eighteen acres of prairie sod ground during that breaking season. He the said defendant then and there faithfully promised the said plaintiff that he the said plaintiff should have the use of said ground so to be broken by the said plaintiff for so long a time as would be necessary to raise a crop of corn, or wheat, at the option of this said plaintiff on the same ground to be broken (sic) by him.*

And this plaintiff complains, and in fact says, that confiding in the promises of said defendant then and there, towit, at &c, on &c as aforesaid, made to this plaintiff as aforesaid, the said plaintiff did break up for said defendant Eighteen and one half acres of prairie sod as he had been specialy requested by said defendant to do, yet the said defendant not regarding his said promise and undertaking as aforesaid but contriving and intending to defraud and deceive said plaintiff, did not, nor would permit said plaintiff to occupy and plant said Eighteen and one half acres so by this plaintiff broken as aforesaid, as the said defendant had faithfully promised and undertaken.

And though often thereunto requested, yet he the said defendant hath forbidden and wrongfully prevented said plaintiff from occupying and cultivating said land; wherefore, &c.

And whereas also afterwards, towit, on the day and year last aforesaid, in the County aforesaid, in consideration that the said plaintiff at the special instance and request of the said defendant, had before that time broken for said defendant, Twenty acres of prairie sod, he the said defendant then and there undertook and faithfully promised the said plaintiff to pay him so much money therefor, as he the said plaintiff reasonably deserved to have of the defendant, when he the said defendant should be thereunto afterward requested, And the said plaintiff avers that he therefor, reasonably deserved to have of the said defendant the sum of fifty Dollars of lawfull money of the United States, whereof the said defendant afterwards, to wit on &c, at &c as aforesaid had due notice.

Yet the said defendant not regarding his said several promises and undertakings but contriving and intending to deceive and defraud the said plaintiff, hath not though thereunto often requested, performed or complied therewith, or any or either of them as in the above counts set forth and declared on, but he hitherto wholly fails to pay and perform the same, and neglects and refuses so to do.

Wherefore this plaintiff saith he is injured and hath sustained damage to the value of one Hundred Dollars and therefore he brings this suit.

Walker & Hewett
Att'is for plaintiff

13   76   47
J. P. Hawthorn
vs) Assumpsit
D. Woolridge

_____

Declaration

_____

Filed July 1st 1836
 Wm Butler Clk

Complaint of Plaintiff in the Suit of Hawthorn vs. Woolridge,
July 1, 1836

State of Illinois
Sangamon County, sc't   }

July term of the
Sangamon Circuit Court
Anno Domini, 1836

James P. Hawthorn complains of David Woolridge, being
in custody &c of a plea of Trespass & vi et armis For that the
said defendant on the Fifth day of June, in the year of our Lord
One thousand eight hundred and thirty-six, at the County of
Sangamon, and State of Illinois, with force and arms, towit at
&c as aforesaid, assaulted the said plaintiff, and then and there
with great violence, struck beat, bruised and knocked down the
said plaintiff, and then and there plucked, pulled and tore divers
large quantities of hair from the head of him the said plaintiff;
and then and there with a stick and with his fists gave and struck
the said plaintiff a great many violent blows and strokes on and
about his head, face, breast, back, shoulders, arms, legs, and
divers other parts of his body and also then and there with great
force and violence, struck, shook, pulled, and knocked him the
said plaintiff down upon the ground, and then and there violently
kicked the said plaintiff, and gave and struck him the said plaintiff
a great many other blows and strokes; and also then and there
did violently thrust his, the said defendant's thumbs and fingers
into the eyes of the said plaintiff and gouge him the said plaintiff,
to his great pain, distress and injury.   By means of which said
several premises, he the said plaintiff was then and there greatly
hurt, bruised, and wounded, and became and was sick sore,
wounded and partially blind; and so remained and continued for
a long space of time towit for the space of six weeks then next
following, during all which time, he the said plaintiff thereby
underwent and suffered great pain, and was much hindered and
prevented from performing and transacting his necessary affairs
and business, by him during that time to be performed and transacted, and also thereby he the said plaintiff was forced and
obliged to, and did necessarily lay out and expend a large sum
of money, towit the sum of   Dollars of lawfull money
of the United States in and about endeavoring to be cured of the
bruises, wounds, sickness, soreness, disorder and blindness aforesaid, occasioned as aforesaid.

And other wrongs to the said plaintiff then and there did,
against the peace of the good people of the State of Illinois, and

to the damage of the said plaintiff of Five Hundred dollars and therefore he brings this suit.

Walker & Hewett
for plaintiff

J. P. Hawthorn

    vs. } Trespass
           vi et armis

D. Woolridge

Declaration

Filed July 1st 1836
  Wm Butler Clk.

The foregoing document, with the exception of the date of filing, was penned by Walker & Hewett. It is included as part of Mr. Lincoln's first law case.

Summons for Lincoln and Others in Suit of Hawthorn vs. Woolridge, September 29, 1836

The People of the State of Illinois, to the Sheriff of Sangamon County . . . Greeting You are hereby commanded to summon David Williams Nelson Asher Bartlett Conyers & A. Lincoln to be and appear before the Circuit Court of Sangamon County, on the 3 day of the next term, to be holden in Springfield, on the 1st Monday, in the month of October next, to testify and the truth to speak in behalf of James P. Hawthorn. In a certain matter of controversy pending in the said Court, wherein Said Hawthorn

      is plaintiff, and David Woolridge
      is defendant; and have then and there this writ.

      Witness the Honorable Stephen T. Logan, Judge of our said Court, at Springfield, this 29th day of Sept. 1836.

Wm Butler Clerk

D. Woolridge
   vs
D. Woolridge
D. Williams
N. Asher
B. Conyers
A. Lincoln

The above summons is a form document filled in at certain places. It is not in the hand of Hewett or Walker, but may be in the hand of Logan or a court clerk other than Butler. While it is signed with the clerk's name, it was not penned in his hand. The presiding judge, Stephen T. Logan, succeeded John T. Stuart as the law partner of Mr. Lincoln, and was succeeded in turn by William H. Herndon.

Plea of Defendant in the Suit of Hawthorn vs. Woolridge, October 5, 1836

Hawthorn ⎫
   vs   ⎬assumpsit
Woolridge ⎭

and the said defendant comes and defends &c. & says he did not undertake & promise in manner & form as the Pltff has above declared against him & this he prays may be inquired of by the county &c

The Pltff will take notice that the ? acct will be exhibited & proven as an offset.

Stuart & Dummer

(48)

Plea

Filed Oct 5th
1836 W. Butler Clk.

This plea and cover notations are in the hand of John T. Stuart, with the exception of the date of filing. His poor penmanship is in marked contrast with the neat hand of Lincoln's legal documents.

Affidavit of Defendant in Suit of Hawthorn vs. Woolridge, October 5 1836

James P. Hawthorn
   vs.   s s   In Trespass
David Woolridge

The defendant, David Woolridge, being sworn says that he verrily believes that the said plaintiff is unable to pay the costs of this suit, and that the officers of this court will be in danger of losing their costs in said suit unless the said plaintiff be ruled to give security therefor. He states that said plaintiff is a young man and without family and that he has not, to the said defendant's knowledge, any real, or personal property out of which the costs could be made.

David Woolridge

Woolridge
ads
Hawthorn
   filed Oct 5. 1836
     Wm Butler, Clk

The words, "In Trespass" in the foregoing affidavit are in the hand of John T. Stuart, while the rest of the document was penned by Mr. Lincoln. The cover notations appear to be by the clerk, Butler. It will be noted that Lincoln spelled "verily" as "verrily." William Butler, was the friend with whom Lincoln resided before his marriage.

Bill of Woolridge in the Suit of Hawthorn vs. Woolridge, After October, 1836

James P. Hawthorn to David Woolridge Dr

To Boarding from the first day of April until the first of November 1835. at $1-50 cents per week being 30 weeks & 4 days   **$45.75**
   To use of waggon & team from first of April till first of November 1836   **$90.00**
   1834 To 11 bushels of wheat at 75   8.25
   1836. Jany 8 Cash lent   100.00
" " " May & June Breaking 10 acres of Prairy   20.00

_____
$264.00

To money lent to enter land, afterwards entered in the name of your brother   50.00

This document is undated, but was obviously written after October, 1836. It was penned by Mr. Lincoln, with the exception of the lines in reference to a loan for the purpose of entering land. These appear to have been the work of John T. Stuart. The document was drawn up as an offset to the action in assumpsit filed by the attorneys for Hawthorn.

Defendant's Answer in the Suit of Hawthorn vs. Woolridge, October 6, 1836

David Woolridge   ⎫   And the said David Woolridge by John
        ats   ⎬   T. Stuart his attorney, comes and defends
James P Hawthorn   ⎭   the force and injury when &c and says
he is not guilty of the supposed trespasses above laid to his
charge *or any or either of them,* in manner and form as the said
plaintiff hath above complained against him, And of this he puts
himself upon the country &c.

Stuart.

James Hawthorn

    vs   ⎬   In Trespass

David Woolridge
Filed Oct 6th 1836
Wm Butler Clk

Stuart signed this document penned by Mr. Lincoln. The cover notations are in the hand of Butler.

Securities for Costs in the Suit of Hawthorn vs. Woolridge, October 6, 1836

James P Hawthorn ⎫
    vs. ⎬ Assumpsit ⎬ In the Sangamon
David Woolridge   ⎭   circuit court

Same
    vs   ⎬   Trespass vi et Armis
Same

I do hereby enter myself as security for the costs in these
causes & acknowledge myself bound to pay or cause to be paid
all costs that may accrue in this cause either to the opposite party
or to any of the officers of the court in pursuance of the Statute
of this State
Dated the 6th Oct. 1836—

John L Hawthorn
John Hawthorn

Hawthorn
    vs
Woolridge
Filed Oct 6th 1836
    Wm Butler Clk.

This bond for security appears to have been penned by Walker or Hewett, and signed by the two Hawthorns. The cover notations were written by Butler.

James P. Hawthorn ⎱
      vs   ⎰   Assumpsit
David Woolridge ⎰

James P. Hawthorn ⎱
      vs   ⎰   Trespass vi et Armis
David Woolridge ⎰

I do hereby enter myself as security for costs in the above titled causes and acknowledge myself bound to pay or bound to be paid all costs that may accrue in either of the above causes, or to any of the officers of the court in pursuance of the Statute of this State
Dated October 7th 1836

                               John Owens

J. P. Hawthorn
         ⎱
  vs   ⎰   Bond for costs
         ⎰
David Woolridge
Filed Oct. 6th 1836
    Wm Butler Clk.

This bond is in the hand of Walker or Hewett, and is signed by Owens. The cover notations were penned by Butler.

Replevin, Affidavit Suit of Hawthorn vs. Woolridge,
October 29, 1836

State of Illinois   ⎱
Sangamon County; &c ⎰

James P. Hawthorn, being first duly sworn, says, that he is the rightfull and bona fide owner of one Black and white spotted yoke of steers, one Black cow & calf, and one Prairie plough. That said property is unlawfully detained from him; he having been compelled to give a delivery bond for its appearance at a certain day; or surrender the use of the same, which he could not conveniently do. That the same was not taken in execution for the payment of debt no judgment having been obtained or execution issued against him, but levied on, to satisfy an execution issued against another man, having no right or interest in said property neither was it taken in payment of taxes. Further this affiant states that he is about to commence an action of replevin to recover the before described property.

James P. Hawthorn

       this 29'' day of Oct 1836

            Wm Butler Clk

James P Hawthorn ⎫ Replevin for one yoke of Black & White
       vs   ⎬ steers four years old. One black cow &
David Woolridge & ⎪ calf & one prairie plough. Value of
Hugh Armstrong ⎭ property of eighty dollars.

                           Damage $20-00

      The Clerk of Sangamon Circuit Court, will issue process in the above case instanter returnable to next term of said Court.

                      Walker & Hewett for plff.

                    Octr, 29th 1836

James P. Hawthorn

          ⎫
    vs   ⎬   Replevin affid't
          ⎭

Woolridge & Armstrong
Filed Oct 29 1836
Wm Butler Clk.

This document is in the hand of Walker or Hewett, and is signed by Hawthorn. The replevin is in another hand than the affidavit. The cover notations, and statement of swearing of the affidavit are in the hand of Butler.

    Statement of Witness' Attendance in Assumpsit Case of
         Hawthorn vs. Woolridge, October 1836

Assumpsit case
James P. Hawthorn

          ⎫   In the Sangamon Circuit Court
    vs   ⎬   October   Term, 1836
          ⎭

David Woolridge

           James B Conyers

being duly sworn, says that he attended Two days as a witness in the above cause, on behalf of the defendant—

    Attest:

                      Wm Butler Clerk

The above is a printed form filled in by the clerk. It is included as part of the history of Lawyer Lincoln's first case.

INCOMPLETE DECLARATION IN THE SUIT OF
HAWTHORN VS. WOOLRIDGE, JULY, 1836

State of Illinois } July Term of the Sangamon Circuit
Sangamon County Sct }   Court, 1836

James P Hawthorn complains of David Woolridge, being in custody &c of plea of Trespass on the case on promises, For that whereas, heretofore, towit on the 15th day of June A. D. 1835 at the County of Sangamon and State aforesaid, in consideration that the said plaintiff, at the special instance and request of the said defendant would break up for the said defendant eighteen acres of prairie sod ground during that breaking season. He the said defendant then and there faithfully promised the said plaintiff that he the

And also undertook and promised that he the said defendant would also furnish two good yoke of work cattle the next season to assist this plaintiff in breaking up so much ground for this plaintiff, as he the said plaintiff, should break up for the said defendant.

&c on &c as aforesaid, made to this plaintiff of as aforesaid, the said plaintiff break up for the said defendant Eighteen and one half acres of prairie sod as he had been specialy requested by said defendant to do. yet the said defendant not regarding his said promise and undertaking as aforesaid but contriving and intending to defraud and deceive said plaintiff, did not, nor

The foregoing document is in the hand of Walker or Hewett, and remains incomplete at the word "nor." It will be seen to continue with the words "would permit said plaintiff" in the complete declaration filed by Walker & Hewett on July 1, 1838. The words following the asterisk in the incomplete declaration are to be placed in the complete declaration at the point marked by an asterisk.

LINCOLN'S FIRST DEBATE OF RECORD, JULY 11, 1836

The first political debate in which Lincoln is known to have participated took place in the court house in Springfield on July 11, 1836. Ninian W. Edwards, a Whig, opened the debate, and was answered by Dr. Jacob M. Early, a Methodist preacher and local Democratic leader under whom Lincoln had served in the Black Hawk War. Then in turn Dan Stone, John Calhoun,

Lincoln and Richard Quinton took part in the discussion. The Sangamo Journal of July 16 printed an account of the meeting by a reporter who signed himself "Up to the Hub" and who included in his account the description reproduced below of Lincoln's methods as a speaker.

"Mr. Lincoln succeeded Mr. Calhoun. At first he appeared embarrassed, and his air was such as modest merit always lends to one who speaks of his own acts. He claimed only so much credit as belonged to one of the members of the Legislature, for getting the State out of debt. He next came to Mr. Calhoun and the land bill. At one fell stroke, he broke the ice upon which we have seen Mr. Calhoun standing, and left him to contend with the chilling waters and merciless waves. His speech became more fluent, and his manner more easy as he progressed. In these degenerate days it seems to be the fashion of the day for all parties to admire even the frailties of the administration. The Van Buren men, particularly, are even taking shelter like ghosts under the rotten bones and tombstones of the dead acts of the administration. Mr. Lincoln, however, lifted the lid, and exposed to the eye the wretched condition of some of the acts of the Van Buren party. A girl might be born and become a mother before the Van Buren men will forget Mr. Lincoln. From beginning to end Mr. Lincoln was frequently interrupted by loud bursts of applause from a generous people."

SPEECHES BY LINCOLN AS A CANDIDATE FOR LEGISLATURE, JULY 16 AND LATER, 1836

At the hamlet of Athens, now in Menard County, the Sangamon County candidates for the General Assembly, seventeen in all, Lincoln among them, began on July 16, 1836, a series of ten speaking engagements at various points in a district twice as large as the State of Rhode Island. "We travelled on horse back from one grove to another," afterward wrote Robert L. Wilson, one of the candidates, shortly to become a member of the famous Long Nine. "The speaking would begin in the forenoon, the candidates speaking alternately until all who could speak had his turn, generally consuming the whole afternoon."

Varsell's farm on Sugar Creek, Mechanicsburg, Cotton Hill, New Salem, Allerton, Berlin, Petersburg, the farms of Thomas Campbell and Isaac Spear in the Springfield district, and finally on the evening of July 30 the town of Springfield were among the points covered by the cavalcade in its itinerary. At Springfield

Lincoln had the sharp encounter with George Forquer dealt with in another place. There is no printed record of any of the other speeches made by him at this time, but Wilson recalled that he espoused "the Whig side of all questions . . . manifesting skill and tact." Two other sources afford interesting glimpses of him in action. James Gourley, afterward a neighbor of the Lincolns in Springfield, was present at the meeting in Mechanicsburg, July 19, and a generation later told Herndon that on that occasion, Lincoln halted his speech long enough to intercede and compel fair play when a gang of roughs picked a fight with his friend and supporter, John Bell.

The other glimpse is afforded by Edmund T. Flagg who, traveling in Illinois in the summer of 1836, in the late afternoon of July 19 halted at the farm eight miles east of Springfield of John Dawson, friend of Lincoln and for six years the latter's associate in the Legislature where he won renown as one of the Long Nine. "Nightfall found me," writes Flagg in the second volume of his The Far West, "at the residence of Mr. D. an intelligent, gentlemanly farmer, with whom I passed an agreeable evening. I was not long in discovering that my host was a candidate for civic honors; and that he had with his friend, Mr. L., whose speech I had subsequently the pleasure of perusing, had just returned from Mechanicsburg, a small village in the vicinity, where they had been exerting themselves upon the stump to win the aura popularis for the coming election." The speech Flagg had "the pleasure of perusing" was the first Lincoln is known to have written out for delivery.

DEBATE WITH EDMUND DICK TAYLOR, JULY OR AUGUST, 1836.

A bombastic and showy political figure during Lincoln's first years in Illinois was Edmund Dick Taylor, born in Virginia in 1788 and a cousin of General Zachary Taylor, who settled in Springfield when the town was young, prospered as an Indian trader and general storekeeper, and in 1832 as a member of the staff of Governor John Reynolds in the Black Hawk War, acquired the title of "Colonel" by which he was known during the remainder of his life.

In 1832 Taylor, as a Democrat, defeated Lincoln for the Legislature. Two years later he was elected to the State Senate, where as one of the Long Nine he helped to secure the removal of the capital to Springfield. He resigned before the end of his term as Senator to accept from President Jackson the appoint-

ment of Receiver of Public Moneys at Chicago, and during the remainder of his long life of eighty-nine years was a resident of that city or of Mendota, active in railroad and canal building and in the development of coal lands.

It was in 1836, when Lincoln was for the third time a candidate for the Legislature, that he had an amusing encounter with Taylor, long talked and laughed about in Sangamon County. Taylor, a lover of fine clothes and costly jewelry and easy master of all the wiles of the demagogue, in the course of one of his meetings with Lincoln on the stump, dwelt at length on the lordly ways and social pretensions of the Whigs which he charged were shared by the young man from New Salem. While he was still speaking Lincoln "quietly slipped to his side, and catching his vest by the lower edge gave it a sharp pull," whereupon the garment opened revealing to Taylor's "astonished hearers a ruffled shirt-front glittering with watch-chain, seals and other jewels. The speaker stood confused and dumbfounded, while the audience roared with laughter." It was now Lincoln's turn to answer, and in words very like those afterward credited to him he completed the colonel's discomfiture. See Herndon's Life of Lincoln, edited by Angle, (New York, 1930), Pp. 157-58.

While Colonel Taylor was making these charges against the Whigs over the country, riding in fine carriages, wearing ruffled shirts, kid gloves, massive gold chains with large gold seals, and flourishing a heavy gold-headed cane, I was a poor boy hired on a flatboat at eight dollars a month, and had only one pair of breeches to my back, and they were buckskin. Now if you know the nature of buckskin when wet and dried by the sun it will shrink; and my breeches kept shrinking until they left several inches of my legs bare between the tops of my socks and the lower part of my breeches; and whilst I was growing taller they were becoming shorter, and so much tighter that they left a blue stream around my legs that can be seen to this day. If you call this aristocracy I plead guilty to the charge.

PETITION FOR SCRAPERS DRAWN BY LINCOLN,
AUGUST, 1836

The original of this petition for scrapers drawn by Lincoln, and in the summer of 1826 signed by him and several score other residents of the New Salem neighborhood, is now in the Illinois State Historical Library at Springfield.

To the Honorable the County Commissioners' Court of Sangamon
County, Illinois

Whereas in the opinion of the undersigned petitioners the
public good requires that said Court take suitable steps to furnish
"scrapers" on the public roads within the county, not solely for
the purpose of economizing labor but for the more necessary and
laudable object of facilitating, cheapening and completing the
business and travelling operations of our (illegible) County. Your
petitioners will not presume to extend remarks or argue the
propriety of the above suggestions, believing that the Court will
fully appreciate this hint sanctioned alike by "Law" and the just
claims of the road-laboring community—

And whereas a "Road Tax" was laid on lands for 1836 by
Sd. Court to labor accruing to roads from which source will be
applied this coming acc. we further suggest the propriety of attending forthwith to this request that we may enjoy the use of
such improvements as may be made in our roads—August, 1836

WILL OF JOSHUA SHORT DRAWN BY LINCOLN

*Joshua Short was a native of Kentucky who lived a few miles
north of New Salem. Lincoln, when he drew Short's will, was a
law student, and seventeen days later, September 9, 1836, a
license to practice was issued to him. On February 8, 1841, the
will, on oath of Lincoln and Little, one of the witnesses to it, was
probated, and when a few months later, the work of the New
Salem student having met all tests, the estate was finally settled,
there remained a tidy sum to be divided among seven heirs. See
"The Will of Joshua Short by Fred E. Trent, Bulletin of the
Abraham Lincoln Association for June, 1929, Pp. 5-7).*

I, Joshua Short, of the County of Sangamon and State of
Illinois, being infirm in body, but of sound mind and memory
do ordain and establish the following as my last will and testament revoking all others.

It is my will that all my debts, if any there be, be immediately paid at my decease.

It is my will that all my property be disposed of at my
decease, as follows (viz)

It is my will that my dearly beloved wife Parthena Short
shall have and retain all the property that she had at the time
of my marriage with her, or that she has since made.

It is further my will that, if she, my said wife, shall, at my decease, desire to go to her relations, she shall be conveyed thence at the expense of my estate.

It is my will that, after the above provisions are carried into effect, all the remaining part of my estate be equally divided between my three sons, Joseph Short, John Short, and William Short, and my three daughters, Sarah Bennett, Chloe Thomas and Elizabeth Short, and my grandson Allen Short, being the son of my deceased son James Short.

It is my will that my son John Short, and my son-in-law James Short be the executors of this my last will and testament.

In testimony whereof I have hereunto set my hand and seal this twenty second day of August, in the year of our Lord one thousand eight hundred and thirty-six.

his
Joshua   X   Short
mark

Attest

    A. Lincoln
    John Little
    Josiah   X   Short
       his mark

LINCOLN TO IRA J. FENN, OCTOBER 6, 1836

Lincoln's practices as postmaster were on occasion free and easy ones. On Sept. 17, 1835, Mathew S. Marsh, a resident of the New Salem neighborhood, wrote as follows to his brother, George M. Marsh: "The Postmaster (Mr. Lincoln) is very careless about leaving his office open and unlocked, during the day; half of the time I go in and get my papers, etc., without anyone being there as was the case yesterday. The letter was only marked twenty-five and even if he had been there and known it was double, he would not have charged me any more—luckily he is a very clever fellow and a particular friend of mine. If he is there when I carry this to the office— I will get him to 'Frank' it." Lincoln franked the letter on request, thereby making himself liable to a fine of ten dollars, for on the outside of it is writ-

ten in his hand: "Free, A.. Lincoln, P. M. New Salem, Ill., Sept. 22"

Mr. Geo. M. Marsh, Portsmouth, N. H.

Springfield, Oct. 6, 1836

Dr Sir: By direction of Judge Lockwood, I send you this with its contents.

Ira I. Fenn Esq

Yours &c

A Lincoln

(On reverse side of sheet)

Free A.. Lincoln P.. M.

New Salem Ill.

SURVEYS FOR ALVIN RINGO MADE BY LINCOLN, NOVEMBER 16 AND 17, 1836.

The certificates of survey here reproduced were of two tracts of land located about four and a half miles west of New Salem. A note by William G. Green in the Herndon-Weik Collection states that the survey of November 17, 1836, was the last made by Mr. Lincoln. On November 30 he left New Salem to be present at the opening of the General Assembly at Vandalia, and a few weeks after his return there on March 8, 1837, he took up his residence in Springfield.

1836 { Surveyed for Ringo a tract of land composed of Sec-
Nov 16 { tions 30 & 31 in Township 18 North of Range 7 West and bounded as follows viz. Beginning on the line dividing Ranges 7 & 8 at a point 6 chains & 81 links North of the North West corner of the said Section 31 at a White Oak 16 inches in diameter bearing N. 43½ E. 48 links. Thence East 14 chains & 93 links to a White Oak 36 inches N 50 W 32 links. Thence South 20 chains & 7 links to a sugar tree 14 inches N 29 W 53 links. Thence West 14 chains & 93 links to a Hickory 14 inches S. 22 E 19 links. North 20 chains & 7 links to the beginning.

T. M. Neale S. S. C.

By A. Lincoln

Novr. 17th{ Surveyed for Ringo a part of the north half of
1836   { section 5 in Township 17 north of range 7 west and bounded as follows—(viz)—Beginning at the most northerly corner of a tract situated on the said section 5 and sold to Lewis L. Cooper by Robert Conover. Thence S 47 W 8 chains & 42 links to a black oak 11 inches Corner—Thence S 70 E-22 chains

& one link to a white oak 16 inches N 26 W 45 links—Thence N
29 E 4 chains & 50 links to a white oak 24 inches S 73 W 20
links—Thence N 61 W 19 chains & 2 links to the beginning.
Also a part of the East half of the South West quarter of said
section 5 and bounded as follows (viz) Beginning at the South
East Corner of Said half quarter at a White Oak 16 inches S
63 W 62 links—a White oak 15 inches N 75 E 76 links—Thence
N 89 W 19 chains & 71 links to a Post & Mound—Thence North
3 chains to a stake—Thence S 89 E 19 chains 71 links to a stake.
Thence south 3 chains to the beginning.

Signed—T. M. Neale SSC
by A Lincoln

RESOLUTION BY LINCOLN REGARDING THE DOOR-KEEPER OF THE HOUSE, DECEMBER 20, 1836

*The proceedings of the Illinois House of Representatives on
December 20, 1836, were marked by two incidents of interest to
the student. One of these was the introduction by Stephen A.
Douglas of a bill to establish a new county to be formed out of
Sangamon. The second is set forth in the appended extract from
the House Journal for 1836-37, Page 86. To lay any measure
"upon the table until the Fourth of July next," meant to end for
good and all discussion of it.*

Mr. Enloe proposed for adoption the following resolution,
viz: Resolved by this General Assembly, That the present Door-keeper
be not allowed one cent more than the ordinary wages
of Door-keeper.

Mr. Lincoln moved to amend the resolution by striking out
all after the word 'Resolved,' and insert the following viz: That
the Door-keeper of this House be now requested to state publicly
to this body whether in his opinion, an Assistant Door-keeper
is necessary:

When, on motion of Mr. Richardson, the resolution and
amendment were laid upon the table, until the 4th of July next.

DISCUSSIONS OF A MINORITY REPORT BY LINCOLN ON THE PROPOSED DIVISION OF SANGAMON COUNTY, DECEMBER 21, 1836

*On January 12, 1937 there was published in the Illinois State
Register two articles reproduced below dealing with the discus-*

sion in the Legislature on December 21, 1836, of the minority report from a select committee prepared by Lincoln and adverse to the proposed division of Sangamon County. The first dealt with debate of a motion that this report should be spread upon the Journal of the House. The second article summarized Lincoln's defense of a bill which had been submitted to the House with the minority report.

Speaker said that on yesterday the report of the minority from the committee on petitions was presented. That he had doubts concerning the course the paper should take in the House. Since yesterday he had examined Jefferson's Manual. The inconvenience of considering minority reports was manifest to all.

Mr. Lincoln then moved that the report of the minority be spread upon the Journal, in order he said that his constituents might see the report.

Mr. Linder said that he would vote against the motion. Needless expense for printing. There were many other ways by which the gentleman from Sangamon could get the report among his constituents.

Mr. Lincoln replied that he claimed the right to know what was due to his constituents as much as any gentleman, & especially as much as one who was not their representative. He had made the motion to spread the report on the Journal, because he thought it due his constituents, and no more than a common act of courtesy from the House, to comply. Mr. L. (sic) said, he hoped that all that had been said on this subject, would go to his constituents. He thought it incourteous, and a departure from the rules of etiquette, for the gentleman from Coles to meddle in the matter at all; but if the House chooses to go by the views of that gentleman so be it; I am content.

Mr. L. (sic) said that he did not think the small expense to the state which the printing of the report would incur, the whole object of the gentleman in opposing his motion—The intention is to affect my constituents. Linder replied at length in sarcastic vein. Decided in negative: Ayes 24, nays 44.

In taking up Lincoln's report from the select committee for division of Sangamon County, Mr. Lincoln said, that as a member of the committee, he would state that the bill before the House was a matter of compromise. He was willing to take the bill, because before any division of Sangamon could take place, the bill declared that the people of Sangamon should themselves decide. He would sustain the bill as it stood; the new county would be too small if lessened. He was opposed to offering to the people a territory too small for their acceptance.

LINCOLN TO JOHN McNAMAR, DECEMBER 24, 1836

Under the name of McNeil, John McNamar was an early and prominent resident of New Salem. In the fall of 1829 in partnership with Samuel Hill, whom Lincoln was to later succeed as postmaster, he opened the first store in the town. This venture proved a profitable one, and enabled McNamar in a comparatively brief period to accumulate considerable property. Meanwhile, boarding at the Rutledge Tavern he fell in love with and became engaged to James Rutledge's daughter Ann, an attractive girl of nineteen. After a time and in confidence he disclosed to her his real name with his reasons for taking an assumed one, and announced that it was necessary for him to return for a time to his old home in New York. Correspondence between them was kept up for some months, but grew formal as McNamar's absence lengthened, and finally came to an end. Then Ann Rutledge died in the summer of 1835. When at the end of three years McNamar returned to New Salem he took up his residence on a farm he had previously purchased on Sand Ridge seven miles north of the village, and there made his home until his death in old age. Recalling after forty years the matter referred to in this letter of December, 1836, McNamar explained that "Lincoln had surveyed the road so as to run in front of his farm, but that the petition would have relocated it a mile or two behind him." Evidently Lincoln's warning was effective, for the 1836-37 Session Laws show no change of route. See Angle, "New Papers and Letters of Lincoln," Boston, 1930, and Thomas, "Lincoln's New Salem," Springfield, 1934.

Vandalia, Dec. 24, 1836

Dear Mack: I write this to notify you that I have the petition for the change of the State road, so as to make it run by Tilmon, Howbacker's, and Bowman's, and that unless you, who are opposed to the change, get up a remonstrance and send it on, I shall be forced to have a bill passed upon the petition. I might write you a long letter of political news, but you will see that as soon in the newspapers, which will save me the trouble.

If you feel any particular interest in this road affair, don't fail to bestir yourself.   Your friend,

A. Lincoln.

John McNamar, Petersburg Sangamon County, Ill.

LETTER TO THE SANGAMO JOURNAL BELIEVED TO HAVE BEEN WRITTEN BY LINCOLN, DECEMBER 24, 1836

When Young was elected Senator of the United States Lincoln, who, with Stuart no longer a member, had now become Whig leader on the floor of the House, voted for his friend Archibald Williams on each of the three ballots. Williams, like Lincoln, tall, angular and uncouth, was a native of Kentucky who in 1828 had come from Tennessee to practice law in Quincy. Lincoln long afterward declared him "the strongest minded and clearest headed man he ever saw," and in 1861 appointed him United States District Judge for the State of Kansas. John A. McClernand, then of Shawneetown and only twenty-four years old, a quarter century later was to serve as a general in the Union Army. James Shields, whom Lincoln dubbed Paddy, was a native of Ireland, then twenty-six years old, and had been dangerously wounded as a soldier in Florida. A hard student he had begun at twenty-two the practice of law at Kaskaskia, and as a member of the House was now on the way to be thrice a Senator of the United States, each time from a different state, and to hold more offices, civil and military, than any other man of his generation. See Reminiscences of the Early Bench and Bar of Illinois by Usher F. Linder (Chicago, 1879), Pp. 238-43, and Life of Major General James Shields by William H. Condon (Chicago, 1900), Page 219.

Vandalia, Dec. 17, 1836

Dear Sir:—This is the close of the twelfth day of the session, and I may with truth say, that little of importance has yet been done—It seems that the progress of business in the legislature, is to be more tardy, in proportion as the number of its members was increased by the last apportionment.

Some things, however, have transpired here which, believing they will not be uninteresting to you, I will now relate, omitting as I go along, an account of the proceedings of the legislature which you must necessarily have received before this reaches you.

On Wednesday last Judge Young was elected to the Senate of the United States upon the third ballot. On the last ballot the vote stood, Young 68, McRoberts 24, Ewing 12, Brown 7, Williams 17. To-day Walter B. Scates was elected Judge for the third Judicial Circuit, and Samuel D. Marshall, prosecuting attorney for the same circuit.

An attempt is being made in the House to make the Board of Canal Commissioners elective by the two Houses. I believe it will succeed in the House, unless some of the Whigs, as they threaten they will, should offer an amendment to make them elective by the people. Would not that be fighting the devil with fire? Would not that be choking democrats with democracy? If I were a member I'd go it. An effort is also making in the House, to make the county commissioner's clerks and county treasurers elective by the people. This also will succeed in the House, though its fate is now doubtful in the Senate.

The most amusing transaction of the present session, has been in relation to the reception of our portion of the surplus revenue.—The Bill for that purpose originated in the Senate, and passed that branch by an almost unanimous vote. The bill; as it came from the Senate, required the governor to demand and receive the money in specie. So soon as it came up for consideration in the House, a motion was made by McClernand of Gallatin, to strike out the words, "in specie," who at first gave as a reason for his motion that a demand for specie might embarrass the Shawneetown Bank, which had a share of the deposites, and which institution, he contended, it was the interest of the people to cherish. This argument was answered by nearly all the Whigs in the House (who by the way were all in favor of retaining the word specie) by an assurance that they would vote for a resolution instructing the governor to deposite in the Shawneetown Bank so much of the money as we might be authorized to draw from it.

This reply seemed for a moment to silence, but by no means to satisfy the anti-specie men. In order to gain time for party drilling, one then moved to adjourn, which motion failed.—They were utterly confounded. Something was to be done, though what, or how they knew not. After a moment's blank staring in each other's faces, it seemed as if they came to the conclusion to occupy the evening in sporting upon the subject, no matter whether to purpose or not. In pursuance of this determination McClernand led off. After about half an hour's gabbing he set down, having in substance said nothing, only that it would be a piece of superlative impudence to the general government for the State of Illinois to ask for specie.

Next came French, of Edgar. The substance of his speech was a repetition of what McClernand had said, together with the additional assertion, that if Illinois should demand specie, all the other states would do the same, and the consequence would be a universal crash of the deposite banks, and dire distress and panic in the monetary concerns of the country, which, he said was what the bloody Whigs most of all things desired. Then followed Nowlen, of Monroe. He said the state had no right to demand any thing from the general government. It was an act of munificence and generosity on the part of the general government, that we were likely to get any thing. Nothing belongs to us, and we had better quietly take all that we could get, and that in any shape we could get it. Beggars, he said must not be choosers. A half a loaf was better than no bread.

McClernand, French, and Nowlen, each took a second round, when, having exhausted their privileges of speaking, they pressed forward a little fellow from Randolph, who by way of distinction I shall hereafter call Paddy Shields. Paddy had discovered that if the word specie was retained, our agent, whoever he might be, he could not be permitted to take a draft of the deposite banks, and consequently he would have to roll the specie from Washington to Illinois, in kegs. And, moreover, he would venture that the general government would not brook such impudence from us. By our folly we should, in the end, get nothing. About this time an adjournment was effected without taking the vote on striking out. Next day the question came up in order, when the word 'specie' was stricken out by a party vote. It is, however, due to the Van Buren men of Morgan to say, that they voted against it. The bill was further amended by striking out the word 'governor' and inserting 'state treasurer' and then returned to the Senate for concurrence. The party whistle was blown, and the Senate concurred in the amendments of the House. Several speeches were made; none, however, of importance except by Turney of Green. He said he knew that demand for specie by all the states, would break every deposite bank in the Nation —that he spoke advisedly and understandingly when he declared that the aggregate of all the specie in the deposite banks would not exceed five dollars for every hundred of the public deposites. This Turney, be it remembered, is a Van Buren man, and one of the worthies who, for the last four or five years, have been laboring to gull and hoodwink the people of Illinois about the speedy commencement of the "Golden Age." According to his declarations two years ago, every substantial man and every substantial man's wife and daughter were now to be traveling upon gold. But now he says, there are not more than five dollars in specie, for every hundred reported in the treasury. I confess no great credit should ordinarily be attached to his assertions, but I believe it is a rule in the court of law, that no man is too great a liar for his own admission to be taken as evidence against him. But to proceed. The bill became a law minus the word "specie." The party on reflection, became alarmed at what they had done, but how were they to repair it? To turn around and repeal or amend the law, would be too ridiculous. Finally an expedient was hit upon. Whiteside of Monroe, introduced a joint resolution in the Senate, requiring the Treasurer, when he should receive a draft upon the Deposite Banks for the money, when presenting the draft for payment, to demand and receive the same in specie.—This resolution passed the Senate unanimously; but when it came to the House the same birds that had shown themselves so hostile to the word "specie" in the bill were seen fluttering again. An adjournment was instantly moved but failed. Up sprang Paddy Shields and moved to amend the resolution by adding "and the Treasurer is particularly forbidden to receive any of the notes of the U. S. Bank." A second motion to adjourn was then made which succeeded. During the interval Paddy was told by his friends that his amendment looked so foolish, he had better withdraw it, which he did at the commencement of the evening session. Then McClernand moved to amend the resolution by striking out the word "receive" so that the resolution thus amended would have required the Treasurer to demand specie, but to receive any thing else if he chose. After receiving a few thumps under the fifth rib for this attempt at duplicity, and a call for the Ayes and Noes upon the amendment, McClernand was forced to withdraw it as Paddy had done his. The question was then taken by Ayes and Noes upon the adoption of the resolution, and carried with but one dissenting voice; though the whole party were as mad and sulky as baited bulls. They voted in so low and surly a tone that the Clerk was continually under the necessity of calling out "How did Mr.———— vote." "Did Mr.———— answer to his name?" and &c, &c.

LETTER TO THE SANGAMO JOURNAL BELIEVED TO HAVE BEEN WRITTEN BY LINCOLN, DECEMBER 30, 1836

Sangamon County, organized in 1821 and named for the river flowing through it, originally embraced the present counties of Sangamon, Cass, Menard, Mason, Tazewell, Logan, and parts of Morgan, McLean, Woodford, Marshall and Putnam, but was somewhat reduced in area in 1825, and in 1839 to its present limits by the setting apart of Menard, Logan and Dane (now Christian) Counties.

Vandalia, Dec. 22, 1836

Dear Sir—The whole day, to-day, has been spent in a struggle upon the question whether a new county should be formed from a part of ours absolutely, or only upon condition that a majority of the people of the county should vote for it. The whole delegation for our county were for the condition—and the establishment of the new county absolutely, was supported upon party grounds purely. Upon the vote being taken, our delegation was sustained by a large majority. It is due to a large portion of Van Buren men in the House to say, that they acted most magnanimously on this occasion; and I write this letter, expressly, to award the meed of honor to them for it, and to tender to them, as I think I may safely do, the thanks of all honorable and independent men.

A Citizen of Sangamon

RECEIPT FOR SERVICES 1836-37

Receipt for services of David Mc Ginnis: File Dated 1836-1837, at the County Commissioners' Court of Sangamon County.
This receipt although not signed by Mr. Lincoln, is manifestly the work of his hands; witness the use of extra spacing which appears in most of his legal papers. David Mc Ginnis was a native of Kentucky, who settled in the Island Grove section of Sangamon County in 1826, and ten years later built one of the first brick houses in the county outside of Springfield. He was also one of the inventors of a device for guiding prairie plows by wheel and lever, which had an important part in bringing the lands of Sangamon County under cultivation. He was killed in old age by being thrown from a buggy by a runaway horse.

The   county of   Sangamon

To

David   McGinniss   Dr.

1836   To   services as   Road Supervisor. $6.00

CHAPTER VIII—LINCOLN IN THE YEAR 1837
SURVEY OF PERIOD

The year 1837 in which fell his twenty-ninth birthday was for Abraham Lincoln a period of increased confidence in his own growing capacity for leadership, and it also marked his advance from one stage to another of an exceptional career. The Tenth General Assembly of Illinois convened at Vandalia on December 5, 1836, and before it adjourned on March 6, 1837, enacted much important legislation. Thus it passed an act providing for a system of internal improvements which included railroads, canals and navigable rivers, to be done at state expense; bills dealing favorably with the state bank at Springfield, and finally legislation which provided that in 1839 the state capital should be removed from Vandalia to Springfield.

Mr. Lincoln as the chosen leader of the Whig minority in the House played a leading and, now and again, a decisive part in the shaping of this legislation. Indeed, it was mainly due to his shrewd management that the members from Sangamon, known to their fellows as the Long Nine, secured the state capital for Springfield. More significant in the retrospect was his reaction to a resolution passed by the General Assembly on January 12, 1837, condemning abolition societies and their activities —a reaction which clearly belongs to the Lincoln of history, whose innate hatred of slavery was in due course to find fit expression in his splendid protest against the repeal of the Missouri Compromise. Not to imperil Springfield's prospects of securing the state capital, he remained silent for the moment, but that matter happily out of the way, on March 3, 1837, three days before the General Assembly adjourned, he joined with one other member in a dignified, restrained and manly protest against its anti-slavery resolution. Mr. Lincoln thus referred to the matter when in 1860 he wrote his third-person autobiography for campaign purposes:

"'March 3, 1837, by a protest entered upon the 'Illinois House Journal' of that date, at pages 817 and 818, Abraham, with Dan Stone, another representative of Sangamon, briefly defined his position on the slavery question; and so far as it goes, it was then the same that it is now. The protest is as follows:

"'Resolutions upon the subject of domestic slavery having passed both branches of the General Assembly at its present session, the undersigned hereby protest against the passage of the same.

" 'They believe that the institution of slavery is founded on both injustice and bad policy, but that the promulgation of Abolition doctrines tends rather to increase that abate its evils.

" 'They believe that the Congress of the United States has no power under the Constitution to interfere with the institution of slavery in the different states.

" 'They believe that the Congress of the United States has the power, under the Constitution, to abolish slavery in the District of Columbia, but that the power ought not to be exercised unless at the request of the people of the District.

" 'The difference between these opinions and those contained in the above resolutions is their reason for entering this protest.

" 'DAN STONE
" 'A. LINCOLN

" 'Representatives from the County of Sangamon.' "

When the General Assembly adjourned in the early days of March, 1837, Mr. Lincoln returned to New Salem to take farewell of the friends he had made during his seven years' residence in the hamlet, and to prepare for his removal to Springfield, where on April 15 he became the law partner of John Todd Stuart. Details of the causes and controversies which filled his first months in Springfield, then a town of about 1200 people, are set forth in other pages of the present volume. Stuart at that period was absorbed in politics, and responsibility for the practice of the firm, "a practice more extensive than lucrative," fell on the junior partner, who soon began going on the circuit to attend the courts of other counties. He likewise found leisure for the making of new friends, and to discuss by letter and at first in a guarded way the subject of marriage with Mary Owens; but in August that high spirited young woman, much to his surprise and chagrin, refused his belated proposal. The rejected suitor, however, on second thought came to regard the affair as a salutary and chastening experience, and a few months later confided to a friend that "he had succeeded only in making a fool of himself."

During his first months in Springfield Mr. Lincoln, without price, shared the bed of his friend, Joshua Fry Speed, and, also without price, had his meals at the home and table of another friend, William Butler. Thus favored, as an individual, he suffered no serious discomfort from the financial panic which in the first half of 1837 swept the country like a tornado, closing banks, bankrupting states and bringing utter disaster to all sorts

*and conditions of men; but that panic was the inevitable sequel
of the bitter political controversy that for eight years had been
waged between Democrats and Whigs, and young Lawyer Lincoln, as a devoted Whig and follower of Clay, was prompt to
condemn the party of Jackson for its causes and consequences.*

*As in New Salem so in Springfield Mr. Lincoln was an
assiduous reader of newspapers, and in their columns followed
the disastrous progress of events, but always from the point-of-
view of a stout Whig partisan. He doubted the wisdom and capacity of Martin Van Buren, who on March 4, 1837, succeeded
Jackson, the latter retiring to his beloved Hermitage to pass
in quiet the few years that remained to him; and he could see
no good in the sub-treasury system which Van Buren, having in
May summoned Congress in special session in September, in a
message of uncommon quality, recommended to that body, as a
cure for the nation's financial ills. Calhoun now severed his late
alliance with the Whigs, and with Wright and Benton gave vig-
orous and in the end effective support to the policy of Van Buren.
And so by slow and gradual stages there was a return to normal
conditions, and ultimate adoption of the sub-treasury system,
developments for which Mr. Lincoln, a stern and still unbending
Whig, gave no credit to a wise, and, as the sequel was to prove,
a far-seeing President.*

*Meanwhile, Mr. Lincoln, no doubt with serious forebodings
as to the future, studied in the newspapers the growing contest
over slavery in and out of Congress. Both in House and Senate
the fight for the right of petition was renewed early in 1837; he
must have read with care the Senate speech of February 7, 1837,
in which Calhoun defended slavery as good for both races in
the South, and gave final form to his doctrine of non-intervention; and soon the demand from the South for recognition of
the independence of Texas, now in successful revolt against
Mexico as a preliminary to its admission to the Union, added a
new and insistent phase to the differences that were to end in
armed conflict. And as signs of what was to come on November
7, 1837, Elijah Parish Lovejoy, an abolition editor, was killed
by a pro-slavery mob in Alton, Illinois; at Faneuil Hall in Boston on December 8, in righteous protest against this outrage,
young Wendell Phillips began his unexampled career as an anti-
slavery orator, while a short fortnight later another debate on
the right of petition in the House at Washington called forth
threats of secession from Robert Barnwell Rhett and other*

Southern members who could devise no other method for throt-
tling the discussion of slavery.

And, a more hopeful herald of nobler things to come which
could not have passed unnoted by Abraham Lincoln, on Novem-
ber 8, 1837, stout-hearted Mary Lyon founded Mount Holyoke
Seminary, and opened a new and broader era in the education
of women.

COMPLAINT OF PLAINTIFF IN SUIT OF CANNON AGAINST KENNEY, JANUARY 4, 1837.

When the complaint of Cannon vs. Kenney was filed in the
Sangamon Circuit Court on January 4, 1837, Lincoln was at
Vandalia serving as a member of the Illinois Legislature and still
a resident of New Salem; but he had already perfected arrange-
ments to become the law partner of John T. Stuart, and it is
probable that it was Stuart who appeared in court in this parti-
cular matter.

January 4, 1837

Manly F. Cannon, plaintiff, complains of Mathew P. Kenney, defendant, being in custody by a plea of trespass: For that
the said defendant on the fourth day of January in the year of
our Lord one thousand eight hundred and thirty-seven, at the
county and circuit aforesaid, with force of arms, seized, took,
and carried away of him, the said plaintiff, one sorrel horse of
great value, to wit: of the value of one hundred dollars, then and
there found and being and converted and disposed of the same
to his own use, and other wrongs to the said plaintiff then and
there did against the peace and dignity of the People of the State
of Illinois and to the damage of the said plaintiff of one hundred
dollars and therefore he sues.

(Signed) Stuart and Lincoln

LETTER TO THE SANGAMO JOURNAL BELIEVED TO HAVE BEEN WRITTEN BY LINCOLN, JANUARY 6, 1837

Internal evidences confirm the belief that this letter was
written by Lincoln. The satire, giving an edge to the pretence
that the writer had been formerly on the staff of the National
Intelligencer at Washington, where he could not make a living,
and that now "with almost murdered conscience" he was com-
pelled to write wholly false reports, was declared by Beveridge
to be "in Lincoln's best vein at that time of his life." See, "Abra-
ham Lincoln" by Beveridge, Volume I, Page 184.

Vandalia, Dec'r. 30, 1836

Dear Brother of the quill:

I have a most unpleasant task to perform.—I am forced to advocate doctrines that I know, if practised on, would destroy the liberties of the country; and to make assertions that I know to be utterly false when I make them. I am compelled even to abuse you week after week, when all my feelings are with you, and when I know your course is the only one to be pursued by an independent man, and that the principles you advocate are the only ones upon which our institutions can be maintained. Can you forgive me for this? I know I do not deserve forgiveness. I feel that I deserve the execration of all mankind, while on earth; and if there be a hotter place for traitors to their country than for any others, I shall be heir to it hereafter. But when I think of my bread and meat—the bread and meat of my family —(there's the tender point) how can I help it?—You must forgive me. I am, heart and soul, with you; and I hope the day is not far distant when I shall be with you "tongue and pen," when, if it be in the range of possibilities, I shall renovate my now almost murdered conscience.

I am induced to write this letter in consequence of my extreme agitation upon the publication of my paper of to-day. Two letters, one by Mr. Thomas, the other by Mr. Hardin, were published in the Patriot; and tho' I knew every word they contained was true, I was surrounded by persons here, and threatened with excommunication, and what was worse, with the election of Hodge as public printer if I did not pronounce them basely false. I was forced to do it; and I am convinced that all that will save me from a severe caning from one or both of them is, that they know nobody will believe what I have said.

When your paper of last Saturday reached here, it was found to contain a communication from your correspondent, which was particularly offensive to ———— ————, ————, and ———— ———— ————. Believing, as they did, that your correspondent was some one of your county delegation, they, with their intimate friends, struck upon a plan, which would, as they thought, array the whole force of the administration party against your county. They wrote a most inflammatory phillipic against the Van Buren party, signed it "Sangamon," and placed in the post office directed to the editor Free Press, not doubting he would publish it, which I believe he would have done had I not given notice of it to one of your members, by which means it was suppressed. I mention this to convince you that I am really with you in feeling. Nothing gives me more pain than the necessity I am under, of continually heaping abuse upon the Governor. My only object in leaving the office of the National Intelligencer was, to gain a livelihood for myself and family, which I had ceased to be able to do there. I have only been successful through the patronage of Governor Duncan; and now, to be compelled to abuse him keeps constantly before my imagination the quotation, "Ingratitude—how sharper than a serpent's tooth it is."

I shall hold on to my present party only long enough to be elected public printer, when, regardless of consequences, I shall give my conscience its own course.

AMENDMENT BY LINCOLN TO AN ACT FOR A STATE ROAD FROM JACKSONVILLE TO BLOOMINGTON, JANUARY 30, 1837

On January 30, 1837, Lincoln introduced in the Legislature the subjoined amendment—copied from original in his handwriting—to an act providing for a State Road from Jacksonville to Bloomington. The amendment was approved and the bill shortly afterward became a law. By substituting John Armstrong for William Montgomery as one of the Sangamon County commissioners for the construction of the road Lincoln agreeably remembered a loyal and lifelong friend.

Amend the third line of the first section, by striking out the name of William Montgomery and inserting John Armstrong. Amend the seventh line of the same section by inserting the words "by way of Greensburg" immediately after the word "thence." Amend the fourth line of the second section by striking out the word "Bloomington" and inserting "intersect the State road leading from Springfield to Bloomington at or near the farm of Lemuel Foster."

BILL REPORTED BY LINCOLN TO RELOCATE A PART OF THE STATE ROAD FROM SPRINGFIELD TO LEWISTOWN, FEBRUARY 10, 1837

On February 10, 1837, Lincoln reported from the House Committee on Finance the bill reproduced below which was duly passed and approved by the governor.

A bill for an act to relocate a part of the State road leading from Springfield to Lewistown:

Be it enacted by the people of Illinois represented in the General Assembly, that so much of the State road leading from Springfield to Lewistown as lies between the Northern boundary of Township No. Eighteen North and the residence of John Jones, shall be so changed as to run due North from the point where said road now crosses the afforesaid Township line, through the center of the South West quarter to Section thirty four, Township Nineteen North Range Seven West, to the Northern boundary of said quarter; thence with the road as now traveled to the residence of the said John Jones.

LINCOLN REPORTS FROM AND ASKS DISCHARGE OF A SELECT COMMITTEE, FEBRUARY 13, 1837

A movement which, as noted elsewhere, took definite shape in 1836 to create three new Illinois counties mainly from the territory of Sangamon at once provoked angry and animated discussion. On February 9, 1837 Stephen A. Douglas presented to the House petitions of numerous citizens of Sangamon County favoring the proposed division and moved their reference to the Committee on Petitions of which he was chairman. Lincoln, however, made a motion, which was adopted, to refer the petitions to a select committee of five. Lincoln was made chairman and Douglas a member of this committee to which was also referred sundry remonstances against the proposed division. On February 13 Lincoln submitted the report reproduced below which was adopted by the House; but this only delayed final and affirmative action in the matter. In 1839 Menard, Logan and Christian counties were set off as a whole or in part from Sangamon County.

Mr. Lincoln, from the select committee to which was referred the petitions of sundry citizens of Sangamon County, praying the establishment of three new counties, principally from the territory of the said county of Sangamon; and the remonstrance of sundry citizens of the same county, against any division or dismemberment of the same, reported that they had the same under consideration, that 1437 names are found on the petition, and 2213 on the remonstrance; upon this fact the committee unanimously agree that the prayer of the petitioners ought not to be granted, and report the same back, and ask to be discharged from the further consideration of the subject.

Which was granted.

Mr. Lincoln, from the same committee to which were also referred the petitions of sundry citizens of Montgomery and Shelby counties, praying the establishment of new counties, reported that they find that a majority of neither county has signed the said petitions, and they therefore report the same back, and ask to be discharged from the further consideration of said petitions.

Which was granted.

REPORT BY LINCOLN OF ANNUAL REVENUE AND EXPENDITURES OF THE STATE OF ILLINOIS, FEBRUARY 16, 1837

Lincoln as a member of the Committee on Finance of the House, agreeable to a directing resolution, prepared and submitted the following report on the receipts of the State in a period of doubt and stress.

The Committee on Finance, who were required by a resolution to ascertain the amount of money annually receivable into the State Treasury by operation of the existing revenue laws; and also, the amount necessary to meet the current expense of the government, report:

That the amount receivable from all sources is	$57,895.15
And the amount required	55,151.97
The different items, forming the above amount of money are as follows (viz)	
From non-resident land tax	$44,395.15
From State Bank	12,000.00
From Shawneetown Bank	1,500.00
Total as above	$57,895.15

As to the amount necessary to meet the current expenditures of the government, the Committee on Finance, have relied on a report made by the Committee on Public Accounts and Expenditures, which, as above is $55,151.97

The Committee on Finance, on looking over the report of the Committee on Public Accounts and Expenditures, discover that, in their judgment, much too small a sum is allowed for a contingent fund; they therefore think it prudent to add $15,000.00

Total	$70,151.97
From which take the revenue	57,695.15
Leaving a deficit of	$12,256.82

AMENDMENT BY LINCOLN TO THE ACT PERMANENTLY LOCATING THE SEAT OF GOVERNMENT OF THE STATE OF ILLINOIS, FEBRUARY 21, 1837

Thanks in large part to Lincoln's adroit management on February 28, 1837, the Legislature of Illinois in joint session chose Springfield as the permanent site of the capital of the state and on April 15 the member from New Salem took up his residence in that town which was to remain his home until he left it in 1861 to assume the Presidency. One of the movements which assured success to the friends of Springfield was this amendment submitted by Lincoln which in due course became a part of the act passed February 28, 1837.

Provided that this act shall be null and void, unless the sum of fifty thousand dollars be donated by individuals, and secured by bonds and security to be approved of by the Governor, and made payable to, the State Treasurer; to become due at such time as the Governor shall direct, which bonds shall be executed and filed with the State Treasurer on or before the first day of May next, and which donation is especially designed to meet the appropriation herein before made, and shall be applied exclusively and immediately to that object; and also, unless a sufficient quantity of ground not less than two acres, upon which to erect public buildings, be donated and conveyed to the State without expense to the State.

NOTE IN THE CASE OF TAYLOR VS. SIMMONS, FEBRUARY 23 AND JULY 8, 1837.
(Herndon-Weik Collection)

This note is in the hand of Taylor, and signed by Simmons. The latter appears to have written "P. Simmons to Note, etc.," on the cover of the note, and Taylor signed it below. Mr. Lincoln penned the notation of the receipt of eighty dollars upon the note. The note was assigned by Taylor to Peyton L. Harrison and furnished grounds for the suit in which Mr. Lincoln filed praecipe in Harrison vs. Simmons on September 16, 1837. The declaration in this assumpsit suit was filed by Mr. Lincoln on September 22, 1837.

Six months after date I promise to pay John Taylor or order Two hundred & thirteen dollars & Sixty two cents to draw

Twelve per cent from the date until paid for value received this
23 of February 1837
$213.62   Pollard Simmons
        Attest
    John W Warner
P Simmons
To Note
    $213.62
    no. 26
John Taylor
Received on the within
$80, July 8. 1837—

BOND OF CHARLES OAKLEY AS FUND COMMISSIONER SIGNED BY MR. LINCOLN AND OTHERS, MARCH 4, 1837

*This bond appears to have been drawn by a clerk, and signed
by the men who became security for Oakley, who was the first
to sign it. The signature of Mr. Lincoln appears fifth in the list
after that of the commissioner. The concluding part of the document was apparently drawn by Judge Smith, a leading Democrat
of the period, and later, with the Whigs, a supporter of the State
Bank of Illinois. Most of the signers of this bond were colleagues of Mr. Lincoln, and some of them demand mention.
Richard N. Cullom was a close friend of Lincoln, a colleague
in the Legislature, and father of Shelby M. Cullom, long United
States Senator from Illinois. The younger Cullom in after years
acted as junior counsel with Lincoln in several cases, and was
the "boy lawyer" in one case with Logan and Lincoln. Murray
McConnel of Jacksonville was one of the outstanding attorneys
of Morgan County, and served as commissioner of the board of
public works for the first judicial circuit. Although the clerk
seemed to write the name, "Jas. Naper", it is likely that Joseph
Naper, state representative from Cook County was meant. Robert
L. Wilson was a member of the Legislature from Sangamon
County and one of the noted Long Nine. Dan Stone will be remembered as a co-signer with Abraham Lincoln of a noted protest against slavery, written the day before they signed the Oakley bond. And in Washington on March 4, 1837, Martin Van
Buren became eighth President of the United States, declaring
in his inaugural address that he should "follow in the steps of
his illustrious predecessor."*

Know all men by these presents that we Charles Oakley M
McConnel Wm. Lane Benj. Mitchell Richd. Bentley A Lincoln L W Wilson Jas. Naper M. Aldrich Robert Storrs Asahel
Ball R N Cullum Jonas Rawalt James Craig and Danl Stone
are held and firmly bound unto Joseph Duncan Governor of the
State of Illinois and his successors in office for the use of said
State in the penal sum of fifty thousand dollars lawful money
of the United States of America for which payment well and
truly to be made we bind ourselves our heirs executors and Administrators Jointly and severally firmly to these presents sealed
with our seals and dated the Fourth day of March A. D. 1837
The condition of the above obligation is such that Whereas,
the said Charles oakley has been elected to the office of Fund
Commissioner under the provisions of an Act of the General
Assembly of the State of Illinois, entitled An Act to establish
and maintain a General System of Internal improvement. approved the 27th day of February A. D. 1837. Now if the said
Charles Oakley shall well and truly and faithfully discharge
the duties of said office of Fund commissioner as aforesaid according to the provisions of said act and shall faithfully account
for all moneys that shall or may come into his hands as such
Fund Commissioner and shall faithfully perform such other duties as shall from time to time be imposed upon him by law as
such commissioner, then this obligation to be void otherwise to
remain in full force and virtue.

Signed Sealed and delivered)
)
in presence of   )

	Chas. Oakley	
	M. M..Connel	(Seal)
	Wm. Lane	(Seal)
	Ben. Mitchell	(Seal)
Approved 4th	Richard Bentley	(Seal)
March 1837	A Lincoln	(Seal)
Joseph Duncan	R. L. Wilson	(Seal)
Govr of Illinois	Jas Naper	(Seal)
	M. Aldrich	(Seal)
	Robert Storrs	(Seal)
	Asahel F. Ball	(Seal)
	Richard N. Cullom	(Seal)
	James Craig	(Seal)
	Dan Stone	(Seal)

State of Illinois on this fourth day of
March 1837 personally appeared before the undersig
one of the Justices   of the Supreme Court of the State
of Illinois   Charles   Oakley   the person named in the
aforegoing   Bond who was duly sworn to support
the Constitution of the United States, and of this State
and to faithfully   honestly and   diligently   discharge
the duties of fund   Commissioner according to Law
and   the best of his   abilities

     In Testimony whereof the undersg
     hath set his name   the day and
     year   aforesaid
        Theophilus   W. Smith

ENTRY FOR E. C. ROSS IN STUART AND LINCOLN FEE BOOK, APRIL, 1837

This entry, in the hand of Mr. Lincoln, is from the fee book of Stuart & Lincoln now in the possession of Mrs. Edna Orendorff Macpherson of Springfield. Her father was Alfred Orendorff, the last law partner of William Henry Herndon, from whom he received a gift of the fee-book. The Ross entry is one of seven entries which appear in Whipple, "The Story-Life of Lincoln," Page 148, but as five of the entries are in the original manuscript form in the Herndon-Weik Collection, this entry is presented as a separate item to prevent repetition of material. The other entry is that for Lucinda Mason, dated October, 1837.
E. C. Ross

   To   Stuart &Lincoln   Dr
1837-April- To attendance at trial of right of
 J. F. Davis property before Moffett $5.00

ENTRY IN THE FEE BOOK OF STUART & LINCOLN, APRIL, 1837

The entry reproduced below is in the hand of the junior partner of Stuart & Lincoln. It is the record kept by the two partners in their well-known fee book now owned by Mrs. Edna Orendorff Macpherson of Springfield. Mr. Lincoln made numerous entries, but upon the departure of the senior partner for Washington on November 2, 1839, he penned the humorous passage in the fee book, "Commencement of Lincoln's Administration."

Mather, Lamb & Co.
To Stuart & Lincoln Dr
1837—April—To attendance at trial of right of J. F. Davis'
   property before Moffett $5.00

LETTER OF LINCOLN TO LEVI DAVIS,
APRIL 19, 1837

*Lawyer Lincoln's first weeks in Springfield in the spring of
1837 were lonely ones. "I am quite as lonesome here as I ever
was anywhere in my life," he wrote Mary Owens in New Salem.
But soon he found new and congenial friends, and activities that
until the end of his days were to have first claim on his time and
energy.   The adoption of nominating conventions was about to
give birth and permanence to the party system, and without delay
the newcomer became a member of the group of half a dozen
Springfield men who shaped Whig affairs in Sangamon County
and were planning to exercise a like influence in the state.*

*One of the members of this group early became a close friend
of Mr. Lincoln This was Dr. Anson G. Henry, who loved a
fight, wielded a sharp pen and had a genius for making enemies.
Early in 1837 Dr. Henry was named a member of a three-man
commission—William Herndon and Archibald Job were his associates—charged with the superintending of construction of the
new state house in Springfield.   True to his urge to rule, Dr.
Henry from the first made this commission a one-man affair
and shaped its course with a high hand.   The letter from Mr.
Lincoln introducing Dr. Henry to Levi Davis, state auditor at
Alton, here reproduced, served its purpose.   Dr. Henry received
$400 on April 22 and returned with it to Springfield, where, a
growing group of his enemies charged he conducted the affairs
of the commission with lavish hand until in 1840 retired from
office by action of the General Assembly.*

*Meanwhile, also in 1837, Dr. Henry was made the Whig
candidate for probate judge in opposition to James Adams, incumbent of that office.   Those who believed that in the construction of the new state house he was recklessly spending the people's
money resolved to accomplish his defeat for the probate judge-
ship.   There followed a bitter personal and political fight, waged
through the newspapers and on the hustings in which Mr. Lincoln, who, as will presently appear, had his own reasons for regarding Dr. Henry's opponent as a rogue, took a leading part.
The election, however, proved that a majority of the voters*

regarded Adams as the victim of unwarranted persecution, for he received 1025 votes to 792 for Henry.

Springfield April 19, 1837

Levi Davis, Esq.,

Friend Davis—The bearer of this, Dr. A. G. Henry, visits you for the purpose of drawing a small amount of money to enable the Commissioners to commence the erection of a State House. He, as you probably recollect, is one of the Building Commissioners. The Bond for the $5000, required by the act locating the Seat of Government, has been executed by several of our Citizens and duly approved by the Governor, and will be filed with the Treasurer by Dr. Henry on his Arrival at your Town. The Dr. being a Stranger to you and the Treasurer, and his duties being of a new kind, he has asked me to request you as friends to render him what assistance you conveniently can. We have, generally in this Country, Peace, Health, and Plenty, and no News. Very respectfully,

A. Lincoln

NOTE AND PRAECIPE IN THE SUIT OF WEBB VS. WATSON, APRIL 21, 1837

The note here reproduced was not drawn by Mr. Lincoln. The "Dam $300" in the lower right hand corner is the only part of it that was the work of his hand. So also were the copy of the instrument sued on, the instructions to Orr, and the praecipe. The cover notations and date of filing are the work of the clerk, Butler. The case when it came before the Sangamon Court for trial on July 6, 1837, was decided in favor of Stuart & Lincoln's client Webb, who was awarded a judgment of $87.70.

Six months after Date I promise to pay Joseph Klein or order the sum of Two Hundred and Thirty four Dollars and Ninety Six cents. For Value Received of him— March 17th 1837. James G. Webb.

Teste (?)

John T. Stuart   Dam $300

James G. Webb's
Note $234.96
due 17th Sept. 1837

A Copy of the instrument sued upon follows:

Know all men by these presents that we Andrew Orr & Benjamin Watson are held and firmly bound unto James Webb assignee of Bell & Tinsley in the penal sum of one hundred and twenty dollars, current money of the United State, for the payment of which well and truly to be made, we bind ourselves, our heirs executors   and administrators,   jointly, severally and firmly by these presents

Witness our hands and seals this 18th day of April A D 1835.   The condition of the above obligation is such, That whereas the said Webb assignee aforesaid, did on this 31st day of March A. D. 1835 before Mordecai Mobley a justice of the peace for the county of Sangamon, recover a judgment against the above bounden Andrew Orr for the sum of $61-50 & Costs from which judgment the said Andrew Orr has taken an appeal to the circuit court for the county of Sangamon aforesaid and State of Illinois, now if the said Andrew Orr shall prosecute his said appeal with effect, and shall pay the said debt and all costs in case the said judgment shall be affirmed or adjudged against him on the trial thereof in the said circuit court, then the above obligation to be void; otherwise to remain in full force and effect

> Taken and entered into before me at my office this 18th day of April 1836

Test C. R. Matheney Clerk   )
    N. W. Matheney.   )
        Andw. Orr   (LS)
        Benjamin Watson (LS)
        State of Illinois   ⎰ In Circuit court
        Sangamon county   ⎱   July Term   1837

                            James Webb   ⎱
                                vs   ⎰
                            Benajamin Watson ⎰
                In Debt
                        Debt $200
                        Damage   100.
            J. T. Stuart for Plff

James G. Webb
            ⎱
    vs   ⎰ Precipe
            ⎰
Benjamin Watson
Filed april 24th
1837
    Wm. Butler clk

REPORT OF COMMISSIONERS DRAWN BY MR. LINCOLN OF THE MARKING AND LOCATION OF A ROAD FROM SPRINGFIELD TO NATHAN HUSSEY'S, MAY 23, 1837

The original of this report drawn by Mr. Lincoln is now in the Illinois State Historical Library. It recalls what was, no doubt, one of his last tasks as deputy surveyor of Sangamon County. George Pasfield was a native of England who settled in Springfield in 1821 and until his death in 1869 at the ripe age of seventy-seven was a leading merchant of the town. Washington Iles came from Kentucky to Illinois in his youth, served in the Black Hawk War, and with Mr. Lincoln had a part in bringing the steamboat Talisman up the Sangamon to a point near Springfield, the only steamboat, as recorded elsewhere, to ever ascend that stream to a point so far from its mouth. John Williams was another native of Kentucky who came in his teens to Springfield, where he was first a clerk in the store of Major Elijah Iles and ere long the successor of that pioneer in business. All three of the commissioners who signed this report were friends and political supporters of Abraham Lincoln.

We, the undersigned, being appointed by the county commissioner's court of Sangamon county, to view a road from the Public Square in Springfield to Nathan Hussey's on the Fort Clark road, report that we have viewed, marked, and located the road as follows (towit) Begining at the Public Square aforesaid, and running from thence with the Peoria road as now traveled, to a point in the middle of said road, from which one of the bearing trees of the South West corner of Section one in Township 16 North of Range 5 West, being a Black Oak 12 inches in diameter, bears N1¼ E 8 chains & 12 links and thence according to the Plot & Field notes returned herewith, to a point on the old road near to the North West corner of the aforesaid Section one Thence with the old road as now traveled to the said Hussey's.

Given under our hands this 23rd of May 1837
We report said road to be of public utility.

Geo. Pasfield
Washington Iles
John Williams

CONTRACT FOR CONTINGENT FEE DRAWN BY LINCOLN, MAY 26, 1837

This contract, now in the Illinois State Historical Library at Springfield, marked the beginning of the most widely discussed suit which fell in Mr. Lincoln's early years as a lawyer. He had been for only a few weeks the partner of John T. Stuart when Mary and Richard Anderson, widow and son of Joseph Anderson, came to Springfiel from their home in Fulton County, to secure possession of and sell ten acres of land lying in the hills near Springfield upon which Oak Ridge Cemetery, the final resting place of Mr. Lincoln was later located, which they claimed belonged to them as heirs of their husband and father.

They found the land occupied by General James Adams, the former attorney of Anderson, who claimed title to it through deeds and other documents of record. Adams, a native of Connecticut where he was born in 1783, had studied for the bar in New York, and in 1821 had become Springfield's first lawyer, soon acquiring what at that time was regarded as an extensive practice. He won the title of general in the Winnebago and Black Hawk Wars, and for fourteen years following 1823 served as justice of the peace. Not a few had occasion in due time to doubt his integrity, but, a hail fellow well met, he fitted easily and happily into pioneer conditions, and, as the sequel was to prove, until the end of his days had more friends than enemies.

Adams, of course refused in May, 1837, to give up the land claimed by the Anderson heirs and the latter applied to Lawyer Lincoln to recover it for them. An examination of the records convinced the young attorney that Adams, in perfecting a title, had resorted to forgery, and he agreed without delay to bring suit for the recovery of the land. His next step was to engage Stephen T. Logan, who was then leader of the Sangamon County bar and who later was to become his partner, to assist in the litigation. Then he drew up a contract for a contingent fee, which on May 26 the widow and son signed, the former with her mark. And on June 22, as will be set forth on a later page, Stuart and Lincoln, together with Logan and Logan's partner, Edward D. Baker, filed suit against Adams for the recovery of the land.

Whereas the heirs of Joseph Anderson deceased are about to commence an action in chancery in the Sangamon Circuit Court, for the recovery of a certain piece of ground (describing the land in controversy); and whereas, Stephen T. Logan, John T. Stuart and A. Lincoln have engaged to prosecute the suit as attorneys for the said heirs, we, the subscribers, being the widow and one of the sons of the said Anderson deceased, agree to give to said Logan, Stuart and Lincoln one-half of the said piece of ground for their services, provided they recover the same; but are not bound to pay anything unless the said piece of ground be recovered.

LETTER OF MR. LINCOLN TO THE THIRD AUDITOR OF THE TREASURY, MAY 30, 1837

This letter, the original of which is now in the Illinois State Historical Library, again testifies to Mr. Lincoln's readiness to aid those who had served with him in the Black Hawk War. On June 28, 1837 the auditor allowed Demmon the sum of $32.68.

Springfield, Illinois, May 30th 1837-

If the claim, founded upon the enclosed papers, be allowed, the money may be forwarded directly to the claimant, "Archelaus Demmon, Springfield, Illinois" If it be *not* allowed, on account of insufficiency of evidence, or for other cause, and the defect, whatever it may be, can be remedied, write back, stating particularly what is lacking, and direct to A. Lincoln, place as above.

The Paymaster or disbursing officer of whom this applicant received pay was, according to recollection, Major Wright of the United States Army. In this there may be a mistake, as there is nothing but memory to refer to. At any rate it was the officer that paid Whiteside's Brigade.

Respectfully

A. Lincoln for

the Applicant

Third Auditor

PRAECIPE AND AFFIDAVIT IN THE SUIT OF ELLIS & COMPANY VS. SMITH, JUNE 9, 1837

The precipe and cover notations and the affidavit here reproduced, except for the date of filing by Clerk Butler and Speed's signature to the affidavit, were drawn by Mr. Lincoln. Speed, then a member of A. Y. Ellis & Company, shared his bed with Mr. Lincoln when in April, 1837, the latter removed from New Salem to Springfield, arriving in his new home on a borrowed horse and with only a few dollars in his pocket; and he was long the young lawyer's closest friend.

State of Illinois ⎱
                  ⎰ ss   In the Sangamon circuit court

Sangamon county ⎰   July Term 1837

A. Y. Ellis, James Bell & Joshua F. Speed
merchants, doing business in the name of

A. Y. Ellis & Co.⎤   In attachment
        vs   ⎬   Debt $62.76 cents
Thomas P. Smith ⎦

> The clerk will issue a writ of attachment herein upon affadavit herewith filed returnable to the next term.

> Stuart & Lincoln, for Plffs

A. Y. Ellis & Co.
    vs.
Thomas P. Smith
    Precipe
Filed June 9th 1837
    Wm. Butler Clk.

State of Illinois ⎤
                  ⎬ss
Sangamon county ⎦

Joshua F Speed being duly sworn saith that he is one of the partners of a firm trading under the style of A. Y. Ellis & Co. which firm is composed of this deponent, Abner Y. Ellis and James Bell: that Thomas P. Smith is justly indebted to the said firm in the sum of sixty two dollars and seventy six cents lawful money of the United States upon a store account: That said Smith has departed from this state, with the intention, as this deponent believes, of having his effects and personal estate removed without the limits of this state, and with the intention, as this deponent believes, of not returning.

That the deponent knows of no other means of collecting said debt but by the process of attachment, may issue &c

> Joshua F Speed

    Sworn to before me
    this 9th day of June 1837
        Wm Butler Clk
A Y Ellis & Co

    vs   ⎬ affa

Thomas P. Smith
Filed June 9th 1837
Wm Butler Clk

AFFIDAVIT OF WILLIAM HERNDON IN THE SUIT OF HERNDON VS. SMITH, JUNE 9, 1837
(Herndon-Weik Collection)

This affidavit was signed by Herndon, but the rest of the paper is in the hand of his attorney, Lincoln. The signing of the affidavit is attested to in the hand of Butler, as are the cover notations. The affidavit signed by Lincoln is in the hand writing of William Herndon, uncle of William H. Herndon, the last law partner of Mr. Lincoln. William H. Herndon was nineteen years old, and a minor in the eyes of the law courts. J. Rowan Herndon, familiarly known as Rowan, was a cousin of William Herndon and it was from him Mr. Lincoln bought an interest in a store at New Salem which later was the subject of much troublesome litigation.

State of Illinois ⎫
Sangamon county ⎬ ss

William Herndon being duly sworn saith that Thomas P. Smith is justly indebted to him in the sum of twentyone dollars and sixty cents lawful money of the United States upon a promissory note made by said Smith to J. R. Herndon and assigned by said J. R. Herndon to the deponent the said William Herndon. The said note being originally made for one hundred dollars, bearing date April 3rd 1837. to become due twentytwo days after date, and to bear twelve per cent interest from the time due until paid, upon which is a credit entered on the 27. May. 1837, for twentynine dollars and seventyfive cents. That said Smith has departed from the state with the intention so this deponent believes of having his effects and personal estate removed without the limits of this state; and with the intention of not returning as this deponent believes

That the deponent knows of no other means of collecting said debt, but by process of attachment and prays that an attachment may issue &c

                                        William Herndon

Sworn to before me this
9th day of July A D 1837
        Wm Butler Clk
William Herndon
            ⎫ 847
    vs   ⎬ affa
            ⎭
Thomas P. Smith

Filed June 9″ 1837
    Wm Butler Clk

PLEA OF COMPLAINANT AND ISSUE OF SUBPOENA IN THE CHANCERY SUIT OF HOUGHTON VS. HART, JUNE 15, 1837
(Herndon-Weik Collection)

The plea of complainant and cover notations here reproduced, except for the date of filing, are in the hand of Mr. Lincoln. The order for issue of subpoena was drawn by his partner, John T. Stuart, whose indifferent penmanship is in marked contrast to the neatness of Mr. Lincoln's handwriting. On the other hand, the word "beginning" is spelled "begining" by Mr. Lincoln, a usage characteristic of his surveys and more than one legal paper. The possessive word "its" is spelled "it's,", the apostrophe being very distinct upon both occasions upon which Mr. Lincoln used the word. The clause, "and render such other and further relief as may seem equitable & your orator &c," is employed rather than the one more frequently used in later documents, towit, "As equity may seem to require and as in duty bound &c." The tract of land which was the bone of contention in this suit consisted of 12:48 acres on the south side of Rock Creek, six miles from New Salem. Mr. Lincoln had surveyed it for David Hart in November, 1834. It may be noted in passing that the day before he began this suit for Houghton Mr. Lincoln had closed his accounts as postmaster of New Salem by paying to William Carpenter, Springfield postmaster, the sum of $248.63, which, in the face of pressing personal needs, he had carefully guarded against the day when demand would be made for it. And likewise on June 14, 1837, he wrote the first of his Sampson Ghost letters of which more on another page.

To the Honorable the Judge of the circuit court for

Sangamon county in chancery sitting—

Respectfully sheweth your orator, Elijah Houghton, that David Hart, being seized of a certain tract of land, being a part of the West half of the South East quarter of Section Thirteen in Township Seventeen North of Range Seven West of the Third Principal Meridian, and bounded as follows, towit, begining at the South East corner of said half quarter; thence West with the Southern boundary line of the same ten chains and seven links; thence North twelve chains and forty links to the centre of the channel of Rock creek; thence down the said creek with its meanderings to the eastern boundary line of said half quarter; thence South with said Eastern boundary line to the place of begining; containing twelve acres and fortyeight hundredths of an acre more or less; and being so seized, sold to your orator, and your orator purchased of him, the said David Hart, the said tract of land, and paid for the same in other land acre for acre, and conveyed the same to the said David Hart. After the time of sale of said land to your orator, to wit, in the month of November in the year 1834 possession of the same was given by the said David Hart to your orator, in whose possession it has ever since remained. Your orator would further state that no deed or memorandum in writing was ever executed by the said David Hart in relation to the sale of said land to your orator— which omission originated in the confidence reposed by your orator in the said David Hart.

That some time in the month of May in the year 1836, the said David Hart died, leaving the following named heirs at law, towit, Jefferson Hart, Melissa Jane Hart, and Rhoda Hart, whom your orators prays may be made defendants to this bill, and required to answer touching all and singular the allegations therein contained.

Your orators prays that upon a final hearing of this case, your Honor would decree, that all the right, title and interest which the heirs at law of the said David Hart, have in that part of the West half of the South East quarter of Section Thirteen in Township Seventeen North of Range Seven West of the Third Principal Meridian which is bounded as follows. towit, begining at the South East corner of said half quarter; thence West with the Southern boundary line of the same, ten chains and seven links; thence North twelve chains and forty links to the centre of the channel of Rock creek; thence down the said creek with it's meanderings to the Eastern boundary line of said half quarter; thence South with said Eastern boundary line to the place of begining; containing twelve acres and fortyeight hundredths of an acre more or less, situated in the county of Sangamon, be conveyed to your orator, and render such other and further relief as may seem equitable & your orator &c

Stuart and Lincoln
Complainant's Solicitors

28

Elijah Houton
        vs
Jefferson Hart   }   In Chancery
Melissa Jane Hart
    Rhoda Hart

    Let a subpoena in Chancery issue for the above Defendants returnable to the next Term

                                  Stuart & Lincoln

June 15th 1837
Houghton
    vs
Harts Heirs
Filed June 15th 1837
    Wm Butler Clk

ANSWER OF SAMUEL H. TREAT AS GUARDIAN AD LITEM IN THE SUIT OF HOUGHTON VS. HART, SANGAMON CIRCUIT COURT, JUNE 15, 1837

This answer of Treat is taken from the original record in the Complete Record book for the case. It is in the hand of the clerk, but no doubt the original was penned by Treat. It is included as a part of the history of the suit of Houghton vs. Hart in which Stuart & Lincoln were counsel for the defendant.

Elijah Houghton   )
        vs.   )
Jefferson   Hart   )   In Chancery
Melissa Jane   Hart &)
Rhoda Hart   )

    Samuel   H Treat   Guardian ad litem of the defendants above named for answer in their behalf to the bill in this cause filed saith   That he knows nothing of the matters & allegations in said bill   contained & requires full proof thereof on the part of the complainant

                                S. H. Treat

AFFIDAVIT IN THE SUIT OF ELLIS & COMPANY VS. SMITH, JUNE 17, 1837

The affidavit here reproduced was drawn by Mr. Lincoln. The attestation and cover notations were penned by Butler.

State of Illinois } s s
Sangamon county }

A. Y. Ellis (alias) Abner Y. Ellis, being duly sworn deposes and says that Thomas P. Smith is justly indebted to him in the sum of one hundred and fifteen dollars lawful money of the United States, the same being upon a promissory note for that sum, bearing date the 8th day of June 1837; that, the said he believes, is having his effects and personal estate removed without the limits of the State; and the said Smith has some personal property in the county aforesaid

Abner Y Ellis

Sworn to before me this
    7" day of June 1837
      Wm. Butler Clk

A Y Ellis

   vs   } affa

Thomas P Smith
Filed June 17" 1837
  Wm Butler Clk

SAMPSON'S GHOST LETTERS BY LINCOLN, JUNE 17, 1837 AND LATER

In 1837 each party, Whig and Democrat, had its organ in Springfield. The Sangamo Journal edited by Simeon Francis, friend and supporter of Mr. Lincoln from the latter's early days at New Salem, was the Whig, and the Illinois Republican, George R. Weber, editor, was the Democratic organ. On June 15, the Republican attacked Dr. Anson G. Henry charging that he had been appointed state house commissioner as a reward for the "dirty work" he had done for the Whigs, and that now the people were paying a heavy price for it. "At the rate he is progressing," said the editor, "it is probable that the $50,000 the people of this town have to pay will about pay the expense of the foundation and the Building itself will not cost the State more than $500,000 if A. G. Henry is allowed to superintend it."

Three days later the Journal, quick to counter in an effective way, charged that the Republican article was prompted by partisan malice, while in another column of the same issue of the Journal Mr. Lincoln in an article signed Sampson's Ghost—the shade of a man who had once owned the land on which Adams lived—gave full reign to an urge for writing anonymous letters to the press which was to remain with him until in 1842 it involved him in serious trouble with James Shields. Circumstantial evidence of a conclusive sort made it plain at the moment that Mr. Lincoln, whose contempt for Adams had become of a bitter and unyielding kind, was the writer of the Sampson's Ghost article, and at a later date he indirectly admitted its authorship. He now inferred that Adams was responsible for the Republican's attempts to injure Henry, and bade him, before assailing the conduct of other men, to study his own—official as well as private, adding that he knew that his own home stood "upon disputed ground." And so began what was to prove a savage but fruitless war of words.

In an address before the Abraham Lincoln Association in 1937 the late Logan Hay recalled that at New Salem, Mr. Lincoln inspired by Jack Kelso, the champion idler of the hamlet, had read Shakespeare, adding that Sampson's Ghost might have been suggested to him by the ghost of Hamlet's father. Be this as it may, there is no doubt that the Sampson's Ghost letters were, with a single exception, the one of his earlier efforts remembered by Mr. Lincoln with least satisfaction in his later years. And it is interesting to recall that when he was writing them in the summer of 1837 in London, Thomas Carlyle, then in the flush of his powers, was publishing his vivid and masterly account of the French Revolution, a book Mr. Lincoln may never have read, but which won and held the admiration of his future partner, William Henry Herndon, while in Cambridge, Massachusetts, on August 31, 1837, Carlyle's friend, Ralph Waldo Emerson, then in his thirty-fourth year, delivered the address on The American Scholar, which was to assure him a high place among the thinkers of his period. And in his native Salem in the summer of 1837, Nathaniel Hawthorne was turning the pages of Twice-Told Tales, his first great work which had just come from the press. A quarter of a century later he was to meet Abraham Lincoln and write of him in an unforgetable way.

Finally in Petersboro, New York, on July 21, 1837, the day before Mr. Lincoln wrote the first of the Sampson's Ghost letters, Gerrit Smith received word that his father's old partner, John Jacob Astor had granted his request for a loan of a quarter million dollars—a loan which, despite the financial panic then at its worst, enabled him to save his great land holdings and to become through a long period of years the chief and unfailing

*almoner of the anti-slavery movement. All this was in the future,
but during the struggle to preserve the Union Abraham Lincoln
was to have no firmer friend than Gerrit Smith.*

FIRST SAMPSON'S GHOST LETTER

To the Editor of the Journal:

To my surprise I find, in looking over the last Illinois
Republican, an article directed against one of the Commissioners appointed by the Legislature to superintend the erection of the State House, well calculated to do Springfield great
injury, and discreditable to the whole delegation of this
County. In justice to the editor I must say that I do not believe that he was able to comprehend its designed effect when
he consented it should appear in his paper. I must think that
it was intended solely to injure Dr. Henry, the commissioner,
who is now a candidate for Probate Justice of the Peace. I
shall not be surprised, if the author can be found out, that it
will fall upon the person of Gen. James Adams, who is likewise a candidate for the same office.—I presume, it is well
known that Gen. Adams has always been opposed to Springfield, as well as her citizens. Before he assails the conduct of
other men, he should take a retrospective view of his own conduct—official as well as private. He must know that his own
house stands upon disputed ground.

Sampson's Ghost.

Springfield, June 14, 1837.

SECOND SAMPSON'S GHOST LETTER

Fork Prairie, July 4, 1837.

To the Editor of the Journal:

In the Illinois Republican of June 15, by accident, I discovered an article which purported to be editorial, designed,
as I believe, to injure your worthy citizen and townsman, Dr.
Henry, who I had understood, was a candidate for Probate
Justice of the Peace. By the time I had finished reading the
article above alluded to, I had come to the conclusion that
the real author was Gen. James Adams, who was likewise a
candidate for Probate Justice of the Peace—as one object was,
by injuring Dr. Henry, to benefit him. I now find over the
General's own signature, in the same paper of June 21, a denial
of the authorship. Be it so; a man may not write an article,
and still circumstances may make him morally responsible
for it. By the bye, the General does not deny that he has al-

ways been opposed to Springfield, as well as to her citizens. The Gen'l. makes some allusions to me, which I do not relish very well; he would have the people believe that I had been mounted upon a rail—better known by soldiers as a wooden horse! and that I had my back scored until the claret flew, all for my toryism in the last war. I must confess that no one better understands the punishment generally inflicted on a tory than the Gen'l. does, if reports be true. The Gen'l. says "as to insinuations on character I leave that with the public." For my own part I am willing that he shall be the keeper of his own character, or leave it with the people, just as he pleases, if he will just tell the people of this county by what authority he holds possession of the property he now lives upon. In conclusion, I will say that I always 'write' my own name, and if any instrument of writing be in existence not written with my own hand, which affects my interest, I hope my heirs will see to it. I feel in hopes that the death of the Justice of the Peace, together with myself, witness, &c will not rob my heirs of their just claims.

Sampson's Ghost.

Sangamo Journal, June 24, 1837.

THIRD SAMPSON'S GHOST LETTER

Fork Prairie, July 4, 1837.

To the Editor of the Journal:

The last production of Gen. Adams, over his signature, which appeared in the Illinois Republican, is quite amusing to some who know him—particularly those who knew him during the last war. Speaking of my communication of June 21st, he says: "And his insinuation leads to the inference, (that Gen. Adams might be his brother in toryism;) as to that then there are too many individuals in this "country to whom my sufferings and losses while in the United States service during the late war are known, to require the least notice."

If reports be true, I will admit that the General suffered great losses, and that his sufferings were great also. But what were the causes of his losses and why did he suffer? Was it while he was acting in defense of his country, or was it from any improper connection with the British in the war referred to? This is a matter of which I know nothing, and if I did it would be no sort of consequence; but I do know something of the General since he arrived in this country, and

I again call upon the General to explain to the citizens of this county by what authority he holds possession of two certain lots of ground in Springfield, upon which he now resides? If he will answer this question fairly, without equivocation, and then the people choose to make him Probate Justice of the Peace, I will acknowledge that Sampson never owned one foot of ground in Springfield. He again says:

"If any person wishes to know the tenor (tenure) of the property on which I reside, it is a leasehold tenement of record, open to all persons, and when Sampson's heirs call for possession of their property, and cannot obtain it by reason that it is legally withheld, it will be early enough to commence complaining of injury."

Why does he refer persons to the record? Will they know any better than they now do? Will they know by looking at the record book whether the instrument of writing be genuine or not? I admire the General for one thing. He appears to wish not to commit himself, for he says when "Sampson's heirs call for possession of their property and cannot obtain it by reason that it is illegally withheld, it will be early enough to commence complaining of injury." Mind, the General does not say, that when Sampson's heirs call for their property which he lives upon, and it shall prove to be theirs, I will immediately surrender it to them. The General thought, perhaps, if he used the latter language, he would be compelled to do an act for which he has no inclination, and thus add another circumstance to those of a very strange character involved in this affair.

In conclusion, I will ask of the General one more favor, and it is simply this—Will he refer the citizens of this county to the citizens of Springfield for information as to his transactons with Sampson, if he ever had any? It would also facilitate this matter if he would state who was public administrator at the time of my death. Perhaps he may know something important to a right understanding of the subject. I consider that there is nothing unreasonable in these requests.

Sampson's Ghost.

Sangamo Journal, July 8, 1837.

FOURTH SAMPSON'S GHOST LETTER

Fork Prairie, July 12, 1837.

To the Editor of the Journal:

I see Gen. Adams or somebody else has published a piece

in the Republican, over the signature of "An Old Soldier."
The General's visit to the editor of that paper on Sunday night,
is now sufficiently explained. The "Old Soldier" writes most
eloquently in praise of himself; for it is well known that no
other person cares enough about him to write such a mess
of stuff for his benefit. I last week called upon the ('old soldier') to say if he was willing to refer the People of this
county to the old citizens of Springfield, to learn the truth
in regard to the manner in which he obtained the lots on
which he now resides. But he has shunned the answer. I
now ask him to publish the lease which he is said to have obtained from me in my lifetime. I want every body should
see it, and know, too, when it was recorded. I want every
thing should come out. The "old soldier" gives us an account
of his feats of chivalry. This is all very well, for if he should
not tell them they might be entirely lost to the world. He
certifies most valorously for his uprightness and good
standing; all very proper for the same reason. He intimates,
too, that he is poor; Gen. Adams sometime ago sold one quarter of his town property at the termination of the canal for
12,000 dollars. The "old soldier" undoubtedly thinks his
disguise a good one—but it is quite too thin to answer the
purpose. When he fixes any more articles over that signature, I would advise him to be more cautious in exposing himself.

Sampson's Ghost.

Sangamo Journal, July 15, 1837.

FIFTH SAMPSON'S GHOST LETTER

Fork Prairie, July 20, 1837.

To the Editor of the Journal:

I am told Gen. Adams has proved most satisfactorily by
affidavits that he was not a tory in the last war. The pains
he has taken to clear up this matter, will show that there
might be grounds for suspicion, particularly as he was formerly a violent advocate of the Hartford Convention candidate
for Presidency.

But I am at a loss to understand what connexion Gen.
Adams' toryism, or support of a tory candidate for the Presidency, has with the property belonging to Sampson's heirs,
and now in the possession of Gen. Adams. I have asked him

to explain the manner in which he came into possession of Sampson's property. You answer that you are not a tory! I still insist upon being referred to some citizens of this town for information touching a lease which I suppose was procured from me since my death. All the answer I can get from you is, that you are not a tory!

Now is not there a little evidence of shuffling here? of a disposition to avoid the question at issue—and to lead the public mind on a false trail? Does it not appear that in this matter that you are anxious to leave "snake holes" out of which to escape?

I must again ask you to give some account of your trade with me—how you came to take advantage of me and draw from me a lease of two lots for ten years, for the great consideration of ten dollars—so as to place beyond my control for ten years, two lots, which I had purchased for my own especial benefit. I must also, again, ask you to refer me to some of the respectable citizens of Springfield who knew of that lease, before I can believe that I could have been so crazy as to give you such a lease. I wish to leave my memory purged from the charge of insanity.

I want, also, that you should publish this lease, so that everybody can see and understand. I wish you would also leave the original lease at the Recorder's Office, or some other public place, for examination. A good deal of evidence material in this matter, can be found in an original document. I hope you will not on any account, lose this lease. A censorious world might say there might be design in losing it. The known care you take of all important documents, will, I doubt not, prevent any such casualty.

I beg, hereafter, that you will let your military career rest in peace. As a ghost, I have done with military affairs. My great object is to find by what tenure you hold my lots— all the circumstances attending their transfer into your hands. Don't parry this call.

Sampson's Ghost.

Sangamo Journal, July 22, 1837.

SIXTH AND LAST SAMPSON'S GHOST LETTER

Fork Prairie, July 26, 1837.

To the Editor of the Journal:

Dear Sir:—I have called and called upon Gen. Adams, to make some statement to this community, in regard to the tenor (tenure), by which he holds possession of my lots. I have called upon him to give to the People a copy of the lease, by which he professes to hold that property. I am anxious that the People should see the lease. I have called upon him also, to refer the People to the old citizens of Springfield, to satisfy them that everything was as it should be. Are not these calls reasonable? Would not a man conscious of his rights, at once respond to these calls? Truth has nothing to fear from examination. I must now, in my turn, refer the People to any and every old citizen of Springfield for information touching this matter—and, further, I now refer you, on the same subject, to Philip and Edward Clark, men well known in this county, now living on the South Fork and with whom Andrew Sampson "lived and died." And I want every man who feels interested in this matter, to ask them for all the information they possess concerning it.

There is another subject which the People wish to understand. I allude to the case of Joseph Anderson. You are aware that a lot of land of ten acres, or thereabouts, which appears to be deeded to you on the Record Books of this county, is claimed by the heirs of the said Joseph Anderson— that they have brought a suit against you in the Circuit Court of this County for the said land.

Information of DEEP IMPORTANCE in this matter will be found in the office of the Circuit Court clerk in Springfield; and if any citizen calls upon the clerk for the purpose, it will be his duty to exhibit the Record to him. I therefore refer to the records and papers in his office for IMPORTANT information in regard to this property which is deeded to Gen. ADAMS, but which is claimed by the heirs of Joseph Anderson.

The charges against me of slander pass unheeded by me as the idle wind. I have pointed out to the People how they can do justice to Gen. Adams and to themselves. Let them do it—and if I am wrong, the examination will result to his advantage.

It is important that the People in selecting a man in whose care to commit DEAD MEN'S ESTATES should be satisfied that a proper disposition will be made of such estates.

My labors have now nearly ceased. I have only sought to promote inquiry. All I ASK—all I WISH is that TRUTH SHOULD PREVAIL. And before I am charged as a slanderer,

I wish all the evidence in the case to be fairly, freely and fully examined.

Sampson's Ghost.

Sangamo Journal, July 29, 1837.

DECLARATION IN THE SUIT OF TRUETT & COMPANY VS. RANSDELL, SANGAMON CIRCUIT COURT, JUNE 22, 1837
(Herndon-Weik Collection)

This is one of the earlier legal papers penned by Mr. Lincoln. The declaration is in his hand, as are the cover notations, with the exception of the file date by Butler. The other cover notation, a duplicate of the first, is by Butler, and he mis-spelled "Truett" as "Trewett" in citing the case. The document is torn badly and blurred in places, and this accounts for the use of parentheses. The context is derived from similar legal papers in the hands of Lincoln, and reveals the care taken by him in the preparation of his documents. It is not as well punctuated as later papers; the words, "Although often requested so to do," are not in parentheses, and the use of first names for plaintiffs and defendants is a characteristic not found in later documents.

Wharton Ransdell, the defendant, was the keeper of a Springfield tavern, while the plaintiff, Henry B. Truett, later was to become defendant in a noted murder case tried by Logan, Baker and Lincoln. The records of cases before the Sangamon County Circuit Court are not complete in all cases, and it is not possible to give a full case history of each case engaged in by Mr. Lincoln. In days of hand copying it was difficult to transcribe every case. Judges Dockets are frequently incomplete, and in many cases no final decision in the case exists. A case history of the suit of Truett & Co. vs. Ransdell does not seem to be available in the records of Sangamon County.

In the Sangamon county circuit court of the July Term 1837

Henry B. Truett and William L. May, trading and doing business under the name of H. B. Truett & Co., complain of Wharton Ransdell being in custody &c. of a plea of tresspass on the case upon promises for that whereas the said Wharton, heretofore, towit, on the twentyfourth day of March in the year eighteen hundred and thirtyseven, at the county and circuit aforesaid, was indebted to the said Henry and William in the sum of thirteen hundred and seventyone dollars and eightyeight cents lawful money of the United States, for divers goods, wares, merchandize and chattels, before that time sold and delivere[d to the] said Wharton, and at his special instance an[d request] , and being so indebted, he the said Wharton, in consideration, afterwards, towit, on the day and year aforesaid, at the county and circuit aforesaid, undertook and then and there faithfully promised the said Henry and William to pay them the said sum of money when he the said Wharton should be thereunto afterwards requested. Nevertheless the said Wharton not regarding his said promise and undertaking, but contriving and fraudulently intending craftily and subtly to defraud and deceive the said Henry and William in this behalf hath not as yet paid the said sum of money or any part thereof to the said Henry and William although often requested so to do, but the said Wharton to pay the same to the said Henry and William, hath hitherto wholly refused and neglected, and still doth refuse and neglect.

To the damage of the said Henry and William in the sum of eighteen hundred dollars and therefore they sue &c.

Logan & Baker for Plff

H. B. Truett & Co.

vs } Decln

Wharton Ransdell
Filed June 22 1837
Wm Butler Clk

COMPLAINT OF PLAINTIFF IN SUIT OF MILLER VS. CHRISMAN ET AL, JUNE 22, 1837
(Herndon-Weik Collection)

The complaint of the plaintiff in this suit, with cover notations, was drawn by Mr. Lincoln, except that Stuart wrote the concluding sentence in which it is stated that Miller had paid the balance of the note against him. Three days before the filing of the Miller complaint Mr. Lincoln had joined in welcoming Daniel Webster to Springfield. The Massachusetts senator, who was touring the West with his family, was accorded a military escort from Berlin to Springfield, and after participating in a barbecue at Porter's Grove in the outskirts of the town delivered a long and stirring address to a great throng.

To the Honorable the Judge of the Sangamon county circuit court in chancery sitting—

Respectfully sheweth your orator, George Miller, that St. Clair Chrisman and Isaac N. Chrisman were seized of the North East quarter of Section Six in Township Seventeen North of

Range Six West of the Third Principal Meridian, and being so seized, they, the said St. Clair Chrisman and Isaac N. Chrisman did, on the 19th day of March in the year 1832, sell the said quarter section of land to your orator, and executed and delivered to your orator, their conditional obligation in writing for the conveyance of the legal title of said land to your orator, which obligation your orator herewith files marked (A) and prays that the same may be taken for, and made a part of this bill. Your orator further states that he has performed the condition of said obligation (the same being the payment of money) on his part, *in part* : and that he is now, and for a long time has been, ready to pay the remaining part. Your orator further states, that at the time he purchased the said land of the said St. Clair Chrisman and Isaac Chrisman, they delivered possession of the same to him your orator, in whose possession it has ever since remained. Your orator further states that some time in the year 1834 the said Isaac N. Chrisman died, leaving the following named heirs at law, towit, Nancy Chrisman and Peyton Chrisman, whom together with Jacob Chrisman, one of the administrators of the estate of the said Isaac N. Chrisman, and St. Clair Chrisman, the surviving obligor in the aforesaid obligation, and also one of the administrators of the estate of the said Isaac N. Chrisman, your orator prays may be made defendants to this bill, and required to answer all and singular the allegations therein contained—

Your orator prays that upon a final hearing of this case your Honor would decree, that all the right, title, and interest which the said Isaac N. Chrisman, have to the North East quarter of Section Six in Township Seventeen North of Range Six West of the Third Principal Meridian, situated in the county of Sangamon, be conveyed to your orator; and grant such other and further relief as may seem equitable, & your orator &c.

Stuart & Lincoln
Complainant's   Solicitors

And the said Complainant states that he has since the filing of his said Bill, paid the whole amount of said Note—

Stuart & Lincoln

30
George Miller
    vs
Nancy Chrisman
Peyton Chrisman

Jacob Chrisman
St. Clair Chrisman
Filed June 22 1837
    Wm Butler Clk

ORDER IN CHANCERY SUIT OF MILLER VS. CHRISMAN ET AL, PROBABLY JUNE 22, 1837
(Herndon-Weik Collection)

As in the case of Moses Martin vs. the Heirs of Martin, this court decree was handed down upon October 16, 1837, the same day upon which petition for partition was filed. It is possible the court decree was dated down in like manner in the preceding case, although the decree is undated. Peyton Chrisman appears as the defendant in both cases and it would appear that the guardian ad litem had been appointed on June 22, 1837. A final decree in the case was rendered on March 17, 1838 and was in favor of George Miller, the plaintiff and client of Stuart and Lincoln.

George Miller Complainant
       against
Nancy Chrisman   In Chancery
Peyton Chrisman
Jacob Chrisman &
St. Clair Chrisman, Defendants

    This day came the complainant by his solicitor, and it appearing to the court that process had been regularly served upon the said Jacob Chrisman and St. Clair Chrisman; and it also appearing to the court that the said Nancy Chrisman and Peyton S. Chrisman are not inhabitants of this state, and that publication of the pendency of this suit has been duly made according to law; and Samuel H. Treat having been appointed *guardian ad litem* to the said Peyton Chrisman, files his answer and says that he has examined the Bill and papers filed and exhibits in said cause, and states that he knows of no reason consistent with the interest of said minor heir why the prayer of said Bill of complaint should not be granted; and the said Nancy Chrisman, Jacob Chrisman, and St. Clair having been three times solemnly called, came not, but made default; it is therefore ordered by the court that as to them the complainants Bill be taken for confessed; and it appearing to the court that the allegations of said Bill are true: It is therefore ordered and decreed by the court that all the right, title and interest which the said St.

Clair Chrisman, and the said Nancy Chrisman and Peyton Chrisman, as heirs at law of Isaac N. Chrisman, deceased, have to the North East quarter of Section Six in Township Seventeen North of Range Six West of the Third Principal Meridian, situated in the county of Sangamon and State of Illinois, be conveyed to George Miller; and that Samuel H. Treat be appointed a commissioner to execute and deliver said conveyance, and that he report his proceedings herein to this court—

COMPLAINT AND REPLICATION IN THE SUIT OF WRIGHT ET AL VS. ADAMS, SANGAMON CIRCUIT COURT, JUNE 23 and OCTOBER 17, 1837.

The suit of Wright et al vs. Adams, as indicated elsewhere, was no doubt the most widely discussed piece of litigation in which Mr. Lincoln had a part during his first years at the bar. Diligent search of the files of the clerk of the Sangamon Circuit Court has failed to disclose the present whereabouts of the original of the complaint in this case filed on June 23, 1837: but it was the joint effort of Stuart & Lincoln and Logan & Baker, who sought to recover a tract of land is was charged illegally held by Adams, and is known to have been in existence in 1926 when the late Albert J. Beveridge was at work on the life of Mr. Lincoln still unfinished when death stayed his pen. "It is curious," wrote Senator Beveridge, "Abraham Lincoln," Boston, 1928, Volume 1:214) "that the bill is in three separate and distinct handwritings of which but six and one half lines—the description of the land by metes and bounds—are that of Lincoln, although there are eight pages of the bill. The signatures of the four solicitors for the complainant, obviously written by the same hand, are somewhat like that of Lincoln, but much bolder. The bill shows that it was the composite product of three lawyers working together at the same time."

Careful search of the files of the clerk of the Sangamon Circuit Court has also failed to locate the replication in this suit filed by Logan and Lincoln on October 17, 1837; but it is not difficult to trace the later stages of a legal contest which at the time provoked statewide comment and discussion, and in the end yielded no tangible results. The suit after an interval was transferred to Schuyler County only to be remanded to Sangamon by Judge Stephen A. Douglas, for the reason that he had been "of counsel" for Adams. Still later depositions were taken, some of which upheld the title of Adams to the land; but the suit was never brought to trial, and, following the death of the defendant in August, 1843, it was abated by the court on the ensuing November 29. Yet it is evident that Mr. Lincoln erred only on the side of needless rancor in treating Adams as a rogue.

CARD OF DR. ANSON G. HENRY WITH COMMENT BY MR. LINCOLN, SANGAMO JOURNAL
JUNE 24, 1837

The attack on Dr. Anson G. Henry by Editor Weber of the Illinois Republican, already referred to, prompted an angry card from the doctor, which appeared in the Sangamo Journal on June 24, 1837, with introductory comment no doubt written by Mr. Lincoln. The meeting requested by Dr. Henry was held the same day in the court room in Springfield. John T. Stuart was chairman of this meeting, and Robert Allen, a Democrat, its secretary. After brief discussion Mr. Lincoln introduced a resolution which was promptly adopted calling for a bi-partisan committee to investigate the charges of the Illinois Republican, and this committee, as set forth in the Sangamo Journal of July 1, 1837, promptly made a report which gave a clean bill of health to Dr. Henry and his associate commissioners charged with the erection of the new state house. Mr. Lincoln's friendship with Dr. Henry was of a close and enduring sort, but one not always regarded with favor by other of his friends.

We call the attention of the citizens of Springfield and of Sangamon county, to the following card,—in which is involved considerations of vital interest to our town and county. If Dr. Henry has been wanting in his duty as a Commissioner, the fact should be known and the evil corrected as speedily as possible. But, on the other hand, if he has done his duty faithfully as a Commissioner, it is due that his conduct should be placed in a true light before the public. This is not only due to Dr. Henry, but it is important to our citizens to correct any error which the public may have fallen into in consequence of the charges made against him in the "Illinois Republican." We hope the card of Dr. Henry will receive the attention it deserves.

⁂   A CARD.—In consequence of charges made in the "Illinois Republican," deeply affecting the interests of Sangamon County, as well as my own character, I would respectfully invite my fellow citizens of Sangamon County, to meet at the Court House, ON THIS DAY (Saturday) at 4 o'clock, for the purpose of enquiring into the truth or falsity of said charges. A general attendance is most earnestly desired.

A. G. Henry

One of the Commissioners for superintending the erection of the public buildings
June 21, 1837.

HERNDON VS. SMITH: LETTER TO CLERK, JULY (?) 1837

This note and cover notations were penned by William Herndon, and are included as part of the history of the case of Herndon vs. Smith. Although, J. W. Weik placed this document with the case of Herndon vs. Smith, the W. H. Herndon signature offers possible conclusion that the document is of later date, and is an undated praocipe from the hand of W. H. Herndon.

Mr. Clerk will you please issue the writ immediately—under seal &c for said defendants.

I have put the term of your court *November* if wrong please alter it

Please ask the sheriff to make a little extra exertion to serve process and I will satisfy him

File the declaration *praeceipe* & copy of note.

Yours &c
W. H. Herndon

Letter to
    Clerk
Lincoln for
    Plaintiff

COMPLAINT IN THE SUIT OF HERNDON VS. SMITH, JULY 6, 1837
(Herndon-Weik Collection)

Mr. Lincoln drew the complaint and cover notations in this case. The "William" of "William Herndon" and that of "William Butler" are clearly in the same hand. The figures are characteristic of the hand of Mr. Lincoln, especially the "6" and "7". It will be noted that the words, "although often requested so to do," are not enclosed in parentheses as in later documents, while the use of the first name of plaintiff and defendant is common in the early legal documents by Mr. Lincoln. The punctuation is more careful than in later legal papers, because the fledgling attorney had time, which busy Lawyer Lincoln did not have at a later period. The division of such words as "twenty-two" is not *found in many of the later papers, and is caused here by reaching the end of the page or quoting from the notes given. The case was decided almost a year later in favor of Stuart and Lincoln. The client of the first Lincoln partnership was awarded a judgment for $280 in the case against Smith. The decision was handed down upon July 3, 1838.*

State of Illinois } ss   In the Sangamon circuit court
Of the July Term 1837

William Herndon complains of Thomas P. Smith of a plea of trespass on the case upon promises for that whereas the said Thomas, heretofore, towit, on the third day of April in the year eighteen hundred and thirty seven, at the county and circuit aforesaid, made his certain promissory note in writing, bearing date the day and year aforesaid, and thereby then and there promised to pay, twentytwo days after the date thereof, to one J. R. Herndon (alias) John R. Herndon or order the sum of one hundred dollars, for value received, with interest at the rate of twelve per cent per annum after due until paid, and then and there delivered the said promissory note to the said John R. Herndon. And the said John R. Herndon to whom or to whose order the payment of the said sum of money in the said promissory note specified, was to be made after the making of the said promissory note, before the payment of the said sum of money therein specified, to wit, on the twenty seventh of May in the year aforesaid, at the county and circuit aforesaid, indorsed the said promissory note, by which said indorsement, he the said John R. Herndon then and there ordered and appointed the said sum of money in the said promissory note specified to be paid to the said William Herndon, and then and there delivered the said promissory note so indorsed as aforesaid to the said William Herndon, by means whereof, and by force of the statute in such case made and provided, the said Thomas then and there became liable to pay to the said William, the said sum of money in the said promissory note specified, according to the tenor and effect of the said promissory note; and being so liable, he the said Thomas, in consideration thereof, afterwards, towit, on the day and year aforesaid, at the county and circuit aforesaid, undertook, and then and there faithfully promised the said William to pay him the said sum of money in the said promissory note specified according to the tenor and effect thereof.

Nevertheless the said Thomas not regarding his said promise and undertaking, but contriving and fraudulently intending craftily and subtly to deceive and defraud the said William in his behalf, hath not as yet paid the said sum of money in the said promissory note specified to the said William, although often requested so to do, and although the time for the payment of the said sum of money according to the tenor and effect of the said promissory note, hath long since elapsed, but the said Thomas to pay the said William the said sum of money hath hitherto wholly refused and neglected, and still doth refuse and neglect. To the damage of the said William in the sum of one hundred and twenty dollars, and therefore he sues &c.

Stuart & Lincoln, for Plff.

The following is a copy of the instrument declared on—
"$100.00   Springfield April 3rd 1837
"Twentytwo days after date I promise to J. R. Herndon or order. One hundred dollars, for value received without defalcation (with 12 per cent Interest after due until paid)

Thos P Smith"

The following is a copy of a credit on said instrument—
"Received on the within note twenty nine dollars and 75 cents—May 27. 1837"
The following is a copy of the indorsement on said instrument—
"Pay to William Herndon, May 27. 1837

J. R. Herndon"

William Herndon
vs.
Thomas P. Smith
Filed July 6th 1837
   William Butler Clk

COMPLAINT IN THE SUIT OF COFFMAN VS. SMITH, SANGAMON CIRCUIT, JULY 6, 1837
(Herndon-Weik Collection)

This complaint, and the notations on the cover are in the hand of young Lawyer Lincoln. The two words, "twenty-one," are run together as "twentyone", a usage by Mr. Lincoln which recurs in many of his documents and letters. In later legal documents, Mr. Lincoln used the last names of complainants and defendants, whereas he uses only first names in this complaint. There is greater brevity and less stilted legal language in this document, than in many others drawn by him at this period. The sum of twenty-one dollars and fifty cents demanded in the complaint was awarded to Coffman, the Stuart and Lincoln client, on October 21, 1837.

| | | In the Sangamon circuit court |
| State of Illinois | s s | of the July Term 1837 |

Aaron Coffman complains of Thomas P. Smith of a plea of tresspass in the case upon promises for that whereas the said Thomas heretofore, towit, on the eighth day of June 1837 at the county and circuit aforesaid was indebted to the said Aaron in the sum of twentyone dollars and fifty cents lawful money of the United States, for work and labour before that time done and performed by the said Aaron in and about removing a certain house for the said Thomas and at his special instance and request, and being so indebted he the said Thomas in consideration thereof, afterwards, towit, on the day and year aforesaid at the county and circuit aforesaid, undertook, and then and there faithfully promised the said Aaron to pay him the said sum of money, when he the said Thomas should be thereunto afterwards requested Nevertheless the said Thomas not regarding his said promise and undertaking, but contriving and fraudulently intending craftily and subtly to deceive and defraud the said Aaron in this behalf, hath not as yet paid the said sum of money or any part thereof to the said Aaron although often requested so to do, but the said Thomas to pay him the same hath hitherto wholly refused and neglected, and still doth refuse and neglect. To the damage of the said Aaron in the sum of fifty dollars and therefore he sues &c.

Stuart & Lincoln
for Plff

Aaron Coffman
vs
Thomas P. Smith
    Filed July 6th 1837
William Butler Clerk

DECLARATION IN THE SUIT OF A. Y. ELLIS VS. SMITH, SANGAMON CIRCUIT COURT, JULY 6, 1937
(Herndon-Weik Collection)

This document, including all notations upon the cover, was penned by Mr. Lincoln. He spelled out the "William" in Butler's name, whereas the clerk abbreviated it. This would lead to the conclusion, as does the handwriting, that Butler signed the file date, and the paragraph beginning, "sworn to before me," in the affidavit of June 9, 1837. The plaintiff, Abner Y. Ellis, who came from Kentucky to Springfield in 1807 was an early and close friend of Mr. Lincoln in his New Salem days and the latter clerked for him at one period. Ellis was a merchant, and for a time a partner of another intimate friend of Lincoln, Joshua Fry Speed. He passed his last days in Quincy, Illinois. Attorney Lincoln wrote and filed the praecipe in this case upon June 9, 1837, and filed the affidavit of Ellis upon June 17, 1837.

State of Illinois } s s   In the Sangamon circuit court
of the July Term 1837

    A. Y. Ellis (alias) Abner Y. Ellis complains of Thomas P. Smith of a plea that he render to him the sum of one hundred and fifteen dollars lawful money of the United States, which he owes to and unjustly detains from him; for that whereas the said Thomas P. Smith heretofore, towit, on the eighth day of June in the year eighteen hundred and thirty seven at the county and circuit aforesaid, by his certain writing obligatory, sealed with his seal, acknowledged himself to be held and firmly bound to the said Abner in the said sum of one hundred and fifteen dollars, above demanded, to be paid to the said Abner one day after the date of the said writing obligatory; yet the said Thomas (although often requested so to do) hath not as yet paid the said sum of one hundred and fifteen dollars, above demanded, or any part thereof to the said Abner, but hath hitherto wholly neglected and refused, and still neglects and refuses so to do. Wherefore the said Abner saith that he is injured, and hath sustained damage to the amount of fifty dollars, and therefore he brings his suit &c. And the said Abner brings here into court the said writing obligatory, sealed as aforesaid, which gives sufficient evidence to the said court here of the debt aforesaid, in form aforesaid, the date whereof is the day and year in that behalf above mentioned.

Stuart & Lincoln
for Plff

The following is a copy of the instrument declared on:

    "One day after date I promise to pay A. Y. Ellis one hundred and fifteen dollars, for value recd this 8th Day of June 1837

A. Y. Ellis   Thomas P. Smith (Seal)

  vs

Thomas P. Smith
Filed July 6th, 1837
William Butler, Clk.

MR. LINCOLN OFFERS BILL FOR A STATE ROAD FROM BEARDSTOWN TO PETERSBURG, JULY 13, 1837

On July 13, 1837, Mr. Lincoln reported from a select committee the bill here reproduced to establish a state road from Beardstown to Petersburg. On his motion the bill was read a second time and engrossed for a third reading. The following day the act was amended on Mr. Lincoln's motion by the insertion of the name of Isham Reavis for Miram Perry and in that form it became a law. Also on July 14 he presented a petition of citizens of Sangamon praying for the establishment of a new county; and, true to his natural inclining to make haste slowly, vainly voted nay on a resolution recommending a vote at the next election for or against a convention to amend the constitution of the state.

Section 1st   Be it enacted by the People of the state of Illinois represented in the General Assembly that Henry Mc Henry, Solomon Perry and Miram Perry be and they are hereby appointed commissioners to view, mark, and locate a state road from Beardstown in Cass county, thence as near as the ground will permit, by way of the town of Richmond, and Robinsons Mill to Petersburg in Sangamon county.

Section 2   Said commissioners, or a majority of them, shall meet at Beardstown on the first Monday in September next, or on any other day which they may agree upon, within six months from the passage of this act, and after being duly sworn by some Justice of the Peace, faithfully to perform the duties herein required, shall proceed to view mark, and locate said road as above described, avoiding as much as the public interest will permit, the injury of private property.

Section 3   Said commissioners shall make out a complete map and report of the location of so much of said road as lies in the county of Cass and file the same with the clerk of the county commissioners court of the said county of Cass; and a like map and report of so much as lies in the county of Sangamon and file the same with the clerk of the county commissioners court of said county of Sangamon.

Sec. 4   Said road shall be and remain a state road, and shall be opened and kept in repair as other state roads are.

Sec. 5   The county commissioners courts of the said counties of Cass and Sangamon shall allow said commissioners such compensation as they may deem reasonable.

ACT INTRODUCED BY MR. LINCOLN AUTHORIZING RHODA HART AND OTHERS TO SELL REAL ESTATE, JULY 15, 1837

On July 12, 1837, Mr. Lincoln gave notice to the House that he would shortly introduce a bill authorizing Rhoda Hart and others—Mrs. Hart was a client of Stuart & Lincoln—to sell certain real estate. The bill here reproduced was introduced July 15, and on the same day its author, true to the faith that was in him, by his vote helped to table an attempt to repeal the internal improvement system which the Legislature had put into effect earlier in the year.

Sec. 1   Be it enacted by the People of the state of Illinois represented in the General Assembly that Rhoda Hart, widow, and Harvey B. Hart, Moses P. Hart, Nancy Hart, John H. Wilson, Martha Wilson, and Rhoda Hart, adult heirs of Moses Hart deceased, all of the county of Sangamon and state of Illinois, be and they are hereby authorized to sell and jointly convey, by a deed or deeds in feesimple, all the real estate of which the said Moses Hart, deceased died seized the same being the South West quarter of Section Twenty four, the East half of the North West quarter of Section Twentyfour, and fifty acres of the South end or part of the East half of the South West quarter of section Thirteen all in Township Seventeen, North of Range Seven West of the Third Principal Meridian, and lying in the said county of Sangamon.

Sec. 2   The said conveyance shall be with this condition, that if the minor heirs of the said Moses Hart deceased shall not execute a release of all their right and title to said real estate, in favor of the purchaser or purchasers, his, her, or their heirs or assigns, within one year after the youngest of them shall arrive at the age of twenty one years, all the above named persons, selling and conveying said real estate as aforesaid, shall be jointly and severally bound to pay to the said purchaser or purchasers, his or her, or their heirs or assigns, double the sum for which the part of the said minor heirs may have been sold, to be recovered in an action of debt against them or either of them; and this act shall be sufficient evidence of said condition, without the same being set forth in the deed of conveyance or any other writing.

Section 3   The duly appointed guardian of the minor heirs of William Everly deceased, late of the county of Edwards and state of Illinois, be authorized to sell and convey the following described tracts of and, towit, the West half of the South West quarter of Section three, and the West half of the South East quarter of Section four, both in Township Seventeen North of Range two West of the Third Principal Meridian and situated in the county of Sangamon and state aforesaid, the same being the property of the said minor heirs, and to apply the proceeds thereof to the maintainance and education of said heirs.

MR. LINCOLN REPORTS AN ACT TO RELOCATE PART OF A STATE ROAD, JULY 19, 1837

On July 19, 1837, Mr. Lincoln reported an act to relocate part of a state road leading from Springfield to Lewiston, and successfully moved the adoption of this amendment which named his old friends of New Salem days, Bowling Green, Bennett Abell and John Bennett commissioners to relocate that part of the road lying between New Salem and Petersburg.

Section 4   That Bowling Green, Bennett Abell, and John Bennett, be and they are hereby authorized to meet at any time within six months from the passage of this act, and to relocate so much of the State road leading from Springfield to Lewiston, as lies between the towns of New Salem and Petersburg, and are required to make a map and report of said relocation and file the same with the clerk of the county commissioner's court of Sangamon county and for their services shall receive such compensation as the county commissioners of said county shall deem reasonable

Agreed to

MR. LINCOLN CONTINUES HIS WAR ON JAMES ADAMS, SANGAMO JOURNAL, JULY 22, 1837

Mr. Lincoln's labors as a legislator during the summer days of 1837 did not interrupt his war of words with James Adams, and on July 15 the Sangamo Journal in its Original Communications gave first place to the skit here reprinted, which, with its author's gift for humor of the broadest sort, lent an amusing turn to that contest. The election referred to in the opening lines resulted in the choice of Jesse B. Thomas Jr. to succeed Stephen T. Logan, resigned, as judge of the first judicial circuit.

A GHOST!   A GHOST!

"Art thou some spirit or goblin damn'd—
"Bringst with thee airs from heaven or blasts from hell?"

Shakespeare.

I am distressed. A wonderful apparition has appeared before

me. I was at the election in Springfield on Saturday, and having taken too heavy a portion of the true democratic drops, on my way home, as if in sympathy with my feelings, I dropped from my horse, and quietly fell into a refreshing and gentle slumber. At midnight I woke, and my brain was clear as the beautiful heavens above me; for they were beautiful;—the moon was just taking its leave in the west, and the stars twinkled gloriously. It was at the "witching time of night," when sprites are flitting through the air, and when music and voices of unearthly sound are whispering in the groves and prairies. I had fancied that I loved scenes like these;—in my ardent imaginings I had often pictured the beautiful prospect that then lay before me. The flowers of the field sent up their exquisite odors, and I at once was revelling in the delights of an imaginary Eden.

But the current of my thoughts was changed.—Gliding through a lengthened and dark vista formed of the growth of the forest, I saw a form coming towards me, with a noiseless tread, that did not rustle a leaf or bend a spire of grass. My blood was chilled, and my hair stood erect as he approached me; but there was a gentleness, a kindness, in the manner of my visitant, that restored me to consciousness and confidence, as the sprite thus addressed me.

Ghost: 'Be jiminys, who are you?"

Stranger: "I am a way faring man, and do harm to no body. Please leave me."

Ghost: "Be St. Patrick, I would not harm you at all at all. The rest of the dead is disturbed by the wicked ness of the living. I loved my wife and children, and left to them my little all. But it is taken away from them—and how can I rest in my grave in pace?"

Stranger: "And what would you have of me?"

Ghost: "Nothing. It is for my own flesh and blood to see to their rights, and if they have a drop of Irish blood in them they will not rest until they have obtained justice! justice! Be jiminys if I were alive how I would do it!"

Stranger: You speak of things I do not comprehend."

Ghost: And do you say you do not comprehend me? Well— I was born in ould Ireland—swate Ireland;—I kem over to Ameriky—to this blessed land. My wife and little ones came with me here—not far from this very spot. We toiled and we labored —I bought a few acres—left it in the care of a friend—went farther and died."

Stranger: And what of all that? Most men die sometime or other."

Ghost: "I left my land in the hands of a friend and that friend—Oh! be jiminys! what shall I say? My very grave cannot contain me.—My spirit wanders about seeking rest and finding none. My acres are in the hands of my friend—signed, sealed and delivered!"

Stranger: "But, perhaps, this transfer was legal."

Ghost: "By the hill of Hoath 'tis a lie!"

Stranger: "Unless all the proceedings are regular no transfer can stand, as you well know."

Ghost: "Jiminys gracious! 'Tis signed with a cross, and I could write my name as well as any can! Oh jiminys! jiminys!"

Stranger: "Rather curious, I confess. But did you not make the assignment?"

At this question my unearthly visitant threw himself into an attitude, that made the cold sweat run down to my feet. There was that in his countenance which made me turn from him with horror.—Anger, indignation, vengeance, flashed from beneath the chilly eyelids of death. I fell to the ground with very affright!

Ghost: "Stranger! You lie! How could I assign a judgment before it was obtained? Be Jimininy Christ it is not so!"

How long I lay in this swoon I do not know. When I rose from it, the sun was just rising over the timber of Sugar Creek, and my horse was grazing near me. I mounted him and returned home, more dead than alive.

Whether there be aught in this epistle that is true, or not—whether I was sleeping or waking—whether it was a hallucination of the brain, or matter of fact—I have no more grounds for judging than yourself. It has, however, made a deep impression on my mind from a real incident, said to have occurred within the limits of Sangamon county.

AN ACT PROPOSED BY MR. LINCOLN TO GOVERN PAYMENTS FOR THE CONSTRUCTION OF THE NEW STATE HOUSE, JULY, 1837

The charges brought forward in June, 1837, that wasteful methods were being employed in the construction of the new state house prompted the friends of Vandalia to renew their efforts to repeal the act which made Springfield the capital of the state. To nullify these efforts Mr. Lincoln in July, 1837, introduced into the Legislature the act here reproduced, but it soon became evi-

dent that there was slight prospect of their success, and so the act did not become a law.

Sec. 1 Be enacted by the People of the state of Illinois represented in the General Assembly: That no money shall hereafter be drawn from the Treasury of the state for the purpose of erecting a State House, execpt such as may hereafter be paid into the said Treasury, by the citizens of Springfield according to the provisions of a certain bond now on file in the Treasurer's office, executed by said citzens for the payment of fifty thousand dollars to be applied to the erection of a State House, or otherwise.

Sec. 2 All monies that have heretofore been drawn from the Treasury by the acting commissioner, for the purpose of erecting a State House at Springfield shall be refunded as soon as the first installment of the bond above mentioned becomes due.

MR. LINCOLN TAKES PART IN A BANQUET AT ATHENS, ILLINOIS, AUGUST 3, 1837

The Illinois Legislature adjourned without date on July 22, 1837, and on August 3 the citizens of Athens, in formal approval of their course during the session lately ended, gave a public dinner to the Sangamon members which a correspondent duly reported in the August 12 issue of the Sangamo Journal. This report throws welcome light on a great state in the making, and on the mood and outlook of its makers. It also records what may have been Abraham Lincoln's first appearance in the role of after-dinner speaker.

Athens, August 3, 1837

The Citizens of this place and vicinity, today gave a public dinner to the Delegation from this County, as a demonstration of approbation of their course in the Legislature. We have to regret that it was not in the power of Mr. Fletcher or Col. Dawson to attend. Mr. J. D. Allen acted as Marshal of the day, assisted by Messrs. Hurt and Grosh as Deputy Marshals. Wm. P. Brown, Esq. presided at the table as President. The Springfield Band kindly volunteered their services on the occasion. At one o'clock about one hundred and fifty gentlemen sat down to an excellent dinner, prepared by Mr. Anderson. After the cloth was removed, the following toasts were disposed of:

REGULAR TOASTS

1. The United States. 'Our country and whole country.'
2. The State of Illinois. Possessed of a fertile soil and salubrious climate, surrounded by navigable rivers and lakes, we

look forward to the brilliant destiny that awaits her, with a confidence undisturbed by the present disastrous condition of our beloved country.

3.   The County of Sangamon. One of the brightest stars in the galaxy which constitute our State. Let her be now and forever one and inseparable.

4.   The recent session of our State Legislature. Its members have performed their duties promptly. Well done good and faithful servants.

5.   The Internal Improvement system—As we have embarked in it, let it be energetically prosecuted. Its results will be felt in the rapid accumulation of wealth and population, and their inseparable concomitants, the advancement of education and the development of the great natural wealth of the State.

6.   Illinois State rights and States men.—May all parties unite in advancing the former and sustaining the latter.

7.   The United States Bank and State Bank of Illinois. Their 'rags' are good in Athens.

8.   John T. Stuart—The voters of the 3d Congressional district appreciate his talents and worth, and will by a triumphant majority next August elect him to represent them in the Congress of the United States.

VOLUNTEERS

By J. K. Hurt.   The 'long nine of old Sangamon.' In the language of Gen. Ewing, 'nine intellectual and physical giants.'—By a long pull a strong pull and a pull altogether, they located the seat of government at Springfield.

By S. B. Esty.   Our political institutions, founded on the natural and immutable laws of man, they have the guarantees of a permanent existence in the patriotism and intelligence of a free people.

By G. Elkin. A Capital gained, and not a foot of territory lost.

By W. B. Brown.   The long nine of Sangamon.   Deservedly popular and influential as members of our Legislature, fearless, talented and upright, they nobly maintained the interests of their constituents, raised the character of our country and reflected honor upon our State. May they, like Crockett, 'go ahead.'

By John B. Taylor.   Illinois, a free State, governed by a judicious legislation, inhabited by an enlightened and free people. Their motto is 'Agriculture, Commerce and Manufactures.'

By H. C. Rogers.   Our delegation of the last General Assembly. Their valuable services merit of their constituents the highest praise. May they be remembered should they offer their services again to the citizens of Sangamon.

Messrs. Herndon and Fletcher, the people's choice. They will glory in sustaining them, while they continue to serve them faithfully.

By J. D. Allen. Illinois—Her course is onward. She has reared the standard of her rights, and proudly assumes that preeminence to which her natural resources and the virtue and intelligence of her people so justly entitle her.

By W. S. Stone. Principles not men.—May the honest supporters of the former always prevail over the slavish advocates of the latter.

By R. L. Wilson. The citizens of Athens. Hospitable, patriotic and intelligent. May it continue the second town in numerical strength in the Key Stone county.

E. D. Baker—The people's choice. They will glory in sustaining him while he serves them faithfully.

A. Lincoln—He has fulfilled the expectations of his friends and disappointed the hopes of his enemies.

By I. G. Hunter. Maj. E. D. Baker—He received a dish thoroughly minced from Mr. Lincoln and baked it until it was thoroughly done! done! Thanks to Major Baker.

By J. D. Allen. N. W. Edwards—A good scion of a noble stock.

A. G. Herndon—Much better than we expected. Must go again.

A. Lincoln—One of nature's nobility.

Robert L. Wilson—A true representative of Sangamon County, and an honest man.

Col. John Dawson—A true friend of democratic principles, and a faithful servant of the people.

Hon. Dan Stone—The citizens of Sangamon will not forget their absent friend.

By H. C. Rogers. Our systems of Internal Improvement and Education. Both eminently calculated to elevate the character, promote the happiness and wealth of the citizens of our State. We wish them the greatest possible success.

Col. Wm. F. Elkin—His merits silence his enemies.

By A. Lincoln—Sangamon County will ever be true to her best interests and never more so than in reciprocating the good feelings of the citizens of Athens and neighborhood.

By A. G. Herndon—Athens: May she continue to increase in population until she ranks with the first towns of the State.

The Springfield Band. Our thanks are due them for their attendance on the present occasion. They merit the greatest praise and commendation.

By Thomas C. Elkin—Education—the pillar which upholds the temple of liberty. Immortality to those who have reared it in Illinois.

Numerous other volunteers were presented, but copies of them were not obtained. The company separated in good time, and nothing occurred to mar the pleasures of the day.

A STORY OF GENERAL ADAMS RELATED BY MR. LINCOLN, SANGAMO JOURNAL, AUGUST 5, 1837

Ou August 5, 1837, there appeared on the streets of Springfield a handbill setting forth at length the history of the controversy between the Anderson heirs and James Adams, a document which can now be found in Nicolay and Hay, "Complete Works" Vol. 1:54--55, 57-64. On the same day the story here reproduced, clearly written by Mr. Lincoln, appeared in the Sangamo Journal. Two days later, August 7, 1837, the contest for probate justice of peace between Adams and Henry ended in the election of the former by a substantial majority, proof that he had not forfeited the confidence of a considerable number of his fellow citizens; but Mr. Lincoln's story of Adams and the calf, caught the popular fancy and quickly found a place in the folk-lore of Sangamon County.

The recent noise and excitement made about the wounds and bruises received by Gen. Adams, reminds me of an adventure which happened to me while travelling to this county many years ago. Not far from this place I met a sucker late in the evening returning to his home. "Good evening friend," said I. "How far is it to Springfield?" "Well, I guess its about five miles." "Are you just from there?" "Well, I am," and said I "What's the news there?" "Well, there's nothing of any account but a sad accident that happened the other day:—you don't know Gineral Adams?—Well, the Gineral went to stoop down to pick some blackberries and John Taylor's calf gave him a butt right —" "You don't say so,—and did the Gineral die?" "No, by G..., but the calf did!"

X .

NOTICE OF TAKING DEPOSITIONS IN THE SUIT OF HOUGHTON VS. HART, SANGAMON CIRCUIT COURT, AUGUST 21, 1937

The notice here reproduced appears in the Complete Record for this case, and is in the hand of the court clerk. There is no evidence that Mr. Lincoln wrote the document, and none that it was the work of Houghton. It may have been penned by Houghton, or it may have been the work of a clerk, which was signed by Houghton. It is probable that Mr. Treat acknowledged the service of the paper in his own hand. It is included as a partial history of the case, and as having relation to the depositions and interrogators of September 2, 1837. These appear in the hand of Lincoln, and were filed on September 6, 1837. Isaac Cogdell was Isaac Cogdal, a friend of Mr. Lincoln's New Salem days and a visitor at the White House in the war years. He is remembered principally as one of the sources for the tale of Lincoln and Ann Rutledge. Thomas Moffett was a friend of Lincoln, and a member of the Young Men's Lyceum which had a not unimportant part in the early history of Springfield.

Samuel H Treat Guardian *ad litem* of Jefferson Hart, Melissa Jane Hart and Rhoda Hart Infant Heirs of David Hart deceased

Sir

You will please take notice that on the Second day of September next between the Hours of ten O clock AM and sun set of said day at the office of Thomas Moffett a Justice of the peace in the Town of Springfield Sangamon County I shall attend for the purpose of taking the deposition of Abraham Lincoln and Isaac Cogdell to be read as evidence in a Suit of Chancery now pending in the Sangamon Circuit Court in which I am complainant and the said Infant Heirs of David Hart Deceased are defendants at which time and place you can attend if you think proper

Elijah Houghton

I acknowledge the Service of the above notice this 21st day of August 1937

S H Treat   Guardian ad
Litem for   Defendants

AFFIDAVIT OF MR. LINCOLN IN THE SUIT OF MILLER VS. CHRISMAN, SANGAMON CIRCUIT COURT, AUGUST 22, 1837.

(Card Files of the Abraham Lincoln Association)

This affidavit was penned and signed by Mr. Lincoln. His friend, William Butler, wrote the attestation to the swearing of the affidavit. It will be noted that Lincoln used the double dot after the letter, "A", a characteristic of many of his legal papers, letters, and documents. A complete history of the case appears in the notes to the court decree, which is dated as possibly being of June 22, 1837.

Abraham Lincoln says that he is advised that Nancy & Peyton Chrisman reside without the state.

A.. Lincoln

Sworn to before me this day
    Wm Butler Clk.

ANSWER OF THOMAS CASSITY DRAWN BY MR. LINCOLN IN THE SUIT OF FOSTER VS. CASSITY, SANGAMON CIRCUIT COURT, AUGUST 28, 1837

This six-page answer filed for the defendant on August 28, 1837, marked the second stage of an interesting and in some ways amusing chancery suit in which the plaintiff Foster contended that the defendant Cassity, whose name his counsel spelled Cassady, contrary to their verbal agreement, had refused to deed a tract of land to him on the ground that both Foster and his agent had trifled with him when he was prepared to make the exchange. On March 6, 1838, leave was given by Judge Jesse B. Thomas to open depositions in the case; on the following July 14 it was agreed that it should be decided in vacation and on October 19 Stuart & Lincoln's client won his case, the complainant being ordered to convey the land involved.

A week after Mr. Lincoln filed Cassity's case, on September 4, 1837, Congress, summoned in special session by President Van Buren to consider ways to abate the financial panic which then afflicted the country, gathered at Washington, and the Democrats by a bare majority of three chose James K. Polk as speaker—an event charged with future meaning for Mr. Lincoln, who nine years later, contrary to prevailing sentiment, was to challenge the war policy of Polk, now become President, and as a consequence lose his seat in Congress.

The answer of Thomas Cassaday defendant to the bill of complaint of Joseph C. Foster complainant.

This defendant reserving to himself all right of exceptions to the said bill of complaint, for answer thereto saith that he admits that the said complainant and defendant were respectively seized of the tracts or parcels of land in the said bill of complaint mentioned, at the time, and in the manner in the said bill alleged but he, the said defendant, denies most positively, that he made any agreement, either with the said complainant, or with any other person as agent for said complainant, to make an exchange of the said tracts or parcels of land.

He, the said defendant, states, that on or about the time mentioned in the said bill of complaint, he did make a verbal agreement with one Seth R. Cutter, to make an exchange of the aforesaid tracts or parcels of land; but that he supposed at the time of making the agreement, the tract of land which, by the agreement, he was to receive, belonged to said Cutter, and that he was not told by said Cutter, or any one else to the contrary. The said defendant further states, that he and the said Cutter, did each, enter upon the possession of the tract of land, which by the said agreement, was to be received of the other, and that he, the said defendant, did commence the cutting of timber on the tract received by him, but that when, very shortly afterwards, he urged upon said Cutter the propriety of their exchanging deeds for the tracts of land respectively, and was told by said Cutter, that the land to be conveyed to him, the said defendant, did not belong to him, the said Cutter, but that it belonged to the said complainant, Joseph F. Foster who then resided, and still resides in Kentucky, he the said defendant, immediately desisted from cutting timber upon, and quitted the possession of the tract of land received by him, and that he had then cut but one tree, and he never since cut any upon the said land.

This defendant further states, that he, the said defendant, having no way left to recover the possession of the same, but the coercive measures of the law; and being a poor man, and ill able to bear the expense of a lawsuit, did not commence suit, but permitted the matter to remain as it was, until the latter part of the year, Eighteen hundred and thirty-two or the beginning of Eighteen hundred and thirtythree, at which time he admits that he agreed with said Cutter, whom he then understood to be acting as the agent of the said complainant, that deeds for the said tracts of land should by the parties be mutually executed and exchanged on the then succeeding first day of March; and that Cutter then told the said defendant to take possession of the land which said defendant was to deed to keep it till deeds were executed.   The defendant further states, that on or about the said first day of March, the said complainant came to the country, and proposed to him, the said defendant, that they should then exchange deeds, and that he, the said defendant, replied that he was ready at the same time asking the said complainand if his wife was with him, to execute a relinquishment of her dower, to which the said complainant assuming an air of solemnity, replied, "O! there has a misfortune happened"; and that one John Calhoun, who was present, addressing himself to the said defendant, said, "Mr. Cassaday, his wife is dead"; and that the said complainant, making no reply to what Calhoun said, he, the said defendant, was induced to believe it was true, and being satisfied on that point, he told the said complainant, that they would go to Springfield and examine and learn whether their respective titles to the said tracts of land were good, and if they were, they would then exchange deeds.

This defendant further states, that both he, and the said complainant then went to Springfield, and, on examination of the records, he, the said defendant, becoming satisfied with the said complainant's title; told him, the said complainant, that he, the said defendant was ready to execute and exchange deeds; and that the said complainant then replied, that, he, said complainant, could not then make a deed in consequence of his wife not being present to relinquish her dower; to which he, the said defendant, in astonishment replied, "I understood you to say your wife was dead." "O" said the complainant, "that was only Calhoun's joke."

This defendant further states that being thus frustrated in his desire to then have the deeds exchanged, he was, at the pressing solicitation of the said complainant, induced to enter into a written agreement, a copy of which, marked (A), this defendant admits to be a true copy .

This defendant further admits, that the indenture which the said complainant has filed with his bill, marked (B) was tendered to him the said defendant, on the said first day of May.

This defendant further admits, that some time afterwards he was informed by Cutter, complainants agent, that said complainant was willing to execute and deliver to him a good and valid deed, and that, conceiving that he had been trifled with, and imposed upon, both by the said complainant and his agent, Cutter;

first, by the agent, Cutter, representing the land he was selling as his own, and thereby getting possession of the said defendant's land; and secondly, by the said complainant representing that his wife was dead, and thereby inducing the said defendant to spend time and money in going to Springfield when it could be of no use; and lastly, by tendering him a deed, misdescribing the land, when his means was so ample for doing it correctly, he, the said defendant, did refuse to accept any deed from the said complainant, or to execute any deed in favour of said complainant, for the other piece of land.

This defendant further states, that he has no recollection of ever having received notice, that said complainant had employed counsel to institute proceedings against him, the said defendant, as is alleged in said bill of complaint.

This defendant further admits, that said complainant's agent, Cutter, did tender to him a second deed, and that the deed filed with the complainant's bill, marked (C) is the same, and that he, the said Cutter, did demand of him a deed for the other piece of land.

But this defendant most positively denies, that he ever did agree, to not insist upon the strict letter of the said written agreement, as is in the said bill of complaint alleged.

And the said defendant further most positively denies, that he ever did, at any time subsequent to the first of May mentioned in the said written agreement, agree to accept and receive a deed from the said complainant, or to execute and deliver one to him for the other piece of land. And this defendant denies that there is any other matter, cause or thing in the said complainant's said bill of complaint contained material or necessary for this defendant to make answer unto and not herein, and hereby well and sufficiently answered, confessed, traversed and avoided or denied, that is true to the knowledge or belief of this defendant; all which matters and things this defendant is ready and willing to aver, maintain and prove as this honorable court shall direct, and humbly prays to be hence dismissed with his reasonable costs and charges in this behalf most wrongfully sustained.

Thomas Cassidy
Stuart & Lincoln for Deft.

This day personally appeared before me, William Butler clerk of the Sangamon circuit court, Thomas Cassiday, whose name is subscribed to the foregoing answer, and being duly sworn, says that all the matters contained in said answer, stated as of his

own knowledge are true and all matters stated upon the information of others he believes to be true.
August 28" 1837

Wm. Butler Clk.

NOTICE OF TAKING DEPOSITIONS IN THE SUIT OF TRAILOR VS. RADFORD, SANGAMON CIRCUIT COURT, SEPTEMBER, 1837,

(Herndon-Weik Collection)

This notice is signed by Reuben Radford, and he appears to have written the entire paper, as well as the cover notations, with one exception. This is the acknowledgement of the service of the notice, which was penned by Mr. Lincoln. He signed the paper in these words, "Lincoln & Stuart Attorneys for A. Trailor." It is interesting to notice that he did not sign the usual Stuart & Lincoln, but reversed the procedure, signing, "Lincoln & Stuart." He also wrote the name of his client with an "or" ending, instead of "er" used by Radford. The Lincoln spelling seems to have been correct. Reuben Radford was a storekeeper at New Salem, but after an encounter with the Clary's Grove boys, he sold out to William G. Greene. Later Lincoln and Berry purchased the interest of Greene in the store. The plaintiff, Archibald Trailor, had an excellent reputation in Springfield, but became involved in a noted murder case handled by Lincoln, and others. He was accused unjustly, but his acquittal failed to help him. He shunned society after the trial, and died at the end of two years. Mr. Lincoln wrote and filed the bond of Reuben Radford and George Forquer on July 6, 1837, and on October 17, 1837 leave was given to open depositions.

The abbreviation, "ads", which appears in this legal paper, and which appears frequently as "ats", is used for the more complete, "ad sectam", meaning at the suit of. It is used when it is found desirable to put the defendant's name first in the filing of legal papers.

Reuben Radford
    ads Chancery
Archibald Trailer

    Mr. Archibald Trailer,
    Sir You will please to take notice that Friday the 15th inst. between the hours of Ten A. M. and Five P. M. of said day, I shall attend at the Clerks Office of the Sangamon Circuit Court for the purpose of taking out a Commission to be directed to

Wilson Primm Esqr, justice of the peace in the City of St. Louis, M'o authorising and empowering him to take the Depositions of John Finney & William Finney, residing in said city. Said Depositions to be read as evidence in the above entitled suit now pending in the Sangamon Court.

Accompanying said Commission will be the following interrogatories

1   Did, or Did not a firm composed of Reuben Radford & Archibald Trailer, under the style of Radford & Trailer, exist in the County of Sangamon about the year 1832, and did, or did not said firm contract a debt with you about that time to the amount of about Four or Five Hundred Dollars. If so State.—

2   How was said debt discharged?—by whom? and at what time? and previous to its being discharged, did or did not partners in said firm execute their joint note to you for the amount.

3   What was the style of the firm to which the aforesaid debt was due?.—

Yours
Reuben Radford

Radford

ads ⎬ Notice

Trailer

....

I acknowledge service of the within notice Sept. 1. 1837. Lincoln & Stuart

Attorneys for A. Trailor

PETITION FOR DIVORCE IN THE SUIT OF NANCY GREEN VS. AARON GREEN, SEPTEMBER 4, 1837

(Herndon-Weik Collection)

This petition and the cover notations are in the hand of Mr. Lincoln except the note of filing which is in that of Butler. The Green case was the first divorce suit in which Mr. Lincoln appeared as attorney. He had this complaint dismissed in the Sangamon Circuit Court on October 10, 1838.

To the Honorable the Judge of Sangamon Circuit court in Chancery sitting.

Humbly complaining sheweth unto your Honor your Oratrix Nancy Green, that on the   day of   in the year of

our Lord one thousand eight hundred and   at the
county and circuit aforesaid, towit, in the county of Sangamon
and State of Illinois, your oratrix was legally married to Aaron
Green, whom your oratrix prays may be made a defendant to this
Bill.   Your oratrix states that after said intermarriage your
oratrix and the said defendant lived together in the county of
Sangamon and State aforesaid, as man and wife, until about the
                    day of   in the year one thousand eight
hundred and thirtyfour your oratrix all that time performing on
her part all the duties of a faithful and affectionate wife—

    She further states that about the said   day of
in the year one thousand eight hundred and thirtyfour said defendant abandoned your oratrix.   She further states that since
said abandonment the said defendant has never returned to your
oratrix, nor furnished her with any support, and, in a word, has
never since performed any of those duties which by his marriage
vow he was bound to do; but in every respect has violated his
marriage contract; all which conduct on the part of the defendant
was contrary to the wishes of your oratrix, and was not brought
about by any fault of her's.   Your oratrix further states that she
has, ever since said marriage and abandonment, resided in the
said county of Sangamon.   She further states that the said defendant, has also, ever since said abandonment, continued, and
still continued to reside in the said county of Sangamon.

    In tender consideration of which your oratrix prays that the
said Aaron Green be summoned to appear and on his oath true
answers make to all and singular the allegations of this Bill;
And that upon a final hearing your Honor will decree that the
Bonds of matrimony existing between the said defendant and
your oratrix may be dissolved; and that such other and further
relief may be granted as the equity of her case may demand: And
as in duty bound she will ever pray &c.

                              Nancy Green
                              By her attorneys
                              Stuart & Lincoln

14
Nancy Green ⎱
    vs   ⎰   Pet. for Divorce
Aaron Green ⎰

Filed Sept. 4, 1837
     Wm Butler Clk
Let Process issue
    Stuart & Lincoln
        (Issued Sept. 4.)

DEPOSITIONS IN THE SUIT OF HOUGHTON VS. HART'S HEIRS, SEPTEMBER 6, 1837

(Herndon-Weik Collection)

This deposition with questions and answers is from the pen of Mr. Lincoln. Justice of the Peace Moffett penned the certification of deposition and appears also to have written the words "The Clerk of the Sangamon Circuit Court." The cover notations are in the hand of Stuart, while Butler wrote the date of filing.

Depositions taken at the office of Thomas Moffett in the town of Springfield on the 2nd day of September in the year 1837 to be read in evidence in the cause now pending in the Sangamon circuit court in which Elijah Houghton is complainant and the heirs of David Hart deceased are defendants.

Abraham Lincoln, who is of lawful age, being duly sworn, gave the annexed answers to the following interrogatories (viz)

Interrogatory 1st. Did you or did you not, by the direction of David Hart, some time in the autumn of 1834, survey and set off by admeasurement to Elijah Houghton the certain tract of land of the following number and boundaries (viz) Begining with the South East corner of the West half of the South East quarter of Section Thirteen in Township Seventeen North of Range Seven West of the Third Principal Meridian; thence West with the Southern boundary line of the same, ten chains and seven links: thence North twelve chains and forty links to the centre of the channel of Rock Creek: then down the said creek with it's meanderings to the Eastern boundary line of said half quarter; thence South with said Eastern boundary line to the place of begining, containing twelve acres and fortyeight hundredths of an acre more or less—

Answer—I did.

Interrogatory 2nd. Did you or did you not then hear said Hart say that he had sold said tract of land to said Houghton, and that said Houghton had paid him for it?

Answer—I did hear him say so a number of different times.

Interrogatory 3rd. Did or did not the said Hart deliver possession of the said land to the said Houghton?

Answer—Said Hart and Houghton were both present and assisting in marking &c at the time of the surveying; and I understood the possession to be delivered to said Houghton by said Hart; but cannot say that I heard it done in express language.

And further deponent saith not

A. Lincoln

State of Illinois } ss
Sangamon County }   This is to certify that on the 2nd day of September A. D. 1837: between the Hours of 6. Oclock A M & 6. Oclock P M of the Same day at my office in Springfield the foregoing Deposition was given & Inscribed by A Lincoln who was duly Sworn thereto according to Law before me.

Thomas Moffett Jus Peace
in & for Sangamon County
State of Illinois

Justice Moffetts fees for taking the above deposition }	340 words	62½
	Certificate	25
		87½

A True Statement of my fees
Attest Thos Moffett J P—

Elijah Houghton   }
        vs   } Depositions
Heirs of David Hart dec }
        The Clerk of Sangamon Circuit
                Court
Filed Sept 6th
1837
    Wm Butler clk

SCISA IN THE SUIT OF HICKMAN VS. BRAUCHER & BRAUCHER, SEPTEMBER 8, 1837

(Herndon-Weik Collection)

This writ beginning with the words, "state of Illinois," and concluding with "the above recited mortgage," was drawn by Mr. Lincoln. The concluding phrase precedes the words, "against Them," at which point John T. Stuart takes up the writing. He concludes with the words "September A.D. 1837," at which point the document is signed by Butler. The cover notations are by Butler down to the point of the beginning of the notations by

Sheriff Elkin, which start with the words, "Executed on Isaac R Brauscher." The word "Scisa" used by Butler seems to have been a variant of scire, and is now obsolete. The two words meant the same thing, investigation or writ for showing cause why a judgment or decision should not be rendered. The name of Rachael Braucher which is given as an interlineation after Isaac R. Braucher is in the hand of Stuart, the only change before Stuart adds the paragraph in his hand. A judgment of $481.96 was rendered in favor of Hickman, the client of Stuart and Lincoln, upon March 5, 1838. Stuart and Lincoln amended their bill of complaint in the case on March 7, 1838. Ten days later, a final decision was in favor of Hickman.

State of Illinois ⎰   The People of the State of Illinois
Sangamon county ⎱ To the Sheriff of Sangamon county Greeting—
Whereas Isaac R. Braucher and Rachel Braucher on the twenty-fourth day of June in the year of our Lord one thousand eight hundred and thirtysix executed the following deed, towit,

"This Indenture made and entered into this twentyfourth day of June A. D. 1836 Between Isaac R. Braucher and Rachel Braucher wife of the said Isaac R. of the county of Sangamon and State of Illinois of the first part, and George Churchill of the county & state aforesaid of the other part Witnesseth That the said party of the first part for and in consideration of the sum of four hundred dollars to them in hand paid by the said party of the second part the receipt whereof is hereby acknowledged, have granted, have gained and sold & by these presents do grant, bargain & Sale unto the said party of the second part all those certain tracts or parcels of land situate lying & being in the county of Sangamon & State of Illinois Known and described as follows Towit, The South West quarter of Section No. Thirtyone in Township Seventeen North of Range four West of the Third Principal Meridian containing one hundred & Seventyeight acres & seventysix hundredths of an acre. Also the West half of the North East quarter of Section, Township and Range aforesaid, and the East half of the North West quarter of the same Section Township and Range both together containing one hundred and & Sixty acres. To have and to hold to him the said party of the second part, his heirs and assigns forever. The above described premises together with all & singular the, privileges, appurtenances and improvements thereunto belonging or in anywise appurtaining. And the said party of the first part do hereby for themselves their heirs executors and administrators Covenant & agree to & with the said party of the second part, forever to warrant and defend the title of said land against the claim or claims of all persons claiming or to claim title to the same. Yet upon this condition, that if the said party of the first part shall well and truly pay to the said party of the second part the said sum of four hundred dollars the consideration above expressed for which the said Braucher hath this day executed his note of hand payable twelve months after date according to the true intent and meaning of said note —then the above Deed to be null and void—Otherwise to remain in full force & virtue—In testimony whereof the said party of the first part have hereunto set their hands & Seals this day & year above written

In presence of   I. R. Braucher (Seal)
Thomas Moffett   Rachel Braucher (Seal)

Which deed above written, was on the day and year aforesaid. duly acknowledged before one Thomas Moffett a Justice of the Peace within & for the county of Sangamon; and which deed was also duly recorded by one (sic) one Benjamin Talbott, Recorder within & for said county, in his office

And whereas afterwards, towit, on or about the third day of May in the year 1837 George Churchill, the grantee in the above deed died, and subsequently, towit, on the 8th day of May 1837 letters testamentary on the estate of the said George Churchhill, with the will annexed were taken out of the office of the Judge of Probate within & for the county of Sangamon, by one William Hickman; and whereas the said note, refered to in the condition to the above deed, the same being in the words and figures following towit, "$400.00 Twelve months after date I "promise to pay to George Churchill or order Four "hundred Dollars with Interest at twelve per cent for 'value received June 24th 1836

I. R. Braucher"

has never been paid, nor any part thereof—

Now therefore we command you to summon Isaac R. Braucher and Rachael Braucher to be and appear on the first day of the next term of the circuit court for the county of Sangamon commencing on the second Monday of October A. D. 1837 at the Court House in Springfield, to show cause, if any they have, why Judgment should not be rendered in favor of William Hickman, Executor of the last Will and Testament of George

Churchhill, deceased, for such sum of money as may be due by virtue of the above recited mortgage—against Them.

And the said William Hickman brings here and shows to the Court his letters Testamentary granted by the Court of Probate in and for the County of Sangamon, dated the 8th day of May 1837. Shewing that he right hath to have & Demand, by the Isaac and Rachael, the sum of money due by said mortgage, as above set forth.

> and have you then there this writ Witness William Butler Clerk of our said Court at Springfield this 8th day of September A.D. 1837.
> Wm Butler Clk

William Hickman
Excr of G. Churchhill

vs } Scisa

I. R. Braucher
& Rachael Braucher

To Oct Term 1837

Executed on Isaac R
Braucher Sept 9—1837

ORIGINAL NOTE OF WILBOURN VS. SIMMONS:
SEPTEMBER 8, 1837

(Herndon-Weik Collection)

The note in this case confirms the fact that Mr. Lincoln erred in his statement that Pollard Simmons in the declaration had signed his note as "P Simmons." It also reveals that his transcription of the name as the signature in the quoted note was correct. Mr. Lincoln frequently copied the notes, even to misspelled words, but it will be seen that he did place a "p" in the "Promise" of the original note.

On or before the 1st day of March next I promise to pay T & J. S. Wilbourn or bearer one hundred and seventy dollars for value recd. this 4th day of Nov. 1836.

P. Simmons

Attest
Bowling Green

NOTICE OF TAKING DEPOSITIONS IN SUIT OF WRIGHT ET AL VS. ADAMS, SEPTEMBER 11, 1837

(Herndon-Weik Collection)

This notice was drawn by Mr. Lincoln and signed by Walker & Hewitt, attorneys for respondent. The declaration in this suit, as noted elsewhere, had been filed on June 22, 1837. Stuart, Lincoln and Logan appeared in the case upon July 5, 1837, as attorneys for the plaintiffs. Logan and Lincoln filed a replication upon October 17, 1837, and upon November 12, 1837, Mr. Lincoln took the deposition of Stephen Dewey, clerk of the Fulton Circuit Court. This contradicted Adams' claim to title to the land in dispute. Adams asked leave to take depositions upon March 8, 1838, and leave was granted by the court. Adams on July 7, 1838, requested leave to withdraw an assignment of judgment which he had filed as an exhibit, and the request was granted the following day. Five days later Adams filed his affidavit and asked for a change of venue to Schuyler County. The case was changed to Schuyler County, but was remanded to Sangamon by Judge Stephen A. Douglas because he had been an attorney for Adams. The case was never brought to trial, but upon November 29, 1843, two months after the death of Adams, it was abated by the court. Mrs. Anderson and the heirs of James Adams received the ten acres of land in question. Lucien Adams who is mentioned in this deposition was the son of James Adams.

Joel Wright et al
   vs   In Chancery
James Adams

Respondent's solicitors in the above entitled cause will please take notice, that on the twenty third day of the present month, between the hours of nine A. M. and five P. M. of said day the complainants in the above cause will attend at the Office of Thomas Moffett in the town of Springfield, Sangamon county, State of Illinois, for the purpose of taking the Deposition of Lucien B. Adams to be read in evidence in the above entitled cause now pending in the Sangamon Circuit Court.

Yours

September 11th 1837

Joel Wright et al
By Stuart & Lincoln
Solicitors

We acknowledge the service of the above notice on the 11th of September 1837

Walker & Hewett
for Respondent

Joel Wright et, al

vs   } Chancery

James Adams

Notice

Filed Sep 11. 1837
       Wm Butler
           ck

BOND FOR COSTS AND SUMMONS IN SUIT OF FLEMING VS. RANSDELL, SEPTEMBER 16-26, 1837

(Herndon-Weik Collection)

This bond for costs is signed by Radford, but the words "Filed Sept 16th 1837" appear to have been penned by Mr. Lincoln, while the signature of Butler is clearly in his hand. The summons for Dorsey was also drawn by Mr. Lincoln. Stuart and Lincoln filed their plea in this case on October 18, 1837. Fleming took a non-suit on July 3, 1838, which means that the case was recorded as having terminated due to the default or failure of the plaintiff to establish a good cause for action.

Sangamon Circuit Court
   October Term 1837.
Samuel Fleming

   vs   } Assumpsit

Wharton Ransdell

I do hereby enter myself security for costs in the above cause, and acknowledge myself bound to pay, or cause to be paid all costs, which shall accrue in the above entitled cause, either to the opposite party, or to any of the officers of this court, in pursuance of the laws of this State.

    Dated Sept. 16th 1837   R. Radford
Fleming

  vs. } Bond for
       } Costs
Ransdell

And also that you bring with you, and produce at the time and place aforesaid a certain mortgage deed which was taken by you from one James Downs to secure the payment of one hundred dollars specified in a certain promissory note taken of the said James Downs by you on the 9th day of June 1836 and since indorsed by you to bearer and passed to Wharton Ransdell—

The People of the State of Illinois to the Sheriff of Tazewell county— Greeting—

You are hereby commanded to summon Charles S Dorsey to be and appear before the Circuit court of Sangamon county on the sixth day of the next term, to be holden in Springfield on the second Monday in the month of October next, to testify and the truth to speak in behalf of Wharton Ransdell in a certain matter of controversy pending in the said court, wherein Samuel Fleming is plaintiff, and the said Wharton Ransdell is defendant; and also to command the said Charles S. Dorsey to bring with him, and to produce at the time and place aforesaid, a certain mortgage deed which was executed and delivered to him by one James Downs to secure the payment of the sum of one hundred dollars specified in a certain promissory note taken by the said Dorsey of the said Downs on the 9th day of June 1836; and since indorsed by said Dorsey to bearer, and passed to Wharton Ransdell— And have there then this writ—

Witness William Butler Clerk of
our said court at Springfield
this 26th day of September 1837
Wm Butler Clk

Fleming
vs
Wharton Ransdell
Filed Oct 14th 1837
Returned Not found
in my county Oct—
10th 1837
Wm A. Tinney Shff SC

PRAECIPE AND BOND IN THE SUIT OF BILLOW VS. WHITE, SEPTEMBER 22, 1837

(Herndon-Weik Collection)

This document is the work of Mr. Lincoln, with the exception of the signature of Robert Irwin, and the date of filing by the clerk. Irwin, long the friend and financial adviser of Mr. Lincoln, was a native of Pennsylvania, who settled in Spring-field in 1834 at the age of twenty-six years. He was first a dry goods merchant, and after that for many years before his death in 1865, in turn secretary and cashier of the Fire and Marine Insurance Company Bank.

State of Illinois   In the circuit court
Sangamon county & circuit October Term 1837

Charles P. Billow
  vs   Tresspass on the case upon premises
Lorance White   Damage $200.00

  The clerk of the Sangamon circuit court will issue process in the above cause returnable to the next term of said court—

Charles P. Billow
  vs
Lorance White

  I do hereby enter myself security for costs in this cause, and acknowledge myself bound to pay or cause to be paid all costs which may accrue in the action, either to the opposite party or to any of the officers of this court, in pursuance of the laws of this state Dated this 22nd of Sept 1837

             Rob . . Irwin

Charles P. Billow
  vs
Lorance White
Precipe & Bond
Filed Sep't 22d 1837
Wm Butler Clk

COMPLAINT IN SUIT OF VON PHUL & MCGILL VS. PORTER, SEPTEMBER 22, 1837

(Herndon-Weik Collection)

* This complaint was drawn by Lincoln, and the cover nota-tions are also his handiwork, with the exception of the file date and the signature of Butler. Lawyer Lincoln spelled "business" as "bussiness" and "trespass" as "tresspass," a common practice in his legal papers. The words, "in the year of our Lord one thousand, eight, hundred and thirtyfour," reveal a punctuation not common to the Lincoln legal papers, but of interest because of his rare misuse of punctuation. A more remarkable char-*

*acteristic of the documents is the rarity of mistakes in punctuation
for an almost unschooled man.*

State of Illinois   }   In the circuit court—
Sangamon county & circuit }   October Term 1837.

Henry Vonphul and Theodore L. McGill, trading and doing
bussiness under the name and style of Vonphul & McGill complain of William Porter being in custody &c in a plea of
Tresspass on the case upon promises; for that whereas the said
defendant (signing his name Wm Porter) heretofore, towit, on
the eighth day of April in the year of our Lord one thousand,
eight, hundred and thirtyfour, at the county and circuit aforesaid,
made his certain promissory note in writing, bearing date the day
and year aforesaid and thereby then and there promised to pay,
to the said plaintiffs or their order, the sum of one hundred and
one dollars with interest at the rate of ten per cent per annum
from date until paid, for value received, and then and there delivered the said promissory note to the said plaintiffs; by means
whereof, and by force of the statute in such case made and provided, the said defendant then and there became liable to pay
to the said plaintiffs the said sum of money in the said promissory note specified according to the tenor and effect of the said
promissory note; and being so liable, he the said defendant, in
consideration thereof, afterwards, towit, on the day and year
aforesaid, at the county and circuit aforesaid, undertook, and
then and there faithfully promised the said plaintiffs to pay them
the said sum of money in the said promissory note specified,
according to the tenor and effect thereof, when he should be
thereunto afterwards requested. Yet the said defendant (although
often requested so to do) hath not as yet paid to the said plaintiffs the said sum of money in the said promissory note specified,
or any part thereof; but so to do, hath hitherto wholly neglected
and refused; and still doth neglect and refuse. To the damage
of the said plaintiffs in the sum of two hundred dollars, and therefore they bring their suit &c.

Stuart & Lincoln for plff

The following is a copy of the instrument declared on—

"Due Vonphul & McGill or order one hundred and one dollars with ten per cent from date till paid—

Springfield, April 8. 1834

Wm Porter"

S 100-00
Vonphul & McGill
   vs
William Porter

Declaration
Filed Sept 22d 1837
Wm Butler Clk

AFFIDAVIT IN THE SUIT OF FOSTER & COMPANY VS. LOCKERMAN, SEPTEMBER 22, 1837

(Herndon-Weik Collection)

This affidavit is in the hand of Mr. Lincoln. Foster signed the paper, and the notations signed by Butler, clerk, are penned by him. The case was dismissed on July 3, 1838 by Stuart & Lincoln, which means for those not in the legal fraternity, that the action was given no further consideration or hearing by the court.

State of Illinois }
Sangamon county }

This day personally appeared before the undersigned, Abner Foster, who, being duly sworn, deposes and says that Stanley Lockerman is justly indebted to Henry T. Foster and Abner Foster trading and doing business under the name and style of H. T. Foster & Co in the sum of eighty dollars and fiftyfour cents lawful money of the United States, for goods sold and delivered; that said Lockerman has departed from this state, with the intention of having his effects and personal estate removed without the limits of this state; and that he believes Absalom Bowling and Riley Clarkston, both residing in the said county of Sangamon are indebted to the said Stanley Lockerman.

Abner Foster

Sworn to before me this
22d day of Sept 1837
   Wm Butler Clk
H. T. Foster & Co.

   vs   } affa

Stanley Lockerman
Filed Sept 22d 1837
Wm Butler Clk

PRAECIPE AND DECLARATION IN THE SUIT OF RUPERT & LINDENBERGER VS. GARRETT, SEPTEMBER 22, 1837

(Herndon-Weik Collection)

This praecipe and declaration are from the pen of Abraham Lincoln, and he wrote the cover notations, with the exception of the filing date by Butler. Mr. Lincoln spelled "Garrett" as "Garret" upon one occasion. He omitted the word "neglected" before "and refused" in this paper, but it may be that Mr. Garrett merely refused to pay the note, without any action of neglect on his part. There is no definite evidence of reason for omission of the usual legal phrase. The defendant filed a plea upon October 12, 1837, and withdrew it upon October 17, 1837. The case was dismissed upon the latter date with costs being assessed against the plaintiff.

State of Illinois   ⎫   In Sangamon circuit court
                                     ⎬ ss
Sangamon county & circuit   ⎭

October Term 1837

Eton W. Dewitt Clinton Rupert and William J. Lindenberger trading and doing bussiness under the style and name of Rupert & Lindenberger complain of Alexander Garrett being in custody &c. of a plea of Trespass on the case upon promises, for that whereas the said Garrett, signing his name Alexr Garrett heretofore, towit, on the seventeenth day of October in the year of our Our Lord one thousand eight hundred and thirty-five, at the city of Louisville, state of Kentucky, towit, at the county and circuit aforesaid, made his certain promissory note in writing, bearing date the day and year aforesaid, and thereby then and there promised to pay, Four months after the date thereof, to the order of the said Rupert and Lindenberger, the sum of one hundred dollars and eight cents, for value received; and then and there delivered the said promissory note to the said Rupert and Lindenberger; by means whereof, and by force of the statute in such case made and provided, the said Garret became liable to pay to the said Rupert and Lindenberger the said sum of money in the said promissory note specified according to the tenor and effect of the said promissory note; and being so liable, he, the said Garrett, in consideration thereof, afterwards, towit, on the day and year aforesaid, at the county and circuit aforesaid, undertook, and then and there faithfully promised the said Rupert and Lindenberger to pay them the said

sum of money in the said promissory note specified according to
the tenor and effect thereof when he should be thereunto lawfully
required.   Yet the said Garrett (although often requested so to
do) hath not as yet paid to the said Rupert and Lindenberger, the
said sum of money in the said promissory note specified or any
part thereof; but so to do, hath hither to wholly refused, and
still doth refuse; to the damage of the said Rupert and Lindenberger in the sum of two hundred dollars; and therefore they
bring suit &c—

Stuart & Lincoln for plff

The following is a copy of the instrument declared on—
"$100 08/100 Louisville October 17th 1835

Four month after date I promise to pay to the order of
Rupert & Lindenberger one hundred and Dollars 08/100 value
received

No. ....   Alexr Garrett"

State of Illinois   In Sangamon circuit court

                 ss

Sangamon county & circuit   October Term 1837

Eton W. De Witt Clinton Rupert & William
J. Lindenberger, trading and doing business   Tresspass on the
under the name and style of Rupert &   case upon promises
Lindenberger

           vs   Damage $200-00
     Alexander Garrett

The clerk of the Sangamon circuit court will issue process
in the above cause, returnable to the next term of said court—

Stuart & Lincoln for plff

I do hereby enter myself security for costs in this cause; and
acknowledge myself bound to pay or cause to be paid all costs
which may accrue in this action either to the opposite party or to
any of the officers of this court in pursuance of the laws of this
state.   Dated this 18 day of Sep 1837

A. Lincoln

Rupert & Lindenberger

    vs   Precipe & Declaration

Alexander Garrett

Sept 22. 1837
Wm Butler Clk

COMPLAINT IN THE SUIT OF RUPERT &
LINDENBERGER VS. GARRETT & COMPANY,
SEPTEMBER 22, 1837

(Herndon-Weik Collection)

This declaration and quoted note are in the hand of Attorney Lincoln. The paper is undated, but as it is known that Mr. Lincoln filed two bills of complaint in the case of Rupert & Lindenberger vs. Garrett upon September 22, 1837, this is obviously the second one. Mr. Lincoln spelled the word, "business" as "bussiness" throughout the paper. "Copy" appears as "coppy." An account of the case, appears in the note to the preceding case of Rupert & Lindenberger vs. Garrett. The bills of complaint in the two cases were filed upon the same day, and the procedure through court, and the final decisions were alike.

State of Illinois   In Sangamon circuit court

Sangamon county & circuit   October Term 1837

Eton W. Dewitt Clinton Rupert and William J. Lindenberger trading and doing bussiness under the name and style of Rupert & Lindenberger complain of Henry Garrett, and Alexander Garrett, trading and doing bussiness under the name and style of H. Garrett & Co being in custody &c of a plea of Tresspass on the case upon promises; for that whereas the said, Henry, and Alexander, heretofore, towit, on the seventeenth day of October in the year of our Lord one thousand eight hundred and thirtyfive, at Louisville, in the state of Kentucky, towit, at the county and circuit aforesaid, made their certain promissory note in writing, bearing date the day and year aforesaid, and thereby then and there promised to pay, Four months after the date thereof, to the order of Rupert & Lindenberger ninetynine dollars and ninetyone cents, for value received; and then and there delivered the said promissory note to the said Rupert & Lindenberger; by means whereof, and by force of the statute in such case made and provided, the said Henry, and Alexander then and there became liable to pay to the said Rupert and Lindenberger the said sum of money in the said promissory note specified, according to the tenor and effect of the said promissory note; and being so liable, they, the said Henry and Alexander, in consideration thereof afterwards, to wit, on the day and year aforesaid, at the county and circuit aforesaid, undertook, and then and there faithfully promised the said Rupert and Lindenberger, to pay them the said sum of money, in the said promissory note specified, according to the tenor and effect thereof, when they should be thereunto lawfully required. Yet the said Henry, and Alexander (although often requested so to do) have not as yet paid to the said Rupert and Lindenberger, the said sum of money in the said promissory note specified, or any part thereof; but so to do, have hitherto wholly refused, and still do refuse; to the damage of the said Rupert and Lindenberger in the sum of two hundred dollars, and therefore they bring their suit &c.

Stuart & Lincoln for plff

The following is a coppy of the instrument declared on—
"99 91/100 Louisville Oct 17 1835.... 183....

Four months after date we promise to pay to the order of Rupert & Lindenberger Ninetynine and Dollars 91/100
Value received
No. .... H. Garrett & Co."

DECLARATION AND PRAECIPE IN SUIT OF MCKEE ET AL VS. THARP, SEPTEMBER 26, 1837

(Herndon-Weik Collection)

The declaration, praecipe and quoted note in this case were penned by Mr. Lincoln. The cover notations are in the small characters used by Butler at times. This paper shows unusual care in its preparation. It is carefully punctuated, and commas and semi-colons are not omitted as in days when Mr. Lincoln tried so many cases that it was a task to file the legal papers in his own hand. Mr. Lincoln varied the spelling of "trespass" spelling it "tresspass" at times, and "trespass" at others. In this legal paper, he used the phrase, "but the same to do," and not "so to do." Stuart used the former phrase upon occasion. Most of the early cases handled by Lincoln were trespass cases, and thus routine litigation, but they offered experience necessary to his growth as an outstanding attorney. Stuart and Lincoln obtained a judgment of $696.26 for MeKee et al upon October 16, 1837. The plaintiff was a resident of St. Louis, Missouri.

State of Illinois ⎫   In the circuit court
                     ⎬ ss
Sangamon county & circuit ⎭   October Term 1837

John McKee, Thomas J. Stewart and Matthew F. Lind, trading and doing business under the name and style of McKee, Stewart & Lind, complain of Reuben Tharp, being in custody &c of a plea of Tresspass on the case upon promises, for that

whereas the said defendant (signing his name R. Tharp) heretofore, towit, on the twenty second day of March in the year of
our Lord one thousand eight hundred and thirtyseven, at St.
Louis Mo. to wit, at the county and circuit aforesaid, made his
certain promissory note in writing, bearing date the day and year
aforesaid, and thereby then and there promised to pay, six months
after date thereof to the order of the said plaintiffs the sum of
six hundred and ninetysix dollars and twentysix cents, for value
received, and then and there delivered the said promissory note
to the said plaintiffs; by means whereof, and by force of the
statute in such case made and provided, the said defendant then
and there became liable to pay to the said plaintiffs the said sum
of money in the said promissory note specified, according to the
tenor and effect of the said promissory note; and being so liable,
he, the said defendant, in consideration thereof, afterwards, towit, on the day and year aforesaid, undertook, and then and there
faithfully promised the said plaintiffs to pay them the said sum
of money in the said promissory note specified, according to the
tenor and effect thereof when he should be thereunto requested—
Yet the said defendant (although often requested so to do) hath
not as yet paid to the said plaintiffs the said sum of money in
the said promissory note specified, or any part thereof; but the
same to do, hath hitherto wholly neglected and refused, and still
doth neglect and refuse—To the damage of the said plaintiffs
in the sum of eight hundred dollars and therefore they bring
their suit &c.

Stuart & Lincoln for plffs

The following is a copy of the instrument declared on—

"$696—26— Saint Louis, March 22nd 1837—

Six months after date I promise to pay to the order of
McKee, Stewart & Lind, Six hundred & ninetysix 26/100 Dollars—value received without defalcation—

R. Tharp"

State of Illinois		In the circuit court
	ss	
Sangamon county & circuit		October Term 1837
John McKee, Thomas J		
Stewart, and Matthew F		Tresspass on the case
Lind, trading and doing		upon promises—
business under the name		Damage $800-00
and style of McKee, Stewart & Lind		

The clerk of the Sangamon circuit court will issue process in the above cause, returnable to the next term of said court—
                         Stuart & Lincoln for plff

McKee, Stewart & Lind ⎫
            vs   ⎬   In the circuit court—
Reuben Tharp   ⎭

I do hereby enter myself security for costs in this cause and acknowledge myself bound to pay or cause to be paid all costs which may accrue in this action, either to the opposite party, or to any of the officers of this court in pursuance of the laws of this state—Dated this 26th of Sept 1837

McKee, Stewart & Lind   A. Lincoln.

            ⎫
   vs   ⎬   Decln &
            ⎭   Precipe
Reuben Tharp

Filed Sept 26, 1837
Wm Butler ck

WILLIAM HERNDON TO STUART & LINCOLN: PAYMENT OF LEGAL FEE, OCTOBER, 1837

This entry in the cash book of Stuart & Lincoln is penned by the junior partner of the firm. The partnership between Stuart & Lincoln began in April, 1837 and terminated on April 14, 1841, although Mr. Lincoln had acted with Judge Logan in cases that were heard several months prior to 1841. The firm of Stuart & Dummer which preceded that of Stuart & Lincoln was the leading firm in Springfield and Stuart and Lincoln retained this position.

William Herndon
            To Stuart & Lincoln Dr
1837—Oct   To Attachment case against Smith $5.00

PETITION FOR PARTITION IN CHANCERY SUIT OF MOSES MARTIN VS. JOHN MARTIN'S HEIRS, OCTOBER 16, 1837

(Herndon-Weik Collection)

This petition for partition is the work of Abraham Lincoln's pen. The cover notations are by Butler, and the figures below appear to be in another hand. Mr. Lincoln erred in his spelling in this legal paper, writing "siting" and "apointed" instead of the spellings accepted for modern usage. He is precise to the quarter cent in his statements of money matters, and corrected several errors in his grammar and spelling by crossing out words.

To the Honorable Judge of the Sangamon circuit court
in chancery siting—

Respectfully sheweth unto your Honor your petitioner Moses M. Martin that about the day of   in the year of our Lord one thousand eight hundred and thirtysix a certain Isaac Martin died in the county of Sangamon—that administration of his estate has been duly granted by the Probate court of said county to your petitioner—that your petitioner has made and duly filed in said Probate court of Sangamon county an inventory, appraisement and sale bill of the personal estate of the said Isaac Martin dec and that your petitioner has applied all the proceeds of the personal estate of said Martin so far as they have come to his hands to the payment of the debts of said Martin—that said personal estate is insufficient for the payment of the debts against the estate of said Martin—that the said personal estate amounts to the sum of four hundred and fifty three dollars and fiftyseven and three quarter cents—and the debts already proved before the late Judge of Probate, now Probate Justice of the Peace, amount to the sum of five hundred and eighty dollars and sixtyfive and one quarter cents—

Your petitioner states that the said Martin died seized of the following lands in the county of Sangamon towit, the West half of the South West quarter of Section Eight in Township Fourteen North of Range Three West; and the South half of the South West quarter of Section Six in the Township and Range aforesaid—Your petitioner further states that the said Martin left at the time of his death Mary Martin his widow and Moses M. Martin, Susan Martin, Eliza Martin, Sara Martin, Meredith Martin, Charity Martin, Patsy Martin, Mahala Martin, Eli Martin, Jacob Martin, and Rebecca Martin children and Heirs at law—the said Eliza, Sarah, Meredith, Charity, Patsy, Mahala, Eli, Jacob, and Rebecca being minors—Your petitioner prays that all the said persons be made defendants to this petition; and that your Honor will apoint a guardian *ad litem* to the said minor heirs, who may be required to answer, on their behalf, to the allegations of this petition; upon a final hearing of which, your petitioner prays an order from your Honorable court, directing, authorizing, and empowering him to sell and convey the aforesaid lands, or so much thereof as may be sufficient to pay the unsatisfied debts of the estate of the said Martin deceased and as in duty bound &c.

Moses M. Martin

administrator of Isaac Martin dec

Exparte Moses M. Martin administrator of Isaac Martin deceased

On Petition to sell real estate—

This day came the said Moses M. Martin, and filed his petition in open court; and Samuel H Treat having been appointed guardian *ad litem* to the minor heirs named in the said petition, files his answer to the said petition, and says that he has examined the said petition and paper therewith filed, and knows no reason why the prayer of the same should not be granted; And it appearing to the court that due notice has been given of this application according to law, and that the allegations of said petition are true. It is therefore considered and ordered by the court that the said Moses M. Martin, administrator of the estate of Isaac Martin dec sell the lands mentioned in the said petition, towit, the West half of the South West quarter of Section Eight; and the South West quarter of Section Six, both in Township Fourteen North of Range Three West of the Third Principal Meridian; situate, lying and being in the county of Sangamon and State of Illinois—And that said sale be made on a credit of six months, after giving due notice according to law and on the terms prescribed by law—And it is further ordered that the said administrator report his proceedings to this court—

Moses Martin

vs   } Pet for Partition

Isaac Martin heirs

Filed oct 16th 1837

Wm Butler Clk

July T. 1838

BRAUCHER & BRAUCHER VS. HICKMAN, OCTOBER 18, 1837

(Herndon-Weik Collection)

A discussion of this case appears in the note to the document of September 8, 1837 reproduced above. The present document is signed by Logan & Baker, but is included as a part of Braucher & Braucher vs. Hickman.

Braucher
   ads   }   Scire Facias to Foreclose
Hickman excr of Churchhill }   Mortgage

And the Defendant comes and defends wrong, and injury when where &c and say the plaintiff his scire facias against him to have and maintain ought not because he says that the plaintiffs scire facias and the matters and things therein contained are not good and sufficient in law for the plaintiff to maintain his scire facias against him and this he is ready to verify wherefore he prays judgment.

Logan & Baker pd

Braucher
      ]
ads   }   [?]
      ]
Hickman
Filed Oct 18th 1837
   Wm Butler Clk

DEFENDANT'S AFFIDAVIT IN SUIT OF FLEMING VS. RANSDELL, OCTOBER 21, 1837

(Herndon-Weik Collection)

This affidavit was drawn by Mr. Lincoln and signed by Wharton Ransdell. William Butler made the notations to Wharton's oath, and he wrote the cover notations. The Butler "7" in 1837 resembled a "9", and a "7" has been placed above in a hand other than of Butler. The "duces tecum" referred to, will be understood by lawyers and students of Latin. It means "thou shalt bring with thee," which in this case meant that Dorsey was to bring the mortgage and his person to court, along with the writ ordering his attendance. As recorded elsewhere in due course the plaintiff took a non-suit. Thus the defendant may be said to have won the case.

Wharton Ransdell }
       ats   }
Samuel Fleming }

This day personally appears Wharton Ransdell who being duly sworn says that he is advised and verrily believes that he can not safely go to trial without the evidence of one Charles S. Dorsey of Tazewell county and a certain Mortgage deed supposed to be in his possession; that he, this affiant has caused to be regularly issued from the clerk's office of this court a Subpoena *duces tecum* requiring the said Dorsey to be and appear at this term of this court and to have with him the said Mortgage deed; that said Subpoena *duces tecum* was directed to the sheriff of Tazewell county and returned by him "not served"; that he expects to be able to procure the evidence of the said Dorsey and Mortgage Deed by the next term of this court, and to prove by them that a certain tract of land lying and being in the said county of Tazewell, is bound by the said Mortgage deed for the payment of the debt for which this suit is brought; and that this application is made for the purpose of justice and not of delay.

W Ransdell

Sworn to me before this
21st day of october A D 1837

W.. Butler Clk

Samuel Fleming

vs } affa deft

Wharton Ransdell
Filed oct 21st 1837
Wm.. Butler Clk

REPORT OF COMMISSIONER IN SUIT OF HOUGHTON VS. HART'S HEIRS, DECEMBER 20, 1837

(Herndon-Weik Collection)

Attorney Lincoln drew this report which was signed by Samuel H. Treat. The cover notations are by Butler. Treat's report shows the decree of the court to have been in favor of Houghton, the client of Stuart and Lincoln. The court ordered that the rights prayed for on June 15, 1837, by Houghton be granted, and title to the tract mentioned in the aforesaid document conveyed to him. This was done at the October term, 1837.

I, Samuel H. Treat, having been appointed by the Sangamon circuit court, at the last October term thereof, a commissioner to make, execute and deliver to Elijah Houghton a deed of conveyance for a certain tract of land, being a part of the West half of the South East quarter of Section Thirteen in Township Seventeen North of Range Seven West of the Third Principal Meridian, and bounded as follows towit: Begining at the South East corner half quarter, thence West to the Southern boundary line, of the same, ten chains and seven links thence North twelve chains and forty links to the centre of the channel of Rock creek; thence down said creek with its meanders to the Eastern boundary line of said half quarter, thence South with said Eastern boundary line to the place of beginning, report:

That I have made, executed and delivered the said deed of conveyance according to the decree of said court.

Given under my hand this 21.st day of December A. D. 1837.

S. H. Treat

Houghton

vs   } Report

Harts heirs

Filed Decr 20th 1837
Wm Butler Clk

CHAPTER IX—LINCOLN IN THE YEAR 1838

SURVEY OF PERIOD

On February 12, 1838 Mr. Lincoln entered his thirtieth year —a year that was to mark his steady advance at the bar and in politics. On January 27 he delivered before the Young Men's Lyceum of Springfield an address on "The Perpetuation of Our Political Institutions," mistakenly placed in the year 1837 by Nicolay and Hay. Suggested perhaps by the recent killing of Elijah Parish Lovejoy by a pro-slavery mob in Alton, although it made only one indirect reference to that tragedy, Mr. Lincoln had devoted much time and labor to this address which stressed and deplored the evil inherent in an increasing disregard for law and remained for a period of years his ablest and most compelling public utterance, admonishing the people "never to violate in the least particular the laws of the country, and never to tolerate their violation by others"—a rule the speaker was to reverently observe until the end of his days.

In Illinois in 1838, however, politics was for Mr. Lincoln an absorbing affair filled with strife and bitterness and sudden death. His partner, John Todd Stuart, was the Whig candidate for Congress in opposition to Stephen A. Douglas, and Lincoln himself headed the Whig legislative ticket in Sangamon—John Calhoun heading the Democratic slate—and was active in the management of Whig interests in the county. Both Stuart and Lincoln triumphed at the end of a contest in which no quarter was asked nor given; and which left a murder trial, the sequel of the killing of Dr. Jacob M. Early by Henry B. Truett, and a world of ill-feeling in its wake. In due course, Mr. Lincoln, who went back to the law after the votes were counted, was one of four Whig lawyers who, with Douglas directing the prosecution, defended Truett and helped to secure his acquittal.

Not less tense during 1838 were conditions in the field of national politics. The Whigs led by Clay, not always with reason or good sense, fought Van Buren and all his works. In March young John Greenleaf Whittier, soon to become the bard of the anti-slavery movement, assumed the editorship of the Pennsylvania Freeman, an abolition journal published in Philadelphia, and two months later witnessed the destruction of the building in which it was housed by a proslavery mob. Sooner or later Mr. Lincoln must have heard of the address delivered by Ralph Waldo Emerson on July 15, 1838, before the divinity school at Cambridge—an address which was to assure fame of a much debated sort to its author and lend a fresh impetus to liberal thought in America. In September, 1838, William Henry Seward, Mr. Lincoln's destined rival for the Presidency, was elected the Whig governor of New York, and a Unitarian congregation in Cincinnati called to its pulpit the younger Channing, a man of exalted purpose who a quarter of a century later was to have friendly and understanding contact with President Lincoln.

And finally in the closing days of September, 1838, there was formed in Manchester the Anti-Corn-Law League, destined to vastly better the lot of English labor, an event of future significance to the young Whig lawyer of Springfield, for two of its founders were Richard Cobden and John Bright, who in a time of doubt and hesitation were to have full faith in a great leader and his unswerving aims, and hold the English masses firm in their support of the Northern cause.

DEFENDANT'S BRIEF IN THE CHANCERY SUIT OF CASSIDY ATS. FOSTER, JANUARY ?, 1838

(Herndon-Weik Collection)

Mr. Lincoln used the spelling, "Cassaday" in the document of January 5, 1838, reproduced below but he now uses Cassidy, a close approach to Cassity as given in Pratt, "Lincoln Day by Day: 1809-1839." The brief is undated, and may have been drawn up as early as August, 1837, at which time Attorney Lincoln wrote a long six-page answer for Cassity, the defendant in the case. It may have been penned after the notice for taking depositions in the case, which Mr. Lincoln wrote on January 5, 1838. The brief and cover notations were penned by Lincoln.

Cassidy
   ats   }   In Chancery—
Foster

In this case the Defendant insists that the force and obligation of the *written agreement* between the parties, expired by its own terms, on the first of May 1833, as will appear by an inspection of the instrument filed with the papers of the cause; that the *subsequent* agreement of the Defendant is of no binding force. *there being no note or memorandum in writing, thereof signed by the party*—that the possession does not take the case out of the statute of frauds, it having been given under the written agreement, and long previous to the making of the subsequent verbal one—

The Defendant also objects that there is no Replication filed by the Complainant—

The Defendant further objects, that there was no sufficient bond for the cost filed, at the commencement of the action—The Bill and exhibits filed by the Complainant, as also the Deposition of Cutter, show that said complainant was not and is not a resident of the state—

The Defendant further insists, that the deed marked (C) and tendered him by Complainants agent, is bad for the following reasons, towit:

First—Because the supposed Justice of the Peace, before whom it purports to have been acknowledged, does not certify that the persons making the acknowledgment *"are personally known to him to be the persons whose names are subscribed to such deed"* whereas the statute requires that he should so certify—

Revised Laws—page 132—Sec. 11—

Second—Because the clerk who certifies that the person taking the acknowledgment, was a Justice of the Peace, does not, either directly or indirectly, show himself to be the *proper* clerk in whose office the official evidence of who are Justices of the Peace, is kept, whereas the statute requires the certificate of the *"'proper clerk."*

Revised Laws—page 138—Sec. 1—

The defendant insists, that by the showing of the complainant, the tendering of a *good deed* to the Defendant was a condition precedent—

Cassidy ⎫
    ats ⎬   Defts Brief—
Foster ⎭

NOTICE OF DEPOSITIONS TO BE TAKEN IN CHANCERY SUIT OF FOSTER VS. CASSIDAY, JANUARY 5, 1838

(Herndon-Weik Collection)

Treat signed his name, and "Atty. of Foster"; otherwise Mr. Lincoln penned this document. Leave was given to open depositions in the case on March 6, 1838. It was ruled on July 14 that it should be decided in vacation. Stuart & Lincoln won on

October 19, *when Foster was ordered to convey the tract of land referred to as deeded to the defendant, Cassity. And at Washington on January 5, 1838, President Van Buren issued a proclamation of neutrality warning American citizens not to aid Canadians then in revolt by hostile acts against Great Britain.*

Joseph C. Foster⎤
          vs   ⎬ In chancery
Thomas Cassaday⎦

The complainant in the above entitled cause will take notice that on Monday the fifteenth day of January Ins between the hours of 10, o'clock A. M. and 5 o'clock P. M. of said day I shall attend at the office of Thomas Moffett Esqr in the town of Springfield for the purpose of taking the depositions of Albert Barger, Levi Tucker, and A. E. Meacham & others to be read in evidence in the above entitled cause now pending in the Sangamon Circuit court—

January 5th 1838   Thomas Cassady

I acknowledge the service of the above notice on this day; and also agree, that the depositions of Seth R. Cutter, John Calhoun and others taken by the above named complainant on the 22nd day of December last, may on the said fifteenth of January, be opened, and the said deponents cross-examined by the said defendant if he choose.

January 5t 1838—

                                        S. H. Treat
                                        Atty of Foster

PRAECIPE AND DECLARATION OF PLAINTIFF IN SUIT OF ANDERSON, BELL & COMPANY VS. GAMBREL, FEBRUARY 2, 1838

(Herndon-Weik Collection)

This document with the exception of the words, "Filed Feby 2d 1838," and the signature of William Butler, is in the hand of Mr. Lincoln. Stuart and Lincoln won this case on July 13, 1838, when a jury awarded the plaintiffs a judgment of $207.65.

State of Illinois   ⎱ In the circuit court of said
Sangamon county & circuit ⎰ county—March Term 1838—

James Anderson Jr, William Bell, and John W. Anderson trading under the name, style, and firm of Anderson Bell & Co

plaintiffs, complain of James Gambrel defendant being in custody
&c of a plea of trespass on the case upon promises: For that
whereas the said defendant, heretofore, towit on the fifth day of
December in the year of our Lord one thousand eight hundred
and thirty six at Springfield, towit, at the county and circuit
aforesaid, made his certain promissory note in writing bearing
date the day and year aforesaid and thereby then and there
promised to pay on or before the fifteenth day of December in
the year one thousand eight hundred and thirty seven to one
Moses Coffman or order the sum of two hundred dollars for
value received, and then and there delivered the said promissory
note to the said Moses Coffman—And the said Moses Coffman, to whom or to whose order, the payment of the said sum of
money in the said promissory note specified was to be made,
after the making of the said promissory note, before the payment
of the said sum of money therein specified to wit, on the day and
year first aforesaid, at the county and circuit aforesaid, assigned
the said promissory note, by which assignment, he the said Moses
Coffman then and there ordered and appointed the said sum of
money in the said promissory note specified to be paid to the said
plaintiffs, and then and there delivered the said promissory note
so assigned to the said plaintiffs: by means whereof and by force
of the statute in such case made and provided, the said defendant
then and there became liable to pay to the said plaintiffs the said
sum of money in the said promissory note specified according to
the tenor and effect of the said promissory note; and being so
liable, he the said defendant, in consideration thereof, afterwards,
towit, on the day and year first aforesaid, undertook, and then
and there faithfully promised the said plaintiffs to pay them the
said sum of money in the said promissory note specified according to the tenor and effect thereof—, Yet the said defendant
(although often requested so to do) hath not as yet paid to the
said plaintiffs the said sum of money in the said promissory note
specified, or any part thereof: but so to do hath hitherto wholly
neglected and refused, and still doth neglect and refuse: To the
damage of the said plaintiffs of the sum of three hundred dollars
and therefore they bring their suit &c

                    Stuart & Lincoln for plffs

The following is a copy of the instrument declared on:
"$200. Springfield 5th December 1836
on or before the 5th day of December 1837 I promise to
pay to Moses Coffman or order two hundred dollars—value rcd
                                               James Gambrel"

On which is the following assignment—
    "Pay to Anderson Bell & Co
              Moses Coffman"

James Anderson Jr ⎫
William Bell &   ⎪   Tresspass on the case upon
John W. Anderson ⎬ promises—
    vs.   ⎪   Damages $300—
James Gambrel   ⎭

The clerk of the Sangamon circuit court will issue process
in the above entitled cause returnable to the next term of said
court—

                              Stuart & Lincoln for plffs

James Anderson Jr ⎫
William Bell &   ⎪
John W. Anderson ⎬ Sangamon Circuit court
    vs.   ⎪
James Gambrel   ⎭

I do hereby enter myself security for costs in this cause and
acknowledge myself bound to pay or cause to be paid all costs
which may accrue in this action, either to the opposite party or
any of the officers of this court in pursuance of the laws of
this state.

Dated this 2nd February A. D 1838—

                                         A. Lincoln

Anderson Bell & Co.
    vs.
James Gambrel

Precipe & Declaration

Filed Feby 2d 1838
Wm Butler Clk

DECLARATION OF PLAINTIFF IN SUIT OF ANDERSON, BELL & COMPANY VS. GARRETT AND GARRETT, FEBRUARY 2, 1838

This declaration, the signature of Stuart and the notation of Butler excepted, is in the hand of Mr. Lincoln. On March 12, 1838, Stuart and Lincoln obtained judgment by confession for $860.48 by Alexander Garrett and a summons to Henry Garrett.

State of Illinois   ⎱   In the circuit court of said
Sangamon county & circuit ⎰   county—March Term 1838—

James Anderson Jr, William Bell, and John W. Anderson trading under the name, style and firm of Anderson, Bell & Co. plaintiffs, complain of Henry Garrett and Alexander Garrett, defendants, being in custody &c. of a plea of tresspass on the case upon promises: For that whereas the said defendants, by and under the name, style and firm of H. Garrett & Co heretofore, towit on the sixteenth day of October in the year of our Lord one thousand eight hundred and thirty five, at Louisville, that is to say at the county and circuit aforesaid, made their certain promissory note in writing, bearing date the day and year aforesaid, and thereby then and there promised to pay, Six months after the date thereof to the order of the said plaintiffs the sum of one thousand and forty nine dollars and seventy two cents, for value received, and then and there delivered the said promissory note to the said plaintiffs; by means whereof, and by force of the statute in such case made and provided, the said defendants then and there became liable to pay to the said plaintiffs the said sum of money in the said promissory note specified, according to the tenor and effect of the said promissory note, and being so liable, they, the said defendants in consideration thereof, afterwards, towit, on the day and year aforesaid; at the county and circuit aforesaid, undertook, and then and there faithfully promised the said plaintiffs to pay them the said sum of money in the said promissory note specified, according to the tenor and effect thereof—Yet the said defendants (although often requested so to do) have not as yet paid to the said plaintiffs, the said sum of money in the said promissory note specified; but so to do, have hitherto neglected and refused; and still do neglect and refuse: To the damage of said plaintiffs of the sum of two thousand dollars, and therefore they bring their suit &c.

Stuart & Lincoln
for Plffs—

The following is a copy of the instrument declared on:

"$1049 72/100 Louisville   Oct. 16th 1835

Six months after date We promise to pay to the order of Anderson Bell & Co. One thousand and Forty nine 72/100 Dollars Without Defalcation, for value received; Negotiable and payable at the — — —

H. Garrett & Co"

On which is the following indorsement—

"Received on the within $305-50 cents Dec 29. 1837"

James Anderson Jr ⎫
William Bell & ⎪
John W. Anderson ⎬ Trespass on the case upon promises—
vs. ⎪   Damage $2000
Henry Garrett & ⎪
Alexander Garrett ⎭

The clerk of the Sangamon circuit court will issue process in the above entitled cause returnable to the next term of said court—

Stuart & Lincoln for plffs—

James Anderson Jr ⎫
William Bell & ⎪
John W. Anderson ⎬ Sangamon circuit court
vs. ⎪
Henry Garrett & ⎪
Alexander Garrett ⎭

I do hereby enter myself security for costs in this cause and acknowledge myself bound to pay or cause to be paid all costs which may accrue in this action either to the opposite party or to any of the officers of the court in pursuance of the laws of this state—Dated this 2nd February A. D. 1838

John T. Stuart

Anderson Bell & Co
vs.
H. Garrett & Co.
Precipe & Declaration
Filed February 2 1838
Wm Butler Clk.

DECLARATION IN THE SUIT OF ANDERSON ET AL VS. PATTERSON ET AL, SANGAMON CIRCUIT COURT, FEBRUARY 2, 1838,

(Herndon-Weik Collection)

The note on which this suit was based is obviously not in the hand of Mr. Lincoln, and the words, "Pattersons note, $200, due 19th Decr 1837" may not be. "Pay to Anderson Bell & Co," and signed "Moses Coffman" below, is in his hand, with the exception of Coffman's signature. The entire legal document was drawn by him. Final decision in the case came on July 5, 1838, when the clerk made entry that the defendant had been duly served with a scire facias by the plaintiff, and " came not but made default." The court then decreed that the plaintiff's scire facias be taken as confessed. It noted also that upon March 9, 1838, the plaintiffs had recovered a judgment of $203.00 in an action of assumpist against Frederick A. Patterson with whom the said George Patterson was impleaded. It decreed in the order of July 5 that George Patterson be made a party to the judgment rendered on March 9, 1838, and that he be liable to pay the same. The plaintiffs were granted execution therefor.

State of Illinois   }   In the circuit court of said

Sangamon county & circuit }   county— March Term 1838—

James Anderson Jr., Wiliam Bell, and John W. Anderson, trading under the name style and firm of Anderson Bell & Co plaintiffs, complain of George Patterson and Frederick A. Patterson defendants, being in custody &c. of a plea of tresspass on the case upon promises: For that whereas the said defendants, heretofore: towit, on the nineteenth day of December in the year of our Lord one thousand eight hundred and thirty six, at the county and circuit aforesaid, made their certain promissory note in writing (the said Frederick A. Patterson signing his name "F. A. X Patterson") bearing date the day and year aforesaid and thereby then and there promised to pay twelve months after the date thereof to one Moses Coffman the sum of two hundred dollars, for value received, and then and there delivered the said promissory note to the said Moses Coffman. And the said Moses Coffman to whom the payment of the said sum of money in the said promissory note specified was to be made, after the making of the said promissory note, before the payment of the said sum of money therein specified, towit, on the day and year aforesaid, at the county and circuit aforesaid, assigned the said promissory note, by which said assignment, he the said Moses Coffman, then and there ordered and appointed the said sum of money in the said promissory note note specified to be paid to the said plaintiffs, and then and there delivered the said promissory note, so assigned as aforesaid to the said plaintiffs; by means whereof, and by force of the statute in such case made and provided, the said defendant then and there became liable to pay to the said plaintiffs the said sum of money in the said promissory note specified, according to the tenor and effect of the said promissory note; and being so liable, they, the said defendants, in consideration thereof, afterwards, towit, on the day and year aforesaid, at the county and circuit aforesaid, undertook, and then and there faithfully promised to pay them the said sum of money in the said promissory note specified, according to the tenor and effect thereof—

Yet the said defendants (although often requested so to do) have not yet paid to the said plaintiffs the said sum of money in the said promissory note specified, or any part thereof; but so to do have hitherto wholly neglected and refused, and still doth neglect and refuse: To the damage of the said plaintiffs of the sum of three hundred dollars; and therefore they bring their suit &c.

Stuart & Lincoln for plffs.

The following is a copy of the instrument declared on:

Twelve months after date we
or either of us promise to pay to moses Coffman two hundred dollars for value received fr him witness our hand and seal this 19 day of december 1836

his
George X Patterson
mark

his
F. A. X Patterson
mark

Patterson's note
   $200
due 19th Decr 1837
Pay to ————
Anderson Bell & Co
   Moses Coffman

BILL IN CHANCERY IN THE SUIT OF GARRETT VS. LEVERING, SANGAMON CIRCUIT COURT, FEBRUARY 6, 1838

(Herndon-Weik Collection)

The date of filing on the cover, and the signature of Butler, are the only parts of this document which were not penned by Attorney Lincoln. Lawrason Levering was the brother of Mercy Levering, the close friend of Mary Todd, who had yet to make her entry into the life of Mr. Lincoln. One sentence in the record offers the result of the case. It reads, "On motion of Complainants counsel ordered that this case be dismissed at the Complainant's cost." The clerk made this entry on October 10, 1838.

To the Honorable the Judge of the Sangamon circuit court in chancery sitting.

Humbly complaining sheweth to your Honor, your orator Alexander Garrett, that on the eighth day of October in the year of our Lord one thousand eight hundred and thirtysix, your orator, together with Jane W. his wife, executed and delivered to one Lawrason Levering, who he prays may be made a defendant to this Bill, a conditional deed of conveyance, of and for a certain tract of land therein discribed, and, a copy of which deed is herewith filed, marked (A), and which your orator prays, may be taken and considered as part of this Bill.

Your orator states that said deed was given only to secure the payment of a certain promissory note therein mentioned; that if the said note were unpaid after it should fall due, the said tract of land was to be sold by the said defendant to satisfy the same, that in case the same should sell for more than sufficient to discharge the said note and pay the expenses of the sale, the overplus was to be paid to your orator by the defendant; that the said note was given for eight hundred and sixtytwo dollars and twentyone cents, to bear interest at the rate of eight per cent per annum from date until paid; and that the said tract of land contains eighty acres, all of which will more fully appear by reference to the copy of the said deed herewith filed.

Your orator further states that some time about one month before the said promissory note fell due, which was twelve months after the date of the said deed, your orators, intending to leave the country on a visit to   had a conversation with the said defendant, in which the said defendant told him that when the said tract of land should be sold, he the said defendant would bid at least as much for it as was due on the said promissory note; and that he, your orator, need give himself no further trouble about the matter, if he was willing to take a full discharge of the said promissory note for the land.

Your orator further states that after the said promissory note fell due, the same remaining unpaid, the said defendant, after giving notice according to the condition of the said deed, did employ an auctioneer to make public sale of the said tract of land; that the said auctioneer did expose the same at public auction, when the said defendant, being the highest and best bidder, the said tract of land was knocked down to him, and he became the purchaser thereof at the rate of price of twelve dollars per acre; and that said sale was made on the eleventh day of October in the year of our Lord one thousand eight hundred and thirtyseven—

Your orator further states ,that, although the said defendant bid the said tract of land off at a price per acre that would have produced a sum more than sufficient to discharge the said note, and pay the expenses of the said sale, he the said defendant has not discharged, nor delivered up to your orator the said promissory note, nor paid to him the said overplus; but to do either wholly refuses.

In tender consideration of all which, your orator prays that the People's writ Subpoena may issue, requiring the said defendant to appear and answer on his corporal oath, all and singular the allegations in this Bill contained, and also that he be required to answer whether he, at the date of answering, has said promissory note in his possession; and that on a final hearing of this cause, your Honor will decree that the said defendant shall deliver up to be cancelled, if the same shall be in his possession, the said promissory note; and also pay to your orator, so much money as his bid at the sale of the said land, exceeded the sum due on the said note, at the time of the said sale, and the expenses of the same; and, in case the said promissory note shall not then be in the possession of the said defendant, your orator prays that he, the said defendant, be decreed by your Honor to pay to your orator the sum of nine hundred and sixty dollars, (being the sum for which he bid off the said tract of land) together with interest from the time of the said sale, and that your Honor will grant such other and further relief as equity may require; and, as in duty bound &c.

Stuart & Lincoln
Solicitors for Complainant

Alexander Garrett   ⎫
     vs.   ⎬ Bill in Chry.
Lawrason Levering ⎭
Filed February 6th 1838
   Wm Butler Clk
The clerk will issue
process hereon—
   Stuart & Lincoln

COMPLAINT OF PLAINTIFF IN CHANCERY SUIT OF WILSON VS. MASTERSON ET AL, FEBRUARY 13, 1838
(Herndon-Weik Collection)

This complaint was drawn by Attorney Lincoln. The date of filing is in the writing of Butler, while "Fee $2.87½" appears to be that of Mr. Lincoln. The other cover notations also come from his pen. Mr. Lincoln omitted the words, "Benjamin F. Masterson," after "thirty-five," in paragraph two of the bill. He hurriedly wrote, "Sanganon," for "Sangamon," but this could not be construed as mis-spelling. He spells the word correctly too frequently to consider this a mistake.

And the day after this complaint was filed in the House at Washington John Quincy Adams presented 350 petitions against slavery and the annexation of Texas which was soon to become a burning issue.

To the Honorable, the Judge of the Sangamon circuit court, in Chancery sitting—

Humbly complaining sheweth to your Honor your Orator George W. Wilson, that one Benjamin F. Masterson did, on the twentyseventh day of June in the year of our Lord one thousand eight hundred and thirtyfive, bargain and sell to your orator the South West quarter of the North East quarter of Section Three in Township Seventeen North, of Range Eight West of the Third Principal Meridian, containing forty acres, and situated in the county of Sangamon and State of Illinois; that your orator paid the said Masterson for the said tract of land; and that the said Masterson obligated himself to convey the legal title of said land to your orator so soon as he. the said Masterson should obtain the United States patent for the same; all of which will appear by reference to the instrument herewith filed, marked (A) and which your orator prays may be taken and considered as part of this Bill—

Your orator further states that some time in the autumn of the year one thousand eight hundred and thirtyfive, Masterson died, without having conveyed the title of said land to your orator; and leaving the following named heirs at law, towit, Lucilla Masterson, (widow) and William B. Masterson and Benjamin F. Masterson, minors. Your orator further states, that the United States patent for the said tract of land is now in his possession, and which he now shows your Honor—Your orator further states that one James Simpson is the legal administrator of the estate of the said Benjamin F. Masterson deceased.

In tender consideration of all which, your orator prays, that the Peoples writ of Subpoena may issue to the said administrator and heirs at law, requiring them to answer all and singular the allegations of this Bill; and that on a final hearing of this case your Honor will decree that the administrator of the estate of Benjamin F. Masterson deceased, convey to your orator, all the right, title, interest and estate in and to the South West quarter of the North East quarter of Section Three in Township Seventeen North of Range Eight West of the Third Principal Medidian, situate in the county of Sanganon and State of Illinois, which the said Benjamin F Masterson had to the same at the time of his decease; and that such other and further relief be granted as equity may require; and your orator as in duty bound &c.

Stuart & Lincoln
Solicitors for Complainant—

George W. Wilson

vs   } Bill in Chy—

James Simpson

Lucilla Masterson
William B. Masterson &
Benjamin F. Masterson
Filed Feby 13th 1838
W. Butler Clk

Fee $2.87½
The clerk will issue
process herein—
    Stuart & Lincoln

BILL OF COMPLAINT IN THE CHANCERY SUIT OF PAYNE VS. BRYAN, SANGAMON CIRCUIT COURT, FEBRUARY 14, 1838

(Herndon-Weik Collection)

The bill of complaint and the bond for costs in this case were penned by Attorney Lincoln. The care exercised by him in most of his legal documents is revealed in the crossing out of "eigth" and replacing it with "eighth." There are no cover notations, but Dr. Harry E. Pratt places the date of the bill of complaint as February 14, 1839. (See Pratt, "Lincoln Day by Day: 1809-1839," Page 120.) The complete record of each case handled by Mr. Lincoln is not available in the records of the Sangamon County Court. There are two volumes of Complete Records for 1835-1840, one taking in the cases of 1835-1840, and the other including the years, 1836-1862. Although entitled, "Complete Records," these volumes contain only a limited number of cases. It is apparent, two volumes could scarcely include the legal business in Sangamon County from 1835 to 1862. There are gaps also in the Records, which are merely the record of the clerk of the action in each case. In view of the numerous discoveries in the field of Lincolniana in recent years, it would be unwise to say that the records will never be found. In the case of Payne vs. Bryan and others, it may be said that present sources do not permit of a complete case history.

To the Honorable the Judge of the Sangamon Circuit court in Chancery sitting:

Humbly complaining sheweth unto your Honor, your Orator, Thomas J. Payne that on the eighth day of December, in the year of our Lord one thousand eight hundred and thirtyfour Nicholas Bryan of the county of Sangamon and State of Illinois, executed a certain mortgage deed, and on the second day of January in the year one thousand eight hundred and thirtyfive, acknowledged the same before one of the Justices of the Peace in and for the said county of Sangamon, and delivered it to your orator; and which mortgage deed was duly recorded in the Recorder's office in and for the said county of Sangamon on the eighth day of January in the year last aforesaid, and is herewith filed marked (A) and which your orator prays may be taken and considered as part of this Bill— Your orator further states that, as will appear by reference to the said mortgage deed, it was given to secure your orator in the payment of Seventeen hundred and one dollars, and interest, due your orator in a certain promissory note; and that the money due on the said promissory note has not as yet been paid, or any part thereof—

In tender consideration of all which your orator prays that said Nicholas Bryan be made defendant to this Bill, by your Honor's Subpoena in Chancery, and that he be required to answer on his corporal oath all and singular the allegations in this Bill contained; and that upon a final hearing of this case, your Honor will Decree that the said defendant pay unto your orator the sum of money due by said mortgage, and that the tract of land mentioned in the said mortgage, and which your orator alleges is a part of the East half of the North West quarter of Section Thirty two in Township Sixteen North of Range Five West be sold to satisfy the debt aforesaid, in said mortgage specified; and that your Honor will grant such other and further relief as equity may require, and as in duty bound &c.

Stuart & Lincoln
Solicitors for complainant—

I do hereby enter myself security for costs in this cause, and acknowledge myself bound to pay or cause to be paid all costs which may accrue in this action, either to the opposite party or to any of the officers of this Court, in pursuance of the laws of this state.

A. Lincoln

dated this 14th day of February

DECLARATION IN THE SUIT OF ROLL VS. ANDERSON, SANGAMON CIRCUIT COURT, FEBRUARY 19, 1838
(Herndon-Weik Collection)

The declaration and cover notations in this case, with the exception of the date of filing, are in the handwriting of Mr. Lincoln. His future partner, Mr. Logan, wrote the plea of the defendant, added the words "the plaintiff doth the like," and signed "Lincoln p q———." The "&" before the plaintiff is not common in the careful work of Mr. Lincoln. It will be noted that he varied the punctuation of the phrase, "negligently, carelessly, and improperly," in each case where he used it, even as he did with the words, "escaped, ran off, and was wholly lost," an indication that he desired to be careful in punctuation, but now and again was uncertain of it. Stuart & Lincoln moved for continuance of the case on March 8, 1838, and it was continued due to a want of summons in time. At this point, the available records in the case end. Studies to the present time have failed to reveal a complete history.

State of Illinois	⎱	Of the March term of the circuit
Sangamon county &	⎬ ss	court for Sangamon county in the
Circuit	⎰	year of our Lord one thousand eight
		hundred thirtyeight—

John E. Roll complains of John Anderson in custody &c of a plea of Trespass on the case: For that whereas heretofore, towit, on   day of October in the year of our Lord one thousand eight hundred and thirtysix, at the county and circuit aforesaid, the said plaintiff delivered to the said defendant a certain Black mare to him the plaintiff of great value, towit, of the value of one hundred dollars, to be by him the said defendant, used without feed or reward for her, use; and to be safely kept by him the said defendant, and returned to the said plaintiff on the same day, and the said defendant then and there had and received the said mare for the purpose aforesaid. Yet the said defendant   not regarding his duty in that behalf, afterwards, towit, on the day and year aforesaid, at the county and circuit aforesaid, conducted himself so negligently, carelessly and improperly in and about the keeping of the said mare, that by and through the mere negligence and improper conduct of the said defendant the said mare escaped, ran off, and became and was wholly lost to the plaintiff, to wit on the day and year aforesaid, at the county and circuit aforesaid—

And whereas afterwards towit, on the day and year aforesaid, at the county and circuit aforesaid, the said plaintiff delivered to the said defendant a certain other black mare, of him the said plaintiff of the value of one hundred dollars to be by the the plaintiff in a reasonable time; and the said defendant then and there had and received the said last mentioned mare of the plaintiff for the purpose last aforesaid— Yet the said defendant not regarding his duty in that behalf afterwards towit, on the day and year aforesaid, at the county and circuit aforesaid conducted himself so negligently, carelessly and improperly in and about the keeping of said last mentioned mare, that by and through the mere negligence and improper conduct of the said defendant in that behalf, the said last mentioned mare, escaped ran off, and was wholly lost to the plaintiff, towit, on the day and year aforesaid, at the county and circuit aforesaid—

And whereas afterwards towit on the day and year aforesaid, at the county and circuit aforesaid the said plaintiff delivered to the said defendant a certain other black mare of the said plaintiff to the value of one hundred dollars, to be by the said defendant safely and securely kept, and the said defendant then and there had and received the said last mentioned mare of the said plaintiff for the purpose last aforesaid— Yet the said defendant not regarding his duty in that behalf, afterwards, towit, on the day and year aforesaid, at the county and circuit aforesaid, conducted himself so negligently, carelessly, and improperly, in and about the keeping of the said last mentioned mare, that by and through the mere negligence and improper conduct of the said defendant in that behalf the said last mentioned mare, escaped, ran off, and was wholly lost to the said plaintiff, towit, on the day and year aforesaid, at the county and circuit aforesaid—

And whereas afterwards towit on the day and year aforesaid, at the county and circuit aforesaid, the plaintiff was lawfully possessed as of his own property of one other black mare of the value of one hundred dollars, and being so possessed thereof he the said plaintiff, afterwards towit, on the day and year last aforesaid at the county and circuit aforesaid came to the possession of the defendant by finding— Yet the said defendant well knowing the said last mentioned black mare to be the property of the plaintiff and of right to belong and appurtain to him hath not as yet delivered the said black mare to the plaintiff although often requested so to do and hath hitherto wholly refused to do so and afterwards towit on the same day and year aforesaid at the county and circuit aforesaid converted and disposed of the said last mentioned mare to his own use—

By reason of all which the plaintiff says he has been injured and sustained damage to one hundred dollars and therefore he brings his suit &c.

Stuart & Lincoln for plff——

And the Defendant comes and defends the wrong and injury, when where &c and says he is not guilty in manner and form as the plaintiff in his declaration hath alleged and of this he puts himself upon the country

Logan & Baker

&the plaintiff doth the like

Lincoln p q——

John E. Roll ⎱
    vs.   ⎰ Decln
John Anderson
Filed Feby 19th 1838
Wm. Butler Clk

PRAECIPE IN THE SUIT OF STONE & COMPANY VS. HUGHES, SANGAMON CIRCUIT COURT, FEBRUARY 21, 1838
(Herndon-Weik Collection)

This praecipe is the forerunner of a declaration, February 23, 1838, in the hand of Mr. Lincoln. It was penned by Stuart, as were the cover notations, with the exception of the date of filing. Stuart spelled "business" correctly from the modern view, and in this was unlike Lincoln. He used "damages," whereas Mr. Lincoln more frequently used "damage." There is marked contrast in the care and neat penmanship of the papers of the junior partner with the hurried scrawl of those by Stuart.

James S. Stone & Zachariah R. Hinckly Trading and doing business under the Style and firm of J. S. Stone & Co. vs. Joel Hughes	Trespass on the case in Assumpsit **Damages. $350.00.**

The Clerk of the Sangamon Circuit Court will issue a summons for the Defendant in the above cause returnable to the next Term of said Court.

                     Stuart & Lincoln
                        Attos for Plffs—

J. S. Stone & Co
     vs.   Precipe
Joel Hughes
Filed Feby 21. 1838
        Wm Butler cx

DECLARATION IN THE SUIT OF WRIGHT VS. BROOKS AND SHACKLEFORD, SANGAMON CIRCUIT COURT, FEBRUARY 23, 1838,
(Herndon-Weik Collection)

This declaration was drawn by Mr. Lincoln, and the cover notations are by him with the exception of the date of filing.

He spelled "whereas" as "wheras," and "tresspass" as "tress-
pass," minor points, but blots on his record as a champion speller.
The note appears to be in the hand of John Taylor. The minute
word, "Dam," and the figure, "$200," are in the hand of Mr.
Lincoln, as are the words upon the cover, "Pay to Erastus
Wright." The concluding part of the cover, beginning with "7
from Taylor" may be the work of Mr. Lincoln's pen, but it is
so small and blurred that it does not offer conclusive evidence
of such a fact. Judgment was rendered in favor of Wright, the
Stuart & Lincoln client, on October 15, 1838. On March 9, 1839,
Shackleford was made a party to the judgment obtained against
Brooks, in the preceding October.

State ofIllinois ⎫   In the circuit court of
Sangamon county ⎬ ss said county
& Circuit ⎭   March Term— 1838—

Erastus Wright plaintiff complains of Charles G. Brooks and
James . . Shackleford being in custody &c. of a plea of Tresspass
on the case upon promises: For that wheras the said defendants,
heretofore, towit, on the third day of August in the year of our
Lord one thousand eight hundred and thirtysix, at the county
and circuit aforesaid made their certain promissory note in writing (the said Brooks signing his name "C..G. Brooks" and the
said Shackelford signing his name "Jas M. Shackelford") bearing date the day and year aforesaid, and thereby then and there
promised to pay, Twelve months after the date thereof to one
John Taylor or order the sum of one hundred dollars to bear
interest at the rate of twelve per cent, per annum, for value received, and then and there delivered the said promissory note to
the said John Taylor—And the said John Taylor to whom or
to whose order the payment of the said sum of money in the
said promissory note specified was to be made, after the making
of the said promissory note, before the payment of the said sum
of money therein specified, towit, on the day and year aforesaid,
at the county and circuit aforesaid, assigned the said promissory
note, by indorsement in writing thereon, by which said assignment, he the said John Taylor then and there ordered and appointed the said sum of money in the said promissory note specified to be paid to the said plaintiff, and then and there delivered
the said promissory note so assigned as aforesaid to the said
plaintiff, by means whereof, and by force of the statute in such
case made and provided, the said defendants then and there became liable to pay to the said plaintiff the said sum of money in

the said promissory note specified according to the tenor and effect of the said promissory note; and being so liable, they the said defendants in consideration thereof, afterwards towit, on the day and year aforesaid, at the county and circuit aforesaid, undertook, and then and there faithfully promised the said plaintiff to pay him the said sum of money in the said promissory note specified, according to the tenor and effect thereof—

Yet the said defendants (although often requested sotodo) have not as yet paid to the said plaintiff the said sum of money in the said promissory note specified, or any part thereof; but so to do have hitherto wholly neglected and refused, and still do neglect and refuse— To the damage of the said plaintiff of two hundred dollars, and therefore he sues &c.

Stuart & Lincoln
for plff—

The following is a copy of the instrument declared on:

$100

Twelve months after date we or either of us promise to pay John Taylor or order one hundred dollars to bear interest at the rate of Twelve per Cent per Annum—August 3d 1836

C. G. Brooks

T. O. C.   Jas M Shackelford
   Dam $200
C. G. Brooks
& J. M Shackelford

          ———

   Note $100

          ———

Pay to Erastus Wright
        John Taylor
    7 from Taylor
  100 Shackelford Note

  178 belongs to
        Morgan & Nigrod [?]
Erastus Wright
        ⎫
  vs   ⎬ Declaration
        ⎭
Charles G. Brooks &
Jas M. Shackelford—
Filed Feby 23, 1838
        Wm Butler ck

DECLARATION IN THE SUIT OF HERNDON VS. SUDDUTH ET AL, SANGAMON CIRCUIT COURT, FEBRUARY 23, 1838
(Herndon-Weik Collection)

This declaration and note are in the hand of Mr. Lincoln. The cover notations with the exception of the date of filing were also penned by him. The mis-spelling of "promise" in the note as "promis" is due to quotation by Lincoln and not his lack of knowledge of the correct spelling. The plaintiff, Archer Herndon, was the rather fiery parent of William H. Herndon, Mr. Lincoln's future partner. The elder Herndon, like his son, was a close friend of Mr. Lincoln. It may be that Mr. Lincoln erred in the penning of "Davis Robertson" in the declaration and quoted note, for the correct person was Davis Robinson. Such mistakes were not common with Mr. Lincoln, and Mr. Robinson must have been known to him, as he was the one nominee of the south fork of the Sangamon to remain in the race for the Legislature against the Whig "Junto" headed by Lincoln, Baker et al in 1838. The entry in the Record book is a long one. Davis Robinson defaulted in the case, whereupon the court ordered a judgment for $365.00, the debt mentioned in the declaration. The clerk assessed damages at four dollars and fifty-six cents, which assessment was approved by the court. Robinson was ordered to pay court costs, and as a final part of the decree of March 9, 1838, the court ordered the issue of a summons in the form of scire facias to Sudduth and Young demanding that they come and show cause why they should not be made parties to the judgment rendered against Robinson.

State of Illinois ⎫
Sangamon county ⎬ ss   In the circuit court of said county—March term— 1838—
& Circuit ⎭

Archer G. Herndon, plaintiff complains of William H. Sudduth, Davis Robertson and Ezekiel S. Young defendants being in custody &c of a plea that they render to the said plaintiff the sum of three hundred and sixtyfive dollars, lawful money &c which they owe to and unjustly detain from him:

For that whereas the said defendants heretofore, towit, on the twentythird day of October in the year of our Lord one thousand eight hundred and thirtyseven at the county and circuit aforesaid, by their certain writing obligatory, sealed with their seals and now shown to the court &c. the date whereof is the day and year aforesaid, acknowledged themselves to be held and firmly bound unto one Leroy L. Hill in the sum of three hundred and sixtyfive dollars above demanded to be paid to the said Leroy L. Hill Sixty days after the date of the said writing obligatory and then and there delivered the same to the said Leroy L. Hill,— And the said Leroy L. Hill to whom the payment of the said sum of money in the said writing obligatory specified was to be made after the making of the said writing obligatory, before the payment of the said sum of money therein specified, towit, on the day and year aforesaid, at the county and circuit aforesaid, assigned the said writing obligatory, by an assignment in writing on the back thereof—by which said assignment he the said Leroy L. Hill then and there ordered and appointed the said sum of money in the said writing obligatory specified to be paid to the said plaintiff, and then and there delivered the said writing obligatory so assigned as aforesaid to the said plaintiff, by means whereof, and by force of the statute in such case made and provided the said defendants then and there became liable to pay to the said plaintiff the said sum of money in the said writing obligatory specified, according to the tenor and effect of the said writing obligatory—

Yet the said defendants (although often requested so to do) have not as yet paid to the said plaintiff the said sum of money in the said writing obligatory specified, or any part thereof; but so to do have hitherto wholly neglected and refused, and still neglect and refuse— To the damage of the said plaintiff of the sum of three hundred dollars and therefore he sues &c.

Stuart & Lincoln
for Plff

The following is a copy of the instrument declared on:
"Oct th 23. 1837

"Sixty days after date we jointly and severally promis to pay Leroy L. Hill three hundred and sixtyfive dollars for value received this day and date above written

William H Sudduth & Davis Robertson (Seal)
E. S Young (Seal)

Archer G. Herndon
vs.
William H. Sudduth &
others ————
Filed Feby 23. 1838
Wm Butler ck

DECLARATION IN THE SUIT OF STONE & COMPANY VS. HUGHES, SANGAMON CIRCUIT COURT, FEBRUARY 23, 1838

(Herndon-Weik Collection)

This declaration and the cover notations were penned by Mr. Lincoln, with the exception of the date of filing. He spelled "business," as "bussiness," a common error in more than one of his legal papers. The informal spelling of the day may have permitted of this, although Mr. Lincoln had gone through Noah Webster's spelling book of the period. The case is listed in some instances as "Stone vs. Hughes," but Lincoln distinctly wrote "Hughs" upon every occasion on which he used the name and it may have been omitted in \the first part of the above docu-name in filing the praecipe in the case. Certain marks of punctuation employed by Mr. Lincoln, and appearing in his other legal papers, may have been omitted in the first part of the above document, but the faded ink does not justify putting them in as an authentic copy of the original paper. The entry by the clerk in this case gives Zenas R. Hinkley instead of Zachariah Hinckley as cited by Mr. Lincoln, but in more than one case, Attorney Lincoln gave a more correct citation than his friend, Butler. On March 7, 1839 the clerk recorded a judgment by default, amounting to $237.37 in debt and damages, with costs assessed against the defendant.

State of Illinois ⎫   In the Circuit Court of said
Sangamon county & ⎬ ss   county— March Term— 1838
Circuit— ⎭

James S. Stone and Zachariah R. Hinckley, trading and doing bussiness under the style and firm of "J. S. Stone & Co" plaintiffs complain of Joel Hughs defendant being in custody &c of a plea of Tresspass on the case in assumpsit: For that whereas the said defendant, heretofore to wit, on the thirtyfirst day of October in the year of our Lord one thousand eight hundred and thirtyseven at Alton that is to say at the county and circuit aforesaid, made his certain promissory note in writing bearing date the day and year aforesaid, and thereby then and there promised to pay, three months after the date thereof, to the said plaintiffs or order, the sum of one hundred and twenty-two dollars and eighty hundredths of a dollar for value received, and then and there delivered the said promissory note to the said plaintiffs; by means whereof, and by force of the statute in such

case made and provided the said defendant became liable to pay
to the said plaintiffs the said sum of money in the said promissory note specified according to the tenor and effect of the said
promissory note; and being so liable, he, the said defendant, in
consideration thereof, afterwards towit, on the day and year
aforesaid, at the county and circuit aforesaid, undertook, and
then and there faithfully promised the said plaintiffs to pay them,
the said sum of money in the said promissory note specified according to the tenor and effect thereof— And whereas the said
defendant also afterwards towit, on the day and year aforesaid,
at Alton, towit, at the county and circuit aforesaid, made his
certain other promissory note in writing, bearing date the day
and year aforesaid, and thereby then and there promised to pay,
Forty days after the date thereof, to the said plaintiffs or order
the sum of one hundred dollars for value received, and then and
there delivered the said last mentioned promissory note to the
said plaintiffs; by means whereof, and by force of the statute
in such case made and provided, the said defendant became liable
to pay to the said plaintiffs the said sum of money in the said
promissory note specified according to the tenor and effect of
the said promissory note; and being so liable he, the said defendant, in consideration thereof afterwards, towit, on the day
and year aforesaid at the county and circuit aforesaid, undertook,
and there faithfully promised the said plaintiffs to pay them the
said sum of money in the said last mentioned promissory note
specified according to the tenor and effect thereof—Yet the said
defendant, (although often requested so to do) hath not as yet
paid the said sums of money in the said several promissory notes
specified, or either of them or any part thereof to the said plaintiffs, but so to do, hath hitherto wholly neglected and refused,
and still doth neglect and refuse: To the damage of the said plaintiffs of three hundred and fifty dollars, and therefore they sue &c.

Stuart & Lincoln
for plaintiffs—

The following are copies of the instruments declared on:
" $ 122. 80/100   Alton   Oct 31. 1837

Three months after date I promise to
pay J. S. Stone &Co or order one hundred
twentytwo 80/100 Dollars value received, paya
ble at the Branch Bank State of Illinois at Alton.

Joel Hughs "

" "100-00   Alton   Oct 31. 1837
          Forty days after date I promise to pay
          J. S. Stone &Co or order one hundred dollars value
          received payable at Branch Bank State of Illinois at
          Alton

                                        Joel Hughs"

J. S. Stone &Co

vs } Declaration

Joel Hughs

Filed Feby 23, 1838
     Wm Butler   ck

DECLARATION IN THE SUIT OF COLBURN VS. WALLACE, SANGAMON CIRCUIT COURT, FEBRUARY 23, 1838

(Herndon-Weik Collection)

This declaration and cover notations, with the exception of the date of filing, were penned by Mr. Lincoln. There seems to be an omission which was to be filled in, as the crossing out of the words, "Yet the said defendant although," leaves the preceding clause, and the following one without meaning. It is said that John T. Stuart amended a paragraph in the document, but the original in the Herndon-Weik Collection reveals no other handwriting than that of Lincoln. William Wallace, defendant, may have been Dr. William Wallace, who married Frances Todd, sister of Mary Todd. This suit occurred about a year before the marriage, and Lawyer Lincoln perhaps caused his future relative more than passing discomfiture. A judgment was rendered by default in favor of Colburn. The sum awarded was $234.60.

This document is incorrectly cited in the Herndon-Weik Collection as a legal paper in the case of Langford vs. Johnson. As such it presents the client of Mr. Lincoln suing himself for recovery of damages. It appears that it may be definitely placed as the amendment to the original declaration in the case of Colburn vs. Wallace, which is dated as of February 23, 1838. There is a star over the word "afterwards" in the amendment, and one preceding the crossed out words, "Yet the said defendant," in the original declaration. There are no instructions as to the use of the two stars, but if the amendment beginning with the words, "And whereas also afterwards Towit," be placed at the star in the

*declaration of February 23, 1838 and followed through to its con-
clusion, it will be seen that it fits into the case of Colburn vs. Wallace. The amendment clarifies that seeming vague meaning of the
original declaration, for now, the words seemingly omitted by
Attorney Lincoln are filled in, and the declaration and amendment give the complete sense of the document.*

*The amendment was the co-operative work of Lawyers Stu-
art and Lincoln. The latter penned the words, "and whereas
also," and after this Stuart took up the work of writing, and continued on the clause, "bearing the day and year aforesaid." Here
Mr. Lincoln resumed with his hand and pen, and went to the
concluding word, "although," at which point the declaration is
resumed in the original declaration.*

State of Illinois ⎫
Sangamon county ⎬ ss   In the circuit court of said
& Circuit ⎭   county—March term— 1838—

    Ebenezer Colburn, plaintiff, complains of William Wallace
defendant, being in custody &c of a plea of Trespass in the case
in assumpsit: For that whereas the said defendant heretofore
towit, on the seventh day of July in the year of our Lord one
thousand eight hundred and thirty seven at the county and circuit aforesaid, made his certain promissory note in writing bearing date the day and year aforesaid, and thereby then and there
promised to pay, on or before the first day of November then
next ensuing, to one E. G. Johns the sum of two hundred and
thirty dollars, for value received, with the condition that the
same might be discharged in lumber and Carpenter's work in
building or finishing off a house in the town of Springfield, unless it should be otherwise agreed, and then and there delivered
the said promissory note to the said E. G. Johns: and the said
E. G. Johns to whom the payment of the said sum of money or
property and labour in the said promissory note specified was to
be made, after the making the said promissory note, and before
the payment of the said sum of money or property and labour
therein specified, towit, on the day and year aforesaid at the
county and circuit aforesaid, assigned the said promissory note
by indorsement in writing thereon, by which said assignment,
he the said E. G. Johns then and there ordered and appointed
the said sum of money or property and labour in the said promissory note specified, to be paid to one James P. Langford, and
then and there delivered the said promissory note so assigned to
the said James P. Langford: and the said James P. Langford to

whom the payment of the said sum of money or property and labour, in the said promissory note specified was by the said assignment directed to be made, after the making of the said promissory note, and before the payment of the said sum of money, or property and labour therein specified, to wit, on the day and year aforesaid, at the county and circuit aforesaid, assigned the said promissory note by indorsement in writing thereon, by which said last mentioned assignment, he the said James P. Langford then and there ordered and appointed the said sum of money, or property and labour, in the said promissory note specified to be paid to the said plaintiff, and then and there delivered the said promissory note to the said plaintiff, by means whereof and by force of the statute in such case made and provided, the said defendant then and there became liable to pay to the said plaintiff the said sum of money or property and labour in the said promissory note specified, according to the tenor and effect of the said promissory note; and being so liable, he the said defendant ,in consideration thereof, afterwards, towit, on the day and year aforesaid, at the county and circuit aforesaid undertook, and then and there faithfully promised the said plaintiff to pay him the said sum of money, or property and labour, in the said promissory note specified, according to the tenor and effect thereof—(often requested so to do) hath not as yet paid to the said plaintiff, the said sum of money or property and labour in the said promissory note specified, or any part thereof; but so to do hath hitherto wholly neglected and refused, and still does neglect and refuse: To the damage of the said plaintiff of the sum of four hundred dollars and therefore he sues &c

Stuart & Lincoln
for plaintiff—

The following is a copy of the instrument declared on:
"On or before the first day of November next I promise to pay E. G. Johns two hundred and &thirty dollars, which may be discharged in lumber and Carpenter's work in building or finishing off a house, for value received this 7th day of July 1837—said work to be done in the town of Springfield unless otherwise agreed hereafter

William Wallace"

(First assignment)

"for value received I assign the within note to James P. Langford   E. G. Johns

(Second assignment)

"for value received I assign the within note to Ebenezer Colburn

J. P. Langford"

104

Ebenezer Colburn

vs. } Declaration

William Wallace

Filed Feby 23, 1838
   Wm Butler clk

PART OF COLBURN VS. WALLACE DECLARATION
(Undated in the Herndon-Weik Collection)

And whereas also afterwards Towit on the Day and year last aforesaid at the County & Circuit aforesaid the said Defendant then & there made his certain other Promissory Note in writing bearing the day and year aforesaid, and thereby then and there promised to pay, on or before the first day of November then next ensuing, to one E. G. Johns the sum of two hundred and thirty dollars, for value received, with the condition that the same might be discharged in lumber and carpenter's work in building or finishing off a house in the town of Springfield, unless it should be otherwise agreed, and then and there delivered the said promissory note to the said E. G. Johns: And the said E. G. Johns to whom the payment of the said sum of money or property and labour in the said promissory note specified, was to be made, after the making of the said promissory note, and before the payment of the said per some of money or property and labour therein specified, towit, on the day and year aforesaid, assigned the said promissory note by indorsement in writing thereon, by which said assignment, he the said E. G. Johns then and there ordered and appointed the said sum of money or property and labour in the said promissory note specified, to be paid to one James P. Langford, and then and there delivered the said promissory note so assigned to the said James P. Langford: And the said James P. Langford to whom the payment of the said promissory note specified, was by the said assignment directed to be made, after the making of the said promissory note, and before the payment of the said sum of money or property and labour therein specified, to wit on the day and year aforesaid, at the county and circuit aforesaid, assigned the said promissory note by indorsement thereon in writing, by which said last mentioned assignment, he the said James P. Langford then and there ordered and appointed the said sum of money, or property and labour in the said promissory note specified to be paid to the said plaintiff, and then and there delivered the said promissory note to the said plaintiff; by means whereof, and by force of the statute in such case made and provided, the said defendant then and there became liable to pay to the said plaintiff the said sum of money, or property and labour, in the said promissory note specified according to the tenor and effect of the said promissory note; and being so liable, he the said defendant, in consideration thereof afterwards towit, on the day and year aforesaid, at the county and circuit aforesaid, undertook, and then and there faithfully promised the said plaintiff to pay him the said sum of money or property and labour in the said promissory note specified according to the tenor and effect thereof— And the said plaintiff in fact saith, that on and before the first day of November in the said promissory note mentioned, he the said plaintiff attended at the said town of Springfield, and demanded of the said defendant, the payment of the said lumber and carpenter's work in the said promissory note mentioned—Yet the said defandant (although

DECLARATION IN THE SUIT OF MASON ET AL VS. RENSHAW ET AL, SANGAMON CIRCUIT COURT, FEBRUARY 23, 1838

(Herndon-Weik Collection)

The declaration and cover notations in this case, the filing date excepted, were drawn by Mr. Lincoln. He mis-spelled 'cattle" in one place, using the word, "cattels." The division of "thirty-three" into two words in the first citation of "one hundred and thirty three" is one of the few instances in which Mr. Lincoln makes a separation of such words. He usually separates them when reaching the margin of the page, or in quoted notes, but in the latter he frequently writes the words as one. The words "were of" preceding James Mason in line two do not give clarity to the sentence, and there is error in "were" for "where". The usual care with which Mr. Lincoln penned his hundreds of legal papers seems lacking to a slight degree, but a few errors in about 1000 is excused by the best critics. The letters, "ss" which follow the county name in many legal papers, are translated most often into the English, "to wit," as they are supposedly a contraction of the Latin word, "scilicet." The case of Mason & Mason vs. the Renshaws was decided in favor of the latter party, on March 7, 1839, when the Masons, through Attorney Lincoln, asked that the case be dismissed.

State of Illinois
Sangamon county
& Circuit—

In the circuit court of said county—March term— 1838—

    Sarah Mason and Paris Mason, plaintiffs, administratrix and administrator of all and singular the goods and chattels, and credits, of James Mason deceased, at the time of his death, who died intestate, complain of Harman Renshaw and Samuel Renshaw defendants, being in custody &c of a plea that they render to the said plaintiffs one hundred and thirtythree dollars and fiftyeight hundreds of a dollar which they unjustly detain from them. For that whereas the said defendant on the second day of November in the year of our Lord one thousand eight hundred and thirty at the county and circuit aforesaid, by their certain writing obligatory sealed with their seals and now shown to the court &c the date whereof is the same day and year aforesaid, acknowledged themselves to be held and firmly bound to the said James Mason in his life time in the said sum of one hundred and thirtythree and fiftyeight hundredths of a dollar above demanded to be paid to the said James Mason or order six months after the date of the said writing obligatory together with interest on the said sum of money therein specified, at the rate of thirtyfive per cent (meaning thirtyfive pre cent per annum) from the time the said sum of money in the said writing obligatory specified should become due until paid—Nevertheless the said defendants (although often requested so to do) have not as yet paid the said sum of one hundred and thirtythree dollars and fiftyeight hundredths of a dollar above demanded, or any part thereof, to the said James Mason in his lifetime, or to the said plaintiffs since the decease of the said James Mason (to which said plaintiffs after the death of the said James Mason, towit on the   day of   in the year of our Lord one thousaind eight hundred and thirty   at Edwardsville, towit, at the county and circuit aforesaid, administration of all singular the goods and chattels and credits which were of the said James Mason deceased at the time of his death who died intestate, by the Judge of Probate of the county of) but they so to do, have hitherto wholly refused and still refuse to pay the same; or any part thereof, to the said plaintiffs as administratrix and administrator aforesaid. To the damage of the said plaintiffs as administratrix and administrator as aforesaid of four hundred dollars, and therefore they bring their suit. &c—And the said plaintiffs bring into court here the letters of Administration of the said Judge of Probate, which give sufficient evidence to the said court here of the grant of administration to the said plaintiffs as aforesaid, the date whereof is the day and year in that behalf above mentioned &c.

Stuart &Lincoln
for plaintiffs—

The following is a copy of the instrument declared on:
"$ 133.58   Sangamo County   2 Nov. 1830
Six months after date we or either of us promise to pay James Mason or order the sum of one hundred &Thirty three 58/100 dollars for value received— This note tc draw thirtyfive per cent interest after it becomes due until paid, witness our hands & seals

Herman Renshaw (Seal)
Samuel Renshaw (Seal)

123

Sarah Mason &
Paris Mason

vs } Declaration

Harman Renshaw
Samuel Renshaw—
Filed Feby 23, 1838
   Wm Butler ck

ENTRY IN THE FEE BOOK OF STUART & LINCOLN

The junior partner made this entry against Harrison as he did many others in the noted fee book of Stuart and Lincoln.
Peyton L. Harrison
To Stuart & Lincoln   Dr.
1838 March —— To case with Dickinson——$10-00

DEFENDANT'S PLEA IN THE SUIT OF FLEMING VS. RANSDELL, MARCH 6, 1838
(Herndon-Weik Collection)

This plea is in the hand of Mr. Lincoln, while the cover notations were penned by Butler. An account of this case will be found in the note to the documents for September 16-26, 1838.

Wharton Ransdell ⎫
     ads   ⎬
Samuel Fleming ⎭

And the said defendant comes and defends the wrong and injury when, where &c. and says he did not undertake or promise in manner and form as the said plaintiff hath above complained against him, and of this he puts himself upon the county—

Stuart & Lincoln

S. Fleming
for Defendant

    ⎫
vs ⎬
    ⎭

Wharton Ransdell
Filed Mar 6th 1838
Wm. Butler Clk

PLEA IN THE SUIT OF SINNARD VS. RANSDELL, SANGAMON CIRCUIT COURT, MARCH 6, 1838

Herndon-Weik Collection)

Mr. Lincoln penned this plea, while the cover notations are in the hand of Butler. The clerk wrote Sinard with one "n" while Mr. Lincoln used the double "nn," for the name of the plaintiff. Stuart & Lincoln asked security for costs from the plaintiff on March 5, 1838, and followed with the plea next day. It is possible that there are further entries regarding this case in the Court Record, but studies to date have not brought them to light.

Joseph Kyle ⎫
    ats   ⎬ And the said Joseph Kyle by his attorney
John L. Sinnard ⎭ comes and defends the wrong and injury, when &c. and says that he is not guilty of the said supposed grienvances above laid to his charge, or any or either of them, in manner and form as the said John L. Sinnard hath above thereof complained against him— And of this the said Joseph Kyle puts himself upon the country &c—

J. L. Sinard
Stuart & Lincoln
for Deft

     ⎫
vs ⎬ plea
     ⎭

Joseph Kyle

Filed Marc 6th 1838
  Wm Butler Clk

LETTER FROM MR. LINCOLN TO LEVI DAVIS
OF VANDALIA

Mr. Lincoln writes his good friend Levi Davis of Vandalia making excuses for delay in attending to the affairs of some of the latter's clients. There has been good reason for the delay, but it has worked no harm. Levi Davis, who like David Davis, was born in Cecil County, Maryland, was then serving as state auditor, but in 1846 took up his residence at Alton where for many years he was a leader at the bar. He died in 1897 in his ninety-first year.

Springfield, March 15, 1838

Levi Davis, Esq.,
     Vandalia, Ill.

Dear Sir: We received yours of the 2nd inst., by due course of mail and have only to offer in excuse for not answering sooner, that we have been in a great state of confusion here ever since the receipt of your letter, and also, that your clients cannot suffer by the delay.   The suit is merely instituted to quiet a title which has passed through Dr. Stapp, but to which he now lays no claim as we understand—he is a mere nominal party to the proceeding—more than all this, we believe nothing will or can be done with the case at this court. We beg your pardon for our neglect in this business; if it had been important to you and your client we would have done better.

Yours truly,
     Stuart and Lincoln.

AFFIDAVIT IN THE SUIT OF GOODACRE VS. SIMP-SON, SANGAMON CIRCUIT COURT, MARCH 17, 1838
(Herndon-Weik Collection)

This affidavit was drawn by Mr. Lincoln, and signed by Goodacre. The notations signed by Butler are in his hand. The case involved the sale of a mare to Simpson, and misrepresentation of her age and condition. As is seen by the affidavit, the case was first tried before a jury in the court of a justice of peace. It was heard by a jury before the Sangamon County Court on March 16, 1838, and a decision rendered in favor of the defendant. The Court Record entries for the July, 1838 and October, 1838 terms reveal no information upon the action taken on this affidavit filed one day after the jury had returned a verdict in favor of Simpson. Mr. Lincoln represented Goodacre, who did not sign his name as penned by Clerk Butler on the cover of the document.

William Goodacre ⎫   Sangamon Circuit court—
             vs   ⎬   On appeal from Justice of the Peace
Simpson   ⎭

    William Goodacre, being duly sworn, says that since going to trial in this court in the above case, he has discovered new testimony, which he is advised and believes would be of materiality in this case, and of the existence of which, he was not before apprised—He states that he is informed and verrily believes that James Weeden will swear that he raised the mare in question in this case, and that she was not more than nine years old at the time this affiant sold her to the said Simpson; and that said James Weeden now resides in Sangamon County, and this affiant believes he will be able to procure his attendance at the next term of this court— This affiant further states that this case, previous to its being brought to this court on appeal was tried by jury before one of the Justices of the Peace of this county, and that on said trial before said Justice of the Peace, no evidence was offered by the defendant Simpson to prove that the said mare was more than nine years old when this affiant sold her to him, said defendant; that from the nature of the case, no written pleadings are necessary, by which this affiant, the plaintiff, might be notified at the defense relied on by the defendant, that in fact, no notice of any kind was given him, that proof of the mare being more than nine years old when he sold her to the defendant would be offered on the trial in this court; and that consequently he was taken wholly by surprise by this part of the defendants testimony, which he believes is untrue, and that he can rebut it by the testimony of the witness above named—

Wm Goodaker

Sworn to and subscribed
before me this 17th day
of March, 1838
       Wm Butler Clk

Goodacre ⎫
      vs   ⎬ affa
Simpson ⎭ Filed Mch 18th, 1838,

      Wm Butler, Clk.

A NOTE WHICH HELPED TO ASSURE THE STATE CAPITAL TO SPRINGFIELD

The note with its imposing array of signers here reproduced had an important part in the removal of the capital of Illinois from Vandalia to Springfield. The bill providing for the transfer approved on February 25, 1837, contained a clause which stipulated that the citizens of the town chosen should contribute at least $50,000 toward the construction of the capital building, and not less than two acres of land as a site for it. Many regarded the $50,000 proviso as placing too heavy a burden on a town of a little more than 1,000 inhabitants, and when the Legislature convened in special session in December, 1839, Stephen A. Douglas, then a member from Morgan County, proposed a bill releasing Springfield from its obligation.

The rest of the story is told in John C. Powers' History of the Early Settlers of Sangamon County, Springfield, 1876. "'The sterling honesty of Abraham Lincoln," writes Mr. Powers, "manifested itself on this, as on all other proper occasions. He interposed his objections, although he fully appreciated the kindly feeling that prompted the proposal; but he insisted that the money should be paid. Arrangements were entered into for paying it in three installments. The two first payments were made without any great difficulty; but the third pressed more heavily, as the financial crash that swept over the whole United States, while the new state house was in course of construction, impoverished many. It became necessary to borrow from the State Bank of Illinois to make the last payment.

"A note for the amount was signed by one hundred and one citizens and deposited with the bank, the money drawn with which internal improvement scrip or stock was purchased and paid into the state treasury, thus paying the last instalment in the state's own evidence of indebtedness. From that time it was a matter between the State Bank and the citizens who signed the note. Soon after the note was given the State Bank failed, and some of the payments were made in its securities, for which it had received par value when it was paid out." Final settlement was made on February 19, 1846, when the principal and interest totalled $17,918. The original note is preserved in a Springfield bank.

$16,666.67   Springfield, March 22, 1838

One year after date, we, the undersigned, or either of us, promise to pay to the President, Directors and Company of the

State Bank of Illinois, sixteen thousand, six hundred and sixty-six dollars and sixty-seven cents, for value received, negotiable and payable at the bank, in Springfield, with interest until paid, at the rate of six per centum per annum, payable semi-annually.

John Hay,
L. Higby,
Joseph Thayer,
William Thornton,
M. O. Reeves,
W. P. Grimsley,
William Wallace,
John B. Watson,
C. H. Ormsby,
Moses Coffman,
Geo. Pasfield,
B. C. Webster,
S. M. Tinsley,
Ephriam Darling,
Jona. Merriam,
Ira Sanford,
Charles Arnold,
John L. Turner,
Joshua F. Amos,
Sullivan Conant,
And. McClellan,
Alexander Shields,
A. Trailor,
C. C. Phelps,
R. B. Zimmerman,
William Hall,
James L. Lamb,
M. L. Knapp,
Thomas Mather,
Tho. Houghan,
D. Prickett,
J. Calhoun,
Josiah Francis,
Washington Iles,

Joel Johnson,
C. B. Francis,
Wm. S. Burch,
J. M. Shackleford,
B. Ferguson,
Benjamin Talbott,
Jesse Cormack,
B. C. Johnson,
Thomas Moffatt,
John F. Rague,
Simeon Francis,
Nathaniel Hay,
Robert Irwin,
Virgil Hickox,
George Trotter,
Stephen T. Logan,
Robert Allen,
James R. Gray,
J. Adams,
J. S. Britton,
W. B. Powell,
F. C. Thompson,
E. M. Henkle,
James W. Keyes,
Wm. Porter,
Wm. H. Marsh,
W. Ransdell,
Joshua S. Hobbs,
John G. Bergen,
B. S. Clement,
C. R. Matheny,
William Butler,
P. C. Canedy,
Jos. Klein,

P. C. Latham,
A. G. Henry,
Ninian W. Edwards,
John T. Stuart,
Jonas Whitney,
Erastus Wright,
John Todd,
E. D. Baker,
A. Lincoln,
Garrett Elkin,
John Capps,
Alexr. Garrett,
Gershom Jayne,
T. M. Neale,
William G. Abrams,
Dewey Whitney,
M. Mobley,
Foley Vaughn,
Abner Y. Ellis,
N. A. Rankin,
S. H. Treat,
Elijah Iles,
Henry F. Luckett,
James P. Langford,
Henry Cassequin,
J. M. Cabaniss,
James Maxcy,
Z. P. Cabaniss,
E. G. Johns,
Amos Camp,
Thos. J. Goforth,
Benj. F. Jewett,
W. M. Cowgill.

GROUNDS FOR APPEAL AND BOND FOR COSTS IN SUIT OF CANNON VS. KINNEY, APRIL 2, 1838

(Herndon-Weik Collection

The documents here reproduced are in the hand of Attorney Lincoln with the exception of the signatures of Joseph Smith and J. P. Anderson. The notations upon the cover are in the hand of William Butler, clerk, who signed himself incorrectly, "Buter." Lincoln writes Kinney clearly as the name of the defendant, while Butler, gives the case as "Cannon vs. Kinney." On March 7, 1838 Cannon had been ordered to give security by March 15. It will be noted that Joseph Smith and J. P. Anderson entered themselves as security, a fact which Lincoln filed with this Document of Error to Sangamon. Stuart and Lincoln had appeared for Cannon when he was ordered to give security, and on July 8, 1841, as will be recorded later, Mr. Lincoln argued this case for his plaintiff, Cannon, before the Supreme Court of Illinois, one of his first appearances before that tribunal.

In the Supreme court for the state of Illinois—

Manly F. **Cannon**
     vs.   **Error to Sangamon**—
Matthew P. **Kinney**

This was an action of Tresspass brought for the seizing and converting of a certain horse—

Plea: Not guilty—At the trial a jury was empanneled; and the plaintiff introduced his witnesses and proved that at a certain time he was the absolute owner of said horse, when he, in the lead-mine country, gratuitously loaned said horse to one John Harris, to be ridden to Sangamon county; that said Harris rode him to Sangamon, and placed him in the hands of one James Harris, his brother to be fed and safely kept, promising to pay for the feeding and keeping, and saying nothing as to who owned him; that said James Harris, after keeping the horse a while placed him in the hands of one Robert Harris, another brother for feeding and safe keeping; that said Robert Harris, so kept him until the rising of grass in the spring, when he turned him on the range with other horses of his own, occasionally giving him salt with his own horses; that while said horse was thus running at large, the defendant seized and took him away; said Robert Harris then telling the defendant that he had understood, that the plaintiff claimed said horse as his property; that the horse at the time of the taking by the defendant, was worth sixtyfive dollars, and here closed his case. The defendant then moved the court to instruct the jury as in case of a non-suit, on the assumed ground that the horse was not taken by the defendant from the possession of the plaintiff; which motion was sustained by the court. To this decision of the court, the plaintiff excepted, and pled his Bill of exceptions thereto, embodying the testimony aforesaid all of which appears by the Record in the cause—

The decision granting a nonsuit as aforesaid, is assigned for error in the causes—

The plaintiff, in the argument of the above cause, will rely on the following points, towit:

1st That as to question of *possession* in the action of Tresspass for injuries to personal property, it is sufficient for the plaintiff to show that he had a *constructive possession* of the property, at the time of the defendants seizing or injuring the same—1st Chitty's Pl. 153.

2nd That in this case, the horse in question was in the *constructive possession* of the plaintiff at the time the defendant seized him 1st Chitty Pl 154—3 John's Digest 575 Bec Ab. tit Ties poss. 577 web 1st Peck Rep. 232—

Lincoln p. q.

Cannon
vs   } Abstract
Kenney

Manly F. Cannon
vs   } Sangamon Circuit Court
Matthew P. Kenney

In Tresspass—

I do hereby enter myself security for costs in this cause and acknowledge myself to pay or cause to be paid all costs which may accrue in this action, either to the opposite party or any of the officers of this court in pursuance of the laws of this state—

Dated this 8th day of February A D 1838

Joseph Smith

Cannon
J P Anderson

vs   } Bond

Kinney

Filed April 2 1838
Wm Butler Clerk

NOTICE FOR TAKING DEPOSITIONS IN THE SUIT
OF McNAIR VS. ADAMS, APRIL 13, 1838
(Herndon-Weik Collection)

The document here reproduced was drawn by Mr. Lincoln. The cover notations are in the hand of Sheriff Elkin, who held that office for four years following 1840, and who earlier as a member of the General Assembly and one of the Long Nine had helped to secure the removal of the state capital from Vandalia to Springfield. In later years his old friend Abraham Lincoln made him registrar of the United States land office at Springfield.

Parmenio Adams was a resident of New York, and one-time member of the New York State Militia, rising from a lieutenancy to be first major. He served in the War of 1812 as major and commandant of New York Volunteers, being stationed on the Niagara frontier. He was twice sheriff of Genesee County, and later served as a representative in Congress from New York, his term extending from January 7, 1824 to March 3, 1827. He died in 1832 at the age of 56 years.

The Dedimus Potestatum was a writ commissioning a private person to execute certain capacities of a judge, in this case, the right to examine a witness. The litigation, as noted elsewhere, continued over a period of years, and on August 9, 1841, the case was changed to the Cass County Circuit Court by agreement of the attorneys for plaintiff and defendant.

Matthew McNair
vs   } In the Sangamon Circuit Court
James Adams   } Assumpsit

The defendant in the above entitled cause will please take notice, that on the fifteenth day of May, next between the hours of 10 o,clock A. M. and 5 o,clock P. M. of said day, the plaintiff herein, will attend at, and sue out from, the clerk's office, in and for the county of Sangamon, state of Illinois, a *dedimus potestatum* for the purpose of taking the depositions of John Grant Jr and others residing in the state of New York; to be read in evidence in the above entitled cause now pending in said court and that the following interrogations are intended to be put to said witnesses—towit;

First—Were you or not acquainted with a man by the name of James Adams, prior to the year 1822?

Second—Where did said Adams reside when you knew him?

Third—Does said Adams still reside there?

Fourth—When did said Adams leave that country?

Fifth—Did said Adams leave that country publicly or privately?

Sixth—About the time the said Adams left the country, did not his family or friends or both circulate a report that he was drowned?

Seventh—State all the particulars, so far as you know, in regard to the general report of the cause and manner of the said Adams' leaving the country at that time—

Eighth—Was or not the said James Adams a reputed brother of one Parmenio Adams, who subsequently was a member of the United States Congress?

Ninth—Was or not the said James Adams usually called "General Adams"?

Tenth—Did or not the said James Adams act in the capacity of an officer in the service of the United States during this last war with Great Britain? and particularly, did he not so act at the capture of Oswego by the British during said war?

April 13th A. D. 1838—   Stuart & Lincoln for Plff

Executed Apl. 14th
1838 on Jas. Adams
by delivering a copy

Service	50
copy	50
Travel	6¼
ritg	12½

$1.18¾

G. Elkin Shff. S. C.

STUART AND LINCOLN AGREE ON A CONTINGENT FEE.

The agreement and note here reproduced were drawn by Mr. Lincoln, who spells balance with two l's; but there is no record of how he and his partner fared in their dealings with their Tazewell county client. The original of the agreement with Crain is now owned by Oliver R. Barrett of Chicago.

Whereas John T. Stuart and Abraham Lincoln have engaged as attorneys in my behalf in a cause now pending in the Chancery side of the Tazewell county circuit court in which I am complainant and the heirs of Lewis H. Crain deceased and others are defendants, therefore if I shall succeed to the full extent of my claim in said case, I promise to pay them the said Stuart & Lincoln the sum of five hundred dollars, but if I should not succeed in the recovery of the property mentioned in said cause as having been purchased of Peter Menard but shall succeed in the recovery of all the ballance claimed in said cause, then I promise to pay them the said Stuart & Lincoln the sum of three hundred dollars—

James W. Crain

April 20. 1838—

Tremont, April 20—1838

Six months after date I promise to pay Stuart & Lincoln twentyfive dollars for value received—

Jas W. Crain

DEBATE BETWEEN LINCOLN AND DOUGLAS AT BLOOMINGTON ABOUT MAY 10, 1838.

During the opening months of 1838 Stuart and Douglas waged a hot fight for a seat in Congress. It had been arranged that they should meet in joint debate at Bloomington during the spring session of the McLean Circuit Court, but Stuart fell ill and Mr. Lincoln took his partner's place. Although there is no record of what passed between Lincoln and Douglas on this occasion, one of those who listened to their debate was Henry Stevens, then a twenty-one year old stage driver, who long afterwards in a letter published in the Bloomington Pantagraph on March 12, 1898, recorded his memories of an encounter of sharp contrasts between two present and future rivals. Mr. Stevens, then in his eighty-second year, wrote in part:

"The old court house is stamped in my memory by its being the theatre of the first contest that I witnessed between Abraham Lincoln and Stephen A. Douglas, who subsequently became so distinguished, the occasion being the canvass for Congress of Douglas & Stewart, Mr. Lincoln having taken the place of the latter on account of illness

"The farmers from the surrounding country had come in (mostly horseback) to hear the debate, and they, with the citizens, gathered on the corner of Main and Front streets (opposite Gridley & Covell's store) and after a preliminary stand up fight (in words) between the Little Giant and David Davis, all with one accord, followed their leaders to the court house. I shall never forget the enthusiasm of the crowd when these giants in debate took the judge's seat, and each in turn (as had been arranged) addressed the audience in half hours alternately, Whigs and Democrats applauding vociferously as their leaders made a score. There was then a more marked difference in the size of the two men than in later years. Douglas had not attained his full stature and tried to make up for it by wearing a tall bell crowned hat which was then worn to some extent."

Four days after Mr. Lincoln met Douglas in Bloomington, on May 14, 1838 at Philadelphia in the presence of a mixed assembly of whites and blacks, Angelina Grimke, who a few years before had left a Quaker household in South Carolina to preach the freedom of the slave in the North, became the wife of Theodore D. Weld. The Welds, which the belated discovery in a New England attic in 1930 of the letters which had been a part of their courtship, instantly won for them a place among the great lovers of history, passed their honeymoon in a New Jersey village they had chosen for it, and during the remainder of the year 1838 the husband, aided by his wife and her sister Sarah, wrote his devastating tract Slavery As It Is, which remained for two decades the favorite text-book of anti-slavery workers. Abraham Lincoln of Springfield may or may not have read Slavery As It Is; but we know that a copy of it fell into the hands of a young housewife and mother of Cincinnati, Harriet Beecher Stowe by name, who later declared that she had found in it motive and material for her Uncle Tom's Cabin. And be it noted, in passing that Mrs. Stowe's story was first published in the National Era, a Washington journal which had for its editor Dr. Gamaliel Bailey, one of Theodore Weld's early converts to abolitionism.

BOND FOR COSTS IN THE SUIT OF NOE VS. CUNNINGHAM, MACON CIRCUIT COURT, MAY 14, 1838
(Lincoln National Life Foundation

The bond here reproduced was penned by Attorney Lincoln, and signed by Findly. Cover notations for the case are the work of the clerk. It will be noted that the bond does not reveal the use of extra spaces which later became characteristic of the Lincoln legal papers. Case records for these recently unearthed documents in the files of the Macon Circuit Court have not been made available; so the cause and result of this case are as yet unknown.

Littleberry Noe ⎫
     vs   ⎬   In the Macon county
James Cunningham ⎭   circuit court

    I do hereby enter myself security for costs in this case and acknowledge myself bound to pay or cause to be paid all costs which may accrue in this action either to the opposite party or to any of the officers of this court in pursuance of the laws of this state—
Dated this 14th day of May A D 1838—

                                     Jasafindly

Noe
  vs
Cunningham

———————

Filed 14th May 1838

    H McGorin clk

AFFIDAVIT OF ADAMS IN THE SUIT OF McNAIR VS. ADAMS, JUNE 13, 1838
(Herndon-Weik Collection)

*   This affidavit and cover notations down to the word, "Affdt.", are in the hand of Samuel H. Treat. James Adams signed the affidavit with a flourish of his pen, and a signature that is full of superfluous lines. Clerk Butler penned the date of filing, while Eastham wrote the note upon the affidavit being sworn before him. Samuel H. Treat, who drew the affidavit, was an able lawyer and jurist. He settled in Springfield in 1834 and in 1839 was appointed judge of the State Circuit Court, being transferred in 1841 to the State Supreme Court. He was chief justice of the Illinois Supreme Court in 1848. President Pierce appointed him United States judge for the Southern District of Illinois, a place he held until his death, in Springfield in 1887, at the age of seventy-six years. The affidavit which he drew is included as part of a long drawn out case, and to give continuity to a study of it.*

Matthew McNair ⎫
     vs   ⎬ In the sangamon circuit court
James Adams ⎭

    James Adams the Defendant in the above entitled cause, being duly sworn saith that he intends taking the depositions of William Arabel Hale, John McFadden, Mary McFadden, Ernest

C. Schryder &——————— Hurd to be read as Evidence on the trial of this cause. That said individuals reside in the county of Peoria & State of Illinois—

Jas Adams

Sworn to before me
this 13 june 1838
     M Eastham J.P.

Adams
  advs.
McNair

———————

Affdt.
Filed June 13, 1838
    Wm Butler ck

DECLARATION OF PLAINTIFF IN THE SUIT OF McNAIR VS. ADAMS, JUNE 19, 1838
(Herndon-Weik Collection)

This declaration, quoted notes, and cover notations were penned by Mr. Lincoln, with the exception of the date of filing, and the concluding notations of "July /41" and "Assumpsit." The last appear to be later notations by another hand. The copy of Adams' signature is distinctly the work of Mr. Lincoln, and he imitates it to the point of enclosing it in the needless frame of flourishes used by the "General." The words enclosed in parentheses, and parts of words so enclosed, are due to fading of the ink and torn places in this legal paper. The words are filled from a context of legal documents of this nature.

When Mr. Lincoln drew and filed this declaration in Springfield in the House at Washington the veteran John Quincy Adams had just begun a historic address on the right of petition and freedom of speech, he was not to conclude until July 7. It is safe to assume that when in due course the text of it reached Springfield it helped not a little to the political thinking along right lines of Abraham Lincoln.

State of Illinois   ⎱   of the July Term of the San-
Sangamon county & Circuit ⎰   gamon county circuit court in the year of our Lord one thousand eight hundred and thirty-eight—

Matthew McNair, plaintiff, complains of James Adams defendant, being in custody &c. of a plea of Tresspass on the case upon promises: For that whereas the said defendant and one

Wight and one Grant, heretofore, towit on the seventeenth day of November in the year of our Lord one thousand eight hundred and seventeen at Oswego that is to say at the county and circuit court aforesaid, made their certain promissory note in writing the said defendant signing his name Jas Adams bearing date the same day and year aforesaid, and by the said promissory note they the said defendant, and the said Wight, and said Grant, jointly and severally promised to pay, one year after date thereof, to the said plaintiff or bearer, one hundred and eighty dollars with interest from the first day of March (then) last (past); and the said defendant, and the said Wight and said Grant then and there delivered the said promissory note to the said plaintiff —By means whereof, and by force of the statute in such case made and provided, the said defendant then and there became liable to pay to the said plaintiff the said sum of money in the said promissory note specified, together with interest as therein mentioned according to the tenor and effect of the said promissory note; and being so liable, he, the said defendant in consideration thereof, afterwards towit, on the day and [ye]ar aforesaid, at Oswego, that is to say at the county [an]d Circuit aforesaid, undertook, and then and there faithfully promised the said plaintiff to pay him the said sum of money in the said promissory note specified, together with interest as therein specified according to the tenor and effect thereof—

And for that whereas also the said defendant, and one Wight and one Grant, afterwards towit, on the same day and year aforesaid, at Oswego, that is to say, at the county and circuit aforesaid, made their certain other promissory note in writing (the said defendant signing his name thus "Jas Adams") bearing date the same day and year aforesaid, and by the said last mentioned promissory note they, the said defendant and the said Wight and said Grant, jointly and severally promised to pay, two years after the date thereof to the said plaintiff or bearer, one hundred and eighty five dollars, with interest from the first day of March (then) last (past); and the said defendant and the said Wight and said Grant then and there delivered the said last mentioned promissory note to the said plaintiff— By means whereof and by force of the statute in such case made and provided, the said defendant then and there became liable to pay to the said plaintiff the said sum of money in the said last mentioned promissory note specified, with interest thereon as therein specified according to the tenor and effect of the said last mentioned promissory note; and being [so] liable, he the said defendant in consideration thereof, afterwards towit on the day and year aforesaid, at Oswego, that is to say at the county and Circuit aforesaid, undertook, and then and there faithfully promised the said plaintiff to pay him the said sum of money in the said last mentioned promissory note specified, according to the tenor and effect thereof—

Nevertheless the said defendant, and the said Wight and the said Grant, nor any or either of them (although often requested so to do; and although the said sever[al] times when the said several sums of money in the [said] several promissory notes specified were to be be paid, [have] long since expired) have not as yet paid the said several sums of money in the said several promissory notes specified, or either of them or any part of either of them; but so to do, have hitherto wholly neglected and refused, and still do neglect and refuse: To the Damage of the said plaintiff of the sum of one thousand dollars; and therefore he brings his suit &c.

Stuart & Lincoln
for Plff

The following are copies of the instruments declared on:
(Copy of note mentioned in first count)

"$180.00   Oswego Novr. 17th 1817

Jointly and severaly we promise to Pay Matthew McNair or Bearer one hundred and eighty dollars one year after date with interest from the first day of March last as witness our hands
Jas Adams
Wight & Grant"
(Copy of note mentioned in second count)

"185.00   Oswego Novr. 17th 1817

Jointly and severaly w[e] promise to pay Matthew McNair or Bearer one hundred and eighty five Dollars two years after date with interest from the first Day of March last as witness our hands

Jas Adams
Wight & Grant"

4

Matthew McNair

vs   } Declaration

James Adams

Filed June 19th 1838
Wm Butler Clk

July /41
Assumpsit

PRAECIPE, BOND FOR COSTS AND DECLARATION OF PLAINTIFF IN SUIT OF HARWOOD VS. FORSYTHE AND BUCKNER, JUNE 19, 1838
(Herndon-Weik Collection)

This praecipe and bond for costs were penned by Abraham Lincoln, the bond being signed by Rankin. The cover notation, "The clerk of the circuit court of Morgan County, Jacksonville, Ills.," is in the hand of Lincoln. The words, "Paid", and "Springfield 11 Jun 19," are stamped on the cover, while other notations are in the hand of Clerk Rockwell. The cover notations in the declaration here reproduced are also in the hand of Rockwell, while the declaration and copy of the note were penned by Attorney Lincoln. In line seven, Mr. Lincoln joined the words, "day and," as he so frequently joined such words "as thirtyeight." This case was decided on October 26, 1838 when Stuart & Lincoln obtained a judgment by default of $508.27 for their client, Lilburn Harwood.

Lilburn Harwood
vs
Newton Forsythe &
Aylett H. Buckner   } Trespass on the case upon
trading under the name   promises—
style and firm of   Damage— $600—
"Forsythe & Buckner"

The clerk of Morgan County circuit court will issue process in the above case returnable to the text term of said court.

Stuart & Lincoln for
Plaintiff

Lilburn Harwood

vs

Newton Forsythe &   In Morgan Circuit Court—

Aylett H. Buckner

I do hereby enter myself security for costs in this cause, and acknowledge myself bound to pay or cause to be paid all costs which may accrue in this action either to the opposite party or to any of the officers of the court in pursuance of the laws of this state.

N. A. Rankin

Dated this 18th day of June A. D. 1838

L. Harwood

vs

Forsythe & Buckner

Precipe & Bond for
    Cost

Filed June 19th
1838

D. Rockwell
        Clk
        Paid

The clerk of the circuit court
    of Morgan county
        Jacksonville
            Ills.

Springfield Il
    Jun
    19

State of Illinois

Morgan County & } ss

Circuit

Of the July term of the Morgan county circuit court in the year one thousand eight hundred and thirtyeight

Lilburn Harwood, plaintiff, complains of Newton Forsythe and Aylett H. Buckner defendants being in custody &c of a plea of Trespass on the case upon promises: For that whereas the said defendants by and under the name style and firm of "Forsythe & Buckner," heretofore towit, on the twentyninth day of March in the year of our Lord one thousand eight hundred and thirtysix, at Philadelphia, that is to say, at the county and circuit aforesaid, made their certain promissory note in writing bearing date the day and year aforesaid, and thereby then and there promised to pay six months after the date thereof, to the order of the plaintiff, by the name of "L. Harwood" the sum of four hundred and fiftytwo dollars, without defalcation, for value received, and then and there delivered the said promissory note to the said plaintiff; by means whereof, and by force of the statute in such case made and provided the said defendants then and there became liable to pay to the said plaintiff the said sum of money in the said promissory note specified according to the tenor and effect of the said promissory note: and being so liable, they, the said defendants in consideration thereof, afterwards towit, on the day and year aforesaid, at the place aforesaid, undertook and then and there faithfully promised the said plaintiff to pay him the said sum of money in the said promissory note specified according to the tenor and effect thereof—

Yet the said defendants (although often requested sotodo) have not as yet paid to the plaintiff the said sum of money in the said promissory note specified, or any part thereof; but so to do have hitherto wholly neglected and refused, and still do neglect and refuse. To the damage of the said plaintiff of the sum of six hundred dollars, and therefore he brings his suit &c.

Stuart &Lincoln for
Plaintiff

The following is a copy of the note sued on:
"$452.   Philadelphia, March 29th 1836

Six months after date we promise to pay to the order of L. Harwood without defalcation, Four hundred and Fifty two Dollars #/100 for value received.

Forsythe &Buckner

143   No 269

Lilburn Harwood
vs
Forsythe & Buckner

_____

Declaration

_____

Filed June 19" 1838
    D Rockwell clk

BILL IN CHANCERY AND BOND IN THE SUIT OF CROW & COMPANY VS. GARRETT, SANGAMON CIRCUIT COURT, JUNE 19, 1838
(Herndon-Weik Collection)

This bill in chancery and bonds are entirely the production of Mr. Lincoln. At the conclusion of the bill the usually careful young attorney slipped into error by asking that, "your orator will grant such other and further relief," when he meant "your Honor." It is not recorded that the judicial dignity was assailed by such an oversight upon the part of Lawyer Lincoln.

To the Honorable the Judge of the Sangamon circuit court in Chancery sitting—

Humbly complaining shew unto your Honor your orators, Edmund Crow, Joshua Tevis, and James W. Brannan, merchants and partners trading and doing business under the firm style and partnership name of Edmund Crow & Co. that Alexander Garrett on the sixth day of December in the year of our Lord one thousand eight hundred and thirtysix, made, executed, and delivered to your orators, the mortgage deed which is herewith filed, marked (A.) and which your orators pray may be made part of this Bill.

They further state that although the time for the payment of the money due upon the promissory note mentioned in said mortgage deed has expired, the said sum of money has not as yet been paid or any part thereof—

In tender consideration of which premises, your orators pray that the said Alexander Garrett may be made defendant to this Bill; and that the People's writ of Subpoena may issue &c; and that on a final hearing of this cause your Honor will decree that the lands mentioned in said mortgage deed be sold to satisfy said debts; and that your orator will grant such other and further relief as Equity may require and as in duty bound &c.

Stuart & Lincoln for
Complainants—

I do hereby enter myself security for all costs to the opposite party or any of the officers of this cause.

A. Lincoln.

DECLARATION OF PLAINTIFF IN SUIT OF STOCKTON VS. TOLLY, JUNE 28, 1838
(Herndon-Weik Collection)

The declaration and cover notations in this case were penned by Lawyer Lincoln. The date of filing is in the hand of Butler.

Stuart and Lincoln filed a rejoinder to the plea of the defendant on July 15, 1839, and a final decision was reached on November 28, 1839 when the case was dismissed with costs assessed against Tolly, the client of Stuart & Lincoln. Two days after this declaration was filed candidates for the Legislature addressed the voters at Water's Camp Ground four miles west of Springfield. It is probable that one of the speakers at this rally was Mr. Lincoln who on February 24, 1838, had caused the Sangamo Journal to announce that he was again a candidate for the Legislature.

State of Illinois ⎫ Of the July term of the circuit court
Sangamon county ⎬ of said county in the year of our Lord
and circuit ⎭ 1839—

George W. Stockton plaintiff complains of James Tolly defendant, being in custody &c. of a plea of Trespass on the case— For that whereas the said defendant before and at the time of the delivery of a certain cooking stove to him, as hereinafter next mentioned, was a common carrier of goods and chattels for him from Beardstown to Springfield towit, at the county and circuit aforesaid. And whereas also the said plaintiff whilst the said defendant was such a common carrier as aforesaid, towit, on the   day of   in the year of our Lord one thousand eight hundred and thirtyseven at Beardstown, towit at the county and circuit aforesaid, caused to be delivered to him the said defendant, and the said defendant then and there accepted and received of and from the said plaintiff a certain cooking stove of the said plaintiff of great value, towit of the value of one hundred dollars to be safely and securely carried and conveyed by him the said defendant from Beardstown aforesaid to Springfield aforesaid, and there towit, at Springfield aforesaid, safely and securely to be delivered for the said plaintiff for certain reasonable reward to him the said defendant in that behalf— Yet the said defendant, not regarding his duty as such common carrier as aforesaid, did not, nor would safely or securely carry or convey the said cooking stove aforesaid, from Beardstown aforesaid to Springfield aforesaid, nor there, towit, at Springfield aforesaid, safely or securely deliver the same for him the said plaintiff; but on the contrary thereof, he the said defendant being such common carrier as aforesaid, so carelessly and negligently behaved and conducted himself in the premises, that by and through the carelessness, negligence, and default of the said defendant in the premises, the said cooking stove, being of the value aforesaid, was broken, destroyed, and rendered wholly valueless, towit, on the day and year aforesaid, at the county and circuit aforesaid—

Wherefore the said plaintiff saith that he is injured and hath sustained damage to the amount of one hundred dollars, and therefore he brings his suit &c.

Stuart & Lincoln p q

George W. Stockton

vs } Decln

James Tolly
Filed June 28, 1838
   Wm Butler clerk

NOTICES FOR TAKING DEPOSITIONS IN THE SUIT OF McNAIR VS. ADAMS, JUNE 13 AND JUNE 29, 1839
(Herndon-Weik Collection)

The first of the notices here reproduced was drawn by Samuel H. Treat, and the only words in the hand of Mr. Lincoln are those acknowledging service of notice. He signed "Stu" apparently as an abbreviation of Stuart. The second notice does not appear to be in the hand of Mitchell, the clerk of Peoria, or of John or George McFadden. It is not in the hand of Butler or Lincoln, and may have been penned by a clerk at Peoria, and signed by Adams. It is the notice to be annexed to the depositions of John and Mary McFadden, and Ernest Schryder. It is placed for this reason as of June 28th or 29th, 1838, but the date may be earlier. It is slightly different in form, but not in context from the first notice.

Messrs Stuart & Lincoln
Attorneys of Matthew McNair

Gentlemen—You will please take notice, that on the twenty Eighth day of June 1838 between the hours of one oclock P. M. & Six oclock P. M. of that day. at the house of William Hale in the county of Peoria & State of Illinois. before Andrew M. Hunt Esq. a Justice of the Peace in & for said county of Peoria, I shall proceed to take the depositions of William Hale. & Arabel Hale & others to be read as Evidence on the trial of a cause now pending & undetermined in the Sangamon circuit court, wherein the said Matthew McNair is Plaintiff & I am Defendant.

You will further take notice that on the 29th day of June 1838 between the hours of one oclock P. M. & Six oclock P. M.

of that day. at the house of John McFadden in the said county of Peoria. before Thomas Tickner a Justice of the Peace for the same county, I shall proceed to take the depositions of John McFadden, Mary McFadden, Ernest C. Schryder &———— Hurt. & others to be read as Evidence in the aforementioned suit in the same manner.

Jas Adams

June 14th 1838

> We acknowledge the service of this notice this
> 13th of June 1838   Stu

Messrs Stuart and Lincoln
Attorneys of Matthew McNair

Gentlemen you will please take notice that on the 28th day of June 1838 between the hours of One Oclock P. M. and Six oclock P. M. of that day at the house of William Hale in the County of Peoria and State of Illinois before Andrew M. Hunt Esqr a Justice of the Peace in and for said County of Peoria I shall proceed to take the depositions of William Hale & Arabel Hale & others to be read as Evidence in the trial of a cause now pending and undetermined in the Sangamon Circuit Court wherein the said Matthew McNair is Plaintiff and I am defendant.

You will also further take notice that on the 29th day of June 1838, between the hours of one oclock P. M. and Six oclock P. M. of that day at the house of John McFadden in the said County of Peoria before Thomas Tickner a Justice of the Peace for the same county I will proceed to take the Depositions of John McFadden Mary McFadden Ernest C. Schryder &———————— Hurd and others to be read as Evidence in the aforementioned suit in the same manner—

Jas Adams

DEPOSITIONS IN THE SUIT OF McNAIR VS. ADAMS, JUNE 29, 1838
(Herndon-Weik Collection)

These depositions, as noted in the statement of Thomas Ticknor, are in the hands of George C. McFadden and John McFadden. The latter appears to have written the statement of Justice of the Peace Ticknor, which was signed in a large scrawl by that official. The document attested by Mitchell is a printed form, which he filled in and signed. The cover notations con-

cerning the case, appear to be in the hand of John McFadden. He seems also to have penned the address upon the envelope or cover which was sent to Butler, with the exception of William Butler. These two words appear to be in the hand of William Mitchell, the clerk at Peoria. The date of filing is in the well-known hand of Clerk Butler. The answers and questions in these depositions, it will be seen, relate closely to the set of interrogatories drawn by Mr. Lincoln in his notice of taking of depositions dated April 13, 1838.

Deposition of John McFadden Mary McFadden & Earnest C. Shryder of the County of Peoria taken on the 29th day of June in the year 1838 between the hours of one oclock P. M. and Six oclock P. M. of Said day at the house of John McFadden pursuant to the anaxed notice, to be read in evidence in a cause pending in the Sangamon Circuit court between Matthew McNair plaintiff and James Adams Defendant.

The said John McFadden being first sworn doth depose and say in answer to the following questions

Ques. 1st Are you acquainted with James Adams late of Oswego New York. known by the title of General Adams. if so when did you first become acquainted with him, and up to what time were you acquainted with him.

Answer I became acquainted with him in the winter of 1812 and my acquaintance with him continued up to the year 1820.

Ques. 2nd Did he remove from Oswego to Illinois.

Ans. I was acquainted with him in Oswego and next saw him in Illinois and I understood that he had removed to Illinois at the time of his removal from Osewgo.

Ques. 3rd When did he leave Oswego for Illinois.

Ans. From the best of my recollection it was in the Spring or Summer of 1820.

Quest 4th Was his intended departure for Illinois a matter of publicity.

Ans. Yes. I frequently and publickly heard it spoken of at Oswego Haniball and Sterling. by himself and others.

Quest 5th Was it subsequently a matter of Publisity that he had—Settled in Illinois.

Ans. Yes. I have heard it frequently spoken of in publick, by Asa Dudley. Mathew McNair James F Wight Alvin & Edward Bronson. William Dolloway & others.

Quest 6 Did McNair speak of it as a matter of publick notoriety.

Ans Yes. he mentioned it publickly in the street in the Vilage of Oswego.

Quest 7 Did you ever hear McNair say that Adams was indetted to him the said McNair.

Ans Not that I recollect.

Quest 8 Did you serve as an officer during any part of the late war with Great Britain.

Ans I did

Quest 9th Was you at any time attacht to the command of said Adams

Ans. I was at the action of the capture of Oswego as I volunteered and was there attached to his command

Quest 10 Did you see McNair at Oswego at that or any other time

Ans. I saw him there on the day of the capture of Oswego, and also on the day previous and frequently from that time up to the year 1835.

Quest 11 Do you know whether he acted as issuing Commissary at that time

Ans. He delt out provisions to this company which I had in command. and also to the other troops. on the west side of the river

Quest 12 Did you hear McNair say he would rather have the British come to Oswego than to have the Malitia come there?

Ans. Yes, I heard him say he would rather have the british come to Oswego than the d—d Malitia

Quest 13 Did McNair ever refuse to Issue to the men under your command, holesom provisions. and had he at the same time salted provisions on hand

Ans. Yes. The beef he dealt out was damaged. and I requested him at the same time to let the troops have pork and he refused and he had at the same time a large quantity of pork in Barrels.

Jno. McFadden

The Said Ernist C. Schryder being first Sworn doth depose and say in Answer to the following questions.

question 1st are you acquainted with James Adams late of Oswego New York known by the title of General Adams if so how long have you been acquainted with him.

Answer I am. I was acquainted with him during the Embargo time and nonimportation. Nonintercourse and in the late war with great Britton and was under his Command at the Repulse of the Britich and at Oswego at the Capture of Oswego.—

Que. 2 was the said Adams then and there an Officer in the United States Service—

Answer he was then in command in the United States Service

question 3d. Do you know that he subsequently went to the State of Illinois

Answer. Yes.

questn 4th. did you Ever hear any person say in New York that said Adams absconded or left Newyork privately.—

Answer I did not

questn 5th did you frequently see and Converse with Matthew McNair of Oswego from the late war up to May in the year 1837.

Answer I did and during that time done a great deal of Business with him

question 6th Did you Ever hear him say said Adams was indebted to him

Answer I never did

question 7th. was or was not Matthew McNair much in the habit in case any person was indebted to him of speaking of it to those with whom he conversed and done Business.

Answer he was

Ernest C. Schryder—

The said Mary McFadden being first Sworn doth depose and say in Answer to the following questions.—

question 1st. are you acquainted with James Adams late of Oswego—known by the title of General Adams—if so State how long you are acquainted with him.—

Answer I was acquainted with him from the fourth of July 1816. to the time he left Oswego for Illinois—

question 2nd do you know Whether it was Spoken of as a matter of Publicity before he left Oswego for Illinois that he was going to Illinois.—

Answer I frequently and Publickly heard it Spoken of both before and after his departure

question 3d. did you Ever hear any person Speak of his departure as having been Secret or Unknown to the Public.—

Answer I never did. but always heard it Spoken of as a matter of Publicity

Mary McFadden

State of Illinois   )
Peoria County ss.   )

I. Thomas Tickner Justice of the peace. do hereby Certify. that John McFadden. Ernist C. Schryder and Mary McFadden was by me Sworn to testify the truth. the whole truth and nothing but the truth. as witnesses in the above named Cause and that the foregoing by them Severally Subscribed was reduced to writing in my presents.   Viz. that of John McFadden by George C. McFadden and that of Ernist C. Schryder and Mary McFadden. by John McFadden being both disinterested persons. and taken at time and place in the annexed notice Specified.—

Thos Ticknor J. Peace

State of Illinois,   )
) ss.
Peoria County   (

I, William Mitchell, Clerk of the county commissioner's court, for said county, do hereby certify, that Thomas Ticknor   Esquire, whose name appears in the foregoing certificate, was, on the day of the date thereof, an acting Justice of the Peace, in and for the county aforesaid, duly commissioned and qualified, as it appears to me of record in my office; and that, as such, full faith and credit are due to all his official acts.

In Testimony Whereof, I have hereunto set my hand, and affixed the seal of said Court, at Peoria this Twenty ninth day of June 1838

William Mitchell Clerk

Sangamon Circuit Court
    Matthew McNair
        vs
    James Adams.—
    Depositions enclosed.—

William Butler Esquire Clerk
Sangamon Circuit Court.—
Springfield. Illinois.—
Filed July 2 1838
Wm Butler Clk

PLEA OF DEFENDANT IN SUIT OF McNAIR VS. ADAMS, JULY 2, 1838

(Herndon-Weik Collection)

These pleas are in the handwriting of Samuel Treat, and Abraham Lincoln has penned the words, "And the said plaintiff doth the like— Stuart & Lincoln for Plff," at the conclusion of the first plea. The "1st Plea," "2nd," "3rd," "4th" and "5th," before each plea are in the hand of Lincoln. The cover notations are by Treat, with the exception of the date of filing. Despite the contention of Treat and Campbell that no cause for suit existed, if ever it had, the litigation continued for several years, indicating that Stuart & Lincoln made out a good case before the court.

James **Adams**
     adm.   }   In the Sangamon Circuit Court.
Matthew **McNair**   In assumpsit

And the said Defendant by his attorney comes & defends the wrong & injury when. &c. & saith that he did not undertake or promise in the manner & form. as the said Plaintiff, hath above thereof alledged against him & of this he puts himself upon the country.

Treat & Campbell
For Deft.

And the said plaintiff doth
the like—   Stuart & Lincoln
for Plff

2nd

And for a further Plea in this behalf the said Defendant. saith that the said Plaintiff ought not to have or maintain his aforesaid action thereof against him, because he saith, that he the said Defendant. did not at any time with in five years next, before the commencement of this suit. undertake or promise in manner & form as the said Plaintiff hath above thereof alleged against him. And this the said Defendant is ready to verify. wherefore he prays Judgment of the said Plaintiff Ought to have or maintain his aforesaid action thereof against him. &c.

Treat & Campbell
For Deft.

3rd

And for a further Plea in this behalf, the said Defendant saith that the said Plaintiff. ought not to have or maintain his aforesaid action thereof against him. because he the said Defendant saith. that the said several supposed causes of action in the said Plaintiffs declaration mentioned. (if any such there were or still are). did not. nor did Either of them accrue to the said Plaintiff at any time within five years next before the commencement of this suit. in manner & form as the said Plaintiff hath above thereof alleged against him the said Defendant. And this the said Defendant is ready to verify. wherefore he prays Judgement. of the said Plaintiff ought to have or maintain his aforesaid action thereof against him, &c.

4th

Treat & Campbell
For Defendant

And for a further Plea in this behalf the said defendant saith that the said Plaintiff ought not to have or maintain his aforesaid action thereof against him.. because he the said Defendant saith. that the said Plaintiff did not commence his suit within five years next after the said several supposed causes of action in the said Plaintiffs declaration mentioned. accrued & this the said Defendant is ready to verify. wherefore he prays Judgement if the said Plaintiff. ought to have or maintain his aforesaid action thereof against him &c.

Treat & Campbell
For Deft.

5th

And for a further Plea in this behalf the said Defendant saith, that the said Plaintiff ought not to have or maintain his aforesaid action thereof against him. because he the said Defendant. saith. that the said several supposed causes of action in the said Plaintiffs Declaration mentioned, if any, accrued on the Seventeenth day of November Eighteen hundred & nineteen, & that the said Plaintiff did not commence his said suit until the   day of   1838. And of this the said Defendant is ready to verify. wherefore he prays Judgement if the said Plaintiff ought not to have or maintain his aforesaid action against him &c.

Treat & Campbell
For Deft.

Adams
  ads
McNair

Pleas.
Filed July 2 1838
Wm. Butler Clk

BILL IN CHANCERY IN THE SUIT OF HART VS. SACKETT ET AL, JULY 3, 1838
(Herndon-Weik Collection)

This bill and cover notations, with the exception of the date of filing, were penned by Mr. Lincoln, who in various ways evinced unusual interest in the litigation in which his client was involved as the widow of Moses Hart.

Rhoda Hart

vs   } Bill

John Sackett & others

Filed July 3, 1838
Wm Butler Clk

To the Honorable the Judge of the Sangamon circuit court in chancery sitting—

Humbly sheweth unto your Honor your oratrix, Rhoda Hart Executrix of Moses Hart deceased, that at the last October term of this court an order was made by this court directing your oratrix to sell the real estate of the said Moses Hart deceased; that in obedience to the said order your oratrix has sold and conveyed the said real estate aforesaid in the parcels and to the persons following, towit; The West half of the South West quarter of Section Twentyfour in Township Seventeen North of Range Seven West, reserving therefrom one eighth of an acre containing a burying ground, to Hiram Penny; The East half of the same quarter Section, Township and Range to Peyton L. Harrison; The West half of the East half of the North West quarter of the same Section Township and Range, to Benjamin McElwain; The East half of the East half of the same quarter, Section, Township and Range to Nancy Hart; and, Fifty acres off the South end of the East half of the South West quarter of Section Thirteen in the same Township and Range to Elisha Bone—Your oratrix further states that John Sackett, and Rhoda Sackett his wife; heirs of the said Moses Hart deceased; and also Jefferson Hart, Melissa Jane Hart, and Rhoda Hart, infant heirs of David Hart deceased, who was also an heir of the said Moses Hart deceased, were omitted to be made parties to the proceeding by which the said real estate of the said Moses Hart deceased was by this court ordered to be sold—

Your oratrix prays that the said John Sackett and Rhoda Sackett his wife, Jefferson Hart, Melissa Jane Hart and Rhoda Hart be made defendants to this Bill; and that the Peoples' writ of Subpoena may issue &c. and that Antrim Campbell be appointed guardian *ad litem* to the said infant defendants, and that he be required to answer &c; and that on a final hearing of this cause your Honor will decree that the said sales of real estate herein before mentioned and described be confirmed as against all defendants to this Bill; and that your Honor will grant such other and further relief as equity may require; and as in duty bound &c.

Stuart & Lincoln
For Compt

ANSWER OF GUARDIAN AD LITEM IN THE SUIT OF HART VS. SACKETT ET AL, SANGAMON CIRCUIT COURT, JULY 3, 1838
(Herndon-Weik Collection)

Mr. Lincoln wrote this answer which was signed by Campbell, and he also penned the cover notations. Rhoda Hart filed her bill on July 10, 1838, and it is probable, as in most cases of this kind, Campbell filed his answer on the same day. Campbell was a native of New Jersey who had lately settled in Springfield, and who until his death in 1860 held an honored place at the Sangamon County bar, serving for many years as a master in chancery in the state and federal courts.

The answer of Antrim Campbell, guardian *ad litem* to Jefferson Hart, Melissa Jane Hart, and Rhoda Hart, infant heirs of David Hart deceased, to a Bill in chancery filed in the circuit court of Sangamon county by Rhoda Hart, Executrix of Moses Hart deceased, against John Sackett, Rhoda Sackett and the aforesaid infant heirs—

This respondent, for answer to said Bill, says that he has examined said Bill, and the facts therein stated and set forth, and that he believes the allegations of said Bill are true; and that he knows no reason, consistent with the interest of said infant heirs, why a decree shall not be rendered in accordance with the prayer of said Bill—

Antrim Campbell
Guardian ad litem for
Infant heirs of David Hart Deceased

FURTHER PLEAS OF DEFENDANT IN THE SUIT OF McNAIR VS. ADAMS, JULY 5, 1838
(Herndon-Weik Collection)

These pleas as in the case of the five pleas, or counts, previously reproduced are in the hand of Treat. The words, "6th Plea," and the numbers, "7th" and "8th" are in the hand of Mr. Lincoln as were the numbers in the first five parts of the plea of July 2, 1838.

6th Plea

Adams
    ads   } In assumpsit
McNair

And the said Defendant for further Plea in this behalf, says that the said Plaintiff ought not to have or maintain his said Defendant did not at any time within *sixteen years* next before the commencement of this suit undertake or promise in manner & form as the said Plaintiff hath above thereof alledged against him, and of this the said Defendant is ready to verify wherefore he prays Judgement if the said Plaintiff ought rather to have or maintain his aforesaid action thereof against him &c.

Treat & Campbell
For Deft.

7th

And the said Defendant for further Plea in this behalf says that the said Plaintiff ought not to have or maintain his aforesaid action thereof against him because he says. that the several supposed causes of action in the said declaration mentioned, (if any there were or still are) did not nor did any or Either of them. accrue to the said Plaintiff at any time within *sixteen years* next before the commencement of this suit, in manner & form as the said Plaintiff hath above thereof complained against him & of this he the said Defendant is ready to verify. wherefore he prays Judgement if the said Plaintiff ought further. to have or maintain his aforesaid action thereof against him.

Treat & Campbell
For Deft.

8th

And the said Defendant for further Plea in this behalf saith that the said Plaintiff ought not to have or maintain his aforesaid action thereof against him because he saith that the said Plaintiff did not commence his suit against this defendant Upon

& for the non performance of the said several promises & undertakings in the said Declaration mentioned *with* in sixteen years next after the same one made & accrued to the said Plaintiff. And this the said Defendant is ready to verify &c. wherefore he prays Judgement if the said Plaintiff ought further to have or maintain his aforesaid action thereof against him—&c

Treat & Campbell
For Deft.

James Adams
    adsm
Matthew McNair

Pleas
Filed July 5th 1838
Wm. Butler Clk

ANSWER OF MR. LINCOLN AS GUARDIAN AD LITEM IN THE SUIT OF THAYER VS. PHILLIPS ET AL, SANGAMON CIRCUIT COURT, JULY 5, 1838

(Herndon-Weik Collection)

The only part of this document in the handwriting of Mr. Lincoln, is the signature, A.. Lincoln. The two periods following the letter, "A," will be noted as a characteristic usage of his early years. He not only placed the two dots after the "A,"but often after the "P" in "P.. M." denoting his title as postmaster at New Salem. Other documents reveal the use of the double period after abbreviations showing that Mr. Lincoln did not use it only after the "A.." for "Abraham." The answer in this case appears to have been the work of four men. Samuel H. Treat seems to have begun the writing with the words "Joseph Thayer," and to have continued down to the clause, "for answer thereto he saith." It appears that John T. Stuart, partner of Lincoln, took up the pen at this point, and concluded with the words, "of July 1838." William Butler signed the notice of the swearing of the answer, and he also wrote the cover notations. Lawyer Lincoln had been appointed guardian ad litem on March 6, 1838. On March 7, 1838, the firm of Stuart & Lincoln filed certificates of publication which was notice that they would make known to the public the fact that an act had been done, or had not been done.

Joseph Thayer complainant   ⎫
         against   ⎬ In chancery
Elizabeth Phillips & others. Defendants. ⎭

    The answer of Abram Lincoln, the guardian *ad litem* of William Phillips. . Infant Defendant herein, to the bill of said complainant.

    For answer thereto he saith. that he has carefully examined the Bill & Exhibits filed in this cause. & believes that all the material allegations. in the complainants Bill. contained. are fully established by the proof and Exhibits in this cause & that he knows of no good reason consistent with the interest of said infant. why the prayer of the complainants Bill should not be granted.

                                            A. . Lincoln

Sworn & Subscribed to
before me this 5th
day of July 1838.
    Wm. Butler Clk

Thayer
    ⎫
vs ⎬ Answer Guardian
    ⎭   ad litem
Elizabeth Phillips

Filed July 5th 1838
    Wm. Butler Clk

REPLICATION OF PLAINTIFF IN SUIT OF McNAIR VS. ADAMS, JULY 6, 1838
(Herndon-Weik Collection)

Mr. Lincoln penned both parts of this replication to the eight pleas entered by Campbell and his partner, Treat. He omitted the word, "state," in the second part of the replication, at the place immediately after the word, "this" and just preceding "towit." It is evident that he was thinking ahead, for he crosses out "Sixteen" in the first part of the replication, replacing it with the word, "five," while he uses it in the term of years in the second part of the document. The cover notations are in the hand of Butler.

Matthew McNair   ⎫
     vs   ⎬   In assumpsit—
James Adams   ⎭

And the said plaintiff as to the said pleas of the said defendant by him secondly, thirdly, fourthly and fifthly pleaded. saith that he the said plaintiff by reason of any thing by the said defendant in those pleas alleged ought not to be barred from having and maintaining his aforesaid action thereof against him the said defendant, because he saith at the time when the said several causes of action in the said declaration mentioned, and each and every of them, did accrue to the said plaintiff, the said plaintiff was beyond the limits of this state, towit, at Oswego in the state of New York, and that the said plaintiff never came within this state from beyond the limits of the state, after the accruing of the said causes of action, and every of them to the said plaintiff, before within five years of the commencement of this action.   And this he the said plaintiff is ready to verify, wherefore he prays judgement and his damage by him sustained on occasion of the non performance of the said several promises and undertakings in the said declaration mentioned to be adjudged to him &c.

Stuart &Lincoln
For Plff

And the said Plaintiff, for further replication in this behalf, as to the said pleas of the said defendant by him sixthly, seventhly and eighthly pleaded saith that he the said plaintiff by reason of any thing by the said defendant in those pleas alleged ought not to be barred from having and maintaining his aforesaid action thereof against him the said defendant, because he saith that at the time when the said several causes of action in the said declaration mentioned, and each and every of them, did accrue to the said plaintiff, the said plaintiff was beyond the limits of this state, to wit, at Oswego in the state of New York; and that the said plaintiff never came within this state from beyond the limits of this state after the accruing of the said causes of action, and every of them to the said plaintiff before within sixteen years of the commencemnt of this action—

And this the said plaintiff is ready to verify, wherefore he prays judgement and his damages by him sustained on occasion of the non-performance of the said promises and undertakings in the said declaration mentioned to be adjudged to him &c.

Stuart & Lincoln
for Plff

Mathew McNair
vs
James Adams

Filed July 6th 1838

Wm. Butler Clk

DEFENDANT'S DEMURRER IN THE SUIT OF McNAIR VS. ADAMS, JULY 6, 1838
(Herndon-Weik Collection)

This demurrer drawn by Treat is reproduced as constituting a sequence of pleas, replication, demurrer and joinder in one of the most widely discussed suits of Mr. Lincoln's first years as a lawyer.

James Adams   } In Sangamon circuit
    adsm   } court
Mathew McNair   }   In assumpsit

And the said James Adams saith that the said replication of the said Plaintiff. to the said second. third, fourth & fifth pleas of him the said Defendant & the matters therein contained, in manner & form as the same are above pleaded & set forth. are not sufficient in law for the said Plaintiff to have or maintain his aforesaid action thereof against him, the said Defendant, & that he the said Defendant is not bound by law. to answer the same, & this he the said Defendant is ready is ready to verify, wherefore for the want of a sufficient Replication in this behalf he the said Defendant prays Judgement, if the said Plaintiff, ought to have or maintain his aforesaid action thereof against him &c

> Treat & Campbell
> For Deft.

And the said Defendant saith that the said Replication of the said Plaintiff to the said sixth. seventh, & Eighth. Pleas of him the said Defendant & the matters therein contained. in manner & form as the same are above pleaded, & set forth are not sufficient in Law. for the said Plaintiff. to have or maintain his aforesaid action thereof against him the said Defendant. & that he the said Defendant is not bound by law. to answer the same, & this he the said Defendant is ready to verify, wherefore for the want of a sufficient replication in this behalf, he the said Defendant prays Judgement if the said Plaintiff, ought to have or maintain his aforesaid action thereof against him &c.

> Treat & Campbell
> For Deft.

James Adams
     adsm
Mathew McNair

Demr.
Filed July 6th 1838
Wm. Butler Clk

JOINDER IN THE SUIT OF McNAIR VS. ADAMS, JULY 7, 1838
(Herndon-Weik Collection)

This joinder was penned by Attorney Lincoln, while the cover notations are by Butler. In the joinder to the second demurrer Mr. Lincoln uses the words, "verry and proved," for the correct phase, "verify and prove." The words are not crossed out, and the mistake is not characteristic of careful Lawyer Lincoln. It merely proves that he made mistakes, but less frequently than most men. A change of venue from Peoria to Sangamon County was agreed on by Stuart & Lincoln for the plaintiff, and Treat for the defendant, on April 2, 1839, and the case continued to be argued with vigor on both sides.

Matthew **McNair**　⎫　　(Joinder to first Demurrer)
　　vs　　　　　⎬　　　　**In Assumpsit**
James Adams　⎭

And the said plaintiff saith that the said replication and the matters therein contained in manner and form as the same are above stated and set forth, are sufficient in law for him the said plaintiff to have and maintain his aforesaid action thereof against him the said defendant; and the said plaintiff is ready to verify and prove the same as this court here shall direct and award; wherefore inasmuch as the said defendant hath not answered the said replication nor hitherto in any manner denied the same the said plaintiff prays judgement, and his damages by reason of the not performing of the said several promises and undertakings in the said declaration mentioned, to be adjudged to him &c.

Stuart &Lincoln, for Plff

(Joinder to second Demurrer)

And the said plaintiff saith that the said replication and the matters therein contained in manner and form as the same are above stated and set forth, are sufficient in law for him the said plaintiff to have and maintain his aforesaid action thereof against him the said defendant; and the said plaintiff is ready to veray and prove the same as the court here shall direct and award; wherefore inasmuch as the said defendant hath not answered the said replication, nor hitherto in any manner denied the same, the said plaintiff prays judgement and his damages by reason of the not performing of the said several promises and undertakings in the said declaration mentioned to be adjudged to him &c.

Stuart & Lincoln for Plff

McNair
    vs   Joinder in
James Adams   Demr

Filed July 7th 1838
Wm Butler Clk

ANSWER OF MR. LINCOLN AS GUARDIAN AD LITEM FOR THE HEIRS OF SAMUEL MUSICK IN THE SUIT OF THE STATE BANK OF ILLINOIS VS. MUSICK, SANGAMON CIRCUIT COURT, JULY 10, 1838

This copy of the answer of Mr. Lincoln appears in the Complete Record of the case penned by the court clerk. The words of Lincoln begin with the phrase, "For answer thereto," and conclude with his signature, "A. Lincoln." The clerk's copy may have been an accurate transcription, but the spelling, "consistent," was not used by Lincoln. He did use the "&" sign in his legal papers, but less frequently than it appears in the copied answer. He rarely capitalized the words, "complainants" and "court," as is done here. Mr. Lincoln was appointed guardian ad litem on July 2, 1838. He knew Samuel Musick as the owner of the ferry which crossed Salt Creek in Sangamon County. On December 9, 1834 he had informed the Legislature that he would propose a bill to permit Musick to build a toll bridge across this stream, and later he introduced various bills to bring road traffic over the Musick bridge. The court record does not permit of definite conclusion, but it is probable that the original answer of A Lincoln was in his hand. It is also probable that there was a double period after the "A," but this is not known. All that is known is that the two dots were most characteristic of the Lincoln of that time.

Circuit Court ⎫
⎬
July 11th 1838 ⎭

Plaintiff ⎫   State Bank of Illinois
         ⎬   against   In Chancery
Defendants ⎭   Samuel Musicks heirs

This day came A. Lincoln guardian ad litem to the infant heirs herein, & swore to and filed his answer to Complainants Bill.—

Answer of ⎫   The answer of Abram Lincoln guardian ad
ALincoln   ⎬litem of Grant Musick, Lewis Musick, & Eliza-
guardn ad litem ⎭beth Musick infant defendants herein to the
                 Complainants Bill.—

For answer thereto he saith that he has carefully examined the pleadings in this cause & that all the material allegations in the Complainants Bill contained are fully established by the Exhibits filed herein & that he knows of no good reason consistent with the interest of said infants why the prayer of the Complainants should not be granted & the mortgage foreclosed & the mortgaged premises sold by the Decree of this Court to pay off & discharge the debt due the Complainants

                                              A. Lincoln

Sworn & subscribed
to before me this 10th day
of July 1838.
Wm Butler, Clk

ANSWER OF DEFENDANT IN THE SUIT OF ANDERSON, BELL & COMPANY VS. GAMBRELL, JULY 12, 1838
(Herndon-Weik Collection)

The words, "And the plaintiff doth the like, Stuart & Lincoln for Plff.," are the only ones in this document penned by Mr. Lincoln. The rest of the answer seems to be in the hands of the opposing attorney, and the careless format and scrawl contrast most unfavorably with the meticulous and neatly penned legal documents of Mr. Lincoln. This opposing attorney was Stephen Arnold Douglas, long the legal and political opponent of Abraham Lincoln, and one of the ablest of his antagonists in either field. There is controversy in regard to the winner of the Lincoln-Douglas debates, but there is no doubt as to the winner of

this case for Stuart & Lincoln's client, Anderson, Bell & Co., was
awarded a judgment of $207.65 upon Friday, July 13, 1838.

Gambril   ⎫   of the July Term of the circuit
                        ⎪   court of Sangamon Illinois the
      vs   ⎬ In case year of our Lord. one thousand
Bell & Co assignees &c ⎭   eight hundred and thirty eight

The defendant James Gambril by his counsel Douglas &
Urquhart; comes and defends the wrong and injury when &
where &c and for plea saith, that the plaintiff his action against
him, in manner and form as in the said declaration alleged—
and set forth ought not to have and maintain because he says,
that he did not assume on himself as the plaintiff hath in his
pleading alleged and of this he puts himself on the country—

Douglas & Urquhart
for the defendant

And the plaintiff doth
the like

Stuart & Lincoln
for Plff.

and the said defendant according to the statute of the State
of Illinois in such cases provided, hereby notifies the plaintiff
that he shall rely in the defence of this action on the following
facts—and causes of defence

First—that the note set out in the plaintiffs declaration
as the inducement to this action was obtained by one
Moses Coffman assignor of the plaintiff from the defendant by misrepresentation by deceit and by suppressing
the truth. The said note was executed for the part
payment of a tract of land lying in Sangamon County Illinois
The said tract of land is was & has been since the sale subject
to a certain disease called & known in common language in the
State of Illinois. as Milk Sickness—which renders it worthless
to the defendant or to any person. for the uses of occupation &
tillage. The defendant expects to prove, the knowledge of the
assignor of the plaintiff of the said fact in regard to the existing
disease in the land—at & before the sale by the plaintiff assignor
to this defendant. Secondly—

The defendant further expects to prove that the settlements
in—about, & around the said land, near the adjoining—have
been long subject to the said disease and unhealthy influences
all of which were known to the plaintiff assignor at and before
the sale of the said tract of land to this defendant—and concealed

by said plaintiff assignor from the defendant in negotiating said
sale, whereby the said defendant was circumvented and induced to
agree to give more for said land than he would otherwise have
done—, as he would not, knowingly have contracted for land to
live on with his family—which is subject to so troublesome a
disease as milk sickness, with a knowledge of the fact—but
whether the plaintiff assignor knew of the disease or not, still
the defendant expects to show the disease to have existed at
and before the contract between the plaintiffs assignor and defendant for the land and that the land is rendered almost useless
to the defendant for occupancy and tillage—

D & U for the
defendant

July Term of the
Sangamon Circuit Court
in year of Lord 1838
Gambril
   vs
Bell & Co
Filed July 12" 1838
Wm Butler Clk

REPORT OF THE ADMINISTRATOR IN THE SUIT OF MOSES M. MARTIN VS. THE HEIRS OF ISAAC MARTIN, SANGAMON CIRCUIT COURT, JULY 14, 1838
(Herndon-Weik Collection)

*This report was penned by Mr. Lincoln, and signed by his
client Moses M. Martin. It is the report which the court had
ordered to be given in its decree of October 16, 1837. One confusing point arises, for Mr. Lincoln cites ownership of the South
half of the South West quarter of Section Six, in the document
of October 16, 1837, while he speaks of the sale of the South
half of the North West quarter in this report. The petition of
partition and court order of October 16, 1837, combine with this
document to afford an almost complete history of the case. The
final report of Moses Martin is not given, but on February 7,
1839, the receipt of Mr. Lincoln for $7.50, the legal fee in the
case, was handed to Moses Martin.*

Exparte, Moses M. Martin   }   On Petition to
Administrator of Isaac Martin decd   sell real estate—

This day comes the said Moses M. Martin and files his report in the above case and says "that in pursuance of the order of the court made in the said case, he did, after due notice of his intention so to do had been given, as will appear by the annexed certificate, on the fifteenth day of January in the year of our Lord one thousand eight hundred and thirtyeight, between the hours of ten o'clock in the forenoon and five o'clock in the afternoon of the same day, expose at public vendue the South half of the North West quarter of Section Six in Township Fourteen North of Range Three West of the Third Principal Meridian containing sixtyone and seventeen hundredths of an acre, and that Daniel Robb, being the highest and best bidder, became the purchaser thereof for the sum of two dollars and twentyfive cents per acre; and that he has executed and delivered to the said Daniel Robb, a deed of conveyance for the said land, and has taken his bond and personal security and a mortgage on the said tract of land to secure the payment of the purchase money thereof—

And further the said Moses M. Martin has not proceeded—

Moses M. Martin

Moses M. Martin

vs } Report

Heirs of
Isaac Martin Decd

Filed July 14th 1838
Wm. Butler Clk

LETTER OF JESSE W. FELL TO LINCOLN AND THE LATTER'S REPLY, JULY 20 AND 25, 1838

The letter here reproduced which Jesse W. Fell wrote to Mr. Lincoln on July 20, 1838, and the latter's reply written on the reverse of it, probably on July 25, 1838, bear early witness to a friendship that in after years was to have weighty issue for the junior partner in the firm of Stuart & Lincoln. Born in 1808, in Chester County, Pennsylvania, Fell studied law and was admitted to the bar at Steubenville, Ohio, and in 1833 became the first lawyer in the infant town of Bloomington. There he quickly claimed a potent place in law and business and in political affairs. In 1855 he led in securing the location of the Chicago & Alton

Railroad through Bloomington, and a year later was one of the founders of the Republican Party in Illinois.

Fell early became the intimate personal and political friend of John T. Stuart and of Abraham Lincoln. In the summer of 1838 Stuart was waging a hectic and stubborn battle with Stephen A. Douglas for a seat in Congress, and from their Springfield law office Lincoln, when he replied to Fell's letter, was giving whole-hearted support to his partner's candidacy. A fortnight later came election day and Mr. Lincoln's return to the legislature for the third time, first in a field of seventeen candidates. It is known that he voted for Cyrus Edwards, losing Whig candidate for governor of Illinois, but more satisfying was his vote for Stuart, which helped the latter defeat Douglas thirty-six votes in a total of 36,495.

Twenty years later, while the Lincoln and Douglas debates were in progress in the summer and fall of 1858. Fell, as ever Lincoln's alert and helpful friend, made a business trip through most of the New England and Middle States, and through Michigan, Ohio and Indiana, taking care as he travelled to feel the political pulse. "Everywhere he found Republicans eager to hear of the man who was successfully defying and answering Douglas," and, "as he sounded the praises of his friend, the conviction grew in him that in a still larger field Lincoln might become the successful rival of Douglas."

When Fell returned home in the late fall of 1858 he proposed to Lincoln, then attending court in Bloomington, "that he should be the next Republican candidate for President. Lincoln professed to think it a foolish idea and declined to write the autobiography for which his friend asked, that he might acquaint people in the East with Lincoln's personal history." Soon, however, Lincoln himself began to think seriously of running for President, especially after visits to Ohio and Kansas in the fall of 1859, and on December 20, when Fell repeated his request for an autobiography, he gave him the desired paper which Fell, without waiting to copy it, mailed to his friend, Joseph J. Lewis in Westchester, Pennsylvania.

What followed forms an interesting chapter in the story of Lincoln's rise to the Presidency. Lewis, a skilled and persuasive writer widely and favorably known in Eastern Pennsylvania, with Lincoln's own story and other material furnished by Fell before him, prepared a sketch in which he stressed Lincoln's Pennsylvania ancestry, his stout advocacy through the years of a protective tariff and other phases of his career sure to appeal to the Republican and anti-slavery Democrats for whom it was intended. It was published in the Chester County Times on February 11, 1860, and, widely copied throughout Pennsylvania and beyond it, helped not a little to shape the decision whereby at the Republican national convention in May the vote of the Pennsylvania delegation was at a decisive moment transferred from Cameron to Lincoln. The manuscript on which it was based was by Lewis duly returned to Fell, who in 1872 published a facsimile of it with an introduction. It is now owned by the Fell estate. In March, 1863, President Lincoln appointed Lewis commissioner of internal revenue. See, "Life of Jesse W. Fell" by Morehouse, pp. 58-64, and "Lincoln in Pennsylvania" by Charles William Heathcote, 1935.

Bloomington July 20th 1838

Dr Sir

I wrote you a few days since a few lines in relation to Stuart —the charges preferred against him about a Government Bank— his coming into this County before the election &c which you have doubtless recd. Do me the favor to reply to it per bearer Mr B. F. Wood of this place—to whom permit me to introduce you. Mr Wood is a fast friend of Stuart and can let you know all about election matters in McLean. We'll do our duty—depend on it.

In great haste
Very respectfully
J. W. Fell

A. Lincoln Esqr.

————————————

Dear Fell.

Yours on the reverse side of this sheet is this moment received. Owing to my absence, the former letter of which you speak was not received until Saturday evening. I answered it yesterday, and doubtless you will have received the answer ere you receive this. I again repeat that you may deny the charges made by Douglass against Stuart in relation to a government Bank. I hope Stuart will pay you the much deserved visit; he is, however, doing well, we are told, where he is. If we do our duty we shall succeed in the congressional election, but if we relax an iota, we shall be beaten.

Your friend
A. Lincoln

MR. LINCOLN ONE OF THE SIGNERS OF A PETITION TO GOVERNOR DUNCAN, JULY 25, 1838

On July 25, 1838, Mr. Lincoln was one of the fourteen signers of the petition here reproduced which asked Governor Joseph Duncan to appoint John Dixon to the vacancy on the important Board of Commissioners of Public Works to succeed James A. Stephenson who had resigned from that body. Dixon, a Whig, and founder of the city which bears his name, was duly appointed by Governor Duncan, and in February, 1839, the Legislature elected him for a full term. Until near the end of his long life of ninety-two years Dixon remained active in politics, and as a delegate to the first Republican state convention held in Illinois, was one of those who listened to and applauded Lincoln's famous Lost Speech. The original of the petition requesting his appointment as commissioner of public works is now owned by one of his descendants, George C. Dixon.

An early and devoted reader of the Washington Globe, Mr. Lincoln, in the month in which he lent a helping hand to a fellow Whig, must have learned from its columns that on August 18, 1838, Lieutenant Charles Wilkes of the Navy had sailed from Hampton Roads on the voyage to Antarctic waters which was to make him famous as an explorer—this in happy ignorance of the fact that three and twenty years later Wilkes by his capture of Mason and Slidell was to supply him with one of the thorny problems of his first year as President.

Springfield July 25, 1838

To His Excelency J. Duncan

Having been informed that a vacancy has occurred in the board of Comrs of Public Works, by the resignation of J. A. Stephenson, we take much pleasure in recommending to your favorable consideration for the vacancy thus created our fellow citizen John Dixon of Ogle County, whom we consider in every way qualified to discharge the duties of such office.

C R Mathews
A G Herndon
A W Edwards
J F Speed
Wm Butler
G Elkin
A Lincoln
Gusshorn Jaquest
Tho C Brown

A G Henry

Jesse B Thomas Jr

Simeon Francis

Jud Wright Comr. Pub Works

EDITORIAL NOTE BY MR. LINCOLN ON BOWLING GREEN, SANGAMO JOURNAL, AUGUST 11, 1838

Mr. Lincoln early found that now and then the penalties of Whig leadership were embarrassing ones. Thus at the August election in 1838, in which Stuart defeated Douglas for Congress and Lincoln was re-elected to the legislature, Archer G. Herndon, Whig, and Bowling Green, Democrat, opposed each other as candidates for the State Senate, and Mr. Lincoln, much to his regret, had to work and vote against his old friend of New Salem days. Herndon was elected by a majority of 47 votes, and the result prompted the editorial note in the Sangamo Journal here reproduced. It is to be noted in passing that although in Sangamon County Mr. Lincoln led the poll in New Salem he received only 31 votes, 70 less than that precinct gave to John Calhoun, the only Democrat to secure election to the legislature. This result was due to two things: New Salem had now become a Democratic stronghold, and Mr. Lincoln's position on the division of Sangamon county, a division hotly opposed by many residents of the hamlet, had lost him a great number of supporters in his former home.

OUR SENATORIAL ELECTION.

At the result of this election, we are both gratified and wounded. We believe the interest of our county required that Herndon should be elected; and, therefore, we are gratified with his selection. On the other hand, to see our old friend, Bowling Green, beaten, and to have been under the necessity of aiding in defeating him, we confess is, and has been, extremely painful to us. Under other circumstances, we would have been glad to do battle for him; but as it was, he threw himself in the ranks of our enemies, and therefore we could do no less than we did.

MR. LINCOLN BECOMES SECURITY FOR COSTS IN THE SUIT OF WILLIAMS VS. CABANISS, SANGAMON CIRCUIT COURT, AUGUST 13, 1838

The original of this document entirely in the hand of Mr. Lincoln is now in the Illinois State Historical Library at Springfield.

Albert G. Williams ⎱
     vs   ⎰ In Covenant
John M. Cabaniss & ⎰ Damage $300
George S. Cabaniss ⎰

    The clerk of the Sangamon circuit court will issue process in the above entitled cause returnable to the next term of said court—

                              Stuart & Lincoln
                                 for Plff—

Albert G. Williams ⎱
     vs   ⎰
John M. Cabaniss & ⎰   Sangamon Circuit Court—
George S. Cabaniss ⎰

    I do hereby enter myself security for costs in this case, and acknowledge myself bound to pay or cause to be paid all costs which may accrue in this action either to the opposite party or to any of the officers of this court in pursuance of the laws of this state.

                                     A. Lincoln
Dated this 13th day of August A. D. 1838

BILL FOR DIVORCE IN THE SUIT OF FOSTER VS. FOSTER, SANGAMON CIRCUIT COURT, AUGUST 13, 1838

(Herndon-Weik Collection)

*   The notation, "Filed August 16th, Wm Butler clk.," is in the hand of the clerk; the rest of this document and notations are from the pen of Mr. Lincoln. On October 20, 1838, the following entry appeared in the Record Book of the Sangamon County Circuit Court: "On motion of Complainant counsel it is ordered that this cause be dismissed at complainant's cost."*
To the Honorable the Judge of the Sangamon circuit court in chancery sitting:

    Humbly complaining sheweth unto your Honor your orator, George W. Foster, that he, your orator was, some time in the month of November in the year of our Lord one thousand eight hundred and thirtyfive, in the county of Sangamon and the state of Illinois, lawfully married to one Charlotte Cooley; that, he your orator, and the said Charlotte continued to live together as man and wife until some time in the month of February in the year of our Lord one thousand eight hundred and thirtysix, at which time, she the said Charlotte, wholly abandoned your orator, and left his bed and board, and has ever since, and for more than the space of two years, wholly refused to return and live with your orator— Your orator states that while he and the said Charlotte lived together, he, your orator, did and performed all and every duty as a faithful and affectionate husband to wards the said Charlotte—

In tender consideration of all which, your orator prays that the said Charlotte Foster be made defendant to this Bill; and that the People's writ of subpoena may issue &c; and that on a final hearing of this cause, your Honor will decree, that the bonds of matrimony heretofore and now existing between your orator and the said Charlotte, be forever dissolved; and that your Honor will grant such other and further relief as equity may seem to require; and your orator as in duty bound &c.—

Stuart & Lincoln
Complts Solicitors

George W. Foster 58

vs } Bill for Divorce

Charlotte Foster

Filed august 16th 1838
     Wm Butler Clk

Let process issue hereon—

Stuart & Lincoln

BILL FOR DIVORCE IN THE SUIT OF SAMUEL ROGERS VS. POLLY ROGERS, AUGUST 14, 1838
(Herndon-Weik Collection)

Mr. Lincoln penned the original bill for divorce in this case. He also penned the cover notations, and the order for issue of process, the one exception being the date of filing. This is probably in the hand of Butler, but is not distinctly his handwriting. Attorney Lincoln omitted the word, "time" after "some" in the line, "some in June or July." It appears that he often thought ahead of his pen, and at such times, omissions were likely to occur. It does not seem that he re-read this paper, as other documents reveal that he put in words which he had omitted. The original bill did not include the adultery charge contained in a later and amended bill and clearly sustains the statement in the affadavit of Lincoln, dated October 20, 1838, *that he dissuaded Rogers from using the adultery charge as grounds for divorce.*

To the Honorable the Judge of the Sangamon circuit court
    in Chancery sitting—

Humbly complaining sheweth unto your Honor, your orator, Samuel Rogers, that some time in the month of October in the year one thousand eight hundred and thirtyfive in the county of Sangamon and state of Illinois, he, your orator, was lawfully married to one Polly Offill; that he, your orator, and the said Polly continued to live together. as man and wife, he your orator, doing and performing every duty on his part, as a tender and affectionate husband, until some in the month of June or July in the year one thousand eight hundred and thirty six, when she the said Polly, left the bed and board of your orator, and has ever since wholly refused to live with him.

In tender consideration of all which, your orator prays, that the said Polly Rogers may be made defendant to this Bill; and that the Peoples writ of Subpoena may issue &c.; and that on a final hearing of the case, your Honor will decree, that the bonds of matrimony now, and heretofore existing between your orator and Polly his wife, be forever dissolved; and that your Honor will grant such other and further relief as equity may require; and your orator, as in duty bound &c.

Stuart & Lincoln
Solicitors for comp

Samuel Rogers

vs   } Bill for Divorce

Polly Rogers

Filed & Issued Aug. 14
1838
        Wm Butler Clk

_____

Let process issue hereon
Stuart and Lincoln

PRAECIPE IN THE SUIT OF HART VS. HARRISON AND HOUGHTON, AUGUST 16, 1838

(Herndon-Weik Collection)

This praecipe is not in the hand of Mr. Lincoln, but appears to have been worded by him. The cover notations down to

"Praecipe" also may have been in his hand as they evidence certain characteristics of his penmanship. Harrison, one of the defendants in this case, was long a friend and political supporter of Mr. Lincoln. Powers in his "Early Settlers of Sangamon County" (Springfield, 1876) repeats some of the piquant stories of pioneer days which Harris, who came from Virginia to Illinois in 1823, delighted to tell in old age.

Rhoda Hart. Executrix of the last will & testament of Moses Hart Deceased. Plaintiff ⎫⎬⎭ In the circuit court for Sangamon county Illinois. to the October term thereof. for the year A. D. 1838

Action of Trespass on the case upon promises Damage Five hundred Dollars.

The clerk of the circuit court aforesaid will issue. summons to the Defendants as above directed to the sheriff of Sangamon county & returnable to the next term of said court.

Lincoln. For Pltff

Aug. 16th 1838.
Rhoda Hart ex. &c
    vs
Peyton L. Harrison &
Elijah Houghton
    Praecipe
Filed August 19th 1838
  Wm Butler Clk

LIST DRAWN BY MR. LINCOLN OF NOTES DUE THE ESTATE OF GEORGE SPEARS, SEPTEMBER 3, 1838

The debtors who figure in this list were residents of the New Salem neighborhood. Thomas Jefferson Nance who had come from Kentucky to be a school-teacher in Illinois, later served in the Legislature. An interesting letter addressed to him by Mr. Lincoln is owned by one of his descendants, but it has not been possible to secure a copy of it for inclusion in these pages. The original of the Spears list is now in the Illinois State Historical Library.

The following is a correct list or inventory of the notes due the estate of George Spears Sen. deceased—viz—

    John Pemberton & T. J. Nance $ 50.
    Joshua Nance & John M. Bigley   " 24.

Jacob Bale & Benjamin Gibbs   "200.
Jacob Bale & Levi Summers   30.
Jacob Bale & James Goldsby   45.
Jacob Bale & Levi Summers   50.
James Goldsby & Levi Summers   80.
                                    _____
                                     $479.
Also one note paid   & 20.
                                    _____
                                     $499.
In addition to the above collected
     interest   60.
                                    _____
                                     $559.

Sept 3—1838   George Spears Jr.
                           Executor of
                           George Spears Sen. decd—

DECLARATION IN THE SUIT OF DURLEY VS. MITTS AND BALL, SANGAMON CIRCUIT COURT, SEPTEMBER 10, 1838
(Herndon-Weik Collection)

The declaration and cover notations in this case, with one exception, are from the pen of Lawyer Lincoln. The one exception is the date of filing in the hand of Butler. The Lincoln handwriting might be construed as giving a possible, "John," as the first name of Mr. Durley, but it appears more like "Jehu." The name of the defendants are penned by Mr. Lincoln as "Mitts and Ball." It is possible that this may have been, "Mills and Ball," but the characteristic Lincoln double "L" is not seen in the word, "Mitts." The double "i," if it be this, is crossed upon three distinct occasions. It is known that Mr. Lincoln infrequently left double "t's" uncrossed, and crossed double "i's" at times. The name is given as it appears in the Lincoln hand. The paragraph preceding the words, "Yet the said defendants (although often requested so to do)," is an unusual feature in this paper and uncommon in the legal documents penned by Mr. Lincoln in his novitiate. Judgment by default was rendered in favor of the plaintiffs on October 15, 1838. Stuart & Lincoln represented them.

State of Illinois   ⎫ ss
                           ⎬   In the circuit court of said county
Sangamon county & circuit ⎭   —October Term, A. D. 1838—

Jehu Durley, plaintiff, complains of Jesse Mitts and Japhet A. Bell, defendants, being in custody &c. of a plea of Tresspass on the case upon promises: For that whereas, the said defendants, heretofore, towit, on the ninth day of May in the year of our Lord one thousand eight hundred and thirtyseven, at the county and circuit aforesaid, made their certain promissory note in writing, the date whereof is the day and year aforesaid, and thereby then and there promised to pay on demand to the said plaintiff the sum of one hundred dollars, drawing twelve per cent interest per annum, for value received, and then and there delivered the said promissory note to the said plaintiff; by means whereof, and by force of the statute in such case made and provided, the said defendants then and there became liable to pay to the said plaintiff the said sum of money in the said promissory note specified, according to the tenor and effect of the said promissory note; and being so liable, they, the said defendants, in consideration thereof, afterwards towit, on the day and year aforesaid undertook and then and there faithfully promised the said plaintiff to pay him the said sum of money in the said promissory note specified, according to the tenor and effect thereof—And the said plaintiff in fact saith that afterwards, towit, on the
day of   in the year
at the county and circuit aforesaid, payment of the said sum of money, in the said promissory note specified was duly demanded by the said plaintiff, of the said defendants according to the tenor and effect of the said promissory note—

Yet the said defendants (although often requested so to do) have not as yet paid to the said plaintiff the said sum of money in the said promissory note specified, or any part thereof; but sotodo have hitherto wholly neglected and refused, and still do neglect and refuse; To the damage of the said plaintiff of the sum of two hundred dollars and therefore he brings his suit &c.

The following is a copy of the instrument declared on— "May 9 1837—

We or either of us promise to pay Jehu Durley one hundred dollars on demand, drawing twelve per cent interest per anom . . . for value received of him as witness our hands and seals this day and date above written—

Jesse Mitts
Japhet A. Ball"

Jehu Durley

vs } Decln

Jesse Mitts &
Japhet A. . Ball
Filed Sep 10th 1838
WButler ck

DECLARATION IN THE SUIT OF ELLIS VS. NAVE, SANGAMON CIRCUIT COURT, SEPTEMBER 10, 1838
(Herndon-Weik Collection)

This declaration and the cover notations are in the hand of Mr. Lincoln, with the exception of the date of filing. One note of interest lies in the omission of the word "our" preceding "Lord" in the second line of the document. On October 19, 1838, Nave defaulted, judgment was rendered in favor of Ellis, and the clerk was ordered to assess the damages.

State of Illinois

}ss

Sangamon county & circuit } In the circuit court of said county
—October Term A. D. 1838

Abner Y. Ellis, plaintiff, complains of Levi Nave defendant being in custody &c of a plea of Tresspass on the case upon promises : For that whereas the said defendant, heretofore, towit ; on the thirtyfirst day of March in the year of Lord one thousand eight hundred and thirtyseven at the county and circuit aforesaid, made his certain promissory note in writing, bearing date the day and year aforesaid, and thereby then and there promised to pay, twelve months after the date thereof, to the said plaintiff on order, the sum of Four hundred and fifty dollars, for value received, and then and there delivered the said promissory note to the said plaintiff ; by means whereof, and by force of the statute in such case made and provided, he, the said defendant, then and there became liable, to pay to the said plaintiff, the said sum of money in the said promissory note specified, according to the tenor and effect of the said promissory note ; and being so liable, he, the said defendant, in consideration thereof, afterward, to wit : on the day and year, and at the place aforesaid, undertook and then and there faithfully promised the said plaintiff to pay him the said sum of money in the said promissory note specified according to the tenor and effect thereof— Yet the said defendant (although often requested so to do ; and although the time specified for the payment of the said sum of money has long since elapsed) hath not as yet paid to the said plaintiff the said sum of money in the said promissory note specified, or any part thereof; but so to do hath hitherto wholly neglected and and refused, and still doth neglect and refuse: To the damage of the said plaintiff Six hundred dollars and therefore he brings his suit &c

Stuart & Lincoln
for Plff.

The following is a copy of the instrument declared on:
"$450

Twelve months after date I promise to pay Abner Y. Ellis on order the sum of Four hundred and fifty dollars value received—Witness my hand. March 31st 1837

Levi Nave"

A. Y. Ellis
}
vs } Decln
}
Levi Nave

Filed Sept 10 1838
        Wm Butler clk

ANTRIM CAMPBELL RECOMMENDED FOR PROSECUTING ATTORNEY BY MR. LINCOLN AND OTHERS, SEPTEMBER 13, 1838

On September 13, 1838, Josephus Hewett, wrote to Governor Joseph Duncan resigning as prosecuting attorney of the first judicial district of Illinois to which post he had been appointed by that official. At the bottom of Hewett's letter the writer, Mr. Lincoln and five other members of the Sangamon County bar joined in a recommendation that Antrim Campbell, who, as noted above, had recently settled in Springfield, be appointed to succeed him. The original of this recommendation is now in the Illinois State Archives.

We the undersigned to hereby certify that Antrim Campbell has been engaged in the practice of the Law in Springfield for eight months last past, and from our knowledge of his character do believe him in every respect worthy of confidence and esteem. And we do also cheerfully recommend him to his Excellency, Joseph Duncan, Governor of the State of Illinois, as fully qualified and competent to fulfill the duties of Prosecuting Attorney and would be much pleased to see him get the Appointment to said office.

Stephen T. Logan,
E. D. Baker,
John T. Stuart,
Ninian W. Edwards,
Samuel H. Treat,
J. Hewett,
A. Lincoln,
Cyrus Walker.

SUMMONS AND DECLARATION IN THE SUIT OF TROTTER VS. PHELPS, SEPTEMBER 15 AND 18, 1838
(Herndon-Weik Collection)

This summons, a printed form filled in and signed by Butler, is reproduced in order to afford full content of the case of Trotter vs. Phelps. "Beareau" was the present Bureau County. The note included in the declaration is in an unknown or unrecognized hand. It was signed by Phelps. The original reveals that Lawyer Lincoln did not transcribe this note in its pristine glory, and one can excuse him. He missed the slightly humorous note of the word, "Severely," for "severally" in the note, but he may have chuckled over it. A comparison of such papers with those of Mr. Lincoln are basis for the tradition of his being a spelling champion. The indorsement of the note was signed by Hill, but the rest of the cover notations were penned by Mr. Lincoln.

The People of the State of Illinois
To the Sheriff of Beareau County—
Greeting

YOU are hereby commanded to summon Ebenezer S. Phelps to be and appear before the Circuit Court of Sangamon County, on the first day of the next term to be holden at Springfield, on the 2nd Monday in the month of October next, to answer to George Trotter In an action of Trespass on the case upon Promises Damages Five hundred Dollars

And have you then there this writ.
(SEAL)

Witness, William Butler Clerk
of our said Court, at Springfield,
this 15 day of Sept A. D. 1838.
Wm Butler Clerk.

Of the October Term of the Sangamon county Circuit
court in the year of our Lord one thousand eight
hundred and thirty eight—

State of Illinois
Sangamon county & circuit } ss

George Trotter, plaintiff, complains of Ebenezer S. Phelps,
defendant, being in custody &c of a plea of Tresspass on the
case upon promises; For that whereas the said, defendant, heretofore, towit, on the twelfth day of March, in the year of our
Lord one thousand eight hundred and thirtyeight, at the county
& circuit aforesaid, made his certain promissory note in writing,
signing his name thereto, "E. S. Phelps" bearing date the day
and year aforesaid, and thereby then and there promised to pay,
Six months after the date thereof, to one Leroy L. Hill or order,
the sum of three hundred and fortyfive dollars with interest
from the date thereof at six per cent (meaning six per cent per
annum till paid, and then and there delivered the said promissory
note to the said Leroy L. Hill; And the said Leroy L. Hill, to
whom, or to whose order, the payment of the said sum of money
in the said promissory note specified was to be made, after the
making of the said promissory note, and before the payment of
the said sum of money therein specified, towit, on the same day
and year and at the same place aforesaid, assigned the said
promissory note by indorsement in writing thereon, by which
said assignment, he the said Leroy L. Hill. then and there ordered and appointed the said sum of money in the said promissory note specified to be paid to the said plaintiff, and then and
there delivered the said promissory note so assigned as aforesaid, to the said plaintiff; by means whereof, and by force of the
statute in such case made and provided. the said defendant, became liable to pay to the said plaintiff, the said sum of money
in the said promissory note specified. according to the tenor and
effect, of the said promissory note; and being so liable, he, the
said defendant, in consideration thereof, afterwards, towit on the
same day & year & at the same place aforesaid, undertook, and
then and there faithfully promised the said plaintiff to pay him
the said sum of money in the said promissory note specified,
with interest according to the tenor and effect of the said promissory note—

Yet the said defendant (although often requested so todo;
and although according to the tenor and effect of the said promissory note, the said sum of money therein specified, has long since

been due) hath not as yet paid to the said plaintiff the said sum of money in the said promissory note specified, or any part thereof; but so to do hath hitherto wholly neglected and refused, and still doth neglect and refuse— To the damage of the said plaintiff of five hundred dollars and therefore he brings his suit &c—

Stuart & Lincoln for Plff

The following is a copy of the instrument declared on:

"Six months after date we Jointly and severely promis to pay Leroy L. Hill or order three hundred and fortyfive dollars with interest from date at six per cent from date till— March th 12. 1838.

E. S. Phelps"

(Assignment thereon)

"Pay to George Trotter

Leroy L. Hill"

George Trotter

vs   }   Decln

Ebenezer S. Phelps

Filed Sept 18th 1838

Wm Butler clerk

Trotter vs. Phelps: Original Note and Indorsement:

Six months after date we Jointly and Severely pomis to pay Leroy L Hill or order three hundred and forty five dollars with in ter- rest from date at Six per cent fom date till paid March th 12 1838

E. S. Phelps

Prin	$345
Int—	12-07½
Amt.	357 07½

Pay to George Trotter

Leroy L. Hill

DECLARATION IN THE SUIT OF FELLOWS VS. KELLAR AND SNYDER, MACON CIRCUIT COURT, SEPTEMBER 19, 1838

With one or two exceptions, the declaration and quoted notes in this case were drawn by Mr. Lincoln. The exceptions will be found in the names, "Abraham H.," and "Albert G.," preceding

*the names "Kellar" and "Snyder" respectively, in the sentence
beginning the document. In the phrase, "complain of Abraham
H. Kellar and Albert G. Snyder," there is a slight departure from
the handwriting of Mr. Lincoln, and it is the same handwriting
that was responsible for the same names in the praecipe and bond
in this case. It appears to be the penmanship of Mr. McGorin,
the clerk, who penned the cover notations. Attorney Lincoln
used the spelling "bussiness" for "business," an error not infrequent in his earlier legal documents. The hyphenated sixty
eight" was caused by reaching the end of the page. The results
of most Macon County cases for this period have not been made
available, but an agreement of March 24 1839, later to be recorded, may be regarded as the end of this suit. Thanks are due
to the Lincoln National Life Foundation of Fort Wayne for
photostats of this and other actions involving the same principals.*

State of Illinois

Macon county & circuit $\rbrace$ ss   In the circuit court of said county
October Term— A. . D. 1838—

William Fellows and Cornelius Fellows, trading and doing
business under the name style and firm of "W. & C. Fellows"
plaintiffs, complain of Abraham H. Kellar and Albert G. Snyder,
defendants, being in custody &c. of a plea that they render to the
said plaintiffs the sum of nine hundred and thirtyseven dollars,
and thirtytwo cents lawful money of the United States, which
they owe to and unjustly detain from them: For that whereas
the said defendants, heretofore towit, on the twentieth day of
July in the year of our Lord one thousand eight hundred and
thirtysix, at the county and circuit aforesaid by their certain
writing obligatory signed "ABR. H. Kellar" & "A. . G Snyder"
sealed with their seals and now shown to the court, the date
whereof is the day and year aforesaid, acknowledged themselves
to be held and firmly bound unto one Willis Oglesby in the sum
of four hundred and sixty-eight dollars and sixtysix cents, parcel
of the sum above demanded, to be paid to the said Willis Oglesby,
six months after the date thereof for value received, and the said
Willis Oglesby to whom the payment of the said sum of money
in the said writing obligatory specified was to be made, after
the making of the said writing obligatory, and before the payment of the said sum of money therein specified, towit on the
sixth day of September in the year and at the place aforesaid,
assigned the said writing obligatory by indorsement in writing

thereon, signing his name thereto, "W. Oglesby" by which said assignment the said Willis Oglesby then and there ordered and appointed the said sum of money in the said writing obligatory specified, to be paid to the said plaintiffs, by their aforesaid style and description of "W. & C.. Fellows" and then and there delivered the said writing obligatory, so assigned as aforesaid, to the said plaintiffs; by means whereof and by force of the statute in such case made and provided, the said sum of money in the said writing obligatory, specified became due and payable to the said plaintiffs, according to the tenor and effect of the said writing obligatory—

And whereas, also afterwards towit, on the same day and year, and at the same place aforesaid, the said defendants, by their certain other writing obligatory, signed "ABR.. H. Kellar" and "A.. G.. Snyder" sealed with their seals and now shown to the court, the date whereof is the day and year aforesaid, acknowledged themselves to be held and firmly bound unto one Willis Oglesby in the sum of four hundred and sixtyeight dollars and sixtysix cents, parcel of the sum above demanded, to be paid to the said Willis Oglesby one year after the date thereof, for value received; and the said Willis Oglesby. to whom the payment of the said sum of money in the said last mentioned writing obligatory specified was to be made, after the making of the said writing obligatory, and before the payment of the said sum of money therein specified, towit, on the same day and year, and at the same place aforesaid, assigned the said writing obligatory, by indorsement in writing thereon, signing his name thereto "W. Oglesby" by which said assignment, the said Willis Oglesby then and there ordered and appointed the said sum of money in the said last mentioned writing obligatory specified to be paid to the plaintiffs, by their aforesaid style and description of "W&C. Fellows" and then and there delivered the said last mentioned writing obligatory so assigned as aforesaid, to the said plaintiffs; by means whereof, and by force of the statute in such case made and provided, the said sum of money in the said last mentioned writing obligatory specified, became due and payable to the said plaintiffs, according to the tenor and effect of the said last-mentioned writing obligatory—

Yet the said defendants (although often requested so to do; and although the time for the payment of the said several sums of money in the said several writings obligatory specified have both long since elapsed) have not as yet paid the said sum of nine hundred and thirtyseven dollars and thirtytwo cents above demanded, or any part thereof to the said plaintiffs; but have hitherto wholly neglected and refused, and still neglect and refuse so to do— To the damage of the said plaintiffs of the sum of one hundred dollars; and therefore they bring their suit &c.

Stuart & Lincoln
for Plffs—

The following are copies of the instruments declared on:

(In first count)

"Six months after date we promise to pay Willis Oglesby Four hundred and sixty eight dollars and sixty six cents for value rcd as witness our hands and seals this 20th day. July 1836

ABR. H. Kellar (Seal)
A. . G. Snyder (Seal)

(Assignment thereon)

"Sept 6. 1836 for value rcd I assign the within to W & C. Fellows.

W. Oglesby"—

(In second count)

"One year after date we promise to pay Willis Oglesby Four hundred and sixtyeight dollars and sixtytwo cents for value rcd as witness our hands and seals this 20th day July 1836

ABR. H. Kellar (Seal)
A. G. Snyder (Seal)

(Indorsement thereon)

"For value rcd I assign the within to W. & C. Fellows—

W Oglesby"

W. & C. Fellows

vs

Abraham H Kellar &
Albert G. Snyder

Filed 19th September
1838

PRAECIPE AND BOND IN THE SUIT OF FELLOWS VS. SNYDER ET AL, MACON CIRCUIT COURT, SEPTEMBER 19, 1838

This praecipe and bond were drawn by Mr. Lincoln with the exception of the names, "Abraham H. Kellar, Albert G. Snyder, and Willis Oglesby," which appear in both praecipe and bond. The cover notations were penned by Clerk McGorin. It will be noted that Attorney Lincoln used the spelling, "oposite," for the correct "opposite." While he made fewer errors in spelling than most of his colleagues, his errors were neither few, nor rare. The double period after A.. in the name "A.. G. Snyder & Co." reveals a Lincolnesque mark, and shows that this double dot was not used alone after the "A" in "A.. Lincoln." As already pointed out complete court records of these recently unearthed Macon County cases have not been made available by studies to date.

William Fellows & Cornelius Fellows
trading and doing business under
the name style and firm of W. & C. Fellows   Trespass on
                          vs   the case upon
Albert G. Snyder   Willis Oglesby   Promises—
and Abraham H Kellar   Damage $6000-00
trading and doing business under the
name style & firm of A.. G. Snyder & Co.

The clerk of the Macon county circuit court will issue process in the above cases returnable to the next term of said court—

Stuart & Lincoln for Plffs—
William Fellows & Cornelius Fellows
                          vs   Macon county
Albert G. Snyder   Willis   circuit court
Oglesby & Abraham H. Kellar

I do hereby enter myself security for costs in this case, and acknowledge myself bound to pay or cause to be paid all costs which may accrue in this action, either to the oposite party or to any of the officers of this court in pursuance of the laws of this state—

                                        A.. Lincoln—
Dated this 15th day of September A. D. 1838

W & C Fellows
    vs
A G. Snyder & Co.

Filed 19th Sept
1838
    H McGorin clk

DECLARATION IN THE SUIT OF FELLOWS VS. SNYDER ET AL, MACON CIRCUIT COURT, PROBABLY SEPTEMBER 19, 1838

As in the case of other documents in this suit, and that of Fellows & Fellows vs. Kellar and Snyder, the names, "Albert G. Snyder, Willis Oglesby and Abraham H. Kellar," were not penned by Mr. Lincoln. With this exception, he was responsible for drawing up the declaration. There is no date of filing given; it was probably September 19, 1838. As the agreement of March 24, 1839, to be recorded later, concerned both the suit of Fellows & Fellows against Kellar & Snyder, and the one against Snyder & Company, it is reasonable to infer that this declaration was filed at the same time as that in the case against Kellar & Snyder. The two cases appear to have been a part of one complete action against Snyder, Kellar, and Oglesby. Attorney Lincoln used "tresspass" for "trespass," and "bussiness" for "business," a not uncommon thing in his earlier legal documents. He is not always consistent in the use of extra spacing, but on the whole, and with consideration of legal documents of the period, it may be said that this "long" Springfield lawyer penned some of the neatest and best worded legal papers of his day.
"$ 358.40

State of Illinois
} ss   In the circuit court of said county
Macon county & circuit   October   Term   A. D. 1838——

William Fellows, and Cornelius Fellows, trading and doing bussiness under the name style and firm of "W&C. Fellows" plaintiffs, complain of Albert G. Snyder Willis Oglesby & Abraham H. Kellar defendants, being in custody &c. of a plea of Trespass on the case upon promises: For that whereas, the said defendants, heretofore, towit on the first day of March in the year of our Lord one thousand and eight hundred and thirtyfive, at Louisville, towit, at the county and circuit aforesaid, by and under the name, style and firm of "A. G. Snyder &Co" made their certain promissory note in writing, the date whereof is the day and year aforesaid, and thereby then and there promised to pay, in six months from the date thereof, to the said plaintiffs by the aforesaid style and description of "W. & C. Fellows" or order, the sum of Eleven hundred and twentyfour dollars and seventynine cents, with interest after for value received; and then and there delivered the said promissory note to the said plaintiffs; by means whereof, and by force of the statute in such case

made and provided, the said defendants then and there became
liable to pay to the said plaintiffs, the said sum of money in the
said promissory note specified, according to the tenor and effect
of the said promissory note; and being so liable, they, the said
defendants, in consideration thereof, afterwards, towit, on the
day and year & at the place aforesaid, undertook, and then and
there faithfully promised the said plaintiffs, to pay them the said
sum of money in the said promissory note specified, according to
the tenor and effect thereof—

And whereas also afterwards, towit, on the seventeenth day
of June in the same year, and at the place aforesaid, the said defendants, by and under the same name style and firm of '"A. G.
Snyder &Co" made their certain other promissory note in writing, bearing date the day and year last aforesaid, and thereby
then and there promised to pay, six months after the date thereof, to the said plaintiffs, by their aforesaid style and description
of "W&C. Fellows," or order, the sum of four hundred and one
dollars and one cent, for value received, and then and there delivered the said promissory note to the said plaintiffs; by means
whereof, and by force of the statute in such case made and provided, the said defendants then and there became liable to pay to
the said plaintiffs the said sum of money in the said last mentioned promissory note specified, according to the tenor and effect of the said last mentioned promissory note; and being so
liable, they, the said defendants, in consideration thereof, afterwards towit, on the same day and year, and at the place last
aforesaid, undertook, and then and there faithfully promised the
said plaintiffs to pay them the said sum of money in the said last
mentioned promissory note specified, according to the tenor and
effect thereof— '

And whereas also afterwards, towit, on the ninth day of
September in the same year, and at the same place aforesaid, the
said defendants, by the aforesaid name, style and firm, of "A. G.
Snyder & Co" made their certain other promissory note in writing, bearing date the day and year last aforesaid, and thereby
then and there promised to pay, Six months after the date thereof, to the said plaintiffs, by the aforesaid style and description of
"W. &C. Fellows" or order, the sum of Twentyseven hundred
and eightythree dollars and seventyfive cents, for value received,
and then and there delivered the said last mentioned promissory
note to the said plaintiffs; by means whereof, and by force of
the statute in such case made and provided, the said defendants,
then and there became liable to pay to the said plaintiffs, the said
sum of money in the said last mentioned promissory note specified, according to the tenor and effect of the said last mentioned

promissory note; and being so liable, they, the said defendants, in consideration thereof, afterwards, towit, on the same day and year, and at the same place aforesaid, undertook, and then and there faithfully promised, the said plaintiffs to pay them the said sum of money in the said last-mentioned promissory note specified, according to the tenor and effect thereof—

And whereas also afterwards, towit, on the seventh day of November in the same year, and at the same place aforesaid the said defendants, by and under, the aforesaid name, style and firm, of "A. G. Snyder &Co" made their certain other promissory note in writing, bearing date the day and year last aforesaid, and thereby then and there, promised to pay, Six months after the date thereof, to the said plaintiffs, by the aforesaid style and description of "W & C. Fellows" or order, the sum of four hundred and fiftyseven dollars and twentytwo cents, for value received, and then and there delivered the said last mentioned promissory note, to the said plaintiffs; by means whereof, and by force of the statute in such case made and provided, the said defendants then and there became liable to pay to the said plaintiffs, the said sum of money in the said last mentioned promissory note specified, according to the tenor and effect of the said last mentioned promissory note; and being so liable, they, the said defendants, in consideration thereof, afterwards, towit, on the same day and year, and at the same place last aforesaid, undertook, and then and there faithfully promised the said plaintiffs to pay them, the said sum of money in the said last mentioned promissory note specified, according to the tenor and effect thereof—

And whereas also afterwards, towit, on the sixteenth day of December in the year of our Lord one thousand eight hundred and thirtyseven, at Decatur, towit, at the county and circuit aforesaid, the said defendants, by and under the aforesaid, name, style and firm of "A. G. Snyder &Co" made their certain other promissory note in writing, bearing date the day and year last aforesaid, and thereby then and there promised to pay, one day after the date thereof, to the said plaintiffs, by their aforesaid, style and description of "W.&.C. Fellows" or order, the sum of eight hundred and eightytwo dollars and one cent, for value received, and then and there delivered the said last-mentioned promissory note to the said plaintiffs; by means whereof and by force of the statute in such case made and provided the said defendants then and there became liable to pay to the said plaintiffs the said sum of money in the said last mentioned promissory note specified, according to the tenor and effect of the said last mentioned promissory note, and being so liable, they the said defendants, in consideration thereof, afterwards, towit, on the same day and year, and at the same place last aforesaid, undertook, and then and there faithfully promised the said plaintiffs to pay them the said sum of money in the said last mentioned promissory note specified, according to the tenor and effect thereof—

Yet the said defendants (although often requested sotodo; and although the said several times for the payment of the said several sums of money in the said several promissory notes specified, have all long since elapsed) have not as yet paid the said several sums of money in the said several promissory notes specified, or either of them, to the said plaintiffs; but so to do have hitherto wholly neglected and refused, and still do neglect and refuse—To the damage of the said plaintiffs of the sum of Six thousand dollars, and therefore they bring their suit &c.

Stuart & Lincoln for Plffs

On the reverse side of this sheet are copies of the notes declared on:

(Note in first count)

"$1121 Dolls. 79 cts Louisville March 1 1835

For value received we the subscribers of Decatur county of Macon and state of Illinois, promise to pay W & C. Fellows or order Eleven hundred & twentyone dollars 79 cents in six months with interest after
Attest

A.. G. Snyder & Co"

(In second count)

"$401 Dolls. $01 cts Louisville June 17 1835

Six months after date we the subscribers of Decatur, county of Macon and state of Illinois promise to pay W & C. Fellows or order Four hundred & one dollars 01 cents for value received
Attest

A.. G. Snyder & Co"

(In third count)

"$2783 Dolls. 75 cts Louisville Sept 9 1835

Six months after date we the subscribers of Decatur, county of Macon and state of Illinois promise to pay W & C. Fellows or order, Twentyseven hundred & eightythree dollars 75 cents for value received
Attest

A.. G. Snyder & Co"

(In fourth count)

"$457 Dolls. 22 cts Louisville 7th Novem. 1835

Six months after date we the subscribers of Decatur, county of Macon and state of Illinois promise to pay W & C. Fellows or order four hundred and fiftyseven dollars 22 cents for value received.

Attest

A.. G. Snyder & Co"

(In fifth count)

"$882. 01/100 Decatur 16 December 1837

One day after date the subscribers of Decatur, county of Macon and state of Illinois promise to pay W & C. Fellows or order eight hundred and eightytwo dollars, one cent for value received—

Attest

A.. G. Snyder & Co"

PRAECIPE AND BOND IN THE SUIT OF FELLOWS ET AL VS. KELLAR AND SNYDER MACON CIRCUIT COURT, SEPTEMBER 19, 1838

Mr. Lincoln drew up this praecipe and bond with the exception of the words "Abraham H." and "Albert G." which precede the names of Kellar and Snyder respectively, in both praecipe and bond. The cover notations are by Clerk McGorin. As is seen in the praecipe, the case was based on collection of a debt, but a more complete picture is given in the declaration of the case, filed on the same day. As in many of the Lincoln legal papers recently unearthed in the Macon County Court files, a case history has not been made available by research to date.

William Fellows & Cornelius Fellows trading and doing business under the name style and firm of W. & C. Fellows vs. Abraham H. Kellar & Albert G. Snyder

In Debt —
Debt—$938-32 cents
Damage "100-00

The clerk of the Macon county circuit court will issue process in the above case, returnable to the next term of said court—

Stuart & Lincoln for Plffs—

Sept. 19, 1838.

William Fellows & Cornelius Fellows vs. Abraham H. Keller & Albert G. Snyder

Macon County Circuit Court—

I do hereby enter myself security for costs in this cause and acknowledge myself bound to pay or cause to be paid all costs which may accrue in this action either to the opposite party or to any of the officers of this court in pursuance of the laws of this state—

Dated this 15th of September A. D. 1838—

A. Lincoln

W. & C. Fellows
vs   }   Precipe &
Kellar & Snyder   Bond

Filed 19th September
1838
    H McGorin clk

PRAECIPE AND BOND IN THE SUIT OF BAUM & SHELDON VS. VAN BERGEN, SANGAMON CIRCUIT COURT, SEPTEMBER 19, 1838

(From the Lincoln National Life Foundation)

This praecipe and bond were drawn by Mr. Loncoln. Peter Van Bergen, a former creditor of Mr. Lincoln, was the defendant in this case. Despite his bringing suit against Lincoln in New Salem days, later on frequent occasions he was the client of Lawyer Lincoln. The record, if any, has not been unearthed yet, as regards this case.

Jacob Baum & John G. Shelton
Trading and doing business under
the name, style and firm of   }   Trespass on the Case
Baum & Shelton   upon Promises
vs.   Damage $250.00
Peter Van Bergen

The clerk of the Sangamon County Circuit Court will issue process herein returnable to the next term of this Court

Stuart &Lincoln
for Plaintiff

Jacob Baum & John G. Shelton
trading and doing business under
the name, style and firm
of Baum & Shelton   }   Sangamon Circuit Court
vs.
Peter Van Bergen

I do hereby enter myself security for costs in this cause, and acknowledge myself bound to pay or cause to be paid all costs which may accrue in this action, either to the opposite party or to any of the officers of this Court, in pursuance of the laws of this State.

A. Lincoln

Dated this 19th day of September, A. D. 1838

DECLARATION IN THE SUIT OF HARLAND VS. MOFFETT ET AL, SANGAMON CIRCUIT COURT, SEPTEMBER 20, 1838
(Herndon-Weik Collection)

The date of filing is in the hand of Clerk Butler, but this declaration and all other notations are in the handwriting of Mr. Lincoln. The case is sometimes cited as Harlan vs. Moffett & Co., but Lawyer Lincoln seems to have added a distinct, "d," after the "n" in "Harlan." Judgment was rendered by the default of the Moffetts, and Stuart and Lincoln added a victory to a most commendable record on October 15, 1838.

State of Illinois

Sangamon county & circuit

} ss

Of the October term of the circuit court for said county in the year 1838—

Silas Harland plaintiff, complains of John B. Moffett and Thomas Moffett defendants being in custody &c of a plea of Tresspass on the case upon promises: For that whereas the said defendants, heretofore towit, on the twenty-eighth day of December in the year of our Lord one thousand eight hundred and thirtyseven at the county and circuit aforesaid, made their certain promissory note in writing, bearing date the day and year aforesaid, and thereby then and there promised to pay on or before the first day of April next ensuing, to the said plaintiff the sum of three hundred and fiftyeight dollars and forty cents with twelve per cent per annum interest thereon from the tenth day of August 1837 till paid—for value received, and then and there delivered the said promissory note to the said plaintiff; by means whereof and by force of the statute in such case made and provided, they, the said defendants, then and there became liable to pay to the said plaintiff, the said sum of money in the said promissory note specified, according to the tenor and effect of the said promissory note; and being so liable, they the said defendants, in consideration thereof, afterwards, towit, on the day and year, and at the place aforesaid, undertook, and then and there faithfully promised the said plaintiff to pay him the said sum of money in the said promissory note specified according to the tenor and effect thereof—

Yet the said defendants (although often requested sotodo) have not as yet paid the said plaintiff the said sum of money in the said promissory note specified or any part thereof; but so to do hath hitherto wholly neglected and refused, and still do neglect and refuse, to the damage of the said plaintiff of the sum of five hundred dollars

And therefore he brings his suit &c Stuart &Lincoln
for Plff

The following is a copy of the instrument declared on:

"On or before the first day of April next we or either of us promise to pay to Silas Harland or order the sum of Three hundred & fiftyeight dollars & 40 cents with twelve per cent per annum interest thereon from the tenth day of August 1837 til paid value recd. Witness our hands this 28th day of December A. D. 1837

John B. Moffett
Thomas Moffett"

Silas Harland

vs } Decln

John B. Moffett &
Thomas Moffett

Filed Sept 20" 1838
  Wm Butler Clk

PRAECIPE AND NOTES IN THE SUIT OF VAN BERGEN VS. NEALE, SANGAMON CIRCUIT COURT, SEPTEMBER 21, 1838
(Herndon-Weik Collection)

Mr. Lincoln drew this praecipe but, as in most cases during his first years at the bar, the cover notations are by Clerk Butler. The word "'Dam" and the figures "400" are in the hand of Attorney Lincoln, and the former, although almost too minute to be seen, is distinctly Lincolnesque in character. In this case, both plaintiff and client were friends of Mr. Lincoln. Van Bergen appears as the client of Stuart & Lincoln, in contrast to having been plaintiff in a suit against Mr. Lincoln. Mr. Henry was James D. Henry. He had been sheriff of Sangamon County, and in 1833, as noted elsewhere, had received judgment against Lincoln and Nelson Alley, for non-payment of a note signed by them. Neale defaulted on October 15, 1838, and Mr. Lincoln gained a triumph, if it may be so called, over his former employer in the surveyor's office.

One day after date we promise to pay Peter
Van Bergen fifty nine dollars & forty cents for value
recd and if not paid to draw fifty per cent
interest untill paid Witness our hands & seals
this 25th of April 1832   T M Neale (Seal)
                        J D Henry (Seal)

The note bears none of the handwriting of Mr. Lincoln.
Neal & Henry

No 26

$ 59.40

Received on the within $ 23.62½
Ap 1837
Amt   207.70
         49.40

         158.30
           1.70

         160.00
           1

None of the writing in this paper appears to be in the hand of Lincoln, although "Ap 1837" was some of the figures are very similar to his handwriting.

Due Peter Van Bergen or order twenty dollars for cash lent April 21st 1837

T M Neale

Dam   400

          Neale
Prin   20
Int   1.70

         21.70
       207.70

       229.40

       228.83
        21.70

       250.53

The words, "Neale, Prin and Int," were penned by Lincoln. The figures are his also, and appear to be computation of the note with interest in the case. There are other figures upon the document which appear to be further figuring upon the part of Lincoln, but which add no knowledge of interest to the paper, which is slightly significant at best.

Peter Van Bergen		In Debt
vs	}	Debt $ 79. 40—
Thomas M. Neale		Damage 300 ——00

The clerk of the Sangamon county circuit court will issue process in the above case returnable to the next term of said

Stuart & Lincoln
for Plff

Peter Van Bergen

vs

Thomas M Neale

Filed Sept 21 1838
WButler

DECLARATION AND PRAECIPE IN THE SUIT OF SHORT VS. QUINTON AND MORGAN, SANGAMON CIRCUIT COURT, SEPTEMBER 21, 1838

(Herndon-Weik Collection)

This praecipe and declaration come from the hand and pen of Abraham Lincoln as do the cover notations, with the exception of the date on which the papers were filed. The word, "copy" is spelled without the double "p" which Mr. Lincoln used often in other documents. Joshua Short, the plaintiff, as elsewhere recorded, was on early and helpful friend of Mr. Lincoln. One of the defendants, Richard Quinton, was an active Democrat politician, who took part in Mr. Lincoln's first debate of political issues on July 11, 1836. Research to the present day has produced no record of this case beyond the filing of the praecipe and declaration.

State of Illinois		Of the October term of the
	ss	circuit court of said county
Sangamon county & circuit		in the year 1837—

Joshua Short plaintiff complains of Richard Quinton and John Morgan defendants being in custody &c of a plea of Tresspass on the case upon promises: For that whereas said defendants, heretofore, towit, on the first day of February in the year of our Lord one thousand eight hundred and thirtysix, at the county & circuit aforesaid made their certain promissory note in writing, bearing date the day and year aforesaid, and thereby then and there promised to pay, one day after the date thereof, to the said plaintiff, or order, the sum of two hundred dollars with twelve per cent interest from date until paid, for value received, and then and there delivered the said promissory note to the said plaintiff; by means whereof, and by force of the statute in such case made and provided, the said defendants then and there became liable to pay to the said plaintiff the said sum of money in

the said promissory note specified according to the tenor and effect of the said promissory note; and being so liable, they, the
said defendants, in consideration thereof, afterwards towit, on the
same day & year, and at the same place aforesaid, undertook, and
then and there faithfully promised the said plaintiff to pay him
the said sum of money in the said promissory note specified, according to the tenor and effect thereof— Yet the said defendants
(although often requested so to do, and although time for the
payment of the said sum of money in the said promissory note
specified, has long since elapsed) have not as yet paid to the said
plaintiff, the said sum of money in the said promissory note specified, or any part thereof; but so to do have hitherto wholly
neglected and refused, and still do, neglect and refuse— To the
damage of the said plaintiff of the sum of three hundred dollars,
and therefore he brings his suit &c.

Stuart &Lincoln
for Plff

The following is a copy of the instrument declared:
"One day after date we or either of us promise to pay Joshua
Short or order two hundred dollars with twelve per—
cent interest from date until paid, it being for value
received of him, so witness our hands this February the
1st 1836
done in the presents of
W. C. Brown
Richard Quinton
his
John + Morgan —"
marks

John Morgan ⎫
vs   ⎬   Tresspass on the case upon promises—
Richard Quinton & ⎬   Damage $ 300-00
Joshua Short ⎭

The clerk of the Sangamon county circuit court will issue
process on the above returnable to the next term of said court—

Stuart &Lincoln
for Plff—

Joshua Short ⎫
vs ⎬ Precipe & Decln
 ⎭

Richard Quinton &
John Morgan——
Filed Sept 21 1838
   Wm Butler ck

DECLARATION IN THE SUIT OF VAN BERGEN VS. NEALE, SANGAMON CIRCUIT COURT, SEPTEMBER 22, 1838

Declaration of the plaintiff in the suit of Van Bergen vs. Neale promptly followed the filing of the praecipe.

Peter Van Bergen plaintiff, complains of Thomas M. Neale, defendant being in custody & of a plea that he the said defendant, render, him the said plaintiff, the sum of seventynine dollars and forty cents, lawful money of the United States, which he owes to and unjustly detains from him: For that whereas the said defendant, together with one J. D. Henry, heretofore, towit, on the twentyfifth day of April in the year of our Lord one thousand eight hundred and thirtytwo, at the county and circuit aforesaid by his certain writing obligatory, signed "T. M. Neale" and "J. D. Henry" sealed with his seal, and also with the seal of the said J. D. Henry, and now shown to the court, the date whereof is the day and year aforesaid, acknowledged himself, to be held and firmly bound unto the said plaintiff in the sum of fiftynine dollars and forty cents, parcel of the sum above demanded to be paid to the plaintiff or order, one day after the date of the said writing obligatory, "and if not paid to draw fifty per cent interest until paid."

And whereas the said defendant, also, afterwards, towit, on the twentyfirst day of April in the year of our Lord one thousand eight hundred and thirtyseven, at the county and circuit aforesaid made his certain promissory note in writing, signing his name thereto "T. M. Neale" bearing date the day and year aforesaid and then and there delivered the said note to the said plaintiff, by which said note he the said defendant then and there promised to pay to the said plaintiff, or order the sum of twenty dollars, for cash lent, other parcel of the sum above demanded, by means whereof, and by force of the statute in such case made and provided the said defendant then and there became liable to pay to the said plaintiff the said sum of money in the said promissory note specified according to the tenor and effect of the said promissory note; and, although the said sum of money in the said writing obligatory, and in the said promissory note specified have both been long since due and payable according to the tenor and effect of the said writing obligatory and of the said promissory note, yet the said plaintiff in fact saith that the said defendant (although often requested so to do) did not, nor would pay the sum of fiftynine dollars and forty cents in the said writing obligatory specified, or the said sum of twenty dollars in the said promissory note specified, or any part of either of them to the

said plaintiff, in manner aforesaid, or otherwise howsoever, but
hath hitherto wholly neglected and refused so to do, whereby an
action hath accrued to the said plaintiff to demand and have of
and from the said defendant the said sum of seventynine dollars
and forty cents above demanded—
To the damage of the said plaintiff of the sum of three hundred
dollars, and therefore he brings this suit &c.

Stuart & Lincoln
for Plff

The following are copies of the instruments declared on:

(In first count)

"One day after date we promise to pay Peter Van Burgen on
order fifty nine dollares & forty cents for value recd. and if not
paid to draw fifty per cent interest untill paid—Witness our
hands & seals this 25th of April 1832

T. M. Neale **
J. D. Henry **

(In second count)

"Due Peter Van Burgen or order twenty dollars for cash lent—
April 21 1837   T. M. Neale"

NOTICE OF SERVICE IN THE SUIT OF TROTTER VS. PHELPS, BUREAU CIRCUIT COURT, SEPTEMBER 24, 1838.

(Herndon-Weik Collection)

*The words beginning with, "Executed by reading to," and
concluding with "state of Illinois," were written by Attorney
Lincoln. "Beareu" was plainly a misspelling of the present day
Bureau County. The grounds for this case are found in the
declaration of September 18, 1838. The summons for Phelps
is the final document in the case as given in the Herndon-Weik
Collection. The defendant, Phelps, defaulted on October 15,
1838, and judgment was rendered in favor of the Stuart & Lincoln's client, Trotter.*

George Trotter

vs   } Sums

Ebenezer S Phelps

To October Term 1838
Executed by reading to
Ebenzer S. Phelps, this

Twenty fourth day of September
    A. D. 1838—
        C. Longworthy
    Sheriff of Beaureau
    county in the state of Illinois—
        Sheriff Fee
        Serving   50
        Returning Sum 12
Princeton
    Sep
    25
Ill.

Wm Butler—
Clerk Circuit Court,
Springfield, Sangamon, Co. Ill.

COMPLAINT IN THE SUIT OF BAKER VS. REEVES & COMPANY, SANGAMON CIRCUIT COURT, SEPTEMBER 24, 1838.

(Herndon-Weik Collection)

This entire document with the exception of the notations on the outside cover by Clerk Butler is in the handwriting of Mr. Lincoln. It is interesting to notice that he ran the hyphenated words "thirty-seven" together as one word, as he did in the case of "sixty-one." The inclusion of the three words "so to do" as "sotodo" is characteristic of many of the legal documents in the hand of Mr. Lincoln. As Edward D. Baker frequently appears throughout the Lincoln letters and legal papers, and is given full attention elsewhere in these volumes, he is here noted merely as an intimate friend of Mr. Lincoln, whose tragic death made a deep impression on a Civil War President. It seems unlikely that a case involving Baker as plaintiff and Lincoln as counsel would be unrecorded in the books of the Sangamon County Circuit Court, but studies up to this time have not made a case history available.

State of Illinois   }   Of the October term of
                    }ss the circuit court of said
Sangamon county & Circuit }   county in the year 1838—

    Edward D. Baker plaintiff complains of Milford O. Reeves, Ephraim Darling defendants, being in custody &c of a plea of Tresspass on the case upon promises. For that whereas the said defendants, by and under the name style and firm of M. O.

Reeves Co heretofore, towit on the nineteenth day of May in the year of our Lord one thousand eight hundred and thirtyseven, at Philada, that is to say, at the county and circuit aforesaid, made their certain promissory note in writing, bearing date the day and year aforesaid, and thereby then and there promised to pay three months after the date thereof, to the order of Abbott & Brothers the sum of eight hundred and sixtyone and three hundredths of a dollar, for value received, and then and there delivered the said promissory note to the said Abbott & Brothers; and the said Abbott & Brothers, to whose order, the payment of said sum of money in the said promissory note specified was to be made, after the making of the said promissory note, and before the payment of the said sum of money therein specified, towit, on the same day and year, and at the same place aforesaid, assigned the said promissory note, by indorsement in writing thereon, signing their names thereto "Abbott & Brothers" by which said assignment, they, the said Abbott & Brothers, then and there ordered and appointed the said sum of money in the said promissory note specified, to be paid to the said plaintiff, by means whereof, and by force of the statute in such cases made and provided, the said defendants, then and there became liable to pay to the said plaintiff, the said sum of money in the said promissory note specified, according to the tenor and effect of the said promissory note; and being so liable; they the said defendants, in consideration thereof, afterwards, towit, on the same day and year, and at the same place aforesaid, undertook, and then and there faithfully promised the said plaintiff to pay him the said sum of money in the said promissory note specified, according to the tenor and effect thereof—

Yet the said defendants (although often requested sotodo; and although the time for the payment of the said sum of money in the said promissory note specified has long since expired) have not as yet paid to the said plaintiff, the said sum of money in the said promissory note specified, or any part thereof; but sotodo have hitherto wholly neglected and refused, and still do neglect and refuse— To the damage of the said plaintiff of the sum of one thousand dollars, and therefore he brings his suit &c.

Logan & Baker for Plffs.

The following is a copy of the instrument declared on:
"$861 03/100 Philada May 19th 1837.

Six months after date we promise to pay to the order of

Abbott & Brothers, Eight hundred & sixtyone 03/100 Dollars #/100 without defalcation for value received.

D. C. Springfield, Ill.   M. O. Reeves & Co."

E

(Assignment thereon)

"Pay to Edward D. Baker

Abbott & Brothers"

Edward D. Baker	
vs.	
Milford O. Reeves	Tresspass on the case
Ephraim Darling trading	upon promises—
and doing business under	Damage $1000-00
the name style & firm of	
M. O. Reeves & co.	

The clerk of the Sangamon circuit court will issue process on the above returnable to the next term of the court—

Logan & Baker for Plffs

184

Edward D. Baker

vs.

M. O. Reeves & Co.

Filed Sept 24 1838

W Butler clk

REPLICATION OF COMPLAINANTS TO ANSWER OF DEFENDANTS IN THE SUIT OF STRINGFIELD HEIRS VS. ORENDORFF HEIRS, SANGAMON CIRCUIT COURT, SEPTEMBER 26, 1838.

This replication is entirely in the hand of Mr. Lincoln. Stuart & Lincoln lost the case on July 20, 1839, when the complainants' bill was dismissed, but two days later, unwilling to accept defeat, they filed the affidavit of one John Strode and, on the allegations there set forth, moved that the court set aside this decree. This motion was sustained, and the case continued with the complainants paying the costs.

These repliants, saving and reserving unto themselves all and all manner of advantage of exception to the manifold insufficiencies of the said answer, for replication thereto say that they will aver and prove their said bill to be true, certain, and sufficient in the law, to be answered unto, and that the said answer of the said defendants is uncertain, untrue and insufficient to be replied unto by this repliant; without this, that any other matter or thing whatsoever in the said answer contained material or effectual in the law to be replied unto confessed and avoided traverned or denied is true; all which matters and things these repliants are and will be ready to aver and prove as this honorable court shall direct, and humbly pray as in and by their said bill they have already prayed—

Stuart & Lincoln for Complts.

Stringfield Heirs

Ads   }   Replication

Orendorff Heirs

Filed Sept 26 1838
  Wm Butler Clk.

PLAINTIFF'S COMPLAINT IN THE SUIT OF WILLIAMS VS. CABANISS AND CABANISS, SEPTEMBER 27, 1838
(Herndon-Weik Collection)

The complaint in this suit was drawn by Mr. Lincoln. The Cabaniss brothers had given their note for $100 current money of Kentucky. Owens, after holding the note for fifteen years, assigned it to Williams, who through Stuart & Lincoln now sought to collect the loan. On August 13, 1838, Mr. Lincoln had filed a notice with the clerk of the Sangamon Circuit Court, the original of which is now in the Illinois State Historical Library, and entered himself security for costs. The defendant filed his plea on October 16, and the case came to trial on July 10, 1839, when the jury, manifestly taking into account the long period of delay that had preceded the effort to effect collection, found for the defendant. James M. Cabaniss, the senior defendant in this case, was one of the group of veterans of the War of 1812 who hailing from Kentucky had helped to settle Sangamon County, and with the rank of captain had served under Harrison at the Battle of the Thames. Later in civilian life he became an active and earnest Whig, and as such a supporter and follower of Mr. Lincoln.

State of Illinois   }   Of the October term of the
                            }ss   circuit court of said county,
Sangamon County & Circuit   }   in the year 1838—

Albert G. Williams, plaintiff, complains of John M. Cabaniss and George Cabaniss, defendants, being in custody &c of a plea of breach of covenant. For that whereas heretofore to wit, on the sixteenth day of August in the year of our Lord one thousand eight hundred and twentytwo, at the county and circuit aforesaid, by a certain instrument in writing then and there made, which instrument, in writing signed by the said John M. Cabaniss, thus, "J. M. Cabaniss" and signed by the said George L. Cabaniss in his full name, and sealed with the seal of each of the said defendants, the said plaintiff now brings here into court, the date whereof is the same day and year aforesaid, it was witnessed, that the said defendants, in consideration of value received by them and from one Nathaniel Owens, then and there jointly and severally bound themselves to pay one day after the date of the said instrument in writing to the said Nathaniel Owens, by the style and description of "Nathl. Owens" one hundred dollars current money of Kentucky. And the said Nathaniel Owens, to whom the payment of the said one hundred dollars current money of Kentucky, in the said instrument in writing specified, was to be made, after the making of the said instrument, in writing and before the payment of the said one hundred dollars current money of Kentucky therein specified was made, towit, on the twentyfifth day of September in the year of our Lord one thousand eight hundred and thirtyseven, at the county and circuit aforesaid, assigned the said instrument in writing by indorsement in writing thereon, signing his name thereto "Nathl. Owens" by whch said assignment, he, the said Nathaniel Owens, then and there ordered and appointed, the said one hundred dollars current money of Kentucky in the said instrument, in writing, specified, to be paid to the said plaintiff, Albert G. Williams, and then and there delivered the said instrument, in writing, so assigned as aforesaid, to the said plaintiff—by means whereof, and by force of the statute in such case made and provided, the said one hundred dollars, current money of Kentucky in the said instrument, in writing, specified, became due and payable, by the said defendants, to the said plaintiff, according to the tenor and effect of the said instrument, in writing. Yet the said defendants (although the time for the payment of the said one hundred dollars, current money of Kentucky, in the said instrument, in writing, specified has long since expired) have not kept their said covenant in the said instrument, in writing, specified, but have broken the same, in this: that they have not as yet paid, either to the said Nathaniel Owens, or to the said plaintiff after the said assigning thereof, the said one hundred dollars current money of Kentucky, or any part thereof or any other money or property in lieu thereof, but so to do have hitherto wholly neglected and refused and, still do neglect and refuse— To the damage of the said plaintiff of the sum of three hundred dollars, and therefore he brings his suit &c

Stuart & Lincoln
for Plff

Sept 27, 1838

The following is a copy of the instrument declared on:

"One day after date we bind ourselves jointly and severally to pay Nathl. Owens one hundred dollars current money of Kentucky. Value recd. witness our hands and seals this 16th of August 1822

J. M. Cabaniss*
George W. Cabaniss*

Test. George W. Davis

(Assignment thereon)

"I assign the within to Albert G. Williams this 25th of Sept. 1837.

Natl. Owens"

PETITION IN THE SUIT OF HURST VS. RAGSDALE, SANGAMON CIRCUIT COURT, SEPTEMBER 28, 1838.

This petition and quoted copies of the notes are in the hand of Abraham Lincoln, who also signs the petition for Charles R. Hurst. The words, "first note," and "second note," in parentheses over the original notes, appear to have been penned by Mr. Lincoln. The notes were signed by Ragsdale, and the assignments by James Bell and Company, but the penmanship of the notes is not clear. It is the same hand that has written the notations concerning the original notes. Lawyer Lincoln was slightly careless as he used a small "i" in interest, where the original note had it as "Interest." He was usually accurate in transcription of these notes, and it will be noted that he wrote "dollars" in note one, but changed it to the "dolls" of the original note. He failed to correct the erroneous grammar of "debts remains unpaid," a fault not customary with him. On motion of the plaintiff's attorney, Mr. Lincoln, the case was dismissed on October 9, 1838.

Sangamon Circuit court, Sct:

Charles R. Hurst, plaintiff states that he holds two notes on the defendant Daniel Ragsdale, in substance as followeth— First.

"$100. Due James Bell & Co one hundred dollars with interest from 1 January 1837 at the rate of 6 per cent per annum— Springfield 16 Sept. 1837.   Daniel Ragsdale"

(Second—)

"212.08 on or before the 1st day of January 1838 I promise to pay James Bell & Co Two hundred twelve dolls, and eight cents for value recd Springfield 16 Sept. 1837.

Daniel Ragsdale"

on the first of which is the following assignment—

"Pay to Charles R. Hurst
                    James Bell & Co"

and on the second of which is the following assignment— and credit—

"Pay to Charles R. Hurst
                    James Bell & Co"

"Dec. 29, 1827 Recd on the within
Note one hundred dolls"

Whereby the plaintiff hath become the proprietor thereof of which the defendant hath had due notice—

Yet the same debts remains unpaid, wherefore he prays judgment for his debt and damages for the detention of the same together with his costs—

Charles R. Hurst—

(first note)

$100—Due James Bell & Co one Hundred dolls with Interest from 1 January 1837 at the rate of 6 per cent per annum— Springfield 16 Sept. 1837.   Daniel Ragsdale

12 p cnt per agreement
2

D. Ragsdale
    $100
Due 1 Jany 1837
Dec 29 1837 Recd
on the within Note
one Hundred doll
pay to Charles R. Hurst
        James Bell & Co

(Second note)

212.08 On or before the 1st day of January 1838 I promise to pay James Bell & Co Two Hundred and Twelve dolls and eight cents for value recd Springfield 16 Sept. 1837.

Daniel Ragsdale

20
Daniel Ragsdale
　212.08
Due 1 Jany 1838.
pay to Charles R. Hurst
　　　James Bell & Co
　53
Charles R Hurst

vs   } Petition

Daniel Ragsdale

Filed Sept 28th 1838
Wm Butler Clk

DECLARATION AND NOTES FOR AN ABSTRACT IN THE SUIT OF THOMPSON VS. OSBORN, SANGAMON CIRCUIT COURT, SEPTEMBER 29, 1838.
(Herndon-Weik Collection)

This declaration is from the pen of Lawyer Lincoln, as are the cover notations, with the exception of the date of filing. The use of "last-mentioned" is not common in his legal papers and he reverts to "last mentioned" near the conclusion of the declaration. He changes the order and monotony of "false, scandalous, malicious, and defamatory words" to another phrasing in his final use of these words. "Trespass" is written "Tresspass," a frequent occurrence as Mr. Lincoln used both spellings for the word. Thompson asked much, and got little, for on March 7, 1839, by agreement, the case was dismissed, court costs being paid by the defendant.

The notes for an Abstract is also in the hand writing of Mr. Lincoln. It is undated, and has no case citation, but there is a striking similarity between it, and the declaration which Lincoln filed in the slander case of Thompson vs. Osborn. It is here placed below the declaration to permit of a comparison of the statements in the undated abstract, and those in the declaration in the case cited.

The day on which this case was begun, September 28, 1838, was a great day in Springfield, for in the afternoon 2,000 Whigs and Conservatives celebrated Stuart's election to Congress with a barbecue and speeches at Porter's Grove. One of the speakers was Mr. Lincoln, who, according to the Alton Telegraph of Octo-

ber 20, was "pithy in his own peculiar style, and showed off some of the prominent features of Mr. Van Buren's administration."

State of Illinois } ss Of the October term of the circuit court of said county
Sangamon county & Circuit in the year 1838—

George W. Thompson, plaintiff, complains of Stephen Osborn, defendant, being in custody &c. of a plea of Tresspass on the case: For that whereas the said plaintiff now is a good, true, honest, just, and faithful citizen of this state, and as such hath always behaved and conducted himself, and until the committing the several grievances by the said defendant, as herein after mentioned, was always reputed, esteemed, and accepted by and amongst all his neighbours and other good and worthy citizens of this state, to whom he was in anywise known, to be a person of good name, fame and credit, towit; at the county and circuit aforesaid. And whereas also, the said plaintiff hath not ever been guilty, or until the time of the committing of the said several grievances by the said defendant, as herein after mentioned, been suspected to have been guilty of swearing falsely, or any other such crime. By means of which said premises, he the said plaintiff, before the committing of the said several grievances by the said defendant as herein after mentioned, had deservedly obtained the good opinion and credit of all his neighbours, and other good citizens of this state, to whom he was in any wise known, towit, at the county and circuit aforesaid. And whereas also, before committing of the said several grievances, by the said defendant, as hereinafter mentioned a certain action had been depending before one of the Justices of the Peace in and for the county of Sangamon aforesaid, wherein one Joel Johnson was plaintiff, and one George Gregory was the defendant, and which said action had been then lately tried at the county aforesaid, and on such trial the said plaintiff in this action, had been, and was examined on oath, and had given his evidence as a witness for and on the part and behalf of the said Johnson towit, at the county and circuit aforesaid. Yet the said defendant in this action, well knowing the premises, but greatly envying the happy state and condition of the said plaintiff, Thompson and contriving, and wickedly and maliciously intending to injure the said plaintiff Thompson in his said good name, fame, and credit, and to bring him into public scandal, infamy and disgrace, with and amongst all his neighbours, and other good and worthy citizens of this state, and to cause it to be suspected and believed by those neighbours and citizens, that he the said plaintiff Thompson had been and was guilty of swearing falsely, and to vex, harrass, and oppress, impoverish, and wholly ruin him the said plaintiff, Thompson heretofore, towit, on the twentyfourth day of September in the year of our Lord one thousand eight hundred and thirtyeight, at the county and circuit aforesaid in a certain discourse which he the said defendant Osborn then and there had with the said Plaintiff, Thompson of and concerning him the said plaintiff, Thompson in the presence and hearing of divers good and worthy citizens of this state, then and there, in the presence of the said last-mentioned citizens, falsely and maliciously spoke and published to, of and concerning the said plaintiff, Thompson and of and concerning the evidence he gave on the aforesaid trial between Johnson & Gregory these false, scandalous, malicious, and defamatory words following; that is to say, "You (meaning the said plaintiff) have been swearing lies for Johnson," thereby, then & there meaning that the said plaintiff Thompson had been guilty of swearing falsely— And afterwards, towit on the same day and year, and at the same place aforesaid, in a certain other discourse which the said defendant Osborn then and there had, in the presence and hearing of one Counsel Sampson and of divers other good and worthy citizens of this state, he the said defendant, further contriving and intending as aforesaid, then and there, in the presence and hearing of the last-mentioned citizens, falsely and maliciously spoke and published, of and concerning the said plaintiff, Thompson of and concerning the evidence he gave in the aforesaid trial between the said Johnson and Gregory, these other false, scandalous, malicious, and defamatory words following, that is to say, "You (meaning the said plaintiff, Thompson) did swear a lie" thereby meaning the said plaintiff, Thompson had been guilty of swearing falsely and afterwards towit, on the same day and year, and at the same place aforesaid, in a certain other discourse the said defendant, Osborn, then and there had in the presence of and hearing of divers good and worthy citizens of this state, he the said defendant, Osborn, further contriving and intending as aforesaid, then and there, in the presence and hearing of the said last metioned citizens, falsely and maliciously spoke and published of and concerning the said plaintiff, Thompson, these other false, malicious, scandalous, and defamatory words following, that is to say "You" (meaning the said plaintiff Thompson) "have been swearing lies" thereby, then and there meaning the

said plaintiff Thompson, had been guilty of swearing falsely—
By means of which several grievances the said plaintiff Thompson, hath been greatly injured, towit, in the sum of one thousand dollars wherefore he brings this suit &c.

Stuart & Lincoln p q.

George W. Thompson

vs   }   Decln

Stephen Osborn—
Filed Sept 29 1838
    Wm Butler ck

NOTES FOR AN ABSTRACT, UNDATED

1. "You swore falsely"
2. "You swore a lie"
3. "You swore a lie" "You swore false" "You swore to a lie and I will have your oath taken away from you before saturday night"
4. "He swore a lie, and he would have his oath taken from him before saturday night"
5. "He swore to a lie, and I will have his oath taken from him before saturday night"

ENTRIES IN THE CASH BOOK OF STUART & LINCOLN, OCTOBER, 1838

Both of the entries here reproduced are in the hand of Mr. Lincoln. His partnership with John T. Stuart which began on April 12, 1837 lasted until April 14, 1841, at which time he became a partner of Stephen T. Logan. It would appear that in the second entry he originally gave the date as "1837," but later corrected the "7" with an "8." The "8" which follows the dash may have been his way of showing that he meant an "8." The second entry is undated except for the year.

Allen & Stone To Stuart & Lincoln Dr
1838 Oct To case with Center $250
         Wiley & Wood
              To Stuart & Lincoln Dr.
1838-8 To defense of Chancery case of Eby $50.00
         Credit by coat to Stuart—   15-00

$35.00

COURT ORDER IN THE SUIT OF HART VS. SACKETT ET AL, SANGAMON CIRCUIT COURT, PROBABLY OCTOBER, 1838.

(Herndon-Weik Collection)

Abraham Lincoln drew both the court order and the cover notations of this document. The cover has no date, and is one of the few Lincoln documents without date of filing. The date is fixed as of October, 1838, because this was the fall term of Sangamon County Circuit Court for that year. Rhoda Hart speaks of John and Rhoda Sackett having confessed the plaintiff's bill at a former term of the court. As her bill in chancery was filed upon July 3, 1838, it was probably confessed at the time. The court order concluded the case in favor of Rhoda Hart, the client of Stuart & Lincoln, insofar as her suit against the Sacketts was concerned.

Rhoda Hart—Complainant
        against
John Sackett
Rhoda Sackett
Jefferson Hart   In chancery
Melissa Jane Hart &
Rhoda Hart
Defendants

This day came the complainant by her solicitor, and the said John Sackett and Rhoda Sackett, having appeared at a former term of this court, and confessed the truth of the complainants Bill, in open court as appears of record; it is therefore ordered by the court that said Bill be taken for confessed as to them; And it appearing to the court that the said Jefferson Hart, Melissa Jane Hart, & Rhoda Hart, have been regularly served with process, and Antrim Campbell having been appointed guardian ad litem to them, files his answer and says that he believes the allegations of said Bill are true, and that he knows no reason consistent with the interest of his said wards why a decree in accordance with the prayer of said Bill should not be rendered; and it appearing to the satisfaction of the court, that the allegations of said Bill are true—It is therefore decreed by the court, that sales of the real estate of Moses Hart deceased, made by the complainant, as executrix of the said Moses Hart, under the order of this court; towit, the sale of the West half of the South West quarter of Section Twentyfour in Township

Seventeen North of Range Seven West (reserving thereupon one eighth of an acre containing a burying ground, to Hiram Penny; of the East half of the same quarter, Section, Township and Range, to Peyton L. Harrison; of the West half of the East half of the North West quarter of the same Section, Township and Range to Benjamin McElwain; of the East half of the East half of the same quarter, Section, Township and Range last aforesaid, to Nancy Hart; and of fifty acres off the South end of the East half of the South West quarter of Section Thirteen, in the same Township and Range, to Elihu Bone, be confirmed as against all the defendants to the said complainants Bill—

Rhoda Hart

vs   Decree

John Sackett & others

PLEA TO SCIRE FACIAS IN THE SUIT OF SAMUEL AND DEMENT VS. MOORE, SANGAMON CIRCUIT COURT, OCTOBER 8, 1838.
(Herndon-Weik Collection)

This document is in the hand of Stuart, and the almost unreadable scrawl is in marked contrast to the neat penmanship of his partner. It is included as a Lincoln legal document, but not as written by him. The cover notations are in Clerk Butler's hand. This is undoubtedly one of the earliest of the legal cases of Mr. Lincoln. As is seen Samuel and Dement sought a judgment against the estate of Sintz. Upon March 15, 1837, Stuart & Lincoln represented Sintz in court. At that time, all defendants in the case were ruled to file their pleas. The following day, Baker & Hewett, attorneys for the plaintiffs, moved for a continuance which was granted. On July 6, 1838, the plaintiffs, informed the court that Sintz had died, and asked that his administrator, Nicholas Moore, be made a party to the suit. This was done, and on October 7, 1838, Stuart & Lincoln moved that the suit be dismissed. This motion was granted, Moore, the client, of Stuart & Lincoln, recovering his costs in the case.

Henry Samuel
& William Dement

vs   Scire Facias

Nicholas Moore
admr. of N. Sintz

This day came the said Nicholas Moore administrator of

Nicholas Sintz. Deceased, and for Plea to said Scire Facias *says Plaintiffs to have* and maintain their action aforesaid against him as administrator aforesaid ought not because he says That the matters and things in said Scire Facias as therein set forth, are not sufficient in law *for the Plffts.* to have and maintain their Scire Facias aforesaid and rebuts scire action *against* him as aforesaid and this he is ready to verify &c.

                                              Stuart & Lincoln
Nicholas Moore   for Deft—
administrator of
Nicholas Sintz—

    ads   } demurrer

Dements
Filed Oct 8 1838
Wm Butler Clk

ANSWER OF GUARDIAN AD LITEM IN THE SUIT OF CASEY'S ADMINISTRATORS VS. CASEY'S HEIRS, OCTOBER 11, 1838
(Herndon-Weik Collection)

In the answer here reproduced, the name "Cyrus Walker," before the words "guardian ad litem" is in the hand of Walker, who also signed it. The rest of this legal paper was penned by Mr. Lincoln. The cover notations are the work of Butler. The court agreed with the guardian ad litem, and decided that the real estate of Casey be sold as prayed in the petition. The final disposition of the land is set forth in the report filed on November 23, 1839, by John W. Patterson and John A. and Jane Casey.

The answer of Cyrus Walker guardian *ad litem* to Polly Ann Casey, Margaret Stone, Alfred Stone, William Casey and Joseph Casey minor heirs of Green Casey deceased, to the Petition of John W. Patterson, John A. Casey and Jane Casey administrators and administratrix of the estate of the said Green Casey deceased, for the sale of the real estate of the said deceased—

This respondent says he has examined the said Petition and papers therewith filed, and knows of no reason consistent with the interest of said minors why the prayer of said Petition should not be granted—

                                              Cyrus Walker
                                              Guardian ad litem

Casey's Heirs
        } Ans
ads   }
        } Guardian
Caseys admns

Filed oct 11th 1838
Wm Butler Clk

ORDER FOR ISSUE OF PROCESS, DECLARATION OF PLAINTIFF AND ANSWER OF THE DEFENDANTS IN THE SUIT OF JUDY VS. MANARY AND CASSITY, SEPTEMBER 19 AND 20, AND OCTOBER 16, 1838

The order for issue of process in this suit was drawn by Mr. Lincoln, and the cover notations by Butler. The declaration and copy of the quoted note were also penned by Mr. Lincoln, but the date of filing is in the hand of Butler, while the words, "Douglass in this case" can be ascribed with reasonable assurance to Herndon or Weik. The plea of the defendants is in the hand of Douglas. The latter's careless scrawl contrasts sharply with the neat penmanship of Mr. Lincoln, who penned the words "And the plaintiff doth the like," signing "Stuart & Lincoln for Pllff." This case was decided on March 12, 1839, when Judy secured a judgment of $168.00, which Manary paid in full on May 30, 1839. Here again there was no doubt of the winner of a Lincoln-Douglas contest, for Lincoln was the victor. Douglas had come to have a high regard for the ability of Abraham Lincoln long before they met in their history making debates.

And it was in the month of September, 1838, that there was paid into the Federal Treasury under the will of James Smithson the sum of $500,000 for the founding of the Smithsonian Institute, in whose affairs Mr. Lincoln when President was to manifest deep and helpful concern.

Eli Judy
     vs   } Tresspass on the case upon promises—
James Manary & } Damage $250-00
William Cassity   }

The clerk of the Sangamon county circuit court will issue process on the above returnable to the next term of said court—

Stuart & Lincoln
for Plff

Stephen A Douglas
appeared for defts.
Eli Judy   862
     vs
James Menary
William Cassity
Filed Sept 19 1838
Wm Butler ck

State of Illinois   ⎫   Of the October term of the
                            ⎬ ss   circuit court of said county
Sangamon county & circuit   ⎭   in the year A. D. 1838—

Eli Judy, plaintiff, complains of James Manary and William
Cassity, defendants, being in custody &c of a plea of Trespass
on the case upon promises: For that whereas, the said defendants,
heretofore, towit, on the twentysixth day of February in the year
of our Lord one thousand. eight hundred and thirtyeight, at the
county and circuit aforesaid, made their certain promissory note
in writing, bearing date the day and year aforesaid, and thereby
then and there promised to pay, on or before the first day of
August then next ensuing, to the said plaintiff the sum of one
hundred and fifty dollars, with twelve per cent interest from
date, and then and there delivered the said promissory note to
the said plaintiff; by means whereof, and by force of the statute
in such case made and provided, the said defendants then and
there became liable to pay to the said plaintiff the said sum of
money in the said promissory note specified, according to the
tenor and effect of the said promissory note; and being so liable,
they the said defendants, in consideration thereof, afterwards towit, on the same day and year and at the same place aforesaid,
undertook, and then and there faithfully promised the said plaintiff to pay him the said sum of money in the said promissory
note specified, according to the tenor and effect thereof— Yet
the said defendants (although often requested so to do, and
although the said sum of money in the said promissory specified
has long since been due) have not as yet paid to the said plaintiff
the said sum of money in the said promissory note specified, or
any part thereof; but sotodo, have hitherto wholly neglected and
refused, and still do neglect and refuse— To the damage of the
said plaintiff of the sum of two hundred and fifty dollars, and
therefore he brings his suit &c

                              Stuart & Lincoln
                                   for Plff

The following is a copy of the instrument declared on in the declaration on the other side of this sheet:
"$150—

On or before the first of August Eighteen hundred and thirtyeight we or either of us promise to pay Eli Judy the sum of one hundred and fifty dollars with twelve per cent interest from date—

Feb. the 26—1838

James Manary
William Cassity"

Witnesseth
David Crouch
180   98

Eli Judy ⎫
    vs   ⎬ Decln
James Manary & ⎪
William Cassity ⎭

Douglass in this case
Filed Sept 20 1838
Wm Butler clk

In the Sangamon circuit court
Oct Term 1838

James Manary et al ⎫
    ads   ⎬
Eli Judah   ⎭

And the said Defendants come and defend the wrong and injury when &c and for pleas say that they did not undertake and promise in manner and form as the said plaintiff hath alleged against him and of this he puts himself upon his country

S. A Douglass
for Defts

And the said Plaintiff doth the like

Stuart & Lincoln
for Pllff

Eli Judah
vs
James Manary
& other
Filed oct 16th 1838
Wm Butler Clk

PLEA IN THE SUIT OF HART VS. PENNY ET AL, SANGAMON CIRCUIT COURT, OCTOBER 16, 1838.

(Herndon-Weik Collection)

In this plea the words, "and the Pltff doth the like &c." are in the same hand which appears in the praecipe of August 16, 1838. The cover notations are similar to the hand of Lincoln, and may be by him. They do not appear to be in the hand of Butler, and the "B" and other letters are in the small script similar to Lincoln's hand and not Butler's. This case stemmed from Rhoda Hart's petition to sell the lands of the deceased Moses Hart. The argument of Penny may be found in that by Peyton L. Harrison of October 20, 1838. The three agreements of July 16, 1841 were all signed by Harrison, Penny and Mc-Elwain, revealing that their cause against Rhoda Hart was a common one. In this case, the cause was dismissed on July 18, 1841 by agreement of Penny to assume the court costs.

Rhoda Hart Exr

vs

Hiram Penny et al

And the defdts come and defends the wrong and injury when &c. and for plea: says that they did not promise and undertake in manner and form as the said plffs in her declaration has alleged and this they pray may be inquired of by the Country.

Logan & Baker p d

and Pltff doth the like &c

Lincoln Pro. Pltff

Harts Execir
    vs.   Plea
Hiram Penny
Filed oct 16 1838
    Wm Butler clk

PLEA OF DEFENDANT AND GENERAL DEMURRER AND JOINDER IN THE SUIT OF RHODA HART VS. PEYTON L. HARRISON, OCTOBER 20, 1838

(Herndon-Weik Collection)

The only words in the document here reproduced penned by Lawyer Lincoln were, "General replication & Joinder, Treat— Logan & Baker," and "General Demurrer & Joinder"—"Treat &

Campbell & Logan & Baker," which last is repeated in slightly different style at its conclusion. The entire document appears to be in the hand of Logan, while Butler penned the date of filing. It is interesting to note that the client of Treat & Campbell, and Logan & Baker was the same Harrison whom Lincoln had acted for as plaintiff in the case of March, 1838 against Dickinson and Taylor.

The case of Hart vs. Harrison was one of several suits and counter suits arising out of the administration of the estate of Moses Hart. Upon July 15, 1837, as noted elsewhere Mr. Lincoln appeared before the Illinois Legislature, and introduced an act to authorize Rhoda Hart to sell and convey certain real estate. In her bill of chancery of July 3, 1838, Rhoda Hart referred to a court decree of the October term, 1837, decreeing the sale of certain real estate. Acting upon this decree, she sold a tract of land described in the bill to Peyton L. Harrison. Harrison's plea as defendant in the case reveals the rest of the story with one exception. Lincoln represented Rhoda Hart, the plaintiff in the case, which upon July 26, 1841 was dismissed by agreement with Harrison paying the court costs.

Hart ⎫
   vs   ⎬
Harrison ⎭

and the Defendant comes and defends the wrong and injury when where &c and says the plaintiff actio non because he says the note in the declaration mentioned was executed without any valuable consideration, and this he is ready to verify wherefore he prays judgment

Logan & Baker pd

General replication & Joinder—

Treat—Logan & Baker—

And for further plea in this behalf the said defendant says the plaintiff actio non because he says that the note sued on was executed for and in consideration of the purchase of a tract of land sold by the plaintiff as administratrix of Moses Hart *decd* under pretense of a certain decree and order rendered by the Circuit Court for Sangamon County on the petition of the said plaintiff as administratrix at the October Term of said court in the year 1837 which decree and order remains of record in said Court & is now here shown and that at the sale made by said plaintiff under pretense of said decree the Defendant supposing said decree and order to be valid and effectual to authorize the sale and conveyance of the land, therein mentioned purchased the tract of land aforesaid and executed the note in the declaration mentioned as part of the purchase money therefor and for no other or further consideration, and the Deft avers that at the time of rendering said decree

Rhoda Hart one of the Heirs of Moses Hart *decd* was an infant under the age of 18 years and that no guardian ad litem was appointed to answer and defend for said infant the plaintiff further avers that Jefferson Hart Melissa Jane Hart & Rhoda Hart infant Heirs of said Moses Hart *decd* children of David Hart *decd* who was one of the sons of said Moses Hart, *decd* and who were entitled to one undivided share of said lands were not in any manner made parties to said petition for the sale of the lands aforesaid wherefore he says that the decree and order aforesaid were null and void And so he says that the consideration for said note has wholly failed

All which he is ready to verify wherefore he prays Judg

Logan & Baker pd

And for further plea in this behalf the Defendant says the plaintiff actio non because he says that the note in the declaration mentioned was executed for and in consideration of a sale made by plaintiff to Defendant of a certain tract of land under pretense of a decree obtained by said plaintiff as admt of Moses Hart *decd* authorizing the plaintiff to sell certain lands therein mentioned which decree remains of record in said Court And the Defendant avers that Jefferson Hart Melissa Jane Hart & Rhoda Hart infant children of David Hart *decd* who was one of the sons Heirs of said Moses Hart *decd* and who were infants at the time of rendering said decree were Heirs of the said Moses Hart *decd* and entitled to one undivided Eighth part of the said tract of land so sold to Defendant and the Defendant avers that Jefferson Hart Melissa Jane Hart & Rhoda Heirs of said Moses Hart *decd* were in no wise made parties to said decree nor were they in any manner bound thereby nor their interest in said lands diverted by said decree and so Defendant says that as to the sum of $ part of the note sued on the consideration of said note has wholly failed All which he is ready to verify wherefore he prays Judgment

Logan & Baker
p d

General Demurrer & joinder
        Treat & Campbell— Logan & Baker—
Rhoda Hart
        vs
Peyton L. Harrison
Filed oct 20" 1838
Wm Butler Clk

AFFIDAVITS OF SAMUEL ROGERS AND ABRAHAM LINCOLN IN THE SUIT OF ROGERS VS. ROGERS, OCTOBER 20, 1838

(Herndon-Weik Collection)

The affidavit of Samuel Rogers here reproduced is signed in the scrawl of the plaintiff, but penned in the neat handwriting of Mr. Lincoln. William Short may have been the son of Joshua Short, who lived a few miles north of New Salem, and whose will, written and attested by Abraham Lincoln, in 1836, reveals a William Short as one of his sons. Joshua Short had a son-in-law, James Short, who may have been a close friend of Mr. Lincoln. James Short, better known as "Uncle Jimmy," lived but a few miles north of New Salem, as did Joshua. There is no conclusive evidence, but perhaps consideration of both Polly Rogers and the Short family may have influenced the action of Lincoln in persuading his client to withhold the charge of adultery. It would appear that Lincoln was not interested in injuring the reputation of a woman, although he later filed the affidavit of Rogers charging adultery, and on the same day, filed his own affidavit stating that he had dissuaded Rogers from using the charge in the original bill.

Mr. Lincoln drew his own affidavit in this case, while the notations of its being sworn, and those citing the case and file date are in the hand of William Butler. The words "as there was other sufficient grounds" may have been current legal phraseology, or they may be regarded as an error in grammar by Lawyer Lincoln.

Rogers vs. Rogers: Affidavit of Samuel Rogers: October 20, 1838

State of **Illinois** }

Sangamon County }

Samuel Rogers }
        vs   } **Divorce**
Polly Rogers }

In this case, Samuel Rogers, being the complainant, being first duly sworn, says upon oath, that large alimony had been decreed against him, that he can prove, and would have proved, had he not been advised to the contrary by counsel that the said Polly Rogers was guilty of adultery with one William Short, while she lived with this affiant; that the allegation of adultery (sic) against the said defendant, was omited (sic) in the complainant's bill, for no other cause, than through tenderness to the said defendant's character—that if he be permitted, he will yet alledge (sic) and prove said charge of adultry against said defendant— He therefore prays a new hearing of the case as to the question of alimony—

Samuel Rogers

Sworn to and
Subscribed before me
this 20" day of oct 1838
     Wm Butler Clk

Rogers

  vs } affa

Rogers

Filed oct 20" 1838
Wm Butler Clk

Samuel Rogers vs. Polly Rogers: Affidavit of A. Lincoln October 20, 1838

State of Illinois }

Sangamon County }

A. Lincoln, being first duly sworn says that he was employed as counsel in the case of Samuel Rogers vs Polly Rogers for a Divorce; that he, this affiant, drew up the complainant's bill; that said complainant at that time told this affiant that he could prove that the said defendant had been guilty of adultery with one William Short—while she lived with said complainant; but that affiant advised said complainant not to make the charge in his bill, as there was other sufficient grounds upon which to obtain a divorce, to wit, absence of more than two years—

A. Lincoln

Sworn to and Subscribed
before me this 20" day of
Oct 20th 1838

Wm Butler Clk

Rogers
    vs   affa
Rogers

Filed Oct 20" 1838
Wm Butler Clk

AMENDED BILL AND JOINDER IN THE DIVORCE SUIT OF ROGERS VS. ROGERS, OCTOBER OR NOVEMBER, 1838.

(Herndon-Weik Collection)

This amended bill of divorce was drawn by John T. Stuart, while the replication and joinder appear to be in the hand of Stephen T. Logan. The only words from the pen of Mr. Lincoln are, "General Replication & Joinder Stuart & Lincoln Logan & Baker." The attorneys for Polly Rogers spelled "allege" correctly, while Mr. Lincoln used "alledge" frequently in his legal papers. The amended bill and replication are undated, but the court gave leave to amend the bill upon October 20, 1838, and it may be assumed that it was changed immediately thereafter. Attorney Stuart used both "Rogers" and "Rodgers" in the amended bill, but his meticulous junior partner used the name "Rogers" consistently in his papers in this case.

Samuel Rogers
    vs
Polly Rogers

The said Complainant Samuel Rodgers by leave of the Court first here files his Amended Bill and for amendment says— That before the filing of his said original Bill To wit on the day of   and at divers other times the said Polly Rogers while living with this complainant in his house was guilty of the sinful and unlawful act of Adultery with one William Short.

He therefore prays Dissolution of the bonds of matrimony as prayed for in his said original Bill—

Saml. Rogers
By Stuart & Lincoln

Rogers

vs   }   Divorce

Rogers

Polly Rogers respondent for answer to said bill and amended bill of complainant says. that it is not true that the said Complt. treated her as an affectionate and true husband although she confesses the marriage alleged nor is it true that she left him without good cause—but on the contrary she was forced to leave him be excessive abuse and unworthy treatment. She denies the adultery by said Complainant falsely charged against her and alleges that she has not violated the marriage contract but she says that the said complainant has himself since the said marriage committed adultery to wit on the   day of with one   To wit in the County of Sangamon She therefore prays the Said Complainants bill may be dismissed—

Polly Rogers
General Replication & Joinder
Stuart & Lincoln
Logan & Baker

MR. LINCOLN URGES THE WHIGS TO NOMINATE HARRISON FOR PRESIDENT, SANGAMO JOURNAL, NOVEMBER 3, 1838.

Mr. Lincoln early became an avowed and earnest supporter of the personal and political fortunes of Henry Clay; but he was also a devoted Whig deeply concerned for the success of his party, and when it became clear to him that to assure that end Harrison not Clay should be the Whig candidate against Van Buren in 1840 he promptly announced that conviction in the editorial columns of the Sangamo Journal.. This editorial furnished one of the opening paragraphs of an unusual chapter in our political history. Whig sentiment decidedly favored the candidacy of Clay in 1840, but a coterie of influential Whigs in New York and Pennsylvania headed by Thurlow Weed were secretly opposed to it, and by adroit maneuvering compassed Clay's defeat in the Whig convention at Harrisburg in December, 1839, when on the grounds of availability he was put aside for Harrison who had a military record and was believed to be a poor man. "My friends," said Clay when informed of his defeat, "are not worth the powder and shot it would take to kill

*them. I am always run when sure to be defeated, and now be-
trayed when I or any one else would be sure of an election."
Confirming this prediction the Whigs triumphed at the polls, Van
Buren receiving only sixty-one electoral votes to 234 cast for
Harrison. But Harrison died on the morrow of taking office,
and his successor Tyler promptly wrecked Whig hopes of great
things.*

We, this week, raise the standard of Gen. Wm. H. Harrison, as a candidate for the Presidency. This stand, we have
not taken without much reflection; but now, that we have taken
it, we shall not be induced to abandon it unless we shall con-
ceive that the harmony of our friends absolutely requires it.

We are aware that offices are not established in this country
for the mere benefit and gratification of the individuals who may
be called to fill them.—We are amongst the foremost to deny,
that any man has just claims to office, unless the People, by
recognizing those claims, can best advance their own interests.
But while we say this, we insist, that so long as human nature
remains as it is—so long as men continue ambitious of distinction—it is not the part of wisdom in any community, to let that
ambition go ungratified, in an individual, who has rendered
arduous and valuable services to that community; for what man
will care to sacrifice his ease and comfort, and spend all the
better part of his life in bearing the burdens and encountering
the dangers of his country, if he shall know, that when he shall
assert his claims to the gratitude of his country, another, who
has toiled not, shall be preferred to him.—When an individual's
hairs have grown grey, and his eyes dim in the service of his
country, it seems to us, if his country-men are wise, and polite,
they will so reward him, as to encourage the youth of that country to follow his example.

If such an individual can now be found in this country; if
the policy we have been urging be sound, and that policy can be
furthered in the person of any one man more than that of any
other, that man, we insist, is Gen. Harrison. Near forty years
ago, when the great North-Western Territory was but one extensive hunting ground of dusky savages, Gen. Harrison tore
himself from all the comforts of civilized life and took up his
abode among those savages, to lay the foundation for all that
population, wealth and independence, that now find a home upon
that fertile and, now, cultivated tract of country. He may, with

great propriety, be called the father of the North Western Territory. There is not an important incident in its history, whether it conduce more to the glory of the past, or to the substantial advantages of the present and future, that does not bear the impress of his untiring hand. Go to the blood-drenched and bone-whitened field of every Indian battle; go to the records of every valuable Indian treaty; go to our most excellent public land system—that system which is so admirably calculated to guard the People of the country where it prevails, against the extremes of aristocratic wealth, and indigent poverty, and, in each and every of them, it will be seen that Harrison has been the man who has done most, suffered most, and profited least, by the respective results.

These services, with thousands of others of minor importance, constitute Gen. Harrison's claims to the gratitude of the American People, and particularly to that of the North Western portion of them. To these claims, there are no drawbacks—no deductions to be made for want of honesty or capability. All his acts bear, as well the marks of profound wisdom, and devoted patriotism, as those of much labor and toil. Unlike most men similarly circumstanced, he has not used the means placed in his power, in acquiring for himself a princely fortune. Though his intellectual powers are in full vigor, age, incessant toil, and long experience in the campaigns and other frontier services in the North West, have very much impaired his physical constitution; to which may be added, he is now poor, and dependent on his own hands for a living.

We repeat, that if the American People wish to honor a patriot and statesman; if they wish to reward a long-tried and faithful friend; if they wish to stimulate the youth of our country to emulation of noble examples; if they wish to proclaim to the world, that poverty shall never arrest virtue and intelligence on their march to distinction; they can, more effectually than in any other way, do all these, by elevating Gen. Wm. H. Harrison to the Presidency.

In expressing a preference for Gen. Harrison, we wish not to be understood, as having, to the smallest extent, lost confidence in the ability or patriotism of those other gentlemen, who are spoken of by our political friends, as candidates for the same high station. We consent to pass by such men as Henry Clay and Daniel Webster, only because their fame is already immortal—because they shine within themselves—because the sickly light reflected by office and power, can add nothing to their splendor—because, come weal or woe, their names will never be forgotten, so long as Cicero, Pitt and our own immortal Washington shall be remembered.

REPORT OF THE COMMISSIONERS IN THE SUIT OF MASON VS. MASON, SANGAMON CIRCUIT COURT, DECEMBER 9, 1838.
(Herndon-Weik Collection)

This report is in the hand of Attorney Lincoln, with the exception of the signature of the commissioners. The cover notations are in another hand. Mr. Lincoln was consistent in the mis-spelling of "beginning" as he spelled it as "begining" from the beginning to the end of the document. The frequent use of numbers such as "eighty seven" and "fifty five," reveals in marked degree the Lincoln habit of running such words into one word, as "fiftyfive." The present document abounds in such Lincolnisms. This report was the final decision, and a double answer in the cases of Lucinda Mason vs. Noah Mason, and Noah Mason, Jr. vs. Lucinda Mason et al. An alias subpoena or second subpoena, was awarded the complainants in both bills, on the motion of Mr. Lincoln, made July 4, 1837. On October 20 of the same year, both bills were taken as confessed, and commissioners appointed to set aside a dower in the case of Lucinda Mason, and to partition the lands on the petition of Noah Mason, Jr. The report below is evidence of the manner in which the court decree of October, 1837 was carried out.

The undersigned having, by an order of the Sangamon circuit court made at the October term thereof in the year of our Lord one thousand eight hundred and thirtyseven, been appointed commissioners to set apart by metes and bounds to Lucinda Mason her Dower in and to certain lands in the said order described; and having by another order of the same court made at the same term, thereof, been appointed commissioners to make partition of certain lands in the said order described (being the same lands described in the first mentioned order) and to set apart by metes and bounds one sixth part of said lands to Caroline Mason and Seth Mason each, and two sixths to Noah Mason and Thomas Mason each, after taking from the same the widow's Dower: Report:

That they have performed the duties enjoined on them by the two said orders, excepting that, by the agreement of the said

Caroline Mason and the guardian of the said Seth Mason, their two sixths were laid off in three bodies or tracts, and not divided or separated from each other. The part alloted to the said Lucinda Mason as her Dower is bounded as follows, towit, Begining at the South West corner of the South East quarter of Section Thirtysix in Township Fourteen North of Range Six West of the Third Principal Meridian: thence East twenty chains: thence North sixty chains and twelve and a half links; thence West nineteen chains and ninety links; thence South six minutes West sixty chains and twelve and a half links to the begining containing ten acres and eightyone hundredths of an acre— Second: Begining at the North East corner of the tract set apart to the said Lucinda Mason: thence North twenty chains, twelve and a half links: thence West nineteen chains and eightyseven and a half links —thence S d 6' W twenty chains and twelve and a half links: thence East nineteen chains and ninety links to the begining, containing forty acres— Third: Begining at the South East corner of the North West quarter of Section one in Township Thirteen North of Range Six West; thence North twenty chains and thirtysix links; thence West twelve chains and seventy eight links: thence South twenty chains and fortysix links: thence N 89d 38 E. twelve chains and seventyeight links to the begining, containing twentysix and seven hundredths of an acre—

The parts set apart to the said Thomas Mason are bounded as follows, towit; First: Begining at the South West corner of the first described tract of Noah Mason: thence North fifteen chains;   thence N 89d 45W six chains and twentyone links; thence South fifteen chains; thence S 89d 45E six chains and twentyone links to the begining, containing nine acres and thirtyone hundredths of an acre— Second: Begining at the North West corner of Noah Masons second tract; thence S d 6' W thirty chains and ten links: thence N 89d 45W nineteen chains and ninety links: thence N17'E. thirty chains and ten links; thence S89d 45'E nineteen chains and eightyseven and a half links to the begining, containing fiftynine acres and eightytwo hundredths of an acre—Third: Begining at the South West corner of Noah Mason's third tract: thence North twenty chains and fortysix links; Thence West twelve chains and seventyeight links; thence South twenty chains and fiftyfive links; thence North 89d 38' E. twelve chains and seventyeight links to the begining, containing twentysix acres and twenty hundredths of an acre — The parts set apart to the said Caroline Mason and Seth Mason are bounded as follows, towit; First: Begining at the South West corner of Thomas Mason's first tract; thence North fifteen chains; thence N 89d 45 W six chains and seventyone links; thence South fifteen chains; thence S 89d 45E six chains and seventyone links to the begining, containing ten acres and six hundredths of an acre— Second: Begining at the North West corner of the first; thence North 17 minutes East thirtyfive chains and fifteen links; thence S 89d 45E. nineteen chains and ninety **links; thence South six minutes** West thirtyfive chains and fifteen links; thence North 89d 45' West twenty chains to the begining, containing seventy acres and twelve hundredths of an acre— Third: Begining at the South West corner of Thomas Masons third tract; thence North twenty chains and fiftyfive links, thence West thirteen chains and fifty three links; thence South twenty chains and sixtyfour links. thence North 89d 38' East thirteen chains and fifty three links to the begining containing twentyseven acres and eightysix hundredths of an acre: All of which metes and bounds will more fully appear by reference to a plat of the survey of the same   herewith filed

The lot set off to Lucinda Mason is numbered on said plat (4) those to Noah Mason 5—1—and 10, those to Thomas Mason 6—2 and 9, those to Caroline and Seth Mason 7— 3 and 8— Given under our hands & seals this 9th day of December 1838

> Job Fletcher J (Seal)
> JaC.. F. Harris (Seal)
> Silas Harlan (Seal)

Lucinda Mason
    1838
Rep of Commiss

MR. LINCOLN OPPOSES A BILL ENABLING A SETTLER TO COLLECT FOR IMPROVEMENTS HE HAS PLACED ON PUBLIC LANDS, DECEMBER 15, 1838.

On August 6, 1838, Mr. Lincoln was elected to the Legislature for the third time, leading the field of seventeen candidates in Sangamon County, and when that body convened at Vandalia on December 3, he was nominated by the Whigs for speaker, only to be defeated on the fourth ballot by William L. D. Ewing, Democrat. But he had now become the Whig leader in the popular branch of the Legislature, and helped to shape its course during a period when it had to face many perplexing problems. Thus the December 27 issue of the Vandalia Free Press reports his part in the discussion of a bill which on the morrow of the panic of 1837 was of vital concern to many an Illinois settler. And there is little doubt that Mr. Lincoln in the closing weeks of 1838 read in the newspapers that the new Whig governor of New York was William H. Seward, who, when Clay and Webster had passed from the scene, was to vainly dispute with him leadership of the successor to that body.

Bill from the Judiciary reported providing for collection of demands growing out of contracts for sales of the possession of public lands. Ficklin moved amendments to Sec. 2 & 3, second amendment adopted. Third that every person who shall purchase of U. S. a tract of land upon which there is an improvement belonging to some person, without making a contract to purchase or pay for same shall be liable to pay what it is worth; or be sued, (if not over $100) before J. P. Value fixed by three disinterested persons of neighborhood.

Mr. Lincoln spoke in opposition to the proposed amendments in which he doubted the right of the Legislature to pass a law enforcing payments for improvements.

Williams also in opposition to amendment. Flood Favorable. Walker Favorable.

REPORT FROM THE MAJORITY OF THE HOUSE COMMITTEE ON FINANCE, DECEMBER 18, 1838, MR. LINCOLN ITS PROBABLE AUTHOR

This report from the Committee on Finance of the House is a printed document, and is unsigned by committee members. As such it is not conclusive evidence that the report is in the words of Abraham Lincoln, but it has been generally attributed to him. Although it was submitted by Archibald Williams of Adams County, an intimate friend of Lincoln, the composition of most of the document, if not all of it, has been credited to Mr. Lincoln. The late Senator Albert J. Beveridge asserted that the styyle and method of reasoning were distinctly Lincolnesque.

Mr. Lincoln had been appointed a member of the standing Committee on Finance, December 8, 1838, and the report was made ten days later. As a report it was an excellent political attack upon the Van Buren sub-treasury plan, and an effective Whig campaign document. The presidential campaign of 1840 was almost two years away, but it was not too early for the

Whigs to stress an issue that was to become an important one in that campaign. The report by Lincoln appears to have been a rehearsal — it was too early for a dress rehearsal — of his speech on the same subject delivered as the last in a series of debates between Illinois Whigs and Democrats on the matter. A comparison of the report with his speech of December 20, 1839, reveals a striking similarity in the treatment of the history of a national bank as given in the address with that in paragraphs two and three of the report. The report does not contain the detailed statistical background of the speech, but it appears to have laid the groundwork for the arguments of the debate. There are few of the "purple patches" of the speech present in the report, but it cannot be denied that the fourth paragraph of th report, while tinged with proud nationalism, was good prose, and at times poetic.

The twenty-nine year old legislator, with "defective education" was not the master of the prose of the Gettysburg Address and the Second Inaugural, but he was revealing flashes of ability that would prove his brief talk on a battlefield no inspiration of a moment. It may be noted in passing that the report had a tendency to lean on passages in the answer of Henry Clay to the Van Buren message suggesting the sub-treasury plan. The Lincoln "beau ideal of a statesman" may have inspired the report of a less well-known Whig in Illinois. The careful reasoning in the report and the speech may be compared with like research upon the slavery problem in the noted Cooper Institute Address. For this, see Nicolay and Hay, Complete Works (New York, 1905), V: 293-328.

The Sub-treasury plan under discussion provided for the building of strong vaults or sub-treasuries in the large cities. These were to be in charge of government officials, and were to divorce the Treasury Department and the banks. Throughout the report runs mention of several important characters. A future President will be recognized in James K. Polk, while Richard M. Johnson was Vice-President under Van Buren. Henry A. Muhlenberg was a noted Pennsylvania politician, and son of Frederick A. Muhlenberg, first Speaker of the House of Representatives in the Congress of the United States. William L. May will be recognized as the Illinois politician, and father-in-law of Henry B. Truett.

Mr. Williams, from the Committee on Finance, made the following report, which was read, viz:

The Committee on Finance, to which was referred that part of the Governor's Inaugural address which relates to currency, have had so much thereof as relates to the establishment of an Independent Treasury and to a National Bank under consideration; and a majority of said committee have directed me to make the following report:

In reviewing the history of the United States, we find that the employment of banks, as fiscal agents, in keeping and disbursing the public moneys, is a practice almost coeval with the very organization of our Government. It was commenced during the administration of Washington, the first President of the Union, and was continued without intermission, through all the changes of administration, until the retirement of President Jackson from office.

For the greater part of this time, the first bank of the United States, chartered by Congress, in 1791, and approved by President Washington, and the second United States Bank, chartered in 1816, and approved by President Madison, were the agents for the discharge of these duties: but during two periods, the banks chartered by the several States substituted for a National Bank, viz: from the expiration of the first United States Bank in 1811, until the creation of the second in 1816; and from the removal of the deposites from the latter bank in 1833, until the end of President Jackson's term of office.

The practice, however, of employing some banks, either State or National, as fiscal agents for the General Government, was uniformly and constantly followed by all the Presidents, until the accession of Mr. Van Buren in 1837.

During this period of nearly half a century, our prosperity was unexampled. The increase of our wealth and population, the development of our resources, and our improvement in all the useful pursuits of civilized life, were extensive and rapid, beyond all parallel in the previous annals of the world. Vast tracts of country were reclaimed from the wilderness—forests were leveled—praries converted into fertile fields—roads opened —rivers explored and the obstructions removed which impeded their navigation. The increase of agricultural products promoted the expansion of other branches of industry. Manufactures of various sorts sprang up and flourished; our commerce was pushed to every quarter of the globe; our sails whitened every sea; and the American flag floated in every breeze, from the Arctic ocean to the southernmost shores of the Pacific. The Old World saw with surprise and admiration our infant colonies, but recently formed into a union of States, advancing with giant strides to the rank of a mighty nation.

Thus it will be seen, from this brief history of the union which, until recently, existed between the General Government and banks, either State or National—and of the extraordinary and unprecedented degree of prosperity which accompanied us in our onward march during the period of this union—that a system, under which we have increased from a mere handful of people to a most powerful confederacy, and under which we have attained a condition so flourishing, cannot in itself be "radically and fundamentally defective." It is, therefore, a matter of no surprise, that a proposition to sever a union so useful and so beneficial should receive, at its very outset, a most decided and signal rebuke.

The first proposition for such a severance was submitted by Mr. Gamble, of Georgia, during the session of Congress held in the winter of 1834 and 1835. This was as follows:

"Resolved, That the Secretary of the Treasury be directed to communicate to this House, whether in his opinion, it is practicable or convenient for that Department to collect, safely keep, and disburse the public moneys of the United States, without the agency of a bank or banks; and, if so, to report to this House the best mode, in his opinion, by which the object can be accomplished."

On motion of Mr. M'Kim, a member of the administration party, the resolution was laid upon the table.

Mr. Gamble, afterwards, on the 6th day of January, 1835, introduced the following resolution:

"Resolved, That the Secretary of Treasury be directed to digest, and prepare, and communicate to this House, a detailed plan by which the public revenue of the United States may be collected, safely kept, and disbursed, without the agency of a bank or banks, either State or National."

On the 11th day of February, at the same session, the bill regulating the deposite of the money of the United States in certain local banks being under consideration, a motion was made by Mr. Robertson, "that the said bill be recommitted to the Committee of Ways and Means, with instructions so to amend the same as to dispense with the agency or instrumentality of banks in the fiscal operations of the Government."

Mr. Gordon moved to amend the said bill, and strike out all thereof after the enacting words, and insert—

"SEC. 1. That from the and after the — day of — in the year —, the collectors of the public revenue, at places where the sums collected shall not exceed the sum of — dollars per annum, shall be the agents of the Treasurer, to keep and disburse the same, and be subject to such rules and regulations, and give bond and security, as he shall prescribe for the faithful execution of their office; and shall receive, in addition to the compensation now allowed by law, — per centum on the sums dispersed, so that it does not exceed the sum of — dollars per annum."

"SEC. 2. And be it further enacted, That at all places, where the amount of public revenue collected shall exceed the sum of — dollars per annum, there shall be appointed by the President, by and with the advice and consent of the Senate, receivers of the public revenue, to be agents of the Treasurer, who shall give such bond and security, to keep and disburse the revenue, and be subject to such rules and regulations, as the Treasurer shall prescribe; and shall receive for their services — per centum per annum of the sums disbursed: Provided, it does not exceed the sum of — dollars per annum."

"SEC. 3. And be it further enacted, That from and after the — day of —, the whole revenue of the United States derived from customs, lands, or other sources, shall be paid in the current coin of the United States."

The yeas and nays were taken upon these several propositions, and, by overwhelming majorities, they were all rejected. Among those who were opposed to their adoption, we find the names of C. C. Cambreling, Zadok Casey, Richard M. Johnson, Wm. L. May, Henry A. Muhlenberg, James K. Polk, John Reynolds, and (with but very few exceptions) all the members friendly to the administration of President Jackson. Every attempt to effect a separation between bank and State was steadily resisted by friends of the party in power. The scheme was disapproved by President Jackson himself, and the official papers at Washington denounced it, as subversive of the settled practice of the Government, as tending to increase, to an alarming extent, the power of the Executive, and exposing the public treasure to be plundered by a hundred hands, where one could not before reach it.

From that time until the special session of Congress, in September, 1837, after the accession of Mr. Van Buren, the project was laid asleep; and the State banks continued to be employed as the fiscal agents of the Government.

At the special session just referred to, the system now familiarly known as the Independent Treasury, or Sub-treasury system was first brought forward as an administration measure. The party which, under President Jackson's administration, had voted against the proposition of Messrs. Gamble, Gordon, and Robertson, were now divided. A majority of the party, coinciding with President Van Buren, supported the measure, while a considerable minority adhered to their original view of the subject.

The bill was defeated at the special session. It was again brought up at the last regular session, and again lost —the Conservative party, as they have been called, remaining firm in their opposition to it.

Your committee do not wish to be understood as resisting, without inquiry or examination, all changes in the fiscal affairs of the Government. They are not hostile to such changes as may be shown to be necessary and proper; but, in view of the high degree of prosperity which the American nation has enjoyed under the system pursued since the foundation of the Government to the present day — when it is proposed to forsake that system and embrace a new and untried plan—they ask, what are the grounds, what are the reasons and considerations which render this change necessary and proper?—and this inquiry is deemed the more important, because of the signal condemnation passed upon this scheme during the session of Congress in 1831-1835, above referred to, with the concurrence of some of those who are now advocating its adoption.

If the example of European nations be quoted, in which plans have been adopted similar to that under consideration— we ask if there be any thing in the character of their governments, or the condition of their subjects, which should excite the envy or challenge the imitation of the American people?

It may be said that it is improper to deposite with the Banks the public money, lest it be used as a fund for banking operations. In the opinion of your committee a sufficient answer to this objection is to be found in a recent vote of this House, declaring it inexpedient to make the collectors of our State revenues the custodiers and disbursers of the same. That vote exhibits, on the part of this House, a preference for banks, over collecting officers, as fiscal agents for the safe keeping and disbursing of moneys, so far as our State revenues are concerned; and your committee are unable to perceive any difference of principle, whether the policy under consideration relates to the revenues of this State or to those of the United States.

A favorite argument in behalf of this scheme is, that it is a divorce of Bank and State, and the creation of an Independent Treasury.

To this your committee answer that it will divorce bank and State only to cement a union still more dangerous—the union of political influence with the influence of money—the Executive patronage with the control of the public purse. It will create a treasury, independent (it is true) of the people, and of their representatives, but dependent upon the President, the Secretary of the Treasury, and thousands of subordinate officers, who hold their appointments at the discretion of the President; among whom are to be included numerous secret agents who, under color of examining into the accounts of collecting and disbursing officers, may be sent into every part of the Union to operate upon elections.

Another fruitful topic of declamation with the advocates of the Sub-treasury system is, the supposed insecurity of the public money in the deposite banks; and this is especially alluded to in that part of Governor Carlin's message which has been referred to this committee. In refutation of this idea, your committee deem it only necessary to quote from a report made by Mr. Woodbury, then and now Secretary of the Treasury, during the session of Congress of 1834 and 1835. He says—"It is a singular fact, in praise of this description of public debtors—the selected banks—that there is not now due on deposite, in the whole of them, which have stopped payment, from the establishment of the Constitution to the present moment, a sum much beyond what is now due to the United States fom one mercantile firm that stopped payment in 1825 or 1826, and of whom ample security was required, and supposed to be taken, under the responsibility of an oath.

"If we include the whole present dues to the Government from discredited banks, at all times, and of all kinds, whether as depositories or not, and embrace even counterfeit bills, and every other species of unavailable funds in the Treasury, they will not exceed what is due from two such firms. Of almost one hundred banks, not depositories, which during all our wars and commercial embarrassments, have heretofore failed in any part of the Union, in debt to the Government, on their bills or otherwise, it will be seen by the above table that the whole of them, except seventeen, have adjusted every thing which they owed, and that the balance due from these, without interest, is less than thirty-two thousand dollars.

"Justice to the State banking institutions as a body, whose conduct, in particular cases, has certainly been objectionable, but whose injuries to the Government have been almost incredibly exaggerated, and whose benefits to it, both during the existence of our two National Banks, and while neither of them has existed, has been almost entirely overlooked, has led me to make this scrutiny, and submit its results, under a hope that it will, in some degree, not only vindicate them from much unmerited censure, but justify this department for the confidence it formerly, and in the great improvement of their condition and of the financial affairs of the Government, has recently reposed in them. Under these circumstances, so very favorable, with the new security and examinations provided for, your former small losses by them in keeping and paying ever the public revenue, under circumstances so very adverse, are compared with our large losses, either in collecting or disbursing that their present safety seems to be as great as is consistent with the usual operations of the paper system, or with the credit which must be always entrusted by the Government, in some way or other, to agents of some kind, in keeping the public money. In considering their safety, it should be constantly recollected that the owners and managers of banks, when properly regulated by legislative provisions in their charters, like other individuals, interested to transact business securely, are desirous of making and not losing money, and that these circumstances, with the preference in the case of failure, belonging to depositors and holders of their bills over the stockholders, united with the security, if not priority, given to the Government, render them, in point of safety, generally, much superior to individual agents of the United States."

The report from which the foregoing quotations are made, was the basis of the late arrangement between the Government and the deposite banks.

What amount of loss has been sustained by the Government committee have no exact means of ascertaining; but from the best sources of information within their reach, they are satisfied since the suspension of specie payments by those institutions, your that the sum is very inconsiderable.

And they deem it not amiss to insert here a passage relating to these banks, from the message of President Van Buren to the present session of Congress, on the 3rd of December, 1838. He says: "It is no more than just to the banks to say that, in the late emergency, most of them firmly resisted the strong temptations to extend their paper issues, when apparently sustained in a suspension of specie payments by public opinion. even though in some cases invited by legislative enactments. To this honorable course, aided by the resistance of the General Government, acting in obedience to the Constitution and laws of the United States, to the introduction of an irredeemable paper medium may be attributed in a great degree, the speedy restoration of our currency to a sound state, and the business of the country to its wonted prosperity."

Your committee are of opinion that this testimony of the President to the honorable and patriotic conduct of the banks, during "the late emergency," furnishes a strong argument in their behalf, in addition to the consideration urged by Mr. Woodbury in the report already quoted; while the force and truth of some of these considerations have been abundantly demonstrated by the frequent and extensive defalcations of "individual agents of the United States."

The report of the Secretary of the Treasury to Congress, at its last session, presented a surprising list of defaulters among the collectors and receivers of the public moneys; and, very recently, the enormous defalcations of the collector at New York, amounting (as reported) to one million two hundred thousand dollars, has been thought worthy of "particular reference" to Congress by Mr. Van Buren.

Your committee, therefore after mature consideration of these passages of Governor Carlin's message which have been referred to them, and of all the important subjects connected therewith, beg leave to submit the following resolution, viz:

Resolved by the General Assembly of the State of Illinois, That the present condition of the currency and the interests of the country, generally, do not seem to require the establishment of an Independent Treasury, and the collection and disbursement of the public revenue is specie.

Resolved, That our Senators in Congress be instructed, and our Representatives requested, to vote against any law or resolution having for its object the adoption of the Independent or Subtreasury System, in any form whatever.

Resolved, further, That they be instructed to use all their efforts to prevent the recharter of the late National Bank, or the chartering of a National Bank of any kind.

Resolved, That the Governor be requested to transmit a copy of the foregoing resolutions to each of our Senators and Representatives in Congress.

MR. LINCOLN DISCUSSES THE ELECTION OF HOUSE MEMBERS TO OFFICE, DECEMBER 20 AND 21, 1838.

Again on December 20, 1838, Mr. Lincoln voted with the majority (44 to 42) in disapproval of a resolution that members of the General Assembly should be eligible to other state offices, declaring that such a practice would be "corrupting in its tendencies.". The following day, December 21, this resolution was brought up for reconsideration, and Mr. Lincoln moved its reference to the committee on internal improvements. There followed a lively debate which was thus reported in the Alton Telegraph of December 29:

Discussion on Dec. 20th and renewed on the 21st. Soon after House met Johnson of Bond moved reconsideration of resolution a vote upon which was taken yesterday, on resolution of gentleman from Adams. Vote considered accordingly, when Murphy of Perry moved to table. He then spoke, and was followed by Happy. Several others spoke and then vote to table decided in negative, yeas 41 nays 43. Webb of White then moved to refer to committee on Judiciary. Several amendments proposed and voted down. Several acrimonious speeches were made.

Mr. Lincoln moved its reference to the committee on Internal Improvements. Mr. Smith of Wabash, and Mr. Thornton, both seemed to regard this as a direct attack on them. They were members of the committee interested in the decision; and they would not allow the insinuation. They would hold the gentleman from Sangamon responsible, &c, &c. Mr. Lincoln, replied, he did not move the reference with any such design as had been attributed to him. He had always been the friend of both of the gentlemen; and at the last extra session he had voted against such a proposition, because his friend from Wabash (Mr. Smith) was personally interested then in the decision, being at that time in the employ of the State. But he would now assure the gentlemen, that the proposition to refer did not originate with him. He was requested to make the motion by one of the especial friends, and a member of the same committee, viz: the gentleman from Perry (Mr. Murphy), and to oblige him he had made the motion. But he was glad he had made it; the hydra was exposed; and all the talk about settling this matter at another tribunal, he had no objection to, if gentlemen insisted on it. He was always ready, and never shrunk from responsibility.

CHAPTER X—LINCOLN IN THE YEAR 1839
SURVEY OF PERIOD

The year 1839, in which fell his thirty-first birthday, was for Abraham Lincoln another period of growth and widening contacts. There was little change in his daily rounds in Springfield. He continued to share with Speed a room over the latter's store, and to eat at the table of his friend Butler; but residence at the capital brought him in friendly touch with influential men from all parts of Illinois, drawn to Springfield by a variety of motives, and during the final session of the General Assembly at Vandalia, which extended from December 3, 1838, to March 4, 1839, although defeated as the Whig candidate for speaker, he was clearly the leader of his party on the floor of the House, and more influential than any other member in shaping its activities.

The House Journal bears witness that Mr. Lincoln was constant in his attendance on the sessions of that body, and to his vigilance and shrewd management were mainly due the thwarting of legislation opposed by his party. Thus he intervened to prevent an attempted repeal of the internal improvement system hopefully adopted by the Legislature in 1837, but now drifting toward the rocks, and to secure instead the appropriation of an additional $800,000 for the improvement of waterways and the construction of railroads. And on January 17, 1839, acting for the House finance committee, he reported, but without results, a plan, set forth elsewhere, for solving the state's financial troubles. He was steadfast and effective in his support of the Illinois state banks when the Democrats threatened their future, and he also had a part in the redistricting of the state for judicial purposes, a process from which issued a new circuit, the Eighth, which, altered from time to time, became the field for most of his labors in the lower courts. It is to be noted in this connection that on December 3, 1839, Mr. Lincoln was by Judge Nathaniel Pope admitted to practice in the federal courts. There was then no Federal Building in Springfield and the courts held their sessions in rented quarters in what was known as the Tinsley Building. There until 1854 Mr. Lincoln tried his Federal cases, and for five years following 1844 his office was on the third floor of the same building.

The session of the Legislature ending in early March, 1839, Mr. Lincoln returned to Springfield, where in June he was elected one of the town's five trustees; in October helped to organize the Whigs for the coming presidential campaign, being named one of the party's electors; and, also in October, if not a little later, met for the first time the young woman who was to become his wife. Mary Ann Todd was the twenty-one year old cousin of Lincoln's partner, John Todd Stuart, "brilliant, vivacious, impulsive" and with a zest for life, who lately had come from her native Kentucky to make her home with an elder sister, Elizabeth Todd Edwards, in Springfield. She quickly found favor with the young men of the town—James Shields and Stephen A. Douglas among them—but at the end of a courtship full of surprises and bewilderment for a suitor, angular, slow of speech and rarely at ease in the company of women, she gave her heart to Abraham Lincoln. The conclusion of that courtship, rudely interrupted and after a time renewed, will be set forth in another place, but here it must be recorded that Mary Todd was beloved of Abraham Lincoln, and that she had her part, and a large one, in shaping the course that led him to the Presidency.

A new and pleasant experience for the people of Springfield in the closing weeks of 1839, was the visit to the town, in anticipation of the convening of the Legislature on December 9, of the McKenzie and Jefferson Company of players, some of whose performances must have been witnessed and enjoyed by Abraham Lincoln and Mary Todd. A religious revival was then in progress in Springfield, and citizens who objected to the drama attempted to prevent the appearance of the players, whose managers had spent a generous portion of their available funds in the erection of a temporary theater; but Mr. Lincoln promptly intervened in their behalf and as one of the town trustees saw to it that there was no interference with their activities. One of the players was a lad of ten, Joseph Jefferson by name, who in after years was to become the most eminent and beloved of American comedians, and who in the Autobiography which, aided by William Winter, he wrote in old age, pays grateful tribute to a future President's aid to strangers in distress. See "Autobiography of Joseph Jefferson," New York 1889, Page 28-39.)

Another visitor to Springfield in November, 1839, with whom it is probable Mr. Lincoln met and talked was Joseph Smith, the Mormon leader then on his way from Nauvoo to Washington to ask President Van Buren and Congress to prevent a threatened persecution of his people by residents of West-

ern Illinois. "It will be a long and lonesome time during my absence from you," Smith wrote from Springfield to his wife in Nauvoo, "but shall I see so many perish and not seek redress? So I will try this once in the name of the Lord." But the Lord did not aid him, and he soon returned to Illinois and to the train of events, not without their effect on the political fortunes of Abraham Lincoln, which on a late afternoon in June, 1844, was to end in his tragic death in Carthage jail.

Now as always keeping in touch with current events through the newspapers which came to the office of Stuart and Lincoln, the junior partner must have read in the last days of January, 1839, of the Buckshot War in Pennsylvania and of the part played in that affair by a saturnine, club-footed lawyer named Thaddeus Stevens, with whom twenty odd years later he was to have many a test of will and purpose. He must have read with sober misgivings as to the future the speech delivered by Henry Clay in the Senate on February 7, 1839, in which that statesman eager to become President with strange shortsightedness reversed his position on the slavery question and destroyed all prospect of realizing his most fondly cherished ambition. And he must have noted, also in February, 1839, the stout defense of the right of petition by Joshua Reed Giddings who a year earlier had been sent to Congress from the Western Reserve of Ohio. Big, burly and fearless, and an energetic and skillful speaker, Giddings remained in the House until 1859, the storm center of ever recurring battles against slavery. He early became the friend of Abraham Lincoln, helped in 1860 to secure his nomination for President, and by Lincoln's appointment was to end his public career as consul-general to Canada.

Finally, for Abraham Lincoln an event of present interest and future command, Quaker Benjamin Lundy, perhaps the first American to devote his life to rescue of the black men from bondage, after a brief illness, died on August 23, 1839, at Lowell, a now deserted hamlet in Putnam County, Illinois where in his last days he was editor of an abolition journal. Born in 1789 and a saddler by trade Lundy in 1815 organized at St. Clairsville, Ohio, the Union Humane Society, one of the first antislavery societies. True to his creed and a man of good-will but unbending purpose, Lundy travelled, often on foot, to all parts of the Union and to Canada and Mexico to write and speak against slavery, and before 1830 had a leading part in the organization of more than a hundred abolition societies. To him be-

longs the credit of being the first abolitionist editor,—Garrison was one of his disciples—and "the first link in a chain to which nearly all the other abolitionists traced their beginnings." Although it is probable that Benjamin Lundy and Abraham Lincoln never met in the flesh there is cause for sober rejoicing in the fact that both take their rest in the soil of the same state.

MR. LINCOLN APPOINTED COMMISSIONER IN THE CHANCERY SUIT OF BUTLER VS. TILFORD ET AL, 1839.

The original of this document, all in pencil, is now in the files of the Sangamon Circuit Court at Springfield. The latter half, as indicated, is in Lincoln's handwriting. The appointment of Mr. Lincoln as surveyor was a co-operative enterprise in pencil work. The clerk wrote the part of the document beginning with the words "William Butler," and concluding with the clause, "bill be taken as confessed." At this point Attorney Lincoln took up the pencil, and beginning with the words, "and it appearing to the satisfaction," concluded the document. The entire paper is in the hand of Mr. Lincoln. William Butler, as elsewhere recorded was one of Lincoln's close friends.

William Butler, Compt.
       vs   } Chy.
William Tilford &c Deft.

This day came the complainant by his counsel and it appearing to the satisfaction of the court that the defendants in this cause had been duly notified of the pendency of this suit by publication and service and they being three times solemnly called came not but made default. It is therefore ordered by the court that the Complainants bill be taken as confessed, and it appearing to the satisfaction of the court, by proof, that the bond filed in said cause, was executed by William Tilford, one of the defendants in this cause. It is therefore ordered and decreed by the court, Abraham Lincoln, be appointed a commissioner to make a survey of the premises in the said cause described, according to the bill and exhibits filed in said cause, and that said commissioner report his proceedings to the next term of this court.

AMENDMENTS OFFERED BY MR. LINCOLN TO THE
BILL CREATING MENARD COUNTY, 1839

These were amendments offered by Mr. Lincoln to the bill passed by the Legislature in 1839 setting off the counties of Menard, Logan and Dane from Sangamon. When the Menard Circuit Court met for the first time at Petersburg on June 17, 1839, Stuart & Lincoln appeared as counsel for the plaintiff in the second case considered by it, the suit of Levi Summers vs. Sears, which was dismissed on their motion.

1st Amend the bill by striking out the names of Richard O. Warrner and Achilles Morris whereof they occur—

2nd Amend the 14th section by adding thereto the following towit:

"And for the collection of the taxes already assessed. All business now pending in the courts of the Justice of the Peace, or of the Probate Justice of the Peace of Sangamon County, or which shall be commenced therein, previous to the organization of the new counties hereby established, shall be finished by said justices and their constables as though no division had taken place."

Amend by adding as a 16th Section the following: "The Justices of the Peace and constables now in office for Sangamon County, who reside in the boundaries of the new counties hereby established, shall continue in office in their respective new counties so long as they would have done if no division had taken place.

Amend the 4th section by adding the following proviso: "Provided that if the said commissioners shall locate the seat of Justice of Menard County on the West or left side of the Sangamon river then, and in that case, the lines of said county, shall be changed as follows, towit: Beginning at the South West corner of sections thirty in Township Eighteen North of Range Six West; thence North two miles, by the surveys; thence East with the survey to the Eastern boundary line of said county as described in this act; thence with the before described boundaries throughout—Provided further, that said commissioners in making the location of the seat of Justice of said county, shall pay no regard whatever, to the above contemplated change of lines—

MR. LINCOLN PROPOSES ADDITIONS TO THE RULES OF THE HOUSE, JANUARY 4 AND 5, 1839.

In the Legislature on January 4, 1839, Mr. Lincoln voted with the majority for a bill to incorporate the town of Danville, with which he was to have intimate and piquant association in future years. And on January 4, and again on the following day Mr. Lincoln with careful regard for the dispatch of business, proposed a total of three additions to the rules of the House. The result is thus recorded on pages 167 and 174 of the House Journal.

Session 1838-39 Jan. 4, 1839

Mr. Lincoln moved to adopt, as an additional rule of this House, the following:

"No bill shall be referred or amended after its engrossment for the third reading, without the consent of two-thirds of the members present."

After two amendments by Mr. Williams it was tabled.

———

Session 1838-39 Jan. 5, 1839

On motion of Mr. Lincoln the following additional rules of the House were adopted:

"Rule—No bill shall be committed or amended, on the question of its passage, except by the consent of two-thirds of all the members present.

"Rule—When any petition, remonstrance, or claim is presented by a member, and such member may not desire its reading he may make the motion to dispense with its reading, and ask its reference at the time of presentation; and the Chair may consider the motion as agreed to unless some member should object, and so state to the House."

REMARKS BY MR. LINCOLN ON HIS PROPOSED APPROPRIATION TO COMPLETE THE STATE HOUSE AT SPRINGFIELD, JANUARY 7, 1839

In the Legislature, January 7, 1839, on motion of Mr. Lincoln the rules were dispensed with and a bill amending the method of summoning grand and petit juros was read a third time and referred to a select committee of which the member from Sangamon was made chairman. On the same day and on Mr. Lincoln's motion, the House resolved itself into a committee of the whole to consider a bill proposed by Lincoln appropriating

$128,300 to complete and furnish the new state house at Spring-field. Friends of Vandalia, still resentful of the clever manner in which in 1837 Lincoln and his fellow members from Sanga-mon had secured the removal of the capital to Springfield, now sought to defeat the bill. Orlando Ficklin of Coles County moved two amendments—one that the amount requested should be do-nated by individuals, and another that at the next legislative elec-tion the people of the state should be permitted to vote for or against the removal of the seat of government to Springfield. When these amendments were voted down, a Vandalia member offered a third to the effect that in the next election the people should record their preference for the capital site. This amend-ment was also defeated, and, Lincoln, leading with vigor and suc-cess the fight for Springfield, caused further motions to defeat the appropriation and to subject it to a popular vote to be voted down, after which his bill was passed in its original form. The story of a winning fight was thus set forth in the Sangamo Journal of January 19, 1839:

Mr. Lincoln said, he believed the majority would agree, that if the work was done at all, it should be well done; and he was willing to submit the question to the House without saying one word more.

Ficklin said that the question of location of the seat of gov-ernment ought to be submitted to the people in 1840. Mr. Lin-coln said, that the people in 1840, would have no better right to decide the question, than the people of 1839. True, the Consti-tution had fixed the seat of government at Vandalia for twenty years, and if the people had made a bad bargain, they had a right to get out of it the best way they could. As to making money in locating the state capital, by selling lots, that matter could be settled by ascertaining how many state capitals had been built by the sale of lots in Vandalia. The idea that money could be made in this way was all illusion.

MR. LINCOLN TAKES PART IN DEBATE OF A BILL FOR COMPLETING THE NEW STATE HOUSE, JANUARY 9, 1839.

During the opening days of January, 1839, there were sharp debates in the House at Vandalia of the heavy cost of the new capital building in process of construction at Springfield, and of a belated proposal to again make Vandalia the seat of govern-

*ment. These debates and Mr. Lincoln's part in them were duly
reported by the Vandalia correspondent of the Sangamo Journal.
Here is his account of the discussion of the "bill making an appropriation for completing the State House:"*

"Mr. Ewing took the floor and moved to strike out all after
the enacting clause of the bill, and insert an amendment, providing that Vandalia shall be the seat of Government until otherwise
ordered. Mr. Ewing said that it was unconstitutional to legislate upon the subject till 1840, and that when the bill passed locating the seat of government at Springfield ,it was supposed
that fifty thousand dollars would cover all the expenses of erecting public buildings. It seemed that it would now require one
hundred and twenty-eight thousand more. He then went into
an examination of the fiscal concerns of the State, and declared
that the State was now in debt six million and a half of dollars;
and it was time members should pause and reflect in making ap-
propriations.

Mr. Lincoln said, he believed the majority would agree, that
if the work was done at all, it should be well done; and he was
willing to submit the question to the House without saying one
word more. Mr. Ewing's amendment was rejected. Mr. Ewing
then proposed another amendment—that a Board of Commissioners should be appointed to locate the seat of government on
vacant land; that they should lay out and sell the lots; and with
the money build a State House. He thought that half a million
might be realized by this measure.

Mr. Ficklin followed and endeavored to show that the State
was not pledged to make the appropriation—that the seat of government ought to remain at Vandalia—that the present capitol
was good enough—and that the question of a location of the seat
of government ought to be submitted to the people in 1840.

Mr. Lincoln said, that the people in 1840, would have no
better right to decide the question, than the people in 1839. True,
the Constitution had fixed the seat of government at Vandalia
for twenty years, and if the people had made a hard bargain,
they had the right to get out of it the best way they could. As
to making money in locating state capitals, by selling lots, that
matter could be settled by ascertaining how many state capitols
had been built by the sale of lots in Vandalia; the idea that money
can be made in this way was all illusion. Mr. Ewing then . . .
said that Springfield could not accommodate the Legislature bet-

ter than Vandalia now does, and could not probably for ten years to come. He wished to see Vandalia remain the seat of government until the interest of the country required its removal. Mr. Ewing's amendment was then rejected.

Mr. Ewing submitted another amendment—that the location should be again submitted to the people—that if there should be no choice, to return to the people the *five* places having the highest number of votes; if there should be no choice out of these, then the *three* highest should be submitted to be voted for the third time; if there then should be no choice, the election to be made between the two highest returned. The amendment was rejected. The committee then arose and reported progress.

Mr. Ficklin proposed an amendment, that the State should lend the corporation of Springfield $128,000 to complete the State House; and at the election in 1840 to submit to the people whether Springfield should remain the seat of government; and, if not, to compel the corporation to reimburse the money thus loaned. An amendment was offered to Mr. Ficklin's amendment by Mr. Carpenter; but both were rejected.

The House adjourned.

BILL DRAWN BY LINCOLN ESTABLISHING THE COUNTIES OF MENARD, LOGAN AND DANE, JANUARY 18, 1839.

The huge area included in Sangamon County, named for the river flowing through it, when it was created in 1821 made certain that, as settlement progressed, it would be subjected to sharp curtailment. Thus is 1824 the present counties of Morgan, Scott and Cass were taken from it; nor did this end the shearing process. Residents of remote parts of the now smaller county, Angle writes, "complained that it took two days, and often longer, to travel to Springfield and return to their homes; and proprietors of town sites which aspired to be county seats abetted their discontent."

In 1838 the people of Springfield had to submit to the demand for another county division, and on January 18, 1839, John Calhoun reported from a select committee of which Mr. Lincoln was a member a bill believed to have been drawn by the latter which from the reduced area of Sangamon created the counties of Menard and Logan to the north and Dane, now Christian, to

the south. Mr. Lincoln, on second thought, offered two amend-
ments which were adopted.   Then the bill as amended was or-
dered engrossed for a third reading. On January 21 it passed
the House, and a few days later, having been approved by the
Senate, was signed by the governor. The text of the bill follows.

A bill for an act to establish the counties of Menard, Logan
and Dane—

Sect 1st Be it enacted by the People of the state of Illinois
represented in the General Assembly that all that tract of country
lying within the following boundaries to wit, Beginning at the
North West corner of Section Twentyseven in Township Seventeen North of Range Eight West of the Third Principal Meridian; thence East to the centre of the Southern boundary of
Section Twentyfour in Township Seventeen North of Range
Seven West; thence North to the middle of the Northern boundary of said sections; thence East to the middle of the Northern
boundary of Section Nineteen in Township Seventeen North of
Range six West; thence North to the centre of Section Eighteen
Township and Range last aforesaid; thence East to the middle
of the Eastern boundary line of said section; thence North to
the channel of Rock Creek, thence down the channel of Rock
Creek to where the Northern boundary line of section Nine,
Township and Range last aforesaid, crosses the same; thence
East to the South West corner of Section Two, Township &
Range last aforesaid; thence North to the South East corner
of Section Twentyseven in Township Eighteen North, Range
aforesaid; thence East to the South East corner of Section Thirty
in Township Eighteen North Range Four West; thence North
to the South East corner of Section Eighteen in Township Nineteen North Range last aforesaid; thence West to the line between Ranges Four & Five; thence North to the Northern boundary line of Sangamon county; thence West with said line to the
Illinois river; thence with the present boundary lines of Sangamon county to the place of beginning shall form and constitute
the county of Menard—

Sec. 2nd That all that tract of country lying within the fol-
lowing boundaries towit, Begining at the North West corner
Township Twenty North of Range Four West; thence South
to the South West corner of Section Eighteen, in Township
Nineteen North of Range aforesaid; thence East one mile, thence
South to the South East corner of the county of Menard; thence

East to the line dividing Ranges Three and Four; thence South to the South West corner of Section Seven Township Seventeen North of Range Three West; thence East to the Eastern boundary lines of Sangamon county; thence with the present boundary lines of Sangamon county to the place of begining shall constitute the county of Logan

Sec. 3rd That all that tract of country lying within the following boundaries, towit; Begining where the Third Principal Meridian crosses the North Fork of the Sangamon river; thence down said river to the line between Sections Nine & Ten in Township Fifteen North of Range Three West; thence South to the South East corner of Section Four in Township Four North Ranges last aforesaid; thence West three miles by the surveys; thence South three miles by the surveys; thence West three miles by the surveys; thence South to the Southern boundary of Township Eleven, Ranges last aforesaid; thence East with the surveys to the Third Principal Meridian; thence North to the place of begining shall constitute the county of Dane—

Sec. 4th That Benjamin Mitchell of Tazewell county, John Henry of Morgan County, Newton Walker of Fulton county, Richard O. Wariner of Montgomery county, and Achilles Morris of Sangamon county be and they are hereby appointed commissioners to locate the seats of Justice of the counties of Menard and Dane— Said commissioners or a majority of them shall meet at Petersburg in Menard county on the first monday of May next, or within twenty days thereafter, and after being first duly sworn by some one authorized to administer oaths, faithfully and impartially discharge the duties imposed on them by this act, shall proceed to explore said county and to locate the seat of Justice thereof with a view to present and future population; which location, when made shall be and remain the Seat of Justice of the county of Menard—

Sec. 5th Said commissioners or a majority of them, shall meet at such place within the county of Dane as may be agreed on by them and at such time as they may agree upon not exceeding twenty days after they shall have located the seat of justice of Menard county, and shall then and there proceed to make the location of the seat of justice of the said county of Dane, in all respects conformably with the fourth section of this act—

Sec. 6th Said commissioners shall make out a certificate of

the location of the seat of justice of each of the said counties of Menard and Dane, stating what tract of land, and what part of the tract each location is made upon; which certificate shall be signed by the said commissioners, and filed in the office of the clerk of the county commissioners' court of Sangamon county, and shall be evidence of the said locations respectively—

Sec. 7th Neither of said locations shall be made on private property unless the owner thereof shall either convey to the county, twenty acres of land, having the location at or near the centre thereof, or donate in money, to be applied to the erection of public buildings, the sum of three thousand dollars—

Sec. 8th That Charles Emmerson of Macon county, Chenney Thomas of McLean county and Charles R. Matheny of Sangamon county, be, and they are hereby appointed commissioners to locate the seat of justice of Logan county; and who, or a majority of whom, shall, in all respects, perform their duties in the manner that the commissioners for the location of county seats of the counties of Menard and Dane, are by the act required to do, and shall meet at the town of Postville in said county of Logan, on the first Monday of May next, or within twenty days thereafter for the purpose of performing the same; and such location when so made shall be and remain the seat of justice of the said county of Logan until the end of the session of the General Assembly in the year 1841—

Sec. 9th Each of said commissioners named in this act, shall receive out of the county treasuries respectively for which he may have served, such per diem allowance, as shall be paid the members of the present General Assembly—

Sec. 10th An election shall be held on the first Monday of April next in each of the counties established by this act, to elect for each of said counties, one Sheriff, One Coroner, one Recorder, one County surveyor, three commissioners, one clerk of the county commissioner's court, and one Probate Justice of the Peace, who shall hold their offices until the next succeeding general election which elections shall be conducted in all respects agreeably to the law regulating elections— Said elections shall be held in the county of Menard, at Petersburg, Sugar Grove, Huron, and Lynchburg; in the county of Logan at Postville and Pulaski; in the county of Dane at Buck Heart Grove, Allenton, and the house of John Durbin, and shall be held by the judges heretofore appointed by the authority of Sangamon county for those precincts respectively, provided that where, any place named in this act for holding said election, has not heretofore been an election precinct, the electors meeting there may choose their own judges and clerks, who shall be qualified according to law, previous to entering upon the discharge of their duties.

Sec. 11th The judges of elections shall deliver to each officer elected a certificate of his election. The poll books shall be retained by them until the clerks of the county commissioner's courts, shall respectively be qualified and then deliver such poll books of each county to its own clerk, who shall make and transmit to the Secretary of State an abstract of the votes given at such election in the same time, manner and form as is required of clerks of county commissioners courts in elections in other counties of this state.

Sec. 12th The said counties hereby established shall be attached to and form part of the first judicial circuit—

Sec. 13th The county of Menard shall be entitled to one representative in the General Assembly, the counties of Logan and Dane together one, the county of Sangamon five, and the four together two Senators and, in case any vacancy shall occur previous to the next election, the four counties shall vote together to fill said vacancy in the same manner as if no division had taken place—

Sec. 14th All business now pending in the Sangamon circuit court, or which shall be commenced therein previous to the organization of the counties hereby established, shall be determined therein, as if no new counties had been established; and the sheriff of Sangamon county is hereby authorized to perform all duties within the boundaries of the said new counties, which may be necessary for the finishing of the aforesaid business.

Sec. 15th The judges of the several elections precincts within the aforesaid counties shall meet at the several places hereinafter named on the second day after said election to compare their respective polls—in the county of Menard, at the town of Petersburg, in the county of Logan at the town of Pulaski, in the county of Dane at the town of Allenton—

LAND RESOLUTIONS DRAWN BY MR. LINCOLN AND PRESENTED TO THE HOUSE, JANUARY, 1839

Diligent search has failed to locate the original manuscript of this report and of the resolutions which gave it effect, but there is little if any doubt that Lincoln was the author of both of them, for they clearly reflect his method of expression and mental processes at this period of his career. As a member of the General Assembly he had done much to fasten upon the people of Illinois a general improvement scheme that called for large and continuing expenditures, and was now drifting toward the rocks; and, to avert threatened disaster, he proposed that Illinois should buy from the General Government all public lands in the State for twenty-five cents an acre, sell them to settlers and other purchasers for one dollar and twenty-five cents an acre—the minimum price at which the Government then sold public lands—and in this way create a fund from which could be paid the interest on the steadily growing General Improvement debt. A majority of the members of the Legislature approved Lincoln's plan; and, the House and Senate concurring, it was duly laid before the Government at Washington, which, however, ignored it.

Mr. Lincoln, from the Committee on Finance, made the following report: The Committee on Finance, to which was referred a resolution of this House instructing them to inquire into the expediency of proposing to purchase of the Government of the United States all the unsold lands lying within the limits of the State of Illinois, have had the same under consideration and report:

That, in their opinion, if such purchase could be made on reasonable terms, two objects of high importance to the State might thereby be effected—first, acquire control over all the territory within the limits of the State—and, second, acquire an important source of revenue.

We will examine these two points in their order, and with special reference to their bearing upon our internal improvement system.

In the first place, then, we are now so far advanced in a general system of internal improvements that, if we would, we cannot retreat from it without disgrace and great loss. The conclusion then is, that we must advance; and if so, the first reason for the State acquiring title to the public land is, that while we are at great expense in improving the country, and thereby enhancing the value of all the real property within its limits, that enhancement may attach exclusively to property owned by *ourselves* as a State, or to its citizens as individuals, and *not* to that owned by the Government of that United States. Again, it is conceded every where, as we believe that Illinois surpasses every other spot of equal extent upon the face of the globe in *fertility* of soil, and in the proportionable amount of the same which is sufficiently level for actual cultivation; and conseqquently that she is endowed by nature with the capacity of sustaining a greater amount of agricultural wealth and population than any other equal extent of territory in the world. To such an amount of wealth and population, our internal improvement system, now so alarming, in view of its having to be borne by our present numbers, and with our present means, would be a burden of no sort of consequence. How important, then, is it that all our energies should be exerted to bring that wealth and population among us as speedily as possible. But what, it may be asked, can the ownership of the land by the State do towards the accomplishment of that desirable object? It may be answered that the chief obstruction to the more rapid settlement of our country is found in the fact that so much of our best lands lie so remote from timber—an obstruction that, did our State but own those lands, our Legislature might do much towards removing, by extending encouragement in the shape of donations, exemptions from ordinary burdens, or otherwise, to the rearing and cultivating of timber, or to the invention of means of building and enclosure that might dispense with the present profuse use of timber. This, then, is another reason why the State should desire the control of all the land within its limits.

Looking to these lands in the second point of view, to wit, as a source of revenue, your committee submit the following: There are now of unsold lands in the State of Illinois, twenty millions of acres, more or less. Should we purchase all of them, at twenty-five cents per acre, they would cost us five millions of dollars. This sum we might borrow, and the proceeds of the sales of the lands, at the present price of $1.25 per acre, would repay the principal, together with the interest thereon, at five per cent, for thirty years, and one-half the lands still be left us.

In a very short time we shall have contracted a very heavy debt for the construction of public works; and yet those works will remain for a time so incomplete as to return us nothing; meanwhile the interest upon our debt must be paid. When this juncture shall arrive (as surely it will) we shall find ourselves at a point which may aptly be likened to the dead point in the steam-engine—a point extremely difficult of turning—but which, when once turned, will present no further difficulty, and all will again be well. The aid that we might derive in that *particular juncture,* by the purchase of public lands, affords, in the openion of the committee, the strongest reason for making that purchase. The annual proceeds of the sales of those lands, should the subsequent sales bear any proportion to those of former times, will pay the interest on the loan created for their own purchase, and also upon many millions of our internal improvement loans; and that, too, at that *particular time* when we shall have but *very small, if any* other means of paying it. And finally, when our public works shall be completed and consequently able to sustain themselves, the proceeds of the sales of the lands may be diverted to the payment of the original debt contracted for the purchase of them. To show that we are not mistaken in saying that the proceeds of the sales of the lands will annually pay the interest on their own loan, and also on a large amount of the internal improvement loan, it is only necessary to state that the interest on the land loan would be but five hundred thousand dollars annually, and that the proceeds of the sales of the public lands in this State have, in one instance, been about three millions a year, (the committee speak from memory only;) so that, should the average of the subsequent sales be half as large, we still should have left one million annually, to pay interest on our internal improvement debt.

The only remaining question is, whether there is any *probability* of the General Government accepting such a proposal. We think there are some reasons for believing it would. It would relieve the General Government from a perpetual source of expensive and vexatious legislation, which, perhaps, annually absorbs one-tenth it receives from that source of revenue. She would receive of us, at once, and without trouble, five millions of dollars—a sum one-third part as large as she paid a foreign government for the Louisiana territory, then including what now are the States of Louisiana, Arkansas, and Missouri—and receive it too, after having received of us, for lands already sold, a sum equal to the whole sum paid for the Louisiana territory; and she would receive that five millions of dollars at a time when she is in most particular need of money.

But should your committee be mistaken; should there be no *probability* of the General Government accepting our proposal, still, it is believed no evil can follow the making it.

The committee, therefore, submit the following resolutions:

Resolved by the General Assembly of the State of Illinois, That the said State propose to purchase of the Government of the United States all the lands not sold or otherwise disposed of, within the limits of said State, at the rate of twenty-five cents per acre, to be paid (unless otherwise agreed upon) at such time as the said Government of the United States shall deliver over to the authorities of the said State of Illinois all the plats, field-notes &c., pertaining to the surveys of said lands.

Resolved, That the faith of the said State of Illinois is hereby irrevocably pledged to carry into effect the foregoing proposal, if the Government of the United States shall accept the same within two years from the passage hereof.

Resolved, That our Senators in Congress be instructed, and our Representatives requested, to use their best exertions to procure the passage of a law or resolution of Congress accepting the foregoing proposal.

Resolved, That the Governor be requested to transmit a copy of the foregoing resolutions to each of our Senators and Representatives in Congress.

Mr. William of Adams said he was not sasisfied with the report.

Mr. Lincoln replied, that as the object had in view by the purchase would be the mitigation of the burthen of taxation, he believed the people would not demand the reduction spoken of by the gentleman. He thought the end proposed by his report would be obtained; that Congress would sell on the terms proposed; and that by holding out inducements for the draining of swamps, and the cultivation of our large prairies, for growing timber, all our lands would sell. He instituted a comparison between Illinois and Indiana ,and showed we were not ten years behind Indiana, and yet she had but 4,000,000 of acres unsold; that Ohio had but say 1,500,000 acres, and yet we were not twenty years behind Ohio; that we might expect Illinois to populate, and her lands to sell more rapidly than in either of these States. He said that at all events he deemed the question worthy of consideration, and for that purpose he had brought in the report.

Mr. Rewalt moved that the report and resolutions be laid on the table and printed, which was done.

ENTRY IN THE FEE BOOK OF STUART & LINCOLN, JANUARY 28, 1839

This entry in the fee book of Stuart & Lincoln was made by the junior partner. It refers to the suit of Kinzie and For-

sythe against Samuel Musick. No legal documents for this suit appear to be available.

Jan. 28, 1839   Sent Kinzie $75. by check.

PROOF OF SUMMONS SERVED IN THE SUIT OF HART VS. HOUGHTON AND HARRISON, SANGAMON CIRCUIT COURT, JANUARY 29, 1839

(Herndon-Weik Collection)

The part of this document beginning with "Executed the within on" and concluding with "this 29th day of Jany 1839" was penned by Mr. Lincoln. It is evident that he was dissatisfied with the notations by the sheriff, as these are crossed out on the cover, and the more exact wording of Mr. Lincoln takes their place—proof of the care exercised by him in legal documents. This summons is a part of a case in which Rhoda Hart, executrix, sued almost everyone with whom she could engage in ligitation. The Sacketts, Harts, Houghton, Harrison, Penny and McElwin were involved. The three last named appear to have had common cause in the case. The suit was settled by written agreement on July 16, 1841, when Harrison agreed to pay court costs, and the case was dismissed. Penny and McElwin joined in the agreement of Harrison.

Rhoda Hart exc &

vs.   } Sum.

Jefferson Hart
Melissa Jane Hart &
Rhoda Hart
To March Term 1839
    (Five lines crossed out)

Service   50
Copy   50
Travel   75
Rtts—   12½
            ─────────
        $1.87½

G. Elkin Shff S. C
By Wm Lavely Deputy
    Executed the within on Jefferson Hart by leaving a copy

thereof at his usual place above, with a white person of the family of the age of ten years and afterwards, towit, with Elijah Houghton, and informing said Houghton of the contents thereof— this 29th of Jany 1839.

G. Elkin Shff s c
By Wm Lavely D. S

MR. LINCOLN INTRODUCES A BILL FOR THE RELIEF OF THE CLERK OF SANGAMON COUNTY, FEBRUARY 6, 1839.

In the opening weeks of 1839 his relations with the State Bank of Illinois, then in deep waters, seriously embarrassed Clerk Charles R. Matheny of Sangamon County, and on February 6, concerned as always for a friend's affairs, Mr. Lincoln introduced into the House a bill for an act for his relief. The original title of this measure was "A bill for an act for the relief of the clerk of the circuit court of Sangamon county," but when it was referred to a select committee for consideration the representatives of other counties demanded like relief, and on February 23, on its author's motion, the measure was amended to include the clerks of the counties of Clinton, Fayette and Franklin. In its more inclusive form the bill in due course became law. It was while this measure was pending that on February 14 Mr. Lincoln requested his partner in Springfield to renew a note of his falling due at the Illinois State Bank, for which he enclosed a new note signed in blank, explaining to Stuart that funds for the renewal were in the hands of their mutual friend, William Butler. And he added in characteristic conclusion: "Ewing won't do anything. He is not worth a damn"—a reference no doubt to the recent and unsuccessful attempt of William L. D. Ewing to repeal the bill removing the state capital to Springfield.

A bill for an act for the relief of the clerk of the circuit court of Sangamon County.

Sec. 1. Be it enacted by the people of the State of Illinois represented in the General Assembly, that whenever the clerk of the circuit court of Sangamon County shall make out a fee bill in due form of law, for services rendered by him or by his predecessor in office, as clerk, in all cases in which the president and directors of the State Bank of Illinois were a party, so far as said services were rendered for said Bank, and for which it is, or would be liable, as such party, and shall transmit the same to the Auditor of Public Accounts, said Auditor shall issue his warrant upon the Treasury in favor of said clerk for such amount as may be so shown to be due him.

Sec. 2. Said clerk, in making out said fee bill shall be liable to the same penalties and forfeitures for any violation of the present law regulating fees as he would be in any other case.

Amend the first section by inserting immediately before the word "state" in the seventh line, the word "old".

"Further amend by adding, as a third section, the following—

Sec. 3. The clerks of the circuit courts of Franklin, Fayette and Clinton counties shall be entitled to the same benefits, subject to the same pre-requisites and liabilities under this act, as the said clerk of Sangamon County.

BOND GIVEN IN THE SUIT OF ADKINS VS. HAINES, MACON CIRCUUIT COURT, FEBRUARY 7, 1839

(Photostat from the National Lincoln Life Foundation)

The spelling, lack of punctuation, and format should prove this a legal work not by Mr. Lincoln. It is included as one of the papers in a case in which he acted as counsel, and in which he wrote a plea on June 4, 1839. The lack of a Judge's Docket for this period in Macon County makes it difficult to locate Lincoln cases, except where his name is cited, but in cases where the documents exist, research thus far has not unearthed a history of this case.

We Robert Haines and John G. Deeds Acknowledge ourselves to be indebted to the People of the State of Illinois in the sum of one hundred dollars to be levied of our respective goods Chattels Lands & tenements for the use of said People

Rendered yet taken upon this Condition that if the said Robert Haines shall personally appear before the Circuit Court of Macon County & State of Ills. on the first day of next term thereof to be holden on the second Monday in the month of May next to Answer David Adkin in a plea In slander

And not depart without leave of the Court then this Reconisance to be void otherwise to Remain in full force and virtue

Witness our hands & seals the 7th day of February A. D. 1839

                his
Robert   x   Haines (Seal)
              mark
John G. Deeds (Seal)

PRAECIPE IN THE SUIT OF VAN BERGEN VS. ARMSTRONG, SANGAMON CIRCUIT COURT, FEBRUARY 12, 1839

(Herndon-Weik Collection)

This praecipe is included with the declaration of February 20, 1839 as part of a case engaged in by Mr. Lincoln, but in which, as he was then in Vandalia, he did not pen the legal papers. The document is in the hand of John T. Stuart, and the notations appear to be in that of William Butler. The filing date is of interest, as Abraham Lincoln celebrated his birthday on that day.

| Peter Van Bergen assignee of Nathaniel A. Rankin— vs. Hugh M. Armstrong &. Hosea I. Armstrong | Action of Debt
Debt $300.00
Damages $100.00 |

The Clerk of the Sangamon Circuit Court will issue a summons for the Defendants in the above entitled cause returnable to the next Term of the Sangamon Circuit Court.

Stuart & Lincoln

February 12th 1839
Peter Van Bergen
assignee of Rankin

vs } Precipe

Hugh M. Armstrong
Hosea I. Armstrong
Filed February 12th 1839

BILL DRAWN AND INTRODUCED BY MR. LINCOLN TO INCORPORATE THE SANTA FE RAILROAD COMPANY, FEBRUARY 19, 1839.

The granting of charters, many of them for enterprises which died in their infancy, was a major activity of the General Assembly of Illinois in the opening weeks of 1839, and in these grants Mr. Lincoln now and again had an important part. Thus on February 19 Edwin B. Webb introduced in the House a bill the member from Sangamon had drawn for the incorporation of the Santa Fe Railroad Company, an ambitious project which never reached the stage of roadbed and rails, but the name of which is preserved in one of the great trans-continental lines of the present time.

And February 19 *was in other ways a busy day for Mr. Lincoln. On his motion the House rules were dispensed with, and a bill to incorporate the Vandalia and Alton Turnpike Road Company ordered to a second reading, while, also on his motion, the counties of Dane, Logan and Menard were added to the eighth judicial circuit. Finally in the evening he attended a joint session of the House and Senate called to elect seven commissioners of the Board of Public Works, and voted for four of the men chosen, one of them a Democrat and three of them Whigs.*

Sec. 1. Be it enacted by the people of the State of Illinois, represented in the General Assembly, That M. I. Newman, R. C. Woolfolk, James C. Mc Pheeters, George Cloud, Wilson Able, Thomas Howard and John Hodgers.   and their associates, successors, and assigns, are hereby created a body corporate and politic, under the name and style of the Santa Fe Rail Road Company for the term of fifty years; and by that name may be and are hereby made capable in law and equity to sue and be sued, plead and be impleaded, defend and be defended, in any court or courts of record; to make, have, and use a common seal, and the same to renew and alter at pleasure, and shall be and are hereby vested with all the powers, privaleges, and immunities which are or may be necessary to carry into effect the purposes and objects of this act as hereinafter set fourth; and the said company are hereby authorized and impowered to locate, construct, and finally complete a rail road from St. A. Fee in Alexander County to the Central Rail Road at some point on said Rail Road south of Jonesboro, upon the most eligible and convenient route and said corporation is hereby authorised to join and connect with the central rail Road, and for this purpose the said company are authorized to lay out their said road wide enough for a double or single track through the whole length; and for the purpose of cutting embankments, stone, and gravel, may take as much more land as may be necessary for the proposed construction and security of said railroad: Provided, All damages that may be occasioned to any person or corporation, by taking such lands or materials for the purposes aforesaid, shall be paid for by the company in the manner hereinafter provided.

Sec.2. The capital stock of said company shall consist of three hundred thousand dollars, to be divided into shares of one hundred dollars each. The immediate government and direction of said company shall be vested in five directors, who shall be

chosen by the stockholders of said company in the manner hereinafter provided, who shall hold their offices for one year after
their election, and until others shall be duly elected and qualified
to take their places as directors, a majority of whom shall form
a quorum for the transaction of business, shall elect one of their
members, president of the board, who shall also be the president
of the company.

Sec. 3. The said corporation is hereby authorized by their
agents, surveyors, and engineers, to cause such examinations and
surveys of the ground and country to be made between said
points as shall be necessary to determine the most advantageous
route for the proper line or course whereon to construct their
said railroad; and it shall be lawful for the said corporation to
enter upon, and take possession of, and use all such lands and
real estate as may be necessary to the construction and maintainance of their said railroad, and the accommodations requisite
and appertaining to the same; and, may also hold such lands as
they may purchase or receive in any manner for the necessary
purpose of said road; Provided, That all lands or real estate
entered upon, and taken possession of, and used by said corporation for the purpose and accommodations of the said railroad,
or upon which the site for the said railroad shall have been located or determined by the said corporation, shall be paid for
by the said corporation in damages, if any be sustained by the
owner or owners thereof, by the use of the same, for the purpose of said railroad, which damages shall be ascertained in the
same manner that damages are ascertained in the case of public
roads running through the lands of individuals, some one of the
directors acting in the stead of the supervisor of the general road
law.

Sec. 4. If any person shall wilfuly, maliciously or wantonly,
and contrary to law, obstruct the passage of any car on said railroad, or any part thereof, or any thing belonging thereto, or shall
damage, brake, or destroy any part of said railroad, or imple-
ments or buildings, he, she, or they, or any persons assisting,
shall forfeit and pay to said company for every such offense
treble the amount of damages that shall be proved before any
court competent to try the same, to be sued for in the manner
and behalf of said company, and such offender or offenders shall
be deemed guilty of a misdemeanor, and shall be liable to an
indictment in the same manner as other indictments are found
in any county or counties where such offence shall have been

committed; and upon conviction, such offender or offenders shall be liable to a fine not exceeding one thousand dollars for the use of the county when such indictment may be found.

Sec. 5. M. I. Newman, R. C. Woolfolk, George Cloud, are hereby appointed commissioners to open subscription books for the stock of said company; and said commissioners or a majority of them, are hereby authorized to open subscription books for said stock, at such places as they may deem proper and shall give at least thirty days' notice of the times and places when and where such books will be opened, in the state paper printed at Vandalia, and shall keep said books open at least five days, unless the whole amount of capital stock shall be subscribed before the expiration of the said five days; and they shall require each subscriber to pay five dollars on each share subscribed, at the time of subscribing; and at the expiration of the said five days, if the whole of the said capital stock shall be subscribed the said commissioners shall call a meeting of the stockholders by giving ten days' notice in a newspaper printed in Vandalia; and at such meeting it shall be lawful to elect the directors of the said Company and when the directors of said company are chosen the said commissioners shall deliver said subscription books, together with all sums of money received by them as such commissioners, to said directors; Provided, That no person shall be a director unless he shall own at least five shares of the capital stock. Said company is hereby authorized to borrow any sum of money not exceeding their capital stock, and to make all such contracts as said corporation may deem necessary to carry into effect the powers and privaleges hereby granted.

Sec. 7. That the rights of way and the real estate purchases for the right of way by said company, whether by mutual agreement between the said corporation and the owner or owners of said land or real estate, or which shall become the property of the said company by operation of law as is in this act provided, shall, upon the payment of the amount belonging to the owner or owners of such lands, as a compensation for the same, become the property of said corporation, absolutely and in fee simple.

Sec. 8. The Legislature reserves to itself the right to purchase the stock of said company at any time by paying the amount actually expended thereon, with the interest at the rate of six per cent per annum; and for the purpose of ascertaining the value thereof, the Legislature may appoint two or more commissioners, who, being duly sworn, shall proceed to ascertain by inspection and the oath of witnesses the actual value of the road, fixtures, apparatus, and cars as aforesaid. The corporation may take and transport on the said railroad any person or persons, merchandize, or other property, by the force and power of steam, or animals, or any combination of them; and may fix and establish, take and receive such rates of toll for all passengers and property transported upon the same, as the directors shall from time to time establish; and the directors are hereby authorised and empowered to make all necessary rules and regulations, by-laws and ordinances, that they may deem necessary and expedient to accomplish the designs and purposes, and to carry into effect the provisions of this act ,and for the transfer and assignment of its stock, which is hereby declared personal property and transferable in such manner as shall be provided for by the by-laws and ordinances of said corporation.

Sec. 9. Said company shall transport the United States mail upon the whole line of said road, whenever required by the Post Master General; Provided, That if the Postmaster General and the company shall be unable to agree upon the compensation to which said company shall be entitled, the Postmaster General may choose one person and the said company shall choose another, who, should they be unable to agree upon the compensation to which said company shall be entitled, shall choose a third person, and the compensation fixed by them or a majority of them, shall be binding upon said company.

Sec. 10. If the said company shall not commence the work in two years from the passage of this act and complete within five years, then this act shall thenceforth cease and be void.

MR. LINCOLN REPORTS A SUPPLEMENT TO THE ACT ESTABLISHING DANE, LOGAN AND MENARD COUNTIES, FEBRURY 20, 1839

Mr. Lincoln wrote and on February 20, 1839, reported from the Committee on Counties this supplement to the act establishing Dane, Logan and Menard Counties. It was at once ordered engrossed for a third reading, passed by the House the same day, duly approved by the Senate and signed by the governor. It will be noted that its purpose was to assure the tenure of office of county officials and members of the House and Senate affected by the creation of the new counties—a departure which, be it said, cost Mr. Lincoln many former supporters in that section of Sangamon which became Menard County.

Sec 1st Be it enacted by the People of the State of Illinois represented in the General Assembly that the officers to be elected under the provisions of the act to which this is supplemental shall hold their offices respectively as long after the next August election as they would do under the general law if they had been elected at said August election—

Sec 2 In all elections for a Senator or Senators in the district composed of the counties of Menard, Logan, Dane and Sangamon, the clerks of the county commissioners courts of the three first named counties shall, within 10 days after each election, return abstracts of the votes given for a Senator or Senators to the Clerk of the County Commissioners' court of Sangamon county, who shall, in presence of two Justices of the Peace, compare said abstracts, together with the votes given for such Senator or Senators in Sangamon County, and shall, as soon as convenient, make out, and deliver a certificate of election to the person so shown to be elected—

Sec. 3 In all elections for a Representative to the General Assembly, in the counties of Logan and Dane, the clerk of the county commissioner's courts of said counties shall, within ten days after each election, meet at the county seat of Logan county, and shall, in the presence of two Justices of the Peace, proceed to compare the votes given in said counties for Representatives, and also to make out a certificate of election for the person so shown to be elected; which certificate shall be delivered to such person as soon thereafter as convenient.—

Sec. 4. Militia duty shall be performed in the counties of Menard, Logan and Dane, and Sangamon, as if no division had been made.

BILL REPORTED BY MR. LINCOLN TO INCORPORATE THE FRANKLIN INSTITUTE, FEBRUARY 20, 1839

At an evening session of the House on February 20, on Mr. Lincoln's motion, the rules were dispensed with, and he reported from the Committee on Elections this act which he had probably drawn to incorporate the Franklin Institute, designed to function at the town of Frankfort in Franklin County. It deserves careful study, for it clearly evidences the measure of skill Mr. Lincoln had acquired as a drafter of proposed legislation.

Sec. 1 Be it enacted by the people of the state of Illinois Represented in the General Assembly

That Solomon Clark Meshack, Morris Williams, A. Roberts,

Isaac Barber, John T. Knox, Ralph Elston, George P. Bayer, Mathew C. Colbay, John B. Maddox, William G. Stephenson and their successors be and they are hereby constituted a body politic and corporate to be known by the name of the Trustees of the Franklin Institute and by that name shall have perpetual succession and have a common seal with power to change the same at pleasure and as such shall be authorized to exercise all powers and privileges that are enjoyed by the Trustees of any Seminary, college or university in this state not herein limited or otherwise directed.

Sec. 2 That the said Trustees shall hold their first stated meeting at the Town of Frankfort in the County of Franklin on the first Monday of June next or so soon thereafter as may be convenient and they or a majority of them shall as soon as they think proper fix upon a permanent seat for said institute and proceed to erect buildings thereon as soon as convenient and the interests of said institution may require.

Sec. 3 The said trustees or their successors by the name aforesaid shall be capable in law to purchase, receive and hold to themselves and their successors for the use and benefit of said institution any land, tenements or rents, good and chatels of what kind soever which shall be given or devised to or purchased by them for the use of the Franklin Institute.

Sec. 4 The said trustees by the name aforesaid may sue and be sued, plead and be impleaded in any court of law or equity in this state.

Sec. 5 In case a sufficient number of members do not attend to constitute a board at any meeting those who do attend may adjourn to any day thereafter or to the next stated meeting and shall give ten days previous notice thereof.

Sec. 6 Five members shall be sufficient to constitute a board for the transaction of all business respecting the said institute excepting those cases particularly excepted.

Sec. 7 The assent of the Majority of the whole number of the members of the Institute shall be necessary to perform the following business: elect and fix the Salary of the President, to fix the permanent seat of the institute, and sell or convey any lands tenements or rents belonging to Said Institute.

Sec. 8 The Trustees shall have power from time to time to establish such by laws and ordinances not contrary to the constitution and laws of this state as they shall deem necessary for the said institute.

Sec. 9 The Trustees shall elect a President, Treasurer & clerk to their own body and so many professors, Tutors or Masters as may be necessary and upon the death, resignation or legal disability of any of the Trustees, President or other officers of the Said institute the board of Trustees shall supply the vacancy by ballott.

Sec. 10 The Treasurer of said Institution always and all other agents when required by the Trustees before entering upon the dutires of their appointments shall give bond for the security of the corporation in such Penal sum and with such security as the board of Trustees shall approve, and all processes against the said corporation shall be by summons and Service of the same shall be by leaving an attested copy with the Treasurer of the institute at least 30 days before the action day thereof.

Sec. 11 The said institute and their preparatory department shall be open to all denominations of christians and the profession of any religious faith shall not be required of those who become students. All persons however may be suspended or expelled from said institution whose habits are evil or vicious or whose moral character is bad.

Sec. 12 The President and other officers of the Said institute shall be subject to the sanction of the board of Trustees and continue in office during good behavior.

Sec. 13. The President of the board of Trustees shall have full powwer to call special meetings of the Said Trustees and it shall be his duty upon the request of three of them to do the same, but upon any call meeting ten days general notice shall be given by the President previous to the meeting.

Sec. 14 The Trustees of the corporation shall have authority from time to time to prescribe and regulate the course of studies to be pursued in said institute and in the preparatory department attached thereto. & fix the rate of Tuitions room rent and other College expences. To appoint instructors and such other officers and agents as shall or may be needed in managing the concerns of the institution & define their powers duties and employments. & fix their compensation, to displace and remove either of the instructors officers and agents. & erect the necessary buildings to purchase books & chemicals & Phylosophical apparatus & other suitable means of instructions to put in operation a System of manual Labour for the purpose of lessening the expence of Education and promoting the health of the Students to make rules for the general management of the officers of the institution and for the regulation of the conduct of the students and to add as the ability of the said corporation shall increase & the interest of the community shall require additional departments for the study of any or all the liberal professions, provided however that nothing herein contained shall authorise the establishment of a Theological department in said institution

Sec. 15 If at any time a member of the board of Trustees shall absent himself for three stated meetings successively or for some disorderly conduct, unless for good cause shown and approved of by the said Trustees in such case, his seat shall be considered vacant and the board instructed to fill his seat with a member provided that the trustees of said institution shall at all times be accountable for their conduct in the management of the business aforesaid in such manner as the Legislature shall by law direct.

312

A Bill for An act to incorporate the Franklin Institute to be Engraved
            Clk H. R.

DECLARATION IN THE SUIT OF VAN BERGEN VS. ARMSTRONG ET AL, SANGAMON CIRCUIT COURT, FEBRUARY 20, 1839.
(Herndon-Weik Collection)

This declaration is included as a Lincoln work, although not in his hand. The document was penned by Stuart, as were the cover notations, with exception of filing date in the hand of Clerk Butler. Mr. Lincoln appeared with Mr. Stuart in the trial of the case. It was decided on March 4, 1839, at which time the suit for collection of $300.00 was dismissed at the defendant's cost, that is, his payment of the court costs in the case.

State of Illinois
Sangamon County   ss   Of the March Term 1839
& Circuit

Peter VanBergen assignee of Nathaniel A. Rankin by his Attorney complains of Hugh M. Armstrong and Hosea I. Armstrong in Custody &c in a Plea that they may render unto him the sum of Three Hundred Dollars which they owe to and unjustly detain from him For that whereas heretofore Towit on the eighth day of February in the year of our Lord one thousand eight Hundred and Thirty eight at the County and Circuit aforesaid the said defendants (the said Hugh M. Armstrong by the style and description of "H. M. Armstrong" and the the said Hosea I. Armstrong by the style and description of "H I Armstrong") by their certain writing obligatory sealed with their seals and now here in Court to be seen the date whereof is the day and year aforesaid acknowledged themselves or either of them to be held and firmly bound unto the said Nathaniel A. Rankin by the style and description of N. A. Rankin his heirs or assigns in the sum of Three Hundred Dollars above demanded to be paid to the said Nathaniel A. Rankin by the description aforesaid on or before the first day of February next ensueing after the date of the said writing obligatory with interest on the same from the date aforesaid of said writing obligatory at the rate of Ten per cent. per annum and if the same was not paid at maturity of said writing obligatory, said defendants bound themselves to pay twelve per Cent interest from that time until paid. Which said writing obligatory by endorsement thereon in writing was on the Twenty seventh day of March in the year of our Lord one thousand eight Hundred and Thirty eight at the County & Circuit aforesaid assigned by the said Nathaniel A. Rankin by the style and description of "N. A. Rankin" to the said Van Bergen of which the said Defendants had notice. Yet the said Defendants though often requested so to do have not as yet paid to the said Plaintiff said sum of Three Hundred Dollars above demanded nor any part thereof but have hitherto wholly neglected and refused and still neglect and refuse so to do. To the Damage of the said Plaintiff   Hundred Dollars and therefore he brings his suit &c.

Stuart & Lincoln—

Copy of Note.

Dollars 300.00

On or before the first day of February next we the undersigned or either of us promise to pay to N. A. Rankin his heirs or assigns Three hundred Dollars for Value Received with interest on same from this date at the rate of ten per Cent per annum and if not paid at maturity we agree to pay twelve per Cent interest from that time until paid

H. M. Armstrong   (Seal)

H. I. Armstrong   (Seal)

Copy of Assignment

For value Received I assign the within to Peter Van Bergen

N. A. Rankin

March 27th 1838.

Peter Van Bergen
assignee of N. A. Rankin

vs.   } Decl

H. M. Armstrong
& H. I. Armstrong
Filed Febry 20 1839
    Wm Butler   ck

RESOLUTION BY MR. LINCOLN PERMITTING THE PEOPLE OF VANDALIA TO USE THE HALL OF THE HOUSE, FEBRUARY 21, 1839

Mr.Lincoln as was his wont mixed social diversion with business during the last session of the Legislature in Vandalia. Witness the resolution which he drew and had adopted on February 21. On the same day, John J. Hardin, then a member of the House from Morgan, reported three amendments drawn by Mr. Lincoln to a bill from the Senate entitled "An act dividing the state into judicial districts" which had been referred to the House Committee on the Judiciary. The amendments were voted on, but only the first, which changed Ogle County from the fifth to the ninth district, was adopted.

Resolved, That the use of the hall of the House of Representatives be tendered to the ladies and gentlemen resident at and visiting the town of Vandalia, on the evening of the 22d of February, instant, for the purpose of any public amusement they may choose to indulge in.

PLAINTIFF'S DECLARATION IN THE SUIT OF LANGFORD VS. DYER ET AL, SANGAMON CIRCUIT COURT, FEBRUARY 22, 1839
(Herndon-Weik Collection)

The declaration and cover notations in this case are in the handwriting of John T. Stuart, and the date of filing is by Butler. The legal paper by the senior member of the two-year-old firm is neater than usual, but still in marked contrast with the meticulous penmanship of the documents of the junior partner. Penmanship is not the mark of a good lawyer, but Mr. Lincoln's writing reveals more clarity of thought and better wording and grammar than that of Stuart. The "so to do" of Mr. Lincoln is "'same to do" with Mr. Stuart. As before noted, Mr. Lincoln was in Vandalia at the time of the filing of the praecipe and dec-

laration in this case. He appeared with Stuart on March 9, 1839,
when, as attorneys for the plaintiff, they asked that the case be
dismissed. The documents are included not as works of Mr.
Lincoln, but as a part of the documentary history of his legal
career.

State of Illinois
Sangamon county   ss   Of the March Term 1839.
& Circuit

James P. Langford by his attorney complains of John Dryer
Robert F. Coffin and Edmund G Johns trading and doing business under the style and form of Dryer Coffin &Co in a Plea of
Trespass on the Case in assumpsit. For that whereas heretofore
To wit on a first day of January in the year of our Lord one
thousand eight hundred and Thirty Nine at the county and circuit aforesaid the said Defendants partners were indebted to the
said Plaintiff in the sum of   Dollars for divers
goods wares merchandise spokes hubs lumber desks goods and
chattels by the said Plaintiff before that time sold and delivered
to the said Defendants and at their special instance and request
and being so indebted they the said Defendants in consideration
thereof afterwards Towit on the day and year last aforesaid at
the County & Circuit aforesaid undertook and then & there faithfully Promised the said Plaintiff to pay him said mentioned
sum of money when they the said Defendants should be thereunto afterwards requested.

And for that whereas also afterwards Towit on the day &
year aforesaid at the County and Circuit aforesaid
                         in consideration that the said Plaintiff at
the special instance and request of the said defendants had before that time sold and delivered divers other goods ware & merchandise spokes hubs lumber desks goods and chattels to the
said defendants they the said Defendants undertook and then
&there faithfully promised the said plaintiff to pay him so much
money as the said last mentioned goods wares merchandise hubs
spokes lumber desks goods & chattels at the time of the sale and
delivery there of were reasonably worth when they the said Defendants should be thereunto afterwards requested. And the said
plaintiff avers that the last mentioned goods wares merchandise
spokes hubs lumber desks goods & chattels at the time of the said
sale & delivery there of were reasonably worth the sum of
               Dollars Towit at the County & Circuit aforesaid on
the day and year aforesaid of which the said Defendants had

notice afterwards Towit on the day and year aforesaid at the County & Circuit aforesaid

Yet the said defendants though often requested have not as yet paid the said several sums of money above demanded or any part thereof to the said plaintiff but the same to do hath hitherto wholly failed and refused and still fails & refuses to the Damage of the said Plaintiff Three Hundred Dollars and therefore he sues &c

Stuart & Lincoln

Jas P. Langford
    vs   Decl.
Dryer Coffin &Co
Filed Feby 22d 1839
    WmButler Clk

AFFIDAVIT AND CAPIAS DRAWN BY MR. LINCOLN IN THE SUIT OF EDWARDS VS. RUSH, SANGAMON CIRCUIT COURT, MARCH 12, 1839

This affidavit and capias tell their own story. On July 12, 1839, the case of Edwards vs. Rush was continued at the request of Stuart & Lincoln, but a search of the files of the Sangamon Circuit Court yield no other facts regarding it.

State of Illinois ⎫
           ⎬
Sangamon County ⎭

This day personally appeared before the undersigned, clerk of the circuit court in and for the county aforesaid, William Edwards of the county aforesaid who is about to commence a suit against Oliver Hazzard Perry Rush, to recover damages for slanderous words spoken by the said Rush, charging this affiant with stealing money; and that the said damages, or the benefit of whatever judgement may be obtained by said affiant, against the said Rush, in the said circuit court, will be in danger of being lost, unless the said Rush be held to bail agreeably to the laws of this state

William Edwards.

Sworn to before me
this 12th day of March
1839

    Wm. Butler, Clk.

William Edwards }

vs. }   Trespass on the case—

Oliver Hazzard Perry Rush. }   Damage $1000.00

The clerk of the Sangamon circuit court will issue a capias on the above, returnable to the next term of said court.

Stuart &Lincoln,

For Plff.

March 12, 1839.

PRAYER OF SAMUEL P. BAILEY DRAWN BY MR. LINCOLN TO INTERPLEAD IN THE SUIT OF GRIDLEY VS. LOW, SANGAMON CIRCUIT COURT, MARCH 12, 1839

On March 7, 1839, Stuart and Lincoln secured a judgment by default for $455.59 against one Hudson Low and in favor of their client, Samuel P. Bailey. Five days later they sought for their client permission to interplead in a suit John Gridley had brought against Low to secure the payment of three notes given by Low and secured by a mortgage on lands owned by him. Careful searching has failed to reveal the outcome of Bailey's prayer to the Sangamon Circuit Court.

To the Honorable the Judge of the Sangamon Circuit Court in Chancery sitting —

Humbly complaining sheweth unto your Honor, your orator Samuel P. Bailey, that one John Gridley has commenced a suit in this court against one Hudson Low, to foreclose a mortgage, on certain lands described in said Gridley's Bill, given to secure the payment of *three* several promissory notes; that said Gridley prays that the lands may be sold to satisfy *two* of said notes only; that your orator is the legal assignee of the other said notes, upon which notes he instituted suit in the common law side of this court, and obtained judgement thereon at this present term—

In tender consideration of which premises your orator prays permission to interplead in the said case of Gridley against Low; and that the decree in said case be so made, that his judgement may be paid out of the proceeds of the sale of the said lands, unless the said proceeds be insufficient to pay the whole amount for which the said lands were mortgaged, in which case your orator prays that a fair distributive share of said proceeds be applied to the payment of his said judgement—

Samuel P. Bailey

by his solicitors
Stuart & Lincoln

Filed Mar 12th 1839.

AGREEMENT OF DISMISSAL OF THE SUITS OF FELLOWS VS. SNYDER, AND OF FELLOWS VS. KELLAR & SNYDER, MACON CIRCUIT COURT, MARCH 24, 1839

(Photostat from the Lincoln National Life Foundation)

This agreement was drawn up by the senior partner in the firm of Stuart & Lincoln, and is included as the final bit of history in the case. The cover notations were the work of Clerk Gorin. Although, as noted, the lack of a judge's docket, and availability of records in cases of this period in the Macon Circuit Court prevent a complete presentation of case histories, in this case, the declarations in both suits mentioned in the agreement, the praecipes and bonds penned by Mr. Lincoln, and the final agreement permit of a complete sketch of the two cases. The declarations drawn by Mr. Lincoln were filed in September and October, 1838, that of Fellows & Fellows vs. A. C. Snyder on a day in October, and that in the suit of Fellows & Fellows vs. Kellar & Snyder on September 19. Reference to these documents, and the praecipes and bonds of September 19, 1838, will present a background for this final agreement.

It is hereby agreed that the suits now pending in the Macon Circuit Court of W. & C. Fellows vs. A. G. Snyder & Co— and The same vs Kellar & Snyder are to be dismissed at the Costs of the Defendants—
March 24th 1839

Stuart & Lincoln
for W. & C. Fellows
Abr H Kellar —

W &C. Fellows
vs.
A G Snyder &Co

Filed   2d April
1839
   M Gorin Ck

SUMMONS AND COMPLAINT IN THE SUIT OF HURST VS. SMITH & TAGGART, JUNE 14, 1839.

The summons and complaint in this case, the attestation of *filing by Clerk Butler excepted, were drawn by Mr. Lincoln. The case quickly ran its course, for on July 13, 1839, Stuart & Lincoln were awarded by default a judgment of $204.07 for their client. Hurst was a native of Philadelphia, born in 1811, who in 1834 settled in Springfield, where he was for many years engaged as a dry goods clerk and merchant. He was long a friend of Mr. Lincoln and active in politics as a Whig.*

Charles R. Hurst
     vs
Samuel **Smith** and
Joseph Taggart—
trading and doing
business under the
name style and firm
of Smith & Taggart

Trespass on the case upon promises—
Damage $400—

    The clerk of the Sangamon circuit court will issue process in the above case directed to the Sheriff of Morgan county—
                    Stuart &Lincoln pq

State of Illinois
Sangamon County
and Circuit

Of the July term of the Sangamon ss circuit court in the year of our Lord one thousand eight hundred and thirty nine

    Charles R. Hurst plaintiff complains of Samuel Smith and Joseph Taggart, both trading and doing business under the name style and firm of Smith & Taggart, defendants, being in custody of a plea of Trespass on the case upon promises: For that whereas the said defendants heretofore, towit, on the eighth day of September in the year of our Lord one thousand eight hundred and thirtyeight at Springfield towit at the county and circuit aforesaid, made their certain promissory note in writing, signing thereto their aforesaid firm name of "Smith & Taggart" bearing date the day and year aforesaid and thereby then and there promised to pay Six months after the date thereof to one John Hammer or order the sum of Two hundred dollars for value received and then and there delivered the said promissory note to the said John Hammer And the said John Hammer, to whom or to whose order the payment of the said sum of the said promissory note specified was to be made, after the making of the said promissory note, and before the payment of the said sum of money therein specified to wit on the day and year aforesaid at the county and circuit aforesaid, assigned the said promissory note by indorsement in writing thereof by which said assignment he the said John Hammer then and there ordered and appointed the said sum of money in the said promissory note specified to be paid to Abner Y. Ellis and Foley Vaughn, then trading and doing business under the name style and firm of Ellis & Vaughn, by their said firm name of Ellis & Vaughn, and then and there delivered the said promissory note, so assigned to the said Ellis & Vaughn and the said Ellis & Vaughn to whom or to whose order the payment of the said sum of money in the said promissory note aforesaid was by the said assignment directed to be made, after the making of the said promissory note, and before the payment of the said sum of money therein specified, towit, on the day and year aforesaid, at the county and circuit aforesaid assigned the said promissory note by indorsement in writing thereon *signing their names* thus "Ellis & Vaughn" by which said last mentioned assignment they the said Ellis & Vaughn then and there ordered and appointed the said sum of money in the said promissory note specified to be paid to the said plaintiff and then and there delivered the said promissory note, so assigned to the said plaintiff—by means whereof, and by force of the statute in such case made and provided, the said difendants became liable to pay to the said plaintiff the said sum of money in the said promissory note specified, according to the tenor and effect of the said promissory note; and being so liable they the said defendants, in consideration thereof, afterwards, towit on the day and year aforesaid, at the county and circuit aforesaid, undertook and then and there faithfully promised the said plaintiff to pay him the said sum of money in the said promissory note specified according to the tenor and effect thereof— And the said plaintiff avers that the said county of Sangamon is the county in which he the said plaintiff resides, that the cause of his aforesaid action accrued in the said county of Sangamon—and that the said defendants reside in the county of Morgan and state aforesaid—Yet the said defendants (although often requested so to do; and although the said promissory note has long since been due) have not as yet paid to the said plaintiff, the said sum of money in the said promissory note specified, or any part thereof; but so to do have hitherto wholly neglected and refused and still do neglect and refuse—To the damage of the said plaintiff of the sum of four hundred dollars, and therefore he sues &c.

Stuart & Lincoln, Plff.

(Copy of note)

"$200.—

Springfield September 8 1838

Six months after date we promise to pay to John Hammer on order two hundred dollars, for value received—

Smith & Taggart."

(1st Assignment)

"Pay to Ellis & Vaughn

John Hammer"

(2nd Assignment)

"Pay to Charles R. Hurst.

Ellis & Vaughn"

Charles R. Hurst

vs } Decln

Smith & Taggart

Filed June 22 1839

Wm Butler Clk

PLAINTIFF'S DECLARATION IN THE SUIT OF McGEE VS. RANSDELL, JUNE 21, 1839.
(Herndon-Weik Collection)

Mr. Lincoln drew the declaration in this case, and he also penned the cover notations with the exception of the date of filing. The case was decided on July 13, 1839, when Stuart & Lincoln received a judgment by default in favor of their client. The award was for $198.30, the balance due McGee.

State of Illinois }
Sangamon county }ss   Of the July term of the Sangamon circuit
anl circuit }   court in the year of our Lord one thousand eight hundred and thirtynine

James McGee plaintiff complains of Wharton Randsdell defendant being in custody &c of a plea of Trespass on the case upon promises: For that whereas the said defendant, heretofore, towit, on the twentysecond day of October in the year of our Lord one thousand eight hundred and thirtyeight, at the county and circuit aforesaid, made his certain promissory note in writing, signing his name thereto "WRansdell" bearing date the day and year aforesaid, and thereby then and there promised to pay on or before the twentieth day of March (then) next (ensuing) to the said plaintiff the sum of two hundred and eight dollars and fifty cents for value received; and then and there delivered the said promissory note to the said plaintiff; by means whereof, and by force of the statute in such case made and provided, the said defendant then and there became liable to pay to the said plaintiff the said sum of money in the said promissory note specified according to the tenor and effect of the said promissory note; and being so liable he the said defendant, in consideration thereof afterwards towit, on the day and year aforesaid, at the county and circuit aforesaid, then and there faithfully promised the said plaintiff to pay him the said sum of money in the said promissory note specified according to the tenor and effect thereof—

Yet the said defendant (although often requested so to do; and although the said promissory note has long since been due) hath not as yet paid to the said plaintiff the said sum of money in the said promissory note specified; but so to do hath hitherto, wholly neglected and refused, and still doth neglect and refuse— to the damage of the said plaintiff of three hundred dollars, and therefore he sues &c.

Stuart & Lincoln p q—

(Copy of note)

"on or before the twentieth day of of March next I will pay James McGee two hundred and Eight dollars and fifty cents for value Recd. this 22d day of October 1838

WRansdell"

James McGee

vs   } Decln

Wharton Ransdell

Filed June 21st, 1839
    Wm Butler clerk

DECLARATION IN THE SUIT OF SPEAR VS.
LINDSAY, JUNE 21, 1839.
(Herndon-Weik Collection)

This declaration was penned by John T. Stuart, as was the quoted note. Abraham Lincoln wrote the words, "David Spear vs Alex Lindsay Decln." on the cover of the legal paper, these being his only contributions to the document. Stuart mis-spelled "promised" and "received," but his errors are few. The document affords an interesting comparison of the writing, grammar, and punctuation of Stuart and Lincoln. Stuart seems to have

*been less meticulous in punctation, word choice, and penmanship
than his partner, but he was the busier lawyer, and at this time
had his mind more upon Congress than the law.*

State of Illinois		Of the July term of the Sangamon
Sangamon County	ss	circuit court in the year of our Lord one
and Circuit		thousand eight hundred and thirty nine

David Spear plaintiff complains by his attorney of Alexander
Lindsay Defendant, being in custody &c of a plea of Trespass on
the case upon promises— For that whereas the said Defendant
heretofore to wit—on the thirtieth day of January in the year
of our Lord one thousand eight hundred and thirty nine: at
Springfield, at the county and circuit aforesaid, made his certain
promissory note in writing, signing his name thereto thus "Alexr
Lindsay" bearing date the day and year aforesaid and thereby
then and there promised to pay, twenty days after the date
thereof to one R. Tharp or Order Two hundred and Eighty five
dollars. with interest at 12 per cent per annum, after three days
from the date thereof, for value received, and then and there
delivered the said promissory to the said R. Tharp—and the said
R. Tharp to whom or to whose order the payment of the said
sum of money in the said promissory note specified was to be
made after the making of the said promissory note, before payment of the said sum of money therein specified, to wit, on the
day and year aforesaid at the county and circuit aforesaid assigned the said promissory note by indorsement in writing
thereon, to David Spear, under the name and description of "D.
Spear" by which said assignment he, the said R. Tharp then and
there appointed the said sum of money in the said promissory
note specified to be paid to the said plaintiff. and then and there
delivered the said promissory note so assigned as aforesaid to
the said plaintiff, by means whereof and by force of the statute
in such cases made and provided the said Defendant then and
there became liable to pay to the said plaintiff the said sum of
money in the said promissory note specified. according to the
tenor and effect of the said promissory note, and being so liable,
he the said defendant. in consideration thereof, afterward to
wit on the day and year aforesaid at the county & circuit aforesaid, undertook and then and there faithfully promised the said
plaintiff to pay him the said sum of money in the said promissory note specified according to the tenor and effect thereof—
Yet the said Defendant (although often requested so to do and
although the said promissory note has long since been due), hath

not as yet paid to the said plaintiff the said sum of money in the said promissory note specified, but so to do hath hitherto wholly neglected and refused and still doth neglect and refuse— to the Damage of the plaintiff of three hundred dollars and therefore he sues

Stuart & Lincoln

(Copy of note)
"Springfield. Jany 30th 1839

$285

Twenty days after date I promise to pay to R. Tharp or order Two hundred Eighty five dollars with int at 12 per cent pr annum after three days from this date, for value received

Alexr.. Lindsay"

David Spear

vs } Decln 849

Alexr.. Lindsay—
Filed June 21st 1839
    Wm Butler clerk

PRECIPE AND DECLARATION IN THE SUIT OF STEWARDSON AND SHOEMAKER VS. DOUGLAS, JUNE 26, 1839.

(Herndon-Weik Collection)

The precipe and cover notations in this case, Butler's date of filing excepted, is in the hand of John T. Stuart, and is included to give continuity to the declaration filed by Mr. Lincoln on the same date. The latter omitted the word, "to," preceding "wit" at the introduction to the declaration, a rare omission on his part, and not found in over thirty documents of the period, 1837-1839. Douglas filed his plea upon July 10, 1839. Stewardson, the client of Stuart & Lincoln, was awarded $1,783.60, by agreement, upon July 15, 1839. It was one of the largest awards won by Stuart & Lincoln during their partnership.

George Stewardson } Trespass on the case
& John W. Shoemaker | in Assumpsit.
    vs } Plaintiffs Damages
Erskine Douglas } Two Thousand Dollars

The Clerk of the Sangamon Circuit Court will issue a summons for the Defendant in the above entitled cause returnable to the next Term of the Sangamon Circuit Court

George Stewardson & John W. Shoemaker vs Erskine Douglas	Stuart &Lincoln of the July Term of the Sangamon Circuit Court in the Year of our Lord 1839.

George Stewardson
& John W. Shoemaker

vs } Precipe

Erskine Douglas

Filed June 26, 1839
William Butler clerk

NOTE: *The precipe and cover notations, with the exception of Butler's date of filing are in the hand of John T. Stuart. It is included to give continuity to the declaration filed by Lincoln upon the same date.*

State of Illinois Sangamon county and circuit	Of the July term of the Sangamo circuit court in the year of our Lord one thousand, eight hundred and thirtynine—

George Stewardson and John W. Shoemaker, plaintiffs complain of Erskine Douglas defendant being in custody &c. of a plea of Trespass on the case in assumpsit: For that whereas heretofore towit, on the twentyseventh day of February in the year of our Lord one thousand eight hundred and thirtyeight, at Springfield, Illinois to wit at the county and circuit aforesaid, the said defendant made his certain promissory note in writing, bearing date the day and year aforesaid, and thereby then and there promised to pay twelve months after the date thereof, to the said plaintiffs, the sum of Fifteen hundred and sixtyeight dollars with ten ten per cent per annum interest thereon from the day of the date of said note till paid, for value received, and then and there delivered the said promissory note to the said plaintiffs; by means whereof, and by force of the statute in such case made and provided, the said defendant, then and there became liable to pay to the said plaintiffs the said sum of money, together with the interest in the said promissory note specified, according to the tenor and effect of the said promissory note; and being so liable, he the said defendant in consideration, thereof, afterwards towit, on the day and year aforesaid, at the county and circuit aforesaid, undertook, and then and there faithfully promised, the said plaintiffs to pay them the said sum of money in the said promissory note specified, according to the tenor and effect thereof— Yet the said defendant (although requested so to do, and although the said note has long since been due) hath not as yet paid to the said plaintiffs the said sum of money in the said promissory note specified, or any part thereof; but so to do hath hitherto wholly neglected and refused, and still doth neglect and refuse— To the damage of the said paintiffs of two thousand dollars, and therefore they sue &c.

Stuart & Lincoln p. q—

(Copy of note)

"$1568— Springfield, Illinois. Feby 27th 1838

Twelve months after date I promise to pay to George Stewardson and John W. Shoemaker or order for value received Fifteen hundred and sixtyeight dollars with ten per cent pr annum interest thereon from this day till paid.

Erskine Douglas"

Stewardson & Shoemaker

vs } Decl

Erskine Douglas
Filed June 26 1839
William Butler ck

PRECIPE AND BOND IN THE SUIT OF PARKER
VS. BRAUCHER, JUNE 26, 1839.
(Herndon-Weik Collection)

The precipe and bond in this case were drawn by Mr. Lincoln, the bond being signed by his partner, John T. Stuart. Butler, as usual at this time, made the cover notations, when Mr. Lincoln did not write a part of them. Lincoln used the word "cost" instead of the more usual "costs" in the bond, and the word "oposite" in the same paper presents a strange figure.

Samuel Parker
vs } Trespass on the case upon promises—
Isaac R. Braucher } Dam—$300.

The clerk of the Sangamon circuit court will issue process in the above cause—

Stuart & Lincoln p. q—

Samuel Parker
vs } In the Sangamon county circuit court—
Isaac R. Braucher

I do hereby enter myself security for costs in this cause, and acknowledge myself bound to pay or cause to be paid all cost which may accrue in this action either to the oposite party or to any of the officers of this court in pursuance of the laws of this state— Dated this 26th of June A. D. 1839—

John T. Stuart

853

Samuel Parker

vs } Sum

Isaac R Braucher

Filed June 26th 1839

William Butler ck

COMPLAINT OF PLAINTIFF IN THE SUIT OF LUCKETT VS. RUCKEL & RUCKEL, JUNE 28, 1839.

Lawyer Lincoln wrote and filed the declaration in this case. The original is now in the Illinois State Historical Society at Springfield. Jacob Ruckel, one of the defendants, was a native of New York who settled in Springfield about the time Mr. Lincoln began the practice of law there, and for more than forty years as cabinet-maker and upholsterer was active in the business affairs of the town.

State of Illinois   }
Sangamon county   }
and circuit   }

Of the July Term of the circuit court of said county A. D. 1839

Henry F. Luckett, plaintiff complains of Daniel E. Ruckel and Jacob Ruckel Jr. late doing business under the name style and firm of "D. E. & J. Ruckel" defendants being in custody &c of a plea that they render unto him the sum of two hundred and thirtyseven dollars which they owe to and unjustly detain from him: For that whereas the said defendants; heretofore, towit, on the fifteenth day of October in the year of our Lord one thousand eight hundred and thirtyeight, at the county and circuit aforesaid, by their certain writing obligatory, signed with their firm name of "D. E. & J. Ruckel" and sealed with their seal, and now shown to the court, the date whereof is the day and year aforesaid, acknowledged themselves to be held and firmly bound unto the said plaintiff by the name of H. F. Luckett, in the sum

of one hundred and eighteen dollars, and fifty cents with twelve
per cent Int. until paid from the 15 day of October 1838, parcel
of the sum above demanded to be paid to the said plaintiff by
his said name of H. F. Luckett, on demand; Yet said defendants
have not as yet paid

And whereas also the said defendants, afterwards towit on
the day and year aforesaid, at the county and circuit aforesaid,
were indebted to the said plaintiff in their aforesaid partnership
capacity, in the further sum of one hundred and eighteen dollars
and fifty cents, parcel of the sum above demanded, for the use
and occupation of a certain Cabinet shop and ware room of the
said plaintiff—by the said defendants, and at their special instance and request, and by the sufferance and permission of the
said plaintiff for a long time before their elapsed had, held used,
occupied, possessed and enjoyed, and to be paid to the said
plaintiff by the said defendants, when they the said defendants
should be thereunto afterwards requested—whereby and by reason of the said last mentioned sum of money, being and remaining wholly unpaid, an action hath accrued to the said plaintiff to demand and have of and from the said defendants the
said sum of one hundred and eighteen dollars and fifty cents,
parcel of the said sum above demanded—

Yet the said defendants (although often requested so to do)
have not as yet paid the said sum of two hundred and thirtyseven
dollars above demanded, or any part thereof, to the said plaintiff; but have hitherto wholly neglected and refused and still
neglect and refuse so to do—To the damage of the said plaintiff
of one hundred dollars and therefore he brings his suit &c

Stuart & Lincoln, p.q.

(Copy of instrument declared on)

"On demand we or either of us promise to pay to H. F.
Luckett his heirs or assigns the sum of one hundred and eighteen
50/100 dollars for the rent of Cabinet & ware room with twelve
per cent Int. until paid from this 15th day of Oct. 1838 as witness our hands & seals

D. E. & J. Ruckell (Seal)

(Copy of account)

"D. E. & J. Ruckel

To Henry F. Luckett—   Dr.

1838 15th Oct. To rent of cabinet shop & ware room $118-50

Henry F. Luckett
   vs   Decl.
D. E. & J. Ruckel
Filed June 28th 1839
   William Butler Clerk

ANSWER OF JOHN D. BEVANS TO THE PETITION OF MARGARET BEVANS, JULY 16, 1839

This interesting document drawn by Lawyer Lincoln and attested by Clerk Butler affords proof of his growing competence as a drafter of legal documents. The original is now in the J. P. Morgan Library in New York.

The answer of John D. Bevans to the petition of Margaret Bevans praying an assignment of Dower of the real estate, and an apportionment of the personal estate of John Bevans, deceased, to which Petition the heirs of the said John Bevans deceased, and the administrator of his estate are made defendants—

This Respondent saving &c for answer to said petition, admits that the said John Bevans departed this life, having first made and published his last Will & Testament, which has since been duly proved, as in Complainants petition stated—He also admits that the said John Bevans deceased, was the husband of the Petitioner; that a provision was made for her in his said will; that she filed with the Probate Justice of the Peace for the county of Sangamon, a written renunciation of the provision aforesaid, the sufficiency of which renunciation, however, this respondent denies—He also admits that the said John Bevans died seized of the lands referred to and described in said Petition; that he also died possessed of the personal estate referred to in said Petition; that James N. Brown has duly administered on the estate of the said John Bevans deceased; that demand of Dower has been duly made by said Petitioner, and that it is withheld from her, but he denies that it was wrongfully withheld—He denies that she is entitled to Dower, because in the year of our Lord one thousand eight hundred and twentynine, the said John Bevans, now deceased settled a separate maintainance upon the said Petitioner, by exercising and delivering to Barnet Giltner, and Nathaniel Tingh of the county of Woodford and state of Kentucky, a deed of trust for two negro girls for the use of the said Petitioner, during her natural life as will more fully appear by referenec to copy of said deed herewith filed, marked (A) and which Respondent prays may be taken as part of this his answer—Respondent further states that said Petitioner accepted said settlement in lieu of all Dower in and to the estate of the said John Bevans deceased; and that said Petitioner has ever since the making of said settlement, received, and now continues to receive, the hire of the said negro girls—

As to the provision made by the said John Bevans in his said will for said Petitioner, and her renunciation thereof, this respondent states that the Petitioner did accept the said provision by receiving and using the property therein designated for her, and that although she has filed her written renunciation to said provision, she has never surrendered the property received under it to the aforesaid administrator or to anyone else

John D. Bevans

State of Illinois
Sangamon County

This day personally appeared before me William Butler Clerk of the Circuit Court of Sangamon County John Bevans who being first duly sworn deposeth and says that the matters and things as stated in the above answers of his own knowledge are true and those stated upon his information of others he believes to be true.

William Butler Clerk

BILL OF EXCEPTIONS IN THE SUIT OF CANNON VS. KENNEY, JULY 16, 1839.
(Herndon-Weik Collection)

The bill of exceptions here reproduced is in the hand of Mr. Lincoln, with the exception of the date of filing by Butler. It should be noted that Mr. Lincoln used Kenney as in the document of February 8, 1839, whereas the clerk used "Kinney." Stuart and Lincoln dismissed the case for the complainant upon July 14, 1838, and on May 29, 1839 wrote and filed a complaint for seizure of Cannon's horse. This bill of exceptions was then filed by Stuart and Lincoln. The case was argued before the Supreme Court of Illinois upon July 8, 1841, with Lincoln appearing for Cannon, and his future partner, Stephen T. Logan, defending the case for Kenney. Later in July, the sorrel horse; the bone of contention, was awarded to the client of Lawyer Lincoln. This case was the second argued before the State Supreme Court by Abraham Lincoln, and has been cited by the courts of Missouri and South Dakota.

Samuel H. Treat, who signed the bill of exceptions in July,
1839, was a native of New York, born in 1811, who at the age
of twenty-three settled in Springfield, where he became the part-
ner of George Forquer. An able lawyer, Treat in 1837 was ap-
pointed a circuit judge, and in 1841 elevated to the Supreme
Court of the State. He served as a member of that body until
1855 when he was named by President Pierce Federal judge for
the Southern District of Illinois, serving in the latter capacity
for thirty-two years. He was long a devoted friend of Mr.
Lincoln.

Manly F Cannon
      vs   }   Tresspass vi et armis—
Matthew P. Kenney

Be it remembered that on the trial of this cause, the plaintiff
proved the absolute property in the horse alleged in his declaration to have been taken by the defendant, to have been in him,
the said plaintiff, at a time when [t]he said plaintiff gratuitously
loaned said horse to one John Harris to be ridden by him from
the lead-mine country to Sangamon county; that said John Harris
did ride said horse to Sangamon county, and then put him into
the hands of his brother James Harris, for feeding and safe
keeping through the winter; without telling him to whom the
horse belonged, and undertaking to pay for the feeding and keeping; that said James Harris, because of his horse food becoming
scarce, put said horse into the hands of Robert Harris, another
brother, who had horse food in greater plenty, to be by him fed
and safely kept through the remainder of the winter; that said
Robert Harris, after feeding and keeping said horse, until the
rising of grass in Spring season of the year, turned him upon
the common with some of his own horses; salting him with his
own horses and all the while supposing him to belong to John
Harris; that while said horse was thus running on the common,
the defendant took and carried him away; Robert Harris
telling plaintiff defendant at the time that he understood plaintiff
claimed said horse said horse was worth sixtyfive dollars at the
time defendant took him, and thereupon the plaintiff closed his
evidence—The defendant then moved the court to instruct the jury
as in case of a non-suit, on the ground that there was no evidence
of the defendant's taking the horse from the *possession* of the
plaintiff, which motion the court sustained, and this plaintiff
accordingly non-suited; and to which opinion of the court the

plaintiff excepts, and prays that this his bill of exception may be signed, sealed, and made part of the record in said cause

Samuel H. Treat (Seal)

Cannon
   vs   Bill Except
Kenney

Filed July 16 1839
Wm Butler Clk

RECEIPT OF PAYMENT BY DAVID PRICKETT, AUGUST 6, 1839

The receipt here reproduced acknowledges payment of $250 on a judgment for $513.49 which on July 13, 1839 Stuart & Lincoln had secured for Kern & Company by default. David Prickett was a native of Georgia who began the practice of law at Edwardsville in 1821 at the age of twenty-one. He served as an officer in the Black Hawk War, and in 1835 settled in Springfield, where he became the first reporter of the Supreme Court of Illinois.. He was an early friend of Mr. Lincoln and like the latter noted for his telling anecdotes.

Received, Springfield, Aug: 6 1839 of David Prickett, two hundred and fifty dollars, to be applied to the discharging of a judgment in the Sangamon Circuit Court against said Prickett, & in favour of the surviving partners of the firm of A. & G. W. Kern & Co.

Stuart & Lincoln
Atty. for Plffs

LETTER TO THOMAS BOHANNAN, AUGUST 7, 1839.

Thomas Bohannan was a Louisville merchant who now and then entrusted Stuart & Lincoln with collection of his Springfield accounts. Josiah Francis, one of the debtors mentioned in Mr. Lincoln's letter of August 7, (mailed two days later) was a native of Pittsfield, Massachusetts, who settled in Springfield in 1836, at the age of thirty-five, and until 1852 with his brother Charles engaged in the manufacture of furniture. He passed his middle and last years on a farm a few miles from Springfield. He and his brother were kinsmen of Simeon Francis, founder of the Sangamo Journal and devoted and helpful friend of Mr. Lincoln.

Springfield, Ill. Aug. 7, 1839

Mr. Thomas Bohannan

Dr Sir

Yours of the 29th ult. is duly received. It was our impression that we had acknowledged the receipt of the two notes of which you speak—one being on Allen & Stone for $117.94 the other on J. Francis for $50.35. We now do so.

We have been receiving promises from time to time of the payment of those notes but which payment has not yet been made. Unless payment is soon made we shall commence suits; though this course we shall regret; for they are honest and honorable men, but they are hard pressed. We regret to say that the entire certainty that we shall need all the means at our command, will not, in justice to ourselves, permit us to authorize you to draw upon us as you suggest. Yours &c.

Stuart & Lincoln.

DEED FROM ABRAHAM LINCOLN TO JOHN HOUSTON, SEPTEMBER 17, 1839.

The deed here reproduced is to be found on Page 632 of Sangamon County Deed Book O. On July 8, 1839, Mr. Lincoln had been appointed by the Sangamon Circuit Court a commissioner to convey to John Houston a tract of land lately owned by Vincent A. Bogue, whose attempt in March, 1832, when young Lincoln served as one of the pilots of the Talisman, to make the Sangamon a navigable stream had ended in disaster and his own flight and bankruptcy. Lincoln's deed to Houston, one of Bogue's creditors, thus served to recall a memorable incident of his New Salem days, and the ill-starred outcome of a venture which had been hailed and applauded by many a Sangamon pioneer.

Abram Lincoln ⎤ Whereas at a Circuit Court in and for the
   to) Deed ⎬ County of Sangamon and the State of
John Houston ⎦ Illinois Begun and held on the Eighth day of July in the year of our Lord one thousand Eight hundred and thirty nine and days following a decree was made by said Court in the words following to wit:

John Houston Complainant ⎤
       against   ⎬ In Chancery
Vincent A. Bogue Defendant ⎦

This day came the complainant By his solicitor and it appearing to the satisfaction of the Court that said Defendant is not a resident of the State of Illinois, and it appearing also to the satisfaction of this Court that notice of the pendency of this suit had been published according to Law, and the said Defendant having failed to enter his appearance and file his answer to said Bill, and he having been three times solemnly called came not, but made default. It is therefore ordered and decreed by the Court that the Bill of said Complainant be taken for confessed and the Court having heard the Testimony and being satisfied that the allegations in said Bill of Complainant are true it is therefore ordered and decreed by the Court that said Defendant convey to said Complainant within Ten days from the rendition of this Decree the Lands in said Bill of Complainant described. To Wit, Being Ten acres of the Twenty three heretofore conveyed by said Houston to said Bogue, said twenty three acres described as follows—to wit—part of the South East fractional quarter of section six in Township Sixteen North of Range Four west, Beginning at the North East corner of said fractional quarter at a point on the South Bank of the Sangamon River bearing North Seventy two degrees, East five chains, thence bearing South fifty seven chains and forty links, and runs from thence South fifty poles, thence west forty poles thence north Eighteen poles, thence west forty eight poles, thence north fifty two poles to the fractional line thence East along said line thirty eight to the River—and thence along the meanderings of said River to the place of beginning, the Ten acres aforesaid to be described as follows To Wit—Beginning at the north west corner of said Tract of twenty three acres on the fractional line of said fractional quarter out of which said Tract of Twenty three acres is taken thence East along said line Forty Eight poles thence South Fifty two poles, thence West forty eight poles, thence North fifty two poles to the place of Beginning. It is further ordered that in default of the said Defendant making the deed aforesaid within the time prescribed by this order then that—A. Lincoln do make and deliver to the said Complainant a Deed conveying to him all the right title and interest which the said Defendant had in and to the Ten acres above described, at the time of the contract set forth in said Bill of Complainant.

Therefore I A.. Lincoln for and in consideration of the premises aforesaid (said Bogue having failed to make said conveyance for more than Ten days from the rendition of said Decree) and by virtue of the authority vested in me by law and by said Decree of Court, do grant bargain and sell unto the said John Houston his heirs and assigns forever, all the right title interest and Estate which the said Vincent A. Bogue had in and to the Ten acres Tract of Land described in said Decree on the twenty fifth day of August in the year of our Lord one thousand eight hundred and thirty one.

To have and to hold to the said John Houston his heirs and assigns forever the above described Ten acre tract of land together with all and singular the privileges and appurtenances thereunto belonging.   In testimony whereof I have hereunto set my hand and seal this seventeenth day of September in the year of our Lord one thousand eight hundred and thirty nine.

A. . Lincoln (seal)

State of Illinois   ⎰ Before me the undersigned Clerk of the
Sangamon County ⎱ Circuit Court of said County personally
appeared Abram Lincoln who is personally known to me to be the real person who executed the above conveyance and in whose name the same is proposed to be acknowledged who then acknowledged the signing of the same to be his free act and Deed for the purpose therein named. Given under my hand and seal at Springfield this 25th Sept. 1839

Wm. Butler Clerk

Recorded September 26th A. D. 1839

Benjamin Talbott R. S. C.

ORDER TO CLERK AND DECLARATION IN THE SUIT OF ILES VS. WHITE, OCTOBER 19 AND NOVEMBER 4, 1839.

(Herndon-Weik Collection)

The order for issuing process in this case was penned by Attorney Lincoln, while the notations appear to be in the hand of Clerk Butler. Mr. Lincoln is also responsible for the declaration of November 4, 1839 except the date of filing by Butler. The care and accuracy of transcription upon the part of Lincoln are seen in his copying of the Funk note with its flagrant errors of spelling. The junior partner of Stuart and Lincoln omitted one or two words in the document, but this paper is an excellent example of the care he took with his work. A judgment by default was rendered in favor of Iles on March 4, 1840. Lincoln represented Iles and the judgment was for $431.92. Isaac Funk who made the note assigned by White to Iles was a widely known and arresting figure in the early history of Sangamon County.

Elijah Iles
vs
Lorence White } Trespass on the case upon promises
Damage $500-00

The clerk of the Sangamon circuit court will issue process in the above cause returnable to the next term of said court—
Stuart & Lincoln p. q.

Elijah Iles
vs
Lorence White

Filed October 19, 1839.
Wm Butler clerk

State of Illinois
Sangamon county
and Circuit } Of the November term of the circuit court of said county A. D. 1839—

Elijah Iles plaintiff complains of Lorence White defendant, in custody &c of a plea of trespass on the case upon promises: For that whereas one Isaac Funk, heretofore, towit, on the eighteenth day of March in the year of our Lord one thousand eight hundred and thirtyseven, at the county and circuit aforesaid, made his certain promissory note in writing, bearing date the day and year aforesaid, and thereby then and there promised to pay, ninety days after the date thereof, to the said defendant, the sum of three hundred and seventy dollars and seventysix cents, and then and there delivered the said promissory note to the said defendant— And the said defendant, to whom the payment of the said sum of money in the said promissory note specified was to be made, after the making of the said promissory note, and before the payment of the sum of money therein specified, towit, on the   day of   in the year of our Lord   assigned the said promissory note by indorsement in writing thereon, by which said assignment, he the said defendant then and there ordered and appointed the said sum of money in the said promissory note specified, to be paid to the said plaintiff And the said plaintiff avers that afterwards towit on the   day of   in the year of our Lord, he instituted a suit upon said promissory note against the said Isaac Funk in the circuit court of McLean in the state of Illinois, and duly prosecuted said suit; and afterwards, towit, at the October term of the said circuit of McLean county in the year of our Lord one thousand eight hundred and thirtynine, the said Isaac Funk appeared and pleaded by notice given according to the statute in such case made & provided to the said action as instituted against him as aforesaid, that said note was not assigned to this said plaintiff until after the same became due; and that the consideration for which the same was given, had wholly failed, upon which the said plaintiff took issue, and the parties went to trial, submitting both matters of law and fact to the court; and that the court after hearing the evidence of the parties, found the said issues for the said Funk, and rendered judgment in his favor for costs in the said cause— By means whereof and by force of the statute in such case made and provided the said defendant, Lorence White, then and there, towit at the county & circuit first aforesaid, became liable to pay to the said plaintiff the said sum of money in the said promissory note specified according to the tenor and effect of the said promissory note, together with the cost of the said suit against the said Funk; and being so liable, he the said defendant in consideration thereof, afterwards towit on the twelfth day of October in the year last aforesaid at the county and circuit first aforesaid, undertook, and then and there faithfully promised the said plaintiff to pay him the said sum of money in the said promissory note specified, according to the tenor and effect thereof, together with the cost of the suit against the said Isaac Funk as aforesaid— Yet the said defendant (although often requested so to do) hath not as yet paid the said sum of money in the said promissory note specified, or any part thereof, or the costs of the said suit against the said Funk or any part thereof; but so to do hath hitherto wholly neglected and refused; and still doth neglect and refuse— To the damage of the plaintiff of five hundred dollars & therefore he sues &c.

Stuart & Lincoln p. q.

(Copy of note sued on)

"Nity days after dait I promis to pay Lorence White three hundred and seventy dollars and seventysix cents, March 18th 1837—

Isaac Funk"

(Copy of assignment)

"For value received I assign the within note to Elijah Iles—
Lorence White"

Elijah Iles

   vs   ⎱   Declaration

Lorence White

Lorence White
Filed Nov 4th 1839
    Wm Butler

DECLARATION AND SECURITY FOR COSTS IN THE SUIT OF HORNSBY VS. RAGSDALE, OCTOBER 22, 1839.
(Herndon-Weik Collection)

The declaration here reproduced was drawn by Mr. Lincoln. It will be noted that he used two words in the case of such words as "twenty five" but only because he had reached the border of the paper; in all other cases he uses the characteristic single word, as "twentyfive," etc. The date of filing is in the hand of Butler, and other cover notations are in that of Mr. Lincoln. The quoted notes, which are listed as seven counts, were also penned by him. For a full discussion of this case, and the ultimate result, see the note to the affidavit of April 2, 1841, filed by Hornsby which appears in a later volume. Hornsby became the client of Lincoln in an eventful month, for it was on October 5, 1839, that the town of Nauvoo, Illinois, was made a stake of the Mormon Church, while it was on October 10, 1839, that the Bank of the United States closed its doors, thus bringing to a costly and disastrous conclusion the conflict of that institution with President Jackson.

State of Illinois ⎫ Of the November term of the
Sangamon county ⎬ss circuit court of said county
and circuit   ⎭ A. D. 1839—

Joseph W. Hornsby plaintiff complains of Daniel Ragsdale, defendant in a plea that he render to the said plaintiff the sum of fourteen hundred and ninetyseven dollars and ninetyone cents which he owes to and unjustly detains from him: For that whereas the said defendant heretofore towit on the first day of December in the year of our Lord one thousand eight hundred and thirtyseven at the county and circuit aforesaid, by his certain writing obligatory sealed with his seal and now shown to the court, the date whereof is the day and year aforesaid, acknowledged himself to be held and firmly bound unto the said plaintiff in the sum of five hundred and fifty dollars, parcel of the sum above demanded to be paid to the said plaintiff on order ten months after the date of said writing with interest at the rate of twelve per cent per annum from the first day of February (then) next (ensuing) until paid for value received—

And whereas also afterwards towit, on the day and year

aforesaid, at the place aforesaid, the said defendant, by his certain other writing obligatory, sealed with his seal and now shown to the court the date whereof is the day and year aforesaid, acknowledged himself to be held and firmly bound unto the said plaintiff in the further sum of five hundred and fifty dollars other parcel of the sum above demanded, to be paid to the said plaintiff on order fourteen months after the date of the said writings with interest from the first day of February (then) next (ensuing) until paid at the rate of twelve per cent per annum, for value received—

And whereas also afterwards, towit, on the second day of December in the year of our Lord one thousand eight hundred and thirtyseven at the county and circuit aforesaid, the said defendant made his certain promissory note in writing, bearing date the day and year last aforesaid, and then and there delivered said note to the said plaintiff, by which said note he the said defendant had then and there promised to pay one day after the date thereof to the said plaintiff by the name of "Jos W Hornsby" or order the sum of seventyone dollars and sixtysix cents, bearing twelve per cent interest, for value received; by means whereof, and by force of the statute in such case made and provided, the said defendant made his certain other promissory note in writing, bearing date the day and year last aforesaid, and then and there delivered the said note to the said plaintiff; by which said note he the said defendant, then and there promised to pay one day after the date thereof to the said plaintiff, by the name of "Jos. W Hornsby" or order the sum of one hundred dollars, for value received, bearing twelve per cent interest until paid: by means whereof, and by force of the statute in such case made and provided, the said defendant then and there became liable to pay to the said plaintiff the said sum of money in the said last mentioned promissory note specified according to the tenor and effect of the said last mentioned promissory note—

And whereas also afterwards towit, on the fourth day of August in the year last aforesaid, at the county & circuit aforesaid the said defendant made his certain other promissory note in writing, bearing date the day and year last aforesaid and then and there delivered the said note to the said plaintiff; by which said note he the said defendant then and there promised to pay, one day after the date thereof to the said plaintiff by the name of "Jos. W Hornsby" or order, one hundred dollars for value received, bearing twelve per cent interest until paid: by means whereof, and by force of the statute in such case made and provided the said defendant then and there became liable to pay to the said plaintiff the said sum of money in the said last mentioned promissory note specified, according to the tenor and effect of the last mentioned promissory note—

And whereas also afterwards towit, on the fourth day of September in the year last aforesaid, at the county and circuit aforesaid, the said defendant made his certain other promissory note in writing, bearing date the day and year last aforesaid, and then and there delivered the said note to the said plaintiff; by which said note he the said defendant then and there promised to pay, five months after the date thereof to the said plaintiff or order the sum of fifty dollars for value received with interest at the rate of twelve per cent from maturity until paid; by means whereof and by force of the statute in such case made and provided, he the said defendant then and there became liable to pay to the said plaintiff the said sum of money in the said last mentioned promissory note specified, according to the tenor and effect of the said last mentioned promissory note—

And whereas also afterwards towit; on the day and year last aforesaid, at the county and circuit aforesaid, the said defendant made his certain other promissory note in writing bearing date the day and year last aforesaid and then and there delivered the said note to the said plaintiff; by which said note he the said defendant then and there promised to pay five months after the date thereof to the said plaintiff by the name of "Jos. W Hornsby" or order, the sum of seventysix dollars and twentyfive cents for value received, to bear twelve per cent interest from maturity until paid; by means whereof and force of the statute in such case made and provided the said defendant then and there became liable to pay to the said plaintiff the said sum of money in the said last mentioned promissory note specified, according to the tenor and effect of the said last mentioned promissory note— And although the said sums of money in the said writings obligatory and said several promissory notes specified, have all been long since due and payable. according to the tenor and effect of the said writings obligatory and said promissory notes, yet the said plaintiff in fact saith, that the said defendant, (although often requested so to do) did not, nor would pay the said sums of money in the said writings obligatory and promissory notes specified, or any of them or any part thereof, to the said plaintiff in manner aforesaid, or otherwise howsoever,

but hath hitherto wholly neglected and refused so to do whereby
an action hath accrued to the said plaintiff to demand and have
of and from the said defendant the said sum of fourteen hundred and ninetyseven dollars and ninetyone cents above demanded— To the damage of the said plaintiff of one thousand
dollars, and therefore he brings his suit &c

Stuart & Lincoln p. q—

(Copies of instruments sued on)

(First count)

"Ten months after date I promise to pay Joseph W Hornsby
or order the sum of Five hundred and fifty dollars, with interest
at the rate of twelve per cent per annum from the first day of
February next until paid for value received—
Dec. 1st 1837

Daniel Ragsdale (Seal)"

(Second count)

"Fourteen months after date I promise to pay Joseph W
Hornsby or order Five hundred and fifty dollars with interest
from the first day of February next until paid at the rate of
twelve per cent for value received—
Dec. 1st 1837—

Daniel Ragsdale (Seal)"

(Third count)

"$71-66
One day after I promise to pay Jos W Hornsby or order
seventyone dollars sixty six cts for value received Bearing 12
per cent Interest—Dec. 2n 1837

Daniel Ragsdale"

(Fourth count)

"$100— One day after date I promise to pay Jos W Hornsby
or order one hundred dollars for val received Bearing 12 per
cent Interest until paid—this 30th day of July 1838

Daniel Ragsdale"

(Fifth count)

"$100— One day after date I promise to pay Jos W Hornsby
or order one hundred dollars for value received bearing 12 per
cent Interest until paid—August 4th 1838—

Daniel Ragsdale"

(Sixth count)

"$50—Five months after date I promise to pay Joseph W Horns-

by or order Fifty dollars for value received with interest at the rate of 12 per cent from maturity until paid—
Sept. 4th 1838

Daniel Ragsdale"

(Seventh count)

"$76-25

Five months after date I promise to pay Jos W Hornsby or order seventysix dollars & twentyfive cents for value received this the 4th of September 1838. this note to bear 12 per cent Interest from maturity untill paid.

Daniel Ragsdale"

Joseph W Hornsby ⎫ In Debt—
vs ⎬ Debt—$1497—91—
Daniel Ragsdale ⎭ Damage—$1000—00

The clerk of the Sangamon circuit court will issue process in the above cause—

Stuart & Lincoln p. q.

Joseph W Hornsby ⎫
vs ⎬ In Sangamon circuit court
Daniel Ragsdale ⎭

I do hereby enter myself security for costs in this cause and acknowledge myself bound to pay or cause to be paid all costs which may accrue in this action either to the opposite party or to any of the officers of this court in pursuance of the laws of this state—

A. .Lincoln

Dated this 22nd of October A. D. 1839
Joseph W Hornsby ⎫
vs ⎬ Declaration
Daniel Ragsdale ⎭
Filed Oct 22d 1839
Wm Butler Clk

PRIECIPE AND DECLARATION IN SUIT OF KENDALL VS. HARDIN AND REAGOR, NOVEMBER 2, 1839.
(Herndon-Weik Collection)

This precipe and declaration are in the hand of Abraham Lincoln, as are the cover notations, with the exception of the date of filing and the figures. The figures at the conclusion of the filing do not appear to have been written by Lincoln, and are distinctly unlike his penned numerals. This case is cited as Kendall vs. Hardin and Reagen, but the hand of Lincoln is not *conclusive evidence of accuracy. "Reagor" as given in line one might be construed as "Reager" or "Reagen", but in the signing of the quoted note, the name is definitely "Reagor", while in the use in the trespass upon the case upon promise it appears to be "Reagor" rather "Reagen." Kendall is given as "Kendoll" and in no case does there appear to be the characteristic small "a" of the hand of Lincoln. The case was continued on March 2, 1840, and a summons issued for the defendants. Hardin and Reagor defaulted upon July 14, 1840, and a judgment of $189.76 damages was rendered in favor of Kendall. Stuart and Lincoln represented the plaintiff, Henry Kendall.*

State of Illinois ⎫   Of the November term of the
Sangamon county ⎬ ss   circuit court of said
& circuit ⎭   county A. D. 1839

Henry Kendall plaintiff complains of James T. Hardin and John R Reagor defendants in custody &c of a plea of Trespass on the case upon promises: For that whereas the said defendants, heretofore towit on the sixth day of September in the year of our Lord one thousand eight hundred and thirtynine at the county and circuit aforesaid, made their certain promissory note in writing bearing date the day and year aforesaid, and then and there promised to pay, on or before the first day of October (then) next (ensuing) to the said plaintiff, the sum of one hundred and eighty dollars and fifty cents for value received and then and there delivered the said promissory note to the said plaintiff; by means whereof and by force of the statute in such case made and provided the said defendants then and there became liable to pay to the said plaintiff the said sum of money in the said promissory note specified according to the tenor and effect of the said promissory note; and being so liable they the said defendants in consideration thereof afterwards towit on the day and year aforesaid, at the county & circuit aforesaid, undertook and then and there faithfully promised the said plaintiff to pay him the said sum of money in the said promissory note specified according to the tenor and effect thereof— Yet the said defendants (although often requested so to do) have not as yet paid to the said plaintiff the said sum of money in the said promissory note specified or any part thereof; but so to do have hitherto wholly neglected and refused and still do neglect and refuse— To the damage of the said plaintiff of the sum of five hudred dollars, and therefore he sues &c—

Stuart & Lincoln p. q.

(Copy of note sued on)

"On or before the first day of October next we or either of us promise to pay Henry Kendoll one hundred and eighty dollars and fifty cents for value received this 6th day of September 1839—

James T. Hardin
John R. Reagor"

180 50
9 00
.20
2½
—————
189.71

Henry Kendoll   ⎫
    vs   ⎬
James T. Hardin   Trespass on the case upon promises
& John R. Reagor ⎭ Damage $500-00—

The clerk of the Sangamon circuit court will issue process in the above cause—

Stuart & Lincoln pq—

20

Henry Kendoll
  vs
James T. Hardin &
John R. Reagor—

Filed Nov 2 1839
    Wm. Butler clek

DECLARATION IN THE SUIT OF KENDALL VS. MOFFETT, NOVEMBER 2, 1839.

(Herndon-Weik Collection)

The declaration and cover notations in this case are in the hand of Attorney Lincoln, with the exception of the date of filing by Butler. The quoted note is copied most accurately, although Mr. Lincoln gives the "undersind" of the note as "undersined." A judgment of $157.90 was rendered in favor of Mr. Lincoln's client, Calvin Kendall, upon November 28, 1839. He agreed to a stay of three months of execution of the judgment. He then took the execution to Schuyler County, but nothing was realized because there were no bidders on the visit on March 25, 1840.

State of Illinois ⎫   Of the **November term of**
Sangamon county ⎬ ss   the circuit court of said
and Circuit   ⎭   county A. D. 1839—

Calvin Kendall, plaintiff, complains of Willis G. Moffett, defendant, being in custody &c of a plea that he render unto the said plaintiff the sum of three hundred dollars which he owes to and unjustly detains from him: For that whereas the said defendant together with one Briscoe, heretofore, towit, on the twentythird day of December in the year of our Lord one thousand eight hundred and thirtysix at the county and circuit aforesaid, by their certain writing obligatory, sealed with their seal and now shown to the court, and signed thus "W. G. Moffett & Briscoe" the date whereof is the day and year aforesaid, acknowledged themselves to be held and firmly bound unto the said plaintiff in the sum of three hundred dollars, above demanded, to be paid to the said plaintiff six months after the date of the said writing obligatory for value received together with interest at the rate of twelve per cent per annum from the date of said writing until paid—

Yet neither plaintiff avers that he resides in the county of Sangamon and that the said cause of action now in the said county of Sangamon.

Yet the said defendant, nor the said Briscoe (although often requested so to do) hath not as yet paid the said sum of money above demanded or any part thereof to the said plaintiff; But hath hitherto wholly neglected and refused, and still neglects and refuses sotodo— To the damage of the said plaintiff of five hundred dollars and therefore he brings his suit &c

Stuart & Lincoln p. q.

(Copy of instrument sued on)

"$300—Six months after date we the undersined promis to pay Calvin Kendoll three hundred dollars it being for value received of him this 23rd day of December A. D. 1836 Bearing 12 per cent intrust untill paid—

W. G. Moffett & Briscoe (Seal)"

Calvin Kendall
          ⎫
vs   ⎬ Declaration
          ⎭
Willis G. Moffett
Filed Nov 2 1839
     Wm Butler ck

PRECIPE AND DECLARATION IN THE SUIT OF HAY
VS. LASWELL, NOVEMBER 4, 1839.
(Herndon-Weik Collection)

*The precipe and declaration in this suit were penned by
Attorney Lincoln down to the end of the words, "Second Count."
The hands of two others are responsible for the balance of the
paper. The cover notations, with exception of filing date, were
written by Lincoln. The cases of Hay vs. Laswell, and Hay vs.
Mock and Laswell, begun on November 5, 1839, appear to have
had close association, although there are slight differences in the
complaints. In the second suit Hay sued for $2.50, the value of
a bridle, and on March 4, 1840, Laswell confessed judgment for
that amount. Mr. Lincoln argued the assumpsit case of Hay vs.
Laswell before a jury on November 27, 1839, but the jury was
unable to agree and was discharged.*

State of Illinois ⎫ Of the November term of the
Sangamon county ⎬ circuit court of said county—
and circuit ⎭ A. D. 1839—

Nathaniel Hay plaintiff, complains of Thomas Laswell defendant, in custody &c of a plea of Trespass on the case upon promises: For that whereas the said defendant, heretofore towit, on the fifteenth day of June in the year of our Lord one thousand eight hundred and thirtyeight, at the county and circuit aforesaid, made his certain note in writing, bearing date the day and year aforesaid, and thereby then and there promised to deliver, on or before the first day of August (then) next (ensuing) to the said plaintiff at Springfield at his brick yard, thirtythree and one third cords of good sound wood split small suitable for burning brick, one third of which was to be four feet long and the ballance eight feet long all to be split wood, for value received, and then and there delivered the said note to the said plaintiff; by means whereof and by force of the statute in such case made and provided, the said defendant then and there became liable to deliver to the said plaintiff the said amount of wood in the said note specified, according to the tenor and effect of the said note: and being so liable, he the said defendant in consideration thereof, afterwards towit, on the day and year aforesaid, at the county and circuit aforesaid, undertook, and then and there faithfully promised the said plaintiff to deliver to him the said wood in the said note specified according to the tenor and effect of said note—

And whereas also afterwards towit, on the day and year

aforesaid, at the county and circuit aforesaid, the said defendant, made his certain other note in writing, bearing date the day and year aforesaid, and thereby then and there promised to deliver, on or before the first day of September (then) next (ensuing) to the said plaintiff, at his brick yard in Springfield, thirtythree and a third cords of good sound wood, one third to be four feet long, and the ballance eight feet long all to be split small and suitable for burning brick, and corded up in close order for value received; and then and there delivered the said last mentioned note to the said plaintiff, by means whereof and by the statute in such case made and provided, the said defendant then and there became liable to deliver to the said plaintiff the said wood in the said last mentioned note specified, according to the tenor and effect of the said last mentioned note: and being so liable, he the said defendant, in consideration thereof, afterwards towit, on the day and year aforesaid, at the county and circuit aforesaid undertook and then and there faithfully promised the said plaintiff to deliver to him the said wood in the said last mentioned note according to the tenor and effect thereof—

And whereas also afterwards towit, on the day and year aforesaid, at the county and circuit aforesaid, the said defendant made his certain other notes in writing bearing date the day and year aforesaid and thereby then and there promised to deliver, on or before the first day of October (then) next (ensuing) to the said plaintiff at his brick yard in Springfield, thirtythree and one third cords of good sound wood one third to be four feet long, and the ballance eight feet long, and all to be split up small suitable for burning brick, for value received; and then and there delivered the said last mentioned note to the said plaintiff; by means whereof and by the statute in such case made and provided, the said defendant then and there became liable to deliver to the said plaintiff the said wood in the said last mentioned note specified according to the tenor and effect of the said last mentioned note; and being so liable he the said defendant in consideration thereof, afterwards towit on the day and year aforesaid, at the county and circuit aforesaid, under took and then and there faithfully promised the said plaintiff to deliver to him the said wood in the said last mentioned note specified, according to the tenor and effect thereof— Yet the said defendant (although often requested so to do; and although the several times for the delivery of the said several lots of wood have long since elapsed; although the said plaintiff hath always been ready to accept and receive the said several lots of wood, according to the tenor and effect of the said notes) hath not as yet delivered to the said plaintiff the said lots of wood or any or either of them, according to the tenor and effect of the said notes or any or either of them, but so to do hath hitherto wholly neglected [and re]fused and still doth neglect and refuse To the damage of the said plaintiff of three hundred dollars, and therefore he sues &c

Stuart & Lincoln p. q.

(Copies of notes sued on)

(First count)

"On or before the first day of August next I bind myself to deliver to Nathaniel Hay in Springfield at his brick yard, thirty three and one third cords of good sound wood split small suitable for burning brick, one third of which is to be four feet long and the ballance eight feet long all to be split wood value received this 15th of June 1838—

Thomas Lasswell"

(Second count)

"On or before the first day of September next I bind myself to deliver to Nathaniel Hay at his brick yard in Springfield thirty three and a third Cords of good sound wood one third to be fore feet long and the balance Eight feet long all to be split small and suitable for burng brick and corded up in close cordes value received this 15th of June 1838

Thomas Laswell"

(Third count)

"On or before the first day of October next I bind myself to deliver to Nathiel Hay at his brick yard in Springfield thirty three and one third Cordes of good sound wood one third to be four feet long and the ballance eight feet long and all to be split up small suitable for burning brick value received this 15th of June 1838

Thomas Laswell"

Nathaniel Hay

vs   } Precipe & Decl

Thomas Lasswell

Filed Nov 4th 1839
    Wm Butler ck

DECLARATION, AFFIDAVITS AND NOTES FOR ARGUMENT IN THE SUIT OF CARMAN VS. GLASCOCK ET AL, NOVEMBER 4, 1839.

(Herndon-Weik Collection)

The documents here reproduced afford informing proof of the methods of Lincoln, the lawyer, during his first years at the bar. The last paragraph of the declaration, which is signed "Logan & Baker pd," is not in the hand of Lincoln. The words, "and the plffs doth the like," are in the same hand as the last paragraph of the document. Mr. Lincoln penned the rest of the document, and the notations upon the cover, with the exception of the date of filing. It will be noted that he mis-spelled "approved" and "whereas" according to modern usage. On November 29, 1839, the plaintiffs asked that one of the defendants, James Strode, be summoned to appear in court as a material witness in the case, and that they be given time to secure his attendance at the next term of court. The jury awarded Carman & Carman a judgment of eighty-five dollars against two of the defendants on March 5, 1840. Stuart & Lincoln took a non-suit in the action against James Strode, and the other defendants in the case recovered their costs. It was a slight return for damages of $1000. and Stuart & Lincoln cannot be credited with a distinctive triumph in the case. Lawyers know, however, that members of the profession are not evaluated in terms of cases won and lost, but in the light of able presentation of a case. Jacob Carman signed the affidavit which he made on November 29. The notations on his being sworn, and the filing date are in the hands of Butler. The rest of this document is in the hand of Attorney Lincoln.

The brackets in the Notes for Argument indicate that they were prepared in 1839. It may have been soon after the filing of the Carman affidavit or at an earlier date. It was not the custom of Attorney Lincoln to prepare notes or long briefs in his legal cases, but several cases reveal such preparation. The computation of costs would indicate that Lincoln had been making estimates of the damages which he asked for in the declaration of November 4th. He made a motion for continuing the case on November 27, 1839, and the motion was granted. It seems clear that the legal brief was prepared for the first arguments in the case, thus placing it before November 27th, and prior to the affidavit before cited. There is no conclusive evidenc in the matter, as the records of the case do not present a brief date.

State of Illinois
Sangamon county and circuit ct. } Of the November Term, 1839

Jacob Carman and Townsend Carman, plaintiffs complain of John Glascock, John Strode William B. Preston, William Hargus and Gored Hendricks, defendants being in custody &s of a plea of Tresspass on the case— For that whereas by an act of the People of the state of Illinois represented in the General Assembly. entitled. "An act declaring the Sangamon river a navigable stream" Approved December 26, 1822 it is enacted as follows towit: "Be it enacted by the People of the state of Illinois represented in the General Assembly: That the Sangaman river from its mouth (following the main channel) to the third principal Meridian be and the same is hereby declared a navigable stream; that no dam of any description or other obstruction shall be placed in the river so as to impede the navigation thereof, or drive the water from its natural channel so as to overflow the bottoms, or produce stagnant waters in any place" and whereas after the making and passing of the said act, and by virtue thereof up to and after the time of committing the several grievances hereinafter mentioned, the said Sangamon river from its mouth following the main channel to the third Principal Meridian, was and of right ought to have been a navigable stream, and was and of right ought to have been a public highway, and was and of right ought to have been free and open for all the good citizens of the state of Illinois and others to navigate the same at all times free from any obstruction, with their canoes, skiffs, periogues, flat boats barges and Steam Boats. And whereas neither the said defendants nor any other person or persons had any right to obstruct or impede the navigation of the said Sangamon River from its mouth following the main channel to the third principal meridian by the erection or maintainence of any mill, mill-dam, mill-house, abutment, buttress, mill-wheel, fish trap, fish trapdam, or any other thing, or things whatever. And whereas before and at the time of committing the several grievances hereinafter mentioned, the said plaintiffs had a flat bottomed boat of great value, towit, of the value of $150, loaded with a large quantity of corn, towit, 2500 bushels of corn, the property of the said plaintiffs, of great value towit, of the value of one thousand dollars proceeding in and upon the said navigable stream upon the main channel thereof, between its mouth and the third principal meridian, towit on the   day of April 1839 at the state, county, and circuit aforesaid: Yet the said defendants well knowing the premises, but contriving and wrongfully and unjustly intending to injure and prejudice the said plaintiffs in this respect and to deprive them of the use and benefit, of the said navigable stream, and to delay hinder and detain the said plaintiffs in navigating the said Sangamon River with their said flat bottomed boat loaded as aforesaid, and to put them to great labour and expense in necessary unloading and reloading their said flat bottomed boat; and to put them to great loss by the necessary exposure of the aforesaid boat load of corn to heavy rains, and to suit[?] detain, injure and destroy their said flat bottomed boat, and the corn loaded therein, towit on the said   day of April, 1839, at the state county and circuit aforesaid, did erect and make in upon and across the main channel of the said Sangamon River between the mouth thereof and the third Principal Meridian, one fish trap, one fish trap dam, and did then and there throw into the main channel of the said Sangamon River between its mouth and the third principal meridian, divers stones, logs, poles, brush, dirt sand and gravel, and other obstructing substances, whereby the navigation of the said navigable stream was greatly impeded, and totally obstructed, and the said obstructions so made, erected, and thrown into said river as aforesaid did keep and continue from that day to the commencement of this suit. By reason whereof whilst the said flat bottomed boat of the plaintiffs loaded with the large quantity of corn aforesaid, was decending the navigable stream aforesaid, towit, the Sangamon River between its mouth and the third principal meridian, the said plaintiffs with their flat bottomed boat aforesaid loaded with the large quantity of corn aforesaid, were stopped, delayed, hindered and detained, from proceeding on down the said navigable stream, by the fish trap, fish-trap dam, stones, logs, poles, brush, dirt, sand, and gravel, and other obstructing substances, by the said defendants made, erected, and thrown in upon and across the said navigable stream as aforesaid; & whereby also the said plaintiffs lost the advantage of proceeding directly to market with their said boat loaded with corn, towit, on the   day of April 1839, at the state county & circuit aforesaid; and by reason which leak their load of corn was greatly injured; and by reason whereof the said plaintiffs, to enable them to proceed to market with their said boat and load of corn, were, afterwards, towit on the   day of April 1839, at the state county and circuit aforesaid, under the necessity of unloading and reloading their said load of corn, and did actually then and there unload and reload their aforesaid load of corn; and by reason of which necessary unloading & reloading of said load of corn, said corn was exposed to the weather, and was then and there wet and thereby greatly injured by the rain, so that a large quantity thereof, towit 400 bushels thereof was destroyed and wholly lost to the said plaintiffs, towit by said hindrance, delay and detention aforesaid. By means of all which the plaintiffs have been injured & sustained damages to the sum of $1000. and therefore they sue &c

Stuart & Lincoln p q.—

And the Defendants come and defend the wrong and injury when where &c and the plaintiffs their action against them to have and maintain ought not because they say they are not guilty in manner and form as the plaintiffs have in their declaration alleged and of this they put themselves upon the country

Logan & Baker pd

And the plffs doth the like

Jacob Carman &   Lincoln pq

Townsend Carman

vs   } Declaration

John Glascock & others
Filed Nov 4th 1839
Wm Butler clerk

DECLARATION OF PLAINTIFF IN THE SUIT OF VAUGHAN VS. RANSDELL, NOVEMBER 4, 1839.

(Herndon-Weik Collection)

The declaration with cover notations here reproduced, Butler's date of filing excepted, was penned by Attorney Lincoln. He corrected errors in more than one case ,and changed "promissed" to "promised" with his usual care, but left an ungrammatical phrase, in the following words, "that a institution of suit . . ." The result of this case will be found in the footnotes to the plea of the defendant of March 6, 1840, which appears to have been the last legal paper filed, before the case went to trial.

State of Illinois ⎫   Of the November term of the
Sangamon county ⎬ ss   Circuit court of said county
and Circuit   ⎭   A. D. 1839—

Foley Vaughn, plaintiff, complains of Wharton Ransdell defendant, being in custody &c. of a plea of Trespass on the case upon promises: For that whereas heretofore towit, on the twentieth day of May in the year of our Lord one thousand eight hundred and thirtysix, at Washington, towit at the county and circuit aforesaid, one Cyrus H. King made his certain promissory note in writing, bearing date the day and year aforesaid, and thereby then and there promised to pay, nine months after the date thereof to one Charles S. Dorsey, by the style and description of "Chs. S. Dorsey", or order, the sum of two hundred and four dollars and seventyfive hundredths of a dollar; for value received, and then and there delivered the said promissory note to the said Charles S. Dorsey; And the said Charles S. Dorsey, to whom or to whose order the payment of the said sum of money in the said promissory note specified was to be made, after the making of the said promissory note, and before the payment of the said sum of money therein specified towit on the seventeenth day of June in the year aforesaid at the county and circuit aforesaid assigned the said promissory note by indorsement in writing thereon, by which said assignment, he the said Charles S. Dorsey then and there ordered and appointed the said sum of money in the said promissory note specified to be paid to one Wharton Ransdell, the defendant in this suit and then and there delivered the said promissory note, so assigned, to the said defendant Wharton Ransdell; And the said Wharton Ransdell to whom the payment of the said sum of money in the said promissory note specified, towit, on the   day of   in the year of our Lord one thousand eight hundred and thirtyeight assigned the said promissory note by indorsement in writing, signing his name to said assignment "W. Ransdell" by which last mentioned assignment the said Wharton Ransdell then and there ordered and appointed the said sum of money in the said promissory note specified to be paid to the plaintiff, Foley Vaughn and then and there delivered the said promissory note so assigned, to the said plaintiff; And the said plaintiff avers that he has used due diligence by the institution and prosecution of a suit against the maker of said note for the recovery of the sum of money therein specified, and has been wholly unable to recover the same by reason of the insolvency of the said maker of the said promissory note— by means whereof, and by force of the statute in such case made and provided, the said defendant then and there became liable to pay to the said plaintiff the said sum of money in the said promissory note specified, together with the costs and charges of his said suit against the said maker of said note; and being so liable he the said defendant, in consideration thereof afterwards towit, on the day and year aforesaid at the county and circuit aforesaid, undertook, and then and there faithfully promised the said plaintiff to pay him the said sum of money in the said promissory note specified according to the tenor and effect thereof together with the costs and charges of the said suit against the maker of said note—And whereas also afterwards, towit on the twentieth day of May in the year of our Lord one thousand eight hundred and thirtysix, at Washington, towit at the county & circuit aforesaid, the said Cyrus H. King made his certain other promissory note in writing, bearing date the day and year aforesaid, and thereby then and there promised to pay nine months after the date thereof, to one Charles S. Dorsey by the style and description of Chs. S. Dorsey or order, the sum of two hundred and four dollars and seventyfive hundredths of a dollar, for value received, and then and there delivered the said promissory note to the said Charles S Dorsey to whom or to whose order the said sum of money in the said promissory note specified was to be made, after the making of the said promissory note, and before the payment of the said sum of money therein specified, towit, on the seventeenth day of June in the year aforesaid, assigned the said promissory note by indorsement in writing thereon, by which said assignment the said Charles S. Dorsey then and there ordered and appointed the said sum of money in the said promissory note specified to be paid to the defendant Wharton Ransdell and then and there delivered said note so assigned to the said Wharton Ransdell; And the said Wharton Ransdell, to whom the said sum of money in the said promissory note specified was by said assignment directed to be paid, after the making said assignment, before the payment of the sum of money in the said promissory note specified; towit on the   day of   in the year of our Lord

assigned the said promissory note by in writing thereon, signing his name thereto, "W. Ransdell" by which said assignment the said Wharton Ransdell then and there ordered and appointed the said sum of money in the said promissory note specified to be paid to the said plaintiff Foley Vaughn, and then and there delivered the said promissory note so assigned as aforesaid to the said plaintiff: And the said plaintiff avers that a institution of suit on said note against the maker thereof would have been wholly unavailing because at the first term of the circuit court of McLean county in which county the maker of said note resided, after said defendant assigned said note to said plaintiff, the maker of said note was wholly insolvent and unable to pay said note or any part thereof— By means whereof and by force of the statute in such case made and provided the said defendant then and there became liable to pay to the said plaintiff the said sum of money in the said promissory note specified, according to the tenor and effect thereof, and being so liable he the said defendant, in consideration thereof, afterwards towit on the day and year aforesaid, at the place aforesaid, undertook, and then and there faithfully promised the said plaintiff to pay him the said sum of money in the said promissory note specified according to the tenor and effect thereof—

Yet the said defendant (Although often requested so to do) hath not as yet paid to the said plaintiff the said sum of money in the said promissory notes specified, or any part thereof, but so to do hath hitherto wholly neglected and refused, and still doth neglect and refuse, to the damage of the plaintiff of five hundred dollars and therefore he sues &c.

Stuart & Lincoln p. q.

(The following is a copy of both notes sued on, both being precisely alike—)

"$204-75. Washington May 20 1836.

Nine months after date I promise to pay Chs. S. Dorsey or order two hundred & four 75/100 dollars, value received, without defalcation—

Cyrus H. King"

(First indorsement)

"June 17 1836. Pay the bearer Wharton Ransdell

Charles S. Dorsey"

(Second indorsement)

"Pay to Foley Vaughn.

W. Ransdell.

Foley Vaughn

vs   } Declaration

Wharton Ransdell—
Filed Nov 4th 1839
Wm Butler, ck

DECLARATION OF THE PLAINTIFF IN THE SUIT OF TROTTER VS. ARNOLD AND FAIRCHILD, NOVEMBER 4, 1839.
(Herndon-Weik Collection)

The declaration, quoted note and cover notations in this case were drawn by Attorney Lincoln, except the filing date which is in the hand of Butler.

State of Illinois ⎫
Sangamon county ⎬   Of the November term of the circuit
and circuit ⎭   court of said county A. D. 1839—

George Trotter plaintiff complains of Robert C. Arnold, and Moses Fairchild defendants in custody &c of a plea of Trespass on the case upon promises: For that whereas the said defendants, heretofore to wit, on the first day of March in the year of our Lord one thousand eight hundred and thirtysix, at Springfield, towit at the county and circuit aforesaid, made their certain promissory note in writing, bearing date the day and year aforesaid, and thereby then and there promised to pay one year after the date thereof, to the said plaintiff or order one hundred dollars with interest from date (meaning the date of said note) until paid at the rate of twelve per cent per annum, the interest to be paid semi annually, for value received, and then and there delivered the said promissory note to the said plaintiff; by means whereof, and by force of the statute in such case made and provided the said defendants then and there became liable to pay to the said plaintiff the said sum of money in the said promissory note specified according to the tenor and effect of the said promissory note; and being so liable, they the said defendants, in consideration thereof, afterwards, towit on the day and year aforesaid, at the county & circuit aforesaid, undertook and then & there faithfully promised the said plaintiff to pay him the said sum of money in the said promissory note specified according to the tenor and effect thereof—

Yet the said defendants (although often requested so to do) have not as yet paid the said sum of money in the said promissory note specified, or any part thereof; but sotodo have hitherto wholly neglected and refused, and still do neglect and refuse, To the damage of the said plaintiff of two hundred dollars and therefore he sues &c.

Stuart & Lincoln p q.

(Copy of note sued on)
"Dolls. $100. Springfield March 1 .. 1836

One year after date we promise to pay to George Trotter or order one hundred dollars with interest from date until paid at the rate of twelve per cent per annum. the interest to be paid semi annually, for value received.

Robert C. Arnold

George Trotter   Moses Fairchild"

vs   }   Decln

R. C. Arnold &
Moses Fairchild
Filed Nov 4th 1839
Wm Butler, ck

PRECIPE, DECLARATION AND BILL OF EXCEPTIONS IN THE SUIT OF HAY VS. MOCK AND LASWELL, NOVEMBER 5 AND 30, 1839.
(Herndon-Weik Collection)

The praecipe and declaration in this case are in the hand of Attorney Lincoln with the exception of the part written in the hand of Logan and Baker in answer to the declaration. The cover notations also appear to have been penned by Lincoln. The care taken by Mr. Lincoln in writing his documents is evidenced by the crossing out of words, which will be found used in their proper place later on in the document. "Always" is spelled as "allways", and the use of "hath not" with the plural defendants is frequently found in the legal documents by Lincoln. He changed to "have" upon occasion. Lincoln listed his employment in the firm fee book in Hay vs. Laswell, and Hay vs. Mock & Laswell. He was more fortunate in the above case as he gained a judgment by consent of $200 for Hay upon March 6, 1840.

The bill of exceptions was penned by Lincoln, and signed by Judge Treat. The cover notations are in Butler's hand. It is of interest to notice that "stalion" is used for the word, "stallion", throughout the bill. As noted elsewhere Laswell confessed judgment for the sum of $2.50, the exact value of the bridle as given in the complaint of Hay vs. Mock and Laswell. This judgment was confessed upon March 4, 1840.

State of Illinois
Sangamon county }   Of the November term of the Circuit
and circuit   court of said county A. D. 1839—

Nathaniel Hay plaintiff, complains of Henry Mock and Thomas Laswell defendants in custody &c of a plea of Trespass on the case upon promises: For that whereas heretofore towit, on the   day of August in the year of our Lord one thousand eight hundred and thirtynine, at the county and circuit aforesaid, the said plaintiff, at the special instance and request of the said defendants, bargained with the said defendants, to buy of them the said defendants, and the said defendants then and there sold to the said plaintiff, a large quantity towit eighty cords of wood, at the rate or price of two dollars and fifty cents for each and every cord thereof, forty cords of which, to be delivered by the said defendants to the said plaintiff, by the fifteenth day of September then next ensuing, at Springfield (meaning Springfield in the county of Sangamon and State of Illinois) and the remaining forty cords to be delivered by the said defendants to the said plaintiff, by the twentyfifth day of December 1839— at Springfield aforesaid; one half of said wood to be four feet in length and the other half to be eight feet in length, the whole of said wood to be well split suitable for burning brick, to be paid for by the said plaintiff to the said defendants at the time and place of making said contract—

And in consideration thereof, and that the said plaintiff at the like special instance and request had then and there under taken and faithfully promised the said defendants to accept and receive the said wood and to pay them for the same at the rate aforesaid; they the said defendants undertook &c. to deliver the said wood to him the said plaintiff as aforesaid; and although the said time for delivery of the said first forty cords of said wood, as aforesaid, hath long since elapsed, and the said plaintiff hath allways been ready and willing to accept and receive the said wood, and although he did, on the day and year and at the place first aforesaid, pay to the said defendants the sum of two hundred dollars, being the amount of two dollars and fifty cents for each cord of wood so to be delivered to him as aforesaid, which fact of payment as aforesaid, the said plaintiff hereby avers to be true; yet the said defendants not regarding &c but contriving &c to deceive and defraud the said plaintiff in this behalf, did not nor would within the time aforesaid, or at any time afterward, deliver the said wood or any part thereof for the said plaintiff at Springfield aforesaid, or elsewhere, but wholly neglected and refused so to do; whereby the said plaintiff hath lost and been deprived of divers great gains and profits, which might and otherwise would have arisen and accrued to him from the delivery of the said wood to him the said plaintiff as aforesaid towit at Springfield aforesaid— To the damage of the said plaintiff of two hundred dollars and therefore he sues &c—

Stuart & Lincoln p q.

2nd count to come in at the star on the other half of this sheet—

And whereas also afterwards towit, on the day and year first aforesaid, at the county and circuit aforesaid the said defendants were indebted to the said plaintiff in the sum of two dollars and fifty cents for a certain bridle by the said plaintiff before that time sold and delivered to the said defendants, and at their special instance and request; and being so indebted, they, the said defendants in consideration thereof afterwards towit, on the day and year aforesaid at the county and circuit aforesaid, undertook and then and there faithfully promised the said plaintiff the said sum of money when they the said defendants should be thereunto afterwards requested—Yet the said defendants (although often requested so to do) hath not as yet paid the said sum of money or any part thereof but so to do hath hitherto wholly neglected and refused—

Hay ⎫ and the Defendants come and
    vs ⎬ defend the wrong and injury when
Mock and Laswell ⎭ where &c and say the Plaintiff

actio non because they say they did not undertake and promise in manner and form as the plaintiff in his declaration hath alleged and of this they put themselves upon the country

Logan & Baker
pd

And the plff. doth the like

Stuart & Lincoln p q.

Nathaniel Hay
    vs
Henry Mock &
Thomas Lasswell

Filed Nov 5th 1839.
    Wm Butler clerk

Nathaniel Hay
   vs
Henry Mock &
Thomas Laswell

Be it remembered that on the trial of the cause, the defendants jointly purchased of the plaintiff a certain stalion or studhorse; that on the consummation of the contract for the purchase of said stalion *one* of the defendants *only*, towit, the said Mock, was present, that said Mock then stated that he and said Laswell had entered into partnership in the keeping of a Livery-stable; that they had purchased said stalion to use at said stable— Plaintiff further proved it was commonly reported that said Mock and Lasswell did keep a Livery stable in partnership commencing about that time; and that said stalion was taken and used at said stable— Plaintiff also proved that at the time of the consummation of the contract aforesaid, said Mock purchased of said plaintiff a certain bridle, which plaintiff had procured for and used upon said stalion, said Mock then stating that he and said Laswell had purchased said stalion to use at the Livery stable, and that they wanted the bridle to go with him; and further that said Mock took said stalion away from the possession of the plaintiff with said bridle upon him— This evidence was offered to support a count in plaintiffs declaration, charging generally that, said defendants purchased said bridle of the plaintiff, and was objected to by the defendants, and the court decided the evidence to be insufficient to charge the defendants jointly, and' thereupon judgment was given for the defendants— To this opinion of the court the plaintiff excepts, & prays that this his bill of exception may be signed, sealed, and made part of the record in the cause—

Samuel H Treat (Seal)

N. Hay
   vs
Mock & Laswell
Filed Nov. 30, 1839
Wm. Butler, Clk

PRECIPE, DECLARATION AND BOND FOR COSTS IN THE SUIT OF HARKNESS VS. TRUETT & COMPANY, NOVEMBER 6, 1839.
(Herndon-Weik Collection)
The file date and Butler's signature are the only parts of the

document and notations in this suit which were not penned by Attorney Lincoln. In one or two cases it appears that Mr. Lincoln had forgotten the words penned by him, and repeated on occasion. These mistakes he crossed out with his usual care. On September 20, 1839 Lincoln recorded the receipt of the note in the case. Harkness, the client of Stuart & Lincoln, received a judgment of $234.50, the amount of the note, and damages of $40.34. Decision was rendered in the Sangamon Circuit Court on November 23, 1839.

State of Illinois Sangamon county and circuit	} ss	Of the November term of the circuit court of said county A. D. 1839

Charles Harkness, plaintiff, complains of Henry B. Truett and William L. May late trading and doing business under the name style and firm of "H. B. Truett & Co" defendants being in custody &c of a plea of Tresspass on the case upon promises; For that whereas the said defendants, heretofore towit, on the fifth day of September in the year of our Lord one thousand eight hundred and thirtysix at Philad towit at the county and circuit aforesaid, by one Miles F. Truett their agent in that behalf, made their certain promissory note in writing, signing thereto their partnership name of "H. B. Truett & Co" bearing date the day and year aforesaid, and thereby then and there promised to pay, Six months after the date thereof, to the order of "Chas. Harkness" the sum of two hundred and thirtyfour dollars and fifty cents, without defalcation for value received, and then and there delivered the said promissory note to the said plaintiff; by means whereof and by force of the statute in such case made and provided, the said defendants then and there became liable, to pay to the said plaintiff the said sum of money in the said promissory note specified according to the tenor and effect of the said promissory note; and being so liable, they the said defendants, in consideration thereof, afterwards towit on the day and year aforesaid at the county and circuit aforesaid, undertook, and then and there faithfully promised the said plaintiff to pay him the said sum of money in the said promissory note specified, according to the tenor and effect thereof— Yet the said defendants (although often requested so to do) have not as yet paid the said sum of money in the said promissory note specified or any part thereof; but sotodo, have hitherto wholly neglected and refused and still do neglect and refuse. To the damage of the said plaintiff of four hundred dollars and therefore he sues &c.

Stuart & Lincoln p q.

(Copy of the note sued on)

"$234. 50/100 Philada Sep 5 1836

Six months after date we promise to pay to the order of Chas. Harkness two hundred thirtyfour Dollars 50/100 without defalcation for value received.

H. B. Truett & Co
pr. Miles F. Truett"

Charles Harkness
vs
Henry B. Truett &
William L May, late
trading and doing business
under the name style
and firm of
H. B. Truett & Co

Trespass on the case upon promises—
Damage $400-00

The clerk of the Sangamon circuit court will issue process in the above cause—

Stuart & Lincoln p. q.

Charles Harkness
vs.
Henry B. Truett &
William L May

In the Sangamon circuit court

I do hereby enter myself security for costs in this cause, and acknowledge myself bound to pay or cause to be paid all costs which may accrue in this action either to the opposite party or to any of the officers of this court in pursuance of the laws of this state—

A. Lincoln

Dated this 6th day of November A. D. 1839

Charles Harkness

vs.
H. B. Truett & Co.

Precipe. decln &
Bond for Costs

Filed Nov 6 1839
Wm Butler Clk

PRAECIPE, DECLARATION AND BOND FOR COSTS IN THE SUIT OF TOWNSEND VS. TRUETT & COMPANY, SANGAMON CIRCUIT COURT, NOVEMBER 6, 1839.

(Herndon-Weik Collection)

There is little in these legal papers that was not penned by Mr. Lincoln. The praecipe, declaration, and bond were his work, as were the cover notations, with exception of the filing date. He changed from "bussiness" to "business" in this document, revealing that he knew the modern and accepted spelling of the word. The declaration contains one of his rare omissions in legal papers devoted to cases of trespass. Near the conclusion of the document, in the line before the beginning of the last paragraph, he writes, "promised the said plaintiff him the said sum of money." The context of other papers in his hand reveals that he omitted the words, "to pay," before "him." The document itself shows a more hurried composition than most of his earlier legal papers, especially in its omission of punctuation, an unusual thing in his later legal papers. The documents presented here are the only evidence of the case as one in which Mr. Lincoln acted as counsel. The record, if it exists, lies in the yet un-searched entries of the Sangamon Circuit Court.

State of Illinois ⎱ Of the November term of
Sangamon county ⎰ ss the circuit court of said
and Circuit   county A. D. 1839

Samuel Townsend, plaintiff, complains of Henry B. Truett and William L May, late trading and doing business under the name style and firm of "H. B. Truett & Co" defendants, in custody &c of a plea of Trespass on the case upon promises For that whereas the said defendants, heretofore towit, on the first day of September in the year of our Lord one thousand, eight hundred and thirtysix. at Philada. towit at the county and circuit aforesaid, by one Miers F. Truett their agent in that behalf, made their certain promissory note in writing, signing thereto their partnership name of "H. B. Truett & Co." bearing date the day and year aforesaid, and thereby then and there promised to pay, Six months after the date thereof to the said plaintiff or order, without defalcation, the sum of one hundred dollars for value received and. then and there delivered the said promissory note to the said plaintiff: by means whereof. and by force of the statute in such case made and provided the said defendants then and there became liable to pay to the said plaintiff the said sum of money in the said promissory note specified, according to the tenor and effect of the said promissory note; and being so liable they the said defendants, in consideration thereof afterwards to-wit, on the day and year aforesaid at the county and circuit aforesaid, undertook and then and there faithfully promised the said plaintiff him the said sum of money in the said promissory note specified according to the tenor and effect thereof—

Yet the said defendants (although often requested sotodo) have not as yet paid the said sum of money in the said promissory note specified or any part thereof; but so todo have hitherto wholly neglected and refused, and still do neglect and refuse; To the damage of the said plaintiff of two hundred dollars and therefore he sues &c.

Stuart & Lincoln p q.

(Copy of note sued on)

"Dolls. 100.00   Philada.   Sept. 1st 1836
Six months after date we promise to pay Samuel Townsend or order without defalcation one hundred dollars for value recd.

H. B. Truett & Co.
pr
Miers F Truett"

Samuel Townsend vs Henry B Truett & William L May late trading and doing business under the name style & firm of H. B Truett & Co	Trespass on the case upon promises— Damage $200---00

The clerk of the Sangamon circuit court will issue process in the above cause—

Stuart & Lincoln p. q—

Samuel Townsend vs Henry B. Truett & William L. May	In the Sangamon circuit court

I do hereby enter myself security for costs in this cause, and acknowledge myself bound to pay or cause to be paid all costs which may accrue in this action either to the opposite party or to any of the officers of this court in pursuance of the laws of the state

A. Lincoln

Dated this 6th day of November A. D. 1839.

Samuel Townsend

vs   } Precipe, Decln
        Bond for costs—

H. B. Truett & Co.

Filed Nov 6th 1839
    Wm Butler clerk

DECLARATION OF PLAINTIFF IN THE SUIT OF NEWSOM VS. NEWTON, NOVEMBER 6, 1839.
(Herndon-Weik Collection)

The declaration in this suit was drawn by Attorney Lincoln, and he wrote the words "David Newsom vs. Joel Newton Declaration," on the cover. These are penned vertically, while the usual horizontal notations are in the hand of Clerk Butler. It does not seem that the fifth count should follow the conclusion of the document, but there are two points to be considered. The original document reveals no point at which the fifth count may be inserted before the words, "Yet the defendant," etc. The words, "5th Count" are placed in the middle of a page unlike the other four counts, which begin at the margin of the page. Finally, in the totalling of the sums for which Newsom was indebted, Mr. Lincoln at first put down the sums of four counts, and gave a total of $4300. That sum was crossed out, a sum of $1000 added, and the total revised to read, $5300. It is possible that Mr. Lincoln, having concluded the document, noted the omission of count five, with the indebtedness, and added it to the document. The original declaration would permit of such a conclusion, but it does not offer conclusive evidence of the paper being penned in this fashion.

State of Illinois   }   Of the November term of the
                    } ss   circuit court of
Sangamon county   }   said county A. D. 1839—

1 David Newsom plaintiff, complains of Joel Newton, defendant, in custody &c of a plea of Trespass on the case upon promises: For that whereas the said defendant heretofore to-wit on the   day of   in the year of our Lord one thousand eight hundred and thirtynine, at the county and state aforesaid, was indebted to the said plaintiff in the sum of one thousand and three hundred dollars for divers goods,

wares, merchandize and chattels by the said plaintiff before that time sold and delivered to the said defendant, and at his special instance and request, and being so indebted, he the said defendant, in consideration thereof, afterwards towit, on the day and year aforesaid, at the county and circuit aforesaid, undertook, and then and there faithfully promised the said plaintiff to pay him the said sum of money when he the said defendant should be thereunto afterwards requested—

2 And whereas also afterwards towit, on the day and year aforesaid, at the county and circuit aforesaid, the said defendant was indebted to the said plaintiff in the further sum of one thousand dollars for so much money by the said plaintiff before that time lent and advanced to the said defendant, at his special instance and request, and being so indebted, he the said defendant, in consideration thereof afterwards, towit, on the day and year aforesaid, undertook, and then and there faithfully promised the said plaintiff to pay him the said last mentioned sum of money when he the said defendant should be thereunto afterwards requested—

3 And whereas also afterwards to wit, on the day and year aforesaid, at the county and circuit aforesaid, the said defendant was indebted to the said plaintiff in the further sum of one thousand dollars, for so much money by the said plaintiff before that time paid, laid out and expended to and for the use of the said defendant at his like special instance and request, and being so indebted, he the said defendant in consideration thereof, afterwards to wit, on the day and year aforesaid, at the county and circuit aforesaid, undertook, and then and there faithfully promised the said plaintiff to pay him the said last mentioned sum of money when he the said defendant should should be thereunto afterwards requested—

4 And whereas also afterwards towit, on the day and year aforesaid at the county and circuit aforesaid, the said defendant was indebted, to the said plaintiff, in the further sum of one thousand dollars, for so much money by the said defendant before that time had and received to and for the use of the said plaintiff; and being so indebted, he the said defendant, in consideration thereof, afterwards towit, on the day and year aforesaid at the county and circuit aforesaid, undertook, and then and there faithfully promised the said plaintiff to pay him the said last mentioned sum of money, when he the said defendant should be thereunto afterwards requested—

Yet the said defendant (although often requested sotodo) hath not as yet paid the said several sums of money or any part thereof, but so to do hath hitherto wholly neglected and refused, and still doth neglect and refuse. To the damage of the said plaintiff of thirteen hundred dollars, and therefore he sues &c.

Stuart & Lincoln p. q.

(Copy of acpt)

Joel Newton

1839—July 1st To goods, wares, merchandize & chattels	$1300-00
To money lent	1000-00
To money paid	1000-00
To money had and received	1000-00
To work & labor done	1000.00
	$5300.00

5 Count

And whereas also afterwards, towit, on the day and year aforesaid at the county and circuit aforesaid, the said defendant was indebted to the said plaintiff in the further sum of one thousand dollars, for the work and labour, care and diligence, of the said plaintiff before that time done performed and bestowed by the said plaintiff, and his servants, and with his horses, oxen, carts, waggons and carriages in and about the business of the said defendant, and at his special instance and request; and being so indebted, he the said defendant in consideration thereof, afterwards towit, on the day and year aforesaid, at the county and circuit aforesaid undertook and then and there faithfully promised the said plaintiff to pay him the said last mentioned sum of money when he the said defendant should be thereunto requested—

David Newsom

vs   } Decln

Joel Newton

Filed Nov 6th 1839
    Wm Butler clerk

ARTICLE BY MR. LINCOLN IN THE SANGAMO JOURNAL, NOVEMBER 8, 1839.

How the public revenues should be raised and guarded never had at any time a congenial or well considered place in the political thinking of Mr. Lincoln, and that fact is clearly in evidence in the article, State Sub-Treasuries—Gold and Silver for Taxes, which he is believed to have contributed to the issue of the Sangamo Journal for November 8, 1839. At that time he was, first of all, a defender of Whig policy and contentions, and so, with voice and pen vigorously, opposed the sub-treasury system brought forward by President Van Buren as a remedy for the financial ills which then afflicted the nation. But despite Whig opposition public sentiment in its favor grew steadily; a new Congress pledged to its enactment was elected, and on July 4, 1840, Van Buren finally signed what the elder Francis P. Blair declared "the second Declaration of Independence." The New Era cited by Lincoln was a New York daily which truculently supported the Van Buren administration and which had for its editor Richard Adams Locke, a clever young Englishman who had come to America a few years before and who is now best remembered as author of the famous Moon Hoax. The Reformer also cited by Lincoln had for its full title The Radical Reformer and Working Man's Advocate, and for its editor Thomas Brothers, an English radical and disciple of William Cobbett, who for a time wrought valiantly to enlist labor in support of the cause of hard money.

The loco foco party are anxious for the establishment of the Sub-Treasury System for the General Government; but few of them have the hardihood to urge the carrying out of the system in the States. This was shown conclusively in our Legislature last winter; where, although very near a majority of the House were in favor of the collection of the public dues in gold and silver, and the establishment of the sub-treasury system by Congress—only NINE of the faithful, if we recollect, were willing to enforce the policy in our State.

While, however, the party are so chary here on the subject, in some parts of the Union they do not hesitate to "go the entire figure." The New York "New Era"—a pattern democratic paper—thus announces its views upon this subject:

"That we are in favor of an entire separation of the fiscal affairs of this State, as well as the United States, from all banks and corporations, and are decidedly in favor of each government being the direct receiver and disburser of the revenue in gold and silver."

This ground is consistent. If the Sub-Treasury System, is

as important to the General Government, as is pretended, it must be equally so to the States. The New York Reformer—another pattern democratic paper—thus reasons upon the subject generally:

"If a National Bank is unconstitutional, so is a State Bank. If a National Bank is dangerous to our liberties, from its immense influence over the government and congress, much more so are the local banks, by their influence over the state governments and legislatures. If the banks are not safe depositories for the funds of the general government, neither are they so for the state. If depreciated bank paper promises, are not a safe currency, in which to receive the revenue of the nation, neither is it, to receive the taxes and tolls belonging to the state."—The parallel holds good throughout. What abnominable mockery is it not then, for any one to pretend to favor the sub-treasury scheme of the general government; to collect all the revenue in the constitutional currency, and for the sake of security to keep it in safes and vaults in charge of receivers appointed specially for the purpose; when at the same time they allow the revenue of the state to be collected in the paper promises of any of the 150 shinplaster manufactories in this state, and deposited in any one of them for safe keeping. Either the measures of the general government are in truth a ridiculous humbug; or the men who support such measures, and at the same time justify a paper currency and are willing to receive it for taxes and tolls, and to keep the state funds deposited in banks, are knaves or fools.

No proposition therefore can be more clear than this, that if we justify and support the sub-treasury project recommended by the President, as a necessary and proper measure; we are equally bound by every motive and consideration, either of consistency or common sense, to support the project of a sub-treasury, and a hard money currency for the state.

If the premises of the Reformer are correct, no man can gainsay its conclusions. To this complexion the Sub-Treasury Scheme must come at last. If the plan has any real and important advantages over the uniform practice which has obtained in this country, since the organization of the government, the low State credit, and exhausted State treasuries, should first feel its renovating influence. Gentlemen Semi Loco Focos, you must go the whole load, or you will be treated as ten times more infamous traitors, than Tallmadge, Rives and others. Reason, common sense, and common decency will not permit you to uphold a FEDERAL Sub-treasury, and at the same time deny your own State its real or pretended advantages.

REPLICATION IN THE SUIT OF ATWOOD & JONES VS. DOUGLAS & WRIGHT, SANGAMON CIRCUIT COURT, NOVEMBER 19, 1839.

This replication is one of the most altered and carved up papers among the Lincoln legal documents. It is a co-operative work. Douglass wrote the replies of Wright, the one beginning with the words, "and the said Wright says," and the other start-ing with the clause "and the said Deft Wright says." It will be noted that he wrote the name of one of the defendants as "Doug-lass," a way in which he wrote his own name in his earlier days. With the exception of these two brief replies by Wright, the replication, with its numerous erasures is from the pen of Mr. Lincoln. Although he cut out almost all of the first part of the replication, he overlooked the word, "no", preceding the crossed out words, "notice had been given." It may be noted in passing that the legal papers of Lincoln were rarely crossed out in such fashion. On March 8, 1839, Asa D. Wright, one of the defen-dants in the case, filed his plea, and on March 9, 1839, the case was continued. As can be seen, the case was one of trespass upon promises, involving a note of a promissory nature. After filing the replication, Mr. Lincoln filed a demurrer on November 22, 1839, in answer to the defendant. The case was finally de-cided on December 2, 1839, at which time a judgment for $568.22 was rendered in favor of Jones and Atwood, the clients of Stuart & Lincoln.

Atwood & Jones   ⎤
       vs   ⎬
Douglas & Wright   ⎦

And the said plaintiffs for Replication to the said first plea of the said Wright by him above pleaded, say *precludi non*, be-cause they say, that at the date of the said note in the said decla-ration mentioned towit on the 23rd day of December A. D. 1837 the said Douglas and Wright were in copartnership with the said Erskine Douglas as alleged in their said declaration under the name style and firm of Douglas & Wright, towit, with Moses Atwood, which were then standing and unsettled, and unsettled, at the time of making of the said note, the plaintiffs aver no notice had been given to the said plaintiffs— And this they are ready to verify, wherefore they pray judgment &c

Stuart & Lincoln p q.

And the said Wright says he was not in partnership as aforesaid on the 8th day of December 1837 with Erskine Douglass &
of this he puts himself upon the country

Douglass for Wright

And plaintiffs do the like

Stuart & Lincoln p q.

And for Replication to the second plea of the said Wright
above pleaded, say *precludi non* because they say, the said Wright
did execute the said note in manner and form as in the said
declaration alleged, and this they are ready to verify, wherefore
they pray judgment &c.

Stuart & Lincoln p q.

And the said Deft Wright says he did not execute said note
as alleged & of this he puts himself upon the country

Douglass for Wright

And the plaintiffs do the like

Stuart & Lincoln p q.

DEMURRER IN THE SUIT OF VAUGHN VS. RANSDELL, NOVEMBER 20, 1839.
(Herndon-Weik Collection)

*This demurrer was penned by Walker, as were the cover
notations. The words, "Joinder in Demurrer, Lincoln p q." and
"Joinder in Demurrer, p q—", are from the pen of Attorney Lincoln, who filed his joinder on November 21, 1839. The court
sustained this in part and gave him leave to amend his declaration of November 21, 1839. The case was continued until the
March, 1840 term of court.*

Vaughan

vs   } Case

Ransdell

And the defendant comes and defends &c & says *actio non*
because he says that each and both of the counts in the plaintiffs
Declaration are insufficient in law to have and maintain said
action nor is he bound by law to answer the Same and this he is
ready to verify

Wherefore he prays Judt &c

Joinder in Demurrer, Lincoln p q.   Walker, pd

For causes of Demurrer he sets down the following viz

1st the first count is blank as to the date of the assignment to Vaughan

2 The 2nd Count does not exhibit any diligence or valid excuse for making it

Joinder in Demurrer p q—   Walker p d

Vaughan
vs
Ransdell

Filed Wednesday
Nov 20th 1839

NOTE OF CONSTANT AND FRANCIS, NOVEMBER 21, 1839.
(Herndon-Weik Collection)

The words, "Constant & Francis" on the cover of the note reproduced below were penned by Attorney Lincoln. A notation below the note refers to it as part of the case of Kerr vs. Constant and Francis. This notation appears to be incorrect, and is incorrect. Abraham Lincoln filed a three-page bill of complaint in the case of Neff, Wanton & Co. vs. Josiah Francis on November 4, 1839. Neff, Wanton & Co. were a group of St. Louis merchants who sought to collect a note of $353.61 from Josiah Francis, a merchant of Athens, Illinois. The note given below does not seem to have been cited at this time, as it was dated more than two weeks after the case. In the final decision of the case on March 25, 1841, judgment was rendered by default of the defendants. The other defendant appears to have been Constant, for the damages awarded were for $397.44, the exact amount of the note given below. It appears that the note was not evidence in the case of Kerr vs. Constant & Francis, but the basis for the award made on December 25, 1841.

$368.—Four months after date we promise to pay to the order of Neff Wanton or order three Hundred and sixty eight Dollars. for Value received.

Nov. 21, 1839   Constant & Francis
        368.
        29 44
    ——————
    397.44
Constant & Francis

REPORT BY JOHN W. PATTERSON AND OTHERS ON
SELLING REAL ESTATE, SANGAMON CIRCUIT
COURT, NOVEMBER 23, 1839.
(Herndon-Weik Collection)

*This report was penned by Mr. Lincoln, as was the cover
notation, concluding with, "to sell Real estate." The date of
filing is not distinctly Lincolnesque, but, "Nov. 23, 1839," appears to have been penned by him, as does, "Butler ck," and it
is possible that the complete document and cover notations were
his work. It is difficult to understand his reason for styling the
cover notation a petition to sell real estate, and then writing a
report of the sale of real estate according to the order of the
court. The petition to sell real estate, brought before the court
by the administrators and administratrix, was granted on October
11, 1838. Stuart and Lincoln appeared for the plaintiffs, the administrators, on March 5, 1838, and Mr. Lincoln then filed this
report of the disposal of the real estate. The case was continued
at the time of the filing of the report. If the records contain a
final decision, research to the present time has not uncovered it.*

John W. Patterson, John A. Casey, and Jane Casey, administrators and administratrix of Green Casey deceased, who were
directed by an order of the Sangamon circuit court to sell the
real estate of the said Green Casey deceased, report that they
have sold lands in obedience to said order after having advertised according to law; and that William Stotts, being the highest
and best bidder became the purchaser of the whole thereof which
are not included in a former report—That is to say, the said
William Stotts purchased The West half of the South West
quarter of Section Twentyfour in Township Nineteen North
Range Five West, the East half of the South East quarter of
Section Thirty in Township Nineteen North of Range Four
West, for the sum of three dollars and eighteen and three quarters cents, per acre, and that they have taken said Stott's notes
with personal security, and a mortgage on the land to secure the
purchase money—

J. W. Patterson
J. A. Casey &
Jane Casey

John W. Patterson & others—
Pet. to sell Real Estate
filed Nov 23 1839
    Wm Butler ck

NEWTON VS. NEWSOM, SANGAMON CIRCUIT COURT, NOVEMBER 26, 1839.
(Herndon-Weik Collection)

This report is not in the hand of Herndon or Henry as their signed names attest. It is not similar to the cover notations by Butler, and seems the work of a clerk in the office of the commissioners. It is included because of its being a part of the history of the case, and as the answer of Herndon and Henry, both well known to Abraham Lincoln. William Herndon will be recognized as the plaintiff in (the case of Herndon vs. Smith, and as the uncle of William H. Herndon. Dr. Anson G. Henry was one of the intimate friends of Mr. Lincoln, and it was he whose medical services were desired by the latter in one of his spells of depression in January, 1841. Newton had sued the two commissioners, but on July 16, 1839, their friend Lincoln obtained costs for them in the case. The case was of Newton vs. Newsom which was submitted to three arbitrators on November 21, 1839. Present studies have revealed no final decision on the answer of the commissioners, nor on the result of the suit brought by Newsom against Newton.

In the matter of Joel Newton, on application for mandamus against W Herndon & A. G. Henry state House cmrs. } Sangamon Circuit Court Of the Nov. T. 1839

And now come into open Court A. G. Henry and William Herndon two of the State House Commissioners of the State of Illinois, and in obedience to a Rule of this Honorable Court, requiring them the said commissioners to shew cause, why a writ of mandamus should not issue against them the said commissioners, compelling them to pay to one Joel Newton, the amount claimed to be due from the said commissioners to the said Newton for timber, lumber and building materials alleged to have been furnished by one David Newsom as agent of the said Joel Newton, to the said commissioners for the use of the aforesaid State House according to the terms of the said Newton & Newsom with said commissioners, and show for cause why said Mandamus should not issue the following facts, viz

It is admitted by these Respondents that they in their capacity as commissioners aforesaid did execute and enter into the covenant set forth by the aforesaid petitioner, Joel Newton, in his petition herein with the said Joel Newton and the said David Newsom as his surety, but these respondents expressly deny that they ever did receive from the said Newton any part or portion of the materials described in said Newton's aforesaid Covenant, according to the terms of said covenant, but admitting that they did receive from the aforesaid David Newsom timber lumber &c, such as is described in the aforesaid Covenant, amounting to the sum of two hundred and sixty eight 65/100 Dollars they expressly charge that such delivery of materials &c was not made by the said petitioner Joel Newton in discharge of his said contract, but by the aforesaid David Newsom, on his own account, or that if delivered in pursuance of the aforesaid Covenant, then that by the agreement of the said Newton & Newsom, with one of your Respondents, William Herndon, the aforesaid David Newsom was authorized to Receive from your respondents, payment in full for the said materials thus delivered and to execute to your Respondents proper receipts & acquittances therefor; and your Respondents allege that on the 4th day of June A D 1839 after the delivery of the aforesaid materials by the said David Newsom, to your Respondents, your Respondent William Herndon, Secretary of the Board of State House commissioners did execute and deliver to the said Newsom at his request five several checks in favor of said Newton & Newsom on the Treasurer of said Board, to wit your respondent A. G. Henry, four of which said checks were for the sum of fifty dollars each, and the remaining one of said checks was was for the sum of Sixty Eight 65/100 Dollars, and that said checks were issued in full and complete payment for the aforesaid materials delivered by the said Newsom as aforesaid; but your respondents further allege that said checks, copies of which are herewith filed marked A. B. C. D and E, and prayed to be taken as part of their response, yet Remain in the hands of the said Newsom outstanding and unpaid.

In further support of the position assumed by your respondents, that by the terms of their agreement with the aforesaid Newton & Newsom, they were not bound in law or equity, upon the delivery of the aforesaid materials, as aforesaid made, to pay the amount due therefor to said Newton, but were required to pay the same to said Newsom alone, or to the said Newsom and Newton, they beg leave to refer to the affidavit of the aforesaid Wm Herndon, herewith filed marked 3 and have only to add that they have no interest whatever in the Result of this controversy but desire that justice may be done, as they believe it has been—

And now your Respondents having fully answered, and sufficient cause why &c shewn pray that the aforesaid Rule may be discharged and they dismissed herein with their reasonable costs

William Herndon
A. G. Henry

Newton ⎱
vs   ⎰ Answer
Newsom of
commrs.

Filed Nov 26" 1839
Wm Butler Clk

WILLIAM D. HERNDON VS. GLASGOW ET AL, NOVEMBER 28, 1839.

Diligent search has failed to disclose the outcome of this suit. It may have been settled out of court. William D. Herndon, the defendant was a widely known pioneer of Sangamon County and a kinsman of William Henry Herndon, Mr. Lincoln's future law partner.

William D. Herndon ⎫
ads ⎬
Glasgow, Shaw & Tatem ⎭

And the said defendant comes and defends the wrong and injury when, where &c and says plaintiffs *actio non* because he says he did not undertake and promise in manner and form as the said plaintiffs in their said declaration have alleged against him; and of this he puts himself upon the country &c

Stuart & Lincoln, p. d.

And the said defendant hereby notifies the said plaintiffs that he will offer to set off the sum of $75.25/100 being the amount of a certain order given by them to one William Speem on the defendant, which the defendant has paid—

Stuart & Lincoln, p. d.

Wm. D. Herndon ⎫
ads ⎬ Plea
Glasgow, Shaw & Tatem ⎭

Filed Nov. 23 1839
Wm Butler Clk.

CARMAN VS. GLASCOCK, NOVEMBER 29, 1839:
AFFIDAVIT

State of Illinois }
Sangamon county }

Jacob Carman one of the plaintiffs in a suit in the circuit court of said county wherein affiant & Townsend Carman are plaintiffs and John Glascock and others are defendants being duly sworn states on oath, that James Strode is a material witness for the plaintiffs on the trial of said suit & that they can not safely go to trial without him that a subpoena was by affiant procured to be issued by the clerk of said court and put in the bands of the sheriff for said witness to attend at this term of court and affiant supposed it was served, seeing the witness in attendance in court on yesterday— Said witness does not attend to day, & affiant can not find the said subpoena to ascertain whether it has been served or not— That said witness resides in this county, and the plaintiffs expect to procure his attendance at the next term of the court, that they expect to prove by him that defendants erected a fish-trap dam across the Sangamon River as charged in the declaration, that affiant knows of no other witness by whom he can prove the same fact, and that this application is not made for delay, but that justice may be done—

Jacob Carman

Sworn to before me
this 27" day of Nov 1837
        Wm Butler Clk

Carman   }
        vs   }   868
Glascock   }   Affidavit
Filed Nov 29t 1839
        Wm Butler Clk

PETITION TO SELL REAL ESTATE AND ANSWER OF GUARDIAN AD LITEM IN SUIT OF REED AND RICHARD VS. EARLY ET AL, NOVEMBER, 1839, TERM OF THE SANGAMON COUNTY CIRCUIT COURT.
(Herndon-Weik Collection)

The petition and cover notations in this case are in the hand of Abraham Lincoln, with the exception of the notations upon the date. These are in two different hands, and are not the work of Butler. They appear to be later notations. Mr. Lincoln used "proced" for "proceeded", and "Thid" for "Third." The errors may have been due to the rapidity of writing, or of thought processes, but there are few such errors in the legal papers drawn by him. The answer of the guardian ad litem is undated, but is the reply of James C. Conkling referred to in that capacity in the court decree of the November, 1839 Term of the Sangamon County Circuit Court, and is therefore placed in that period of time.

To the Honorable the Judge of the Sangamon circuit court—

Your petitioners, James F. Reed, and Peter Rickard, represent that in the month of March A D. 1838, Jacob M Early died, having duly made and executed his last Will and Testament, and appointed therein your Petitioners as executors thereof; that they have taken out letters testamentary from the office of the Probate Justice of the Peace in and for the county of Sangamon; that they have proced, so far as possible to the settlement and adjustment of said estate; that the personal property and available debts due said estate are insufficient to pay the debts duly established against said estate by the sum of t[went]y one hundred and nineteen dollars & thirtyone cents and that they know of no means of paying said debts, except by the sale of the real estate of the said deceased— They further state that said Early died seized of the West half of the South East quarter of Section Six, eighty acres; the South West quarter Section Six, one hundred and thirty acres; The North West quarter of the North West quarter of Section Seven thirtytwo acres; the North East fractional part of the North East quarter of Section Seventeen, eighteen acres and forty hundredths of an acre; all in Township Nineteen North, of Range Eight West of the Third Principal Meridian—and situated in the county of Menard & state of Illinois— And also one undivided half of the East half of the South West quarter of Section Twentytwo, in Township Sixteen North of Range Four West of the Third principal meridian—situated in the county of Sangamon— They further state that said Early died, leaving his widow Catharine Early and George N. Early, (then born,) and Jacob M. Early (since born) infant children and heirs at law, all of whom your Petitioners pray may be made parties to this petition and that James C. Conkling be appointed guardian *ad litem* to the said infant defendants— They further pray that your Honor will order them to sell the said real estate, to pay the debts aforesaid—

James F. Reed
Peter Rickard—

James F. Reed &
Peter Rickard

vs   } Petn to sell real estate—

Heirs of Jacob M. Early
    Nov. T. 1839
       Nov/ 39

The answer of James C. Conkling, guardian *ad litem* to George N. Early and Jacob M. Early, infant heirs of Jacob M. Early deceased, to the Petition of James F. Reed, and Peter Rickard, to sell the real estate of said Jacob M. Early deceased—

This respondent for answer to said Petition, says that he has examined said Petition and the papers therewith filed, and that he knows of no reason consistent with the interest of the said infant heirs, why the prayer of said Petition should not be granted—

Jas C. Conkling

CARMAN VS. GLASCOCK: NOTES FOR ARGUMENT
NOVEMBER [?], 1839

1st Prove that River is declared navigable—
2nd That defendants obstructed it in Sangamon county and between mouth and meridian line—
3rd That plaintiffs had a boat load of corn on the river above the dam; that said boat ran on the dam,
    1 Sprang a leak—corn wet thereby—amt of damage—
    2 Could'nt get off without unloading—
    3 Water falling & boat would break if not got off—
    4 Did unload—corn got rained on & amount of damage thereby
       Amount of labor in unloading & reloading and the value of it—
11 hands 2 days—22$
175 bushels of corn at 37½
  3

8.525.65   65.62½
  48   22.00

45   87.62½
Carman
vs.
Glascock
[1839]

COMPLAINT IN THE SUIT OF FOUCH VS. THOMAS ET AL, SANGAMON CIRCUIT COURT, NOVEMBER, 1839.
(Herndon-Weik Collection)

This document was penned by Attorney Lincoln. There is a slight variation in usage, for he writes, "so to do" as the words, "so todo," a difference from running the three words together or separating them in modern usage. The complaint of Fouch is the only known evidence of his participation in an interesting case. Future research may unearth a case history, but it is non-existent at present.

State of Illinois ⎤   Of the November term of
Sangamon county ⎬ ss   of the circuit court of
and circuit   ⎦   said county A. D. 1839—

John Fouch, plaintiff, complains of Wesley Thomas, Andrew Scott, and William Underwood, defendants, being in custody &c of a plea of Trespass on the case upon promises: For that whereas the said defendants, heretofore, towit, on the fifteenth day of March in the year of our Lord one thousand eight hundred and thirtynine at Berlin. Illinois. towit at the county & circuit aforesaid, made their certain promissory note in writing (said Underwood signing his name thereto "Wm. Underwood") bearing date the day and year aforesaid, and thereby then and there, the first as principal, and the others as securities, promised to pay one day after the date thereof to the said plaintiff. the sum of Three hundred dollars with interest at the rate of twelve per cent per annum, and then and there delivered the said promissory note to the said plaintiff; by means whereof, and by force of the statute in such case made and provided the said defendants then and there became liable to pay to the said plaintiff the said sum of money together with interest in the said promissory note specified according to the tenor and effect of the said promissory note; and being so liable, they, the defendants afterwards towit, on the day and year & at the place aforesaid undertook, and then faithfully promised the said plaintiff to pay him the said sum of money together with interest, in the said promissory note specified, according to the tenor & effect thereof— Yet the said defendants (although often requested so todo) have not as yet paid to the said plaintiff the said sum of money in the said promissory note specified or any part thereof, but so to do hath hitherto wholly neglected and refused, and still do neglect and refuse: To the damage of the said plaintiff of the sum of five hundred dollars, and therefore he sues &c

Stuart & Lincoln p q.

(Copy of the note sued on)

"Berlin Illinois March 15th 1839

One day after date we the undersigned, the first as principal and the other as securities, promise to pay John Fouch Three hundred dollars with interest at the rate of twelve per cent per annum.

Wesley Thomas
Andrew Scott
Wm. Underwood"

SUPPLEMENTAL BILL IN THE SUIT OF SPEAR VS. NEWTON, SANGAMON CIRCUIT COURT, DECEMBER 3, 1839.

(Herndon-Weik Collection)

With the exception of Clerk Butler's notation of the withdrawal of the bill from the papers, this supplemental bill and cover notations were drawn by Mr. Lincoln. The date given by Butler places the document as of the year 1839. The withdrawal was probably made from the newspapers which published the bill. The defendant filed his demurrer to the supplemental bill, August, 1840. Mr. Lincoln spelled "operation" as "opperation", an error characterized by a student of his legal documents "as one of his few mistakes in spelling." It is curious that "begining" was overlooked, for he used it twice, as he did in almost every survey and legal document containing survey reports which he penned from 1837 to 1841. The legal papers will never dispel any of the great qualities of Mr. Lincoln, but a complete check of the errors in spelling, might cause a reasonable doubt as to his capacity in the field of spelling, as viewed in terms of fixed and formal methods. As seen from the content of the supplemental bill, suit was instituted on June 25, 1839. On July 18, 1839, the defendant was ruled to answer, and I. S. Britton appointed as auditor in the case. The auditor was a judicial listener, and today, as in Massa-

chusetts, it was his duty to take accounts in the case and report to the court. On August 1, 1840, the defendant moved that the supplemental bill be dismissed and filed his reasons. The court overruled the motion of the defendant, whereupon he filed his bill of exceptions. On November 14, 1840, the court ordered Britton to pay $820.39 to David Spear and $350.00 to the defendant's plea. The court heard the case on November 30, 1841. In the case of Spear vs. Newton & Lewis, the court sustained Mr. Lincoln's demurrer to the defendant's plea. The court heard the case on November 30, 1841; awarded the plaintiff $75.00, and granted an appeal to the Supreme Court. At last, on December 2, 1841, the case of Spear vs. Newton was ordered stricken from the docket. As the defendants in Spear vs. Newton & Lewis had been granted an appeal to the Supreme Court of Illinois, it was no doubt for this reason that the case was stricken from the court record. It would seem that Spear vs. Newton and Spear vs. Newton & Lewis were one and the same case, or parts of it.

To the Honorable the Judge of the Sangamon circuit court in Chancery sitting—

Humbly complaining sheweth unto your Honor, your orator David Spear, that he as the administrator of the estate of Thomas J. Luster, filed a Bill in chancery in this court against Joel Newton, on the 25th day of June 1839— He now alleges that the allegations of said bill are true. He further states that said defendant has filed his answer to said Bill, in which he alleges that the terms upon which he entered into partnership with your orator's intestate, were, that said intestate sold to him one half of certain lands, which are of the description following, towit.

The West part of the North East fractional half of Section Five, in Township Sixteen North of Range Four West. 141 acres— the South part of the North East fractional quarter of Section Six, same Township and Range 31 acres— A part of the South East fractional quarter of Section Six, in the same Township and Range & bounded as follows, towit:

Begining at the North East corner of said fractional quarter at a point on the Sangamon River thence South 50 poles; thence West 40 poles; thence North 52 poles; to the East & West section line, thence East with said line 38 poles to the River; thence with the River to the begining 23. acres. ten acres bought of Solomon Blue— North East fourth of the North East quarter of Section Seven, same township & Range; 40 acres; Sixteen acres off the South part of the North East fractional quarter of

Section One in Township # Sixteen North of Range Five West— A part of the South part of the North East fractional quarter of Section Six, Township Sixteen North of Range Four West 20 acres— South West fourth of the South West quarter of Section Six same Township & Range last mentioned. 40 acres— West part of the South East fractional quarter of Section Five in same Township & Range 105 50/100—for which he was to pay twenty five hundred dollars, to said intestate, that a saw mill was to be erected on said land at the equal cost of the parties. to be run by said Newton at five hundred dollars, per year, that the profits of said mill were to be divided equally between said parties, and that the said Newton was to pay the aforesaid twentyfive hundred dollars out of his half of the profits of said mill— Said answer alleges that said mill was put in opperation on the first of May 1838, and admits that said intestate advanced to said Newton the sum of $1638— Now may it please your Honor although, by the said Newton's own showing the said saw mill has been running for more than a year and a half, said Newton has as yet paid nothing, either to the said Luster or to any of his representatives, either on the said twenty-five hundred dollars due for said land, or on said Luster's part of the profits of said mill— Your orator further states that he believes said Newton to be insolvent, and wholly unable to pay the other just debts due by him—that he continues to run said mill and to cut and use timber off the aforesaid land, both for lumber, and fuel for said mill, the same being a steam mill—that in consequence of the said running of said mill, the same is continually being worn, and is in great danger of being worn out & rendered wholly valueless, and of being burned down, to the great damage of your said orator in his said character & capacity of administrator— that in consequence of the said cutting of timber, the said land is daily decreasing in value, and, unless the same be stopped, will soon be almost entirely valueless, it being of but little value but for the timber—

In tender consideration of all which, your orator prays that an injunction may issue, restraining said Newton from further running said mill, and from cutting any more timber on the land aforesaid— He further prays that the partnership between his intestate and said Newton be dissolved, and said Newton compelled to deliver over to said Receiver, all property belonging to said copartnership, and all books papers, and evidences of debts due the same, and that said debts be collected, and said property sold, by said Receiver, and that from the proceeds of the same, all that is fairly due your orator in his aforesaid capacity of administrator, be paid over to him and that said receiver be authorized to rent out said mill & the dwelling house & coal bank on said land— He further prays that said Newton be compelled to account with your orator for all waste done upon the land aforesaid, and for reasonable rent of the said mill—

He further prays that said Newton be enjoined and restrained from collecting any debt due said copartnership, or for any lumber made at saw mill—

Your orator states that the legal title to said land rests in him—your orator— in his individual capacity

Your orator further states that his intestate, died leaving the following named heirs at law, towit Sarah Luster, since married to one Dr Ann Sherrill, Thomas M. Luster and Perrin D. Luster— whom he prays may be made parties to this Bill— He prays that such other further relief be granted, as equity may require, and as in duty bound &c.

Sworn to before me
this 3d day Decr 1839
    Wm Butler Clk

David Spear

vs   } Sup. Bill

Joel Newton
Withdrawn from
Papers July 31. 1840
    Wm Butler Clk

MR. LINCOLN SPEAKS ON KERR-LOVE CONTEST FOR SEAT IN THE HOUSE OF REPRESENTATIVES, DECEMBER 9, 1839.

The Illinois Legislature met in Springfield for the first time on December 9, 1839, the House, of which Mr. Lincoln was the Whig leader, convening in the Second Presbyterian Church. One of the first matters to claim the attention of the House was the rival claims to a seat of Oscar Love and Richard Kerr of Pike. The report of the ensuing debate is from the Alton Telegraph of December 21. In the evening Mr. Lincoln attended a meeting of the Springfield town board, of which he had been chosen a member on June 21, 1839, to succeed Samuel H. Treat. Discussion of the Kerr-Love contest was continued by the House on December 16, when Love lost his seat by a tie vote, much to the satisfaction of Mr. Lincoln and his fellow Whig members.

Several members elected to fill vacancies appeared. Among them Mr. Love presented a certificate of his election from Pike County to succeed Richard Kerr. Williams of Adams moved that the case be referred to the Committee on Elections, with instructions to enquire whether Mr. Kerr had vacated his seat or not. Kerr had told him he had not resigned.

Resn agreed to and Mr. Love retired.

Shortly afterwards, Mr. Walker of Vermilion, moved to reconsider the vote upon the resolution.

Upon this motion an animated debate took place, in which Messrs. Walker of Vermilion, Happy, English, Carpenter, Ficklin and R. Smith, supported the motion, and Messrs, Williams, Webb, Marshall, Lincoln and others opposed it.

SUIT OF DAVID BAILEY VS. THE ADMINISTRATORS OF NATHAN CROMWELL, DECEASED, APPEAL FROM TAZEWELL TO THE ILLINOIS SUPREME COURT, DECEMBER 9, 1839.
(Herndon-Weik Collection)

*The document here reproduced, beginning with the words "David Bailey appelant" and ending with the signature "Lincoln p-q" was written by Lawyer Lincoln. The rest of the document is in the hands of Stephen T. Logan and Duncan, clerk of the court. This appeal from Tazewell began one of the more important cases which Mr. Lincoln tried before the Supreme Court of Illinois during his early years at the bar. Stephen T. Logan appeared for the appellees, and Mr. Lincoln alone for the appellant securing a reversal of the Circuit Court in a decision afterward cited in both state and federal courts. In accordance with the contention of Mr. Lincoln, the court held "that it was presumption of law in the State of Illinois that every person is free without regard to color; that where the consideration of a promissory note was shown to have been the sale of a negro girl, and that at the time of the sale it was agreed between the parties that, before payment of the note should be demanded, the payee should produce the necessary papers and indenture to prove that the girl was a slave or bound to service under the laws of the State of Illinois, and such papers were not produced though **demanded**,*

*that there was no consideration for the note and that it was void,
as the sale of a free person was illegal." See "Abraham Lincoln;
The Lawyer Statesman" by John T. Richards, Boston, 1916,
Page 208.*

David Bailey appelant ⎫
       vs. ⎪
The administrators of ⎬ Appeal from Tazewell—
Nathan Cromwell ⎪
deceased—appellees ⎭

And now comes the appellant, and says that in the Record
and proceedings in the cause aforesaid, there is manifest error
in this, towit:

1st That the court below erred in sustaining the Demurrer
to the fourth plea—

2nd That the said court erred in giving judgment for the
plaintiffs below on the issues and evidence submitted—

Lincoln p- q-

And the said appellee denies that there is any such error—
nor any others:

Logan for appellee

Administrators of
Nathan Cromwell
    ads
David Bailey
    Transcript
    192
Filed Decr. 9. 1839
J. M. Duncan ck
Jim Matheny D C.
Fee for Transcript $7.04
Certificate and Seal 50
       ——
      $7 54

BILLS INTRODUCED BY MR. LINCOLN IN THE HOUSE, DECEMBER 10, 1839, AND LATER.

*On December 10, 1839, the rule of the House on Mr. Lin-
coln's motion was dispensed with and he introduced a bill authorizing the collectors of an unnamed county "to collect all taxes
now due." The bill was read twice and on his motion referred
to a committee of three. On the same day Mr. Lincoln introduced a bill for "an act relative to the taking of depositions and*

*to the Collector of Menard County." Both of these bills are here
reproduced. It may also be noted in passing that on December
10, 1839, John Calhoun, whom Mr. Lincoln had served as deputy
county surveyor, was elected clerk of the House. Mr. Lincoln,
however, voted for Andrew Johnston, with whom he was to conduct an interesting correspondence in later years.*

A Bill for an act to authorize the Collector of
county to collect certain taxes therein named—

Be it enacted by the people of the state of Illinois represented in the (General Assembly) that the collector of
county be authorized to collect all taxes now due from the inhabitants of that portion of Sangamon count lying within the
following bounds towit Beginning at the South West corner of
Section Three in Township Seventeen North of Range Six West
thence North four miles by the surveys, thence East with the
surveys ten miles thence South with the surveys two miles thence
West with the surveys nine miles thence South with the surveys
two miles, thence West with the surveys one mile to the begining.

A bill for an act relative to the taking of depositions, and to
the Collector of Menard county—

Be it enacted by the People of the State of Illinois, represented in the General Assembly That hereafter in any suit at
law or in Equity wherein the defendant or defendants shall reside without the limits of this state, or shall have gone without
the limits of this state with the intention of removing himself
or themselves, or his or their personal property and effects without the limits of the same, and shall have no attorney known to
the plaintiff or complainant within the limits of this state, it shall
be lawful for the plaintiff or complainant in such suit to take
depositions to be used in the same, in the same manner, as is
now provided by law, excepting that the notice now required
by law to be served on such defendant or defendants shall not
be required to be given; Provided that in every such case the
plaintiff or complainant shall, before taking such deposition, file
with the clerk of the court wherein such suit shall be depending
the affidavit of himself or some other credible person, stating
that he verily believes that said defendant or defendants resides
without the limits of this state, or has gone beyond the limits
of this state with the intention of removing himself or his personal property or effects beyond the limits of the same, and has
no known attorney residing in this state

Sec. 2nd That the collector of Menard county be authorized to collect all taxes now due for the year 1839 from the inhabitants of or on real estate situated within that portion of Sangamon county, which lies within the following boundaries, towit, Beginning at the South West corner of Section Three in Township Seventeen North of Range Six West, thence North four miles by the surveys; thence East ten miles by the surveys; thence South two miles by the surveys; thence West nine miles by the surveys; thence South two miles by the surveys; thence West one mile by the surveys to the beginning.

Sec. 3rd That said collection shall be made in accordance with the assessment heretofore made under the authority of Menard county; and said collector shall pay over the state revenue collected in said district to the state as in other cases; and shall pay one half collected therefrom for county purposes into the county Treasury of Sangamon county, and the other half, into the county Treasury of Menard county—

RESOLUTIONS OFFERED BY MR. LINCOLN AND ADOPTED AT A WHIG MEETING IN SPRINGFIELD, DECEMBER 11, 1839.

Aside from his responsibiliteis as Whig leader in the lower branch of the Illinois Legislature the last weeks of 1839 held much of interest for politically-minded Abraham Lincoln. No doubt near the end of November he read in the Louisville Journal that a section of the Abolitionists had organized the Liberty Party pledged to immediate emancipation and named James G. Birney as its candidate for the Presidency—a diversion which four years later, when Clay was their nominee, was to spell defeat for the Whigs. On December 6, 1839, Harrison, as stated elsewhere, was made the choice of the Whig national convention.

Meanwhile party lines were becoming tightly drawn in Illinois and the Whigs following reluctantly the example set them by their Democratic rivals, adopted the convention system in state and county and set up a central committee to operate the party machinery. This committee, composed almost entirely of Springfield men, called a convention to meet in that town on December 11, 1839, a day after a like assembly by the Democrats, and to this body following a round of speeches by Baker, Browning and others, Mr. Lincoln offered a preamble and resolutions which had prompt and unanimous adoption, but which until the present time have failed to find a place in collections of his writ-

ings. It may be noted that the Democrats did not accept the invitation Mr. Lincoln held out to them; also that in the afternoon of December 11, 1839, he attended a meeting of the town trustees of Springfield and voted for a resolution granting licenses to applicants to keep "groceries" for two months, each applicant giving bond and paying a fee of $50.

Whereas, The Van Buren State Convention, which adjourned on the 10th inst., passed various resolutions denouncing Whig individuals, Whig policy, and the Whig party in general.

Therefore.

Resolved, That every member of that Convention, who introduced any such resolution, or resolutions, or any amendment thereto, be respectfully requested to bring the same, or a correct copy thereof, into this Hall, and to attempt to sustain it by facts and arguments.

Resolved, That on the discussion of said resolutions, we will meet their authors, man for man, and speech for speech, in order that the public may see with whom are the facts, and with whom the arguments.

Resolved, That for the purpose of discussing said resolutions, we will meet their authors on tomorrow evening at 7 o'clock p.m. in this Hall, or at any other time and place that may better suit their convenience.

MR. LINCOLN SUBMITS TO THE HOUSE A PETITION TO VACATE PART OF BENNETT'S ADDITION TO THE TOWN OF PETERSBURG, DECEMBER 17, 1839.

John Bennett, Lincoln's old friend of New Salem days, early in the history of Petersburg laid out an addition to that town bearing his name. Lots apparently did not sell as readily as Bennett had anticipated and so on December 17, 1839, Mr. Lincoln wrote and signed for him a petition to the Legislature praying vacation of a part of the addition. This petition was referred to a House committee of which Mr. Lincoln was made chairman, and in due course its favorable report was approved by the Legislature, the Senate adding to the title of the act, House Bill No. 58, "and for the assessment and collection of taxes in certain counties." It is also to be noted that in the evening of the day in which Mr. Lincoln lent a helping hand to an over-hopeful promoter he also served as one of the managers of a cotillion at the American House, which Elijah Iles had built the previous year and which the people of Springfield proudly proclaimed the *"most imposing structure of its kind west of the Alleghenies."*

A Bill for an act to vacate a part of the town plat of Bennett's addition to the town of Petersburg.

Be it enacted by the people of the state of Illinois represented in the General Assembly that the town plat for Blocks numbered two, three, four and five, in Bennett's Addition to the town of Petersburg, be vacated, Provided that this act shall be null and void as against any individual proprietor or proprietors (if any such there be) of the part of said town hereby proposed to be vacated.

And be it further enacted that it shall be the duty of the county commissioners courts of the counties of Green and to assess a tax for state purposes for the year 1840 which tax shall be thirty cents upon every hundred dollars worth of taxable property and shall be assessed and collected in the same manner and paid into the State treasury at the time and under the same conditions as other State taxes are.

Sec. The auditor of Public accounts at the next session of the General Assembly shall report the amount of taxes which may have been assessed during the year 1840 in the said counties under the provisions of the foregoing Section and compute according to the best data in his possession the difference between the amount of taxes assessed during the said year and the amount of the taxes which under the provisions of the act concerning Public Revenue in force Feb 26 1839 should have been assessed during the years 1839 and 1840. The provisions of this Bill shall apply to all the counties in this state which have failed to make an assessment & collection of taxes for the year 1839.

The Petition of John Bennett praying the vacation of the plat of part of Bennett's addition to the town of Petersburg

Lincoln
Dawson
Gilham

Amd. adopted by
Senate Jany 30th
1840
   B. B.
     Secy

MR. LINCOLN PROPOSES AMENDMENT TO A PENDING LIQUOR BILL, DECEMBER 28, 1839

According to the House Journal for 1839-40 on December

26, 1839 *Mr. Lincoln proposed the amendment set forth below to the liquor bill then pending before that body. Better remembered is the speech Mr. Lincoln had delivered six nights before on the political issues then absorbing public attention, in particular Van Buren's proposed sub-treasury system. This speech climaxed a series of debates between Whig and Democratic contenders which took place between December 14 and 20, 1839, Douglas, Calhoun and Lamborn speaking for the Van Buren Administration, and Logan, Baker and Lincoln for the Whigs. The address prepared with meticulous care by Mr. Lincoln, and again revised for publication was repeated in substance in the more than half a hundred speeches which he delivered during the presidential campaign of 1840, and may be fairly accounted its author's ablest and most effective effort up to that time. And it won him a statewide reputation as a Whig leader from whom great things were to be expected in the future.*

Mr. Webb from the committee on the Judiciary, to whom was referred "A bill for an act to repeal an act, entitled 'An act, regulating tavern and grocery license, and for other purposes; reported a substitute for the bill entitled 'A bill for an act concerning groceries', and recommended its passage. Mr. Henry moved to amend the report by striking out one quart wherever it occurs in the report; which was not agreed to. Mr. Lincoln moved to amend the report by striking out the third section, and the words 'and trustees of incorporated towns,' whenever they occur in the report; which was agreed to.

CHAPTER XI—MR. LINCOLN IN THE YEAR 1840
SURVEY OF PERIOD

The year 1840 in which fell his thirty-second birthday was for Abraham Lincoln another period of steady advance at the bar and in political affairs. Its opening days found him occupied with his duties as leader of the Whigs in the popular branch of the State Legislature which, as already recorded, had met in Springfield for the first time on October 19, 1839; and also appealing to John T. Stuart, his law partner then in Congress, to bring his proposal for Illinois to buy all public lands in the state for twenty-five cents an acre to the attention of John C. Calhoun—an appeal which proved a fruitless one.

The long session of the Legislature which did not adjourn until February 3, 1840, was afterward described by Governor Ford as full of "bitterness and personal hatred." National politics had little if any part in its discussions. Instead the first and chief concern of its members was how to rescue the state from the "financial quick sands in which it had sunk deeply and was still sinking." One remedy was set forth in a series of scathing resolutions offered in the House by Wyatt B. Stapp which declared that a costly system of internal improvements had been imposed upon the people without their knowledge or consent, bringing "ruin and desolation" in its train, and moved repeal of the law which had brought it into being. Thirty-nine members voted with Stapp for its repeal, and the law was saved by an opposing majority of only three, one of whom was Mr. Lincoln.

The fight thus begun continued until the end of the session. Party lines were for the moment lost sight of, and resolution followed resolution, attended in each instance by prolonged and angry debate. Now and then Mr. Lincoln failed to vote on a particular resolution, and his recorded votes reveal a confused state of mind, although he did not falter in his support of a system of which he had been one of the creators. After weeks of futile debate, and equally futile balloting, the doctor father of John A. Logan, then a member from Jackson county, moved that, as the House appeared inclined to break down the internal improvement system at the expense of the State and its banks, this when no proof of corruption was before it, that body should give instant and exclusive attention to the subjects of banks and improvements and adjourn on February 3. Dr. Logan's demand was

*not formally approved by the House, but it spurred that body to
action, and on February 1 it enacted a law which abolished the old
and created a new Board of Public Works and one Fund Commissioner instead of the existing board.*

*Mr. Lincoln's chief concern during a troubled session, how-
ever, was the affairs of the State Bank at Springfield, threatened
with a loss of its charter. "The Legislature," he wrote Stuart in
the closing days of 1839, "has suffered the bank to forfeit its
charter without benefit of clergy," adding "there seems to be little
disposition to resuscitate it." These fears proved without foundation. In the end, Mr. Lincoln, laboring with skill and tact for
the bank, a new law was passed by the Legislature, which set
aside forfeiture of its charter for refusing specie payments, renewed that charter, and "suspended" the laws which forbade the
Bank's continuing in business. Moreover, the restrictions now
placed on conduct of its affairs, restrictions for which Mr. Lincoln voted, were sane and salutary ones. Mr. Lincoln likewise
helped in the passage of measures which assured continuance of
work on the Illinois and Michigan Canal, and temporary settlement of the internal improvement debts.*

*He was also a member of a select committee chosen to pre-
pare and report a bill for the reincorporation of the town of
Springfield, which bill became a law just before adjournment—
"another strand binding Springfield more firmly to the ambitious
young politician and lawyer"; and he took an active and effective
part in the shaping of new and more equitable liquor legislation
for the state. Bills of individual members dealing with this debated subject were duly referred to the House Judiciary Committee, headed by Mr. Lincoln's friend Edwin B. Webb, which
in the last days of December, 1839, reported a substitute for them.
This substitute provided that a high license fee should be exacted
from all liquor dealers, and for a period of weeks provoked a
keen and angry discussion in which Mr. Lincoln, who seconded
another friend, Edward D. Baker, in hearty support of the bill,
was now and again a leading participant. An amendment offered
by him giving county commissioners sole power in the granting
of licenses was agreed to without a vote, and his was one of the
fifty-two ayes to twenty-nine nays which assured final passage
of the bill.*

*The session of the Legislature ended, Mr. Lincoln plunged
into one of the most noisy and picturesque presidential campaigns
in our history. The Whigs, on the plea of availability, had put*

aside Clay for Harrison, but they had adopted no platform, agreeing only in hostility to Van Buren and his party. Daniel Webster wrote of his own party "as made up of different opinions and principles, of gentlemen of every political complexion, uniting to make a change in the administration." But the Whigs felt that they were on the way to a resounding triumph at the polls, and after a brief speaking trip in western Massachusetts and Vermont, Webster in early July reported to a friend: "The general spirit where I have been is extraordinary, marvelous, unprecedented. We are on the high road to the greatest civil revolution ever yet achieved in this country."

Young Mr. Lincoln shared in the confidence of 'the great Whig leader, fanned as it was by volcanic, volatile, and noisy eruptions of not always intelligent sentiment. The story of the speeches he made in all parts of Illinois is set forth at length on later pages. He also found time to play a shaping part in the "monster" Whig demonstration which took place in Springfield on June 4, 1840—"We never before saw such an exhibition of humbug" wrote one Democratic editor;—helped to edit a party paper called The Old Soldier, and led in thoroughly organizing the Whig electorate county by county. "I have never seen the prospects of our party so bright in these parts as they are now," he wrote his partner at Washington. The result of the election confirmed his confidence. Thanks to the dexterity and resourcefulness of which Stephen A. Douglas was to give so many proofs in later years, the Democrats carried Illinois, but the Whigs triumphed in the nation, and Harrison secured 234 out of 294 electoral votes—only to be claimed by death soon after he took office and to be succeeded by John Tyler, by birth and inclining a states right Democrat of the first order.

Called by Governor Carlin two weeks in advance of the regular date the Illinois Legislature assembled on November 23 for the last session of that body which Mr. Lincoln, who had been reelected earlier in the month, ever was to attend as a member. The Democrats had a majority in both branches of the Legislature, but he again received his party's vote for speaker and was its leader on the floor of the House, where, as the governor informed its members, the task first in order was to find means for paying the interest on the state debt falling due on January 1, 1841. There followed weeks of noisy wrangling and confusion, and of unsatisfactory accomplishment, in which Mr. Lincoln and his Whig associates in the House played an unavailing and more than once contradictory part. The result at the year's end was the enactment of two brief laws which repealed the act for the settlement of the internal improvement debts passed at the previous session; directed the state treasurer to take charge of all improvements, and called for the hypothecation of state bonds to raise money for the payment of interest on the improvement debt. Governor Ford, to whom, called from his duties as a justice of the State Supreme Court, shortly fell the handling of an impossible situation, bears angry and regretful witness to the fact that after 1841 no further attempt was made to pay even interest on the state debt and Illinois "became a stench in the nostrils of the civilized world."

PROPOSED AMENDMENT BY MR. LINCOLN TO AN ACT FOR THE RELIEF OF INCORPORATED TOWNS, JANUARY, 1840.

The proposed amendment here reproduced was copied from the original in Mr. Lincoln's hand. The House Journal for 1839-40 shows that it was promptly tabled when submitted to that body.

Strike out the second Section, and insert the following: Sec. 2 The collector of said court shall pay over to the President and Trustees of such incorporated town within his county one half of the county tax collected by him off of property and personal within the limits of such incorporated town.

AMENDMENT TO THE PUBLIC REVENUE ACT INTRODUCED BY MR. LINCOLN, JANUARY 2, 1840

The paragraphs here reproduced were an amendment submitted by Mr. Lincoln on January 2, 1840, to the public revenue act, which duly passed the House. They reveal Mr. Lincoln's careful regard for the interests and welfare of veterans of the Revolution.

That hereafter all Revolutionary pensioners within this state, shall be permitted to loan all or any part of the money which they may have acquired exclusively by means of their pensions, without paying any tax whatever, therefor—

The assessors of the several counties within this state, shall take the production of the regular pension certificate from the War office of the United States as sufficient evidence that the person therein shown to be a Revolutionary pensioner is a Revolutionary pensioner, and shall then take the statement upon honor of such pensioner, as sufficient evidence of the facts whether he has any money loaned other than that acquired by means of his pension, and if so, how much, and on all other questions deemed necessary and proper under this act —

BILL REPORTED BY MR. LINCOLN FOR A STATE ROAD FROM PETERSBURG TO WAVERLY, JANUARY 9, 1840 AND LATER

In the House on January 9, 1840, Mr. Lincoln, mindful of the comfort and convenience of old friends in the New Salem section, presented a petition of citizens of Sangamon and Menard counties for a state road from Petersburg in Menard County to Waverly in Morgan County. The petition on his motion was referred to a select committee of himself and two others which duly reported House Bill 117 here reproduced from the original in Mr. Lincoln's handwriting. John B. Broadwell, one of the commissioners who located this road, was a Sangamon County pioneer, three of whose sons in later years served in the Union Army.

A bill for an act to establish a state road from Petersburg in Menard County to Waverly in Morgan County.

Sec 1st. Be it enacted by the People of the State of Illinois represented in the General Assembly: That John B. Broadwell, John J. Lemon (some one has crossed out Lemon and written in Franklin Minor) and Achilles Morris, be and they are hereby appointed commissioners to view, mark, and locate a state road from Petersburg in Menard County by way of John B. Broadwell's, Berlin, New Berlin and the railroad depot in Sangamon County to Waverly in Morgan County.

Sec 2nd. That said commissioners or a majority of them shall meet in Petersburg on the first Monday of March next or any time within sixty days thereafter and after being first duly sworn, shall proceed to locate said said (sic) road, avoiding as much as possible all injury to private property.

Sec. 3rd. That said commissioners shall make out a separate report of so much of the location of said road as lies in each of said counties, and file the same with the clerk of the county commissioners court of the proper county.

Sec 4th. That said commissioners shall have such compensation out of the Treasuries of said counties as shall be just and reasonable.

UNIDENTIFIED AMENDMENT PROPOSED BY MR. LINCOLN IN THE HOUSE, JANUARY, 1840

This unidentified amendment proposed by Mr. Lincoln and in his handwriting may have had association with the recurring bill for internal improvements discussed by the Legislature in the first half of January, 1840. He remained a strong advocate of the general system established in 1837, and when on January 28, 1840 a bill was passed repealing it he was one of those who voted against it. Two day later he made an earnest but unavailing appeal for reconsideration of this action.

Amend the eighth section by adding thereto the following towit. 'nor upon any contracts except those existing at the passage of this act.'

Provided that contracts which may be transferred from one contractor to another without any change in their terms, shall not be construed to be new contracts.

Provided that no more than five hundred thuosand dollars of said certificates shall at any one time be outstanding.

PROTEST SIGNED BY MR. LINCOLN AGAINST THE HOUSE'S REFUSAL TO IMPEACH JUDGE JOHN PEARSON, JANUARY 11, 1840

Subjects of sharp discussion in Northern Illinois at the close of 1839 and the opening of 1840 were the alleged misconduct of Judge John Pearson of Chicago and the attempt by members of the bar of that city to secure his removal from the bench. It was alleged that as judge he had failed to heed a mandamus issued by the Illinois Supreme Court and at Springfield the House on January 6, 1840, devoted the day to debate on the request for his impeachment. In the end the House refused to impeach Pearson, and on January 17, thirty-two members, a majority of them Whigs, signed a stinging protest against its action. Mr. Lincoln, who was greatly interested in an affair charged with the partisan animosities of Whigs and Democrats, is believed to have had a hand in the framing of this protest, set forth below. After his name, the last on the list, he wrote, with characteristic caution, "True as I believe."

The undersigned Members of the House have seen with unalloyed regret the decision of this House, in favor of the resolution against impeaching John Pearson, Judge 7th Judicial Circuit justly professed against him,

Those charges were of a high and grave character, and as evidence that they were so considered by the house it will be seen that the house resolved by a very large majority to hear the proof relied upon to sustain them.

That proof has been heard — it has not only contended to sustain but is has established by the highest grade of testimony every specification alleged against the respondent. Nor is there one fact stated in those specifications which has not been proved either by the records of the Circuit Courts or the oaths of the Two respectable and intelligent witnesses — And we here embody in this protest some of the facts thus established. It has been proved, that John Pearson, Judge 7th Judicial Circuit, has violated the right of trial by jury. by refusing to permit the Counsel for the prisoner a peremptory challenge to a juror his prescribed number of Challenges not being exhausted — alleging as the reason therefor, a rule of practice of the circuit which was unrecognizable against the forms of the law, and the letter and spirit of the Constitution, He has prevented an appeal from his decisions to a higher tribunal, by refusing in numerous cases to sign "bills of exceptions" containing a statement of his decision and the testimony on which such decision was based, when he as well as the counsel in whose favor he decided admitted these statements to be true. And when the statutes of the state expressly making it his duty to sign such bills of exception have been made to him he still persisted in his refusal, saying that such statutes were but a "legislative flourish."

He has arrogated to himself the right of final decision subject to no appeal by refusing to hear and disobeying the process of the Supreme Court of the State of Illinois, commanding him to sign a bill of exception, thereby treating the mandates of the superior court with contempt, and denying an appeal from the tribunal over which he presided.

He has treated with Contempt and scorn the process of a court of the United States, which he was bound to obey by refusing to hear it and by treating it with utter neglect.

He has acted in an arbitrary and oppressive manner, by threatening to punish counsel for presenting in a respectful manner the process of the Supreme Court and the Circuit Court of the US, and by actually punishing them for so doing, not once only but repeatedly under the influence of passion and excitement, thereby perverting the power placed as a sacred trust in his hands to the indulgence of personal feeling and private resentment,

He has shown culpable ignorance of the law, by quashing an indictment for the sole reason that the clerk had left out one word in the copy delivered to the prisoner and by quashing twenty indictments at one term for the single reason that the date in the caption was in figures when the statute of the State, expressly directs the caption to be so written, thereby permitting crime to have a free course, obstructing public justice, and degrading the character of the Judiciary in the eyes of the world.

These facts have been proved in the presence of this house, and every candid observer will bear us witness that they have received no darker coloring from our statement. And yet with these startling facts fresh in the recollection of the House, it has been solemnly decided by a majority in which was included every number agreeing in political sentiments with the respondent that they did not afford reason that the said John Pearson should be impeached. The decision is final; he is again to ascend the bench, again to be entrusted with the "issues of life and death", again to officiate not merely as minister of stern and impartial justice, but as the representative of the majesty and dignity of the law,

To permit this result, without the formality of a trial, is in our estimation dangerous, if not fatal, to the purity of the judicial character. We have ever struggled to maintain the independence of the judiciary, and to place it high above the assaults of party violence and political feeling, but we have also desired to see all judges, amenable to the law they are called upon to administer, and subject to those restraints wisely provided for in the practice of other countries and the constitution of our own. We believe that in this case the authority of precedent, the usages of the past and the dictates of the constitution have been alike disregarded, and being firmly of opinion that the decision of this house will tend to render our judges irresponsible, and to bring our courts into contempt, to destroy the rights of individuals and cast disrespect on the administration of public justice we therefore present, this remonstrance against the judgment of the house.

And if as citizens of the state rejoicing in her honor ,and sorrowing in her shame, we shall find these predictions fulfilled, and be compelled to look back to the action of this honorable house as a source of judicial tyranny and apprehension, casting a stain upon public character and bringing ruin to individual interests, we at least desire, that all men may know that as we have not assented to the decision so we are not answerable for the consequence. Wherefore against the resolution of this house declaring that the Hon P. Judge should not be impeached and brought to trial, we do most respectfully but earnestly protest

C. B Baker
Archibald Williams
Jas. H. Murphy
Vital Jarrot
Saml. D. Marshall
Wm. H. Henderson
Richard Kerr
Joseph G. Bowman
Wyatt B. Stapp
Allen Emerson
Alexander Phillips
Robert McMullen
John J. Hardin
John W. Read
John Dawson
Wm. Orwell
Jesse K. Dubois
S. Dunn
James Craig
Alden Hull
James G. Cunningham
Rich W. Starr
Wm. F. Elkin
Germanicus Kent
John Henry
Andrew M. Emmick
Moses Harlan
Cheney Thomas
E. B. Webb
W. B. Archer
J. H. Lyons
A. Lincoln (True as I believe)

MR. LINCOLN PRESENTS THE PETITION OF SARAH MARTIN FOR A DIVORCE, JANUARY 16, 1840

One of the clients of Stuart & Lincoln, in 1839 was Sarah Martin who for good and sufficient reasons sought a divorce from her husband, which at that time could only be secured with des-

patch by action of the Legislature. Accordingly Mr. Lincoln drafted the necessary petition, a document filled with human touches of an intimate and revealing sort; had it signed by his client, and on January 16, 1840 presented it to the Legislature. There it was read and on Mr. Lincoln's motion referred to a committee composed of himself and two friends. This committee on January 25, reported the bill reproduced below, and in due course the Legislature dissolved the bonds of matrimony between Nathaniel and Sarah Martin. One wonders what befell this much-enduring wife in after years.

The petition of Sarah Martin late Sarah James to the Hon. the Senate and House of Representatives of the State of Illinois Your Petitioner

would humbly represent to your Honl. Bodies That previous to the 30th day of October, 1839 She was living on the Premises where her first husband had lived and where he died; That She has the care support & education of two little boys confided to her, the children of her deceased husband one of the age of eight years and the other five — That by her care & industry she would have been enabled to support herself and the two little boys But that at the time first above named your Petitioner was married to a man by the name of Nathaniel B. Martin who after six days left her house without assigning any sufficient cause intending as he said to go to Alton and St. Louis and then to return to carry on his business as Blacksmithing in the Town of Springfield, and said he had rented a shop from Wm. Hinkle for that Purpose all which has turned out to be a mere pretence. He has never returned since and is now residing, as she is informed, somewhere in the Iowa Territory. He has never even written to her and moreover he owed when he left her a large amount for some of his debts & she has been called on and greatly harassed. Her first husband was an industrious & practical man as well as a Kind Husband and by his business of Blacksmithing supported his family decently and left a House and lot and a Small personal estate. That all of his personal estate except what was assigned to your petitioner as her dower has been expended for the ntrture & Education of her children. But your petitioner would be assured that what she might in future earn should be her own. She still believes she could by the helping of Providence support herself and children and live in comparative peace and comfort again. But this She thinks cannot possibly be the case while She is bound by the Marriage relation to Said

Martin. That she has now no hopes that he will ever be a helper but a hindrance to her in providing for her family She is sorry to say that he has proved himself utterly unworthy of the confidence she once reposed in him. Your petitioner would wait the ordinary proof of the Law and obtain a divorce at the end of two years on account of his absence But she feels that by so doing She is hazarding her happiness and that of her children and standing liable to have all her property taken by him and his Creditors and thus become a wretched child of want cast on the cold charity of a world too indifferent to the wants or the woes of others. Your petitioner thinks she has learned a sufficient lesson by this sad experience not again to hazard her happiness, her property, her all by a similar act, but by a life of quiet industry and domestic care to render herself worthy of the respect of her neighbors and the regard of those whom she now Petitions. In tender consideration of the Assembly She Prays that your Hon!. Bodies will grant her a divorce from her husband the said Nathaniel B. Martin and thus restore to peace & comfort in some degree one who is doubly a widow — And for this your Petitioner will ever Pray &c

Sarah Martin

A bill for an act to dissolve the bonds of matrimony between Nathaniel B. Martin, and Sarah Martin his wife —

Be it enacted by the people of the state of Illinois represented in the General Assembly That the bonds of matrimony existing between Nathaniel B. Martin and Sarah Martin, his wife, be and they are hereby forever dissolved.

A BILL FOR AN ACT TO AMEND EXISTING ACTS IN RELATION TO CONSTABLES INTRODUCED BY MR. LINCOLN, JANUARY 20, 1840

Mr. Lincoln's activities as Whig leader of the House in the session of 1839-40 covered a wide range. One of them was the introduction by him on January 20, 1840, of a measure of minor importance reproduced below, House Bill 188, which appears to have been written by another hand. It was duly referred to the committee on judiciary but there is no further reference to it in the House Journal.

A Bill for an act to amend the Several acts in Relation to
Constables —

Sec. 1. Be it enacted by the People of the State of Illinois

Represented in General Assembly — That from and after the first day of August next Each and Every Constable elected Shall before he Enters upon the duties of his office Execute in the Presence of the Clerk of the County Commissioners Court of the County for which he was Elected an Instrument in writing Signed by himself and one or more Persons as his Sureties who Shall be free-holders and Residents of Said County To be approved by such Clerk and the approval Endorsed thereon — by which such Constable and his Sureties shall jointly and Severally agree to Pay to Each and Every Person or Person all Sums of Money that the Said Constable may become Liable to Pay by Reason of his neglecting or Refusing Justly and fairly to account for and Pay over all monies which may Come to his hands under any Process or Otherwise by virtue of his Office — which Bond or Instrument of writing shall Remain on file in the office of the Said Clerk for the Benefit of all Persons who may become injured by the Official Conduct of Said Constable — and a Copy of the Instrument of writing aforesaid Certified by the Clerk of the County Commissioners Court of the County Shall be Prima-Facia Evidence of the Execution Thereof —

Sec. 2 If any Constable Shall fail or neglect to Return any Execution with Ten days after the Return day thereof The Party in whose favour the same was issued may maintain an action against the Constable and his Sureties before the Justice who Issued the same or Some Other Justice of the Peace and Recover the amount thereof with Interest from the date of the Judgment upon which said Execution Issued —

Sec. 3 Any Constable to whom any Execution Shall have been delivered and whose Term of Office shall Expire before the Expiration of the Time within which the Collection or Return of Such Execution is Required by law Shall Proceed in all Matters Relating to said Execution and in the Same manner to collect the same that he might have done had the Time of Office of such Constable not Expired and the Constable and his Sureties Shall be liable for any Neglect of duty and for all monies Collected upon Such Executions in the Same manner and to the same Extent that they would have been If the term of Office of Such Constable had not expired —

Sec. 4 On the Return of all Executions the Constable Shall Pay over to the Justice who Issued the Same all money Collected by virtue thereof not Previously Paid to the Plaintiff

Sec. 5 In all actions against Constables and their Sureties

for the Recovery of money Collected by the Constable by virtue of Executions If the Paintiff Recover he Shall be Entitled to Recover Interest from the date of the Judgment upon which the Executions were Issued or If Collected upon Other Process from the date of Such Process — and Execution Shall Issue forthwith upon all Judgments Rendered in Pursuance of this act.

Sec. 6 All actions against Constables and their Sureties Shall be . . . Commenced within Two years from the Expiration of the Office of the Constable —

Sec. 7 All acts and Parts of acts Coming within the Purview of this act be and the same is hereby repealed.

RECEIPT BY MR. LINCOLN FOR FEE DUE STUART & LINCOLN, JANUARY 21, 1840

The fees charged by the firm of Stuart & Lincoln as a rule were extremely modest ones; witness this receipt given by Mr. Lincoln to T. R. Skinner on January 21, 1840.

STUART & LINCOLN

Received, Springfield, Jan. 21st, 1840 of T. R. Skinner, five dollars, being in full of our fee for attending in court to procuring an assignment of Dower to Harriet L. Langston late widow of Isaac L. Skinner.

STUART & LINCOLN

(On back of document)
No. 11. Stuart & Lincoln. Rect. $5.00

REPORT PREPARED IN PART BY MR. LINCOLN OF A JOINT SELECT COMMITTEE TO INQUIRE INTO THE CONDITION OF THE STATE BANK OF ILLINOIS. READ IN BOTH HOUSES AND LAID ON TABLE, JANUARY 21, 1840

When, called by Governnor Carlin, the Illinois Legislature met in special session on December 9, 1839, its chief task was to devise means for mending the finances of the state then in desperate condition. The state's threatened bankruptcy was charged by the Democrats in part to mismanagement of the State Bank of Illinois with headquarters at Springfield, and on the second day of the session one of the Democratic leaders in the Legislature, Orlando B. Ficklin, then at the threshold of a long and brilliant career in politics and at the bar, offered resolutions for a legislative investigation of the bank and of any charges that might be preferred against it.

These resolutions were adopted without opposition and a committee appointed which included Ficklin and Lincoln. Then an alarmist message from Governor Carlin gave a sharper edge to public uneasiness and partisan differences — the country was still suffering from the panic of 1837 — and a fight over proposed remedies began which lasted throughout the session of the Legislature. Meanwhile the Ficklin committee industriously pushed its labors and on January 21, 1840, submitted a majority report. here reproduced, in the preparation of which Lincoln appears to have exercised a directing hand. This report cleverly put forward by inference a compromise course calculated to appeal to perplexed legislators, and although promptly laid on the table in both houses, it helped ten days later, January 31, 1840, to the enactment of a bill which could be fairly accounted a victory for Lincoln and other friends of the bank for it set aside forfeiture of its charter for refusing specie payments; suspended laws against it continuing business, and placed new but not rigid restrictions on its methods.

The undersigned, members of the committee to which was referred the joint resolution of both branches of the Legislature, submit the following report to the Senate:

In obedience to the joint resolution of both branches of the General Assembly, the undersigned proceeded to examine into the condition of the State Bank of Illinois, and into such charges preferred against the Bank as they deemed of sufficient importance, in their bearing upon the interests of the community, to claim the time and attention of the undersigned.

As a reason for not going more minutely into an examination of the condition and conduct of the several Branches of this institution, the undersigned would state, that time has not been afforded them to visit the several Branches, and their information, therefore, relative to the Branches, is derived, in part, from witnesses called before and examined by the undersigned, but mainly from the statements under oath of the President and Cashier of the Parent Bank.

It will be recollected that, during the session of 1836-37, a joint select committee was appointed by the Legislature of Illinois to examine into the condition of the State Bank, with a view of ascertaining, among other things, whether said institution would constitute a safe depository for the funds of the State.

On the 18th day of February, 1837, that committee submitted a report to the House of Representatives, and about the same time a report was also submitted to the Senate, which reports occupied most of the ground, from the organization of the Bank, in 1835, to the then present time.

The undersigned deemed it an act of inutility, not to say of supererogation, to re-investigate and re-examine the same charges examined and reported upon by the former committee, and have therefore directed their attention more particularly to the actings and doings of the Bank since February, 1837.

After a laborious and attentive investigation, the undersigned have prepared the following report, which they beg leave to submit.

As the undersigned believed that the Legislature wished information to enlighten their judgment, and to assist them in coming to a conclusion as to the propriety of renewing the forfeited charter of the Bank, they deemed it not improper to bestow most of their attention upon the following inquiries:

1st.   Whether there had been any circumstances of mismanagement of the affairs of the Bank, or mal-practices on the part of her officers, or any of them, against which future legislation might guard, or which would render the institution unworthy of public confidence?

2d.   Whether the stock in said Bank, owned by the State, is safe; and whether the interest of the State and the interests of the People would be consulted by a renewal of the charter of the Bank?

By reference to the joint resolution of both houses, it will be seen that the first inquiry is, "whether the Bank has forfeited its charter?"

The 25th section of the charter, as amended, provides that if the Bank shall, for sixty days after demand, neglect or refuse to pay its evidences of debt in specie, it shall forthwith close all its business except the collecting and securing of its debts, and the charter shall be forfeited.

More than sixty days have elapsed since the Bank announced that it had suspended specie payments, and, as applications for the specie redemption of its liabilities have doubtless since been made and refused, the undersigned have no doubt that the charter of the Bank would be declared forfeited by the proper court, on proof of such demand and refusal. The forfeiture, they believe, would date on the sixtieth day from the day of refusal. The charter, therefore, although not yet adjudicated upon, must certainly be forfeited, when the subject is brought before the proper tribunal.

The next inquiry which the committee is directed to make is, "what rates of the discounts of the Bank have been to persons living out of the State?"

The examination of the statements of the Bank has produced in our minds some surprises at the smallness of the business which the Bank has done with non-residents. The amount now due the Bank on loans and discounts to non-residents, amounts to but four per cent of the whole sum of the debt due the Bank. The documents which form a part of this report, give information as to the distribution and character of this debt.

The committee are next instructed to inquire as to the character of the transactions of the Bank with the house of Nevins, Townsend & Co., of New York.

The object of the inquiries on this subject appears to be to ascertain if the Bank, in its transactions with this house, has loaned them money, either without or at a low rate of interest; or has suffered any portion of the stock which they own in the Bank to remain unpaid; and, whether the Bank did not keep in their hands, for their advantage, large sums of money, while our citizens who applied to the Bank for funds in New York, were refused them.

A full examination of the accounts of this house with the Bank, has assured the undersigned that none of these abuses have existed.

This house has been employed by the Bank as its agent in New York for the transaction of most, if not all, of its business to be done through an agent in that city. Their agency commenced, as appears from the documents herewith submitted, by the transfer to them from the Phoenix Bank, of New York, out of the funds received by that Bank in payment of the capital stock of the State Bank, paid in by individuals of one hundred thousand dollars; which they were instructed to invest in gold coin for the use of the Bank, and one half of which they shortly afterwards forwarded to the Bank in gold. The funds of the Bank having accumulated at this time in New York, from the paying in of the capital stock, and the Phoenix Bank having refused to allow any interest thereon, a portion of it was deposited with Nevins, Townsend & Co., who gave security and allowed six per cent interest on it. It did not remain long in their hands, however; a demand for eastern exchange arising at home which occasioned its withdrawal. For some time past this house has constantly been the creditor of the Bank for large sums of money paid on the checks of the Bank; and, at the present time, the Bank is their debtor in the sum of $150,000.

The undersigned have not been able to discover any thing objectionable in these transactions. It would seem that this house was not only able but willing to make large advances to the Bank, and that some advantage must have resulted to those whom the Bank was, by these means enabled to accommodate with checks on New York. The necessity of some agency of the Bank in New York is obvious; and no reason is seen for the preference of a bank over private bankers, if they are not able to give satisfactory security, as is the case with the house of Nevins, Townsend & Co., who are bankers of high character.

The committee are next instructed to inquire if the capital stock subscribed by Samuel Wiggins, of Cincinnati, has been paid in?

In prosecuting this inquiry, they have ascertained that Samuel Wiggins was the original holder of the stock of the Bank, to the amount of nearly $200,000, on which he paid several of the earlier instalments; but that, being disappointed in the sale of his stock, he applied to the Bank and obtained loans to the amount of $108,000, for the refunding of which he pledged his bank stock; which money, so obtained, was applied in paying up the calls made by the Bank on the purchasers of its stock. This is said to be the only instance, except an amount of about $3,000 to other individuals, in which this odious practice has been resorted to — a subterfuge and evasion of the law of this character has been practised in other States to an alarming extent, so as to make the capital of particular banks rest upon a paper instead of a metallic basis. While the undersigned regret that any, even a solitary case of this sort, should have been tolerated by the Directors of the State Bank and do not incline to offer for it any palliation whatever, they at the same time feel highly gratified that this practice, so obnoxious to well founded institutions, has not been general; but that all the other payments of subscriptions upon stock have been made in gold and silver, or in such funds as were authorized to be received by the charter of the Bank.

It has also been made the duty of the committee to ascertain the nature of the transactions of the Bank with the house of Denman, of Philadelphia; whether any loans were made by them; whether they were permitted the free use of money collected by the falling due of bills drawn on them on account of pork, bacon, lard and lead, shipped them by the Bank, and whether any bills drawn on them have been renewed to prevent protest.

The undersigned have not been able, in their examination, to find the slightest trace of any connection between the Bank and the house in question, other than that which has grown out of the purchase by the Parent Bank and the Alton Branch, from our citizens, of bills of exchange drawn on said house. Mr. Denman is believed, by the undersigned, to be a responsible and wealthy commission merchant, a part of whose business is, dealing in western produce, as agent for the shippers, and they feel it is due to him to state that all the bills on him, held by the Bank, have been fully paid when due.

The next subject of inquiry is, the transactions of the Bank with the house of Grigg & Weld, of Boston.

It appears that the Bank was the holder of about $70,000 of the acceptances of this house, of drafts drawn on them at Alton, and negotiated by the Branch of the Bank there, when they failed, and since that time this debt has been reduced to $23,000, which sum is considered by the officers of the Bank as being pretty well secured.

Intimately connected with this branch of the inquiry is the transactions of the Bank with the house of Godfrey, Gilman & Co., of Alton.

The tabular statement of the cashier shows the amount of the liabilities of this house as drawers, discounters and endorsers, to have swollen to the immense amount of $800,748.00 which has since been reduced to the sum of $419,358.00. This debt also is considered to be made safe by collateral security.

The undersigned feel reluctance in introducing the names of these individuals and their private accounts with the Bank from the fact that public rumor was rife with reports and charges against them, and had not failed to set forth the facts in as glowing colors, at least, as they merited.

These two cases are deemed sufficient to demonstrate the impolicy of the Bank extending such large accommodations to individuals or firms; many objections might be urged to this course. The undersigned, however, will proceed to notice only a few of them.

1st.   It deprives the Bank of the power of fulfilling one of its important functions, to wit: the extending its accommodations to the community generally.

2d. It is exceedingly hazardous to risk so much upon the solvency of a single individual or firm, as a single failure may result in the loss of the entire debt.

3d. The individual or firm having access to the Bank and being permitted the free use of its funds may monopolize the trade in any speculation or enterprise in which he chooses to embark.

4th. Nothing is better calculated to engender heart-burnings and to enlist enemies of the most hostile character against a Bank than for the community to entertain the belief that the institution is used for the benefit of the few to the exclusion of the many. It will be recollected that a charge similar to this was made against the late Bank of the United States, and to sustain that charge it was urged that Mr. T. Biddle, in October, 1830, was indebted to that institution in the sum of $1,120,000. If the objection had any weight in it as applied to the United States Bank, with its immense capital and circulation, with how much greater force does the objection apply to our Bank having a circulation less than $3,000,000.

It is understood that the Directors of the Parent Board, aware of the impropriety of this course, have adopted measures to restrain Directors of Branches in again making such excessive loans. While the undersigned decidedly disapprobate this practice of extending such large accommodations to individuals or firms, they are gratified to have the opportunity to bear testimony that the Bank in a large majority of cases has made her discounts to dealers wanting small sums for immediate use, as will be seen by reference to a tabular statement furnished by the Bank and herewith presented.

For the nature and extent of the loan to the Bank of Missouri, reference is made to the copy of contracts between the two banks, which is herewith presented.

The transaction was not fully carried out, and the amount loaned was soon returned. The arrangement seems to have been made from a desire on the part of this Bank to cultivate friendly relations with a neighboring institution which was about to go into operation. It was a part of the contract with the Missouri Bank that she should redeem in specie, if necessary, the paper of the State Bank loaned to her. The undersigned see nothing objectionable in this transaction.

The undersigned is also charged with the inquiry, whether the Bank has dealt or speculated in lead, lands, or any other commodity. So far as the undersigned have been able to hear and ascertain the facts, the Bank has not engaged in speculation in lead, lands or any other commodity. In relation to this charge the undersigned have availed themselves of the testimony of the officers of the Bank, of correspondence touching these transactions, and of the testimony of respectable gentlemen residing at the point where these abuses are said to have occurred.

The Bank professing to be desirous to enhance the price of lead in the hands of the miner or smelter, and to give the profits incident to its reshipment, to the commission merchants of Alton, rather than to those of St. Louis, who had hitherto monopolized the trade, made arrangements to have lead shipped to J. G. Lamb, of Alton, who was to act as the mutual agent of the owner of the lead and the Bank, in its reshipment and sale. Upon the sale of the lead, after refunding the money advanced, where the shipment was first made to the agent, say about three-fourths of the market price of the lead, together with interest, commissions and other costs, and charges incident to the operation, the overplus accruing from the sale thereof was to be paid to the fomer owner, thereby making the Bank neither gainer or loser by the fluctuation in price of the article so shipped.

The statements of the officers of the Bank is corrobated by the testimony of the other witnesses examined as to this point as will more fully appear by the accompanying depositions.

While the undersigned fully acquit the Bank of the charge of speculating or dealing in lead, they are constrained to animadvert upon the course as being unwise and improper on the part of the Bank. It is most obvious that as soon as the arrangement above alluded to was made public, (and its publicity could not easily be prevented), the commission merchants in St. Louis, and the keen-eyed speculator of the mineral region, whose interests would be affected injuriously by this operation of the Bank, would wage a simultaneous war against the institution, and, prompted by the ever living principle of cupidity, each would try to excel the other in the malignity of the attack and the ferocity of its prosecution.

Experience has shown us that such was the result of this enterprise; and the avowed good intentions of the Bank have not only been thwarted, but much odium has been brought to bear against the institution in consequence of the lead operation.

The undersigned believe that a bank should pursue the "even tenor of her way," without lending her influence and her funds to stimulate any particular individual in any particular branch of business; and whenever she departs from her plain path of duty, she is likely to awaken the vigilant jealousy of the people, and bring upon her own head either ruin or a loss of confidence, which, to a Bank, is infinitely worse.

In relation to the charge of the Bank dealing in pork, the undersigned would say, that they have no evidence of that fact; but, on the contrary, if such had been the case, those cognizant of it have failed to make the proof. There is one circumstance, however, connected with this charge, to which the undersigned will advert.

The cashier of the Chicago Branch, with a view of engaging in the purchase of pork with Mr. E. K. Hubbard, and Mr. Dole, procured their note to be discounted, and obtained funds for the purpose aforesaid.

Although the undersigned do not deny the right of any officer of the Bank, in common with other citizens, to receive accommodations, yet they deem it inexpedient to embark in speculations of the staple commodities of the country, and more especially so when the Bank is not prepared to accommodate all who might desire to obtain its paper.

If the Bank at the time referred to had been prepared to discount the notes of all who applied, this circumstance would probably have excited no remark, but so soon as the notes of others were rejected the disappointed applicants bitterly complain of favoritism being extended to Bank officers.

If there is any one subject of which the people are more easily excited than any other, and in regard to which their jealousy never slumbers, it is as to the privileges and powers of Banks. Therefore, every precaution should be used by those institutions to guard against such charges, or at least to furnish them no foundation to rest upon.

The undersigned have not been able to ascertain that the Bank has dealt or speculated in lands further than was absolutely necessary for the erection of her banking houses.

The next inquiry relates to the suspended debts of the Bank at the branches of Alton, Galena, and Chicago. As the examination in prosecution of this inquiry necessarily involves an exhibition to the undersigned of the transaction of the Bank with a number of private individuals and as publication of their names and accounts would effect no public good, they have declined doing so, and will only state the general results of the examination.

A considerable amount of debt exists at these Branches which, at the present, is unproductive, and must require much time in the collection.

Although a portion of these debts will in all probability be lost, it is not believed that the loss will be sufficiently heavy to impair eventually the capital stock of the Bank.

It will be seen by a reference to an exhibit furnished by the Bank that a contingent fund of about $170,000 has been set apart, which, the undersigned believe, will indemnify the Bank in any losses on her suspended debt, and the other debts due the Bank and Branches are believed to be well secured.

In answer to the inquiry, what portions of the loans of the Bank have been made to Bank Directors, the undersigned refer to a statement made by the officers of the Bank, and accompanying this report.

The amount due from Bank Directors was heretofore larger than it now is, and has been reduced by the going out of office of some who were largely indebted. The undersigned do not believe that the liability of the present Directors is greater than might be safely extended to other individuals of equal number and responsibility not connected with the Bank.

The committee next proceeded to investigate the charge contained in the following portion of the resolution, to wit: "also the character of the transaction between the Acting Fund Commissioner and the President of the Bank" in negotiation of the bonds sold to constitute the stock owned by the State in that institution, and if the bonds, at or since the time of their purchase by the Bank, could not have been sold for cash at or above par, and whether any money has been paid in to represent the stock of the State.

The answer of the officers of the Bank to this inquiry is, that after fruitless efforts to sell the stock at par, it was offered to the Bank in payment of the subscription of the State stock, and was accepted by that institution, and that the bonds have ever since been offered at par but have not been sold.

The amount of stock so sold to the Bank was $1,665,000, and the sum of $335,000 was paid in cash, making in all $2,000,000.

While it is granted that the sale of the State bonds owned by the Bank would have enabled that institution to enlarge her circulation, and thereby accommodate more persons, it is deemed very questionable whether, in the present crisis, the stockholders and note holders of the Bank are not in a better condition than if the State bonds had been sold, for the reason that they can be used to obtain funds either by sale or hypothecation.

The next inquiry is, "whether the Bank has not dealt unfairly in declaring dividends and reporting means as available which are in reality unavailable and in bad debts?"

The question of the propriety or impropriety of dividends of the Bank must depend on the amount of its bad debts as compared with its surplus fund and reserved profits.

These latter the officers of the Bank have stated on their oaths they believe to equal or exceed the former, and the undersigned have no reason to differ from them in opinion on this subject.

Some of the committee are aware that there has been a great anxiety with some persons connected with the public works, that the dividends should be as large as possible, and were fearful that this influence might have operated on the Directors, but they have no evidence of such a result.

The last inquiry which the committee are directed to make is, "whether houses connected with some of the principal officers of the Bank have not been accommodated largely to the exclusion of others equally solvent?"

The undersigned feel it to be their duty to state, without hesitation, that there is not the slightest evidence to support a charge of this character.

The undersigned, before passing on, will offer some reflections upon the causes of the suspension of specie payments by the Bank. It will be recollected that when the Banks of Philadelphia and New York suspended specie payments in 1837, that the western and southern Banks almost simultaneously followed in their train.

When the Philadelphia Banks suspended specie payments last fall, many of the western and southern banks also found it necessary to close business. There is a chain of connexion between the banks of the interior and those of the Atlantic cities which obliges the former to follow the course of the latter, and the suspension of the banks located in the centre of trade is felt by all the banks in the Union.

This is not attributable to any organic defects of the institions themselves, but to the irresistible law of trade and exchange, which cannot be controlled by country banks.

The position of our banks is doubly unfortunate; they have not only to guard against the accumulation of their paper in the eastern cities but have also to keep an eye upon St. Louis, at which point much of the trade of the west centres.

When we superadd to those causes the fact that the funds (mostly gold and silver) of the General Government collected in the land offices in this State, have (with the exception of a limited deposite in the Branch at Chicago) been transported to and deposited in the Banks of Kentucky and the Bank of Missouri, it must therefore be admitted that the Banks of this State have had a peculiarly difficult task to perform in keeping up the credit of their paper.

Under this view of the subject, unless it is first shown that our Banks had some agency in bringing about the suspension by the Banks of the Atlantic cities in 1837 & '39 your committee percieves but little cause to visit any very heavy denunciations upon our institutions for doing an act which they were urged to by the most imperious necessity.

An opinion as to the solvency of the Bank to meet and to pay all demands against it, will, no doubt, be expected from the committee.

It will be perceived from the statement of the condition of the Bank filed herewith, that her entire circulation amounts to $2,786,315, and that her whole liabilities are $3,924,002 84; while she has on hand $2,464,750 of Illinois State bonds; $2,710,476 76 of notes discounted and due from individuals to the Bank; $440,182 10 of money loaned to individuals by the Bank, and secured by mortgage on real estate; bills of exchange $786,974 89; real estate $72,611 33; due from other Banks $435,624 27; due by State of Illinois $141,089 46; notes of other Banks $152,275; of gold and silver coin $173,869 32; making in all $7,677,794 13. This sum your committee deems amply sufficient to indemnify not only note holders and other creditors of the Bank, but also to secure the State for all the stock which she owns in the institution; and in the event of the Bank not being resuscitated, your committee apprehend no danger of the State sustaining any loss upon its Bank stock.

Before closing this report it is but an act of justice due from the undersigned to the officers of the Parent Bank, to state, that they afforded the committee every facility in their power to aid them in a free and full investigation into the condition of the Bank and into the conduct of its various officers.

B. Monroe
Jno. D. Woods
  Of the Senate.
Orlando B. Ficklin,
A. Lincoln.
  Of the House of Representatives.

BILL AUTHORIZING THE PURCHASE OF A HOUSE FOR THE USE OF THE GOVERNOR REPORTED BY MR. LINCOLN, JANUARY 24, 1840

When Springfield supplanted Vandalia as capital of the state and construction of a new capital building began there was promptly voiced a popular demand for the proper housing of the governor of the state. Accordingly Mr. Lincoln drew and on January 24, 1840, reported from the House committee on finance the bill here reproduced authorizing the purchase by the auditor of public accounts of a house for the use of the governor. This bill was duly enacted and carried into effect, but after 1856 the governor was housed in a mansion to which his occupancy gave a name — a fine structure which long remained one of the show places of Springfield.

Sec. 1st Be it enacted by the People of the state of Illinois represented in the General Assembly, That the Auditor of Public Accounts be and he is hereby authorized to purchase a suitable house and lot within the town of Springfield, for a residence for the Governor of the state, Provided the same shall not cost more than eight thousand dollars.

Sec. 2nd The Auditor shall issue his warrant on the Treasury for the amount agreed on by him for said purchase, in favour of the person of whom said purchase shall have been made. —

Sec. 3rd Before issuing his warrant as aforesaid, the Auditor shall particularly enquire into and ascertain that a clear and unencumbered title to the house and lot so purchased can be made, and moreover shall actually take a conveyance of such title to the Governor of the state of Illinois for the use of the People of said state.

Sec. 4th Upon the completion of such purchase and conveyance, the Auditor shall notify the Governor thereof; and after one month subsequent to said notice, no allowance for house rent, or traveling expenses shall be made to the Governor.

MR. LINCOLN AND OTHERS DISCUSS THE SUBJECT OF INTERNAL IMPROVEMENTS, JANUARY 30, 1840

The issue of the Sangamo Journal for February 7, 1840, contained this report of the House discussion of internal improvements on January 30, 1840, to which reference has been made in another place. It is again to be noted that the Whig leader's plea proved an unavailing one.

Hardin said this measure had been before the House in a dozen different shapes, every day for a month and he hoped it would be pressed upon the attention of the House no longer. Mr. Lincoln said, he thought this a question of sufficient importance to justify this last effort in behalf of a proposition, to save something to the State, from the general wreck. It was very true that similar propositions had before been voted down in this House by large majorities; but it might be a returning sense of justice, would induce this House to acknowledge, upon this last opportunity, that at least some portion of our internal improvement should be carried on. That after the immense debt, we have incurred in carrying these works almost to completion, at least one work calculated to yield something towards defraying its expense, should be finished and put in operation. Everybody acknowledged that this much, if no more, should be done; and why not come up to the question here, with the same candor that we do out of doors?

AMENDMENT BY MR. LINCOLN OF AN ACT IN RELATION TO PROMISSORY NOTES, JANUARY 30, 1840

Below is given an entry from the House Journal for January 30, 1840, which deals with Mr. Lincoln's final activities in the session of 1839-40.

Engrossed bill for "An act in relation to promissory notes was read a 3rd time and on motion of Mr. Lincoln, amended as follows; Provided, that nothing should be construed to legalize the taking of more than 12% interest annum, in any case whatever." Bill passed with this amendment. (No record vote).

AN ACT TO AMEND THE SEVERAL LAWS IN RELATION TO THE ILLINOIS AND MICHIGAN CANAL, BELIEVED TO HAVE BEEN DRAWN BY MR. LINCOLN, APPROVED FEBRUARY 1, 1840.

As this is a printed document in the Laws of Illinois, there is no evidence that it is the work of Abraham Lincoln, for it does not bear the signature of its author. Internal evidence of the wording does not lead to the conclusion that he composed the law, for there were several men in Illinois who were as capable with words as Mr. Lincoln, and a routine enactment permits of little clue to the author. The same can be said of many of the legal papers of Mr. Lincoln; anyone might have written them. In them, however, we have evidence of his handwriting, his usage of extra spacing, and at times he strays from the formal wording of a legal paper.

The possibility that Mr. Lincoln was the author of this bill either in part or in whole, is based on the fact that he reported it from the select committee, and one of his biographers has stated "that he probably wrote the bill that was finally passed." Mr. Lincoln was chairman of the Select Committee for further prosecution of the canal, and as he reported an amendment providing for the pursuit of work on it, it is possible that he may have had a hand in the composition of an act to amend other laws on the matter. The report was made on January 22, 1840, ten days before final enactment of the bill.

The canal had been proposed in a report in 1835, suggesting construction of an artificial waterway to connect Lake Michigan and the Illinois River. Mr. Lincoln supported the plan as part of a program of internal improvements that, as is known, almost bankrupted the State of Illinois. The law of February 1, 1840, is included with the works of Mr. Lincoln, but with the qualifications given above, which permit the possibility of its being his handiwork, but which allow no definite conclusion in the matter.

SEC. 1. Be it enacted by the People of the State of Illinois, represented in the General Assembly, That it shall be the duty of the commissioners of the Illinois and Michigan Canal to sell so much of the canal lands and lots, the present year as may be required to pay the interest on the loans made for canal purposes; sales made under this act shall be conducted and under the same restrictions as required by the act to which this is an amendment: Provided, however, if the commissioners shall be of opinion the interest of the State requires more than ten per cent. to be paid at the time of sale, they shall state in their advertisements the amount that will be required to be paid at the time of purchase.

SEC. 2. Where timber land is selected for sale, it shall be the duty of the commissioners to divide it into small lots, not to exceed forty acres in one lot, and to require one fourth of the purchase money to be paid at the time of purchase, and the balance to be paid in three annual installments, with six per cent. interest, paid in advance for the first year. Sales made under the provisions of this act shall be subject to the same forfeitures and restrictions as required in the several acts authorizing the sales of canal lands.

SEC. 3. There shall be one principal engineer, who shall have a salary of two thousand dollars per annum; there shall be one resident engineer, who shall have fifteen hundred dollars per annum; there shall be seven assistant engineers, who shall each have a salary of one thousand dollars per annum. And the engineers aforesaid shall not receive any other compensation for their services, under any pretence whatever: Provided, that the work on the canal progresses. But it shall be the duty of the board of canal commissioners to discharge such assistant engineers, whenever said work is suspended.

SEC. 4. It shall be the duty of the commissioners, when any person or persons claim damages that they may have sustained, by the construction of the Illinois and Michigan canal, to settle with any such person or persons for the damages they may have received, and pay the same: Provided, If the commissioners are of opinion the claim is too high, and the claimant will not take a fair compensation, they shall call the appraisers as required in the act to which this is an amendment, and they shall proceed, as required in said act. Said appraisers shall receive a reasonable compensation, not to exceed five dollars per day, for their services, for the time necessary to perform the duties required of them as such appraisers and shall be paid out of the canal fund.

SEC. 5. That the board of public works of this State, whose appointment is provided for in a bill, entitled "An act to provide for the settlement of debts and liabilities incurred on account of internal improvements, in the State of Illinois," shall be, and they are hereby, authorized to employ not exceeding four assistant engineers, at a salary not exceeding one thousand dollars per annum.

SEC. 6 That the compensation of the chief engineer, whose appointment is provided for in the bill referred to in the preceding section, shall be two thousand dollars per annum, any bill or law to the contrary notwithstanding.

SEC. 7. The act passed February 27, 1839, entitled "An act to provide for a loan for canal purposes," is hereby so changed as to authorize the interest on bonds hereafter sold under the provisions of said act to be paid semi-annually.

SEC. 8. The Governor, Auditor, and Treasurer of this State, shall settle the accounts of the several agents employed by the Governor, within the last year, to negotiate canal loans, or to convey funds from Eastern cities to this State, and allow them respectively, a compensation of five dollars a day for the time occupied by them in the performance of these services; except in cases where a different agreement has been made with them by the Governor; and if any such agent has retained a greater compensation than herein allowed, he shall be required to refund the overplus, and the same shall be added to the canal fund: Provided, That no person shall be entitled to receive from the State a per diem compensation for services performed in two or more different capacities at the same period of time.

SEC. 9. Should there be no funds on hand to meet the liabilities of the State to the contractor, for labor done on the Illinois and Michigan canal, at the estimate to be made on the first of March next, it shall be the duty of the commissioners of said canal to issue their checks to contractors for such amount as may be found then due, as now provided by law, and payable whenever funds have been deposited for that purpose, bearing an interest at the rate of six per cent: Provided, that this provision shall not extend to estimates made after said first day of March next: Provided, also, That in no case shall such checks be issued for a smaller amount than one hundred dollars.

Approved, February 1, 1840

CHARTER OF THE SPRINGFIELD MECHANICS UNION DRAWN BY MR. LINCOLN AND GRANTED FEBRUARY 3, 1840.

This charter of the Springfield Mechanics Union, granted on the last day of the first session of the Illinois Legislature held in Springfield, has an interesting story behind it. Three movements in the middle decades of the last century helped to shape public opinion in all parts of the land. These were the temperance movement, the uprising against slavery, and organized efforts to better the condition and widen the outlook of the average man. Each of the three had earnest supporters in Springfield.

The Washington Temperance Society of the town had 700 members, including Abraham Lincoln, and its Colonization Society held weekly meetings and collected funds for the settlement of negroes in Liberia, hoping in this way to solve the slavery question, while in April, 1837, following the example of other towns of the Middle West, the Springfield Mechanics Institute was established with John F. Rogue, architect of the new state house, as its president. The Institute had a short and uneventful career, and in 1839 was succeeded by the Springfield Mechanics Union for which, at the request of its projectors, Mr. Lincoln drew the charter reproduced in this place.

The efforts of the Mechanics Union, which soon counted 200 members drawn from nearly two score callings, to help the artisans of Springfield were varied ones, and covered an eight-year period. There was only one college graduate, it may be noted, among its members—Calvin Goudy, a printer. Simeon Francis, editor of the Sangamo Journal, was the first president of the Mechanics Union, and among its other founders were George R. Weber, editor of the Illinois Journal, who later was to see service in both the Mexican and Civil Wars; Edmund R. Wiley, a tailor, whose son and namesake was to become colonel of one of the first colored regiments enrolled under President Lincoln; Caleb Birchall, a bookbinder; Thomas Lewis, a New Jersey shoemaker who settled in Springfield in 1837, and in after years had a long and eventful career; William D. Herndon, a brick mason; John E. Roll, a plasterer, who, when a growing lad at Sangamo Town, had helped young Lincoln build the flatboat in which the latter made the trip to New Orleans which preceded his settlement at New Salem; and finally Charles Ludlum, a mason, who was to rent the Lincoln home while Mr. Lincoln was in Congress.

The Mechanics Union flourished for seven and a half years, and during that period collected nearly $1,000 in dues and fines with which in 1842 it bought a building and established a school for the children of its members. The school's principal in its third year was Francis Springer, later president of Illinois University, whose annual salary in a day of first things was $800. The Mechanics Union also held monthly meetings which were addressed now and then by prominent men willing to contribute their services. Thus Abraham Lincoln was asked to be the speaker on the evening of July 29, 1841. He accepted the invitation, but no record has been found of his topic or how he handled it.

Be it enacted by the people of the state of Illinois, represented in the General Assembly, That . . .
and their associates, and successors be, and they are hereby con-

stituted, a body politic and corporate, under the name of The Springfield Mechanics Union, for the purpose of affording relief to the sick and disabled members thereof, and to the widows and orphans of deceased members; for the establishment of a common school, and a public library; and for the promotion of literature, science, and the mechanic arts; and for no other purpose whatever.

Sec. 2 The said corporation, on the establishment of their common school, shall receive from the school commissioners of the county the same amount of money, in the same proportion, and apply the same to such tuition in the same manner, as other common schools are paid and kept: Provided that the teachers or instructors, of said school shall be selected by the corporation, and be under the control of its by-laws.

Sec. 3 The said corporation by the name of The Springfield Mechanics Union, is declared and hereby made capable in law to sue and be sued, plead and be impleaded; to have a common seal, and the same to alter or rename at pleasure, to make and adopt a constitution and by-laws for the government of the corporation, not inconsistent with the laws of this state, or the Constitution of the United States, and the same to alter or amend whenever it may be deemed necessary; provided that the said corporation shall not hold more than five acres of land with the improvements thereon, for a longer term than one year, except such as may be donated to, and for the sole use and behoof of the corporation.

Sec. 4 The officers of this corporation shall consist of a President, Vice President, Secretary, Treasurer, and a board of seven directors, who shall continue in offiec for the term of one year, and until their successors are elected, together with such other officers as may be provided for by the constitution and by-laws of the corporation. The duties, rights, privileges, and liabilities of the aforesaid officers to be defined by the constitution and by-laws of said corporation.

Sec. 5 All fines and forfeitures for non attendance, delinquency imposed by the constitution and by-laws provided for in third section of this act, not exceeding twenty five dollars, in any individual case, shall be recoverable by action of debt, before any justice of the peace of the proper County, by the said Company in their corporate capacity, which shall be for the use of the corporation.

Sec. 6 This corporation shall not be dissolved nor a dividend made of its funds, while there are seven resident members in favor of continuance.

Sec. 7 The legislature hereby reserve the right to amend or repeal this act whenever in their opinion the public good may require it.

Sec. 8 This act to be in force from and after its passage.

Amend the bill by filling the blank in the first section with Caleb Bundell, Thomas Lewis, Edmund R. Wiley, William D. Herndon, Simeon Francis, George R. Weber, Walter Davis, George Wood, and R. H. Coflin.

PLAINTIFF'S DECLARATION IN THE SUIT OF HOOD VS. GRAY, FEBRUARY 6, 1840

(Herndon-Weik Collection)

Mr. Lincoln drew the declaration in this case. The cover notations, the date of filing by Butler excepted, are also in his hand. The decision of the court is rendered in the footnote to the plea of March 5, 1840, in his case. Work on the new state house was in progress when this suit was brought, and familiar sights on the streets of Springfield in summer and autumn days were long chains of oxen, ten and twelve to a team, drawing heavy blocks of stone to Springfield from a quarry not far from the town. The Hood-Gray litigation may have had its birth in this state of things, for the John F. Rogue mentioned in Hood's complaint was the baker turned architect who designed the state house and had a hand in its erection.

Archibald Hood

vs } Decln

John W. Gray

Filed Febry. 6" 1840
Wm. Butler clerk

State of Illinois }
Sangamon county }   Of the March term of the circuit
and circuit }   court of said county A. D. 1840

Archibald Hood, plaintiff, complains of John W. Gray, defendant, in custody &c. of a plea in assumpsit: For that whereas heretofore, towit on the   day of October   in the year of our Lord one thousand eight hundred and thirtynine, at the county and circuit aforesaid the said defendant bargained for and bought of the said plaintiff, and the said plaintiff at the special instance and request of the said defendant, then and there sold to the said defendant a certain   lot of   cut stone, at the price of three hundred dollars

to be by the said plaintiff, cut according to a certain draft procured by the said defendant to be made and delivered to the said plaintiff by one John F. Rogue, and the said lot of stone to be ready for delivery by the said plaintiff to the said defendant at the said plaintiffs shop   in   Springfield   in the county and circuit aforesaid, within the three weeks then next ensuing and to be paid for by the said defendant as follows to wit, one hundred dollars to be paid by the said defendant to the said plaintiff on or before the said plaintiff should be ready to deliver the said lot of stone, and the remaining two hundred dollars to be paid by the said defendant to the said plaintiff within the nine months then next ensuing; and in consideration thereof, and that the said plaintiff, at the like special instance and request of the said defendant, had then and there undertaken and faithfully promised the said defendant to cut the said lot of stone, according to the draft aforesaid, and to have the same ready for delivery to the said defendant in the time   and at   the place aforesaid, he, the said defendant undertook and then and there faithfully promised the said plaintiff to accept the said lot of stone, of and from him the said plaintiff and to fetch the said lot of stone away from the aforesaid shop of the said plaintiff for the same at the times and in the manner aforesaid. And although the said plaintiff afterwards and within the three weeks next after the making of the said promise and undertaking of the said defendant to wit, on the day and at the place aforesaid, was ready and willing to deliver the said lot of stone to him the said defendant. Yet the said defendant, not regarding his said promise and undertaking, but contriving and craftily and subtly intending to deceive and defraud the said plaintiff in this behalf, did not, nor would at the time the said plaintiff was ready as aforesaid, to deliver to him the said defendant, the said lot of stone, or at any time before or afterwards, accept the said lot of stone, or any part thereof of and from the said plaintiff, or pay him for the same as aforesaid, but then and there wholly neglected and refused so to do—

And whereas also, the said defendant, afterwards, towit, on the first day February in the year of our Lord one thousand eight hundred and forty, at the county and circuit aforesaid, was indebted to the said plaintiff in the further sum of three hundred dollars for the work and labour by him the said plaintiff before that time done, performed and bestowed in and about the business of the said defendant, and for the said defendant, and at his special instance and request.

And also for divers materials and other necessary by the said plaintiff before that time found and provided, and used and applied, in and about the work and labour for the said defendant, and at his like special instance and request— And being, so indebted to the said defendant in consideration thereof afterwards to wit on the day and year and at the place aforesaid undertook and then and there faithfully promised the said plaintiff to pay him the said last mentioned sum of money when he the said defendant should be thereunto afterwards requested— Yet the said defendant (although often requested so todo) has not as yet paid to the said plaintiff the said last mentioned sum of money, or any part thereof; but so to do has hitherto wholly neglected and refused, and still does neglect and refuse—To the damage of the plaintiff of five hundred dollars, and therefore he sues &c.

Stuart & Lincoln p. q.

(Copy of the account sued on)

r—

"1840   John W. Gray   To Archibald Hood   D

    st

Feb 1   To work and labour done & materials found. $300.00"

Archibald Hood

vs   } Decln

John W. Gray

Filed Febry 6" 1840

Wm. . Butler clerk

MR. LINCOLN BECOMES SECURITY FOR COSTS IN THE SUIT OF TYDINGS ET AL VS HATHAWAY ET AL, FEBRUARY 16, 1840.

Litigants in the Illinois of Mr. Lincoln's early years at the bar, now and again were without money and the lawyer employed in a case became security for court costs. Mr. Lincoln followed this practice in the document here reproduced, the original of

*which is now in the library of Brown University at Providence.
It appearrs to have been wrongly dated, for February* 16, 1840,
*fell on a Sunday. On motion of the plaintiff's attorney this case
was dismissed on March* 2, 1840.

John W. Tydings &
James H. Widney
     vs   Sangamon Circuit court
Wesley Hathaway &
Samuel N. Fullinwider

I do hereby enter myself security for costs in this cause, and
acknowledge myself bound to pay or cause to be paid all costs
which may accrue in this action either to the opposite party, or
to any of the officers of the court in pursuance of the laws of
the state   Dated this 16th day of February A. D. 1840
                                   A..Lincoln

DECLARATION AND PRAECIPE IN THE SUIT OF TYDINGS VS. HATHAWAY & FULLINWIDER, FEBRUARY 17, 1840.
(Herndon-Weik Collection)

*This declaration and quoted note are from the pen of Mr.
Lincoln, but the cover notations are in two other hands. The
clerk seems to have added the word "praecipe", as there is in
evidence no request or order to issue a process or at least none
in the handwriting of Mr. Lincoln. The latter neglected his
usual desire for harmony in the use of the clause, "and still neglects and refuses so'todo," with the plural subject, "the said defendants." Such an error is not common to his legal papers, but
occurs from time to time. The declaration and praecipe represent the only evidence of Mr. Lincoln's connection with a case,
the history of which has not been made known by studies up to
the present time.*

State of Illinois
Sangamon county &   Of the March term of the
circuit   circuit court of said county
                             A. D. 1840.

John W. Tydings and James H. Widney, plaintiffs, trading
and doing business under the name style and firm of Tydings &
Widney, complain of Wesley Hathaway and Samuel N. Fullinwider being in custody &c of a plea that they render unto the
said plaintiffs the sum of eleven hundred and eight dollars, and
twentyfour cents, which they owe to and unjustly detain from

them: For that whereas the said defendants, heretofore, towit, on the eleventh day of May in the year of our Lord one thousand eight hundred and thirtyseven, at the county and circuit aforesaid, by their certain writing obligatory, sealed with their seal ,and signed thus "W. Hathaway" "S. N. Fullinwider" and now shown to the court, the date whereof is the day and year aforesaid, acknowledged themselves to be held and firmly bound unto the said plaintiffs by their firm name of Tydings & Widney in the sum of eleven hundred and eight dollars and twenty-four cents above demanded, to be paid to the said plaintiffs twelve months after the date of the said writing obligatory; yet the said defendants, (although often requested sotodo) have not as yet paid the said sum above demanded to the said plaintiffs; but have hitherto wholly neglected and refused, and still neglects and refuses soto do. To the damage of the said plaintiffs of one hundred dollars, and therefore they bring their suit &c.

Stuart & Lincoln p. q.

(Copy of the instrument sued on)

"Twelve months after date we or either of us promise to pay Tydings & Widney or order Eleven hundred and eight dollars and twentyfour cents, for value recd. as witness our hands and seals this eleventh day of May 1837—

W. Hathaway (Seal
S. N. Fullinwider (Seal)"

Tydings & Widney

vs   } Decl & precipe

Hathaway & Fullinwider

filed Feby 17th 1840
Wm Butler clk

DECLARATION IN THE SUIT OF TROTTER VS. LASWELL AND ELKIN, SANGAMON CIRCUIT COURT, FEBRUARY 18, 1840.

(Herndon-Weik Collection)

Mr. Lincoln penned this declaration, praecipe, and quoted note. The cover notations are also in his hand, but the date of filing is in another handwriting, not characteristic of Butler's usual large and bold hand. The comma after the words, "one thousand," preceding "eight hundred and thirtyeight," is not com-

mon with Mr. Lincoln, but it appears in more than one of his legal documents. It will be noted that he used a double "s" in "Lasswell", whereas the clerk used "Laswell" in other cases to which this gentleman was a party. The quoted note used the double "s", leading to speculation as to the way in which Laswell spelled his name. Lawyer Lincoln gave both spellings of "Garret" in his legal documents using the first name of the one-time sheriff of Sangamon County. Dr. Elkin, who is listed as "Garret Elkin" in many cases, was elected sheriff in 1834, but Mr. Lincoln voted for his friend, Deputy-Sheriff Dickinson. The case was continued on March 6, 1840; research up to this time has made no further record available.

State of Illinois   ⎫   Of the March term of the
Sangamon county   ⎬   circuit court of said
and Circuit   ⎭   county A. D. 1840—

George Trotter, plaintiff, complains of Thomas Lasswell and Garrett Elkin, defendants, being in custody &c of a plea of Trespass on the case upon promises: For that whereas heretofore towit, on the twentyfourth day of December in the year of our Lord one thousand, eight hundred and thirtyeight, at the county and circuit aforesaid, the said defendants made their certain promissory note in writing, said Elkin signing his name thereto "G. Elkin" bearing date the day and year aforesaid, and thereby then and there promised to pay, on or before the first day of February (then) next (ensuing) to the said plaintiff or order, the sum of one hundred and five dollars with twelve per cent interest from the date of said promissory note till paid, for value received, and then and there delivered the said promissory note to the said plaintiff; by means whereof, and by force of the statute in such case made and provided, the said defendants, then and there became liable, to pay to the said plaintiff the said sum of money in the said promissory note specified according to the tenor and effect of the said promissory note, and being so liable, they, the said defendants, in consideration thereof, afterwards towit on the same day of the making of the said promissory note at the county and circuit aforesaid, undertook, and then and there faithfully promised the said plaintiff to pay him the said sum of money in the said promissory note specified, according to the tenor and effect thereof— Yet the said defendants (although often requested sotodo) have not as yet paid to the said plaintiff the said sum of money in the said promissory note specified, or any part thereof; but so to do, have hitherto wholly neglected and refused, and still do neglect and refuse so to do. To the damage of the said plaintiff of two hundred dollars, and therefore he sues &c.

Stuart & Lincoln p q

(Copy of the note used on)

"On or before the first day of February next we promise to pay George Trotter or order one hundred & five dollars with 12 per cent interest from this date till paid value received this 24th day of December, 1838

Thomas Lasswell
G Elkin"

George Trotter vs Thomas Lasswell & Garrett Elkin	Trespass on the case promises— Damage $200.00—

The clerk of the Sangamon circuit court will issue process in the above cause—

Stuart & Lincoln p. q—

George Trotter

vs   Decln Precipe

Thomas Lasswell

Garrett Elkin—

Filed Feby 18 1840

   Wm Butler clck

PLAINTIFF'S DECLARATION IN THE SUIT OF SPEAR VS. CAMP, FEBRUARY 20, 1840
(Herndon-Weik Collection)

The declaration in this suit, including quoted note, endorsements, and cover notations, the date of filing excepted, are in the hand of Attorney Lincoln. The unusual separation of the words, "eighty four," may be a quotation from the note, as the same separation appears in the quoted note. The usual joining of such words is found in other Lincoln documents. Mr. Lincoln wrote "non-payment" in his first use of the word, but thereafter employed the two words, "no payment." It will be noted that he made a slight error in the omission of the word, "avers", in the phrase, "and the plaintiff that said Ragsdale being so liable," as he did in leaving out the word "there", in the clause, "and then and faithfully promised the said plaintiff . . ." The spelling of judgment" as "judgement" appears to have been habitual with Mr. Lincoln in these early legal papers, as does "ballance" for "balance." This case was tried before Judge Treat on March 13, 1840, and in due time a decision was rendered in favor of Spear, whose friendship for Mr. Lincoln dated from the latter's first years in New Salem.

State of Illinois ⎱
Sangamon county ⎰ ss   Of the March term of the circuit
and circuit   court of said county A. D. 1840—

　　　Isaac P. Spear, plaintiff, complains of William Camp defendant, being in custody &c of a plea of Trespass on the case upon promises: For that whereas on the fifth day of January in the year of our Lord one thousand eight hundred and thirtyeight, at the county and circuit aforesaid, one Frederick

A. Patterson, by the name and style of   F. A. x Patterson
　　　　　　　　　　　　　　　　　　　　　　　 his
　　　　　　　　　　　　　　　　　　　　　　　mark

made his certain promissory note in writing   bearing date the day and year aforesaid and thereby   then and there promised to pay, on or before the first day of October next after the date of the said promissory note, to the said defendant William Camp or order, one hundred and fiftyfour dollars and eight four cents; for value receive of him, and then and there delivered the said promissory note to the said defendant— And afterwards, towit, on the first day of September in the year of our Lord one thousand eight hundred and thirtyeight at the county and circuit aforesaid, the said defendant, to whom or to whose order the   said sum of money in the said promissory note specified was to be paid, by his endorsement in writing on the back of the   said promissory note, signed with his hand and dated the same day and year last aforesaid, assigned the said promissory note to the said plaintiff Isaac P. Spear— And afterwards, towit on the tenth day of October in the year aforesaid, the said plaintiff Isaac P. Spear, by his endorsement in writing on the back of said promissory note, signed with his hand, the date whereof is the day and year last aforesaid, assigned the said promissory note to one Daniel Ragsdale.   And afterwards, towit on the sixth day of December, in year aforesaid the said Ragsdale by endorsement in writing on the back of the said promissory note, signed with

his hand, the date whereof is the same day and year last aforesaid, assigned the said promissory note to Grimsley & Levering— And the plaintiff avers that afterwards towit on the
eighth day of December in the year aforesaid, William P. Grimsley and Lawrison Levering merchants and partners, trading under and known by the name style and firm of Grimsley & Levering sued out from the clerks office of the circuit court for
Sangamon county a summons in an action of Trespass on the
case against the said Frederick A. Patterson for the non-payment
of the said sum of money in the said promissory note specified. And that such proceedings were had on the said summons
and in the suit thereby instituted, that at the   March term
of the circuit court for Sangamon county, in the year of our
Lord one thousand eight hundred and thirtynine, on the sixth day
of said term, the said William P. Grimsley and Lawrison
Levering recovered Judgement against the said Frederick A Patterson for the non payment of the promissory note aforesaid,
for the sum of one hundred and fiftyeight dollars and ninetysix
cents damages, being the amount of principal and interest due
on the promissory note aforesaid,— And afterwards towit, on
the twentyseventh day of March in the year aforesaid an
execution of Fieri Facias, issued on said Judgement from the
clerks office of the circuit court for Sangamon county, directed to the Sheriff of Sangamon county against the estate of
the said Frederick A. Patterson for the said sum of one hundred and fiftyeight dollars and ninetysix cents damages and seven
dollars and twelve and a half cents costs of said suit— Which
execution afterwards towit, on the first day of April in the year
last aforesaid, at the county and circuit aforesaid came to the
hands of Garrett Elkin who then was and still is Sheriff of
Sangamon county— And afterwards, towit on the fourteenth
day of June in the year last aforesaid, the said Garrett Elkin
Sheriff of Sangamon county aforesaid returned said execution to the clerks office of the circuit court for Sangamon county
with an endorsement thereon, that he had made by the sale of
property the sum of thirty dollars, and fifty cents and that
there was no other property found to satisfy said execution, all
of which more fully, and at large appears by the record and proceedings in said suit now of record in this court— By means
whereof the said Daniel Ragsdale became liable to pay to the
said Lawrison Levering and William P. Grimsley the sum of
one hundred, and fortyfive dollars

being the balance of principal, interest, and costs due on said judgment after deducting the said sum of thirty dollars and fifty cents made on said execution, and the plaintiff, said Ragsdale being so liable, he did on the said fourteenth day of June in the year last aforesaid, at the county and circuit aforesaid, the said Ragsdale paid to the said William P. Grimsley and Lawrison Levering Merchants trading under, and known by the name style and firm of Grimsley & Levering the said last mentioned sum of money

By means of all which and by force of the statute in such case made and provided the said plaintiff Isaac P. Spear, became liable and bound to pay to the said Ragsdale the said sum of money last aforesaid, being the ballance due on the judgement aforesaid— And the plaintiff avers, that afterwards towit on the fourteenth day of June in the year last aforesaid, the said Daniel Ragsdale sued out from the clerks office of the circuit court for Sangamon county a summons in an action of Tresspass on the case against the said plaintiff Isaac P. Spear for the non payment of the sum of money last aforesaid, and that such proceedings were had on the said last mentioned summons and in the suit thereby instituted that at the July term of the circuit court for Sangamon county in the year last aforesaid, on the seventh day of said term, the said Daniel Ragsdale recovered judgment against the said plaintiff, Isaac P. Spear, for the non payment of the sum of money last aforesaid, for the sum of one hundred and fortyfour dollars and twentyfive cents   damages, being the amount for which he was then liable to the said Ragsdale upon the premises aforesaid and afterwards towit, on the first day of August in the year last aforesaid, an execution of Fieri facias issued on said last mentioned judgement from the clerks office of the circuit court for Sangamon county directed to the Sheriff of Sangamon county. against the estate   of the said plaintiff Isaac P. Spear, for the said sum of one hundred and fortyfour dollars & twentyfive cents debt and fourteen dollars and sixtyeight and three quarters cents costs of said last mentioned suit— Which execution afterwards, to wit on the fifteen day of August in the year last aforesaid at the county and circuit aforesaid came to the hands of Sheriff Elkin who then was and still is Sheriff of Sangamon county— And afterwards towit on the twentysixth day of October in the year last aforesaid returned said execution to the clerks office of the circuit court for Sangamon county, with an endorsement thereon that the same was satisfied all of which more fully and at large appears by the record and proceedings in said last mentioned suit now of record in this court— By means of all which the plaintiff avers that he has fully paid the damages, interest, and costs, of the said last mentioned judgment, towit, on the said ninteenth day of October in the year last aforesaid, at the county and circuit aforesaid—

By means of all which, and by force of the statute in such case made and provided, the said defendant became liable to pay to the said plaintiff the sum of one hundred and seventyone dollars & thirtyfour cents being the sum paid by said plaintiff on the said last mentioned execution, and being so liable, he the said defendant, in consideration thereof afterwards towit on the day and year last aforesaid, at the county and circuit aforesaid undertook and then and faithfully promised the said plaintiff to pay him the said last mentioned sum of money when he should be thereunto afterwards requested—

Yet the said defendant (although often requested so to do) hath not paid to the said plaintiff the said last mentioned sum of money or any part thereof, but so to do hath hitherto wholly neglected and refused and still doth neglect and refuse— To the damage of the said plaintiff of two hundred and fifty dollars, and therefore he sues &c

Stuart & Lincoln p q—

Copy of note and endorsements

"January 5th 1838
On or before the first day of October next
I promis to pay to William Camp or order one hundred & fiftyfour dollars and eighty four cts for value
received of him

	his
Test	F. A. x Patterson"
	mark

N. W. Matheny
(Endorsements on note)
I assign the within note to Isaac P. Spear, Sept. 1st 1838
William Camp
Value recd I assign the within note to Dan
iel Ragsdale
Oct. 10th 1838 Isaac P. Spear"
Value received I assign the within note to
Grimsley & Levering. Dec. 6 1838. Daniel Ragsdale"

Isaac P. Spear

vs } Decln

William Camp

Filed Feby 20th. 1840
Wm. Butler   Clk

APPEAL BELIEVED TO HAVE BEEN ADDRESSED BY LINCOLN TO THE READERS OF THE OLD SOLDIER, FEBRUARY 28, 1840

One of the methods employed by the Whig leaders in Illinois to secure votes for the Harrison electors in 1840 was a campaign sheet to which, in honor of their candidate, they gave the title The Old Soldier. Published from the office of the Sangamo Journal the first number appeared on February 1, and the last of its seventeen numbers on September 30. Lincoln was one of its five editors and is believed to have written the article To the Readers of the Old Soldier which appeared in the issue of February 28 and which reveals the flamboyant phrasing and the methods as an uncompromising partisan employed by him at that stage of his career.

The circular to which reference is made in the opening sentences was sent out about February 4, and will be found in Nicolay and Hay's Works 1:142-145. That Springfield in the late winter of 1840 was a place and period much given to short tempers, and quick resentment of imagined offense has amusing proof in a letter Lincoln sent off to Stuart the day after the appeal here reproduced appeared in The Old Soldier. "Douglas," the Whig champion wrote his partner in Washington, "having chosen to consider himself insulted by something in the Journal undertook to cane Francis (its editor) in the street. Francis caught him by the hair and jammed him back against a market-cart, where the affair ended by Francis being pulled away." And the Missouri Republican reporting the incident on March 16, added this excuse for the editor of the Journal: "Francis, who is a good-natured, fat, hearty, clever man, loves a laugh much better than personal difficulty."

Some time since the undersigned sent a Circular to particular individuals in several Counties of this State, urging them to use their best exertions to organize, and form into "battle array" the friends of Gen. Harrison, for the approaching contest. This Cir-

cular we marked "Confidential." We did so, because we knew,
that nothing short of utmost secrecy, on the part of even our own
friends, could enable it to "clear the clutches" of the Post Office,
and reach any tolerable portion of its points of destination.
As we anticipated, it has been pirated from the mail, and published by the Van Buren papers. Of course, all copies of it,
which have not reached their addresses, will not *now* be permitted to do so. We therefore urge upon our friends in those
counties which this circular has never reached, (if the paper
containing the article shall ever reach them) to go to work and
organize themselves in the most efficient manner, for routing the
enemies of the country and of Gen. Harrison, from the councils
of the nation.

But again, it is objected that we, the undersigned, are the
The Van Buren papers raise many objections to the Circular in question. They affect the greatest horror, that it should
have been marked "Confidential". Had they not better reserve
their horror for the contemplation of the fact, that *their friends*
"robbed the mail" to get hold of it? And does not the fact that
they did thus rob the mail, justify, nay, even imperiously require,
every honest man to use every possible precaution, to enable his
communications to pass unembezzled through the post offices,
to their destination?

But, again, it is objected that we, the undersigned, are the
editors of "The Old Soldier," as it is urged appears from this
confidential Circular. This assumption the Circular does not
warrant. In it, we say "The Old Soldier" will be *superintended*
by us. Of course we are responsible for its contents; and we
desire to shun no part of the responsibility, arising from its
management. But while we say this, we also say to the friends
of Gen. Harrison every where, that they, as well as we, are the
editors of "The Old Soldier." And we now invite them—particularly those who have seen Gen. Harrison, where cowards
dared not show their heads — where storms of "leaden rain and
iron hail" carried death and desolation in their course — where
his erect figure, stationed in the loftiest rampart, and seen from
every part of the theatre of action; and his voice, rising in
trumpet tones above the roaring of the death-dealing tempest, —
gave "'form and spirit to the war"; them, we invite to aid us,
in filling its columns with such "burning truths" and "confound-
ing arguments" as will stop the ears of the Old hero's thous-
and tongued caluminators.

What credit or discredit "The Old Soldier" may derive from

our names, is not for us to determine. We have not thrust those names upon the public; but now that our enemies have, we only say: "There they are; let those assail them who can." Upon the authority of those names, (whether that authority be good or bad,) we assure the readers of "The Old Soldier," that nothing shall appear in the columns, *as facts,* which we do not, on the fullest investigation in our power to make, believe to be true. No *"vile falsehood"* shall enter them. It is our intention, that our friends every where may, without fear of successful contradiction, repeat whatever they may find, *stated as a fact,* in the columns of "The Old Soldier."

But the Van Buren papers object to the friends of Gen. Harrison organizing. We urge that organization; and we insist that it is not for our opponents to inveigh against it. *They* set us the example of organization; and we, in self defense, are driven into it. If *they* now wish *disbanding,* let them set the example. Let them *disband* their double-drilled-army of "forty thousand office holders," a part of whose regular tactics it is, to pilfer letters and papers from the mails, lest the old soldiers, who have fought and bled with Gen. Harrison may all learn that he is now a candidate for the Presidency.

With our own friends, we justify — we urge —organization on the score of necessity. A disbanded yeomanry cannot successfully meet an organized soldiery.

The old soldiers of the War of 1812-13 - and 1814, remember, that previous to that war, there was no organization amongst them; but immediately on learning that an organized foe was invading their land, they, too organized — met — conquered — killed and drove the foe beyond the "world of waters." To those old soldiers we say — An organized army of office-holders is now fitting out an expedition against your old commander. They are coming armed — (not with bristling steel, because that bedazzles their eyes — not with powder and balls, because the smell of sulphur offends their nostrils, but) with falsehood, slander, and detraction, upon the characters of yourselves and your chieftain, established in the hard and bloody conflicts with your country's invading enemies. That army too, must be met. Organization must again be had. We, your sons and younger brothers, will form the rank and file; you shall be the generals, and commanders-in-chief. Thus organized we shall meet, conquer, and disperse Gen. Harrison's and the country's enemies, and place him in the chair, now disgraced by their effeminate and luxury-loving chief.

> A. C. Henry
> R. F. Barrett *
> E. D. Baker
> J. F. Speed
> A. Lincoln

* Dr. Barrett having taken the office of Fund Commissioner, does not think it proper for him to longer participate in the superintendence of "The Old Soldier," and he, therefore, withdraws from it.

DEFENDANT'S AFFIDAVIT DRAWN BY MR. LINCOLN IN THE SUIT OF RAGSDALE & ASHBERRY VS. SPEAR, MARCH 2, 1840

Here Mr. Lincoln again appears as counsel for David Spear, a friend of his New Salem days. The original of this affidavit is now in the Illinois State Historical Library at Springfield. The affidavit was drawn by Lincoln, and signed by Spear. The attestation was by Butler, but the writing before this is not his. A complete history of the case has not been made available.

State of Illinois }

Sangamon County }

David Spear, the defendant in a certain suit now pending in the Sangamon Circuit Court, wherein Daniel Ragsdale and Monroe Ashberry are plaintiffs, being first duly sworn, states on oath, that he verily believes the said Ragsdale is unable to pay the costs of said suit and that since the commencement of said suit, the said Ashberry has become a nonresident of this state and that he verrily (sie) believes the officers of said court will be endangered with respect to their legal demands unless said plaintiffs be ruled to give security for costs in said suit.

David Spear

Sworn to & subscribed before
me March 2d   1840
  Wm Butler Clk

AFFIDAVIT OF DEFENDANT IN THE SUIT OF RAGSDALE AND ASHBERRY VS. SPEAR, SANGAMON CIRCUIT COURT, MARCH 2, 1840.

This affidavit and demand that security for costs be given is in the hand of Mr. Lincoln. Spear signed the affidavit, while the filing of the document was attested by Clerk Butler. The handwriting which is signed with the name of Butler is not conclusively like that of the clerk and friend of Lincoln, but the hand may be his. A history of this suit has not been made available by research to the present time.

State of Illinois } ss
Sangamon county }

David Spear, the defendant in a certain suit now pending in the Sangamon Circuit court, wherein Daniel Radgsdale and Monroe Ashberry are plaintiffs, being first duly sworn, states on oath, that the said Ragsdale is unable to pay the costs of said suit and that since the commencement of said suit, the said Ashberry has become a non-resident of this state and that he verrily believes the officers of said court will be endangered with respect to their legal demands unless said plaintiffs be ruled to give security for costs in said suit—

David Spear

Sworn to & Subscribed before
me March 2d 1840
    W Butler ck

COURT ORDER DRAWN BY MR. LINCOLN FOR ADMINISTRATORS OF THE ESTATE OF CHARLES R. MATHENY TO SELL REAL ESTATE, MARCH 3, 1840

This order, drawn by Mr. Lincoln and approved by Judge Samuel H. Treat, permitted settlement of the estate of an outstanding pioneer of Sangamon County. Charles R. Matheny was born in 1786 in Loudon County, Virginia; became in early manhood a Methodist Episcopal minister, and in 1805 as a missionary of that church settled in what later became St. Clair County, Illinois. There in addition to preaching, he studied and practiced law, and in 1820 served as a representative in the Territorial Legislature. When Sangamon County was organized in 1821, Matheny accepted an invitation to become its clerk and auditor, and clerk of the circuit court, and with his wife Jemima Ogle settled in Springfield. There he was repeatedly re-elected county clerk, and held that office at the time of his death in October, 1839. Noah W. Matheney, fifth of the eleven children of Charles R. and Jemima Matheny, by appointment succeeded his father as county clerk, and by successive re-elections held that office for thirty-four years. In his last days he was president of the First National Bank of Springfield. James H., another son of Charles R. Matheny, served in the Civil War as a lieutenant-colonel of volunteers and following 1874 was for a period of years judge of Sangamon County. All three of the Mathenys were close and trusted friends of Abraham Lincoln, the father from the latter's settlement at New Salem.

Gersham Keys &
Noah W. Matheny
administrators of
Charles R. Matheny
deceased

vs

The heirs of Charles
R. Matheny deceased

On Petition to sell

Real Estate —

This day came the Petitioners and filed their Petition in open court, and it appearing to the court, that due notice of this application has been given according to law, and Milton Hay, guardian *ad litem* to the minor heirs in said Petition mentioned, having filed his answer stating that he knows of no reason consistent with the interest of said minors, why the prayer of said Petition should not be granted, and it also appearing to the satisfaction of the court that the obligation of said Petition are true — It is therefore ordered by the court that the said Petitioners sell the real estate described in said Petition, towit: A part of the South East fractional quarter of Section Twentyone in Township Sixteen North of Range Four West, in Sangamon county; also Lots, Four, Five and Six in Block Fortyfive in Petersburg in Menard county — also, Lot one ,and four feet off of the North side of Lot Two, in Block One, in Enos' addition to the town of Springfield — or so much thereof as will pay the debts of said estate; that it be sold in a credit of six and twelve months, and bond or bonds and security, and a mortgage or morgages taken on the premises, to secure the purchase money — and that said Petitioners report their proceedings herein to this court—

Adm of Matheny

vs

Heirs of Matheny   Order

PLEA OF DEFENDANT IN THE SUIT OF HOOD VS. GRAY, SANGAMON CIRCUIT COURT, MARCH 5, 1840.

This plea is in the hand of Stephen A. Douglas, as are the cover notations, with the exception of the date of filing. It is

*included as a part of the case of Hood vs. Gray, and a document
in the hand of Mr. Lincoln's most renowned opponent. Mr.
Lincoln appears to have been far more careful in drawing up
his legal papers than Douglas, for the latter scrawled his on
paper with little or no form. It is interesting to note that he
spelled, "alleged", as "alledged", a spelling frequently used by
Mr. Lincoln. The declaration of February 6, 1840 and this plea
are the only known evidenec of Mr. Lincoln's connection with
a case the history of which has not yet been made available by
search of court records.*

Sangamon Co March Term 1840

Archibald Hood }
     vs   } assumpsit
John W Gray }

And the said defendant comes & defends the wrong & injury when &c and for plea says *actio non* because he says that he did not undertake and promise in manner as alledged and of this he puts himself upon the country for trial &c

                    S A Douglass for
                          Deft

Hood }
  vs } assumpsit
    }
Gray

Filed Mar 5th 1840
Wm. Butler Clk

DEFENDANT'S PLEA IN THE SUIT OF VAUGHN VS. RANSDELL, MARCH 6, 1840
(Herndon-Weik Collection)

*The defendant's plea in this suit is not the work of Walker,
who was a hurried and awkward penman. It appears to be in
another hand, possibly that of an associate of Walker, or of a
clerk in the court house. Clerk Butler made the cover notation
as to date of filing, and Mr. Lincoln penned the words, "And the
plaintiff doth the like Stuart & Lincoln p q." The jury awarded
Vaughn, the Stuart & Lincoln client, a judgment of $245.86. On
March 7, 1840. Walker, attorney for Ransdell, entered a motion
for a new trial, but the court denied this motion on March 12,
1840.*

State of Illinois

    Of the November Term of the Sangamon Circuit Court

Sangamon County   eighteen hundred and thirty nine

Foley Vaughn   ⎫

      vs   ⎬   Assumpsit

Wharton Ransdell⎭

    And the said Wharton Ransdell by his attorney comes and defends the wrong and injury when &c and saith that he did not undertake or promise in manner and form as the said Foley Vaughan hath above thereof complained against him and of this he puts himself upon the country &c

                           Cyrus Walker for Deft

And the plaintiff doth the like

      Stuart & Lincoln p q.

Sangamon Circut Court

    November Term 1839

Foley Vaughn   ⎫

      vs   ⎬   Plea

Wharton Ransdell⎭

Filed Mar 6. 1840

    WmButler ck

AFFIDAVIT IN THE SUIT OF WEBSTER & HICKOX VS. COGDAL, SANGAMON CIRCUIT COURT, MARCH 7, 1840.

(Herndon-Weik Collection)

This affidavit is the work of Mr. Lincoln, and was signed by his friend and client, Isaac Cogdal. The swearing of the affidavit was attested by Butler who also wrote the cover notations, in which he appears to have erred in giving "Cogdall" as the name of the defendant. The affidavit offers additional evidence of the use of extra spacing to emphasize words and phrases, as the writing of Mr. Lincoln at many points reveals a distinct separation of words and phrases. Twenty odd years later Cogdal, the defendant in the case visited Mr. Lincoln in Washington, and on this visit he supposedly heard the President say that he had left his heart at the grave of Ann Rutledge—a good story for those who delight in romance connected with great men, but Isaac Cogdal is the only authority for it. Mr. Lincoln recorded on December 4, 1839, in the fee book of Stuart & Lincoln, a

*notation of his employment by Cogdal, in the case, but this entry
with the affidavit of March 7 are the only known records of its
existence. Studies to date have not made known its history, with
exception of Cogdal's statement that judgment had been rendered
against him on March 7, 1840 in the sum of ninety odd dollars.
This is clear from internal evidence in the affidavit. Virgil
Hickox was known to Abraham Lincoln from New Salem days,
for it was he who was witness to the drawing of the note which
began the ventures in that place of Denton Offutt, young Mr.
Lincoln's one-time employer.*

State of Illinois   }
                } ss
Sangamon county }

    Isaac Cogdal, the defendant in an appeal case in the Sanga-
mon circuit court, wherein Bela C. Webster and Virgil Hickox,
trading and doing business under the firm name of "Webster &
Hickox" are plaintiffs, being first duly sworn, states on oath,
that he arrived at the court house on this day, and was surprised
to learn that judgment for ninety odd dollars had been rendered
against him in his absence; that the reason of his being absent
was, that the summons in the case was read to him notifying
him to appear on the second monday of March; that he was
making all due preparation for a trial on that day; that he had,
at considerable labour and expense, procured witnesses to be in
attendance on that day from another county; that he verrily believes on a fair and just settlement of accounts between the plaintiffs and him, the plaintiffs are indebted to him, and that he
will be able to prove it so, in case he can have a fair trial of the
cause; that this application is made for the purpose that justice
may be done; and for no other purpose whatever— In order
that no hardship may be imposed upon the plaintiffs by the granting of a new trial, the defendant proposes to admit on the trial
that their charges *against* him are correct, and only insist upon
his payments and set offs—

Subscribed & sworn to before me   Isaac. Cogdal
this 7th day March. 1840
    Wm Butler Clk

Cogdall
        }
   ads } affa
        }
W & Hickox

filed Mar 7th 1840
    Wm Butler Ck

PLEA OF THE DEFENDANT IN THE SUIT OF SPEAR VS. CAMP, SANGAMON CIRCUIT COURT, MARCH 7, 1840.
(Herndon-Weik Collection)

Stephen Trigg Logan, later the law partner of Mr. Lincoln, drew the plea and cover notations in this case, while Clerk Butler wrote the date of filing. Mr. Lincoln made the customary answer to the plea, "And the plaintiff doth the like," and signed it for Stuart & Lincoln, p. q. The Logan handwriting is easy to read, but less neat than that of Mr. Lincoln... The able lawyer and judge was careless of small and capital letters, as were most of the attorneys of his day. As seen by the declaration of February 20, 1838 this was an action brought for trespass upon the case upon promises. On March 6, 1840 the plaintiff made his joinder to this plea which was filed March 7, 1840. The court heard the case on Friday, March 13, 1840 after having given permission to Stuart & Lincoln to amend their declaration. The court heard the case, and took time to consider, but the result of that consideration has not been made known by study up to this time.

Isaac P. Spear
    vs   In assumpsit
William Camp

And the defendant comes and defends the wrong and injury when where &c and says he did not undertake and promise in manner and form as the plaintiff in his declaration hath alleged and of this he puts himself upon the country

Logan pd—

And the plaintiff
doth the like—

Stuart & Lincoln. p. q.

I. P. Spear

    vs   plea

W Camp

Filed Mar 7th 1840
Wm Butler Clk

AFFIDAVITS IN APPEAL FOR A NEW TRIAL IN THE SUIT OF MANNING VS. MORGAN, MARCH 9, 1840

(Herndon-Weik Collection)

The first and second of the three affidavits here reproduced are not in the hand of Stuart or Lincoln, attorneys for the defendant, except possibly the signature of Hall; but William Butler wrote the cover notations, and attested to the swearing of all three affidavits. The only handwriting in the third affidavit by Attorney Lincoln is found in the signature, "Abner x Hall." A. Lincoln signed the "A. Lincoln" of the second affidavit, and the "Abner x Hall" in the first affidavit appears to be in his hand. It would appear that in this case Mr. Lincoln was seeking to regain ground lost through an error of judgment, and filed the three affidavits in an attempt to regain it.

William Manning ⎫
  vs   ⎬
Martin L Morgan &c ⎭   In Debts

The Defendant, Hall States on oath. that he was surprized on the trial of this Cause by the Court refusing to allow him to prove that the writing obligatory sued on was delivered by him as an escrow, in consequence of his affidavit not being filed before the Jury were Sworn. He states that he believed and was so advised by his counsel, that the affidavit filed after the jury was sworn would be in time, else he would have filed his affidavit before the Jury sworn.

He states that he could & would have proven by Ambury Rankin, if the Court had permitted, and if a new trial be granted he will prove, that he delivered the writing sued on as an escrow, to said Rankin upon condition that it should not be delivered as his act and deed until other responsible men had signed & delivered the same on sureties, which [the] condition has not been performed—— He asks a new trial not for delay but Justice

          his
        Abner x Hall
         mark

  Sworn to before me this
9" day of March 1840
    Wm Butler   clk

In the above case Abram Lincoln states he was attorney for Defendant Hall & that he was informed before the trial, of the defense set out by Deft Hall in foregoing affidavit, and that he did not believe that it was necessary to file any affidavit denying the execution of the writing sued on before the jury were sworn, or he would have done so, and he was the more confirmed in such being the case by the fact that he mentioned the defense of an escrow, before the trial & the plaintiff's counsel refused to have the jury sworn until the Subscribing Witness was present—Affidavit states that he was surprized at the decision given as aforesaid.   A Lincoln

Sworn to before me this
9" day of March 1840
Wm Butler clk

Hall   ⎫
   ads   ⎬ affa
Manning ⎭
Filed 9th March 1840
Wm..Butler Clk

———:———

William Manning ⎫
        vs   ⎬   Debts
Martin L Morgan &c ⎭

Abner Hall one of the Defendants makes oath that he has filed his plea of *non est factum* in this s[uit] denying that the instrument sued on is his deed, & now according to the act of assembly [?] in such case provided states on oath that the writing described in plaintiffs declaration & sued on is not his act & deed. March 9th 1840

Sworn   to   this 9th   his
                                 Abner   x   Hall
                                        mark
   day of March 1840
      Wm..Butler Clk

PLEAS IN THE SUIT OF MANNING VS. MORGAN ET AL, SANGAMON CIRCUIT COURT, UNDATED BUT PROBABLY MARCH 9, 1840.
(Herndon-Weik Collection)

This plea and cover notations are the work of Mr. Lincoln with two exceptions. Stephen T. Logan, his second partner, wrote the words, "And the plaintiff doth the like," and signed his

name thereto. He also penned the words, "Demurrer in short by consent," and "Joinder," signing for himself, and Lincoln p. d. The word, "oyer," is merely the legal court term for a hearing. The demurrer was an assertion that granting the previous pleading to be true, there was insufficient evidence to proceed further in the case. Hall stated in his affidavit of March 9, 1840 that his plea had been filed, and it seems probable that it was filed on the same day, when Mr. Lincoln signed it in his name.

William Manning ⎫
      vs ⎪
Martin M. Morgan ⎬   In Debt
Samuel Sackett & ⎪
Abner Hall ⎭

And the said defendant Hall, comes and defends the wrong and injury where, when &c and craves oyer of the said supposed writing obligatory &c &c and says that the said writing obligatory is not his deed; and of this he puts himself upon the country &c.

And the plaintiff doth the like

Logan pq

And for further plea in this behalf the said defendant, Hall, comes and defends the wrong and injury when &c. and craves oyer of the said supposed writing obligatory &c &c. and says the said writing obligatory was executed without any consideration— that on the thirteenth day of November in the year of our Lord one thousand eight hundred and thirty two, the said plaintiff sold without any previous request of the said Hall, to one Martin M. Morgan goods amounting in value to two hundred and sixty-eight dollars and thirtyfive cents, upon which sale the plaintiff gave the said Morgan a credit of six months from the thirteenth day of November aforesaid; that afterwards, towit, on the twentysecond day of December in the same year aforesaid, the said plaintiff applied to the said Hall to secure the debts contracted by the said Morgan as aforesaid, whereupon the said Hall executed the said writing obligatory declared on binding himself with the said Morgan to pay the sum of money aforesaid at the expiration of six months from the said thirteenth day of November in the year aforesaid, and this he is ready to verify, wherefore &c. &c.

Stuart & Lincoln p. d.

Demurrer in short by consent
Joinder

Logan pq

Hall
}
ats } Pleas
}
Manning

LINCOLN AS COMMISSIONER DEEDS LAND TO WILLIAM BUTLER, MARCH 9, 1840

On July 8, 1839, Judge Treat appointed Mr. Lincoln commissioner to convey the land involved in the suit of Butler vs. Tilford and others, dealt with in another place. What followed this action of the court is set forth in the order and deed reproduced below.

March 9, 1840

Whereas at the November Term, in the year of our Lord One thousand eight hundred and thirty nine of the Sangamon County Circuit Court, a decree was made by said Court in the words following to Wit:

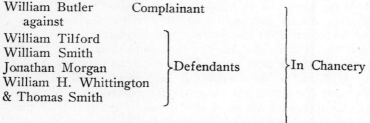

William Butler   Complainant
   against
William Tilford
William Smith
Jonathan Morgan   }Defendants   }In Chancery
William H. Whittington
& Thomas Smith

This day came the Complainant by his solicitor and in his motion. It is ordered that his bill be dismissed as to the defendant William Smith, and it appearing to the satisfaction of the Court that the subpoena in this cause has been duly served on the defendant William Tilford, and that notice of the pendancy of this suit has been given to the defendants Jonathan Morgan, William H. Whittington and Thomas Smith by publishing the same for five weeks successively in the Sangamo Journal, a newspaper printed in Springfield, Illinois, the first publication on the first day of April the last on the twenty second day of said month in the year Eighteen hundred and thirty seven, and the said defendants having failed to enter their appearance herein, and to answer to the complainant's Bill, it is ordered that the same be taken as confessed against them: and it appearing to the court that Abraham Lincoln who was appointed to make a survey of the premises in the Bill and exhibits mentioned has made and filed his report of said survey which report is approved by the Court — and the cause now come in to be heard on the Bill and exhibits filed, and the said report and the Court being sufficiently advised of and concerning the premises and being satisfied that the allegations of Complainant's Bill are true It is now ordered, that the defendants, Thomas Smith and William Tilford convey to the complainant the tract of land in the Bill exhibits and said report mentioned and described, to Wit: That part of the North half of the North East quarter Section five in Township Fifteen North Range seven West of the third principal meridian which is bounded as follows,

Beginning at the North West corner of said quarter section thence East six chains and forty links to a rock at a point intersecting a fence owned by Elkanah Butler in his life time; and being thirty three chains and forty nine links west of the North East corner of said quarter, thence south two degrees West twenty nine chains and seventy links to the southern boundary of said quarter thence West five chains and forty links to the South West corner of said half quarter Section, thence North twenty nine chains and sixty four links to the beginning, containing seventeen acres and seventy two hundredths of an acre, and that they convey said land to the complainant on or before the first day of the next term of this court, and if they do not convey said land to the complainant on or before the first day of the next Term of this court, It is ordered that Abraham Lincoln be appointed commissioner to convey the same and that he convey to complainant by deed, all the right which the said William Tilford, William H. Whittington, and Thomas Smith, or either of them had to said land at the commencement of this suit— and it is further advised that complainant recover of said Defendants his costs in this suit expended.

And, It is further ordered that Abraham Lincoln be allowed the sum of seven dollars for his services as surveyor in surveying, and make Report of the proceeding in pursuance of an order of this Court.

And whereas the said defendants Thomas Smith and William Tilford failed to convey to the said complainant the said tract of land in the said decree described on or before the first day of the term of said Court next after the making of said decree as by the said decree they were ordered to do.

Now therefore I, Abraham Lincoln by virtue of the authority by law, and by the aforesaid decree in me vested, and in consideration of the premises aforesaid, do hereby grant, bargain and sell unto the said complainant William Butler, and to his heirs and assigns forever, all the right which the said William Tilford, William H. Whittington and Thomas Smith, or either of them had to the tract of land in said Decree described at the time of the commencement of the suit on which said decree was rendered.

To have and to hold, to the said William Butler his heirs and assigns forever the aforesaid tract of land together with all and singular the privileges and appurtances thereunto belonging —

In testimony whereof I have hereunto set my hand and seal this ninth day of March in the year of our Lord one thousand eight hundred and forty. —

A. Lincoln

State of Illinois ⎱
             ⎰ SS
Sangamon County ⎰

Be it known that on this 9th day of March, 1840 Before the undersigned Judge of the circuit court for the county aforesaid, personally appeared Abraham Lincoln to me personally known to be the identical person described in & who executed the foregoing deed as grantor and commissioner and who duly acknowledged that he Executed the said deed as grantor & commissioner for the uses & purposes therein Expressed.

Saml. H. Treat

Smith & Tilford

Deed ⎱
  to ⎰
by A. Lincoln
   commissioner
William Butler
Filed for Record at 3 o'clock
P.M.   March 18th 1840
      Fee $1-50

State of Illinois ⎱
             ⎰ SS
Sangamon County ⎰

Recorders office Springfield
March 20th 1840—
I, Benjamin Talbott Recorder in

and for said County do certify that the within deed of conveyance is Recorded in my office in Book P.V — pages 409 up to
412 —

Benjamin Talbott RS C

DECLARATION AND NOTES IN THE SUIT OF KERR VS. HILL, SANGAMON CIRCUIT COURT, MARCH 14, 1840.
(Herndon-Weik Collection)

*This declaration and the cover notations, with the exception
of Clerk Butler's date of filing, are the work of Mr. Lincoln.
Kerr & Company was a St. Louis concern, for which he frequently acted as attorney. As is seen from the declaration and
copies of the notes, Hill had given three notes to Kerr & Co. of
a total value of $2045.67. On November 9, 1839, Mr. Lincoln
made record of taking them for collection, by entry of such fact
in the Stuart & Lincoln fee book. The entry in the fee book and
the declaration comprise the known history of the case, as research to date had not unearthed the court record of it.*

State of Illinois ⎫
Sangamon county ⎬ ss
and circuit ⎭

Of the March term of the
circuit court of said county
A. D. 1840—

John Kerr and Augustus Kerr, surviving partners of the
late George Washington Kerr, who is now deceased, complain
of Daniel B. Hill, being in custody &c. of a plea of Trespass on
the case upon promises: For that whereas the said defendant,
heretofore, towit, on the third day of November in the year of
our Lord one thousand, eight hundred and thirtyeight, at St.
Louis, towit, in the county and circuit aforesaid, made his certain promissory note in writing, signing his name thereto "D. B.
Hill" bearing date the day and year aforesaid and thereby then
and there promised to pay six months after the date thereof, to
the order of the said plaintiffs, and their said partner since deceased, by their said firm name of A. & G. W. Kerr & Co, Five
hundred and eight dollars and fifty four hundredths of a dollar,
with interest at ten per cent per annum after maturity, for value
received, and then and there delivered the said promissory note
to the said plaintiffs and their aforesaid partner since deceased.
And the plaintiffs aver that the said George W. Kerr, has since
deceased; by means whereof, and by force of the statute in
such case made and provided, the said defendant then and there
became liable, to pay to the said plaintiffs the said sum of money

in the said promissory note specified, according to the tenor and effect of the said promissory note; and being so liable, he the said defendant, in consideration thereof, afterwards, towit, on the day and year aforesaid, at the county and circuit aforesaid, undertook and then and there faithfully promised the said plaintiffs to pay them the said sum of money in the said promissory note specified according to the tenor and effect thereof— Yet the said defendant (although often requested sotodo) hath not as yet paid the said sum of money in the said promissory note specified, or any part thereof; but so to do hath hitherto wholly neglected and refused and still doth neglect and refuse. To the damage of the said plaintiffs of six hundred dollars, and therefore they sue &c.

Stuart& Lincoln pq

John & Augustus Kerr

vs   }   Decln

D. B. Hill
Filed Mar 14th 1840
Wm Butler Clk

Notes Sued On

"$225 55/100 St. Louis, May 7th 1839

Two Months after date, I promise to Pay to the Order of John & Augustus Kerr,

Two Hundred & twenty five Dollars, 55/100 without defalcation, for value received, with interest at the rate of Ten per cent. per annum, after maturity, until paid

D. B. Hill"

Int to 5th March 1840. $54.64

This is a printed note which is filled in, but the words, "Int. to 17th March 1840," and "$15.04," were added by Mr. Lincoln. Despite their minute form the characters of these words are distinctly Lincolnesque.

Int to 5th March 1840, $54.64

$"1311 38/100   St. Louis   April 5th. 1839
Six Months   after date I Promise to Pay to the Order of John & Augustus Kerr Thirteen Hundred & Eleven Dollars 58/100 Without defalcation for Value received with interest at the rate of ten per cent pr anum after due until paid

B. D. Hill"

This note is also a printed form which was filled in, but the notation "Int to 5th March 1840. $54.64," is in the hand of Mr. Lincoln.

BILL OF EXCEPTIONS IN THE SUIT OF MANNING VS. MORGAN ET AL SANGAMON CIRCUIT COURT, MARCH 14, 1840.
(Herndon-Weik Collection)

This bill of exceptions was drawn by Mr. Lincoln. The cover notations with the exception of the familiar signature of Clerk Butler, and date of filing, were also penned by him. The words, "Non est factum," mean that the defendant excepted on the ground that the instrument sued on was not his own act and deed. The record in the case goes no further. As will be seen from the bill of exceptions, the jury found for the plaintiff, and the court refused the defendant's motion for a new trial. William Manning may have been the owner of the one book store in Springfield at the time. The paper drawn by Mr. Lincoln gives the name as William Manning, whereas the owner of the book store was listed as William Manning, Jr.

William Manning   }
     vs   }
Martin M. Morgan }   In Debt—
and others   }

Be it remembered, that this cause came on to be tried upon issue joined upon the plea of *Non est factum,* of one of the defendants: Abner Hall, that the jury was called and sworn, that the plaintiff produced the instrument. sued on, being a sealed note, whereupon the said defendant Hall offered to file an affidavit verifying the truth of his plea of *Non est factum,* to the filing of which the plaintiff objected, on the ground that it was then too late, which objection was sustained by the court, and said affidavit forbidden to be filed; that the plaintiff then offered to read said sealed note to the jury, without proof of it's execution, to which said defendant objected, but which objection was overruled by the court, and the plaintiff read the said sealed note to the jury; that the defendant then offered to prove by a witness, that said sealed note had been delivered by him as an escrow, and that the condition it was so delivered upon had never been performed; to which evidence the plaintiff objected, and which objection was sustained by the court, and the evidence rejected; that the jury then found a verdict for the plaintiff, whereupon, the defendant filed the following affidavits, and reasons in writing, copies of which were given to the opposite party & to the court towit: (here insert them) and moved the court for a new trial, which motion was overruled by the court— To all of which opinions of the court the defendant excepts, and prays that this his bill of exceptions may be signed sealed and made part of the record in the cause—

Saml. H Treat (Seal)

Manning

vs   }   Bill of

Hall }   Exceptions

Filed Mar. 14, 1840
Wm. Butler, Clk

PETITION AND WAIVER IN THE SUIT OF BARRETT VS. WARREN, MORGAN CIRCUIT COURT, MARCH 24, 1840.
(Herndon-Weik Collection)

This entire petition is the work of Mr. Lincoln, as the signature for Baker appears to be in his hand. The notations on the cover are also in his hand, with the exception of those by the clerk concerning the date of filing. It will be noted that "judgment" is spelled "judgement." Mr. Lincoln used both spellings, a habit justified by modern dictionaries. The waver, with the exception of "Barrett Warren &c" is also in the hand of Mr. Lincoln, who apparently wrote these papers for his good friend, Baker. Present day records reveal no other connection with the case, and studies to the present time have not made a case history available.

State of Illoiois

Morgan circuit Sct.

William O. Barret, plaintiff states that he holds these several notes on the defendant William B. Warren, in substance as followeth

1st "$354.00 One year after date I promise to pay Richd F Barret three hundred & fiftyfour dollars with interest at eight per cent from this date for value recd this 1st of November 1836

W. B. Warren"

2nd "$354.00 Two years after date I promise to pay Richd F Barret Three hundred & fiftyfour dollars with eight per cent interest from this date for value recd this 1st of November 1836.

W. B. Warren"

3rd "$354.00 Three years after date I promise to pay Richd F. Barrett Three hundred & fiftyfour dollars with eight per cent interest per annum from this date for value recd this 1st of November 1836.

W. B. Warren"

On the first of which notes is the following assignment— "Pay to Wm D. Barret, July 14th, 1837

Richd F. Barret"

(Over)

And on the third of which notes is the following assignment— "Pay to Wm D. Barrett, July 14th, 1837

Richd F. Barret"

And on the second of which notes is the following assignment— "Pay to Wm D. Barret, July 17th 1837.

Richd F. Barret"

Whereby the plaintiff hath become the proprietor thereof of which the defendant hath had due notice. Yet the same debt remains unpaid, wherefore he prays judgment for his debt and damages for the detention of the same, together with his costs—

Wm D. Barret
By E. D. Baker
his attorney—

Wm D. Barret

vs. } Petition

Wm B. Warren— No 1
Filed March 24 1840
    D Rockwell
        Clerk

————0————

William D. Barret }
    vs. } On Petition & Summons.
William Miller }

This day came the plaintiff and filed his Petition and notes, and the defendant appeared in open court, and waved the necessity of filing the Petition and notes ten days before the day of trial, and the service of process, and consents that the case shall be placed upon the docket, to stand in all respects, as if all legal steps had been taken to bring it to trial at this term of this court—

William D. Barret   ⎤
   vs.   ⎬ On Petition & Summons.
Horatio G. Rew ⎦
  Same order as above—
William D. Barret   ⎤
   vs.   ⎬ On Petition & Summons.
William B. Warren ⎦
Barret
Warren &c

BILL OF COMPLAINT AND STATEMENT OF PLAIN-
TIFF IN SUIT OF BAKER VS. ADDINGTON ET AL
FILED AT TAYLORVILLE, CHRISTIAN
COUNTY, APRIL 2, 1840
(Herndon-Weik Collection)

The bill of complaint and statement here reproduced are in the hand of Attorney Lincoln, as are the notations on the outside of the complaint. The only portion of either document not written by him is the notation of filing by the clerk of Christian County. There is no other evidence of Mr. Lincoln being in Taylorville on April 2, 1840 and, as four days later he addressed a Whig rally at Carlinville, it has been suggested that the Baker complaint and statement were sent from Springfield by mail or messenger.

To the Honorable the Judge of the Christian
County circuit court in chancery sitting

Humbly complaining sheweth unto your Honor your orator James Baker that on the 25 day of October A. D. 1834. One Thomas Johnson, being lawfully seized of the East half of the North West quarter of Section Twenty and the South East quarter of the South West quarter of Section Seven, both in Township Fifteen North Range Two West of the Third Principal Meridian, then in Sangamon, now in Christian county, and being desirous of selling the same, constituted one Drury Bondurant his agent to sell the same, and gave him the authority in writing for so doing which is herewith filed, marked (A.); that on the 27 day of September A. D. 1838, in pursuance of his authority from said Johnson, said Bondurant sold to your orator the land aforesaid, for the sum of five hundred dollars, undertaking for the said Johnson that a deed of conveyance should be made to your orator for said land when the money as aforesaid, should be paid, or be ready for payment, and as evidence thereof gave your orator the bond herewith filed marked

(B.)—your orator further states that in pursuance of said contract, he moved upon the said land and has resided there ever since, and made divers valuable improvements on the same, amounting at least in value; to one hundred dollars, and that he has fully paid to the said Bondurant the said sum of five hundred dollars, in payment for said land— He further states, that shortly after said Johnson appointed said Bondurant his agent as aforesaid, he said Johnson removed from the State of Illinois; and that since the purchase of said land by your orator, said Johnson died, leaving his widow Rebecca Johnson, who has since intermarried with one John Addington, and Eli Johnson a minor his son, all of whom your orator prays may be made defendants to this bill.

And in as much as your orator is, in equity entitled to said land, but is without remedy at common law, he prays that the Peoples writ of subpoena may issue upon the aforesaid defendants, requiring them to answer &c, and that in a final hearing of the cause your Honor will decree that the said defendants convey to your orator all their right title interest and estate in and to the lands aforesaid, and grant such other and further relief as equity may require, and as in duty bound, &c—

                              A Lincoln for Complainant—

James Baker
      vs
Rebecca Addington
John Addington &
Eli Johnson, as heirs
of Thomas Johnson
deceased—
The Clerk of Christian
county will issue a
subpoena in chancery
on the above—
         A Lincoln for
            Compl
Filed April 2nd A. D. 1840
         H. M. Vandeveer Clerk
              ——:——

Baker vs. Addington et al: Statement of Baker: April 2, 1840

State of Illinois   ⎞
                    ⎬
Christian County   ⎠

James Baker who is about to commence a suit in chancery in the circuit court of the county aforesaid against Rebecca Addington, John Addington, **and Eli Johnson** as heirs of Thomas Johnson deceased, being first duly sworn states on oath, that all of said defendants reside out of this state as he verily believes—

James Baker

Subscribed & sworn ⎫
to before me this 2nd day of ⎪
April 1840— ⎪
    H. M. Vandeveer Clerk ⎭

PLAINTIFF'S DECLARATION IN THE SUIT OF RANSDELL VS. CALHOUN,
APRIL 21, 1840
(Herndon-Weik Collection)

The declaration and praecipe in this suit are in the hand-writing of Attorney Lincoln. He also penned the cover notations, with the exception of the date of filing, and the note upon the issuance of a summons in the case. Mr. Lincoln separated the words, "thiry nine", which he later changed to "thirty six", one of the few instances of such a division, with the exception of necessary division caused by reaching the margin of a page. He also seems to have a surplus of periods in the use of one after the word, "Lincoln," and in the final, "Stuart & Lincoln,, p.q." Wharton Ransdell was a Springfield hotel keeper, owner of Ransdell's Tavern, where Lincoln and other Whigs had a banquet honoring William Henry Harrison on October 5, 1836. The defendant, John Calhoun, had appointed Lincoln as his deputy surveyor in the fall of 1833, when Lincoln needed work, but it may be said that the latter opposed friend and foe alike in his court battles. He sued against Ransdell almost as often as he acted as attorney for him. In this case, on motion of the plaintiff, a writ of inquiry was granted July 16, 1840. One week later, the jury called in the case rendered a judgment for $245.95 in favor of Ransdell, the client of Stuart & Lincoln.

State of Illinois ⎫   Of the July term of the circuit
Sangamon county ⎬   court for the said county
and circuit ⎭   A. D. 1840—

Wharton Ransdell, plaintiff complains of John Calhoun defendant being in custody &c of a plea of Trespass on the case upon premises— For that whereas heretofore towit on the

day of   in the year of our Lord one thousand eight
hundred and thirty six, the said defendant was indebted to the
said plaintiff in the sum of two hundred and forty dollars and
twentyfive cents for meat, drink, washing, lodging and other
necessaries, by the said plaintiff before that time found and provided, for the said defendant, and at his special instance and
request; and for the meat, drink. washing, lodging, and other
necessaries before that time found and provided by the said
plaintiff for other persons, and at the like special   instance and
request of   the said defendant; and for horse meat, stabling, care
and attendance by the said plaintiff before that time provided and
bestowed for, in, and about the feeding and keeping of divers
horses, mares, and geldings, of and for the said defendant, and
at his like special instance and request; and being so indebted,
he the said defendant in consideration thereof afterwards to wit,
on the day and year & at the place aforesaid undertook, and then
and there faithfully promised the said plaintiff to pay him the said
sum of money aforesaid, when he should be thereunto afterwards requested—

   Yet the said defendant (although often requested so to do)
hath not as yet paid the said sum of money, or any part thereof; but so to do hath hitherto wholly neglected and refused— To
the damage of the said plaintiff of four hundred dollars, and
therefore he sues &c.

Stuart & Lincoln p. q.

Wharton Ransdell⎫
        vs   ⎬   Trespass on the case upon
John Calhoun ⎭   premises — Damage $400-00

   The clerk of   the Sangamon Circuit court will issue process
in the above entitled cause —

Stuart & Lincoln. p. q.

Wharton Ransdell
              ⎫
  vs   ⎬ Decln
              ⎭
John Calhoun

Filed Apl 21, 1840
      Wm Butler clk

   (Summons issued 22 Apr 1840)

AMENDED DECLARATION BY LINCOLN IN THE SUIT OF CARTER VS. BENNETT & RANSDELL, SANGAMON CIRCUIT COURT, FILED APRIL 21, 1840

As noted elsewhere Mr. Lincoln filed the declaration in the suit of Siloam S. Carter vs. William T. Bennett and Wharton Ransdell in the Sangamon Circuit Court on February 4, 1840 — the same day on which a circular he had written as a member of the Whig State Committee and which urged organized support of Harrison was mailed out to leading Whigs of the state. (See Nicolay and Hay 1: 142-45.) On April 21, 1840, Mr. Lincoln on motion granted by the court wrote and filed the amended declaration reproduced below, the original of which is now owned by Joseph De Castro of Springfield, Illinois.

Siloam S. Carter
      vs.   Sangamon Circuit Court
William T. Bennett &   In Debt
Wharton Ransdell

Amendments to the declaration in the case above referred to —

Amendment to the first count to come in at the letter (A)

Which writing obligatory was and is subject to a certain condition thereunder written, whereby after reciting to the effect following, towit, "that whereas the said Siloam S. Carter did on the 10th day of September A.D. 1839 before William Savely, a Justice of the Peace for the county of Sangamon, recover a judgement against the above bounden William T. Bennett for the sum of $90.80/100 & costs dollars, from which judgement the said William T. Bennett, had taken an appeal to the circuit court for the county of Sangamon aforesaid, and state of Illinois, the parties to the said writing obligatory agreed that if the said William T. Bennett should prosecute his said appeal with effect, and should pay the said debt and costs, in case the said judgement should be affirmed or adjudged against him on the trial thereof in the said circuit court, then the said writing obligatory was to be void; otherwise to remain in full force and effect."

And the plaintiff avers that the said appeal was adjudged against the said William T. Bennett, on the trial thereof in the said circuit court at the November term thereof in the year 1839, for the sum of one hundred and one dollars and fifty cents, together with five dollars and seven cents damages, and also for the costs of the said plaintiff expended in the said cause, as well before the Justice of the Peace, as in the said circuit court — And the plaintiff further avers, that the said William T. Bennett, has hitherto wholly neglected and refused to pay the said debt and costs so adjudged against him by the said circuit court as aforesaid, and still neglects and refuses so to do —

(Amendment to the second count to come in at the letter (B)

Which, writing obligatory was and is the subject to a certain condition thereunder written, whereby, after reciting to the effect following towit "That whereas the said Siloam S. Carter, did on the 10th day of September A.D. 1839 before William Savely, a justice of the Peace for the county of Sangamon, recover a judgement against the above bounden William T. Bennett, for the sum of $25 & costs dollars, from which Judgement the said William T. Bennett had taken an appeal to the Circuit Court for the county of Sangamon aforesaid and state of Illinois, the parties to the said last mentioned writing obligatory agreed that if the said William T. Bennett should prosecute his said appeal with effect, and should pay the said debt and costs, in the case the said judgment should be affirmed or adjudged against him on the trial thereof in the said Circuit court, then the said writing obligatory was to be void, otherwise to remain in full force and effect." And the said plaintiff avers, that the said appeal was adjudged against the said William T. Bennett, on the trial thereof in the said Circuit court, at the November term thereof in the year 1839, for the sum of fifty nine dollars, and also for the costs of the plaintiff by him expended in said case as well before the justice of the Peace, as in the said circuit court — And the said plaintiff further avers, that the said William T. Bennett has, hitherto wholly neglected and refused to pay the said debt and costs so adjudged against him by the said circuit court as aforesaid, and still neglects and refuses so to do —

(Amendment to third count, to come in at the letter (C)

Which writing obligatory was and is subject to a certain condition thereunder written whereby, after reciting to the effect following, towit, "That whereas the said Siloam S. Carter did on the 10th day of September A.D. 1839, before William Savely, a Justice of the Peace for the county of Sangamon, recover a judgement against the above bounden William T. Bennett for the sum of $50. 50/100 & costs, dollars, from which judgement

the said William T. Bennett had taken an appeal to the circuit
court for the county of Sangamon aforesaid, and State of Illinois, the parties to the said last mentioned writing obligatory
agreed, that if the said William T. Bennett should prosecute his
said appeal with effect, and should pay the said debt and costs,
in case the said judgement should be affirmed, or adjudged
against him on the trial thereof in the said circuit court, then the
said writing obligatory was to be void, otherwise to remain in full
force and effect" — And the said plaintiff avers, that the said
appeal was adjudged against the said William T. Bennett, on
the trial thereof in the said circuit court at the November term
thereof in the year 1839. for the sum of fifty one dollars together with two dollars and fifty cents damages, and also for
the costs of the said plaintiff by him expended in said case, as
well before the justice of the Peace, as in the said Circuit court
— And the plaintiff further avers, that the said William T. Bennett has hitherto wholly neglected and refused to pay the debt
and costs, so adjudged against him by the said circuit court as
aforesaid, and still neglects and refuses so to do—
Siloam S. Carter

vs.

Wm. T. Bennett & Wharton Ransdell
Amendments to Declaration —
Filed April 21st 1840
  Wm. Butler Clk.

DECLARATION BY MR. LINCOLN IN THE SUIT OF RANSDELL VS. LIGHTFOOT AND LIGHTFOOT, SANGAMON CIRCUIT COURT, FILED APRIL 21, 1840

*There is proof that Lawyer Lincoln was ready to serve all
worthy clients without regard for past or present relations in
the fact that on the same April 21, 1840 when he filed an
amended declaration in a suit in which Wharton Ransdell was one
of the defendants he also wrote and filed the declaration reproduced below in a suit brought by Ransdell against Goodrich and
Henry Lightfoot. This latter suit was tried by the court on
July 21, 1840, and judgment awarded Ransdell, Lincoln's client.*

State of Illinois ⎫ Of the July term of the circuit
Sangamon County ⎬ court of said County AD 1840
and Circuit ⎭

Wharton Ransdell plaintiff complains of Goodrich Lightfoot

and Henry Lightfoot, defendants being in custody & of a plea of Trespass on the case upon premises: For that whereas the said defendants, heretofore towit, on the eighteenth day of September in the year of our Lord one thousand eight hundred and thirty nine, at the county and circuit aforesaid made their certain promissory note in writing, (the said Henry signing his name thereto "Henry Lightfot") bearing date the day and year aforesaid, and thereby then and there promised to pay on or before the first day of April (then) next (ensuing) to the said plaintiff by the style & description of "W. Ransdell" the sum of one hundred and twenty dollars and seventynine cents, bearing interest at the rate of twelve per cent per annum from date, and then and there delivered the said promissory note to the plaintiff, by means whereof, and by force of the statute in such case made and provided, the said defendants then and there became liable to pay to the said plaintiff the said sum of money in the said promissory note specified according to the tenor and effect of the said promissory note, and being so liable they, the said defendants, in consideration thereof, afterwards, towit, on the day and year aforesaid, at the county and circuit aforesaid, undertook, and then and there faithfully promised to said plaintiff to pay him the said sum of money in the said promissory note specified according to the tenor and effect thereof —

Yet the said defendants (although often requested so to do) have not as yet paid the said sum of money in the said promissory note specified, or any part thereof; but so to do have hitherto wholly neglected and refused, and still do neglect and refuse. To the damage of the said plaintiff of two hundred dollars, and therefore he sues &C.

Copy of note sued on

"On or before the first day of April next one or either of us promise to pay W. Ransdell, or order, one hundred and twenty dollars and seventy nine cents bearing interest at the rate of twelve per cent per annum from this date as witness our hands this 18th day of Sept 1839.

> Goodrich Lightfoot
> Henry Lightfot"

GRANT OF APPEAL TO THE ILLINOIS SUPREME
COURT AND CONTINUANCE ORDER IN THE
SUIT OF SCAMMON VS. CLINE,
MAY 12 AND 21, 1840

(Herndon-Weik Collection)

*The grant of appeal and continuance order here reproduced
had a part in the history of one of Mr. Lincoln's earliest cases
before the Illinois Supreme Court, but he had no part in the penning of them. Norman Buel Judd, who figured in this case, was
a leading membber of the Chicago bar and long a helpful if not
wholly trusted friend of Mr. Lincoln. He was one of the founders of the Republican Party in Illinois, and to him, after David
Davis, belongs chief credit for Mr. Lincoln's first nomination
for the Presidency. Judd was disappointed in his efforts to secure a place in the Cabinet, but was appointed minister to Ger-
many, the first diplomatic post to be filled by President Lincoln.
(See Intimate Memories of Lincoln by Wilson, Pages 3-4.)*

*The first days of May 1840, brought with them, two incidents
charged with future meaning for Mr. Lincoln. In New York
on the first day of that month Horace Greeley, moved thereto by
Thurlow Weed, founded The Log Cabin, a weekly journal perhaps read by Mr. Lincoln in which its still youthful editor
championed the election of Harrison and at the same time began
the career as a moulder of public opinion that, despite erratic
ways that often provoked or confounded his political associates,
made him for a generation a dominant influence in shaping the
history and policies first of the Whig and later of the Republican
Party. Thus, while he aided in the first nomination of Mr. Lincoln, he thereafter as a ready fault finder too often proved a
thorn in the flesh of a beset and troubled President.*

*Again it was on May 11, 1840, that James Gillespie Birney,
a native of the South and former owner of slaves now pledged
to fight for their freedom, became the presidential nominee of
the newly formed Liberty Party. The vote he received did not
affect the result of the election in 1840, but a second candidacy
in 1844 cost the Whigs the electoral vote of New York and
snatched the Presidency from Henry Clay, the leader most admired by Abraham Lincoln in early manhood.*

J. Y. Scammon vs. Cornelius Cline: Grant of Appeal to Illinois
Supreme Court: May 12, 1840

Jonathan Y. Scammon ⎫ April Term 1840
      vs ⎬
Cornelius Cline ⎭ Appeal

    It is ordered for reasons on file that this appeal be dismissed. to which the Plaintiff takes exception. It is therefore. ordered that an appeal be taken to the Supreme Court upon the Plaintiff's entering into bond, with Norman B. Judd as security in the sum of one hundred dollars within thirty days after the adjournment of this court.

    I S. S. Whitman, Clerk of the cir. court of the Courts of Boone, certify that the above is a true copy from the records of said court in regard to the above entitled suit. And that the appeal Bond to the supreme court has been duly entered into, and this day filed in the Clerk's office of said Court.

> In testimony whereof I have hereunto set my hand and private seal, (there being no seal of office) at Belvidere in said County this 12th day of May A. D. 1840

(Seal)   attest   S. S. Whitman. clerk

---o---

Scammon vs. Cline: Continuance Order: May 21, 1840

Jonathan Y. Scammon ⎫ Boone Cir. Court April term 1839
      vs ⎬
Cornelius Cline ⎭ Appeal

It appearing that the summons in this cause had not been served ten days before the sitting of this court. it is ordered that this cause be continued to the next term.
Supreme Court
July Term 1840

Jonathan Y. Scammon
    plff. in error
      v.
Cornelius Cline
    deft.in error

    Error to Boone
  Filed May 21. 1841
        J M Duncan
  Rec. Dec. T. 1840
    Scammon

LINCOLN AT PONTIAC ASKS FOR A SUMMONS IN THE SUIT OF POPEJOY VS. WILSON, MAY 19, 1840

The request for summons here reproduced is an interesting reminder of Mr. Lincoln's experiences on the circuit. The first of the six circuits into which Illinois was divided in 1835 was the scene of his practice from 1837 to 1839, but on March 2 of the latter year, the swift and steady increase in the population of the state — twenty-seven new counties were created between 1836 and 1839 — caused the reorganization of the existing six into nine circuits. Thus the six northern counties of the first with the counties of Menard, Dane and De Witt became the new eighth circuit, and it was on this circuit, altered from time to time as to its constituent units, that for a score of years Mr. Lincoln traveled as a circuit lawyer.

Courts in each of the circuits began on the first or second Monday in March and continued in a majority of the circuits counties, an added July term in some of them. After 1848 David Davis of Bloomington was judge of the eighth circuit, until June. Fall as well as spring terms were held in all of the and Mr. Lincoln was one of the three or four lawyers who kept him company to all of the county seats included in his spring and fall journeys. Thus, until the coming of the railway made possible week-end returns to Springfield, Mr. Lincoln was absent from his home and office a full half of each year; but there is abundant proof that he keenly enjoyed the primitive albeit diverting conditions of life on the circuit, while his liking for all sorts and conditions of men and his unfailing supply of pat and humorous anecdote assured him a cordial welcome in each of its county seats. They also raised up for him an army of friends who played an effective part in the furtherance and fulfilment of his political ambitions; and he was ever and always an ambitious man.

The suit of Popejoy vs. Wilson which was one of the matters which took Mr. Lincoln to Pontiac in May, 1840, was a case of trespass and had a long and varied history to be dealt with in another place. Having filed his request to the clerk to issue a summons he went on from Pontiac to Clinton, where on May 23 he successfully defended one Spencer Turner indicted for murder, receiving for his fee a ninety-day note for $200. But this note he did not succeed in collecting until April, 1846, and then only after long litigation.

William Popejoy Jr. ⎱
         vs.   ⎰   Trespass on the case
Isaac Wilson   ⎰   Damage $2000.

The clerk of the Livingston county circuit court will please issue a summons in the above entitled cause returnable to the next term of said court — He will also issue subpoenas on behalf of the plaintiff for Michael Murray, Maranda Murray (his wife), John Falky, and Dorcas Moore —

May 19th 1840   Lincoln Pffs.

INSTRUCTIONS TO THE JURY WRITTEN BY LINCOLN IN THE SUIT OF CLARY VS. HARRISON, MENARD CIRCUIT COURT, 1840

When on March 2, 1839, Menard was set off from Sangamon County with Petersburg as its county seat and made a part of the new eighth circuit, Mr. Lincoln became one of the lawyers in regular attendance at the spring and fall sessions of its circuit court, finding many clients among the friends he had made in his New Salem days, as the document here reproduced bears witness. John Clary, the plaintiff in the suit of Clary vs. Harrison, was a Sangamon County pioneer and gave his name to the section known as Clary's Grove.

Instructions to the jury written by Lincoln in suit of Clary v. Harrison, in Menard Circuit Court.
The plaintiff having introduced the affidavit of the defendant are the jury bound to hear and consider the whole of it as evidence, and to give it so much weight, as when taken in connection with all the other evidence in the case they shall think entitled to.
(Marked "granted" on the edge)

PETITION OF ADMINISTRATORS OF JOHN McGEE TO SELL REAL ESTATE, DEWITT CIRCUIT COURT, MAY 22, 1840.

(Photostat from the Lincoln National Life Foundation)
The document here presented gives a complete history of the case with one or two exceptions. It is known that Mr. Lincoln was appointed as guardian ad litem to the heirs of John McGee on May 22, 1840. The court decree on the petition to sell real estate appears to be from the pen of one J. J. McGraw, and the paper is presented because it is part of the record of a case in

which Mr. Lincoln was a party to the suit, and because it pre-sents his answer as guardian ad litem in resume form. The clerk of the court was Kersey H. Fell, brother of Jesse W. Fell, intimate of Mr. Lincoln, while Attorney Benedick was Kirby Benedict who later appeared with Douglas and Lincoln as de-fense counsel for one Spencer Turner, accused of murder. As related in another place Mr. Lincoln spent several years trying to collect his fee from Turner.

State of Illinois	Circuit Court DeWitt
DeWitt County	County May Term 1840
ex parte	
Thomas Fruit and	Petition to sell real estate of
John Walker Admin	the Estate of John McGee

On this day May 22nd 1840 came the complainants by their solicitor Benedick and files their petition and presented the same to the court praying for authority to sell the following real estate Situated lying and being in the county of DeWitt and state of Illinois to wit, The west half of the South East quarter of Section number thirteen in Township number nineteen North of Range numbered One East of the third principal Meander Meredian containing eight acres

And it appearing to the Satisfaction of the court that notice of the time of presenting said petition has been duly published according to Law

And it also appearing by the abstract of the Probate Records from the Probate office of the County of Macon that the debts established against the said estate before the probate Justice of the Peace of said county exceed the assets arising from the sale of the personal property of said estate the sum of Two Hundred and fifty one Dollars and seventeen and three fourths cents and It also appearing that the said Administrators have duly filed in said Justice office an Inventory and sale Bill of the Personal property of said Estate

And Abram Lincoln having been appointed Guardian Ad-litem of James Milissa McGee Elizabeth McGee Sampson McGee George McGee and Rosanna McGee Infant heirs of said John McGee Deceased who having Answer filed to said Petition showing that he sees no reason why the prayer of said Petition should not be granted

Therefore it is ordered adjudged and decreed by the court that Thomas Fruit and John Walker Administrators of the Estate of John McGee Deceased be and they are hereby appointed authorized and empowered to sell the real Estate above described upon a credit Six and Twelve months the purchasers giving security sufficient and Mortguage upon the premises to Secure the payment of the same that they make conveyance to the purchasers and they report their proceedings as well to this court as to the probate Justice of the Peace

State of Illinois }
DeWitt County }

I hereby certify that the above is a true copy from the record of the case to sell Real Estate exparte Thomas Fruit and John Walker Administrator of the Estate of John McGee Decd—

(Seal)

Given under my hand and private seal there being no official seal provided dated at Clinton May the 30th A D 1840

K H Fell clk
pr J J McGraw Dept ck

ANSWER OF MR. LINCOLN AS GUARDIAN AD LITEM FOR MARY ELIZABETH FINLEY, MAY 26, 1840.

(Photostat from the Lincoln National Life Foundation)

Little or none of this document was penned by Mr. Lincoln. He merely signed his name to an answer which he did not write, and added the words, "guardian ad litem." It is probable that he acted only as guardian ad litem, although research to the present date sheds no light on the history of the suit, or the part played in it by Lawyer Lincoln. His answer is the only known evidence of his connection with the case.

Answer of Abram Lincoln Guardian ad litem of Mary Elizabeth Finley infant heir of Alvin Finley deceased

And this respondent Abram Lincoln comes and for answer saith that he has examined the petition presented to the court in this cause and the proceedings related thereto and that he knows of no good reason why the prayer contained in the premises should not be granted and the land there in described ordered to be sold for the purpose therein Expressed—

A Lincoln
Guardian ad litem

PLEAS IN THE SUIT OF YOUNG VS. COX, MACON CIRCUIT COURT, MAY 26, 1840.

(Photostat from the Lincoln National Life Foundation)

These pleas were drawn by Mr. Lincoln, and the cover nota-

tions which cite the case are in his handwriting. It will be noted that he used the spelling "alledged" for "alleged", and he seems to have alternated between the two spellings, using the incorrect form less frequently in later legal papers. As can be seen from the phraseology of the pleas, the case involved a note, and a suit for trespass upon the case upon promises. The final record in the case reads as follows:

Macon County

Tues. May 26 1840

Parties by atty. & deft. withdraws plea & saith nothing further in bar or preclusion of pltfs action whereby the pltf. against him stands wholly undisputed. Action brot on a promissory note for payment of money only. Ordered that pltf have $154.99

Charles Emmerson, who was an associate of Mr. Lincoln in other cases, opposed him in this suit, and emerged with a judgment in favor of his client, Young.

Ephraim Cox   ⎫
      ads   ⎬
William M Young ⎭

And the said defendant comes and defends the wrong and injury when, where &c. and says plaintiff *actio non,* because he says he did not undertake and promise in manner and form as the said plaintiff in his said declaration hath alledged against him; and of this he puts himself upon the country &c—

Lincoln p- d-

And for further plea in this behalf the said defendant by application to the court comes and defends the wrong & injury when &c and says plaintiff *actio non,* because he says that a greater rate of interest was reserved in taking the note in the plaintiff's declaration mentioned, than twelve per cent per annum, and this he is ready to verify; wherefore he prays judgment &c.

Lincoln p. d.

And for further plea in this behalf the said defendant by application to the court comes and defends the wrong and injury where &c. and says plaintiff *actio non* because he says that a greater rate of interest was reserved in taking the note in the plaintiff's declaration mentioned, than twelve per cent pre annum, in the manner following towit: That said defendant borrowed of the said Thomas Devin, on or about the fifteenth of April A D. 1839, one hundred dollars, for which he gave said Devin his note for one hundred and thirteen dollars with interest at twelve per cent per annum from date; that afterwards; towit on the day of the date of the note in plaintiffs declaration mentioned for no consideration whatever excepting the discharge of the note first above mentioned; and this he is ready to verify wherefore he prays judgment &c.

Lincoln p. d.

Cox

ads } Pleas—

Young
Filed May 28th 1840
H. McGorin clk

ANSWER OF JAMES C. CONKLING IN THE SUIT OF BAKER VS. ADDINGTON ET AL, CHRISTIAN CIRCUIT COURT, JUNE 1, 1840.
(Herndon-Weik Collection)

This answer, with the exception of the signature of Conkling and the note on the date of filing signed by the clerk, is in the hand of Attorney Lincoln. The defendants in this case defaulted in the Dane (Christian) County Circuit Court on June 1, 1840. The court examined the exhibit of Baker, and then appointed Levi W. Goodan commissioner to convey the land described in the bill filed by Lincoln on April 2, 1840. Goodan's report of conveyance of the property was approved on June 2, 1842. Conkling was a Springfield lawyer and in turn Whig and Republican associate of Abraham Lincoln. He married Mercy Levering, a close friend of Mary Lincoln, and husband and wife watched and recorded the progress of a historic courtship. (See Mary Lincoln, Wife and Widow, Sandburg and Angle, New York, 1832, Pages 170 to 185.)

The answer of James Conkling guardian *ad litem* to Eli Johnson, to a bill in chancery filed against him and others by James Baker, in the circuit court for Christian county —

This respondent, for answer to said Bill, says that he knows nothing about the truth of the allegations of the same and that he demands that full proof be made thereof to the satisfaction of the court —

Ja C. Conkling
Guardian at Litem

James Baker
    vs.
Rebecca Addington *et al* } Answer of guardian &c.

al
Filed June first 1840
     H. H. Vandeveer Clerk

REPORT OF THE YOUNG MEN'S CONVENTION AND SOLDIERS' MEETING HELD IN SPRINGFIELD, JUNE 3 AND 4, 1840, PROBABLY WRITTEN BY MR. LINCOLN.

For the Whigs of Illinois the outstanding events of the noisy and boisterous presidential campaign of 1840 were the Young Men's Convention and Old Soldiers' Meeting held at Springfield on June 3 and 4. On June 2 delegations from all parts of the state began arriving at the capital, and we are told that "the spectator who looked on and saw the long lines of wagons and canoes filled with men, and the hundreds on horseback, might well have supposed that the whole sucker state had broken loose." (Transactions of the Illinois State Historical Society, 20: 160.)

The convention organized at eight o'clock in the morning of June 3, and two hours later a grand procession took up its line of march. The procession was two and a half miles long, divided into 1463 sections, each containing six or more paraders. At its head were soldiers of the Revolution and the War of 1812. Then followed imposing delegations which had come from the neighboring states of Indiana, Missouri, and Iowa to have their part in the affair, and these were trailed by delegations from fifty-nine counties of Illinois, at their head Cook County with a band and a miniature brig thirty feet in length. On the second day, June 4, there was a barbecue at which the delegations about to depart were fed on roasted ox; and then an afternoon and evening of continuous speaking by earnest champions of the Whig cause. Among the speakers were Samuel Lisle Smith, then twenty-three years old, a witty and eloquent Chicago lawyer, who had lately come to the West from his native Philadelphia, and who was to die of cholera in 1854; John Hogan, a Methodist preacehr turned lawyer, who was to fill many public posts and live to the great age of eighty-seven years; Fletcher, son of Daniel Webster, who was to fall in battle during the Civil War; John J. Hardin, Edward D. Baker, and their friend Abraham Lincoln, whose speech was recalled in an after time by a youth-

ful listener, John M. Scott, for half a century a member of the McLean County bar:

"Mr. Lincoln stood in a wagon from which he addressed the mass of people that surrounded it. He was tall, and perhaps a little more slender than in later life, and more homely than after he became stouter in person. He was then only thirty-one years of age, and yet he was already regarded as one of the ablest of the Whig speakers in that campaign. There was that in him that attracted public attention. Even then he was the subject of popular regard because of his candid and simple mode of discussing and illustrating political questions. At times he was intensely logical, and always most convincing in his arguments. Much time was devoted to telling stories to illustrate some phase of his argument. One story he told on that occasion was not one that it would be seemly to publish, yet the manner of telling was so peculiarly his own that it gave no offense. On the contrary it was much liked by the vast assembly that surrounded the temporary platform from which he spoke, was received with loud bursts of laughter and applause, and gave him a most favorable hearing for the arguments he later made in support of the measures he was sustaining."

And on June 15 the tenth issue of The Old Soldier, the Whig campaign newspaper of which Abraham Lincoln was one of the editors, devoted all of its four pages to the events of June 3 and 4. There is little doubt that its introductory account of the rally here reproduced was written by Mr. Lincoln, for it is just the sort of story that could have been reasonably looked for from him in his thirty-second year.

It is difficult to find language expressive enough to convey any thing like a correct idea of the proud and exciting scene which has just closed in this place. Much as we expected from the whigs of Illinois—wide spread and intense as we knew the enthusiasm and zeal for the cause of Harrison, Tyler and Reform,—yet with those facts before us, the Convention just closed exceeded every thing we had anticipated. It was an outpouring of the people! The assembly of themselces! They came like the rush of the mountain torrent—like the gathering together of a mighty army. They came in parties of tens, of hundreds, and of thousands, from the north, the south, and the east, and the west—delegations poured in and swelled the vast multitude. They came in conveyances and by means which bespoke their precincts and the sections from whence they hailed. They came not like "the silk stocking gentry" (as they are frequently called by their opponents;) but as farmers, mechanics, and sturdy laborers would be expected to come, in their own farm wagons, on horseback, and by such other means as they individually had at command. Every thing about them indicated that they were the sturdy yeomanry of the country, her bone and sinew, the men who do their own work, their own fighting, and their own voting. They came with their camps and camp equipage, sleeping on the ground at night and preparing their own food by the way, thus manifesting, in the strongest possible manner, that no toil or exposure could quench or slacken the spirit of patriotism and the love of country which burns in every whig bosom. Some of the delegations came over roads now unusually bad for the season, being deep and miry, and were from eight to ten days on the way, having to journey from one to two hundred and fifty miles. Can language convey any just conception of the zeal of men who thus regardless of toil march to the rescue of their country?

With them came hoary headed veterans of the revolution, grey headed soldiers who had served under Gen. Wayne, and the soldiers of the last war. Some of these war-worn veterans had journeyed a long distance and exposed their aged and venerable forms to many privations and toils by the way.—Their attendance was numerous, there being near two hundred and fifty in all present at their meeting. The animating and stirring scene around them appeared to light up afresh the spirit which in days past had called them to the tented field, to protect and defend their country. These witnesses of Gen. Harrison's history of the Government from its organization to the present day, with one heart and one voice, joined in the loud cry for—reform, Reform REFORM!

Nature smiled upon the assemblage. Tuesday was clear and brilliant, and at an early hour in the afternoon of that day delegations from remote parts of the State came in, and pitched their tents and formed their encampments. The day following the sun arose clear, but at an early hour clouds gathered up and for a time it was apprehended that there would be rain, but they passed off. At an early hour delegations with flags flying and banners streaming to the breeze, came in. The spectator who looked on and saw the long lines of wagons, canoes, &c., filled with men and the hundreds on horseback, might well have supposed that the whole Sucker land had broken loose.

For the particulars of the reception of the delegations, the proceedings of the Young Men's Convention, the various addresses, the meeting of The Old Soldier's Convention, their proceedings and processions, and the addresses on Thursday, we refer the reader to a subsequent account.

Justly may the whole proceedings be said to be the proudest and greatest exhibition ever witnessed in Illinois; and when the season of the year is considered,—now the busiest for the farmer, —the sparsely settled character of the country; the fact that our city is alone to be reached by land conveyance, and that over roads none of the best; we feel that we have the right to claim for this the palm of being the greatest Convention yet held in the West.

The propitious smiles of heaven were but repaid in the order and decorum which characterised the whole proceedings. Notwithstanding the number present was so great, the enthusiasm so general, and the excitement so extended, everything was conducted with perfect order and propriety. Speech on speech was listened to by the crowd with undivided attention, and for hours of each day the whole concourse stood upon their feet, listening and responding to the flood of eloquence which was poured out by the different gentlemen called upon the stands. A fact or two will best attest the attention and intelligence of the audience and the ability of the orators who addressed them. On Wednesday the Convention was organized and the speakers called to the stand about 2 o'clock;—from that hour until about 12 o'clock at night, with the exception of a short adjournment for supper, the crowd continued attentive listeners of the speeches—sometimes two or more speaking at the same time from stands in different parts of the grounds. On Thursday a like exhibition was given of their attention; and throughout the two days not the slightest disturbance arose to mar the harmony of the assembly, nor was there a single delegate or whig on the ground, intoxicated. Intelligence, attention and sobriety were the distinguishing features of the crowd and their conduct. Never did an assembly of equal magnitude conduct themselves with greater honor to themselves, their country and their cause.

PRAECIPE AND DECLARATION IN THE SUIT OF WAGGENER VS. PORTER, SANGAMON CIRCUIT COURT, JUNE 5, 1840.
(Herndon-Weik Collection)
The date of the filing of this document is in the hand of

Clerk Butler, but the declaration and quoted note, with its misspelling of "ballance" for "balance", are from the pen of Attorney Lincoln. The proecipe appears to be missing. Mr. Lincoln listed it in citing the case, but there is no order to issue process in his hand. William Porter, the defendant in this suit, was a friend of Mr. Lincoln dating from the latter's New Salem years. He was also a devoted Whig, and on November 22, 1841 served with Lincoln and Simeon Francis on a committee of the Sangamon County Whig Convention which endorsed Joseph Duncan for governor.

State of Illinois	Of the July term of the
Sangamon county	circuit court of said county
and circuit	A. D. 1840 —

George Waggener plaintiff complains of William Porter defendant, being in custody &c of a plea of Trespass on the case upon premises: For that whereas the said defendant, heretofore towit; on the fourteenth day of November in the year of our Lord one thousand eight hundred and thirtyeight, at Springfield in the county and circuit aforesaid, made his certain promissory note in writing, signing his name thereto "Wm Porter" bearing date the day and year aforesaid, and thereby then and there promised to pay one day after the date thereof to the said plaintiff the sum of six hundred and fifty dollars, and interest at twelve per cent till paid, for value received, and then & there delivered the said promissory note to the said plaintiff; by means whereof, and by force of the statute in such case made and provided, the said defendant then and there became liable to pay to the said plaintiff the said sum of money, together with the interest in the said promissory note specified according to the tenor and effect of the said promissory note; and being so liable, he the said defendant, in consideration thereof, afterwards, towit, on the day and year aforesaid, at the county and circuit aforesaid, undertook, and then and there faithfully promised the said plaintiff to pay him the said sum of money in the said promissory note specified according to the tenor and effect thereof —

Yet the said defendant (although often requested so to do) hath not as yet paid to the said plaintiff the said sum of money in the said promissory note specified, or any part thereof; but so to do hath hitherto wholly neglected and refused & still doth neglect and refuse— To the damage of the said plaintiff of one thousand dollars, and therefore he sues &c.

Stuart & Lincoln p. q.

————o————

Copy of note sued on
"Springfield November 14.   1838.
"   One day after date I promise to pay to George Waggener
six hundred & fifty dollars and interest at twelve per cent till
paid value received, being the ballance due him on a final settlement of all our business —

                                                    Wm Porter   "

George Waggener ⎫
      vs.   ⎬   Precipe & Decln
Wm. Porter   ⎭
Filed June 5 1840
      Wm. Butler clerk

MR. LINCOLN'S FIRST APPEARANCES BEFORE THE ILLINOIS SUPREME COURT, DECEMBER, 1839 AND JUNE 6 AND 18, 1840.

*Mr. Lincoln made his first appearances in the Illinois Su-
preme Court in December, 1839 and on June 6, 1840 when he
moved to have the cases of Gibbs vs. Ingraham and Thomas vs.
Broadwell stricken from the docket. One was an appeal from
Pike and the other from Morgan County, and both after due
consideration were dismissed by the court.*

*Mr. Lincoln made his first argument before the Illinois
Supreme Court on June 18, 1840, when he appeared for the de-
fendant in the suit of Scammon vs. Cline, which had been ap-
pealed from a justice of the peace to the Boone Circuit Court.
Mr. Lincoln in his argument contended that the appeal should have
been to the circuit court of Jo. Daviess instead of Boone County.
The decision of the Boone Circuit Court was reversed by the
Supreme Court. (See Third Illinois, Page 456).*

*The record proves that both in the number and importance
of the cases in which he appeared, and also in the number which
he won, Mr. Lincoln was one of the foremost lawyers in practice
before the Illinois Supreme Court between the summer of 1840
and that of 1860. A study made by Dr. Harry E. Pratt in 1843
shows that during the period indicated he appeared alone or as
joint counsel in not less than 243 cases, and he won the greater
number of them, for he was at his best when given abundant
time for study of the facts and scrutiny of the law underlying
a particular case. Indeed, one has only to consider the causes*

*which he argued before the Illinois Supreme Court to reach the
conclusion that in his gift for analysis, strong and unfailing
grasp of fundamentals, and ability to give them lucid and persuasive expression Abraham Lincoln either in or out of Illinois,
was one of the ablest lawyers in a period of great lawyers. (See
Lincoln's Supreme Court Cases, Compiled by Harry E. Pratt,
Illinois Bar Journal, September 1843.)*

ANSWER OF GUARDIAN AD LITEM IN THE SUIT OF SEARS VS. SUMMERS, SANGAMON CIRCUIT COURT, JUNE 9, 1840.
(Herndon-Weik Collection)

*This answer by Rutledge was drawn by Mr. Lincoln and
signed by the guardian ad litem. The cover notations are in the
hand of Clerk Butler. He appears to have written "Siemers"
as did Mr. Lincoln in the court decree of June 9, 1840, but in
this answer Attorney Lincoln has clearly placed a dot over the
"i" in the name of Maria Siemers and one over the "m" in that
of her husband. Careless placement of that dot over the "i"
seems to have been characteristic of Mr. Lincoln, and from his
penmanship one may interpret the name either as "Siemers"
or "Seimers". And it will be noted that he wrote "refered"
for "referred". David Rutledge was a brother of Ann Rutledge, and on June 8, 1840 Mr. Lincoln had asked for his appointment as guardian ad litem. He was one of Petersburg's
first attorneys and opposed his dead sister's friend in a number
of cases. (See Lincoln's New Salem by Thomas, Springfield,
1834, Page 94.)*

The answer of David H. Rutledge, guardan *ad litem,* to
Melvina Summers, & Levi Summers to a bill filed against them
& Maria Seimers, & Henry Seimers, by Henry Sears, George
Close, Rebecca Close, and Levi Summers, administrator &c.

This Respondent, for answer to the allegations of the bill
in the case above referred to, says he knows nothing of the
truth thereof, and requires full proof of the same to be made —

D. H. Rutledge

Henry Sears	
and others	answer
vs.	of guardian
Maria Siemers	ad litem
& others	
Filed June 9th 1840	

COURT DECREE IN THE SUIT OF HENRY SEARS ET AL VS. MELVINA SUMMERS ET AL, SANGAMON CIRCUIT COURT, JUNE 9, 1840.

(Herndon-Weik Collection)

Attorney Lincoln drew the court decree in this case. He spelled "beginning" as "begining", an error common in his early legal papers. The decree is undated in the Herndon-Weik Collection, but as the court handed down its decision on June 9, 1840, Mr. Lincoln no doubt drew the order at that time. The case was begun by a bill in chancery asking conveyance of the land, and on November 11, 1839, Mr. Lincoln moved that it be continued to the June, 1840, term of the court. The motion was granted, and on June 9, 1840, this decree in favor of Lincoln's clients was handed down. Levi Summers, administrator of the estate of Alfred Summers, had known Mr. Lincoln in his New Salemn days. Henry Sears, complainant with him, was defendant in the case of trespass sued on by Mr. Lincoln for Summers in June, 1839, and Summers the litigant to whom Mr. Lincoln makes familiar reference in his letter of May 30, 1839, addressed to Nathan Dresser given in another place.

Henry Sears
George Close
Rebecca Close &
Levi Summers, administrator of the estate of Alfred Summers deceased

     vs

Maria Siemers
Melvina Summers
Levi Summers &
Henry Siemers

In chancery—

This day came the complainants, and it appearing to the satisfaction of the court, that all defendants had been regularly served with process, and they being three times solemnly called, came not but made default— It is therefore decreed by the court, that said Complainant's bill be taken for confessed, as against the said Maria Siemers and Henry Siemers— And David H. Rutledge having been appointed guardian *ad litem* to the said minor heirs, Melvina Summers and Levi Summers, having filed his answer, saying that he knows nothing of the truth of the allegations of the said complainant's bill, and requires full proof of the same to be made, and the court hearing the allegations and proofs of the said complainants, and being satisfied that said allegations are true— It is therefore decreed by the court, that the deeds, filed with the bill in this cause, and marked (A.) (B.) & (C) be cancelled, and forever annulled; and that the said Complainants George Close and Rebecca Close his wife, convey to the said Henry Sears, the legal title in and to the West half of the South East quarter of Section Seventeen, in Township Twenty North of Range Seven West of the Third Principal Meridian, situate, lying and being in the county of Menard and state of Illinois, excepting therefrom a lot containing two acres and thirty poles and bounded as follows, to wit; Beginning seventyeight poles South of the North West corner of said tract; thence East fourteen poles; thence South twenty poles; thence West fourteen poles; thence North to the beginning.

ASSIGNMENT OF ERRORS IN THE SUPREME COURT CASE OF SCAMMON VS. CLINE
(Undated in Herndon-Weik Collection But Probably June 10, 1840)

The portion signed by Mr. Lincoln of the document here reproduced was not penned by him. The wording was his, but not the hand. The misuse of capitals and lack of punctuation indicate it is a poor copy of the original replication. The words "in propria persona" means "in his own person", and as Jonathan Young Scammon, at that time reporter of the Illinois Supreme Court and a lawyer of large practice, was the plaintiff in this case, it is reasonable to assume that he drew his assignment of errors in person.

Supreme Court of the State of Illinois, June Term A. D. 1840.

Jonathan Y. Scammon v. Cornelius Cline, Error to Boone

And the said plaintiff in error comes and says that in the Record and proceedings aforesaid, and in the rendition of the judgment aforesaid there is manifest error to wit.

1st.   The court erred in dismissing said Appeal.

2nd.   the judgment of the Court below was for the defendant, whereas it should have been for the plaintiff in the Court below.

Scammon in propria persona.

And the said defendant in Error comes and Says that there

are   no such Errors in the Record of the proceedings of the
Court below in this Cause as the said Plaintiff in Error hath
alleged Wherefore he prays that the Judgment of the Court below may be affirmed

> Lincoln   for   Defendant
> in   Error.

> Tm,

ABSTRACT IN THE SUIT OF SCAMMON VS. CLINE, POSSIBLY JUNE, 1840, TERM OF ILLINOIS SUPREME COURT.
(Undated in Herndon-Weik Collection)

*This abstract is not in the hand of Mr. Lincooln, and ap-
pears to have been drawn by Giles Spring, who appeared for
Scammon. It is included with other attendant documents in order
to give a partial history of this early Illinois Supreme Court case
in which Mr. Lincoln was the counsel for Cline.*

J Y Scammon
    vs   Supreme Court
Cornelius Cline   June Term 1840

This cause was tried before a Justice of the peace Feb 21
1839 and judgment rendered against the plaintiff an appeal was
taken by the plff to the Boon cir ct and filed an appeal bond on
the first Day of March 1839 and a supersedeas was issued on
the second day returnable to the April Term of said court— A
preacipe for a summons to the defendant was filed April 26-
1839 returnable to said April Term. & the cause at the time was
continued

The cause came on for trial in the boon circuit court at the
April Term 1840—an affidavit was filed that the bond had been
on the files of the Clerks office from 1st March up to the present
time

The defendant moved to dismiss the appeal— Because the
said appeal was taken to the circuit court of Boon county before any court was appointed in said county and whilst Boon
was attached to Jo Davess county for judicial purposes.

Which motion was sustained and is now object [?] for
Error
Scammon
   vs
Cline

Act of 1837 attaches
Boon Cty to Jo Davess —
9 RT [?] page of agts 1838 sec 9—
— Till county is organized
Judj. on the 21st Feb.
Appeal on the 1st of March
supersedeas issued after
Appeal taken one day before the law fixed
the time for holding the Boon C. Court

LETTER OF MR. LINCOLN TO JONATHAN G. RANDALL. JUNE 16, 1840

This whimsical yet appealing letter was for one father and son a disturbing echo of the Young Men's Whig Convention which for three days in early June of 1840 brought to Springfield delegations from all parts of Illinois, and aroused much noisy enthusiasm for the candidacy of General Harrison. By the same token it enabled Abraham Lincoln to reap a goodly number of new and devoted friends among the youthful Whig voters of the state. It is also safe to assume that Jonathan Randall without delay and in satisfying fashion restored the lost or stolen outfit of his son Richard.

Springfield,
June 16 — 1840.

Jonathan G. Randall,
    Rushville, Ill.
My Dear Sir:
    Your son Richard has just told me of his great loss. The rascally Whigs, through a mistake, took his trunk containing all his clothes off to Chicago, and his heart is almost broken. Make him up some new ones just as you know he needs and make his heart glad.

Yours Respectfully
A. Lincoln.

ORDER OF PAYMENT AND RECEIPT FOR SERVICES OF SCHUYLER STRONG AND ABRAHAM LINCOLN, JUNE 17, 1840.

This order and receipt, the originals of which are in the Illinois State Archives, are neither the words, nor penmanship of Mr. Lincoln, but form a part of his works, as the receipt was *signed by proxy for him. The copy of the order appears to be the work of William Prentiss, while the receipt may be the handiwork of John Hogan, as order and receipt are in two different handwritings. Mr. Lincoln voted for Hogan as a member of the Board of Public Works, casting his vote on February 19, 1839. He probably voted for Prentiss for alderman of Springfield as the latter was a Whig who was elected to office on April 20, 1840. The services rendered were those of a legal nature, and the $50 for Mr. Lincoln represented attorney's fees. Schuyler Strong, a Springfield attorney, and friend of Mr. Lincoln and his opponent in court, signed the receipt in his strong scrawl. His imitation of Abraham Lincoln's "A. Lincoln", was a poor one.*

Office of the Board of Public Works
Springfield Ills. June 17th 1840

The following is a copy of an Order adopted by the Board of Public Works this day, to wit:

"Ordered, that the sum of One hundred dollars be allowed to Schuyler Strong Esq and Fifty dollars to A Lincoln Esq for professional services rendered the Board of Public Works

Wm Prentiss
Secy Bd Pub Works

Received Springfield June 17th 1840 of John Hogan Comr of the Board of Public Works. One Hundred and fifty Dollars in full for the above order of the Board Pub. Works— $150—

Schuyler Strong
A. Lincoln

AGREEMENT BETWEEN REUBEN RADFORD AND JAMES F. REED DRAWN BY MR. LINCOLN
JUNE 17, 1840

This agreement drawn by Mr. Lincoln had to do with the division of $1000 involved in a lawsuit then pending between Radford as defendant and John L. Roberts. The day after it was drawn, June 17, Mr. Lincoln made one of his first arguments in the Illinois Supreme Court when he appeared for the defendant in the suit of Scammon vs. Cline, an appeal from Boone County which that body decided against his client on February 24, 1841. It is also proper to recall that two days later, June 20, 1840, Samuel F. B. Morse received a patent for the telegraph, and in the class graduated at West Point were two young men,

*George Henry Thomas of Virginia and William Tecumseh
Sherman of Ohio who twenty odd years later were to hold high
place among the generals who made it possible for President
Lincoln to subdue the Confederacy.*

It is hereby agreed by and between James F. Reed and Reuben Radford, that the sum of one thousand dollars in state script be deposited with William Prentiss by the Board of Internal Improvements, of the sum due said Radford through said Reed, by said Board, to indemnify said Reed for what he may have to pay for said Radford in case wherein he said Reed has been served a garnishee in a suit by John S. Roberts against said Radford— It is further agreed, that when the said case of Roberts against Radford shall be determined, said Prentiss is to pay to said Roberts so much of the said one thousand dollars as the court may have decided to be paid by Reed to Roberts, and the remainder, if any there be, is to be paid to said Radford by said Prentiss.

P. Radford
James F. Reed

June 17th 1840

ASSIGNMENT OF ERRORS IN THE SUIT OF JAMES & LEONARD VS. HUGHILL, APPEAL TO THE STATE SUPREME COURT, JUNE TERM, 1840, FROM TAZEWELL COUNTY.

Stuart & Lincoln were attorneys for the appellants in this case which is reported in Third Illinois, Page 362. The opposing counsel was Stephen T. Logan.

In the Supreme Court of the State of Illinois —

June Term 1840

James &
Leonard
vs
Hughill
} Appeal from
Tazewell

And the said plaintiff assigns for error, in the record, decree, and proceedings therein, the following towit:

First—The court below erred in rendering the interlocutory decree, as by the default of the defendants below, and subsequently the final decree, because the said defendants below, do not appear by the record, to have been regularly served with process —

Second—The court below erred, in that it decreed in said cause, for appelee, whereas it should have decreed for the appelants (sic); and also for other errors in the record and decrees aforesaid.

                                    Stuart & Lincoln for
                                          appellants

James &   ⎫
Leonard   ⎪   Assignment of
  vs   ⎬   Errors —
Hughill   ⎭

Filed June 19, 1840
    J. M. Druman

COMPLAINT IN THE SUIT OF DITSON VS. McMURRY, SANGAMON CIRCUIT COURT, JULY TERM, 1840.

In this case Stuart & Lincoln were counsel for the plaintiff, who on July 17 secured a judgment by default. On the same day Stuart & Lincoln secured judgments in three other cases, and the junior member of the firm gave notice in the Sangamo Journal that at one o'clock in the afternoon of Monday, July 20, he would address the people of Springfield at the court house. It was then that he had the debate with Jesse B. Thomas dealt with in another place.

State of Illinois   ⎫   Of the July term of the
Sangamon County   ⎬   circuit court of said
& Circuit   ⎭   county A.D. 1840

Jesse Ditson plaintiff, complains of Logan McMurry defendant being in custody &c of a plea that he render unto the said plaintiff the sum of one hundred dollars which he owes to and unjustly detains from him. For that whereas the said defendant, heretofore towit, on the twentyeighth day of April in the year of our Lord one thousand eight hundred and twenty eight at the county and circuit aforesaid by his certain writing obligatory sealed with his seal, and now shown to the court the date whereof is the day and year aforesaid acknowledged himself to be held and firmly unto the said plaintiff in the sum of one hundred dollars, above demanded, to be paid to the said plaintiff one day after the date of the said writing obligatory, with twelve per cent interest from (the) date (of the said writing obligatory) until paid for value received—

Yet the said defendant (although often requested sotodo) hath not as yet paid the said sum of one hundred dollars above demanded or any part there of to the said plaintiff, but hath hitherto wholly neglected and refused and still neglects and refuses so to do. To the damage of the said plaintiff of one hundred dollars and therefore he brings suit &c

Stuart & Lincoln pq

Copy of writing sued on

"Sangamon City April 28th 1838

"On day after date I promise to pay Jesse Ditson or order one hundred dollars with twelve per cent interest from date until paid for value recd."

DECLARATION AND PRAECIPE IN THE SUIT OF TROTTER VS. THOMAS, SANGAMON CIRCUIT COURT, JULY 1, 1840.
(Herndon-Weik Collection)

The hand of Attorney Lincoln is evident throughout the documents in this case. The date of filing purports to be signed by Clerk Butler, but does not appear to be in his hand. Mr. Lincoln, it will be noted, was guilty of one or two slight sins of omission, but these may be pardoned in a busy lawyer pho penned more legal documents than most men of his day. Ninian W. Edwards, to whom the note sued on was made, was the son and namesake of a man who had studied law under William Wirt, and by appointment of President Madison had served as governor of Illinois when it was still a territory, later becoming one of its representatives in the Federal Senate and in 1826 its governor for four years.

The younger Edwards, a lawyer by profession, was the brother-in-law of Mary Todd Lincoln, having married her sister Elizabeth, and it was at their home in Springfield that in 1842 Abraham Lincoln and Mary Todd were united in marriage. First a Whig and later a Democrat, Edwards served several terms in the Illinois Legislature, in 1836 as a colleague of Mr. Lincoln, when as one of the famous Long Nine he helped to secure the removal of the state capital from Vandalia to Springfield. For three years following 1854, by appointment of Governor Matteson he was superintendent of public instruction, and was in a

*large measure responsible for the establishment of the state
system of public schooling in Illinois. He performed his last
public service as captain commissary of subsistence to which
post he was appointed in June, 1861, by President Lincoln. The
career of Jesse B. Thomas who made the note sued on by Trotter
is set forth in another place.*

State of Illinois			Of the July term of the
Sangamon county	}	ss	Circuit court of said
& Circuit			county A. D. 1840.

George Trotter, plaintiff, complains of Jesse B. Thomas Jr.
defendant, being in custody &c of a plea of trespass on the case
upon premises: For that whereas the said defendant heretofore
towit, on the twelfth day of October in the year of our Lord one
thousand eight hundred and thirtyeight, at the county and circuit
aforesaid, made his certain promissory note in writing, bearing
date the day and year aforesaid, and thereby then and there
promised to pay, one year after date thereof to Ninian W. Edwards or order, the sum of seven hundred dollars, with twelve
per cent interest per annum, from and after the expiration of
the year until paid, for value received, and then and there delivered the said promissory note to the said Ninian W. Edwards
And the said Ninian W. Edwards to whom or to whose order
the payment of the said sum of money in the said promissory
note specified was to be made, after the making of the said
promissory note, and before the payment of the said sum of
money therein specified, towit, on the day and year aforesaid,
at the county and circuit aforesaid, assigned the said promissory
note, by indorsement thereon in writing, by which assignment,
he the said Ninian W. Edwards, then and there ordered and
appointed the said sum of money in the said promissory specified to be paid to the said plaintiff, and then and there delivered
the said promissory note, so assigned as aforesaid, to the said
plaintiff; by means whereof, and by force of the statute in such
cases made and provided, the said defendant then and there became liable to pay to the said plaintiff the said sum of money
in the said promissory note specified, according to the tenor and
effect of the said promissory note; and being so liable, he the
said defendant, in consideration thereof, afterwards, towit, on
the day and year aforesaid, undertook, and then and there faithfully promised the said plaintiff to pay him the said sum of
money in the said promissory note specified according to the
tenor and effect thereof—

Yet the said defendant (although often requested sotodo) hath not as yet paid the said plaintiff the said sum of money in the said promissory note specified, or any part thereof; but so to do hath hitherto wholly neglected and refused, and still doth neglect and refuse. To the damage of the said plaintiff of one thousand dollars; and therefore he brings suit &c.

Stuart & Lincoln p q.

George Trotter
vs } Declaration & Precipe
Jesse B Thomas Jr

Filed July 1st 1840
Butler Clerk

Original Note of Thomas, October 12, 1838

"One year after date I promise to pay to Ninian W. Edwards or order seven hundred dollars with twelve per cent interest per annum from and after the expiration of the year until paid for value received this 12th October 1838—

Jesse B Thomas Jr"

Note for $700 —
Jesse B Thomas Junr
12th Oct 1838
Pay to George Trotter
Ninian W Edwards

COMPLAINT IN THE SUIT OF ILES VS. LYMAN AND LYMAN, SANGAMON CIRCUIT COURT, JULY 2, 1840.

Available records do not indicate the outcome of this suit in which Stuart & Lincoln appeared as counsel for the plaintiff; but it serves to recall an arresting figure in the early history of Sangamon County and of Springfield. Elijah Iles was a native of Kentucky who settled in Illinois in 1821 at the age of twenty-five just after Springfield, a hamlet of less than a dozen families, had been made the county seat of the lately created county of Sangamon. He set up as a merchant in Springfield with a growing measure of success, served with his future attorneys in the Black Hawk War, and, a leader in all that made for the growth of Springfield, in 1839 built the American Hotel, for a period of years the largest hotel in Illinois. He also helped to secure the removal of the state capital from Vandalia to Springfield;

*built and conducted the first grain elevator in the town, and do-
nated the ground for the graveyard where in ripe age he was
laid to rest.*

State of Illinois ⎫ Sangamon County ⎬ & Circuit ⎭	Of the July Term of the Circuit court of said county A.D. 1840 —

Elijah Iles, plaintiff, complains of Cornelius S. Lyman and
Cornelius Lyman, defendants, being in custody &c of a plea of
trespass on the case upon premises: For that whereas the said
defendants, heretofore towit, on the first day of May in the year
of our Lord one thousand eight hundred and thirtynine, at the
county and circuit aforesaid, made their certain promissory note
in writing, bearing date the day and year aforesaid, and thereby
then and there promised to pay, twelve months after the date
thereof to one Eddin Lewis, the sum of one hundred and twenty
dollars, bearing twelve per cent interest from the date of the
said note until paid, for value received and then and there delivered the said promissory note to the said Eddin Lewis, and
the said Eddin Lewis, to whom the payment of the said sum
of money in the said promissory note specified was to be made,
after the making of the said promissory note, and before the
payment of the said sum of money therein specified towit, on
the tenth day of January in the year of our Lord one thousand
eight hundred and forty, at the county and circuit aforesaid,
assigned the said promissory note by indorsement in writing
thereon, by which said assignment he the said Eddin Lewis then
and there ordered and appointed the said sum of money in the
said promissory note specified to be paid to the said plaintiff and
then and there delivered the said promissory note, so assigned
as aforesaid to the said plaintiff; by means whereof, and by force
of the statute in such case made and provided they the said defendants, then and there became liable to pay to the said plaintiff
the said sum of money in the said promissory note specified according to the tenor and effect of the said promissory note; and
being so liable they the said defendants, in consideration thereof,
afterwards towit, on the day and year last aforesaid, at the
county and circuit aforesaid undertook and then and there faithfully promised the said plaintiff to pay him the said sum of
money in the said promissory note specified according to the
tenor and effect thereof —

Yet the said defendants (although often requested so to do)
have not as yet paid to the said plaintiff the said sum of money

in the said promissory note specified, or any part thereof, but so to do have hitherto wholly neglected and refused, and still do neglect and refuse so to do — To the damage of the said plaintiff two hundred and fifty dollars and therefore he sues &c

Stuart & Lincoln pq

Copy of note sued on

"Twelve months after date we or either of us promise to pay Eddin Lewis one hundred and twenty dollars for value received of him Bearing twelve per cent from this date until paid this first day of May 1839 —

Cornelius S. Lyman
C Lyman"

Copy of assignment

"'For value received, I assigne the within note to Elijah Iles, 10th January 1840.

Eddin Lewis"

COMPLAINT IN THE SUIT OF STOCKTON VS. TOLLY, SANGAMON CIRCUIT COURT, JULY 2, 1840

This is another case in which Stuart & Lincoln appeared as counsel for the plaintiff where available records are silent as to the result, but Stockton, the plaintiff, was a man much given to litigation and appeared at frequent intervals in the courts, sometimes with Attorney Lincoln as his counsel and now and again opposing him. One hopes that in this instance he was awarded damages for the stove Carrier Tolly apparently had handled in so careless a manner.

State of Illinois }
Sangamon County } Of the July term of the circuit
And Circuit   } court of said county A.D. 1840

George W. Stockton plaintiff complains of James Tolly defendant, being in custody &c. of a plea in assumpsit For that whereas the said defendant before and at the time of the making of his promise and undertaking hereinafter mentioned, was a common carrier of goods and merchandise for him in and by a certain waggon, or cart, from Beardstown to Springfield towit at the county and circuit aforesaid — And the said defendant being such carrier as aforesaid, the said plaintiff, heretofore towit

on the nineteenth day of February in the year of our Lord one
thousand eight hundred and thirtyseven at Beardstown towit,
at the county and circuit aforesaid at the special instance and
request of the said defendant caused to be delivered to him the
said defendant, so being such carrier as aforesaid at Beardstown
aforesaid a certain stove of the said plaintiff of great value towit of the value of seventyfive dollars to be taken care of, and
securely carried and conveyed by the said defendant as such
carrier as aforesaid, in and by the said waggon or cart from
Beardstown aforesaid to Springfield aforesaid and then, towit
at Springfield aforesaid to be safely and securely delivered by
the said defendant for the said plaintiff; and in consideration
thereof, and of certain reward to him the said defendant, in that
behalf, he the said defendant, being such carrier as aforesaid
then and there towit on the day and year aforesaid, at the county
and circuit aforesaid, undertook and faithfully promised the said
plaintiff to take care of the said *stove* aforesaid, and safely and
securely carry and convey the same in and by said waggon or
cart from Beardstown aforesaid to Springfield aforesaid, and
there, to wit at Springfield aforesaid, safely and securely to deliver the same for the said plaintiff — And although the said
defendant received the said *stove* aforesaid for the purpose aforesaid, yet the said defendant as such carrier not regarding his duty
as such carrier nor his said promise and undertaking so made as
aforesaid, but contriving and fraudulently intending craftily and
subtly to deceive the said plaintiff in this behalf, hath not taken
care of the said *stove* aforesaid or safely or securely carried or
conveyed the same from Beardstown aforesaid, to Springfield
aforesaid, nor hath then, towit, at Springfield aforesaid, safely
and securely delivered the same for the said plaintiff, but on the
contrary thereof he, the said defendant being such carrier as
aforesaid so carelessly and negligbly behaved and conducted himself with respect to the said *stove* aforesaid, that by and through
the mere carelessness, negligence, and improper conduct of the
said defendant in this behalf, the said *stove* aforesaid being of the
value aforesaid, afterwards, towit on the day and year aforesaid,
at the county and circuit aforesaid, became and was wholly broken
to pieces, destroyed and lost to the said plaintiff, towit at Springfield aforesaid — To the damage of the said plaintiff of one
hundred dollars and therefore he sues &c

                                              Stuart & Lincoln pq

PLAN OF CAMPAIGN DRAWN BY MR. LINCOLN, JULY, 1840, OR EARLIER.

This plan drawn by Mr. Lincoln, the original of which is now owned by the Missouri Historical Society, shows the care he gave in the summer of 1840 to details of the campaign to assure the choice of Whig electors in Illinois. The concluding line in the document, beginning with the words, "It shall be," and ending with the incomplete phrase, "to make a," is not his work. This last sentence is minute in character of writing, but appears to be the work of John T. Stuart. The use of the small "m" in "monday" is not common with Lincoln, although his incorrect use of small letters in place of capital letters is found from time to time. The plan reveals a characteristic usage of extra spacing.

The underlined word, "task", does not seem to have significance but it is interesting to consider the importance of getting votes stressed by a man who has too often been pictured as a naive gentleman who sat back and permitted himself to be nominated for the Presidency. The document throws little new light on the Lincoln known to students, but it may reveal Lincoln, the Illinois politician, to many a reader. Be it noted again that, while Harrison was elected, the skill and adroitness of Stephen A. Douglas, who was chiefly responsible for the conduct of the Van Buren campaign in Illinois, assured the election in that state of Democratic electors—an outcome in no way pleasing to Mr. Lincoln and his Whig associates.

1st Appoint one person in each county as county captain, and take his pledge to perform promptly all the duties assigned him—

Duties of the county captain

1st To procure from the poll-books a separate list for each Precinct of all the names of all those persons who voted the Whig ticket in August—

2nd To appoint one person in each Precinct as Precinct Captain, and, by a personal interview with him procure his pledge, to perform promptly all the duties assigned him—

3rd To deliver to each Precinct Captain the list of names as above, belonging to his Precinct; and also a written list of his duties—

Duties of the Precinct Captain

1st To divide the list of names delivered him by the county captain, into Sections of ten who reside most convenient to each other—

2nd To appoint one person of each Section as Section Captain, and by a personal interview with him, procure his pledge to perform promptly all the duties assigned him—

3rd To deliver to each Section Captain the list of names belonging to his Section and also a written list of his duties—

Duties of the Section Captain

1st To see each man of his Section face to face, and procure his pledge that he will for no consideration (impossibilities excepted) stay from the polls on the first monday in November; and that he will record his vote as early in the day as possible—

2nd To add to his Section the name of every person in his vicinity who did not vote with us in August, but who will vote with us in the fall, and take the same pledge of him, as from others—

3rd To *task* himself to procure at least such additional names to his Section—

PLEA AND SET OFF IN THE SUIT OF MOCK VS. LASWELL, SANGAMON CIRCUIT COURT, JULY 28, 1840.
(Herndon-Weik Collection)

This plea and set off were penned for Baker & Strong by Mr. Lincoln who signed their firm name to the papers in the case. He wrote the cover notations, with the exception of the date of filing. It may be noted that these two papers are incorrectly filed in the Herndon-Weik Collection, being under "Saswell ads. Mock." Studies to date present no court record in this case. The affidavit of July 20, 1840, the account rendered, and this plea represent the known evidence of Mr. Lincoln having played a part in it.

Thomas Laswell   ⎫
    ads   ⎬   In Assumpsit
Henry Mock   ⎭

And the said defendant comes and defends the wrong and injury when &c. and says plaintiff *actio non* because he says he did not undertake and promise in manner and form as the plaintiff in his said declaration hath alleged against him; and of this he puts himself upon the country &c.

Baker & Strong p. d.

And the said defendant hereby gives notice to the said plaintiff, that he will, on the trial of the above cause, offer to prove and set off the annexed account of the said defendant against said **plaintiff.**

Baker & Strong p. d.

Thomas Laswell

)

   ads   } Plea &

       J   Setoff

Henry Mock

   Plea & Notice

Filed July 28, 1840

   Wm. Butler Clk

SPEECHES OF MR. LINCOLN IN SUPPORT OF HARRISON, FEBRUARY 10 TO OCTOBER 20, 1840.

Although the records at command are slight in volume and of secondary value it is not difficult to shape a fairly accurate account of Mr. Lincoln's part as a Whig speaker in the presidential campaign of 1840, for, with timely adaptation in each instance to local conditions, in the sixty-odd appeals for the election of Harrison which he made in Illinois and Kentucky between March 10 and October 20, he closely followed the carefully prepared address delivered by him in Springfield on November 20, 1839, and which, promptly printed in pamphlet form for general distribution, can be found in Volume I, Pages 100 to 141 of Nicolay and Hay's Complete Works.

Mr. Lincoln made his first appeal for the election of Harrison at a dinner which closed an all-day Whig rally in Peoria on February 10, and five days later the Peoria Register and Northwestern Gazette praised him for "fearlessly and eloquently exposing the iniquities of the sub-treasury scheme" then being urged by the Van Buren administration. And it is also interesting to recall that on the other side of the Atlantic on February 10, 1840, Queen Victoria of England became the wife of her cousin, Prince Albert of Saxe Coburg and Gotha — a union charged with fateful import for a future President, for it was the intervention of the prince consort, a friend and well-wisher of the North that, just before his death in December, 1861, prevented a disastrous break over the Trent Affair between Washington and London where a quarrelsome Palmerston then headed the British Cabinet.

A three-day political debate between Whigs and Democrats began at Jacksonville on March 16. It was opened by Edward

Dickinson Baker who was replied to in a two-hour speech next day by Josiah Lamborn. What followed was thus reported on March 27 not without bias by the Democratic Register of Springfield:

When Mr. Lamborn concluded, the meeting adjourned to the market house to hear a speech from Mr. Lincoln, who had come there for the sole purpose of making a speech. Lincoln proceeded in his speech, dealing out the usual quantum of abuse upon the administration of Gen. Jackson, to convince the people that Martin Van Buren ought not to be elected President: when, the signs not appearing very favorable, he was requested to postpone the balance of his speech until night, which he consented to do. Mr. Douglas was then called to address the people, which call he obeyed. As powerful and convincing speeches as Mr. Douglas has made, never upon any former occasion did he so completely triumph over a political opponent. This was not only the opinion of his friends, but also that of his political opponents. At night Mr. Lincoln again led off to a crowded audience. at the court-house, and spoke about two hours, with only tolerable success — we say only tolerable success, for his friends confessed their disappointment and mortification. Mr. Douglas followed . . . and completely used up Mr. Lincoln and his speech. When Mr. Lincoln read from the Report of the Secretary of the Treasury the long list of defaulters, to prove that *Mr. Van Buren's* administration is corrupt, Mr. Douglas defied him to show that any one officer appointed by Mr. Van Buren had ever proved a defaulter, whilst hundreds had occurred under every other administration.

Mr. Lincoln spoke at a Whig rally in Carlinville on April 6, and three days later, he addressed the people of Alton. his address being thus reported on April 11 by the Telegraph of that town:

A. Lincoln, Esq. of Sangamon county, one of the Presidential Electors, addressed the citizens of Alton. on last Thursday evening at the old Court room, on the great questions at issue between the people and the office-holders. Although not more than two or three hours previous notice could be given of the intended meeting, the room, which is very spacious, was crowded to excess; and his speech, which, although highly argumentative and logical, was enlivened by numerous anecdotes. was received with unbounded applause, and left a very favorable impression on the minds of his auditors.

On April 11, Mr. Lincoln was one of ten speakers at an all-day and evening rally at Belleville. Two days later the Missouri Republican declared his speech "lucible, forcible, and effective," but in its next issue the Advocate, a Democratic newspaper lately set-up in Belleville, which championed the cause of its party with spirit and energy, had this curt reference to it:

Mr. Lincoln followed a federal candidate for elector. His speech was weak, puerile, and feeble. "How different" remarked many of the Whigs, "to what we had expected." Poor Lincoln! he should have rested his fame upon his printed speech, going the rounds of the federal papers, as purported to have been delivered by him at Springfield. He predicated his whole speech upon the sale of the one-eyed horse for twenty-seven dollars, that happened to be sold by a constable during the day. To what slight accidents are we frequently indebted for our great things! How very fortunate for the Whigs that *Mr.* Lincoln saw the sale of the *one-eyed* horse that day! He was thus enabled to prove that Mr. Van Buren caused it, together with all the other ills in life that us poor morals "are heir to."

On May 2 at Tremont in Tazewell County there was a four-cornered debate in which Lincoln and Douglas had a part. One of the Whigs who helped to make up an audience that filled the course-house put on paper this lively account of the meeting published on May 15 in the Sangamo Journal:

The debate was opened by Mr. Lincoln, who after some general and appropriate remarks concerning the design and object of all Governments, drew a vivid picture of our prospects and happy condition previous to the time of the war which was waged against the U. S. Bank, the constitutionality ,as well as the great utility of which he vindicated in a most triumphant manner. He next turned his attention to the Sub-Treasury, the hideous deformity and injurious effects of which were exposed in a masterly style. He then reviewed the political course of Mr. Van Buren, and especially his votes in the New York Convention in allowing Free Negroes the right of suffrage, and his Janus-faced policy in relation to the war. In this part of his speech Mr. Lincoln was particularly felicitous, and the frequent and spontaneous bursts of applause from the People, gave evidence that their hopes were with him. He related many highly amusing anecdotes which convulsed the house with laughter: and concluded his eloquent address with a successful vindication of the civil and military reputation of the Hero of Tippencanoe. —

During the whole of Lincoln's address Douglass manifested the utmost petulancy and want of gentlemanly decorum, frequently interrupting the speaker, and reminding one forcibly by his manner of "a tempest in a teapot." At the close of Lincoln's speech which was responded to by three hearty cheers, the Little Giant ascended the rostrum, but it was no go. The Big Giant had effectually used his candidate up, and he only raved incoherently about high tariff, people's money (which by the bye has all been stolen by his own friend) U. S. Bank, blasphemy, Tom Benton, &c.

Mr. Lincoln spoke on June 27 at Shelbyville, where according to a correspondent of the Democratic Register, "he had but a thin audience." A larger crowd, however, greeted him in his home town of Springfield on July 20. After the fiery Douglas the Democratic leader with whom he appears to have been keenest to break a lance in the campaign of 1840 was Jesse Burgess Thomas, nephew and namesake of an early federal senator from Illinois, and himself a man of parts, who in 1843 succeeded Douglas on the bench of the State Supreme Court and who, at the time of his death in 1850 at the age of fourty-four, was a leader of the Chicago bar. When Lincoln and Thomas met in joint debate at the Springfield court-house on July 20 the former charged his opponent with the authorship of the letters signed "Conservative" which had appeared some time before in the Sangamo Journal, and Lincoln retorted in such savage fashion that the Register, in its issue of July 24, regretfully recorded that he had "descended to such low, vulgar abuse that many of the Whigs were disgusted and openly avowed 'decided disapprobation' of his conduct" — a view of the matter, however, not shared by the Sangamo Journal and a majority of Mr. Lincoln's friends who felt that he had only returned in full measure the fare dealt him by Thomas.

At Waterloo on August 25 Mr. Lincoln participated in a joint debate with Adam Wilson Snyder, a Democratic elector who had come from Pennsylvania to Illinois twenty-five years before, and who had studied law while working as a wool-curler, later winning a noteworthy place at the bar and in politics. Mr Lincoln spoke for two hours to an intent and "crowded audience." Mr. Snyder followed in an address of equal length, and according to a report from the Waterloo correspondent of the Springfield Register which appeared in that journal on Septem-

*ber 4 had much the best of the war-of-words. This correspond-
ent wrote as follows:*

Early on Monday morning a notice was placed on the court-
house that A. Lincoln, Esq. would address the people on Tuesday. There was present to hear him a crowded audience. From
his heretofore printed speech, and the high qualifications the
Whigs had attributed to the man, public expectation was excited in a great degree. — The Whigs were chuckling, as usual,
with the anticipated triumph of their orator. The Democrats of
this county had on the ground their old favorite, A. W. Snyder,
one of the electors, and felt confident that Lincoln would be well
answered. — Mr. Lincoln commenced his speech, and a more
soft milk and cider thing was rarely ever heard. He seemed
like a man traveling over unknown ground, hesitating, feeling
his way, lest he should fall into some quick sand. He spoke
about two hours, going over much of the slang that you see
every day in the Federal papers. On the whole, the speech was
any thing but what it was expected to be. Both parties were
disappointed at the effort.

*But still ready to meet all comers Mr. Lincoln about August
28 in an unfinished church at Mount Vernon met John Alexander Mc Clernand in joint debate. Mr. Mc Clernand was a
native of Kentucky born in 1812 who had passed his youth in
Shawneetown, where at the age of twenty he was admitted to
the bar and volunteered for service in the Black Hawk War.
Thereafter his rapid advancement in politics included three
terms in the Illinois Legislature and four terms in Congress.
There is no extant account of how Lincoln and Mc Clernand
fared in their meeting at Mount Vernon, but following 1856,
when Mc Clernand became a resident of Springfield and three
years later the representative of that district in Congress, their
relations were lively and for Mr. Lincoln now and again perplexing ones. In 1861, McClernand, ever intent on being in the
thick of things, left Congress to become first a brigadier and then
a major general of volunteers, but his clashes with Grant in the
Vicksburg campaign and his general reluctance to take orders
presented a continuing problem to President Lincoln until in
1864 he resigned from the service and returned to politics and
the practice of law.*

*Mr. Lincoln on September 1 spoke at a Whig barbecue in
Carmi where he was the guest of his friend Edwin B. Webb,
who was also serving as a Whig elector. It is probable that he*

spoke two days later at Mt. Carmel and on September 5 he again met Mc Clernand in joint debate at Shawneetown. He spoke at Morganfield, Kentucky, across the Ohio River from Shawnee-town, on September 8, and between September 7 and 17 he debated at Shawneetown and Equality with Josiah Lamborn, an adroit and truculent antagonist. The Springfield Register of October 2 thus commented on their meeting at Equality:

We learn from a gentleman who was present at the late political discussion at Equality, that after Mr. Lamborn had concluded an eloquent and powerful speech, showing the identity of modern Whiggery and ancient Federalism, Mr. Lincoln rose and told the people that if they would attend on the next day, he would prove to their satisfaction that the Van Buren party was the old Federal party, and that the Whigs were the old-fashioned Democrats. At this moment an aged, gray-headed gentleman by the name of Wilson ,arose in the crowd and said to Mr. Lincoln: "Stop my young friend, I listened to your speech yesterday with the deepest interest, and admired it as a true exposition of the principles by which our party has always been governed. I lived in the days of John Adams and Thomas Jefferson, and was a Federalist then and wore the Black Cockade. I am a Whig now, and support Harrison for the reason that he has always belonged to our party and will carry out our principles. I cherish the names of Federalist and Whig as meaning the same thing and alike applicable to our party. I beseech you, therefore, my young friend, not to cast disgrace upon our party, by denying its name, origin, or integrity."

Mr. Lincoln took his aged friend's advice. — He made a speech the next day without alluding to the name of Federalist once. He entered into an elaborate defence of Federal principles under the name of Whiggery, and when he had concluded, his venerable grey-headed friend advanced and gave him his hand, saying: "Well done, my young friend! Our cause is safe in your hands."

There is a local tradition that Mr. Lincoln spoke at Marshall-town in the afternoon and at Casey in the evening of September 19. On the afternoon of October 20 he debated at Albion with Isaac P. Walker, a Democrat elector, and George W. Harris recalled in old age that he devoted a part of the morning hours of that day to a copy of Byron's poems which he had borrowed from the log school house of the village. (See "My Recollections of Abraham Lincoln" by Harris in Farm and Fireside, Decem-

ber 1, 1904.)   *There is no record that Mr. Lincoln voted in the presidential election, November 2. He was in Lawrenceville on that day and was paid a fee for carrying the election returns of Lawrence county to Springfield there to be filed with the Secretary of State.*

Mr. Lincoln was in his thirty-second year when in 1840 he first won a statewide reputation as an individual and persuasive champion of the Whig cause. How at that time was each of the group of unusual men born in the same year as the Springfield lawyer shaping his career? Kit Carson at Bent's Fort was taking to wife a Cheyenne girl and winning fame as a Guardian of the Trail. In England Charles Darwin had lately published his A Naturalist's Voyage Around the World, and, happily married, was soon to make his home at Down House in Kent and begin the long years of labor which in 1871 bore epoch-making fruit in The Descent of Man. William Ewart Gladstone, born to wealth and station, was already a member of Parliament and fairly started on the career which, despite his much-lamented misreading of the signs during the Civil War, was to give him first place among two generations of British statesmen.

In Boston Oliver Wendell Holmes was gaining repute as a physician of skill and quality, and had to his credit a volume of verse which included The Last Leaf, long one of the favorite poems of Abraham Lincoln. In his native Virginia Cyrus Hall Mc Cormick was perfecting the reaper begun by his father which a few years later was to transform farm life in the Illinois of his own and Lincoln's time. In 1840 Edgar Allan Poe was a magazine editor in Philadelphia and putting forth some of the best prose and verse produced by him during a career that nine years later was to reach a sordid and tragic end in Baltimore.

And in October, 1840, Alfred Tennyson, in the quiet of an English village, was slowly giving shape to the Idylls of the King and other verse which gathered in 1842 in two volumes of Poems, new and old, were to win him universal fame. But it was not until 1850 that he published In Memorian, on which he had been engaged for many years and some of whose noblest passages, born of a great friendship, recall for men and women of a later time Abraham Lincoln's rise from humble origins to undying renown.

ASSIGNMENT OF JUDGMENT BY GEORGE TROTTER VS. JAMES DUNLAP, NOVEMBER 24, 1840.
(Herndon-Weik Collection)

This assignment beginning with the words "George Trotter vs. Jesse B. Thomas, Judgment obtained in action of assumpsit," and concluding with the phrase "November 24, 1840" was drawn by Attorney Lincoln. The other part of the document was penned by William Butler. George Trotter signed both parts, and Clerk Butler penned the cover notations to complete this three-handed work. The papers of July 1, 1840 and November 13, 1840 include a comprehensive history of this case, and it need only be noted that Mr. Lincoln asked upon July 18, 1840 that it be continued due to the failure to serve process in time. As will be seen by the court decree of a judgment of $792.75, Attorney Lincoln won a decisive victory over his political opponent, Thomas. The interlocutory decree which is referred to was an intermediate decree, and not the final decree in the case. Mr. Lincoln erred in one point in the penning of this legal paper, for he wrote "Sagamon" for "Sangamon", a mistake that is found in few of his legal documents.

George Trotter vs. Jesse B. Thomas: Assignment of Judgment: November 24, 1840

George Trotter
vs
Jesse B. Thomas, Jr. } Judgment obtained in action of assumpsit

George Trotter
vs
Jesse B. Thomas, Jr. } In chancery to foreclose a mortgage
Interlocutory decree taken—

I assign the benefit of the above entitled judgment, and also of the mortgage in the said chancery case, with the use of my name to a final decree, both of which cases are in the circuit court of Sagamon county, to James Dunlap for value received

Nov. 24th A. D. 1840—
George Trotter

Rd from William Butler for James Dunlap Seven hundred & Eighty six dollars & thirty three cents.
Nov. 20" 1840
George Trotter

Trotter

vs } assignment

Thomas

To James Dunlap

MR. LINCOLN OPPOSES A BILL FOR THE RELIEF OF WILLIAM NORMANDY, DECEMBER 21, 1840.

There was perhaps a fair measure of partisanship in Mr. Lincoln's opposition in the House session of December 21, 1840, to a bill for the relief of William Normandy who had suffered loss through the destruction of certain notes of the State Bank. Set forth below is the report which appeared in the Sangamo Journal of December 25 of a spirited debate of the proposal by Whigs and Democrats. Mr. Lincoln's last recorded participation in the 1840 proceedings of the House occurred on December 31 when he voted in favor of an unsuccessful attempt to repeal the existing premium on wolf scalps. The following day brought his broken engagement with Mary Todd and a period of acute mental anguish for Mr. Lincoln.

Mr. Murphy of Cook, from the select committee to which was referred the petition of Mr. Dormandy for remuneration for the destruction of certain notes, of the State Bank, reported a Bill for his relief—authorising the auditor to issue his warrant in favor of Mr. Dormandy in the proportion to $600 that the amount of stock owned by the bank, is to the whole stock.

Mr. Murphy then explained why he believed Dormandy should be paid—at same time casting slurs on courts who had refused relief.

Mr. Lincoln said, as wholesale charges of fraud had been dealt out by the gentleman from Cook, which involved many of his constituents, he felt it his duty to say something in regard to this case.

It was not true, as the gentleman had stated, that the petitioner had been defrauded through the chicanery of the law, or of the courts. He would inform the House that since this Legislature had met, the naked question of fact, of the actual destruction of these notes, accompanied by any question of law, had been submitted to a jury, of the petitioner's own choice, and that a majority of this jury had solemnly decided that it was an attempt on the part of Normandy to impose upon the Bank. Under such circumstances, was it not assuming too much for the gentleman from Cook to get up here and tell us, without examination on his part, that the facts were as he had stated them, and that there was fraud and perjury on the part of the Bank, the court, and the jury?

Mr. Murphy, in reply, said, it was somewhat strange the gentleman should impute fraud to one of his own constituents. He supposed Mr. Normandy was a loco, and did not vote for the gentleman, (Mr. Lincoln) which accounted for his offering the petition. He did not charge the jury with perjury—it was nothing unusual for a jury to disagree about a just claim, especially where they had the instructions of a judge to help them, against right. It might be that Mr. Normandy was unable to procure such testimony as was necessary in a court of law. Mr. M. recapitulated the circumstances of the case which he contended were sufficient to justify the House in passing the bill.

Mr. Lincoln said, he did not know whether Mr. N. voted for him or not—he presumed he did not. If there were those in this House who thought this fact would have any influence on his conduct in regard to this bill, he should not stop to enlighten them as to his motives; he was careless of the opinion of such. The gentleman from Cook persisted in reciting what he termed the facts of this case. He would say to the House that the trial, to which he had before alluded, was presided over by Judge Breese, whom the gentleman would not charge with partiality to the Bank—that this jury was composed in part by Dr. N's own political friends—that he had able counsel to assist him, and that upon the naked question as to whether these notes were burnt or not, a majority of that jury had determined, after hearing under oath all the testimony, and the arguments of counsel, that these notes were not burnt.—And yet the gentleman, without investigation, assumed that for granted, which the jury found otherwise, and upon this assumption charged fraud and dishonesty upon the Bank, and all who had any thing to do with the case. He thought it better that one man should rest under the imputation of fraud than one hundred.

CHAPTER XII—SUPPLEMENTARY ITEMS, 1833 TO 1839.

In this final chapter there are assembled in chronological order some fifty items of varying interest, ranging from 1833 to 1839, which for divers reasons—belated acquisition and difficulties in accurate transcription among them—it was not practicable to give their more fitting place in earlier chapters. All of them, however, are charged with meaning for the Lincoln student. Here is the bond executed in 1833 which permitted Berry & Lincoln to sell liquor in New Salem, a venture not wholly to the liking of the junior partner, which a quarter of a century later was to claim an odd place in his memorable and next to the last contest with Douglas. Here also are recurring evidence in the shape of letters and newspaper editorials of the ill-relish blended with envy with which an ambitious Lincoln watched the swift advance of his rival Douglas from local to state and national leadership.

Entries from the famous fee book of Stuart & Lincoln show that the firm's financial returns from its large and growing practice were modest ones—both partners were always moderate in their charges to clients of narrow means—while legal documents of divers sorts make clear how in the shaping of them Mr. Lincoln mastered without delay the tools of a new trade. General James Adams, friend of Douglas and Mormon Joe Smith, but despised by Lincoln, reecives final dismissal from the stage in the letter of An Old Settler and in a savage review of his manifest and varied shortcomings. On the other hand there are letters, some of them of a whimsical and amusing sort, which bear convincing witness to Mr. Lincoln's rare gift for winning friends and retaining them through the years despite the wear and tear of every-day life.

Finally there are convention resolutions and editorials from the Sangamo Journal which prove that for upward of fifteen years Mr. Lincoln was a stout and unyielding Whig partisan who could see no good of any sort in the Democratic party and its leaders. Growth in breadth of political vision, as in other matters, was with Mr. Lnicoln a gradual but inevitable process. In the end his outlook became a national one, and his regard for parties governed by their will and purpose to serve common and beneficient ends. All this was in the future during his first years in Springfield, but even then discerning ones came to share the belief that he had uncommon gifts and had before him an uncomman career.

Among those who early came to hold young Mr. Lincoln and his qualities in high regard and to predict great things for him was Nathaniel Pope, honest, blunt spoken and a shrewd judge of men, who for thirty-one years following 1819 was a federal judge in Illinois. Judge Pope was no respector of persons, but Mr. Lincoln early became a prime favorite with him, and he had no inconsiderable part in shaping the younger man's career at the bar. When Judge Pope died in 1850 Mr. Lincoln's epoch-making years were still in the future, but when they came they confirmed in full and rounded measure a strong man's early faith in him.

BOND FILED BY BERRY AND LINCOLN WHEN LICENSED TO KEEP A TAVERN AT NEW SALEM, MARCH 6, 1833

In order to stimulate scanty sales in their grocery store Berry and Lincoln in the spring of 1833 applied to and received from the County Commissioners' Court of Sangamon County a license to keep a tavern at New Salem. Doubtless the firm's purpose in procuring this license was not to keep a tavern, but to retail in varying quantities a generous supply of the liquors they had in stock as a result of their purchase of three groceries—this in quick succession and on credit. Only under these conditions did Lincoln ever sell liquor. When granted a license the applicants therefor were required by law to file a bond, and below is reproduced the bond given by Berry and Lincoln. This bond, in which Lincoln's good friend, Bowling Green, joined, appears to have been written by the clerk of the commissioners' court, and Lincoln's name signed by another, probably by his partner Berry.

Know all men by these presents, we William F. Berry, Abraham Lincoln and John Bowling Green, are held and firmly bound unto the County Commissioners of Sangamon County in the full sum of three hundred dollars to which payment well and truly to be made we bind ourselves, our heirs, executors and administrators firmly by these presents, sealed with our seal and dated this 6th day of March, A.D. 1833. Now the condition of this obligation is such that Whereas the said Berry & Lincoln has obtained license from the County Commissioners' Court to keep a tavern in the Town of New Salem to continue one year. Now if the said Berry & Lincoln shall be of good behaviour and observe all the laws of this State relative to tavern keepers—then this obligation to be void or otherwise remain in full force.

Abraham Lincoln   (Seal)

Wm. F. Berry (Seal)
Bowling Green (Seal)

DECLARATION AND PRAECIPE IN THE SUIT OF T. AND J. S. WILBOURN VS. POLLARD SIMMONS, SANGAMON CIRCUIT COURT, SEPTEMBER 8, 1837
(Herndon-Weik Collection)

This declaration, quoted note, and praecipe are in the handwriting of Mr. Lincoln, while the cover notations were penned by Butler. Lawyer Lincoln spelled "business" as "bussiness" and "trespass" as "tresspass" whenever he used these words in this document, a common error in most of his early legal papers. The use of the first names of plaintiffs and defendants is common also to the early documents, and disappears about 1838 to 1839. There is a lack of the usual Lincoln accuracy in spelling "Simmons" as "Simons" as given in the original note in the case. Mr. Lincoln's quoted copy gives the name as "Simmons" in the signature to the note. A change of the usual phrase "so to do" is noted near the conclusion of the declaration, where Attorney Lincoln has penned the words, "But he to do this." Pollard Simmons was an early resident of the New Salem neighborhood, and as a Democrat aided in securing the appointment of Mr. Lincoln as deputy surveyor of Sangamon County. The case was decided upon October 18, 1837, when a judgment of $175.60 was rendered in favor of the Wilbourns.

State of Illinois ⎫ In Sangamon circuit court
⎬ ss
Sangamon County & Circuit ⎭ October Term 1837

Thomas Wilbourn and John S. Wilbourn trading and doing business in the name and style of "T & J. S Wilbourn" complain of Pollard Simmons (signing his name P. Simons) being in custody &c of a plea of Tresspass on the case upon promises: for that whereas heretofore, towit, on the fourth day of November in the year of our Lord one thusand, eight hundred and thirtysix, the said Pollard made his certain promissory note in writing, bearing date the day and year aforesaid, and thereby then and there promised to pay, on or before the first day of March next ensuing, to the said Thomas and John or bearer the sum of one hundred and seventy dollars lawful money of the United States for value received, and then and there delivered the said promissory note to the said Thomas and John, by means

whereof and by force of the statute in such case made and provided, the said Pollard then and there became liable to pay to
the said Thomas and John the said sum of money in the said
promissory note specified, according to the tenor and effect of
the said promissory note, and being so liable, he, the said Pollard
in consideration thereof afterwards, towit, on the day and year
aforesaid at the county and circuit aforesaid undertook, and then
and there faithfuly promised the said Thomas and John to pay
them the said sum of money in the said promissory note specified
according to the tenor and effect thereof when he should be thereunto afterwards lawfully required. Yet the said Pollard (although
often requested so to do) hath not as yet paid the said sum of
money in the said promissory note specified or any part thereof
to the said Thomas and John. But he to do this hath hitherto
wholly refused and still doth refuse—To the damage of the said
Thomas and John of two hundred and fifty dollars and therefore
they bring their suit &c—

Stuart &Lincoln
for plaintiffs

The following is a copy of the instrument declared on:

"On or before the 1st day of March next I promise to pay to
J & J. S. Wilbourn or bearer one hundred and seventy dollars for
value recd. this 4th day of Nov. 1836   P. Simmons"

Attest

Bowling Green

State of Illinois	} ss	In Sangamon circuit court
Sangamon county & circuit		October Term 19937

Thomas Wilbourn &		
John S. Wilbourn trading &		Trespass on the case
doing business in the name & style of	}	upon promises
T. and J. S. Wilbourn		
vs		Damages $ 250—00
Pollard Simmons		

The clerk of the circuit court will issue process in the above
case returnable to the next term of said court—

Stuart &Lincoln
for plaintiffs—

T & J. S. Wilbourn

vs } Decl

Pollard Simmons
Filed Sept 8th 1837
Wm. Butler Clk

MR. LINCOLN REPLIES TO GENERAL ADAMS' PRO-
TESTATIONS OF INNOCENCE, SANGAMO
JOURNAL, SEPTEMBER 9, 1837

Re-election as probate justice of the peace gave General James Adams a fresh stock of self-confidence, and in a letter published in the Illinois Journal on September 6, 1837, he again loudly proclaimed his innocence of the charges of dishonest practices that had been brought against him, and sought by methods wholly his own to prove that they were without foundation. Mr. Lincoln the same day drew up a savage answer to the Adams letter which appeared in the Sangamo Journal on September 9 and which tore to bits his defense of his conduct, declaring his noisy protestations "all as false as hell, as all in this community must know." This retort no doubt gave a full measure of satisfaction to its author. It ended for the moment a profitless war of words, and when Mr. Lincoln again assailed Adams he found a more congenial and droller subject for his pen.

In the Republican of this morning a publication of Gen. Adam's appears, in which my name is used quite unreservedly. For this I thank the General. I thank him, because it gives me an opportunity, without appearing obtrusive, of explaining a part of a former publication of mine, which appears to me to have been misunderstood by many.

In the former publication alluded to, I stated in substance, that Mr. Talbott got a deed from the son of Gen. Adams for the purpose of correcting a mistake that had occurred on the record of the said deed in the Recorder's office—that he corrected the record, and brought the deed and handed it to me—and that, on opening the deed, another paper, being the assignment of a judgment, fell out of it. This statement Gen. Adams and the editor of the Republican have seized upon as a most palpable evidence of fabrication and falsehood. They set themselves gravely about proving that the assignment could not have been in the deed when Talbott got it from young Adams, as he, Talbott, would have seen it when he opened the deed to correct the record. Now the truth is, Talbott did see the assignment when he opened the deed, or at least he told me he did on the same day: and I only omitted to say so, in my former publication, because it was a matter of such palpable and necessary inference. I had stated that Talbott had corrected the record by the deed; and of course he must have opened it: and, just as the General and his friends argue, must have seen the assignment. I omitted to state the fact of Talbott's seeing the assignment, because its existence was so necessarily connected with other facts which I did state that I thought the greatest dunce could not but understand it. Did I say Talbott had not seen it? Did I say anything that was inconsistent with his having seen it before? Most certainly I did neither; and if I did not, what becomes of the argument? These logical gentlemen cannot sustain their argument only by assuming that I did say *negatively* everything that I *did not* say affirmatively, and upon the same assumption, we may expect to find the General, if a little harder pressed for argument, saying that I said Talbott came to our office with his head downwards; not that I actually said so, but because I omitted to say he came feet downward.

In his publication to-day, the Genl. produces the affidavit of Reuben Radford, in which it is said that Talbott told Radford that he did not find the assignment in the deed in the recording of which the error was committed, but that he found it wrapped in another paper in the Recorder's office, upon which statement the Genl. comments, as follows, to wit:—"If it be true as stated by Talbott to Radford, that he found the assignment wrapped up in another paper at his office, that contradicts the statement of Lincoln that it fell out of the deed."

Is common sense to be abused with such sophistry? Did I say what Talbott found it in? If Talbott did find it in another paper at his office, is that any reason why he could not have folded it in a deed and brought it to my office? Can any one be so far duped, as to be made to believe that what may have happened at *Talbott's* office at one time, is inconsistent with what happened at my office at another time?

Now Talbott's statement of the case as he makes it to me is this, that he got a bunch of deeds from young Adams, and that he knows he found the assignment in the bunch, but he is not certain which particular deed it was in, nor is he certain whether it was folded in the same deed out of which it was took (Sic) or another one, when it was brought to my office. Is this a mysterious story? Is there any thing suspicious about it?

But it is useless to dwell longer on this point—Any man who is not wilfully blind can see at a blush, that there is no discrepancy between Talbott and myself.

In regard to the Genl's. concluding statement that "Having thus reviewed in my own way, the statements of Messrs. Talbott and Lincoln and shown that they are not only inconsistent with truth, but each other" I can only say, that I have shown that he has done no such thing: and if the reader is disposed to require any other evidence than the General's assertion, he will be of my opinion.

Excepting the General's most flimsy attempt at mystification, in regard to a discrepancy between Talbott and myself, he has not denied a single statement that I made in my handbill. Every material statement that I made has been sworn to by men who, in former times, were thought as respectable as General Adams. I stated that an assignment of a Judgement, a copy of which I gave, had existed—Benj. Talbott, C. R. Matheny, Wm. Butler, and Judge Logan, swore to its existence. I stated that it was said to be in Gen. Adam's handwriting—the same men swore it was in his handwriting. I stated that Talbott would swear that he got it out of Gen. Adam's possession—Talbott came forward and did swear it.

Bidding adieu to the former publication, I now propose to examine the General's last gigantic production. I now propose to point out some discrepancies in the General's address: and such too, as he shall not be able to escape from. Speaking of the famous assignment the Gen. says: "This last charge, which was their last resort, their dying effort to render my character infamous among my fellow-citizens, was manufactured at a certain lawyer's office in the town, printed at the office of the Sangamo Journal, and found its way into the world some time between two days *just before the last election.*" Now turn to the Key's affidavit in which you will find the following: (viz) "I certify that some time in May or the early part of June, 1837, I saw at Williams' corner a paper purporting to be an assignment from Joseph Anderson to James Adams, which assignment, was signed by a mark to Anderson's name, "&c. Now mark, if Keys saw the assignment on the last of May or 1st of June, Gen. Adams tells a falsehood when he says it was manufactured just before the election, which was on the 7th of August; and if it was manu-

factured just before the election Keys tells a falsehood when he
says he saw it on the last of May or 1st of June. Either Keys
or the General is irretrievably in for it; and in the General's very
condescending language, I say "let them settle it between them."

Now again, let the reader, bearing in mind that Gen. Adams
has unequivocally said, in one part of his address, that the charge
in relation to the assignment was *manufactured just before the
election;* turn to the affidavit of Peter S. Weber, where the following will be found (viz) "I Peter S. Weber do certify, that
from the best of my recollection on the day or day after Gen.
Adams and wife started for the Illinois Rapids, in May last, that
I was at the house of Gen. Adams, sitting in the Kitchen, situated
on the back part of the house, it being in the afternoon, and that
Benjamin Talbott came round the house, back into the Kitchen,
and appeared wild and confused, and that he laid a package of
papers on the kitchen table and requested that they should be
handed to Lucien. He made no apology for coming to the
kitchen, nor for not handing them to Lucien himself, but showed
the token of being frightened and confused both in demeanor and
speech, and for what cause I could not apprehend."

Commenting upon Weber's affidavit, Gen. Adams asks:
"Why this fright and confusion?" I reply that this is a question for the General himself. Weber says that it was in May,
and if so, it is most clear, that Talbott was not frightened on
account of the assignment, unless the General lies when he says
the assignment charge was manufactured *just before the election.*
Is it not a strong evidence that the General is not travelling with
the pole-star of truth in his front, to see him in one part of his
address roundly asserting that the assignment was manufactured
just before the election and then, forgetting that position, procuring Weber's most foolish affidavit, to prove that Talbott had
been angaged in manufacturing it *two months before?*

In another part of his address, Gen Adams says, "That I
hold an assignment of said judgement, dated the 20th of May,
1828, and signed by said Anderson, I have never pretended to
deny or conceal, but stated that fact in one of my circulars previous to the election, and also in answer *to a Bill in Chancery!*"
Now I pronounce this statement unqualifiedly false; and shall
not rely on the word or oath of any man to sustain me in what
I say; but will let the whole be decided by reference to the Circular and answer in Chancery of which the General speaks. In
his circular he did speak of an assignment; but he did not say

it bore date 20th of May 1838; nor did he say it bore any date. In his answer in Chancery, he did say that he had an assignment; but he did not say that it bore date the 20th of May 1828; but so far from it, he said on oath (for he swore to the answer) that as well as recollected, he obtained it in 1827. If any one doubts, let him examine the Circular and answer for himself. They are both accessible.

It will readily be observed that the principal part of Adams' defence, rests upon the argument, that if he had been base enough to forge an assignment, he would not have been fool enough to forge one that would not cover the case. This argument he used in his circular before the election. The Republican has used it at least once, since then; and Adams uses it again in his publication of today. Now I pledge myself to show, that he is just such a fool as he and his friends have contended it was impossible for him to be. Recollect—he says he has a genuine assignment; and that he got Joseph Klein's affidavit, stating that he had seen it, and that he believed the signature to have been executed by the same hand, that signed Anderson's name to the answer in Chancery. Luckily Klein took a copy of this genuine assignment, which I have been permitted to see; and hence I know it does not cover the case. In the first place it is headed "Joseph Anderson vs. Joseph Miller," and leads off "Judgment in Sangamon Circuit Court." Now, mark, there never was a case in Sangamon Circuit Court entitled Joseph Anderson vs. Joseph Miller. The case mentioned in my former publication and the only one between these parties that ever existed in the Circuit Court was entitled Joseph Miller vs, Joseph Anderson, Miller being the plaintiff. What then becomes of all their sophistry about Adams not being *fool enough* to forge an assignment that would not cover the case? It is certain that the present one does not cover the case; and if he can get it honestly, it is still clear that he *was fool enough* to pay for an assignment that does not cover the case.

The General asks for the proof of disinterested witnesses. Who does he consider disinterested? None can be more so than those who have already testified against him. No one of them had the least interest on earth, so far as I can learn, to injure him. True, he says they had conspired against him; but if the testimony of an angel from heaven were introduced against him, he would make the same charge of conspiracy. And I now put the question to every reflecting man, do you believe that Benjamin Talbott, Charles R. Matheny, William Butler and Stephen T. Logan, all sustaining high and spotless characters and justly proud of them, would deliberately perjure themselves, without any motive whatever, except to injure a man's election; and that too, a man who had been a candidate, time out of mind, and yet who had never been elected to any office?

Adams' assurance in demanding disinterested testimony, is surpassing. He brings in the affidavit of his own son, and even of Peter S. Weber, with whom I am not acquainted, but who, I suppose is some black or mulatto boy, from his being kept in the Kitchen, to prove his points; but when such a man as Talbott, a man who, but two years ago run against Gen. Adams for the office of Recorder, and beat him more than four votes to one, is introduced against him, he asks the community with all the consequence of a Lord, to reject his testimony.

I might easily write a volume, pointing out inconsistencies between the statements in Adams' last address with one another, and with other known facts, but I am aware the reader must already be tired with the length of this article. His opening statement, that he was first accused of being a tory, and that he refuted that, that then the Sampson's Ghost story was got up, and he refuted that; and that as a last resort, a dying effort, the assignment charge was got up, is all as false as hell, as all this community must know. Sampson's Ghost first made its appearance in print, and that too, after Keys swears he saw the assignment, as any one may see by reference to the files of papers; and Gen. Adams himself, in reply to the Sampson's Ghost story was the first man that raised the cry of toryism, and it was only by way of set-off and never in seriousness, that it was bandied back at him. His effort is to make the impression that his enemies first made the charge of toryism, and he drove them from that; then Sampson's Ghost, he drove them from that; then finally the assignment charge was manufactured *just before the election.* Now the only general reply he ever made to the Sampson's Ghost and tory charges, he made at *one and the same time,* and not in succession as he states; and the date of that reply will show, that it was made at least a month *after* the date which Key's swears he saw the Anderson assignment. But enough. In conclusion I will only say that I have a character to defend as well as Gen. Adams, but I disdain to whine about it as he does. It is true I have no children nor Kitchen boys; and if I had, I should scorn to lug them in to make affidavit for me.

A. Lincoln.

Sept. 6, 1837.

LETTER OF MR. LINCOLN TO THE THIRD AUDITOR OF THE TREASURY SEPTEMBER 9, 1837

The original of this letter to the third auditor of the treasury is now in the Illinois State Historical Library at Springfield. It again proves Mr. Lincoln's continuing concern for the men with whom he had served in the Black Hawk War, and no doubt effected its purpose.

Springfield, Illinois, Sept 9th 1837

To the Third Auditor
    Sir

Enclosed are the proofs made for procuring payment for a horse lost by John W. Warnsing on the Black Hawk campaign. Warnsing has sold the claim to one Thomas Epperson; and both Warnsing and Epperson tell me there is a Power of Attorney from Warnsing to Epperson now on file in your office. If this be true, I suppose the award & Draft may be made directly to Epperson; if not let them be made to Warnsing. In either case, if not inconsistent with your regulations, let the letter, enclosing the Draft, be directed to me at the above place—The disbursing officer that paid Warnsing was serving with J. D. Henry's Brigade. We do not recollect his name.

Respectfully your Obt Servt
A. Lincoln.

Third Auditor
    Washington City
        District of Columbia
Mailed on Sept. 14, 1837.

DECLARATION IN THE SUIT OF BILLOW VS. WHITE, SANGAMON CIRCUIT COURT, SEPTEMBER 22, 1837
(Herndon-Weik Collection)

This document is in the hand of Attorney Lincoln, with the exception of the number, "109" and the date of filing in the hand of Butler. The characteristic habit of Lincoln in writing the two words such as "twenty four" in one word, thus "twentyfour," is most apparent in this document.. The words "whereas" and "effect," are misspelled, reading "wheras" and "efect." Such *errors were infrequent in the legal documents. The case is cited as Billan vs. White, but the writing of Mr. Lincoln appears to read more like, "'Billow vs. White." Judgment was rendered in favor of Billow upon the default of White, the client of Stuart and Lincoln being awarded the sum of $154.34.*

State of Illinois
Sangamon county & circuit } ss

In the circuit court

October Term 1837

Charles P. Billow complains of Lorance White being in custody &c in a plea of Tresspass in the case upon promises; for that whereas the said defendant, heretofore, towit, on the first day of July in the year of our Lord one thousand eight hundred and thirtyseven, at the county and circuit aforesaid, made his certain promissory note in writing, bearing date the day and year aforesaid, and thereby then and there promised to pay, at the State Bank of Illinois at Springfield, twenty days after the date thereof, to the order of the said plaintiff, the sum of one hundred and fortythree dollars and twentyfour cents for value received, and then and there delivered the said promissory note to the said plaintiff; and the said plaintiff in fact saith, that afterwards, towit, on the twentyfourth day of July in the year aforesaid, at the said State Bank of Illinois at Springfield aforesaid, towit, at the county and circuit aforesaid, the said promissory was duly presented and shown at the said State Bank of Illinois aforesaid, for payment thereof, and payment of the said sum of money therein specified was then and there duly required according to the tenor and effect of the said promissory note; but that neither the said State Bank of Illinois, nor the said defendant, nor any other person or persons on behalf of the said defendant, did or would at the said time when the said promissory note was so presented and shown for payment thereof as aforesaid, or at any time before or afterwards, pay the said sum of money therein specified, or any part thereof, but wholly neglected and refused so to do, of all which said several premises the said defendant, afterwards, towit, on the day and year last aforesaid, at the county and circuit aforesaid, had notice. By means whereof, and force of the statute in such cases made and provided, the said defendant then and there became liable to pay to the said plaintiff the said sum of money in the said promissory note specified, when he the said defendant should be thereunto afterwards requested; and being so liable, he, said defendant, in consideration, thereof, afterwards, towit, on this day and year last aforesaid, and at the county and circuit aforesaid, undertook, and then and there faithfully promised the said plaintiff to pay the said sum of money in the said promissory note specified when he, the said defendant should be thereunto afterwards requested.

And for that wheras also afterwards, towit, on the first day of July in the year aforesaid, at the county and circuit aforesaid, the said defendant made his other certain promissory note in writing, bearing date the day and year last aforesaid, and thereby then and there promised to pay, twenty days after the date thereof, to the order of the said plaintiff the sum of one hundred and forty three dollars and twenty four cents for value received, and then and there delivered the said promissory note to the said plaintiff; by means whereof, and by force of the statute in such case made and provided, the said defendant then and there became liable to pay to the said plaintiff the said sum of money in the said promissory note specified, according to the tenor and effect of the said promissory note; and being so liable he, the said defendant in consideration thereof, afterwards, towit, on the day and year last aforesaid, at the county and circuit aforesaid, undertook, and then and there faithfully promised the said plaintiff to pay him the said sum in the said promissory note specified, according and efect thereof, when thereunto lawfully required—

Yet the said defendant (although often requested so to do) hath not as yet paid to the said plaintiff, the said sum of money in the said promissory notes specified, or either of them, or any part thereof; but sotodo, hath hitherto wholly neglected and refused, and still doth neglect and refuse. To the damage of the said plaintiff, in the sum of two hundred dollars, and therefore he brings his suit

Stuart & Lincoln for plff—

The following is a copy of the instrument declared on:

"$143-24   Springfield July 1st 1837

Twenty days after date I promise to pay to the order of Chas. P. Billow one hundred . . & fortythree Dollars & twentyfour cents, for value received, payable and negociable at the State Bank of Illinois at Springfield without defalcation

Lorence White"

109
Charles P Billow
vs
Lorence White

Declaration
Filed Sept 22d 1837
Wm Butler Clk

_____

NOTE BY MR. LINCOLN SIGNED AN OLD SETTLER, SANGAMO JOURNAL SEPTEMBER 30, 1837

In the issue of the Sangamo Journal for September 30, 1837, Mr. Lincoln returned to his prodding of General James Adams in a new and amusing way. His fresh assault took the form of a note signed An Old Settler, but no doubt penned by Mr .Lincoln, in which claim is made that the writer has read the Sampson's Ghost Letters, and understands that there are irregularities in the handling of certain lots and a plot of ten acres by Adams. He has examined these matters with care, and shortly will give his conclusions regarding them.

TO THE PUBLIC

Some time in May last, I discovered an article in the Journal, over the signature of 'Sampson's Ghost,' rather insinuating that Gen. Adams had been guilty of some improper conduct in relation to a certain piece of property which he then lived upon. Shortly after it was intimated that he might have fraudulently obtained a deed to a certain piece of land near Springfield, containing ten acres—which in right, as was said, belonged to a widow woman and her children, by the name of Anderson. Again he was charged with having in his possession an assignment of a judgment, which assignment was thought to be a forgery. All the above charges I have examined impartially—also the defence of General Adams—with the view, if possible, of arriving at correct conclusions as to his guilt or innocence—and have come to the conclusion that Adam's conduct will not bear the test of scrutiny. I will, hereafter, give to the public, in Numbers, a full history of the matter; and should I fail to convince the public that I have arrived at correct conclusions, I will never again dip my pen in ink to expose the villainy of any man.

An Old Settler.

ENTRY FOR LUCINDA MASON IN STUART AND LINCOLN FEE BOOK, OCTOBER, 1837
(Whipple, Story Life of Lincoln, Page 149)

As mentioned in the notes to the Ross entry of April, 1837, this is one of the two items listed in the Whipple book which do

*not appear in the original manuscript items in the Herndon-Weik
Collection. The obtaining of the assignment of dower was given
by court decree at the October term, 1837, and the final report
and allotment of dower appear in the document of December
9, 1838, elsewhere reproduced in the present volume.*

Lucinda Mason
          To Stuart & Lincoln   Dr
1837 Oct. To obtaining assignment of Dower $ 5.00

OLD SETTLER LETTER NO. 1 WRITTEN BY MR. LINCOLN, SANGAMO JOURNAL OCTOBER 7, 1837

*True to his promise of September 30, 1837, the first of the
Old Settler letters written by Mr. Lincoln appeared in the October 7 issue of the Sangamo Journal. General Adams is charged
with dishonest practises in acquiring title to certain lots in Springfield. And Mr. Lincoln includes a letter from Elijah Iles, one of
Springfield's leading citizens, which sets forth details of another
case in which Adams resorted to unfair methods.*

I have promised if possible, to convince the public, that General Adams has been guilty of improper conduct in several instances. In this task, I feel confident that I am doing no more
than every honest man is bound to do, when he becomes satisfied
that a public officer has forfeited the support of a free and generous people.

I feel myself bound to make good my promises: and I will
assure the public that in doing so, I shall make no attempt at un-
fairness—I shall make no statement except from my own knowledge, or from a source entitled to credit.

I cannot do my duty in this matter, without going back to
the time when Adams first made his appearance in this place,
which, if I have not been misinformed, was in the year 1821 or
'22. On his arrival here, he professed to be a lawyer, and as such
he was frequently employed. At that time he was considered a
good one—as a counsellor I have heard no objections made by his
clients; and, for a time, as a citizen, no particular objection was
raised against him. But his real character soon discovered itself.
His first attempt at knavery was made upon a gentleman who
has since left this State,—whose present residence I will not mention in this number; but will, hereafter give a full statement of
the affair as it took place. I will now say it grew out of his setting up a claim to some lots, to which I will prove, before I get
through, he had no earthly claim whatever. The matter was then

compromised by the owner paying Adams a certain sum of money.

He then set up a claim to other property in this place, to which he had no right, as I have been told by a number of respectable gentlemen of this town.

I have called on Elijah Iles, Esq. and he has furnished me with a statement of this man's extraordinary conduct, which is as follows:

"Springfield, 3d October, 1837

Sir:

Agreeable to your request, I give you a statement of the cause of the difference between Gen. Adams and myself.

Previous to the Land Sales I purchased a claim to the lot of land on which the temporary County Seat of Sangamon County was located; and as individuals settled in the town, they were told by me, that if I was successful in the purchase, that I would donate to them a lot or lots, according to circumstances. Among those who came to the town was Gen. Adams; and from the favorable opinion I had of the General I agreed to let him have more than others. After the purchase was made by me, and I was making the conveyances to the different individuals, the Gen. claimed a greater amount than I had promised to donate him, and insisted that it was as I had promised, which was altogether different to my understanding. To all others to whom I made deeds, I know of no misunderstanding.

Another circumstance was the case of R. Burden, to whom I donated one lot, and sold him another. I acknowledged the deed to Burden before Adams; and some months after, Burden sold the lots to James Strode, and requested me to make a deed to said Strode—which I did, forgetting that I had already made a deed to Burden. Strode had his deed recorded, after which Burden presented his deed for record and through the influence of Squire Matheny, Burden agreed not to have his deed recorded, but would deliver it to me and let me destroy it.

Burden made the following statement, as far as now recollected, in presence of Matheny and myself: That he did not know that I had made him a deed until General Adams wrote him while at work at Clark's Mills urging the necessity of his coming to town forthwith—that he had something to communicate to him that would be greatly to his advantage and much to his disadvantage if he failed;—and when he called on Adams, he, (Adams) presented him the deed from me, and influenced him to present the deed for record; and by encouragement of gain, or worth to that amount held out, induced him to take the course he did. Burden acknowledged he was wrong, and that it was a mean act.

Respectfully Yours,

E. Iles

N.B. I do not now recollect whether I saw the letter from Adams to Burden, but will refer you to Squire Matheny or Messrs. Clark. E. I."

I may make some very strong statements to the public, and quite unpleasant to General Adams before I close. He may wince, and screw as other men of the same character usually do, under the lash of Justice and the power of Truth, still he shall not escape. His duplicity shall not be covered over by the mantle of religion.

ANSWER OF MR. LINCOLN AS GUARDIAN AD LITEM OF WILLIAM NELSON IN THE SUIT OF WHITE VS. HARRIS ET AL, SANGAMON CIRCUIT COURT, OCTOBER 10, 1837

Mr. Lincoln played no part in this case, except as guardian ad litem. The answer given by him is taken from the court record in the hand of the clerk. It may be said that these are the words of Abraham Lincoln, but they are not in his hand. It is probable that the clerk transcribed the original answer in the hand of Lincoln, although exact transcription may be questioned. Mr. Lincoln was not given to capitalizing words like "should," unless they were at the beginning of a sentence. The notice of the appointment of Lincoln as guardian is in the hand of the clerk.

Craig White	Complainant	
against		on Petition
David P. Harris & Others	Defendants	for Partition

This day came the Petitioner by his counsel and filed his Petition and the printers Certificate of the Publication of the notice of the presentation of his said Petition herein, and on his motion. It is ordered by the court that A. Lincoln be appointed guardian *ad litem* to William Nelson an infant defendant herein

Craig White		
vs		
David P. Harris & Polly his wife		on Petition
Betsey Nelson & William Nelson		for Partition

Abraham Lincoln guardian *ad litem* to the said William Nelson a minor states that he has examined the papers in this cause & that he knows of no good reason consistent with the interest of said William why the prayer of the Petition Should not be granted.

A. Lincoln

LAST OF THE OLD SETTLER LETTERS

Mr. Lincoln's controversy with General Adams appears to have been one of his chief concerns during the year 1837, but in this brief letter which appeared in the Sangamo Journal on October 14, 1837, he ceased to air the affair in the newspapers, thus heeding the criticism to which he had been subjected that there were more seemly and effective ways of trying a law suit.

The Republican of this week, the mouth-piece of a purchased set of politicians, says: "We have received a long and able document from Gen. Adams, for publication, which will be given in our next."

I will wait and see this celebrated defense of the General before I say much more upon the subject—satisfied in my own mind that every attempt which he makes to remove the cloud of suspicion which hangs over his character, will add new proofs of guilt.

It may be that he has sent his defense to the writing Judge, for the purpose of soliciting his opinion. If so, I shall expect quite an able document—perhaps upon corporations.

An Old Settler.

MR. LINCOLN TAKES DEPOSITIONS IN THE SUIT OF WRIGHT VS. ADAMS SANGAMON CIRCUIT COURT, NOVEMBER 11 AND 12, 1837

On November 11 and 12, 1837, the suit of the Anderson heirs against James Adams in which Joel Wright appeared as plaintiff again occupied the attention of Mr. Lincoln. On the first day he took the deposition of Isaiah Stillman, and on the second day that of Stephen Dewey, clerk of the Fulton Circuit Court. The originals of these depositions have disappeared, but it is known that "Stillman swore that in 1832, several years after the assignment by Anderson to Adams alleged by the latter, Anderson learning that Stillman was about to make a trip to Springfield, asked him to see Adams and find out if Joseph Miller had paid him any money for Anderson, and, if so, to get it; that he did see Adams and delivered the message, but was told by Adams that he had collected no money for Anderson from any one. Stillman further stated that in their talk Adams said nothing about Anderson having already assigned to him the claim of Joseph Miller. The deposition of Dewey on the following day contradicted Adams on several important points. The record indicates that beside the depositions of Stillman and Dewey several others were taken by Mr. Lincoln, but these also are now missing from the files." See Lincoln the Litigant by Townsend, Boston, 1925, Pp. 103-04.

And the good-neighbor phase of Mr. Lincoln's labors as a lawyer was again in evidence on November 20, 1837, when he took "from Joshua Hobbs his written order on William Butler to pay Thomas Hunter $4.75 for hauling thirty-eight loads of manure." Photostat in the possession of the Abraham Lincoln Association, Springfield, Illinois.

LETTER OF MR. LINCOLN TO WILLIAM A. MINSHALL, DECEMBER 7, 1837

Busy as he was as a lawyer, Mr. Lincoln could always spare a half hour for politics. Hence this characteristic letter of December 7, 1837, to a fellow Whig, William A. Minshall of Rushville. Minshall, who was born and had studied law in Ohio, settled in Rushville when the town was young and early became a leader at the bar and in politics. He served three terms in the General Assembly, and in 1847 sat in the convention which framed a new constitution for the State of Illinois. Under that instrument he was in 1848 elected judge of the circuit court for his district, dying five years later in office.

Usher F. Linder tells a story of Minshall which must have been greeted with approving laughter by their mutual friend Lincoln when he heard it for the first time. "Minshall in his early days," writes Linder, "was given to dissipation. He courted a most beautiful woman, and on proposing marriage to her, she promptly rejected him, on the strength of which Minshall got most gloriously drunk; in his crazy mood put on seven clean shirts, and in that condition, he went over to see her again, letting her know that it was impossible for him to live without her. The young lady, who was far from being indifferent to the suit of Minshall, finally concluded that she would try to make a man of him; so she said to him: 'Mr. Minshall, I will never marry a drunkard, and if I had a husband and he was to become one I would leave him on the instant if I loved him as I love life; but I have come to the conclusion that I will marry you upon one condition: If you will reform your habits, give me satisfactory proof of the same, and make a solemn vow that you will never drink again. So now go home and divest yourself of all those shirts but one, come back in a month from now and we will consummate this agreement.' Minshall gladly took her at her word. After a month's probation he returned, took the vow and they were married. And he religiously lived up to his pledge to the day of his death." (See Usher F. Linder, "Reminiscences of the Early Bench and Bar of Illinois," Chicago, 1879, Page 361-62)

Nor did a policy of silence on the part of his Whig opponents avail to halt the swift advance of Stephen A. Douglas. Friend Minshall.

I write this to say that it is Stuart's intention to be a candidate for congress again; and that he will be publicly announced before long. I would suggest to you the propriety of your letting our friends in your parts know, that he is to be the candidate.

On the receipt of this, write me all you know, and all you think, in regard to our prospects for the same.

I believe we have nothing here that would be news to you. I am ashamed to write so short a letter; but lack of material, you know will (explain?) my being short.

Your sincere friend
A. Lincoln

P. S. We have adopted it as part of our policy here, to never speak of Douglas at all. Isn't that the best mode of treating so small a matter?

PRAECIPE AND DECLARATION IN THE SUIT OF REED AND WIFE VS. ARNOLD AND BUTLER, SANGAMON CIRCUIT COURT, JANUARY 12, 1838
(Herndon-Weik Collection)

The praecipe and declaration in this case are from the pen of Mr. Lincoln, as are the cover notations, with the exception of Butler's notation upon the file date. The case is cited at times as James F. Reed and Eliza Reed vs. Arnold and Butler, but the Court Record of Sangamon County gives it as James E. Reed and Eliza, his wife, vs. Charles Arnold and William Butler. Attorney Lincoln used "James E. Reed" upon every occasion in reference to the plaintiff. The "E" of this case differs measurably from the "F" in the "James F. Reed" of the case of Reed and Rickard vs. Early et al, dated, November, 1839. It is possible that Mr. Lincoln erred in the middle initial; he did upon occasion. James E. Reed was a leader of the Reed-Donner trek to California, being one of the few survivors of the expedition. William Butler was probably the friend at whose house Attorney Lincoln was taking meals at the time. If so, it will be seen that in law cases, Abraham Lincoln treated friend and foe alike. The well preserved and neatly penned Court Record Book of Sangamon County contains this entry: "It is adjudged by the Court that the said Plaintiff recover of the said Defendants the sum of Two Hundred and fifty dollars the Damages assessed as aforesaid and also their Costs herein expended and that he have execution therefor." Stuart & Lincoln represented the plaintiffs in the case and the judgment in favor of their client was rendered on March 9, 1838.

State of Illinois ⎱ In the Circuit court of said
⎰ county—
Sangamon county & circuit ⎰ March Term 1838

James E. Reed and Eliza A. (late Eliza A. Kindoll) his wife, plaintiffs, complain of Charles Arnold and William Butler defendants, being in custody &c. for that whereas the said defendants, heretofore, and whilst the said Eliza A. was sole and unmarried, towit, on the twenty third day of December in the year of our Lord one thousand eight hundred and thirtysix, at the county and circuit aforesaid, made their certain promissory note in writing, bearing date the day and year aforesaid, and thereby then and there promised to pay twelve months after the date thereof to the said Eliza A. now the wife of the said James E. Reed (by her then name of Eliza A. Kindoll) the sum of two hundred and fifty dollars, for value received, and then and there delivered the said promissory note to the said Eliza A. ; by means whereof, and by force of the statute in such case made and provided, they, the said defendants then and there became liable to pay to the said Eliza A. whilst she was sole and unmarried the said sum of money in the said promissory note specified according to the tenor and effect of the said promissory note specified according to the tenor and effect of the said promissory note; and being so liable, they, the said defendants in consideration thereof, afterwards, towit, on the day and year aforesaid, at the county and circuit aforesaid, undertook, and then and there faithfully promised the said Eliza

money in the said promissory note specified according to the tenor
and effect thereof when they should be thereunto afterwards lawfully requested. Yet the said defendants (although often requested
so to do) have not as yet paid the said sum of money in the said
promissory note specified, or any part thereof, to the said Eliza A.
whilst she was sole and unmarried, or to the said James E. Reed
and Eliza A. his wife, or either of them since their intermarriage.
But they to do this have hitherto wholly refused, and still do
refuse to pay the same; or any part thereof, to the said James E.
Reed, and Eliza A. his wife.

To the damage of the said James E. Reed and Eliza A. his
wife, of four hundred dollars, and therefore they bring their suit
&c.

Stuart & Lincoln
for Plff

The following is a copy of the instrument declared on:

"Twelve months after date we or either of us jointly and
severally promise to pay Eliza A. Kindoll the sum of Two
hundred and fifty dollars good and lawful money, for value
received without interest.

Witness our hands and seals this 23d day of Decr 1836

Charles Arnold
William Butler"

State of Illinois	In the circuit court of said county
Sangamon county & circuit	March term 1838

James E. Reed & Eliza A. his wife vs Charles Arnold William Butler	In Assumpsit Damage $400—

The clerk of the Sangamon circuit court will issue process in
the above entitled cause returnable to the next term of said court—

Stuart & Lincoln for
Plff

James E Reed & Wife
vs
Charles Arnold &
William Butler

Precipe & Decln
Filed Jany 12th 1838
  Wm. Butler Clk

LETTERS OF "A CONSERVATIVE" WRITTEN IN PART BY LINCOLN, SANGAMO JOURNAL, JANUARY 12, JANUARY 27, FEBRUARY 3 AND FEBRUARY 10, 1838

During January and February, 1838, a series of four letters were published in the Sangamo Journal signed "A Conservative." They purported to come from a conservative Democrat, and deplored the conduct of affairs in his party. After a careful study of the four letters, Dr. Glenn H. Seymour, in an article published in the July, 1936, issue of the Journal of the Illinois State Historical Society, recorded his conclusions that, while the first A Conservative letter might be reasonably ascribed to Francis, editor of the Sangamo Journal, the remaining three were written in whole or in part by Abraham Lincoln. He pointed out that Mr. Lincoln was in Springfield during the period the letters appeared in the Journal; that "the cadence and rhythm of the prose was that of the early Lincoln, and that the arrangement of the argument is peculiarly in his manner."

Conservative No. 2 letter, here reproduced, appeared in the Sangamo Journal on January 27, 1837, and was a scorching attack on the nomination by a Democratic convention held in Peoria of Stephen A. Douglas to contest with John T. Stuart, Mr. Lincoln's partner, for the seat in Congress then held by William L. May.

A CONSERVATIVE — NO. 2

The present number will be devoted to the Peoria Convention. And while I admit that conventions really gotten up by the People, unpacked and fairly conducted throughout, are highly proper, and strictly democratic in every just sense of the word; I shall attempt to show that the one lately held at Peoria, was gotten up and conducted in such a manner, as to render it both injurious and disgraceful to the party if they attempt to sustain it.

In the first place, a certain gentleman who resides in Sangamon county, and who has followed a variety of occupations, both here and elsewhere, for a living and failed in all, cast about for some desperate manovre (sic) that might save him, when he should be called upon to close up his loafing operations. After some considerable wandering, his eyes were finally settled upon a Land Office; and to remove the incumbent, and place himself in his stead, all the powers of his mind were put to the torture. He first made a set at the Receiver's Office in Springfield, but the Receiver seeing nothing in prospect that he liked better, and preferring himself to the best of his friends, chose not to be jostled from his place. Next he turned to the Register's Office. It was filled by a young man of respectable talents for one of his age, who had received rather an extraordinary succession of favors from his party, and who, mistaking those favors, which were merely designed to give him the means of living, as evidence of a high admiration of his talents, was more completely assailable on the score of vanity, and more susceptible of flattery than is often the lot of man to be.

Long practice enabled him to discover the vulnerable point of the Register; and there he directed his attack. He commenced, as is supposed by telling him that he regretted to see him confined to the dry and laborious occupation of writing answers to the endless and silly enquiries of every applicant about N. W. of S. E. of 23, T. 24 R. 3W., etc., etc.; that for one whom nature designed for nothing else but to be

"'Fixed to one certain spot,
To draw nutrition, propagate, and rot."
such a plodding occupation was well enough; but that for one of his towering genius, it was absolutely intolerable. "You," continued he, "may be President of these United States just as well as not. A seat in Congress is not worthy to be your abiding place, though you might with propriety serve one term in the capacity of Representative—not that it would at all become you; but merely in imitation of some king, who being called to the throne from obscurity, lodges for one night in a hovel as he journies to the palace. History gives no account of a man of your age occupying such high ground as you do now. At twenty-four Bonaparte was unheard of; and in fact so it has been with all great men in former times. Of the history of all of them, Mr. Van Buren alone approaches rivalship to yours. Indeed, the similarity is striking. The only difference, perhaps, is, that his own was but the miniature of what you's is the life size."

"But", said the Register, "do you really think a seat in Congress within my reach?"

"'Within your reach! What a question!—How strange it is, that while true genius can place a true estimate upon everything else, it never can upon its own powers. There is no doubt of a seat in Congress being within your reach. The only question is whether you will condescend to occupy it. Our party have the majority in this District, and all you have to do is to get nominated at a District Convention as a party candidate. Get the nomination, place this office in my hands, (which I would by no means accept, only for the opportunity it will afford me of serving you) and take the field boldly, and make a regular electioneering campaign of it from this time to the election, and, depend upon it, success is certain."

"Done," says the Register. "'Procure me the nomination of the District Convention, and the office is yours."

"I fear you mistake my motive," says the man of expedients. "I only proposed to take the office as a means of serving you."

"Just so I understand you," says the Register.

"So let it be then."

"Agreed."

Steps were immediately taken to get up a Convention. The "man of expedients" was seen to be the prime mover of all, or nearly all, the primary meetings this side of the river.—As many delegates were to be appointed from each county, as the county was entitled to senators and representative (sic) in the legislature —In Sangamon I know precisely how the matter was managed. Nine men were appointed delegates care being taken to get as many of them pledged to the Register as possible, and the remainder made up of men who it was known, would not attend, and their vacancies of course were to be filled by those who did. And it is a fact not to be denied, that in filling these vacancies, no man would or could be accepted unless he would pledge himself to go for the Register. There was much difficulty in getting all these places filled; and I know that several respectable members of the party as can be found in the county, voluntarily offered to go, but were rejected in consequence of expressing a preference for other men over him who finally received the nomination; while others who accepted and did attend, had their stage fare and expenses paid to Peoria and back from a source they knew not whence; for no other reason than their being pleased to vote for the Register. This same spouting prime mover, attended the horse races at Jacksonville, and got up a meeting there, which I have every reason to believe, was conducted precisely, or at least, very nearly, in the same manner as that in Sangamon. Anon the Convention is in session at Peoria. This same man is there taking the lead. Discovering that matters are so arranged, that his man can succeed if the vote be immediately taken, he announces to the Convention that some of his family are dangerously ill, and that he must of necessity leave before the next day, and therefore requests that the nomination be immediately made. Through kindness to him the unsuspecting members consent, and the nomination is made, when, to the astonishment of all, this man again rises in a blaze of good humor, and proposes that the Convention shall adjourn the next day, that the members may have the pleasure of a better acquaintance!—He was detected in, and castigated for his duplicity on the spot by a talented young gentleman, Mr. Hodge, of Galena; but even then, little did the members think that a majority of them were at that very moment the dupes of this man; and that they had actually made a nomination, which, but for his exertions, from motives now apparent, would never have been thought of. But the nomination was made; and, according to contract, I presume, at this time, a correspondence is going on between Washington and this place, in regard to the regular transfer of the Land Office.

I have said the nomination, if adhered to by the party, would both injure and disgrace them. I maintain the points. It will injure them because it will lose them the district. Abstractly speaking, the nominee is a clever enough young man; but he cannot be elected. He has not a personal acquaintance with the one-hundredth man in the District; and by those to whom he is known, he is not remarkably favorably known: If there were no other evidence, the profound silence and disregard, with which the whig press treat him, are sufficient to prove that his claims to a seat in Congress, are beneath the dignity of contempt. God knows they are never slow in the abuse and slander of any democrat, that is worth slandering and abusing: and yet, although he has been before the people of the district some six or eight weeks, no one of them has even condescended to notice him in any way, except the Chicago American; and I have no doubt that if the editor could see the man, he would beg pardon for what he has done, and promise faithfully to do so no more.

But an attempt to sustain this nomination will both injure and disgrace the party on another account. Our party have ever declared and I hope conscientiously too, that they were actuated only by the purest motives. On the other hand, the whigs are ever charging us with corruption; and I confess if we attempt to sustain the Peoria nomination with all the foul and corrupt transactions that attended it in its incipient and subsequent stages, it will put them to little trouble to prove it on us. If such ill-begotten assemblages as that, be permitted to pass as regular Democratic Conventions, it will not be long, till the honest of all parties will need only to be informed that a candidate has been nominated by a Convention, to determine them to vote against him. They will receive, as they should, the scorn and contempt of the world.

In conclusion, I will say, I can not vote, for the Peoria nominee, and I will not vote for a whig. I go for a new District Convention, to be really gotten up by the people, that shall not be a disgrace upon the word; and that will nominate some member of the party who will stand some chance of success.

A Conservative

Three days later, on January 30, 1837, an angry Douglas answered this attack with a long letter in the Illinois Republican in which he demanded the name of the "Conservative." His demand prompted this "Addendum to Conservative No. 2, published in the Sangamo Journal on February 3:

ADDENDUM — TO CONSERVATIVE NO. 2

In looking over the loco foco paper published here, I discover that my last number has called forth a very ill-natured, and to my judgment, a very silly article from Mr. Douglas. Mr. D. has either mistaken my object, or designs to lead me from it. If the latter, he will not succeed for more reasons than one. In the first place, I am on terms of friendship with him, and wish to remain so. As to his abuse of (   ) it, as the fulmination of (   ) to give up my name (   ) (it designs to divert) public attention from what I consider a very important, to a mere personal difficulty between him and me.

My object was not to assail him; nor would I have even referred to him, if it had been possible to avoid it. I did not even mean to charge him with culpability in contracting the land office. Under ordinary circumstances, I would regard such a transaction as culpable; but I hold if a man is flattered out of his sense, he is no more responsible than when he is insane from other causes. My object was, and still is, to stay, if possible, the strong adverse current which is now setting against the cause of equal rights. Taking advantage of the destructive schemes of the loco foco party, as a weapon against the whole, the high-toned blue-light federalists have swept State after State from our ranks, till we are left with a mere fragment of strength among the people; but which, if prudently used, may be again swelled to a majority ere the present term of Mr. Van Buren expires. This being the case, my object is to snatch back from the federalists, this Congressional District, into whose grasp it is almost gone. But, in these trying times, instead of some man of talent and acquaintance with the people, and possessing other suitable qualifications presented as our candidate, we have a young man who is not only the very spawn of that loco focoism which has crushed and destroyed our party in New York and several other smaller States; but who was actually foisted upon the party by the influence of a land office. That this last was the fact, Mr. D. denies; but I believe it to be true for what appears to me to be the best of reasons. It is not my purpose to denounce him; but I will say to him, that when he explains to me why he, that I heretofore called the man of expedients, felt so deep an interest in procuring his nomination, as to attend the primary meetings out of his own county; to have all the appointed delegates pledged to him before he would appoint them; to tell a falsehood in the Convention which he knew must be detected within a few hours at most; to communicate with a land officer in the north, urging him to be a candidate, and then deceiving him; and lastly, to go to Vandalia at a most disagreeable season to procure the nomination of Colonel Stephenson, to appease his friends, whose complaints it was feared might be sufficiently loud to drive the Peoria nominee from the track—I say, when he will explain all these things, I pledge myself then to furnish him with some others which he knows to be in my possession, and which will readily enough occur to him on reading this.

I now again say to the Democratic party of this District, that if they wish their principles to continue in the ascendant; if they wish to again, as they have heretofore done, defeat the designs of the federalist party; if they wish to preserve true democracy as well in reality as in name, some other candidate must be placed upon the track. I have already given it as my opinion that a Convention fairly gotten up would be the proper method of bringing such a candidate before the people.

The Conservative

The last of the four Conservative letters appeard in the Sangamo Journal on February 10, 1837, and was made up of protests purporting to come from Democrats of the district hostile to the nomination of Douglas. The only one of these protests having a signature bore that of William L. May, who wrote from Dixon's Ferry under date of December 1, 1837, setting forth the unfair manner in which Douglas had wrested the nomination for Con-

gress from him. The conclusion of this series of protests, however, sounds very like Mr. Lincoln:

Without admitting that those articles are slanderous, I answer that I refuse to sign my name to them, because I am no candidate for public favor, and consequently the people have no interest in my character; because, if my statements are false, Mr. Douglass can as easily show them to be so, without knowing my name as with it; and, particularly, because I know Mr. Douglass knows those statements are true ,and is therefore inordinately desirous to divert public attention from them by getting into a personal quarrel with me.

DECLARATION AND PRAECIPE IN THE SUIT OF HARRISON VS. DICKINSON AND TAYLOR, SANGAMON CIRCUIT COURT, JANUARY 27, 1838
(Herndon-Weik Collection)

This declaration and praecipe were penned by Attorney Lincoln, as were the cover notations, excepting the date of filing in the hand of Butler. David Dickinson, one of the defendants, was a former deputy-sheriff of Sangamon County, and well known to Mr. Lincoln, who in 1834 had voted for him for sheriff. The co-defendant, John Taylor, was a man of much property, being owner of a large part of the town of Petersburg. The case was decided on March 9, 1838, at which time the clerk made entry of the default of the defendants, and a judgment by default of five hundred and sixty dollars debts and damages, the costs being also assessed against the defendants. Once again, Attorney Lincoln is seen acting against an old friend of New Salem days.

State of Illinois⎫
⎬ In the circuit court of said
Sangamon county & circuit ⎭ county—March Term. 1838—

Peyton L. Harrison, plaintiff, complains of David Dickinson and John Taylor, defendants, being in custody &c. of a plea that they render to the said plaintiff the sum of five hundred dollars and interest lawful money which they owe to and unjustly detain from him: For that whereas the said defendants, heretofore, towit, on the fifteenth day of March in the year of our Lord one thousand eight hundred and thirty seven, at the county and circuit aforesaid, by their certain writing obligatory (the said David Dickinson signing his name D. Dicknson) sealed wth their seals and now shown to the court &c. the date whereof is the day and year aforesaid, acknowledged themselves to be held and firmly bound unto the said plaintiff in the sum of five hundred dollars above demanded to be paid to the said plaintiff on order on or before the twentyfifth day of December then next ensuing, to draw twelve per cent until paid. Yet the said defendants (although often requested so to do) have not as yet paid the said sum of five hundred dollars above demanded or any part thereof, to the said plaintiff; but have hitherto wholly neglected and refused, and still neglects and refuses so to do,— To the damage of the said plaintiff of two hundred dollars, and therefore he brings his suit—

Stuart & Lincoln for Plffs—

The following is a copy of the instrument declared on:
"On or before the 25th December next we or either of us promise to pay to Peyton L. Harrison, or order five hundred dollars value received drawing Twelve per cent until paid—

March 15th 1837   D. Dickinson (Seal)
Witness our hands & seals   John Taylor (Seal)"

Peyton L. Harrison
        ⎤ In Debt
    vs ⎬
        ⎦

David Dickinson & Debt—$500-00
David Dickinson &   Debt— $5500-00
John Taylor .   Damage   ..200-00

The clerk of the Sangamon circuit court will issue process in the above entitled cause returnable to the next term of said court—

Stuart & Lincoln for Plff

P. L. Harrison
    vs
David Dickinson &
John Taylor—
  Declaration & Precipe
Filed Jany 27 1838
  Wm Butler Clk

NOTES IN THE SUIT OF STAFFORD VS. WHITNEY & WHITNEY, JANUARY 28, 1838
(Herndon-Weik Collection)
These notes are in the hand of Lawyer Lincoln, and signed

by Jonas and Dewey Whitney. The cover notations are from the pen of Mr. Lincoln, but the word, "to," may be viewed as suspect, as it is not distinctly Lincolnesque. In view of the fact that the signatures of the two Whitneys are the only marks of penmanship not by Lincoln, it is possible that the word, "to", was penned rapidly by him. These notes are part of the suit of Stafford vs. Whitney and Whitney, March 4, 1841, dealt with in another place.

Jonas & Dewey Whitney

to   } Notes

1

DanStafford

$85- 41—

$85- 41—

"Springfield Ills: January-29-1838

Seven months after date we or either of us promise to pay Daniel Stafford Junior or order the sum of eightyfive dollars and fortyone cents with six per cent interest from date until paid; for value received—

Jonas Whitney
Dewey Whitney"

"Springfield, Ills. January 29-1838

Nine months after date we or either of us promise to pay Daniel Stafford Junior, or order eightyfive dollars and fortyone cents, with six per cent interest from date until paid; for value received—

Jonas Whitney
Dewey Whitney"

PRAECIPE AND DECLARATION IN THE SUIT OF ELLIS & VAUGHN VS. RANSDELL, SANGAMON CIRCUIT COURT, JANUARY 29, 1838,

(Herndon-Weik Collection)

This praecipe and declaration are in the hand of Mr. Lincoln. The figures and cover notations, with the exception of the file date, are also in his hand. He spells "style" as "stile," an infrequent usage by him. Abner Y. Ellis was a close friend of Mr. Lincoln in the latter's New Salem days, and afterward a partner of another Lincoln intimate, Joshua Fry Speed. Wharton Ransdell, as noted in another place, was the keeper of a tavern in Springfield. On March 9, 1838, the clerk entered a final decision in the Record Book of Sangamon County, noting that the defendant had defaulted, and that the court had decreed judgment in favor of the clients of Stuart & Lincoln in the sum of One hundred thirty one dollars and forty five cents damages, not including costs, which were to be paid by Ransdell.

State of Illinois
}
ss   In the circuit court of said
Sangamon county and circuit
county—March Term 1838

Abner Y. Ellis and Foley Vaughn, late trading under the name, stile and firm of Ellis & Vaughn, plaintiffs, complain of Wharton Ransdell, defendant, being in custody &c of a plea of tresspass on the case upon promises: For that whereas the said defendant, heretofore towit, on the fourth day of October in the year of our Lord one thousand eight hundred and thirty seven, at the county and circuit aforesaid, made his certain promissory note in writing (signing his name thereto "W. Ransdell") bearing date the day and year aforesaid, and thereby then and there promised to pay to one Robert C. Arnold, on demand, the sum of one hundred and twentyeight dollars and twentyfive (meaning one hundred and twentyeight dollars and twentyfive cents) for value received, and then and there delivered the said promissory note to the said Robert C. Arnold— And the said Robert C. Arnold, to whom the payment of the said sum of money in the said promissory note specified was to be made, after the making of the said promissory note, before the payment of the said sum of money therein specified, towit on the first day of January in the year of our Lord one thousand eight hundred and thirtyeight, at the county and circuit aforesaid, assigned the said promissory note, by which said assignment, he the said Robert C. Arnold then and there ordered and appointed the said sum of money in the said promissory note specified, to be paid to the said plaintiffs, and then and there delivered the said promissory note so assigned as aforesaid to the said plaintiffs, by means whereof, and by force of the statute in such case made and provided, the said defendant then and there became liable to pay to the said plaintiffs the said sum of money in the said promissory note specified according to the tenor and effect of the said promissory note; and being so liable he the said defendant, in consideration thereof, afterwards, towit, on the day and year last aforesaid, at the county and circuit aforesaid, undertook, and then and there faithfully promised the said plaintiffs to pay them the said sum of money in the said promissory note specified, according to the tenor and effect thereof—

Yet the said defendant (although often requested so to do) hath not as yet paid to the said plaintiffs the said sum of money in the said promissory note specified, or any part thereof, but so to do hath hitherto wholly neglected and refused, and still doth neglect and refuse— To the damage of the said plaintiffs of the sum of two hundred dollars; and therefore they bring their suit &c.

Stuart & Lincoln for Plff

The following is a copy of the instrument declared on:

"Due Robert C. Arnold one hundred and twentyeight dollars and twentyfive cents for value Rcd this 4th October 1837

W. Ransdell"

$$\begin{array}{r} 12825 \\ 2\frac{1}{2} \\ \hline 25650 \\ 64 \\ \hline 320 \\ 12825 \\ \hline 131.45 \end{array}$$

| Albert Y. Ellis & Foley Vaughn vs Wharton Ransdell | Tresspass on the case upon promises— Damage $200-00— |

The clerk of the Sangamon circuit court will issue process in the above case returnable to the next term of said court—

Stuart & Lincoln—

Ellis & Vaughn
   vs   .
W. Ransdell

Precipe & Declaration
Filed Jany 29th 1838
  Wm. Butler Clk

THE LEGISLATURE VOTES MONEY TO COMPLETE THE STATE HOUSE AT SPRINGFIELD, JANUARY 10, 1839

Following the debate of January 9 there was a shrewd rallying of forces by Mr. Lincoln and the other Whig leaders in the Legislature concerned for Springfield's future; and on January 10 a bill, in the drafting of which, it is safe to assume he had participated, and which made an adequate appropriation for completing the new state house, was passed by the House. The text of this bill, duly approved by the Senate and signed by the governor, follows. Three days after its passage by the House, in the Senate at Washington Silas Wright of New York called up President Van Buren's sub-treasury bill and started it on the way to final enactment—a course which in the months just ahead was to call forth in angry protest much unavailing oratory from Abraham Lincoln of Springfield.

Be it enacted by the people of the State of Illinois represented in General Assembly, That the sum of $128,300 be, and the same is hereby appropriated, to defray the expenses of finishing the State House at Springfield and furnishing the same, and the offices attached thereto, with all the necessary furniture for the use of the said house and offices—said sum payable out of any money in the treasury not otherwise appropriated.

Sec. 2. The Commissioners appointed to superintend the erection of the public buildings at Springfield, shall proceed, without delay to cause the said buildings to be completed in the manner, upon the plan, and with the materials heretofore agreed upon by said Commissioners.

Sec. 3. The appropriation hereby made shall be paid out in the manner and at the times hereinafter specified. The Commissioners shall upon the passage of this act, and quarterly thereafter, make a report to the Governor, stating to him the amount of money which will be required for use during the next three months, and the amount expended during the preceding three, and upon the reception of said report, the Governor shall make an order upon the auditor, requiring him to issue an order upon the Treasury for the amount so required. The warrant shall be payable at the State Bank of Illinois to the order of the commissioners.

Sec. 4. The Commissioners shall deposit all orders issued in their favor in the State Bank, and the money shall be paid out by the Bank upon the orders of said Commissioners.

Sec. 5. The commissioners shall, instead of paying out money, make orders or checks upon the Bank, in favor of all persons to whom money may be due, and shall state on the face of such orders or checks, the consideration for which they were given, and shall be so written as that the signature of the payee upon the back shall make the order or check operate as a receipt from the payee to the State as well as to the Bank.

Sec. 6. In case any, or all the Commissioners appointed to superintend the erection of public buildings shall die, resign or refuse to act, the governor shall appoint a successor or successors.

JURY DECISION AND DECREE OF THE COURT IN THE DIVORCE SUIT OF ROGERS VS. ROGERS, SANGAMON CIRCUIT COURT, ABOUT MARCH 15, 1839.
(Herndon-Weik Collection)

The last paragraph of this decree appears to have been penned by John T. Stuart. Mr. Lincoln wrote no part of the jury decision, but the document is included as the end of an unwholesome divorce case. Its history appears in the legal papers for August 14, October 20, the amended bill of October or November, 1838, and this decision. The case cannot be considered a victory for Stuart & Lincoln, for although Rogers gained a divorce on grounds of desertion, as charged in a bill for divorce of August 14, 1838, Polly Rogers was absolved of the charge of adultery, and received an alimony payment of $78.00 per year, and immediate payment of a sum that must have displeased Rogers. He had complained of the original alimony award of $1,000. The jury remained silent on the counter charge of adultery by Mrs. Rogers against her husband.

Samuel Rogers

vs } Petition for divorce

Polly Rogers

This day came the parties and issues being joined upon the bill of Said Complainant and the answer of said defendant,— The Court directed a jury to be sworn to try the said issues, Whereupon came a jury, To wit A. R. Robinson (and eleven others), who after being duly sworn to try Said issues. And after hearing the evidence and argument of counsel, retired to consider of their verdict and then coming again into court say. "we of the jury find the defendant did desert and abandon the said Complainant as set forth in said bill, and that said defendant has not been guilty of adultery as charged in Said bill nor other improper conduct." Whereupon it is ordered and decreed by the Court that the bonds of matrimony now existing between the said Samuel Rogers and the said Polly be and the same are forever broken and dissolved. And the court having heard evidence as to the property of said Complainant and the condition of said defendant—it is further ordered and adjudged that the said Complainant pay to the said defendant as alimony the sum of one hundred and thirty nine dollars, on the first day of Sept. 1838 and that he pay her the further sum of thirty nine dollars, on each first day of March and first day of September thereafter until the further order of the court. Said payments are hereby required to be made to the clerk of this court at his office, and the court doth further order that compt. & deft. pay their other costs of this court.

CHANGE OF VENUE AND LETTER IN THE SUIT OF McNAIR VS. ADAMS, PEORIA CIRCUIT COURT, APRIL 2 AND 8, 1839.
(Herndon-Weik Collection)

The words "Stuart & Lincoln Attys for Plff" in the agreement for change of venue are in the handwriting of Mr. Lincoln. The letter was penned by Samuel H. Treat, as was "Wm. Mitchell, Peoria, Illinois" on the cover notation. "McNair vs. Adams" is in a different hand, and Clerk Mitchell penned the date of filing. Agreement and letter are part of a prolonged and bitter contest instigated, as set forth on earlier pages, by Mr. Lincoln, On August 9, 1841, there was another change of venue, this time to the Cass County Circuit Court. There the matter rested until the death of Adams in August, 1843, put an end to further proceedings.

Mathew McNair. Pltff.   In the Peoria circuit
       vs.   court. on change of venue
James Adams.   Deft.   from Sangamon

It is hereby stipulated & agreed that the venue in this cause be changed from Peoria county to sangamon county.

                Stuart & Lincoln
                Attys for Plff
                S. H. Treat attorney
                deft. Adams.

————0————

Letter for Change of Venue: April 8, 1839.

Springfield April 8th 1839—

Wm Mitchell Esq..

Dear Sir.

You will find on your Docket a case of Matthew McNair vs James Adams—

Will you have the goodness to file the Enclosed agreement & when the cause is called up, have the venue changed to this county. By so doing you will much oblige Messrs Stuart & Lincoln. & your Obet. Servant

S. H. Treat.

McNair
   vs
Adams
Paid 10
Paid
Wm Mitchell Esquire
        Peoria—
        Illinois
Filed April 10th 1839
Wm Mitchell Clerk

AFFIDAVIT BY MR. LINCOLN IN THE SUIT OF LUSK VS. COON, TAZEWELL CIRCUIT COURT, PROBABLY MAY, 1839.

No doubt an interesting story lies behind this affidavit of Mr. Lincoln, but it has not been possible, despite much labor, to obtain the details of it. The same regret attaches to many other incidents of his first years at the bar.

State of Illinois)
Tazewell County (

On of the defendants in an action of trespass pending in the circuit court of the county aforesaid, wherein Robert Lusk is plaintiff, being first duly sworn, states on oath, that he does not know, nor can he learn of any Robert Lusk residing in the State of Illinois; that he has heard of a man by the name of Lusk residing in the State of Tennessee, whom, from circumstances, affiant supposes to be the plaintiff in said suit—Affiant therefore states that he verily believes said plaintiff was not, at the commencement of this suit, nor is now, a resident of this state—

DECLARATION, PRAECIPE AND BOND FOR SECURITY IN THE SUIT OF FORSYTH VS. TRUETT & MAY, SANGAMON CIRCUIT COURT, MAY 22, 1839.

(Herndon-Weik Collection)

This declaration and praecipe were drawn by Mr. Lincoln The notations on the cover, signed by Walker, are also in his hand, as are those signed by Butler. The others were penned by Lincoln. The repetition of the word "the" as in "the the" and of "in", as in the case of "in in" should be noted. Mr. Lincoln usually crossed out such superfluous words, but repetitions are found in a few of his documents. The signature of Irwin and the notations on the cover are the only parts of the bond for security not in Mr. Lincoln's hand. Mr. Lincoln gave the case as "Forsyth & Forsyth vs. Truett & May" and brings out the fact that John and Jacob Forsyth traded as "Jacob Forsyth & Co." Clerk Butler files the case as Forsyth & Co. vs. Truett & Co. Truett and May entered their pleas as defendants on July 10, 1839. Stuart and Lincoln acted for the plaintiffs, and Mr. Lincoln bid in lots 3 and 4 in Taylor's Addition to Springfield. The cost was $961.06, and the former owner of the lots was William L. May. This was in satisfaction of the judgment obtained against him. Truett was May's son-in-law, and Mr. Lincoln was one of the attorneys who in the previous year had saved him from conviction for the murder of Dr. Jacob M. Early.

State of Illinois
Sangamon County   } S S
& Circuit—

Jacob Forsyth and John A. Forsyth, trading and doing business under the style and firm-name of "Jacob Forsyth & Co" plaintiffs, complain of Henry B. Truett and William L. May, defendants, being in custody &c. of a plea of tresspass on the case upon promises: For that whereas; heretofore, towit, on the first day of July in the year of our Lord one thousand eight hundred and thirtyseven at Springfield Ill. towit, at the county and circuit aforesaid, made their certain promissory note in writing, bearing date the day and year aforesaid, and thereby then and there promised to pay, six months after the date thereof, to the order of the said plaintiffs, by their said firm-name of "Jacob Forsyth & Co" the sum of eight hundred dollars, for value received, with interest at the rate of six pr ct (meaning six per cent) from the date of the said promissory note, and then and there delivered the said promissory note to the said plaintiffs; by means whereof, and force, of the statute in such case made and provided, the said defendants then and there became liable to pay to the said plaintiffs the said sum of money in the said promissory note specified, according to the tenor and effect of the said promissory note; and being so liable, they, the said defendants, in consideration thereof, afterwards, towit, on the day and year, and at the place aforesaid, undertook, and then and there faithfully promised the said plaintiffs to pay them the said sum of money in the said promissory note specified according to the tenor and effect thereof— Yet the said defendants (although often requested so to do; and although the time for the payment of the said sum of money in the said promissory note specified has long since expired) have not as yet paid to the said plaintiffs, or to their order, the said sum of money in the said promissory note specified, or any part thereof; but sotodo have hitherto wholly neglected and refused, and still do neglect and refuse, to the damage of the said plaintiffs of fifteen hundred dollars, and therefore they sue &c.

Stuart & Lincoln p.q—

(Copy of the note sued on)

"$800—Springfield Ill July 1st 1837—

Six months after date we promise to pay to the order to Jacob Forsyth & Co Eight hundred Dollars 100 for value received with interest at the rate of six per. ct from this date—

Henry B. Truett
William L. May"

Jacob Forsyth & John A. Forsyth trading and doing business under the style and firm-name of "Jacob Forsyth & Co" vs Henry B. Truett & William L. May	Trespass on the case upon promises— Damage $1500-00—

The clerk of the Sangamon circuit court will issue process in in the above case returnable to the next term of said court—

Stuart & Lincoln p q—

Forsyth &c vs Truett & May	In Case

And the Defendant May comes & defends & says he did not assume upon himself in manner & form as plaintiffs have alleged & of this he puts himself upon the country

Walker p d

And the Plff. doth the like.

Stuart & Lincoln

Jacob Forsyth & Co

vs } Declaration &
Precipe—

Henry B Truett and
William L. May—
Filed May 22d 1839
Wm Butler clerk

———0———

Jacob Forsyth & John A. Forsyth
vs } In S
Henry B. Truett & William L. May

I do hereby enter myself security for costs in this cause, and acknowledge myself bound to pay all costs which may accrue in this action, either to the opposite party or to any of the officers of this court in pursuance of the laws of this state—

John Irwin

Dated this 20th day of May A D. 1839.

Forsyth & Co
vs
Truett & Co
Filed May 22 1838
Wm Butler ck
$898.00

LETTER OF MR. LINCOLN TO NATHAN DRESSER, MAY 30, 1839.

(From the Herndon-Weik Collection)

The letter here reproduced was addressed to Nathan Dresser, clerk of the Menard Circuit Court, and instituted a trespass suit for $200 damages for Levi Summers, administrator for Alfred Summers vs. Henry Sears. When the Menard Circuit Court met for the first time at Petersburg on June 17 this suit was second on the docket, but was dismissed on motion of Stuart & Lincoln. On November 11, 1839, Mr. Lincoln asked for a continuance, filing a petition to make title to a tract of land, and on June 8, 1840, he moved that David H. Rutledge, a brother of the well known Ann, be appointed as guardian ad litem for Levi *and Melvina Summers. The judge ordered that the land be transferred as prayed for in the petition by Summers, the costs to be paid by him.*

Springfield May 30, 1839.

Mr. Dresser:

Enclosed are the papers to commence a suit for old man Summers against H. Sears. You will find one of Butler's blank summons filled up by me which you can copy and it will be right in this case—It would do for itself but for its having the Sangamon seal to it—

Also on the other side of this sheet you find a petition for an order to have the land involved in this matter conveyed to Sears— It, together with the bond, (also enclosed) you will file & docket among your Chancery cases—No process to issue in it.—

————0————

The above writing is true and genuine and was written by Mr. Lincoln himself.

Wm. H. Herndon

Aug 20th 87

DECLARATION AND PRAECIPE IN THE SUIT OF SUMMERS VS. SEARS, MENARD CIRCUIT COURT, MAY 31, 1839.

(Herndon-Weik Collection)

This declaration, quoted note, and precipe are from the pen of Mr. Lincoln, and the cover notations are his work. The care exercised by him as an attorney will be seen in the crossing of the word, "Alfred," and the substitution of the correct name, "Alford." It is a minor change, but it reveals an important characteristic of Mr. Lincoln. He erred at times, and overlooked a few mistakes, but on the whole, was careful in the drafting of his legal papers. This may account for an orderly process of thinking in court, and an ability before the bench surpassed by few, if any, of the Illinois attorneys of his period. As recorded above this case was second on the docket of the Menard Circuit Court when it convened on June 17, 1839, and was dismissed on the motion of Stuart & Lincoln, attorneys for Summers.

State of Illinois		Of the June term of the
Menard county	}	circuit court for said county
and circuit		A. D. 1839—

Levi Summers, administrator of the estate of Alford Summers deceased, plaintiff complains of Henry Sears defendant, being in custody &c of a plea of trespass on the case upon promises: For that whereas the said defendant, heretofore, and in the life time of the said Alford Summers since deceased, to-wit on the twentyseventh day of December in the year of our Lord on thousand eight hundred and thirtyseven at the county and circuit aforesaid made his certain promissory note in writing signing his name thereto thus Henry (his + mark) Sears bearing date the day and year aforesaid, and thereby then and there promised to pay on or before the first day of April in the year of our Lord one thousand eight hundred and thirtynine to the order of the said Alford Summers the sum of one hundred and thirty dollars for value received, and then and there delivered the said promissory note to the said Alford Summers: by means whereof, and by force of the statute in such case made and provided, he, the said defendant then and there became liable to pay to the said Alford Summers in his lifetime since deceased, the said sum of money in the said promissory note specified, according to the tenor and effect of the said promissory note, and being so liable, he, the said defendant, in consideration thereof, afterwards, towit, on the day and year aforesaid, and at the place aforesaid, undertook, and then and there faithfully promised the said Alford Summers in his lifetime to pay him the said sum of money in the said promissory note specified, according to the tenor and effect of the said note— Yet the said defendant not regarding &c. but contriving &c. to deceive and defraud the said Alford Summers in his life time, and the said Levi Summers, plaintiff, as administrator as aforesaid after the death of the said Alford Summers (to which said Levi Summers, after the death of the said Alford Summers, towit on the   day of in the year of our Lord one thousand eight hundred and thirty-eight, at the county of Sangamon and state aforesaid, administration of all and singular the goods and chttels and credits, which were of the said Alford Summers deceased, at the time of his death, who died intestate, by the Probate Justice of the Peace for the county of Sangamon aforesaid, in due form of law was granted in this behalf hath not as yet paid the said sum of money to the said Alford Summers in his lifetime, or to the said Levi Summers administrator as aforesaid, since the death of the said Alford Summers (although often requested sotodo;) but he so to do, hath hitherto wholly refused, and still refuses to pay the same, to the said Levi Summers, administrator as aforesaid. To the damage of the said plaintiff, as administrator as aforesaid of two hundred dollars, and therefore he brings his suit &c. And the said plaintiff brings into court here the letters of administration of the said Probate Justice of the Peace of Sangamon county, which give sufficient evidence to the said court here, of the grant of administration to the said plaintiff as aforesaid, the date whereof is the day and year in that behalf mentioned—

Stuart & Lincoln p. q.

(Copy of the note declared on)

"$130.00.

On or before the first day of April 1839 I promise to pay to the order of Alford Summers the sum of one hundred & thirty dollars for value received this 27th December 1837

his
Henry   +   Sears"
mark

Levi Summers, administrator of Alford Summers deceased vs Henry Sears	Trespass on the case upon promises— Damage— $200-00—

The clerk of the Menard county circuit court will issue process in the above entitled cause returnable to the next term of said court—

Stuart & Lincoln p. q.

Levi Summers adsr &c.

vs   Decln & precipe

Henry Sears—

Filed May 31st
   1839

AGREEMENT IN THE SUIT OF SAWYER VS. CORDELL, MACON CIRCUIT COURT, JUNE 3, 1839.

(Photostat from the Lincoln National Life Foundation)

The agreement in this case was drawn by Mr. Lincoln, attorney. It was signed by John Sawyer, but the signature of David Cordell was in the handwriting of Mr. Lincoln. The word, "appeal" indicates that the suit was an appeal from a decision of a Justice of Peace court, as appeals from the Circuit Courts went to the State Supreme Court. As the original or first decision in the case is not known, we are ignorant of its nature. As in other Macon Circuit Court cases of 1839, research has not made records available, and all that is known is that Mr. Lincoln acted as attorney for one party and that neither party to the suit emerged victorious.

John Sawyer ⎫
    vs   ⎬ Appeal—
David Cordell ⎭

In this case the parties agree that the suit shall be dismissed each party paying half of the cost

June 3, 1839
John Sawyer
David Cordell

Sawyer

   vs   ⎬ Agreement

Cordell

PLEA IN THE SUIT OF ADKIN VS. HINES, MACON CIRCUIT COURT, JUNE 4, 1839.
(Photostat from the Lincoln National Life Foundation)

Although the pleas in this case were signed with the name of Emmerson, they were drawn by Mr. Lincoln. The only words, not in his hand, are "David Stutesman." The cover notations are by Clerk Gorin. Although research to date offers no record of this case, it appears to have been a slander suit brought by Adkin on the ground that Hines had openly and falsely charged that he had stolen goods. An interesting fact in this connection is the appointment of Mr. Lincoln on October 31, 1839 to act as attorney for David Adkin. The latter had been indicted at Decatur for larceny, but the jury found him not guilty, on the day Mr. Lincoln was appointed to defend him.

Robert Hines ⎫
    ats   ⎬ Macon Circuit Court
David Adkin ⎭

And the said defendant comes and defends the wrong and injury when where &c. as to the speaking and publishing of the said several words of and concerning the said plaintiff, as in his said declaration mentioned the said defendant by leave of the court here for this purpose first had and obtained according to the form of the statute in such case made and provided, saith that the said plaintiff ought to have or maintain his aforesaid action thereof against him, because he says that the said plaintiff as in his said declaration mentioned, to wit, on the fifteenth day of March in the year of our Lord one thousand eight hundred and thirtyeight, at the county of Macon in the state of Illinois, did feloniously steal, take and carry away certain goods and chattels towit, five pigs and five hogs of one George G. Deeds of great value towit of the value of fifty dollars—Wherefore he the said defendant afterwards towit at the said several times when &c. in the said declaration mentioned at the county of Macon aforesaid, did speak and publish the said words of and concerning the said plaintiff as in the said declaration mentioned as he lawfully might for the cause aforesaid—

And this he the said defendant is ready to verify, wherefore he prays judgment if the said plaintiff ought to have or maintain his aforesaid action thereof against him &c.

And for further plea in this behalf as to the speaking and publishing of the said several words of and concerning the said plaintiff, as in his declaration mentioned, the said defendant, by leave of the court here for this purpose first had and obtained according to the form of the statute in such case made and provided, saith that the said plaintiff ought not to have or maintain his aforesaid action thereof against him because he says that the said plaintiff, before the speaking and publishing of the said words of and concerning the said plaintiff as in his said declaration mentioned, towit on the fifteenth day of March in the year of our Lord one thousand eight hundred and thirtyeight at the county of Macon in the state of Illinois did feloniously steal, take and carry away certain goods and chattels, towit five pigs and five hogs of one David Stutesman of great value towit of the value of fifty dollars— Wherefore he the said defendant afterwards towit, at the said several times when &c. in the said declaration mentioned at the county of Macon aforesaid, did speak and publish the said words of and concerning the said plaintiff, as in the said declaration mentioned as he lawfully might for the cause aforesaid— And this he is ready to verify where fore he prays judgment if the said plaintiff ought to have or maintain his aforesaid action thereof against him—

Emmerson for Deft

Hines

> ats } Plea

Adkin
Filed 4th June 1839
Wm Gorin clk

DECLARATION BY MR. LINCOLN IN THE SUIT OF LOCKWOOD VS. WERNWAG, SANGAMON CIRCUIT COURT, JUNE 20, 1839.

This declaration, the original of which is now in the Illinois State Historical Library, was drawn by Mr. Lincoln. It marks the beginning of one of a trio of suits which in the spring and summer of 1839 beset William H. Wernwag who had encountered financial disaster while carrying out a contract for the construction of a bridge over the Sangamon river north of Springfield. An adjustment of some sort having been reached out of court, the case, on motion of Mr. Lincoln, was dismissed on November 30, 1839.

State of Illinois   Of the July term of the Sangamon
Sangamon county } Ss circuit court in the year of our Lord one
and circuit   thousand eight hundred and thirtynine—

Benjamin H. Lockwood, plaintiff, complains of William H. Wernwag defendant, being in custody &c of a plea in assumpsit: For that whereas heretofore towit on the   day of   in the year of our Lord one thousand eight hundred and thirtynine at the county and circuit aforesaid, the said defendant was indebted to the said plaintiff in the sum of one hundred and four dollars and thirtyeight cents lawful money of the United States, for the work and labour, care and diligence of the said plaintiff, by him the said plaintiff before that time done, performed and bestowed in and about the business of the said defendant, and for the said defendant, and at his special instance and request; and being so indebted, he the said defendant, in consideration thereof, aforesaid, towit on the day and year aforesaid, at the county and circuit aforesaid, undertook and then and there faithfully promised the said plaintiff to pay him the aforesaid sum of money when he the said defendant should be thereunto afterwards requested—

Yet the said defendant (although often requested so to do) hath not as yet paid to the said plaintiff the said sum of money or any part thereof; but so to do hath hitherto wholly neglected and refused and still doth refuse—To the damage of the said plaintiff of the sum of two hundred dollars, and therefore he sues &c.

Stuart & Lincoln pq.

(Copy of Acpt)

William H. Wernwag
> To Benjamin H. Lockwood   Dr

1939 To labour done on and about the Sangamon bridge $104.38

Benjamin H. Lockwood

vs   } Decl.

William H. Wernwag
Filed June 20 1839
> Wm Butler Clk

DECLARATION BY MR. LINCOLN IN THE SUIT OF HURT VS. WINTERS, SANGAMON CIRCUIT COURT, JUNE 20, 1839.

This declaration was drawn by Mr. Lincoln. Reuben Winters had refused to pay for a horse he had bought from John M. Hurt, and the latter sought a judgment for $100. Diligent search has failed to disclose the outcome of the action.

State of Illinois } Of the July term of the Sangamon
Sangamon county } Sc Circuit court, in the year of our Lord one
and Circuit } thousand eight hundred and thirtynine—

John M. Hurt, plaintiff, complains of Reuben Winters defendant, being in custody of a plea of assumpsit; For that whereas heretofore towit, on the   day of   in the year of our Lord one thousand, eight hundred and thirtynine, at the county and circuit aforesaid, the said defendant was indebted to the said plaintiff, in the sum of sixtyone dollars, for a certain horse by the said plaintiff before that time sold and delivered to the said defendant, and at his special instance and request, and being so indebted, he the said defendant, in consideration thereof, afterward, towit, on the day and year aforesaid, at the county and circuit aforesaid, undertook, and then and there faithfully promised the said plaintiff to pay him the aforesaid sum of money when he the said defendant should be thereunto afterwards requested—

Yet the said defendant (although often requested so to do) hath not as yet paid to the said plaintiff, the said sum of money, or any part thereof; but so to do hath hitherto wholly neglected and refused and still doth neglect and refuse— To the damage of the said plaintiff of the sum of one hundred dollars, and therefor he sues &c.

Stuart & Lincoln, p. q.

(Copy of account)

Reuben Winters

To. John M. Hurt   Dr.

1839   To 1 horse $61.00

DECLARATION IN THE SUIT OF HURST VS. SMITH ET AL, SANGAMON CIRCUIT COURT, JUNE 22, 1839.

The declaration and quoted notes in this case were drawn by Mr. Lincoln as was the citation of the case upon the cover notations. The date of filing was penned by Clerk Butler. There is unusual emphasis of the extra spacing used by Mr. Lincoln and it is most marked in this legal paper. It will be noted that he omitted the word "money" in the sentence which begins, "and the said John Hammer, to whom or to whose order the payment of the said sum." There are too many legal papers in which Mr. Lincoln spelled the word, "defendants", in correct fashion, to admit of his not knowing the correct spelling, but in the sentence beginning, "by means whereof, and by force of the statute," contains the word, "difendants," as there is a definite dotted "i", in place of Lawyer Lincoln's usual first "e". The plaintiff in the suit, Charles R. Hurst, was a merchant in Springfield, but little or nothing has been unearthed in regard to the defendant. On July 13, 1839, Stuart & Lincoln won this case by default, their client Hurst, being granted a judgment of $204.07.

State of Illinois ⎫   Of the July term of the Sangamon
Sangamon county ⎬ Sc Circuit court, in the year of our Lord one
and Circuit   ⎭   thousand eight hundred and thirtynine—

Charles R. Hurst, plaintiff complains of Samuel Smith and Joseph Taggart, late trading and doing business under the name style and firm of Smith & Taggart, defendants, being in custody &c. of a plea of Trespass on the case upon promises: For that whereas the said defendants, heretofore, towit, on the eighth day of September in the year of our Lord one thousand eight hundred and thirtyeight at Springfield, towit at the county and circuit aforesaid, made their certain promissory note in writing, signing thereto their aforesaid firm name of "Smith & Taggart" bearing date the day and year aforesaid, and thereby then and there promised to pay Six months after the date thereof to one John Hammer or order the sum of two hundred dollars for value received, and then and there delivered the said promissory note to the said John Hammer And the said John Hammer, to whom or to whose order the payment of the said sum of in the said promissory note specified was to be made, after the making of the said promissory note, and before the payment of the said sum of money therein specified, to wit on the day and year aforesaid at the county and circuit aforesaid, assigned the said promissory note by indorsement in writing thereon, by which said assignment he the said John Hammer then and there ordered and appointed the said sum of money in the said promissory note specified, to be paid to Abner Y. Ellis and Foley Vaughn, then trading and doing business under the name style and firm of Ellis & Vaughn, by their said firm name of Ellis & Vaughn, and then and there delivered the said promissory note, so assigned, to the said Ellis & Vaughn and the said Ellis & Vaughn to whom or to whose order the payment of the said sum of money in the said promissory note specified was by the said assignment directed to be made, after the making of the said promissory note, and before the payment of the said sum of money therein specified, towit, on the day and year aforesaid, at the county and circuit aforesaid assigned the said promissory note by indorsement in writing thereon, signing their names thus "Ellis & Vaughn" which said last mentioned assignment they the said Ellis & Vaughn then and there ordered, and appointed the said sum of money in the said promissory note specified to be paid to the said plaintiff and then and there delivered the said promissory note specified to be paid to the said plaintiff— by means whereof, and by force of the statute in such case made and provided, the said difendants became liable to pay to the said plaintiff the said sum of money in the said promissory note specified, according to the tenor and effect of the said promissory note; and being so liable, they the said defendants, in consideration thereof, afterwards, towit, on the day and year aforesaid, at the county and circuit aforesaid, undertook and then and there faithfully promised the said plaintiff to pay him the said sum of money in the said promissory note specified according to the tenor and effect thereof— And the said plaintiff avers that the said county of Sangamon is the county in which he the said plaintiff resides; and that the cause of his aforesaid action accrued in the said county of Sangamon—and that the said defendants reside in the county of Morgan and state aforesaid— Yet the said defendants (although often requested so to do; and although the said promissory note has long since been due) have not as yet paid to the said plaintiff the said sum of money in the said promissory note specified, or any part thereof; but so to do have hitherto wholly neglected and refused, and still do neglect and refuse— To the damage of the said plaintiff of the sum of four hundred dollars, and therefore he sues &c.

Stuart & Lincoln, p. q.

(Copy of note)

"$200 100

Springfield September 7 1838

Six months after date we promise to pay to John Hammer or order two hundred dollars, for value received—

Smith & Taggart"

(1st assignment)
"Pay to Ellis & Vaughn
John Hammer"

(2nd assignment)
"Pay to Charles R. Hurst
Ellis & Vaughn"

Charles R. Hurst
    vs   } Decln
Smith & Taggart

Filed June 22 1839
  Wm Butler ck

PRAECIPE AND BOND IN THE SUIT OF LANE & WEBB VS. WEBBER, SANGAMON CIRCUIT COURT, JUNE 24, 1839.
(Herndon-Weik Collection)

This praecipe and bond were drawn by Mr. Lincoln. The cover notations also are in his hand with the exception of the date of filing. It will be noted that he omitted the word, "be", in the phrase "cause to paid," an infrequent error upon his part. The case was one of debt as seen from the praecipe, and on July 20, 1839, it was dismissed on the motion of the plaintinff, made

*through Stuart & Lincoln. Although Mr. Lincoln rarely made
mistakes in the names of the persons connected with a suit, it is
possible that John B. Webber was the John B. Weber who made
a knife attack on Garret Elkin and D. Cutright. For a complete
account of that affair see, Angle, Here I Have Lived (Springfield, Illinois, 1935, Page 67). The day on which this praecipe
and bond were written was an eventful one for Mr. Lincoln.
Fearful that an angry and disgruntled Douglas would go to
Washington and contest Stuart's seat in Congress he and four
other Springfield Whigs joined in a letter to the editor of the
Chicago American requesting certain information from the poll
books of that town. (See Nicolay and Hay 1:96) that would
refute the claims of Douglas, while Samuel H. Treat, having been
appointed by Governor Carlin to succeed Stephen T. Logan as
circuit judge, in the evening of June 24 Mr. Lincoln was chosen
Treat's successor on the town board of Springfield.*

John N. Lane & Willoughby L. Webb trading under the style of John N Lane & Webb vs John B. Webber	In Debt. Debt $673.78 Damages $200.00

The Clerk of the Sangamon Circuit Court will issue a summons for the Defendant in the above entitled cause returnable
to the next Term of the Sangamon Circuit Court.

Stuart & Lincoln

John N Lane and Willoughby L. Webb trading under the style of John N Lane & Webb vs. John B. Webber	In Debt of the July Term of the Sangamon Circuit Court 1839

I do hereby enter myself security for Costs in this Cause
and acknowledge myself bound to pay or cause to be paid all Costs
which accrue in this action either to the opposite party or to any
of the officers of this Court in pursuance of the Laws of this
State. Dated this 24th Day of June 1839.

A. Lincoln—

John N. Lane & Webb

vs   } Precipe

John B. Webber

Filed June 24 1839
William Butler ck

SUIT OF JOHN A. McCLERNAND VS. ROBERT IRWIN & COMPANY, SANGAMON CIRCUIT COURT, JULY 8 AND 16, 1839.

The papers here reproduced have to do with a contest for office that in the first half of 1839 greatly excited the people of Illinois and at the same time added to Abraham Lincoln's growing repute as a lawyer of promise and capacity. This contest became a matter of absorbing interest to the Whigs and Democrats of Springfield, when early in July the Supreme Court of Illinois met for the first time in that town, and took under consideration the case of Alexander P. Field vs. The People, appealed from the Fayette Circuit Court. A native of Kentucky and a nephew of Nathaniel Pope, for a generation judge of the United States District Court, Field, also a lawyer, had settled in Illinois about the time of its admission into the Union, locating in Union County where he quickly won prominence in politics and at the bar.

Field served three terms in the General Assembly and early in 1829 was by Governor Edwards appointed secretary of state, which post he continued to hold under Governors Reynolds and Duncan. But when the Whig Party came into being, Field, originally a Democrat, assumed leadership in the new organization, and on the election of Thomas Carlin, a Democrat, as governor, in August, 1838, he was by the new executive replaced as secretary of state by John A. McClernand. Contending that the Illinois Senate had not confirmed McClernand's appointment, he refused to give up the office, and in April, 1839, the Fayette Circuit Court ousted him, the case, by agreement, being appealed to the Supreme Court.

While the case was pending in the latter body, the state offices on July 4, 1839, were removed from Vandalia to Springfield, where Field stored his books and papers as secretary with Robert Irwin & Company, whereupon McClernand undertook to replevin them, and on July 5 was granted authority to do so by the Sanga-

mon Circuit Court. At this point, Mr. Lincoln, prompt to aid a friend and fellow Whig, became one of the attorneys for the defendants in the suit of McClernand vs. Irwin & Company and helped to draft the petition reproduced below, which, along with a motion to quash the writ of replevin, was on July 8 presented to the Sangamon Circuit Court. The motion was opposed by Stephen A. Douglas as attorney for McClernand, but on July 16 Judge Samuel H. Treat, as recorded in the two documents also given below, quashed the writ of replevin, and ordered McClernand to pay the costs. Six days later the Supreme Court denied McClernand's contention and upheld Field's right to the office of secretary of state.

In the end, however, neither of the contestants profited by these developments for in November, 1840, the Illinois Senate confirmed Governor Carlin's appointment not of McClernand but of Stephen A. Douglas in place of Field. As sequel to an unusual suit it may be recorded that the then youthful Douglas held the post only until February, 1841, when he resigned to take a place on the Illinois Supreme Court on his way, as events proved, first to the House and then to the Senate in Washington. Nor was Field long out of office, for also early in 1841, President Harrison appointed him secretary of Wisconsin Territory. Later he removed to St. Louis and then to New Orleans where he practised law for the remainder of his days. In December, 1862, he appeared in Washington as a member-elect of the House from Louisiana, but despite his claim that he had been a stout Union man, put forth in an eloquent and persuasive speech, he was refused his seat. He died fifteen years later in New Orleans.

The friendship between Mr. Lincoln and Field continued until the former's death, and in 1859 was marked by an incident that reflected in an appealing way the future President's attitude toward slavery during his latter Springfield days. "A man named Hinckel," as William H. Herndon more than once recalled the affair, "had brought here from Kentucky an old woman named Polly Mack. In 1859 her son, a free negro, going down on a steamer to New Orleans had been fined, and imprisoned, and finally advertised, for sale. Polly came to Mr. Lincoln with her trouble, and Lincoln wrote to Alexander P. Field, then in practice at New Orleans, begging him to get the poor fellow off, and promising money for costs and services. There were, of course, a good many difficulties, and one day Mr. Lincoln sent me to Governor Bissell to ask his interposition. The Governor answered that he did not think he had any authority in the case.

'By God!' said Mr. Lincoln, starting up, 'before I have done, I will make the road so hot that he shall find authority'." Mr. Lincoln did not succeed in convincing the Governor that he had authority to act in the matter. Instead he headed an adequate subscription fund which in due course was sent to Field in New Orleans, and restored young Mack to his mother.

It is also to be noted that during the weeks in which Field's fight for place reached a climax, to be exact, on July 6. 1839, John A. Sutter, who had come from his native Switzerland to engage briefly in the Santa Fe trade, travelling by way of Oregon, Honolulu and Alaska landed at Yerba Buena, soon to become San Francisco, and began the career which was to end in the discovery of gold by one of his workmen and the great migration which hastened by a generation the settlement of the Farther West.

To the Honorable the Judge of the Sangamon Circuit Court—

Humbly complaining sheweth unto your Honor, your orator Alexander F. Field, that on the twentythird day of January in the year of our Lord one thousand eight hundred and twentynine the then Governor of the State of Illinois, by and with the advice and consent of the Senate of the State of Illinois duly appointed your orator Secretary of State of the State of Illinois; that he has, ever since until the fifth day of April in the present year of our Lord one thousand eight hundred and thirtynine, and subsequently held, exercised and performed the said office of Secretary of State, and the duties thereof; that on the said fifth day of April A.D. 1839 the then Governor of the said State, without the advice and consent of the Senate of the said State, appointed John A. McClernand to be Secretary of State of the said State of Illinois; that on the eighteenth day of April in the year last aforesaid, the People of the State of Illinois, at the relation of the said John A. McClernand, filed in the Circuit court of Fayette county in said state, an information in the nature of a *Quo Warranto* against the said Field, your orator, for illegally and without warrant, grant or right, holding and exercising the said office of Secretary of State of the said State of Illinois; that afterwards, at the April term of the said circuit court of Fayette county, being the same term at which the said information was filed, your orator filed in said court his plea to the said information, to which plea the said People of the State of Illinois then and there filed their Replication, to which Replication your orator then and there demurred, which demurrer the said People then and there joined that the questions raised by the pleadings in the case, is, whether the Governor possesses the constitutional power of removing your orator from said office of Secretary of State; that afterwards, towit, at the same term of the said circuit court of Fayette county said demurrer was overruled by the said court and judgment entered up that your orator be ousted from the said office of Secretary of State, that by the agreement of the parties an appeal from said judgment has been taken to the Supreme Court of the said State of Illinois which appeal is still pending and undecided in that court, that on the day of July in the present year 1839, the said John A. McClernand commenced an action of Replevin in the Sangamon circuit court, and procured to be issued from the office of the clerk of the circuit court of Sangamon county a writ of Replevin to take from the possession of Robert Irwin and John Irwin, with whom your orator had deposited them for temporary safe keeping, on his arrival with them at Springfield from Vandalia in pursuance of law—the books, papers, seal, and boxes containing them, belonging to the said office of Secretary of State; that said writ has been placed in the hands of the Sheriff of Sangamon county to be issued: that the said John A. McClernand is attempting to intrude himself into the said office of Secretary of State without any lawful right so to do; that he has taken and continued to take from the Post office at Springfield such letters, papers and documents addressed to the Secretary of the State of Illinois or to your orator as Secretary of State and threatens and gives out as your orator is informed, that he will get possession of the Books, papers and documents belonging to the said office of the Secretary of State and procure and exercise the duties of the said office under color of his said pretended appointment and in defiance of the rights of your orator as secretary of state.

————0————

July 8, 1839

John A. McClernand, Sec. of State ⎫
                vs.   ⎬ Replevin
Robert Irwin & Co.   ⎭

This day came the defendants by their attorney and filed their grounds, and moved the court to quash the writ of Replevin issued in this cause. (The writ was issued on July 5, 1839). The motion was taken up later in the day by their attornies (Douglas for McClernand and Lincoln for Irwin & Co.) The Court takes time to consider until the next morning.

———0———

July 16, 1839

This day came the parties by their attorneys and the court being now sufficiently advised (Judge S. H. Treat) and having materially considered the motion entered on a former day of this term to quash the writ of replevin issued herein, orders that the said writ be quashed and that the defendants recover of the pltf. their costs expended.

(January 2, 1840 McClernand paid $5.00 of the total costs of $7.50).

PLEA IN THE SUIT OR PARKER VS. BRAUCHER, SANGAMON CIRCUIT COURT, JULY 16, 1839.
(Herndon-Weik Collection)

This case was submitted to the court on July 16, 1839, and a judgment of $242.68 was rendered in favor of Braucher, the client of Stuart & Lincoln. An appeal was granted on condition that a bond of security be made with Alex Lindsay within thirty days. The plea is in the hand of the firm of Douglas & Urquhart, probably by Douglas. It is the usual scrawl common to most of that firm's legal papers, but both partners were capable attorneys in the court room. Stuart wrote, "and the plaintiff doth the like," but Mr. Lincoln signed "Stuart & Lincoln," for the signature is clearly in his hand. The cover notations below appear to have been penned by Douglas. It was during the early July days of 1839 that Jacob Bunn, of Hunterdon County, New Jersey, who was to become the trusted and helpful friend of Mr. Lincoln, made his first visit to Springfield. A year later, at the age of twenty-six, he engaged in business in the town as junior member of a firm of wholesale and retail grocers. In the spring of 1843 he set up in business for himself, afterward becoming for thirty-five years Springfield's principal private banker.

Braucher

at the suit of } In Trespass on the case

C Parker

The defendant by his attorney comes and defends the & injury when &c and for plea saith that he did not assume in manner and form as the plaintiff hath alleged in his declaration and of this he puts himself on the country. July Term 1839.

Douglas & Urquhart
attorneys for plaintiff

and the plaintiff doth the like

Stuart & Lincoln

Samuel Parker

vs

Isaac R Braucher

Filed July 16th, 1839.

PREAMBLE AND RESOLUTIONS PROBABLY DRAFTED IN PART BY MR. LINCOLN AND ADOPTED BY THE FIRST WHIG STATE CONVENTION OF ILLINOIS HELD IN SPRINGFIELD, OCTOBER 7 AND 8, 1839.

Mr. Lincoln was not a delegate to the first Whig State Convention of Illinois which brought a goodly assembly to Springfield on October 7 and 8, 1839, the Whig leaders having somewhat reluctantly adopted the custom set afoot by the Democrats of functioning through county and state conventions; but he was one of its leaders, was named one of the five presidential electors, and appointed one of the five members of a state central committee, along with his friends Speed, Baker and Doctor Henry. Moreover, there is every reason to believe that he had an important part in shaping the preamble and resolutions which his partner Stuart submitted to the convention in the afternoon of its second day, and which were promptly and unanimously adopted by that body.

WHEREAS, the assembling of delegates in the *first* State Convention of the Whig party of Illinois, presents a fit and interesting occasion for an interchange and expression of views on the political condition and prospects of our country:—and whereas the period is again rapidly approaching when the people of these United States will be called on to render their verdict on the measures and character of the administration party. And whereas this Convention in common with all opposed to the administration of Martin Van Buren, believe, in the emphatic language of Henry Clay, that there is a radical mal-administration of the Government: that the great interests of our country are trodden down: that new and dangerous principles and practices have been introduced and continued: that a fearful conjunction of the purse and the sword in the same hands already alarmingly strong is perseveringly attempted: that the Constitution has been grossly violated: and that by the vast accumulation of executive power, our system is rapidly tending to an

Elective Monarchy: that the principles of democracy are so mutilated and disfigured by the administration party of the present day, that the democrats of '76 cannot recognize it in its modern disguise: that for promises of retrenchment and reform —of purity and integrity in the administration of the general government, the Van Buren party have exhibited the most unbounded extravagance, daring corruption and contempt of the wishes and interests of the people: and whereas we believe that to *effect a change of measures;* we must *effect a change of rulers*:

Therefore, *Resolved,* That we have full and entire confidence in the talents, patriotism and political integrity of the two distinguished statesmen spoken of as candidates for the presidency, the Hon. HENRY CLAY, of Kentucky, and Gen. WM. HENRY HARRISON, of Ohio—both favorite "Harries of the West," and that in opposition to Martin Van Buren.

Resolved, That Martin Van Buren came into office on the strength of his predecessor, and not on the strength of his own popularity—though long in public life he has identified himself with no deed of good or glory to his country—an artful politician, but not a profound statesman—an ambitious and selfish experimenter on the resources, credit and prosperity of the people, he deserves not their support, and especially of the West, whose interests he has repeatedly and uniformly opposed.

3d Resolved, That the scheme of a Sub-treasury, still continued to be forced by the President upon the people in defiance of their will repeatedly expressed, is a daring and dangerous attempt to concentrate all power in the Executive—to unite in his hands the purse and the sword—to create two species of currency, *gold* and *silver* for pampered office-holders, and *rags* for the people, the laborers and producers of the country; and that it will fasten a swarm of Sub-treasurers as leeches on the public monies, whose security to the government after they are glutted will be like that of Price and Swartwout—*leg-bail* in a foreign land.

4th, Resolved, That in the opinion of the Convention, the State Bank system, the former favorite measure of the administration party, has signally failed to accomplish the object intended, and that although the charter of the State Bank of Illinois was recommended by the acting Van Buren Governor, and passed by a legislature whose members almost entirely belonged to the administration party, the Whigs, after its creation, actuated by their great principle to preserve rather than to destroy the established institutions of the country, supported the Bank in common with the administration party, as an experiment of the State to provide against the want of a National Bank; they distinctly repel the attempt now made by the Van Buren party to cast, for political purposes, the origin of this State Institution on the Whig party, and here distinctly disclaim its paternity.

5th, Resolved, That while this Convention distinctly repels the charge made by the Van Buren press that the Whigs of this State are in favor of life offices, and believes that it is constitutional and expedient for the legislature to define the tenure of the office of Secretary of State, it also must express its conviction that in the many recent appointments to the offices of Secretary of State and Treasurer of the Illinois and Michigan Canal, the present Governor has exhibited a want of wisdom and vacillation of purpose unworthy the character of Chief Magistrate.

6th Resolved, That Samuel Marshall, Edwin D. Baker, Abraham Lincoln, Cyrus Walker and Buckner S. Morris, be recommended by this Convention as candidates for Electors to be supported by the Whig party of this State at the next Presidential election; that they be pledged to support the nominees of the Whig National Convention, and are requested and expected to address in person the people in different portions of the State on the subjects to be involved in that great contest.

7th Resolved, That it is the deliberate opinion of this Convention, that a majority of the People of the United States are opposed to the corrupt and destructive measures of the present national administration, and that a complete combination of the strength and votes of the Whig party, is alone wanting to wrest the sceptre of unhallowed power from the unprincipled dynasty that wields it, and to restore to our beloved country the halcyon reign of individual and national prosperity.

8th, Resolved, That to effect this desirable organization, the Whig party in this State and throughout the Union, must merge all personal predilections, all local questions and all minor differences of opinion, in consideration of the general weal; that they must look at men through principles, rather than at principles through men, and under the broad banner of organization and union go out to battle, firm in the righteousness of their cause, and ardent in their hope of victory.

ENTRY IN STUART & LINCOLN FEE BOOK, OCTOBER 10, 1839.

This entry in the Stuart & Lincoln Fee Book was made by Lincoln. It apparently had to do with a check Stuart was supposed to have drawn in favor of Robert A. Kinzie, and about which on December 23, the maker of the check being then in Washington, his partner made inquiry, at the same time asking about some lost deeds "belonging to old Mr. Wright." It is manifest that at times, John T. Stuart had the carelessness of a large nature.

Oct 10 1839 By check on Chicago Bank $80.00

SUIT OF HOOPER ET AL VS. HAINES, UNITED STATES CIRCUIT COURT, OCTOBER 19, 1839.

On October 19, 1839, Mr. Lincoln asked the clerk of the United States Circuit Court to issue a summons on a plea of trespass in the suit of Hooper, Marlin and Smith against Benjamin Haines, surviving partner of B. Haines & Son. This was his first case in the Federal Courts, although he was not admitted to practice before them until December 3, 1839. On November 9 he filed a declaration against Haines, alleging his failure to pay a promissory note for $567.28 and a debt of $12.64. The defendant defaulted, and on December 5, Mr. Lincoln's clients were awarded $626.82 damages.

It is to be regretted that there survive few documents concerned with Mr. Lincoln's activities in the federal courts, but his practice before them early became an important and steadily growing one, and a survey of it demands a place in any adequate account of his career as a lawyer. Such a survey will be found in a comprehensive and carefully considered article entitled "Lincoln's Earlier Practice in the Federal Courts (1839-1854)" contributed by Benjamin P. Thomas to the June, 1835 Bulletin of the Abraham Lincoln Association. Soon after Illinois' admission to the Union, Congress made the state a federal judicial district, and the court thus created held two yearly sessions at Vandalia as long as that town remained the capital of the state. When the state offices were removed to Springfield in 1839 the federal courts followed them, and in the new capital for fifteen years Mr. Lincoln tried his federal cases. Finally in February, 1855, moved thereto by the rapid growth of Northern Illinois, the state was divided into two federal districts, the Northern District holding its sessions in Chicago and the Southern Dis-

trict in Springfield; and during his five remaining years at the bar, Mr. Lincoln had a part in many important cases before both courts.

Transcripts of the records of the federal courts prior to 1855 reveal twenty-nine cases in which Mr. Lincoln was retained as sole or associate counsel, representing the defendants in eleven and the plaintiffs in eighteen cases. He won nineteen cases— ten by default or dismissal, lost six and settled three out of court. There is no record of the result in the twenty-ninth case. Most of these actions had to do with the collection of debts and were of a routine nature, but now and again Mr. Lincoln was counsel in cases of unusual interest and importance, some of them dealing with contested patents and others with the general welfare, such as the famous Effie Afton case, and these will be dealt with in later volumes.

The judge of the district court of Illinois from March, 1819 until his death in 1850, when he was succeeded by Thomas Drummond, was Nathaniel Pope, a diamond in the rough, whose part in Mr. Lincoln's legal career was a major one. The Springfield lawyer was from first to last a prime favorite with Judge Pope. The traits of the two men and the relations between them were described in a revealing and authoritative way by Judge Anson S. Miller of Rockford, whose recollections given to Moses Coit Tyler were published on March 28, 1868, in the New York Independent. "Judge Pope, father of General John Pope," Judge Miller recalled, "was a most remarkable man, one of the patriarchs of Illinois; and it used to seem to me that Lincoln was an idol with him. The Judge was a strong, original character. He had a head like a half-bushel, with brain enough for six men. He was learned, but rough and gruff. He had a wonderful knowledge of human nature, and was utterly without fear. Gen. Pope has many of his father's qualities; and these qualities have made him the bold energetic soldier and the indomitable administrator. They say that the General has a sort of genius for swearing. Well, he comes by it honestly. His father had the gift of speaking decidedly plain English, even in court . . . I have said that Judge Pope loved Lincoln. His affection for Lincoln was very marked. He would snub Logan. He didn't like Col. Baker. He was what Dr. Johnson calls a good hater. In fact, he was strong in everything—his likes and his dislikes. Lincoln was one of his likes. He told me that he thought Lincoln was a very able and promising man. The Judge was rough toward every-

one; but his roughness toward Lincoln had a touch of tenderness in it. He would sometimes rebuke him, but in a sort of fatherly way. I remember that once Judge Pope called a case in which Lincoln was engaged; called again, no answer. 'Where's Lincoln?' roared the Judge in his severe fashion; 'why don't he attend to his business?' Soon Lincoln came shambling into court. 'O, Mr. Lincoln you've come at last, have you? Well, I've been calling for you a long time.' Many persons wondered at the favor shown to John Pope by Mr. Lincoln during the war. I understand it. Mr. Lincoln remembered John Pope's father with gratitude and reverence; he knew John Pope too. He knew that he was made of good stuff, as indeed he is. We had no better soldier than Pope. It was treachery in the rear, not the enemy in the front, that defeated him. Lincoln understood the sort of roar in John Pope's proclamations which many people thought gasconade. That roar he got from his gruff old father; it was the roar of the lion, and Lincoln had heard it a thousand times. It was the most natural thing in the world for Lincoln to stand up for Judge Pope's son."

NOTE ON REMITTANCE TO THOMAS BOHANNAN, OCTOBER 23, 1839.

(Herndon-Weik Collection)

The note here reproduced was signed by Joshua Speed, but it came from the pen of Lincoln. There is no evidence that it was payment in any case, but it may have been a collection upon notes of Allen & Stone and Josiah Francis. In August, 1839, as already noted, the attorneys for Bohannan & Company had written that he had received nothing on these notes, and intended to start suit if payment was not forthcoming.

I hereby certify that I on this day deposited in the Post Office at this place a letter of Stuart & Lincoln directed to Messrs. Thos. Bohannan & Co. of Louisville Ky—enclosing $126.—

Joshua F. Speed.

Springfield, Ills. Oct. 23, 1839—

PLEA IN THE SUIT OF NESBITT & NESBITT VS. SCHULTZ, MACON CIRCUIT COURT, OCTOBER 28, 1839.

(Photostat from the Lincoln National Life Foundation)

The wording of this plea might permit the belief that it was a case of trespass upon the case upon promises, but research to

*date does not justify such conclusion. The part played by Mr.
Lincoln in the case is not clear, although he drew up the plea,
with the exception of the signature, "Burdick p d." He may
have been associated with Charles Emmerson.*

Schultz ⎫
     ats ⎬
Nesbitt & Nesbitt ⎭

And the defendant comes and defends the wrong & injury
when where, &c. and says plaintiffs *actio non* because he says he
did not undertake and promise in manner and form as the said
plaintiffs have declared against him; and of this he puts himself
upon the country &c.

Burdick p d

And the plaintiffs do the like
Emmerson p. q.

Schults ⎫
     ats ⎩ Plea
Nesbitt & ⎰
Nesbitt ⎭
Filed October 2t8h
1839.
    H McGorin
    By McLelen DC.

A NOTABLE ENTRY IN THE FEE BOOK OF STUART & LINCOLN, NOVEMBER 2, 1839.

*On November 2, 1839, John T. Stuart left Springfield for
Washington to take his seat in Congress, and Mr. Lincoln noted
his partner's departure with this jocose entry in the fee-book of
the firm. It would be difficult to exactly determine what he was
earning in 1839 but, with his salary as a member of the Legislature, his income enabled him to pay his expenses and reduce
the debts that had trailed him from New Salem, and that no
doubt was "his only ambition in money matters" in his third
year at the bar.*

Commencement of Lincoln's administration
1839 Nov 2

       Henry Kendoll ⎫
           vs ⎬ Note
       Hardin & Reagon ⎭ $180.50

DECLARATION IN THE SUIT OF O'NEAL VS. GATTEN, SANGAMON CIRCUIT COURT, NOVEMBER 4, 1839.

(Herndon-Weik Collection)

This declaration and the words, "Saml. O,Neal vs. Josephus Gatten Decln", are in the handwriting of Mr. Lincoln. The cover notations other than those cited, are by Clerk Butler. Mr. Lincoln hurried "towit" into "twit", and a characteristic use of a comma in words like "O,Neal" is to be noted. He did the same thing in his spelling of "o'clock" as "o,clock." A comparison of the declaration with that for Hawthorn in the case of Hawthorn vs. Wooldridge will show that Lawyer Lincoln followed rather closely a formal legal wording. O'Neal suffered not only physical damage, but was handled roughly by the court for the case was dismissed at the defendant's cost on November 22, 1839. The plaintiff sustained a good beating, and that was about all he got out of the case.

State of Illinois
Sangamon county } ss   Of the November term of the circuit court of said county
and Circuit   A. D. 1839—

Samuel O,Neal plaintiff complains of Josephus Gatten, defendant, being in custody &c. of a plea of Trespass— For that whereas the said defendant heretofore towit, on the   day of September in the year of our Lord one thousand eight hundred and thirtynine, at the county and circuit aforesaid, with force & arms assaulted the said plaintiff, and then and there, with great force and violence, with divers sticks, clubs, hoes, hoe-handles, malls wedges, logs of wood and with his fists gave and struck the said plaintiff a great many violent blows and strokes, on and about his head, face, breast, back, shoulders, arms, legs and divers other parts of his body— By means of which said several premises, he the said plaintiff was then and there greatly hurt, bruised and wounded, and became and was sick, sore, lame and disordered, and so remained and continued for a long space of time to wit for the space of four weeks then next following during all of which time he the said plaintiff thereby suffered and underwent great pain, and was hindered and prevented from performing and transacting his necessary affairs and business by him during that time to be performed and transacted, and also thereby he the said plaintiff was forced and obliged to, and did necessarily pay, lay out, and expend a large sum of money twit the sum of $100—in and about endeavouring to be cured of the

bruises, wounds, sickness, soreness, lameness, and disorder aforesaid, occasioned as aforesaid to wit at the county & circuit aforesaid: And other wrongs to the said plaintiff then and there did,
against the peace &c. and to the damage of the said plaintiff of
five hundred dollars, and therefore he brings his suit &c.

Stuart & Lincoln p-q-

Saml. O,Neal

vs   }   Decln

Josephus Gatten

Filed Nov 4th 1839
Wm Butler ck
Nov 13th 1839— Recd
on this cause $5.00
to be applied to the
costs in this cause
        Wm Butler clerk

COURT ORDER IN THE SUIT OF REED & RICKARD VS. EARLY ET AL, SANGAMON CIRCUIT COURT, NOVEMBER, 1839.
(Herndon-Weik Collection)

Attorney Lincoln penned this court order, and the word, "order," on the cover. The order is undated, but as it refers to the fact that the petitioners appeared with their petition upon the same day, it may be assumed that it was decreed at the November, 1839 term of the court. Mr. Lincoln scanned this paper carefully, for he makes interlineations, and changes the word "named" to "described" as having a better meaning in the document. The precise accuracy of his survey reports for his legal documents reveals the care he took in surveying tracts when he was a deputy surveyor. Peter Rickard of the case was the father of Sarah Rickard, with whom Mr. Lincoln or his friend Joshua Speed had a romance about 1841. Two Lincoln letters of June 19, 1841 and February 3, 1842, contain mention of Sarah, but the last name is omitted. Miss Rickard was a sister-in-law of William Butler, intimate friend of Lincoln. The petition of November, 1838 reveals the cause of the case. The petition and court order reveal the outcome. It was one of many actions against Early's heirs which were brought after Early's death at the hands of Henry B. Truett.

James F Reed &
Peter Rickard
executors of Jacob
M Early deceased Complainants   On Petition to
                    against   sell real estate—
Catherine Early
George N. Early &
Jacob M Early Defendants

This day came the Petitioners, and filed their Petition in open court, and it appearing to the court that notice of this application had been given according to law, and James C. Conkling, having been appointed guardian *ad litem* to the said George N. Early and Jacob M. Early, files his answer and says he knows no reason consistent with the interest of his said wards why the prayer of said Petition should not be granted; and it also appearing to the satisfaction of the court that the allegations of said Petition are true— It is therefore ordered by the court, that the said Petitioners sell the real estate described in the Petition, towit, The West half of the South East quarter of Section Six, eighty acres; the South West quarter of Section Six, one hundred and thirty acres; the North West quarter of the North West quarter of Section Seven, thirtytwo acres; the North East fractional part of the North East quarter of Section Seventeen, eighteen acres and forty hundredths of an acre, all in Township Nineteen North of Range Eight West of the Third Principal Meridian situated in the county of Menard and [st]ate of Illinois;— And also one undivided half of the East half of the South West quarter of Section Twentytwo, in Township Sixteen North of Range Four West of the Third Principal Meridian situated in the county of Sangamon; that they sell said land at public vendue on a credit of six and twelve months, and that they take bond and security, & a mortage on the premises to secure the purchase money; and that they report their proceedings herein to this court.

Order—

A LETTER SIGNED "A LOOKER-ON", BUT PROBABLY WRITTEN BY MR. LINCOLN, SANGAMO JOURNAL, NOVEMBER 8, 1839.

The letter here reproduced appeared in the Sangamo Journal on November 8, 1839. It was titled The State Bank, dated Clinton County, Ill., Oct. 28, 1839 and signed A Looker-On.

In his issue of November 16, 1839, *the editor of the Illinois State Journal charged that the article had been written "by the Longest of the long-nine"— his customary nickname for Lincoln—and there is little doubt that the latter was its author.   It was the work of a stout Whig who could see no good in the course of his opponents, and one may doubt if Mr. Lincoln ever fairly measured the good-sense and firmness of Jackson's successor in seeking to remedy the conditions that had led to the panic of* 1837 *until in* 1861 *he himself headed an administration compelled to find ways to meet the mounting costs of a mighty struggle between the sections.   Yet in* 1839 *he had already learned how to fight political enemies with their own weapons.*

The administration party are again exulting.   The cry is now the Banks are broken.   Suspension has again overwhelmed the dynasty of Banks.

And, as is usual, no matter what happens, the Whigs are again blamed for this matter!

It is very advantageous for the Locos to have some one to blame for everything.   If the States are to have local banks, to supply a vacuum occasioned by the withdrawing of the paper of the United States Bank, the Locos create State Banks; and while they do well, the administration obtain the credit of supplying a better currency; but when the crash comes as predicted by the Whigs, then the Loco Focos must free themselves from the odium, and throw it upon the Whigs.

But the people are not so gullible as these would-be dictators would seem to suppose.—An intelligent people will not be always misled.   They are beginning to see the game playing on their confidence and will assuredly hurl back on those, their deceivers, their just indignation.

I am led to these reflections by an attentive perusal of several of the late numbers of the "Illinois State Register."   This reckless print has been for some time pursuing a course which its editors suppose will aid what they are pleased to call democracy; and I doubt not it will subserve the true democracy; but they have certainly been overshooting the mark, for the confiding people of Southern Illinois are too intelligent to be led into the absurdities which it presents to them.

The State Bank of Illinois, and its creation, are charged by this paper on the Whigs!   I know no other apology for the ignorance of this assertion, than that the *worthy* editor was not then a citizen of the State,—for surely if he was he would have known better.

I was in the State long before the State Bank was erected. I was at Vandalia when it was established, and I know those who figured—those who aided—and the grounds upon which its establishment was urged.

Gen. W. L. D. Ewing was then a Senator, and Acting Governor, and urged the establishment of a State Bank, on the ground that the General Government would put down the United States Bank, and General Jackson, Mr. Taney and Mr. Woodbury, and the whole party, urged the establishment of Banks, to supply a "better currency." Senator Ewing introduced his project—it was democratic;—Senator Will, another democrat, brought forward his project—and while it was pending, letters were said to be received from Washington, urging the passage of Will's bill, and promising the deposites to the Bank. Judge Smith urged it as a democratic measure, as did many other equally distinguished members of the party.

The few Whigs in the Legislature divided on the measure, and most of those who supported it, have since become Van Buren men. Well, the next measure the Banks wanted was the power to suspend in 1837. Governor Duncan was urged to convene the Legislature to grant this aid to the Bank, by Col. John A. McClernand, and Col. J. Fry, *both distinguished democrats,* and Canal Commissioners; and in the House of Representatives of that year, there were but eighteen Whigs. R. G. Murphy, of Perry, and Jas. Shields, then of Randolph, now of St. Clair, were the great champions, aided by Milton Carpenter of Hamilton, who carried through the suspension law. All these were democrats, as they call themselves, and with numerous others, were for legalizing the suspension.

Thus, I believe, I have given you simple facts, to show that the State Bank was created by the Loco Foco party on instructions from Washington;—they have nourished and sustained it;—they legalized its suspension in 1837, and will doubtless do it again in 1839, and, as it is their own dog, they may whip it, and, I trust, the Whigs will only stand by and see it well done.

A Looker-On.

Clinton County, Ill. Oct. 28, 1839

AFFIDAVIT BY MR. LINCOLN IN THE SUIT OF BRAUCHER VS. HEIRS OF JAMES SAYLES, SANGAMON CIRCUIT COURT, 1839 or 1840

This affidavit by Mr. Lincoln had to do with a suit for the partition of real estate owned by the heirs of James Sayles deceased. A petition for the desired partition was granted and three commissioners to effect it were appointed by the Sangamon Circuit Court on July 16, 1840, but on November 12 these commissioners reported that the property was not suitable for partition, and the court appointed William F. Elkin a commissioner to sell. it.

State of Illinois

Sangamon County

Isaac R. Braucher   In Chancery

vs.

Heirs of James
Sales Deceased

A. Lincoln being first duly sworn says on oath, that he is informed and verily believes that Jemima Arminda Sales, son of the defendants to the Bill hereto attached, resides out of the state of Illinois—   A. Lincoln

ARTICLE ON CLAIM OF DOUGLAS TO STUART'S SEAT IN CONGRESS BELIEVED TO HAVE BEEN WRITTEN BY LINCOLN, SANGAMO JOURNAL, NOVEMBER 28, 1839.

At the state election held on August 6, 1838, John Todd Stuart, after a hard-fought and bitter contest, defeated Stephen A. Douglas for Congress by thirty-six votes in a total of 36, 495 polled, so narrow a margin that Douglas, with some reason, angrily contended that he had been defeated by fraud. There followed a sharp exchange of letters between Douglas and Stuart, the latter on March 13, 1839, declining to canvass again the votes cast in the election of August 6, or to resign his claim to the office of representative and run the race over again. The reported plan of Douglas to contest the election troubled the Whig leaders in Springfield and Lincoln, alert to the interests of his partner, prompted five of them to join him late in June, 1839, in a confidential letter to various Whig editors in the Congressional district, including the editor of the Chicago Daily American (See "Complete Works" by Nicolay and Hay 1:96) requesting them to find out and report to Stuart and Lincoln if mistakes had been made in adding the votes, and if minors, non-residents or unnaturalized foreigners had voted for Douglas. The latter in the end gave up the idea of trying to unseat Stuart, who on November 2, 1839, left for Washington to take his seat. Lincoln, however, declaring that if one "heard Douglas say that he had abandoned the contest it would not be very authentic," for a time kept a watchful eye on the guileful young Democrat, (See Lincoln to Stuart November 14, 1839), and is believed to have penned this caustic editorial headed The Contested Election which appeared in the Sangamo Journal on November 28, 1839. Douglas had already become one of the few men whom Lincoln regarded through the years with abiding distrust and ill-will.

Why has not Mr. Douglas gone on to Washington to contest the seat of John T. Stuart in Congress? Can any living mortal tell? Surely, if the loco foco papers of this State are to be believed—he had a majority of the votes given for Representative to Congress last fall in this District? Why then, has he not gone to claim his seat?

Can it be possible that the loco foco press has been engaged, for the last six months, in deceiving their readers upon this subject?—How often they have asserted that Mr. Douglas had a majority—a clear and decided majority of the votes? and how often have they denounced the State officers for giving Mr. Stuart a certificate of election to which they said he was not entitled? How often have they charged Clerks of Counties with baseness and corruption in transmitting false returns?

Was all this merely to deceive what is called "the democratic party",—to give Mr. Douglas some little political capital —and to produce excitement in the community? Were these the high and holy motives of Mr. Douglass and his presses?

If Mr. Douglas has a majority of the votes, it is his most solemn duty to repair to Washington and claim his seat. If he has not that majority; and if he has either through design, or mistake given currency to wrong statements, affecting the character of our public officers, and misleading the people, it is just and proper that he should make all the atonement in his power; —and at once undeceive the public.

We are inclined to the belief that the denouments in this case, will show to the public what reliance is to be placed upon the statements of the loco foco press in this State, when their party interests are concerned.

INDEX TO PERSONS, PLACES AND SUBJECTS

INDEX TO DOCUMENTS AND LEGAL PAPERS